Casebook on Interpersonal Behavior

in Organizations

Casebook on

Interpersonal Behavior

in Organizations

Abraham Zaleznik

Professor of Organizational Behavior
Graduate School of Business Administration
Harvard University

David Moment

Associate Professor of Organizational Behavior
Graduate School of Business Administration
Harvard University

John Wiley & Sons, Inc., New York · London · Sydney

Library of Congress Catalog Card Number: 64-23866
Printed in the United States of America

Preface

T HE CASES in this book have been used in courses at the Harvard Business School and elsewhere. Until quite recently, these courses were thought of, and generally taught, as courses in human relations. The students were candidates for graduate degrees in business administration, members of executive training programs, and, in a few instances, industrial foremen and supervisors. Consistent with the human relations approach, they were being taught to be more competent in working with people.

Within the past few years, however, there has been developing a significant difference in the ways that we, the researchers who collected some of these cases, and the teachers who use them in our courses, are thinking about what we are doing. This difference is reflected in the change in course titles; as of the academic year 1963–1964, the courses formerly titled Administrative Practices and Human Relations at the Harvard Business School have been changed in content, purpose, and name, although they still deal with people at work. The new names are Human Behavior in Organizations and Interpersonal Behavior. The new teachers, as well as some of the old, have had professional training in the behavioral sciences, but some of them, significantly, have *not* had training in business administration. We, the authors, have both kinds of background, but we personally approve of and welcome this real change in emphasis toward a behavioral scientific approach to the understanding of human behavior at work. This point of view is evident in the content of the cases here.

We have neither abandoned nor renounced the goals of human relations training, but rather have attempted to look at the goals of this training within the context of what is known about the processes of individual development. At this point in our experience, we have concluded that there are two separable aspects of training for improved interpersonal competence. One of these involves personality and behavior change, relatively deep-seated processes within the private life of the individual. This kind of learning and experience cannot be transferred from one person to another. The other aspect is cognitive learning—the acquisition of more valid, public, and communicable thinking processes. As long as these two vastly different kinds of learning goals are pursued together in a single course or training program, the two processes may actually interfere each with the other. Emotional insight and personal learning can be used as a defense against the development of cognitive clarity. Similarly, cognitive learning can be used as an intellectual shield against the more deep-seated, private learning. The manner in which these two forms of defense actually take place when particular persons are involved in particular courses and programs depends heavily upon the individual's current stage of personality development and the social context of the experience.

To facilitate development of both kinds of learning, we propose separating them one from the other in the design of courses and training programs. For example, we have offered courses where the individual is assigned readings, hears lectures, and takes part in discussions of readings and cases, all of which are oriented toward learning content and methodologies. This kind of experience draws upon the accomplishments of behavioral scientific inquiry and theory. Separate from this experience, and either during the same academic term or the one immediately preceding or following, the individual is involved in a more personal and emotional small-group laboratory experience, where the intent is to contribute toward the private kind of learning. The integration of these two different kinds of experience is left up to the individual, as it must be, given the divergent nature of the processes involved. We cannot talk the individual into making the integration.

These comments explain why we advocate a behavioral scientific approach to the cases in interpersonal behavior contained in this book. They also will explain some important differences between the kinds of cases presented here and the kinds of cases which may be found in various casebooks on human relations or administrative problems. The major difference is that our cases do not tend to be organized around a particular management problem, and do not demand superficial decisions or remedial action from the reader. They are heavily laden with action implications, but not of the kind that are directly appropriate to a managerial decision-making orientation.

Cases may be used in a variety of ways, by both teachers and students. To a sophisticated theoretician, or a formal researcher, they may be seen as "instances of" certain principles or uniformities, specific examples of more general ideas. Or they may be used as data confining or denying certain theories. At another extreme, cases may be used as projective stimuli, the "inkblots" of a Rorschach test, or the ambiguous pictures in a Thematic Apperception Test. When used in this manner, the students, and possibly their teacher, respond with the feelings and fantasies evoked in themselves by the cases, including their personal recollections of similar experiences. Some training settings deliberately pursue this "displacement" or "projective" approach. A third use of cases is as material on which to practice inductive analysis. In this approach, the student attempts to build his own "currently useful generalizations" from the experience simulated in the cases he studies. This latter approach was advocated by the early adherents to the case method at the Harvard Business School, which is one of the traditions behind us. Our observation is that you can use experience, either real or as simulated in a case study, only once for purely inductive analysis; as soon as you have made your generalization, the particular case or real experience becomes an "instance of" that generalization. Hence, although the students may use the case material inductively, and the instructor may do so the first time he reads it, in case teaching the students often become more preoccupied with trying to guess what their teacher is trying to get at in the case than with inductive analysis.

We do not like playing games with our students or with our readers. We honestly think, for example, that the generalizations and analytical methods of competent professionals trained in the behavioral sciences are far more valid for communicating knowledge than those of the untrained student. We do not like to force a student to "re-invent the wheel." On the other hand, we are also aware that his personal learning will have more validity when he does it himself, and that it is a good thing for the student to learn to be realistically independent of "experts," whether they be witch doctors or doctors of philosophy. In order to balance these two values—transferable behavioral scientific knowledge and methodologies on the one hand and the value of the individual's learning from his own experience on the other hand—we strongly advocate innovative teaching around the use of cases, theoretical materials, and real personal experiences. With respect to cases, especially those in this book, we strongly recommend that the teacher and student be aware of what they are and are not doing with the case material.

These cases contain descriptions of behavior at the most concrete levels which are practical for the case form. They describe what people do and say. In some cases, the descriptions are summarized in quantified forms. All these cases are the results of research activities. Some of them contain interpretive comments. The others primarily contain data with little or no interpretation. The particular researchers, authors, case writers, and interpretive analysts are identified in the Case Source Acknowledgments, which follow this Preface.

In marked contrast to many human relations or administrative training cases, the cases in this book do not take someone's perception of a problem at face value and give data from which the student is supposed to arrive at a solution. The people in the cases, at a variety of organizational levels, do verbalize problems. However, rather than taking their definitions of problems as "orders," telling us how we should define our problems, or as requests for answers to which we must respond, we take them as data, as parts of the personal and social situations we are trying to understand. For the individual looking for situations that challenge the man of action, many of these cases will be disappointing.

The cases were not written as instances of unusual, dramatic, or stupendous problems. The events described in them are quite commonplace in the working world. On the other hand, the cases do not pretend to be representative of all of the working world. They were not written, or included in this book, to represent "typical" behavior patterns or classes of problems. They were written, and are included here, because the case writer was engaged in research in the situations, and because they provide good opportunities for analyzing interpersonal behavior.

A wide variety of settings is represented: assembly lines, job shops, managerial and professional group meetings, a sales force, a grocery store, an advertising agency, a hotel staff. While the reader can get some feel for the unique cultures involved, he will also be able to see uniformities such as social control taking place regardless of the setting. He will see managers and professionals subject to the same determinants of behavior as blue-collar worker groups. By comparing cases, he will be able to see the importance of particular technologies and tasks as partial determinants of behavior. The cases may be dealt with as discrete units for analysis, or they may be clustered together for comparative analysis. The table of contents suggests one such grouping. The general theoretical considerations underlying this organization appear in a companion volume, *The Dynamics of Interpersonal Behavior*, by the same authors and publisher.

We advocate two different modes of investigating these cases. The first mode is that of exploration and discovery. A correlate of competent learning behavior is the capacity to be surprised, to deal head-on with the unexpected. This mode poses two challenges: (1) what events, specifically, were surprising—that is, unpredicted on the basis of our prior knowledge and expectations—and (2) what underlying uniformity, of which we were obviously unaware if we were surprised at all, makes sense of the events. Once we discover and understand the underlying uniformities, similar events will be more predictable to us in the future. Furthermore, when we catalog these uniformities, we have come up with a deliberately thought-out personal theory of behavior. This mode of investigation is primarily inductive, but draws heavily on past experience and expectations; the new event is initially interpreted in terms of old theories. It is only when we encounter dissonance, surprise, or personal dismay that we have an immediate opportunity to revise our theories and learn.

The exploratory mode has its dangers. We do not always revise theories to close up the discrepancies evidenced by surprise or dismay. Sometimes we behave defensively, and dispose of the dissonance by moral evaluation. If we are not careful, we will dispose of these events, which were not supposed to happen according to our usual theories, by moralizing. Thus, the not uncommon phenomenon of group norms restricting output can be disposed of by calling the occurrence "bad," and labeling the group as a "bad" group. Similarly, behavior at higher levels in organizations could be disposed of as instances of managerial exploitation and selfishness. Clearly, moral judgment does not explain a thing. It may make us feel better, but it does not make the world more predictable. Hence, the exploratory mode must be tempered with a patient, understanding need to learn, rather than a need to defend. This mode is not, and cannot, be incorporated into the case material; it exists, or does not exist, in the orientation of the reader.

The second mode of investigation is more intellectual, theoretical, and general. Once we learn to explain the events in the cases in terms of other events, facts, or characteristics evident in the *same* case, we have to lift our explanation to a higher, more general and universal level. Thus, the idea of group norms which restrict productivity, for example, comes up as a manifestation of social control, a more generally applicable idea. Once the idea of social control is understood, a larger range of events than just group restriction of output is encompassed by our theories. These broader events would include, in this example, similarities among managers in the language they use and do not use with each other, differences between one group's language system and another's, the student's reluctance and embarrassment at using the professor's, or textbook's, language in the presence of other students, and so forth. Once this higher-level concept is understood, new events can be seen as instances of this or that process, and a more detailed and exhaustive inquiry into the specifics of the particular case may be undertaken.

There is nothing we can do to facilitate the first mode—that of inductive exploration—by writing words. That mode has to be set by the real students and teachers as they work together. We can, however, contribute toward the second mode—that of generalization —by citing references in the literature on interpersonal behavior and organizations. This will be the major strategy of the introductory comments that will appear at the beginning of each group of cases. In these commentaries, certain themes which unite the cases will be suggested. References are made to the literature in the field in the Introduction, pages 3–5.

Finally, we must acknowledge that every teacher, and every student, will see different aspects of the cases. Each will be discovering some things that are new and particularly relevant to himself, and not seeing some things that others find important. A student or teacher concerned with political behavior and power will interpret the cases quite differently from persons concerned with the more poetic, aesthetic, or humanistic aspects of experience. Although we advocate a behavioral scientific approach to the cases, and have found them particularly suitable to that approach, we believe there is something in them for everyone, regardless of discipline or interests.

We take a great deal of pleasure in acknowledging the help of friends and colleagues in the preparation of this book. The administrative officers of the Harvard Business School (Deans Stanley F. Teele and George P. Baker and Associate Deans Russell H. Hassler and George F. F. Lombard) provided encouragement during its completion. We thank them for their interest and also for granting permission to use case material copyrighted by the President and Fellows of Harvard College. In this connection we express our appreciation as well to Andrew R. Towl and Harvey P. Bishop, officers responsible respectively for case development and case distribution at the Harvard Business School.

Associate Dean George F. F. Lombard, before he undertook administrative duties at the School, was a colleague in the field of organizational behavior. He located and assumed responsibility for organizing a number of the case studies included in this volume; we wish to thank him for his help. Professor F. J. Roethlisberger and the senior author of this volume collaborated in the initial design and teaching of the course that ultimately led to this casebook and its theoretical companion. We take pleasure in thanking Professor Roethlisberger for his many contributions to this volume in particular and to our thinking in general. Mrs. Ruth C. Hetherston edited many of the cases and added considerably to their clarity. Miss Ann Allen assisted in the final work with the manuscript and proofs. The individual authors of the cases are acknowledged on page xiii, but we wish to thank them as a group here for diligent field work and the patience it takes to execute a piece of field research. Only those who have experienced this process understand the demands it makes of the researchers.

ABRAHAM ZALEZNIK
DAVID MOMENT

Boston, Massachusetts
Spring 1964

Case Source Acknowledgments

E XCEPT for the two cases indicated below, the cases in this volume are copyrighted by the President and Fellows of Harvard College and are used by express permission. In most instances the name of the company has been disguised. Also, in various cases, certain dates, quantitative data, and the identification of individuals, locations, organizations, and products have been disguised. Disguises so employed leave unaltered the salient characteristics of the problems which confronted the individuals, groups, and organizations involved. Case material of the Harvard Graduate School of Business Administration is prepared as a basis for class discussion. Cases are not designed to present illustrations of either effective or ineffective handling of administrative problems.

We gratefully acknowledge its authors' permission to include The Eastern Electronic Company case, and the permission of Northwestern University to use the Lightner Company series of cases. We also wish to acknowledge the work of the original field researchers, case-writers, editors, and supervisors who each had a part in one or more of the cases. They were Louis B. Barnes, Philip Borden, Hugh Cabot, C. Roland Christensen, James V. Clark, Peter P. Gil, Ruth Hetherston, Richard C. Hodgson, J. B. Kassarjian, Paul R. Lawrence, George F. F. Lombard, Thomas Miller, Walter Milne, David Moment, R. K. Ready, Fritz J. Roethlisberger, Samuel Robbins, A. H. Rubinstein, H. A. Shepard, Harold S. Spear, Dan Sydiaha, Marjorie Van Leuvan, T. North Whitehead, William F. Whyte, and Abraham Zaleznik.

Several cases are adaptations of material which also appears in separate research publications. These include Roethlisberger, F. J., and Dickson, W. J., *Management and the Worker*, Cambridge, Massachusetts; Harvard University Press, 1939, and three volumes published by the Division of Research of the Harvard Business School: Zaleznik, A., *Foreman Training in a Growing Enterprise*, 1951; Zaleznik, A., *Worker Satisfaction and Development*, 1956; and Zaleznik, A., Christensen, C. R., and Roethlisberger, F. J., *The Motivation, Productivity, and Satisfaction of Workers: A Prediction Study*, 1958.

ABRAHAM ZALEZNIK
DAVID MOMENT

xiii

Contents

Introduction   1

PART ONE   THE BROAD VIEW   7

Spofford Fabricated Products Company (B)   10
The Webbing Line   15
The Crandell Watch Company   41
The Eastern Electronic Company:
     A Problem in Liaison   51

PART TWO   GROUP PROCESSES   59

Observations and Interviews
     with a Small Group of Workers   63
Agricultural Equipment Company   119
The Briggs Box Company   154

PART THREE   INTERPERSONAL DYNAMICS   255

Howard Atkins and Joseph Wexler   259
Margaret Mahoney and Richard Carleton   266
Grosvenor House   282
Community Church (A)   314

PART FOUR   ENVIRONMENTAL CONSTRAINTS   323

The Watkins and Worster Agency (B):
     A Study of Interpersonal Relations
     in an Advertising Agency   325
New England Markets, Inc.   401

PART FIVE   LEADERSHIP AND CHANGE   453

The Lightner Company (A)   456
The Lightner Company (B)   469

The Lightner Company (F)   479
The Lightner Company (G)   490
Cold-Air Corporation (A)   501
Cold-Air Corporation (B)   514
Cold-Air Corporation (C)   528
Tremont Hotel (A)   534
Allmetal Steel Corporation   546

List of Cases   587

Casebook on Interpersonal Behavior

in Organizations

Introduction
Cases on Interpersonal Behavior
in Organizations

THE cases that appear in this book were selected, edited, and arranged in sequence while the authors were working on a companion textbook, *The Dynamics of Interpersonal Behavior*.[1] Although the casebook may be used in a variety of courses for many different purposes, the authors feel some responsibility for divulging their intentions, since this may help the user of the cases make sense in their grouping and sequence, whether or not this ordering is followed in practice.

Our over-all theoretical framework attempts to place the study of the individual, the group, and the organization in a logical relationship to each other. We are cutting across the boundaries of established disciplines in doing so. We are not unique in this—the approach is well documented as an interdisciplinary, problem-centered point of view. The foundation of our approach is our definition of the problems in which we are interested. Here we may diverge significantly from other problem-centered theoretical frameworks, similarly based on personality theory and sociological theory.

Our definition of the problem derives from outside of personality and sociological theories themselves. One historical origin is in the relatively atheoretical, or even antitheoretical, problem-centered approach exemplified in the early days of the case method at the Harvard

[1] Published by John Wiley and Sons, 1964.

1

Business School.[2]   A major emphasis here was, and still is, training prospective managers to be effective decision makers. In this approach, making decisions is the crucial operation; deliberate analysis, explanation, and prediction, the bases of scientific theorization, are tolerated only insofar as they help the individual make a decision. Idle speculation, or a divergent interest in truths that have no immediately relevant application, are confronted with demands such as, "What difference does the idea make—how does it affect your decision?" or, more bluntly, "So what?"

While our Business School colleagues have been working and reworking their programs aimed at improving the quality of business decisions, therapists and consultants of various schools of thought have been attending to the importance of the choice processes in the development of effective individuals and groups, regardless of occupational settings.[3]   Certain pathological conditions in groups, individuals, and organizations are accompanied by marked inability to make decisions or choices. It is around this strategic problem—the need for the individual to improve his capacity for making choices, and the parallel need for decision in groups and organizations—that our theoretical framework is constructed.

The individual is our center of attention. We are most interested in his processes of choosing. This is what we want to learn more about in our research, and what we want to influence by our courses and expositional writings. In writing as behavioral scientists there appears superficially a contradiction between individual choice and determination. If the behavioral event is determined, it would seem as though the event were not an instance of choice. As scientists, we study all behavior as if it were completely "determined." Our position is that it is only by understanding the determinants of behavior that one can conceive of *alternatives:* we can make choices only in situations where we perceive alternatives. When we do not see alternatives, our behavior is determined not by ourselves, but by forces of which we are unaware and which we cannot control directly.

The choice process marks the location of our central problem. Our strategy is to approach it through increasing understanding of the determinants of behavior—individual, group, and organizational. The ultimate actor, or chooser, or decision maker, is the individual, even when we are interested in group and organizational problems. In

[2] See, for example, McNair, Malcolm P., Editor, *The Case Method at the Harvard Business School,* New York: McGraw-Hill, 1954.
[3] See, for example, the final chapter in Robert W. White, *Lives in Progress,* New York: Dryden Press, 1952.

this respect, groups and organizations do not "behave" any more than numbers, such as stock prices, "behave"—the terms "group behavior" and "organizational behavior" refer to the behavior of *individuals* in groups and organizations, for the purposes dictated by *our* definition of "the problem."

To understand an individual's behavior, we need to understand the ways in which his personality is influenced by attributes of the groups in which he works and lives, the other individuals with whom he interacts, the organization within which he and his group work, and the cultures in which they all live. The organization of the casebook follows the direction set forth in the textbook, where the theory and its supporting research findings are discussed in detail. We start by looking at group processes and move on to personality and interpersonal processes, then to the organization and the culture, and finally to problems of leadership and change. This sequence reflects some of the realities of the phases of the individual's life cycle. He starts life in a group—the family—and his individuality emerges from the interaction between social processes and his biological constitution. Specific persons and his relationships to them influence him, and in turn are influenced by him. As his world and his self broaden, he is increasingly concerned with the environment beyond his immediate, face-to-face groups. Problems of leadership and change engage the working, living person as he attempts to cause effects on the world.

All the cases involve all the classes of determinants indicated by the section headings. Some courses may wish to use the cases in a different sequence, and may wish to use them for purposes other than those which our section titles suggest. In any event, each group of cases is introduced by comments which present our views of relevant themes in the cases included in that particular section. A listing of references follows.

REFERENCES

General

References which discuss the use of cases for learning:

Andrews, Kenneth R. (editor), *The Case Method of Teaching Human Relations and Administration,* Cambridge: Harvard University Press, 1953.

Benne, Kenneth D., "Case Methods in the Training of Administrators," p. 631 ff., and Slater, Philip E., "Displacement in Groups," pp. 725 ff., both in Bennis, W. G.; Benne K. D.; and

Chin, R. (editors), *The Planning of Change*, New York: Holt, Rinehart, and Winston, 1961.

Knudson, Harry R., Jr., *Human Elements of Administration*, New York: Holt, Rinehart, and Winston, 1963, Introduction, pp. 1–11.

Examples of case analysis:

Homans, G. C., *The Human Group*, New York: Harcourt, Brace, 1950, Chapters 3, 7, 13, and 14.

Zaleznik and Moment, *Dynamics of Interpersonal Behavior*, New York: Wiley, 1964, contains sample analyses in most chapters.

Zaleznik, Abraham, *Worker Satisfaction and Development*, Boston: Division of Research, Harvard Business School, 1956.

See also the Watkins and Worster case in this book, Section IV, p. 325.

Behavioral scientific theory and methods:

Zaleznik and Moment, *op. cit.*

Homans, *The Human Group*

Homans, George C., *Social Behavior: Its Elementary Forms*, New York: Harcourt, Brace, and World Inc., 1961. This volume also contains examples of analyses of case data.

Krech, D.; Crutchfield, R. S.; and Ballachey, E. L., *Individual in Society*, New York: McGraw-Hill, 1962.

Part I: The Broad View

Zaleznik and Moment, *op. cit.*, Chapter 1.

Homans, G. C., *The Human Group*, Chapters 1 and 2.

Part II: Group Processes

Homans, *The Human Group*, entire book.

Zaleznik and Moment, *op. cit.*, Chapters 2 through 5.

Roethlisberger, F. J., and Dickson, W. J., *Management and the Worker*, Cambridge, Mass.: Harvard University Press, 1939, pp. 379–548. This is a description and analysis of the Bank Wiring Room, from which the "Interviews and Observations on a Small Group of Workers" was taken.

Homans, *The Human Group*, pp. 48–80. This is another discussion of the Bank Wiring Room.

Zaleznik and Moment, *op. cit.*, Chapter IX—more on the Bank Wiring Room.

Part III: Interpersonal Dynamics

General:
  Zaleznik and Moment, *op. cit.*, Chapters V through VIII.
  Leary, Timothy, *Interpersonal Diagnosis of Personality*, New York
    Ronald Press, 1957.
  Sullivan, Harry Stack, *The Interpersonal Theory of Psychiatry*,
    New York: W. W. Norton, 1953.
The self-fulfilling prophecy:
  See, for example, Merton, Robert K., *Social Theory and Social
    Structure*, Glencoe, Ill.: Free Press 1957, pp. 421–436.
The interpersonal reflex:
  Leary, *op. cit.*, pp. 91–131.
  For detailed and interpreted case studies of individual development
    related to the study of interpersonal dynamics, see Robert
    White, *Lives in Progress*, New York: The Dryden Press, 1952.
The authority dilemma:
  See the history of Little Hans in Sigmund Freud's "Analysis of a
    Phobia in a Five-Year Old Boy," in *The Standard Edition of
    the Complete Psychological Works of Sigmund Freud*, Volume
    X, London: The Hogarth Press, 1955.
  Also see "The Interpretation of Dreams," in Freud, *op. cit.*, Volume
    IV, 1953, pp. 260–266.

Part IV: Environmental Constraints

  Homans, *The Human Group*, Chapter 4, "The External System."
  Homans, *Social Behavior: Its Elementary Forms*, Chapter 11, "The
    Nature of the Givens."
  Zaleznik and Moment, *op cit.*, Chapters IX through XI.
  Roethlisberger and Dickson, *op. cit.*, Chapter XXXIII, "Formal vs.
    Informal Organization," and Chapter XXIV, "An Industrial
    Organization as a Social System," pp. 525–568.

Part V: Leadership and Change

  Homans, *The Human Group*, Chapter 8, "The Position of the
    Leader."
  Homans, *Social Behavior: Its Elementary Forms*, Chapters 8,
    "Esteem," and 16, "Status, Conformity, and Innovation."
  Zaleznik and Moment, *op. cit.*, Chapters XII and XIII.
  Bennis, W. G.; Benne, K. D.; and Chin, R., *The Planning of Change*,
    New York: Holt, Rinehart, and Winston, 1961.

Part One

The Broad View

To lay the groundwork for this book, the four cases constituting this opening section anticipate the range of problems and processes covered in the remainder of the contents. The cases in subsequent sections will deal with four specific aspects of interpersonal behavior— group processes, interpersonal dynamics, environmental constraints, and leadership and change.[1]

Of the cases in this general introduction, the first, Spofford Fabricated Products Company, consists of five conversational events. In each of these, people in and around the work situation describe events in which they have participated, and present their reactions and interpretations concerning them. Although *individuals* do the talking, the challenge is to detect sentiments and evaluations that refer to *group* processes. To what extent, and in what specific ways, does a disturbance or "problem" within an individual reflect a group or interpersonal influence? What demonstrates that individuals are *not* disconnected, isolated persons on the job, but are tied to each other by bonds of shared feelings and social processes? What is the content of these shared feelings? What are the "social messages" carried by ostracism and one's efforts to influence others? These and other

[1] The sequence follows the theoretical scheme of a companion volume, Zaleznik, A. and Moment, D., *The Dynamics of Interpersonal Behavior*, New York: John Wiley, 1964.

questions may be pursued to help separate individual from group processes and attributes.

The Webbing Line case introduces the spectrum of analytical dimensions for group analysis—technological influences, job requirements, leadership, change, social status inside and outside the group, motivation, satisfaction, and productivity. Its data ideally allow the use of George Homans' conceptual scheme for the analysis of small groups.[2] It emphasizes the social meanings of technological objects and activities.

The data in the Webbing Line case also allow examination of relationships between personality and other factors. It is possible to detect how the unique individual "uses" the social and technical aspects of his work environment in his personal life style and defense mechanisms. Thus, the personal meaning of work and the group to the specific individuals can be examined in relation to the social demands placed upon them by the work group, and the technical and organizational demands made by the company's representatives. The social aspects of the individual's motivations, as well as the nonsocial, "job achievement" aspects, can be compared with each other and with the motives of the company, as represented by the group's external authority figures.

The Crandell Watch Company case provides an opportunity to analyze the differences among various groups' values, norms, and behaviors with respect to a presumably common technological item, time standards. Here we have industrial engineers, foremen, and workers from different groups expressing what work means to them and what the standards mean. The difference between the intentions of a plan and its consequences becomes clearly visible. Differences in the supervisory styles, or orientations, of different foremen stand out. The workers' actual motivations contrast sharply with some other groups' ideas of what their motives are, or should be. The social meanings of different kinds of jobs—"craft" work *versus* "production line" work, managerial "work" *versus* production work—appear. Similarly, the relationship between sentiments and social positions is clearly evident. We not only see "in-group" sentiments and behavior patterns, but also get a feel for intergroup relations, especially around conflict and communications problems. In this instance, "communications problems" are not simply language, semantics, "public speaking," or other "logical" issues: they get inextricably tangled

[2] See George Homans, *The Human Group*, New York: Harcourt, Brace, 1950, Chapters 1–6; see also Zaleznik and Moment, *The Dynamics of Interpersonal Behavior*, New York: John Wiley, 1964, Chapters 2–4.

with motives, group membership, and orientations toward authority. Their resolution requires considerably more than "using the right words."

The final introductory case—The Eastern Electronic Company: A Problem in Liaison—is strikingly different from the others. It involves higher-educated people, whose very jobs require of them an orientation toward problem-solving inquiry. The meeting described in the case has a beginning and an end and allows clear differentiation between "here-and-now" events and sentiments and "there-and-then" happenings. To some degree, the participants' actions may be seen as the political behavior of representatives of absent groups. Yet, at the same time, it contains a here-and-now reality of people doing things to each other in the meeting, socially and interpersonally. To some students, it may be appropriate to try to separate the problem-solving aspects from other aspects of the behavior in the meeting and describe more clearly some of the specifics of these other social and interpersonal aspects of the behaviors. At the same time, it is possible to see the processes and issues of the earlier cases manifested in different form within the world of science and engineering, among interacting scientists and engineers.

Spofford Fabricated Products Company (B)

At the Spofford Fabricated Products Company, which manufactures war products, Tom Jones, a member of the Standards Department, was speaking to Margaret Redcliff, a member of the Personnel Department. The date was May 3, 1943.

MRS. REDCLIFF: I see you're putting in a sliding scale of guarantees on the new AB job.

MR. JONES: We're having trouble in that group, getting the girls to make the rate. They're complaining the rate is too stiff and they can't make it. So we're guaranteeing 20 cents an hour extra the first week to any girl who makes the rate, 15 cents an hour the second week, 10 cents an hour the third week, and so forth. It's a swell system and works like a charm. One girl will crack through and then watch them all follow. It works, I know; I tried it before in a ticklish situation. Believe me, that other situation was plenty hot, and I thought I might get my fingers burned. I was plenty worried, but the girls cracked through. It worked swell.

MRS. REDCLIFF: Tell me about that previous situation and how it worked. I'd like to know.

MR. JONES: You know that CD job down on the first floor—that job on which there are seven girls. Well, they started that job last December. It settled down in a few weeks, so we took studies and set the rate sometime in February. It was a fair rate, not too stiff at all. But the girls claimed that they couldn't make a living wage on it. They all grumble in the beginning about any rate, so I didn't bother about it. I felt that in time one of the operators would decide to make the rate and then the others would follow her. But nothing happened; a month passed, so I got a little worried and had the operation studied again. We couldn't find anything wrong with the rate. It wasn't too tight. Well, believe it or not, in spite of this the girls took their case to the union sometime in

March. All the big shots got interested in the problem. I was plenty worried. Even Mr. Milton, the division head, came down to the floor and watched one of the girls for two hours. Finally I recommended a sliding scale of guarantees over a period of a number of weeks. I had my fingers crossed for a while. Wasn't sure it was going to work. But you know what? Within three weeks all the girls were making the rate; first one operator and then another gave in. Believe me, it works. At first I thought the division head was going to blame me. Instead he complimented me for making a good study and sticking by it. The rate I set was right. All that was needed was a little psychology to sell it. Well, that the way it goes, one damn' problem after another, but that one's over, thank God.

EVENT TWO

On May 5, 1943, Mary McDonnell, age 20, a member of the CD group, was sent to talk to Mrs. Redcliff because Mary decided to quit her job. Part of their conversation was as follows:

MRS. REDCLIFF: So you're planning to leave us, Mary. Why?

MISS MCDONNELL: I'm not feeling well. Don't know what's the matter, but the job's got me down. I went to my doctor, who said if I didn't have a rest I'd have a nervous collapse.

MRS. REDCLIFF: What's the matter with the job, Mary?

MISS MCDONNELL: Oh, I don't know. It's all right as jobs go. I guess it's me. I guess it's gotten under my skin.

MRS. REDCLIFF: What do you mean?

MISS MCDONNELL: Well, it's never been the same since I went to the union for the girls about the rate. I never did anything like that before. Perhaps I shouldn't have done it. I wanted to become an instructor, but killed my chance by going to the union about the rate.

MRS. REDCLIFF: What is this about the union and the rate, Mary?

MISS MCDONNELL: Well, you know last February, when they put a rate on that job, we felt it was too stiff. We told our foreman that, but he didn't pay any attention. They timed me on the job, and I didn't work too fast—just right, if you know what I mean. I liked the girls I was working with. We had good times together and they were working hard. We had no loafers on the job. It was a good bunch of kids until Angelina came along. Do you know her? She came in about two months ago, and before we knew it, she was getting out more than the rest of us. Boy, can she work—

and good quality, too. It isn't fair, though. It makes us look silly. We spoke to her about it, but she says she's not working for money. If the contract had been for anyone but the Navy, she'd have stuck with us, but for the Navy she says she'd do anything—just anything.

Just anything. Say where was I? I was telling you about the rate and the union. Well, the kids were sore about the rate, and when the foreman wouldn't listen, they said we ought to take it up with the union and asked me to be their spokesman. Well, I did, and believe me, did things jump around for a few days. Mr. Milton, the big boss, came down and watched me. He watched me for two hours. It was awful. I was trembling so much I couldn't work. I finally had to leave the floor and before I knew it I was crying and crying. Did anyone ever watch you for two hours? Well, it's a terrible experience. It gives me the creeps just to think about it.

They didn't change the rate. Said it was fair and offered us a bonus if we made it. The gang's never been the same since. It used to be a swell bunch of kids. We don't have any fun any more. No one speaks to Angelina. Say, you know Angelina, don't you? She's a funny kid, isn't she? She isn't eating her lunch at her bench any more. I guess we are pretty mean to her. But she did make us look silly—the way she made the rate and then some. . . .

EVENT THREE

On May 6, 1943, Mrs. Redcliff met Angelina Ricco, age 20, in the lavatory. Part of their conversation went as follows:

MRS. REDCLIFF: How's it going? Still pushing 'em out?

MISS RICCO (speaking quite fast and excitedly): I don't care what the girls think. I'd do anything for the Navy.

MRS. REDCLIFF: Have you a boy friend in the Navy?

MISS RICCO: Hell, I got a lot of boy friends in the Navy. I don't care if the girls don't speak to me. See if I care. Hell, I'm just nuts about the Navy. I can't help it if I work fast, can I? . . .

EVENT FOUR

On May 25, 1943, Mrs. Redcliff, while walking through the department, noticed that Miss Ricco had a new job. Inasmuch as in the opinion of the operators this job was considered to be one of the worst in the department, she was interested and went to Josephine Lunt, age 35, the forelady of the department of which the CD was a part.

MRS. REDCLIFF: I see Angelina has a new job. How come?

MRS. LUNT: Her quality was bad.

MRS. REDCLIFF: Really? I thought Angelina did a good job, both on output and quality.

MRS. LUNT: Well, her quality was slipping.

MRS. REDCLIFF: Come clean, Josephine. There's more to this than quality. You remember that you told me, when I was making my breakdown on that job, to watch Angelina, as she was your best operator, not only for speed but for the right method. I'm just interested, as this looks like a situation that I have seen in other factories. I'm interested in how you solved it. I'm not talking to anybody.

MRS. LUNT (dragging Mrs. Redcliff to a corner of the room): Well, let me tell you, Margaret, I think I can trust you. This business got me down. I spent nights lying awake about it. I had to do something. The girls on CD were upset. You know Mary almost left. I couldn't have it anymore. The morale of that group was shot to hell. Angelina was beating the rate. Do you know she turned out x units one day. Can you believe it? Finally I decided to check her work. Believe me, I had a hell of a time finding anything wrong. But for two weeks I spent several hours after work, checking her work. The slightest thing I could criticize I brought to her attention the next morning, saying if she didn't improve her quality, I'd have to transfer her to another job. I kept this up for two weeks, and finally I thought I had enough on her to transfer her. Honestly, Margaret, I had to do it. The situation couldn't go on any longer.

MRS. REDCLIFF: How did Angelina feel about it?

MRS. LUNT: She took it without complaining too much. I had to do it. And do you know within a week after the transfer, the girls were eating lunch with her and she was going over to them during rest periods. Can you believe it! I saw them walking down the aisles arm in arm.

EVENT FIVE

On June 1, 1943, Mrs. Redcliff happened to meet in the lavatory a group of girls from C department on the first floor. Miss Ricco and her sister were present.

MRS. REDCLIFF (addressing the group): I hear the testing department sent back a lot of your work today. What's the matter, the stock bad?

MISS RICCO (who had been combing her hair, began to gesticulate with the comb in her hand and pointed it at Mrs. Redcliff): You

don't think I'd tell you. I don't mean you personally; you know
what I mean. I've learned to keep my mouth shut around here.
Hell, every operator in the department knows what's wrong but
they're not talking—not to any supervisor, anyway. I'm sick of
the job I'm on. The company is a big gyp. I'm no machine.
They can't treat me like one, either. I'm flesh and blood too, but
nobody seems to know it. Josephine's not too bad. She's giving
me a break this week; she's letting me do some inspecting while
Rita is out on vacation. I'm going to be inspecting all next week
too. Am I scared!

OLDER WOMAN, but a new employee: Well, I hope you do a better job
than you've been doing on your old job. Half your stuff comes
through to me not finished, and I've got to take time fixing it up.

MISS RICCO: That's not true. I'm a good operator. I know every job
around here.

OLDER WOMAN: Just because you know the jobs doesn't make you a
good operator. One trouble with you is you're erratic. If you
don't feel like doing a good job, you don't.

SECOND GIRL: That's telling her.

OLDER WOMAN: I'm not saying you can't do a good job. You can
when you want to but. . . .

MISS RICCO: So that's your story. Hell, what if I am, you haven't
learned like I have to keep your mouth shut around here.

MISS RICCO'S SISTER: Come on, Angel, stop fixing your hair, let's get the
hell out of here.

Angelina and her sister left.

SECOND GIRL (to older woman): Well, you certainly talked up to her.
That's what she needs, somebody to tell her where she gets off. She
talks too much.

OLDER WOMAN (to Mrs. Redcliff): She's a loudmouth. I walked up
to the corner with her for lunch the other day and she talked
so loud I was embarrassed. And her language is vile, too. I'm
not used to so much swearing.

MRS. REDCLIFF: I know that's so, but she's not a bad kid. You can't
take her words too seriously. She's had a bad break in the last
few weeks.

The Webbing Line

W<small>HEN</small> Frank Waugh, a young member of the Harvard Business School research staff, had an opportunity to spend three days in the Lincoln-Harvey Manufacturing Company, he decided to devote his attention to the operations on a new conveyor which had been installed in the company three months previously. The conveyor, called the webbing line, was the only operation of its kind in the plant.

When Walter Hutton, production manager, had talked to Mr. Waugh about the webbing line during his first day in the plant, he had said, "You will probably see all kinds of problems on that line. I think that those problems arise, in part, because the line is so new and also because of the very fact that it is a conveyor. We have had no experience with that kind of an operation. The supervisor of the webbing line is one of our best foremen, but he has never had to run a conveyor. He is a craftsman, like everyone else here. He is still supervising the line himself directly. He has a large department, however, and will probably need some supervisory help eventually in running the line. The question is, what kind of help and who? We have to answer that one. I think the foreman has one answer, but I don't know whether it is the best answer. We still have many mechanical bugs in the line. We have difficulty ironing some of them out. We have had high personnel turnover on the line, all instigated by ourselves. We haven't yet settled on any permanent personnel for the line or even any definite personnel policies for those jobs. We have yet to make job evaluations and set a wage system for the line. So you see, we have many things to think about. Should we try to think about all of them at the same time, or are there some of them we should be thinking more about than others? After you finish your study, I'd like to hear your ideas."

THE WORK ENVIRONMENT

Lincoln-Harvey Manufacturing Company was one of the old companies in a medium-sized New England town. Control of the company was still in the family which had founded it.   There had never been a president with a name other than Harvey.

The company employed 1000 people, nearly all of whom lived in the town and its immediate environs.   Several of the people in the company were second- and third-generation employees, and members of the same families worked in the plant and office.   Management thought that the company had a "good reputation" in the community and pointed to its ability to hire "good, high-class" workers during the labor shortages of the Second World War and to the number of "old-timers" in the work force.   Over one-fourth of the employees had been with the company 15 years or longer.   The ethnic distribution of the work force reflected closely the pattern of the town: one-third Irish, one-third French-Canadian, one-third Yankee.

Most of the work performed at Lincoln-Harvey called for individual craft skills.   The employees in the manufacturing division were represented by three craft unions.   Mr. Waugh was impressed, in his overall view of the manufacturing operations, with the near absence of anything resembling assembly-line production.   There were a few areas with tables at which two or more people performed operations in sequence on a product, and some machines required the labor of two or three people.   But most of the work was of an individual nature in which the employee produced for either finished or in-process stock.   Many of those jobs called for varying levels of craft skills.   All employees were paid on the basis of either individual piece-work or an hourly rate; no group incentive rates were offered by the company.

The new conveyor was installed in the Finishing Department, which, in general, performed the finishing operations on all products produced by the company.   The other two departments produced parts but few finished products.   The superintendent of the Finishing Department was Paul Mathenet.   Henri Bouvier was the foreman directly responsible for the webbing line.   He had three group leaders under him, but he had turned over none of the responsibilities for the webbing line to any of his group leaders.   Both Mr. Mathenet and Mr. Bouvier were French-Canadian, as were 90 per cent of the employees in the department.   Exhibit 1 is a layout of the section of the Finishing Department for which Mr. Bouvier was responsible.   Exhibit 2 is a drawing of the webbing line.

The webbing line has been engineered by one of Lincoln-Harvey's large customers for the production of a new model of the customer's product.   The customer had insisted on the new design, and Lincoln-Harvey, lacking the equipment to produce the product, was presented

EXHIBIT 1

THE WEBBING LINE

Finishing Department—Henri Bouvier's Section

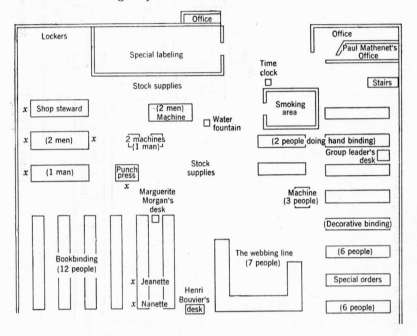

with the alternative of installing the webbing line in its plant or losing the customer's business to another firm. The name of the new conveyor was descriptive of the special feature of the customer's product as redesigned, and the product came to be known as a "web."

Installation of the webbing line in Mr. Mathenet's department began in the late spring, and the line was in operation after July 15. The company originally hired, with one exception, high school students on summer vacation to perform the jobs on the line. The top management of the company spoke to Mr. Waugh of the "bang-up job those high school students did on that line. They learned their jobs quickly and worked hard all summer." When the high-school students returned to school, Mr. Bouvier and Mr. Mathenet replaced them on the webbing line with permanent employees in the company.

Mr. Waugh observed the line one month after the change in personnel. The people named in Exhibit 2 are those who held the jobs at the time Mr. Waugh made his visit to Lincoln-Harvey. Management did not mention to him five of the jobs by any job title, nor did it

EXHIBIT 2

THE WEBBING LINE

Layout of the Webbing Line

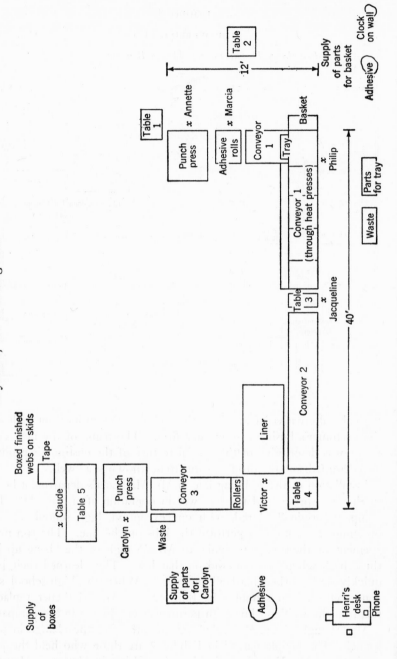

18

use names for many of the machines on the line. In Exhibit 2 the labels "punch press," "adhesive rolls," "basket," "tray," and the numbering of the conveyors were terms used only by Mr. Waugh in writing up his observations. Management did call Claude a "boxer" and Victor a "liner"; but it also called Victor's machine a "liner."

WEBBING LINE JOBS

Annette's chief job was to operate a punch press. She did this punch-press work on small metal strips; the total operation required approximately five seconds. When she had finished with a piece, she placed it on her side of the adhesive rolls.

Annette was also responsible for keeping the "basket" filled with parts, a supply of which was located nearby. The basket held approximately 100 parts and was emptied in 15 minutes. When there were only a few parts left in the basket, Philip usually called it to her attention and she would leave her punch press to get them. She also filled the basket whenever there were breaks in the work resulting from brief shutdowns of the whole conveyor. Annette always kept a small supply of finished work from her punch press on Table 1 so that pieces were available for the adhesive rolls when she left the punch press to fill the basket.

Marcia pushed the metal pieces through the rolls which applied adhesive and then, with a special instrument, spread the adhesive evenly over the strips. Management spoke of the adhesive rolls as "one of the bugs in the line." They hoped to be able to redesign them so that no operator would be required at that position on the line. In the fall, however, other "bugs" in the line were requiring management's more immediate attention, and no one was specifically working on the problem of the adhesive rolls. When Annette left her punch press to get parts for the basket, Marcia continued her work by getting pieces from Annette's finished supply on Table 1. When Marcia had completed her work on the metal strip, she placed it on Conveyor 1. Three or four times during a shift, Marcia had to fill the adhesive rolls with adhesive.

Philip's position on the line was referred to by Mr. Bouvier as a "key" position. Conveyor 1 was constructed to move the metal strips which Marcia had placed on the conveyor and the parts from the basket to this position at regular intervals. It also moved his completed work away from him and through the heat presses. The timing of the conyevor allowed him approximately 10 seconds to perform his operations on the product. His job was to place the metal strip on the part from the basket and to place over the metal strip a small part which he picked from the "tray." At Philip's position was a foot pedal which could be pressed to start and stop Conveyor 1 but gave him no control over its speed.

Philip was also responsible for keeping the "tray" filled with parts; this had to be done approximately once every two hours. To fill the "tray," Philip had to stop the conveyor so he could leave his work position; he also filled the tray whenever the conveyor was stopped for other reasons. If the conveyor was stopped for more than 30 or 40 seconds, the parts would scorch in the heat presses unless that section of the conveyor had been cleared.

Jacqueline inspected the product and scraped off any excess adhesive which had been squeezed out in the heat presses. At the time of Mr. Waugh's visit, excess adhesive had to be scraped from every one of the units on the webbing line. Jacqueline told him, "Scraping off the adhesive takes all the time I have, and I do very little inspecting." She did inspect some units, usually units which had been scorched in the heat presses when the conveyor had been stopped, and she threw those units into a box near her. When Jacqueline finished her work on a piece, she placed it on Conveyor 2. Conveyor 2 ran at the same speed as Conveyor 1 but could be stopped and started separately. The switch for Conveyor 2 was at Jacqueline's position.

The liner, like the punch presses, was not a machine unique to the webbing line. Its operation was regarded, however, as a relatively skilled job in contrast to the operation of a punch press. The wage rate for the liner operator was 60 to 75 cents an hour more than that for the other positions on the webbing line. Victor was responsible for operating the liner and for making setups and performing minor maintenance on the machine. The liner could be set to operate at the same speed as parts came to it from Conveyor 2. After the liner operation, Victor placed the unit on Conveyor 3.

Conveyors 1 and 2 were moving belts; Conveyor 3 was stationary and was connected to the table of Carolyn's punch press. At Victor's end of Conveyor 3 were two cylindrical rollers, much like the wringer on a washing machine. Victor guided the nearly completed "webs" into the rollers. Each "web" was pushed along the conveyor by the "webs" behind going through the rollers. When the conveyor was full, there were approximately 20 "webs" on it. If the liner operator were to send more units through the rollers than were being removed from the conveyor by the punch press operator, the units would jam on the line and in the punch press. The rate at which Victor put units on Conveyor 3 had to be regulated, therefore, according to the rate at which Carolyn performed her job. If units were coming to Victor at a faster rate than Carolyn was operating, Victor was to stack them on Table 4 and put them through the liner at Carolyn's rate.

Carolyn's job was to place an additional metal part on the product and to operate her punch press. When she finished her operations, she placed the "webs" on Table 5.

Claude put the "webs" in boxes, 60 per box, and piled the boxes on skids. He also supplied Carolyn's workplace with the necessary parts approximately once every hour. Claude filled in for the other operators on their jobs when they had to leave the line for short periods.

Management planned to establish an incentive wage payment system for the webbing line jobs, but no effort had been made to do so by the fall. The company wage and rate administrator told Mr. Waugh, "There is no point in my making job evaluations and setting an incentive system for that line until the jobs settle down into some more stable and permanent routine. They don't even have the machines operating as they want them yet."

THE WEBBING LINE PERSONNEL

Victor was the only employee who had been on the line since it had been put into operation on July 15; the other six had been on the line only one month when Mr. Waugh visited the plant. Philip and Claude had just been hired when they went to the webbing line. The others had been "borrowed" from other jobs where work was slack at that time—Annette from bookbinding, Marcia from decorative binding, Jacqueline and Carolyn from the sewing section. All those jobs had been in Mr. Mathenet's department, but only bookbinding and decorative binding were under Mr. Bouvier. Mr. Mathenet planned to transfer the girls back to their old jobs when there was work for them there. The four women suffered a loss of 30 to 60 cents an hour when they accepted the jobs on the webbing line.

Mr. Waugh asked Mr. Mathenet, "Do you think of those people as being only temporary on the webbing line, then?"

MR. MATHENET: Some of those people are too valuable to be left on the line. Take Marcia, for instance. She is much too valuable to us as a decorative binder to spend her time permanently on that job on the line. She will go back to decorative binding as soon as we get work for her in that section. She is wasting her skills now. This is true of Annette also. She is much more valuable to us in bookbinding. For most of the jobs on the webbing line, we can pick anybody off the street and have her doing a satisfactory job in an hour, so there is no sense in our using skilled people on the line unless we do it to keep from losing them entirely from the company during short periods when work is slack in their regular jobs.

MR. WAUGH: How long do you think the seven people now on the line will stay on the line?

MR. MATHENET: That's hard to say. Whenever work picks up in their old sections, then we will send them back. Philip and Claude are different, of course. This is their only job in the company, and we intend to keep them on the line. I hope Victor stays on the line too. He is doing essentially the same thing he did in his old department, and we need him on the line. His old job is gone permanently, so he should stay on the line. Jacqueline and Carolyn may be on the line longer than Annette and Marcia will be. Work in the sewing section holds out only about six months out of the year, so we always have to do something else with those people during the six months' shutdown in that section.

Mr. Waugh talked also to Mr. Bouvier about his plans for manning the webbing line.

MR. BOUVIER: I can hire anybody to come in and take over most of those jobs. I have those three boys who will be my key permanent people on the line. For the other positions, I can take anybody. When we have not much work in some sections, I can move some of those workers for short times to the webbing line.

MR. WAUGH: So the four positions where the women now are on the line will probably be high turnover positions.

MR. BOUVIER: Yes, there will be high turnover. In this company we always have heavy work in some sections and slack work in others at the same time. We will use those four jobs on the line for people who don't have work in their regular jobs. If we get filled up all over and have no one in the company to move to those jobs, we can always pull in some young kids for the work on the line.

Exhibit 3 presents certain personal information about the seven people who worked on the webbing line.

Mr. Waugh spent nearly all one day with Annette, Marcia, and Philip. Annette and Marcia were in their late thirties, married, and each had two children in high school. Annette had worked at Lin-

EXHIBIT 3

THE WEBBING LINE

Personal data

Name	Age	Service	Nationality Origin	Marital Status	Prior Occupation in Lincoln-Harvey
Annette	37	15 yrs.	French-Canadian	Married	Bookbinder and others
Marcia	39	19 yrs.	French-Canadian	Married	Decorative Binder
Philip	17	1 mo.	French-Canadian	Single	—
Jacqueline	20	14 mos.	French-Canadian	Married	Sewing machine operator
Victor	26	8 yrs.	French-Canadian	Single	Liner operator
Carolyn	18	7 mos.	American	Single	Sewing machine operator
Claude	19	1 mo.	French-Canadian	Single	—

coln-Harvey for 15 years; Marcia, 19 years. Both had left the company 2 years previously and had returned within the last year, so neither had more than several months' seniority at the time Frank made his visit to the plant. Annette's husband was in the regular army and had been stationed overseas much of his 13 years in the service. She lived alone with her children. Marcia's husband was credit manager for another local manufacturing company.

Before working on the webbing line Annette had worked in bookbinding, and she called herself a bookbinder. During her 15 years' service with the company she had worked, however, on nearly a dozen different jobs. Marcia had been in decorative binding during her 19 years in the company before going on the webbing line. Both bookbinding and decorative binding were regarded as crafts; in both, the work involved the skills of making a product by hand. Annette had two older sisters, Jeanette and Nanette, who worked in bookbinding. When she had been in that job, she had worked at the same table with her sisters. During smoking breaks, Annette spent her time talking to her sisters while they worked. Marcia always went with Annette during the smoking breaks. Marcia's father had been a foreman of one of the craft sections at Lincoln-Harvey and had retired the previous January after 57 years' service in the company.

Philip was 17 and on his first permanent job. He had been in school with Marcia's son but had quit school before graduating.

Annette and Marcia maintained almost a constant flow of conversation while Mr. Waugh was with them. Philip entered into the conversation several times but usually at his own initiative. Mr. Waugh was interested in the pattern of the conversation when Philip entered into the discussion. On one occasion Marcia had asked Mr. Waugh what his occupation was.

MR. WAUGH: I am a teacher.

MARCIA: A teacher! Oh, how nice! I really mean that. We really need teachers. My husband is on the school board—he has been for 15 years—and I have always been very close with teachers.

PHILIP: You say you are a teacher?

MR. WAUGH: Yes.

PHILIP: A teacher! Gosh! I don't like teachers.

MR. WAUGH: You've never gotten along too well with teachers, huh?

PHILIP: No, sir! I steer clear of them. I never did like school.

MARCIA: You know, Philip, you are really only hurting yourself by not staying in school.

PHILIP: I never made any money going to school.

MARCIA: Maybe not, but you are hurting yourself in the long run. You know that school really is good for you, and some day you will regret that you don't have more education.

PHILIP: I always hated to see school come around. I only went about two days a week. I never got caught either.

MARCIA: Maybe you never got caught, but it was only yourself you were hurting.

PHILIP: Your son cut a couple of times with me.

ANNETTE: My boy was very happy when school started this fall. He was getting tired of sitting around all summer.

MARCIA: Yes, so was my boy. He was very happy to go back to school. He really likes it very much. (To Philip) You'll realize these things some day yourself, Philip.

ANNETTE: Yes, what do you want to do? Work at that job all your life?

PHILIP: I don't mind it. This is easy. I am making some money at it too.

ANNETTE: Yes, but you wouldn't want to do it all your life.

PHILIP: I don't care. I think it's easy.

MARCIA (to Mr. Waugh): That job really isn't very easy.

ANNETTE: I'll say it isn't. Henri (the foreman) wanted to put me on that job when he first brought me over here. I tried it for just a day, and I said that that job was not for me.

MARCIA: You know, Annette, your son and mine are about as alike as night and day. Your son plays football and mine is a musician. [To Mr. Waugh]: My son plays in the band.

ANNETTE (to Mr. Waugh): My son wants to be a draftsman. (She elaborated at some length about her son's interest and training in drafting.)

During the day Philip entered into discussion with Annette and Marcia when they discussed local high school football, the World Series, and cars. On other topics, however, most of the conversation was between Annette and Marcia.

About 30 minutes before the lunch period[1] Marcia said to Annette, "I think I will go out for lunch today. I think I'd like to have a manhattan this noon." Fifteen minutes before lunch break Marcia asked Claude to take her place on the line, and she left the plant. When Mr. Waugh returned to the webbing line after his lunch, the operators were all back at work.

ANNETTE: Did you have a good lunch?

MR. WAUGH: Yes, did you?

ANNETTE: I always have a terrible lunch. I'm too lazy to fix more for myself than a cheese sandwich.

MARCIA: I enjoyed my manhattan.

ANNETTE (laughing): We are going to have to watch Marcia this afternoon. She isn't too steady.

MARCIA (laughing): I remember once when you had a manhattan.

ANNETTE: When was that?

MARCIA: I don't know, but I remember seeing you drinking a manhattan one night.

ANNETTE: At the Washington (Hotel)?

MARCIA: Yes, that's where it was.

ANNETTE: Well, that was a special occasion.

Marcia left the plant for lunch each of the three days Mr. Waugh was there, although the first day was the only day she was gone longer than 30 minutes. Annette brought her own lunch each day and ate with her sisters in the bookbinding area. Marcia talked to Mr. Waugh about her husband's company: "I talked to my husband about you, and he said he would be happy to have you come over to see his company." She also talked about going to a nearby city to see several popular shows and about other topics not related to her work at Lincoln-Harvey.

[1] Employees were allowed 30 minutes for lunch.

Annette talked much more about Lincoln-Harvey, particularly about her job in bookbinding. Very seldom during Mr. Waugh's day with the two women, however, did he feel that he was talking to either of them alone. Each woman talked as much as the other, and they usually talked to him together. They traded jobs several times during the day and never complained to each other about the other's work. Attitudes about the company and their jobs, as expressed by Annette and Marcia, are included below.

ANNETTE: My sisters have been bookbinders for 25 years, and I have been for 15 years. I guess it's just in the family. . . . I don't like this job I have now at all. I liked my job in bookbinding much better; in fact, I think that this is the worst job of any I have had. This is the worst job in the company. . . . It may be true, of course, that when they finally set the rates on this job, if I can make as much money as I could on other jobs I would like to have, I might change my mind about this job. Certainly one of the worst things about the job now is that I am making much less money than I was, and I don't like this cut in pay. So I do wish they would hurry and set the rates, because I'm not happy about the money I am making now. There are a lot of other things I don't like about this job, too, but if I could make more money, then I might change my mind about staying here. Right now, I wish I were back in bookbinding, but there's no work there for me now. I sure wish the salesmen would get on the ball and sell. That's the reason I have to be on this job now. . . . Don't get me wrong about the company though. This really is a wonderful company to work for. I've always worked for Lincoln-Harvey. Even after I had quit work, when I decided to work again, I had to come back to Lincoln-Harvey. I really don't worry too much about this job on the line because I'm sure that at Lincoln-Harvey everything will come out all right. . . . I don't know why it is that I feel this way about the company. Of course, my sisters and my friends are here. I didn't use to go out much at all, but lately I have started going out with Marcia and Jeanette and the girls they go out with. I'm a new member in that group. . . . I've known Marcia for a long time. I never knew any of the other people on this line, however, until we all started to work on it. I did know Victor a little before I took this job. He's an old-timer too.

MARCIA: This job gets me down. I don't like the monotony of it, just doing the same thing all the time. There is just nothing interesting in this job. This job holds you down to your position so much. Over in decorative binding it was so much easier. I could work as I pleased there. I could start when I pleased, stop when I pleased, take breaks when I wished. I was pretty much on my own. This is so much different here. . . . This is a good company to work in, however. The Harveys are very nice people to work for. They are a very good family . . . . I don't know why I like this company so much, but I do. A couple of years ago I quit. I thought I'd like a rest, and also I wanted a change. But I got tired sitting around home; there wasn't anything to do there. So I decided to work again, and I came back here. There's something about this place that drives a person back to it. I can't stay away. Of course, my father worked here. And my friends are here too. My closest friends here are Jeanette, Marguerite Morgan (group leader over bookbinding), Marie Henrion (timekeeper), and Annette.[2] Annette started going out with us only lately. . . . I really wanted to come back to work when I did. If I have to stay on this job, though, I don't know how long I will stay here. The worst thing about it, of course, is that I'm not getting as much money as I was. But still, I don't like the job anyway, and I don't know whether I'll stay here if I have to stay on this job. It's hard to leave this company, though.[3]

Mr. Waugh did not talk with other operators on the webbing line as much as he did with Annette and Marcia. Whenever he talked to Philip, Annette and Marcia joined into the conversation. He spent approximately eight hours standing near and watching the other operators, but they did not converse with him as Annette and Marcia had done. His observation was that Jacqueline conversed very little with anyone at work. A few times when the line was stopped, she walked over to talk briefly to Philip or to Victor and Carolyn around Table 4. She called over to Carolyn a few times at work, particularly on Mr. Waugh's third day there. Her remarks to Carolyn that day generally concerned thoughts about the company party, which was set for that night. Jacqueline was approximately 20 and had been married at the end of the summer. She talked to Mr. Waugh only in

[2] Mr. Waugh observed that Jeanette, Marguerite, and Marcia were among the best dressed women at work in the plant. They wore hose, heels, blouses or sweaters, and wool skirts at work. Marguerite wore a wool suit one day. He never met Marie Henrion. Annette was dressed nearly a well as the others the third day Mr. Waugh was in the plant, but the first two days she wore an old cotton blouse, slacks, flat heel shoes, and socks.
[3] On the third day Mr. Mathenet told Mr. Waugh that Marcia had requested a transfer to the Advertising Department.

answer to questions, and her remarks were always brief. One time he overheard her say to Philip, "When they set the rate on this line, they will probably set it at 5,000." Philip responded, "Oh, no, if they do that, I will owe the company money." Mr. Waugh later decided to talk to Jacqueline about the rate.

MR. WAUGH: Do you wish they would hurry and set the rate for this job?

JACQUELINE: I don't know. I don't know whether I'll like the rate or not.

MR. WAUGH: Are you a bit worried that they will set the rate too high?

JACQUELINE: They won't set it too low. (Pause) Oh, yes, I wish they would get the rate set just so we will know. I don't know that I'll be happier with the pay though.

During Mr. Waugh's three days around the webbing line, the work activities of Victor, Carolyn, and Claude were hampered by mechanical difficulties with Carolyn's machine. Her press was not punching the rivets properly. Her machine was "down" several times while new adjustments were made in the setup on the jig on the press; rejects at this position, however, continued to be high through the time Frank Waugh was in the department. Work did not flow through the last three stations on the line at the same rate as it did to Victor's position. At the end of the first day, Frank estimated that approximately two-and-a-half hours' work was stacked on and near Table 4, and at no time during his three days in the plant did Victor, Carolyn, and Claude catch up with the units produced by the others on the line. Carolyn's machine was watched and worked on several times by Mr. Bouvier, Mr. Mathenet, or a man from the maintenance department. During every smoking break a maintenance man also made adjustments on the press.

Carolyn received help with her job much of the time that her press was operating. Victor once explained to Mr. Waugh that "Carolyn has the toughest job on the line. She has more operations to perform than any of the rest of us, and the troubles she has been having so far with that press have slowed her down in doing the work she has to do, too. All those rejects break up the rhythm." The help she received consisted of someone's standing along Conveyor 3 and putting the parts on the web for her so that she had only to operate the press. She received this help several times from Claude and from Mr. Bouvier and Mr. Mathenet. A few times they operated her punch press, and on those occasions Carolyn put the parts on the web for them. When Mr. Bouvier was working with Carolyn there was little conversation between them. When Mr. Mathenet operated the press, the work was consistently of high quality.

MR. MATHENET: (smiling, to Carolyn): I can't seem to make it punch out any bad ones.

CAROLYN (smiling): Maybe it's me.

MR. MATHENET (smiling): Maybe that is it.

CAROLYN (after a pause): Come on and hurry up. We are falling behind. (Mr. Mathenet and Carolyn smiled at each other again.)

Mr. Mathenet talked briefly to Mr. Waugh about the difficulties they were having with Carolyn's machine.

MR. MATHENET: We are certainly having our troubles with that last machine on the line. I was down there this morning to see what I could learn about it. I like to do that because before I became superintendent, I knew nothing about the work in this department. I still have much to learn about the operations here. We still have a lot of bugs in the webbing line, but that last machine on the line is the biggest right now.

MR. WAUGH: It has occupied much of Henri's time, I have noted.

MR. MATHENET: Yes, it is a tough problem to lick, and I know that Henri has been working hard on it. Several people are trying to figure it out. We don't know what the trouble is yet, but I suppose we will lick it eventually.

Aside from the interactions which took place around the difficulties with Carolyn's punch press, Mr. Waugh observed few others on that side of the line. Victor talked very little to anyone. Only a few times did he overload Conveyor 3 so that the webs jammed in Carolyn's press, and each time he stopped loading the conveyor quickly and smiled at Carolyn. Carolyn and Claude talked together occasionally. On Mr. Waugh's third day in the plant, there was some talk, particularly between Carolyn and Victor and Carolyn and Jacqueline, about the company party they were going to that night. Several times Carolyn called out, "Tonight's the night," and Jacqueline responded, "That's right. Tonight's the night." One time Victor said to Carolyn, "Is tonight the night, Carolyn?"

CAROLYN: Yes, tonight's the night.

VICTOR: I'll bring a bottle of Seagram's Seven and fill you up tonight.

CAROLYN: You think so, do you? You'll probably just fill yourself up.

VICTOR: If that happens, I'll probably not even look at you then.

CAROLYN: No, you probably won't.

VICTOR: If I get that drunk, I won't be any good to you, so I had just as well not look at you.

CAROLYN: I guess not.

Victor told Mr. Waugh: "Tonight will be the first party in this company for Carolyn. I'll be interested to see how she makes out at the party. I don't know whether she knows what she is saying sometimes or not, but I'd sure like to find out tonight. If she's like she talks, a man would be a fool to pass that up. It should be a good party tonight."

Mr. Waugh estimated Victor to be approximately 26 and Carolyn, 18. Neither was married. Victor had worked as a liner for Lincoln-Harvey for eight years. Carolyn had worked for the company seven months. She was the only non-French-Canadian on the webbing line.

Claude was approximately 19. He had been in the United States for only two years. All other operators on the line had lived all their lives in the town in which Lincoln-Harvey was located. It was part of Claude's job to fill in for the other operators on the line when they had to be away from their work for short periods. While Mr. Waugh was around the line, Claude filled in for Annette, Marcia, and Philip a few times. Each time it was the operators who asked Claude to fill in for them. When Claude took the job at the adhesive rolls, however, he asked to trade jobs so he could operate Annette's punch press instead. Those requests occurred whether it was Annette or Marcia who was operating the punch press at the time. Claude was asked to fill in for Philip only once. He was unable at that position to operate at the speed of the conveyor and stopped the line to perform his operation on each piece. All of his work was scorched in the heat process and Jacqueline called that to his attention several times.

Claude served also to relay information to the people on the line, and at the end of the shift he told all the operators what the day's output had been. One time he told Annette and Marcia about the difficulties with Carolyn's press and later showed Annette two webs, one with the rivets properly punched by Carolyn's press and the other with the rivets incorrectly punched.

ANNETTE: Then it was all the fault of Carolyn's machine and not mine.

CLAUDE: Oh, it's all the fault of Carolyn's machine. Your machine is all right.

MR. WAUGH (to Annette): You were worried that poor quality might be your fault?

ANNETTE: I certainly was. I don't want to be responsible for that bad work. I don't want it to be at my machine.

When Mr. Bouvier talked to Mr. Waugh about Claude, he spoke of some changes he planned to make in Claude's duties. "Claude is a boy I am training to help me supervise the line. Next week I am going to put him on Philip's job. I want him to know all the jobs, and I think he needs more experience in Philip's job. When he knows that job, he will be able to fill in for any of the people on the line when they go to the washroom or when they are sick. When he is able to help out that way, then I shall teach him to keep some of the records for me. He can keep the work schedules for me, and he can order the materials we need at each position on the line. I have spent a lot of my time on the line because I wanted to learn the jobs. Now I am ready to have Claude begin to take over the direct supervision of the line and handle the paper work I have to do in connection with that work."

THE SUPERVISOR

While Mr. Waugh was observing the operations on the webbing line, he became interested in knowing more about the foreman, Mr. Bouvier. He had noticed that Mr. Bouvier was kept busy attending to the technical problems of the jobs under his supervision. Mr. Bouvier devoted much of his time to the problems of Carolyn's punch press, often standing beside Conveyor 3 putting parts on the webs for Carolyn. He also inspected all the webs Carolyn rejected because of defective operation of her machine and hammered many of the rivets down by hand so that the web could pass inspection. He spent much of his time looking at parts and finished work in all sections of his department. He was seldom at his desk.

Annette, Marcia, Victor, Jeanette (Annette's sister in bookbinding), and Marguerite Morgan (group leader in bookbinding) told Mr. Waugh that they thought Mr. Bouvier took his job too seriously and worked too hard, and they all expressed sympathy for him.

Mr. Mathenet and Nils Bjornstrom, the personnel manager, also talked to Mr. Waugh about Mr. Bouvier.

MR. MATHENET: Henri works very hard, too hard in fact. Not too long ago he was working here from 7:00 A.M. until 9:30 P.M. I called him in a few times and told him, "Look, Henri, you've got to stop working so hard. You are going to wreck your health. I want you to get out of the plant in the evenings." Well, I don't think he stays around until 9:30 too often any more, although he is here until 6:30 quite often. Sometimes now, though, he will leave at the end of the shift at 4:30. He is still working too hard, however, any way I look at it. Henri is a good foreman, however. He's good with the people, and he certainly knows bookbinding and the other operations in his section. He's one of the real old-timers here and full of skill.

MR. BJORNSTROM: Henri is a very hard-working fellow, always busy. He will always find problems to tackle. Henri is a very, very skilled man. He knows his jobs thoroughly, particularly book-binding. He is good to his people, too. He's not easy with them, he's a good disciplinarian, but I think they respect him. I think that Henri is our best foreman, over all. He is very conscientious and he does a good job. If he has a fault, it is that he works too hard. In fact, we have had to call him in a few times and practically order him not to work so hard. We have some foremen in the plant who would not work a minute of overtime, but for Henri, overtime is the rule. I think he is hurting his health. He doesn't look as well as he used to.

With these comments in mind, Mr. Waugh was pleased when Mr. Bouvier told him that he had some time to sit down and talk. Mr. Waugh's record of his conversation with Henri is summarized below. In all Mr. Waugh and Mr. Bouvier talked together a total of three hours.

MR. BOUVIER: Well, we have Carolyn's machine running now. It really has been causing us trouble, and it isn't settled yet. I just don't know what it is, although I do have one idea. (He described his idea for the solution of the problems with Carolyn's machine). I don't know, though. That's only an idea I have.

MR. WAUGH: I guess you've had a couple of quite difficult problems the last few days. I understand that you've had some trouble with the glue over in the bookbinding section too.

MR. BOUVIER: Oh, yes, that's been a very great headache. We've had to remake a thousand books. (He talked about the problems of the glue in bookbinding.) I know what to do, usually, when these things come up, though. I've had lots of experience, and I know these problems. I have to give my supervisors a lot of help on these problems because they don't know some of these things. But I have very good supervisors under me. They all do a very good job, all help me a lot. The people are very good too. We have very high-class people in here. These are all very good people, very dependable, very good workers. They all know their jobs very well. They can be trusted very much and they really don't require much supervision.

MR. WAUGH: How do you see the contribution you make to this operation as a supervisor then? What do you see your job as being?

MR. BOUVIER: I see my job as training my supervisors. That's my first job. And the thing I have to train them in first is how to get along with people. You know, some people are very sensitive, and you have to behave around them in a certain way. You just can't go up to them and start banging on the table and ordering them to do this or that. You have to be nice to them, take it easy with them, go slow with them. They're good workers if you know how to handle them. There are other types that will take advantage of you, and you have to know that type. You can't play around with them; you have to be direct and give them their orders and insist on them right from the start. You have to know the type that cries. There's always the type that will go off and cry, and you always have to know that type. It is very important for a supervisor to be able to know what types of people his workers are. I've always been very good at telling what kinds of characters people have. My wife always asks, "How do you do it?" She often tells me that she doesn't understand how I can do it so quickly with some people. I tell her I can just look at some people and I can tell what type they are. And I know how to handle those people. I can be tough with some of them if they're the type that you have to be tough with. I had one of those types once, a woman. Her supervisor would give her jobs to do, and she would say, "I won't do it." She would also tell the people around her, "Don't do that." She was definitely a bad type to have because she was not only not cooperating herself, but she was infecting some of the others around her. The supervisor couldn't do anything with her, so I said, "I'll go in and straighten this thing out." So I went up to her one day and said, "Now look, you can't behave this way. You were told to do this job this way, and now you not only are saying you won't do it, but you are trying to tell the others not to do it too. You can't behave this way." She said something or other sassy back to me, and I said, "Either you do it this way or we don't need you. We don't have to have you at all." Well, I left and when I came back later she was crying. But I knew this was only an act. I knew she was only doing this to soften me up so that I would get easy and let her have her way. Well, I didn't yield, and I said again, "You either do it this way, or we'll have to get rid of you." Well, we eventually did get rid of her. We had a hard time, but we finally found someone on the top floor who said he was willing to take her. I think he's always been sorry he ever did that, too. No, I've always been very good at telling what kinds of people I have under me and how I should handle them. This is very important for the supervisor to know.

MR. WAUGH: Would you be interested in telling me about these people on the webbing line?

MR. BOUVIER: Yes, I'd like to do that very much. Let's start with that first girl.

MR. WAUGH: Annette.

MR. BOUVIER: She is a very good type. She's a very good worker. She's a little slow, not the fastest worker we have, but she will get the job done. You can always depend upon her to do the job, and she will do it well. She's very good on quality. She's a very good type. Now let's take the second girl.

MR. WAUGH: Marcia.

MR. BOUVIER: Now, she is very smart, very clever. In a way, she's too smart. She is the type that will take advantage of you. She has to be watched. She's very smart and very fast and very skilled. But I'd much rather have that first girl than the second girl. The first girl I can always depend on. She'll always do a good job. She'll never take advantage of me. But that second girl is too smart for her own good. She'll take advantage of you in all kinds of little ways. If I didn't keep an eye on her, I know that she would be taking all kinds of advantages. Give her an inch, and she'd take everything. She wouldn't come to work until 8:30 in the morning if we ever let her get away with it. She's got to be watched. Now, Philip. (Mr. Bouvier leaned back in his chair.) Philip is a very good kid. He tries hard, does a good job, does what he's told, puts forth effort, is dependable, a very good kid. He has just one problem. I've talked to him about this one. He can't be a good worker, I've told him, as long as he stays out until two o'clock in the morning. He's got to get more sleep at night. Philip says to me, "How do you know I stay out?" I tell him, "I can tell just by looking at you in the morning. I can tell you've been out till two o'clock. You haven't had enough sleep, and you're fighting that. You are conscientious, and you want to do a good job, and you're fighting that. The two of them together, they're clashing, and I can tell it when I see you in the morning." Now, he's a good kid, he's trying hard, capable of doing a good job, but he's got to learn he can't stay out until two o'clock in the morning. Something else, he used to go to the smoking area a lot.   One day I went to him and said, "Now, Philip, I suppose you think you're getting a rest when you come in this smoking area. You are only kidding yourself. You're not getting a rest in here. Look at how small this area is and how little air circulates in this smoking pen. And all the cigarette smoke in this air. You are smoking, and you are not getting a rest. You are just kidding yourself. You are really tearing yourself down." Philip has to learn these things. He has a big future for himself, though. He is trying hard, he does have a lot of skill, a lot of ability, and he can do a good job. If he will just watch himself on some of these things, like staying out too late at night, he will make a fine worker.

MR. WAUGH: So you see him as a type you probably would like to have in your department, but a type whose character is not yet set. You want to help him mold that character so that he will be a good type permanently.

MR. BOUVIER: Yes, that's right. I want to help him get that character set so that he'll be the right type. He is at the spot right now where he could break either way, could go the wrong way. And then he wouldn't be any use to us at all. But if he can just keep away from staying out until two o'clock in the morning, build himself up, take care of himself, keep on doing a good job, trying hard, then he will really be a good worker. But I have to watch him closely now, not because he's doing a bad job, but because as you say, his character isn't set. I want to make sure it's set right. Now this next girl.

MR. WAUGH: Jacqueline.

MR. BOUVIER: Yes. She's the touchy type. I think her problem is that she's not strong.

MR. WAUGH: You mean not physically strong?

MR. BOUVIER: Yes. I think she needs a rest. She needs more good food and a rest. She's touchy now. I have to go very easy with her. I can't come right out and talk with her straight. She's very touchy, very sensitive. I have to be careful with her. Well, let's go to this next fellow here.

MR. WAUGH: Victor.

MR. BOUVIER: Victor is a very hard worker. He does a good job. He knows that machine. He ran one before he came here, and he's a very good worker. There's only one thing I have to watch in Victor. I think he drinks. He's the sort of person who I have to watch on Friday mornings after payday. I'm afraid he will come in drunk sometime. That is what is wrong with Victor. Otherwise, he is a very hard worker and does a good day's work for me. There is something else about him, however, too. You notice that he is between two girls. I think I will have to watch him in that spot. If those two girls get dissatisfied, I think they can probably work on Victor and lead him astray with them. He is also the kind who is not yet set, and I can't be sure that he will always be a good worker. I think maybe he could be led astray. If those two girls became dissatisfied, they could work on Victor and it would probably be Victor who would come to me with the complaint. The girls could work on him that way, so I'm going to have to watch this situation, I think. Something else about Victor, too, is that he is the sort of fellow who doesn't want to get ahead. He is probably satisfied to stay in that job. I don't think he wants to learn anything new. He is a good man on this job, but I don't see much else for him. Now that next fellow.

MR. WAUGH: Claude.

MR. BOUVIER: Yes, now he's different. He is very intelligent. As a matter of fact, he fooled me. I didn't think he was as smart as he is. But he has learned some little things around here that I never thought he could pick up. He has proved himself to me, so I have changed my mind about him. For him to learn those things he did, he had to hunt and dig for them. If something big comes along, learning that will be easy for him. If he can dig down and get the little things, the big things will come easy for him. So I'm training him. I think I can develop him. (Mr. Bouvier told Mr. Waugh what new jobs he planned for Claude during the next few months.) Yes, he's a fellow I can train. He has a good character, he works hard, he tries, he does a good job, he is smart. As I say, he fooled me; he is smarter than I thought he was. He would like to learn something new every day. He picks up new things all the time. That is how he is different from Victor.

MR. WAUGH: What about Carolyn?

MR. BOUVIER: Carolyn is a very good worker. She works very hard, does a good job. I think she works better alone, however; I don't think this is quite the job for her. The thing about Carolyn is that she calls attention to herself. You notice how she will talk to the others and call attention to herself. This is distracting to the other workers. I think she works better when she is alone where she can't disturb the other people so much. On this job, however, she's always calling to the other people. She is a good worker, however, and I think she will do a good job for me on this line. That is a hard job she has. We've had trouble with that machine, but she has done a good job all along and worked hard. She's

young, however, and like all these young kids; you have to watch
them. I'll have to see to it that she doesn't break the wrong
way. I want to keep her doing right. Of course, I will never
talk to her about how she calls attention to herself. I never talk
to the people about their private personalities like that. I just keep
aware of those traits myself and see to it that they don't get out
of hand.

MR. WAUGH: As you talk about all these workers, I get a picture of
a group of people you are going to have to keep your eye on but
who are, as a whole, doing a pretty good job.

MR. BOUVIER: Oh, yes, they are all doing a good job. And I like
them all and respect them. All the people in this company are
good people, I think. (Mr. Bouvier talked about the workers in
bookbinding.) I have no trouble with any of them. They are all
very high-type workers. (He then began to speak of his relationship, as a foreman, to the people under him.) I believe that a
supervisor should know the jobs, not just know how they are done,
but he should actually be able to do them himself. I can't do
any of these jobs as fast as the people on them can, but I can do
them, and I think that's very important. That's why you see
me working on some of those jobs on the webbing line. If you
know how to do the jobs and can show the people that you can
do them, then they will respect you more. It is important that
your employees respect you. Something else important for a
supervisor is that he be on the floor. Some of the supervisors
sit at their desks; I don't beleive in that. You never get to know
the jobs or the people if you sit at your desk. The supervisor
has to be on the floor; he has to be seen. That, too, will lead
him to be respected by his people. He can get around; he knows
what's going on; he can talk to them.

MR. WAUGH: Being on the floor and knowing how to do the jobs
helps you know the people as well as the machines better.

MR. BOUVIER: Yes, I have to do the jobs so I can learn something
about the machines. I don't know a lot about the machines so
I have to work on them to learn. I know a lot about books.
My work has always been in bookbinding, and I know books. I
can talk to the people about the books. I don't know the machines
very well, however. Something else that's very important about
my job and one of the things I teach my supervisors is how to read
this production schedule sheet. It is very important to be able to
read this form. After a supervisor has read several of these sheets,
maybe he thinks he knows everything. But I always tell my super-

visors that they should read every word of each sheet and should
then read it over again to be sure that they haven't missed something. Because sometimes there are small changes in an order
which, on the surface, look very familiar. (Mr. Bouvier gave an
example of a standard order which had had one minor change in
the specifications.) Some of the supervisors think this order sheet
isn't very important. It is just as important as the rest of the
job; just as important as knowing how to handle the people. Some
people think a supervisor shouldn't spend his time doing all this
paperwork, but it's something he has to do.

MR. WAUGH: So your job requires you to know people and how to
handle them, to know books and how to put them together, to
know machines and how to operate them, and to know the paperwork and the things required by the company.

MR. BOUVIER: Yes, those are all very important, and they are all part
of my job. Those are the things I train my supervisors in. It
is very important that they know all of those things.

MR. WAUGH: And I get a picture that you like this job very much and
are very interested in it.

MR. BOUVIER: Oh, yes, I'm very interested in this job. The part I
like best, of course, is studying the characters of these people.
That's a very fascinating study, you know. All my life, I've been
very interested in people. You know, when I was young, I wanted
to be a doctor. I liked people, and I wanted to help them. I
thought that if I were a doctor I could do the most to help people.
But my father died, and one thing came after another, and I never
did get to be a doctor. That is still what I would like, though.
I want to help these people. That's what I try most of all to do.
So I study their characters, study their jobs, study the books—I
try to keep things going right. I think that is the way I help the
people. That is what I am most interested in.

MR. WAUGH: This is the way you can be a doctor even now.

MR. BOUVIER: Yes, that's very much so. This is the way I can help
the people like I always wanted. You know, sometimes, and I'll
say this is true, sometimes I probably work much too hard on
this job. Some people have told me that I'm foolish for working
so hard. I admit that there have been times when I have been in
here late at night; I have worked long hours and I have worked hard.
I have been told several times that I should not stay here at work
so long, that I should go home at the end of the shift and rest.
But this is the way I help these people. I can't work too hard
because everything I do is to help the people. As long as I'm
helping the people, then I'm getting satisfaction. I'm not like

some people who worry about the job all night. I can go out with my wife, I can pick up a book and read, and I can enjoy the book and enjoy talking to my wife. I'm not worried about the job because I have stayed here until I have been satisfied. Yes, it is very important to me to be able to help these people. That is why I do all these things.

MR. WAUGH: I don't want to switch things on you too much, but you've been talking a lot about the things that give you satisfaction on the job. I am sure that they are very real satisfactions. I wonder if there are some things about the job that you don't like to handle. I wonder if we could talk about some of the things that you like least about the job.

MR. BOUVIER: I don't think there is anything like that. The part of the job that I know least, I suppose, is the machines. But I get a lot of help from my boss on that.

MR. WAUGH: Mathenet?

MR. BOUVIER: Yes, he knows machines. He used to be a tool and die maker. He knows how the machines and tools are put together and how they operate. He can think of a lot of things about the machines that I wouldn't think of. I can tell him a lot about books. When he came here, he didn't know anything about bookbinding. All of his training was in machines. He knew that. So I train him in books, and he teaches me about the machines.

MR. WAUGH: I'm getting the picture then that you and Mathenet get along very well together and complement each other very satisfactorily.

MR. BOUVIER: Oh, yes, we get along very well together. He helps me on the machines; I help him on the books. And I know the people too.

MR. WAUGH: As you talk, I get a picture that you don't feel much pressure on you from the management above you. The pressure you feel, in a way, is keeping on top of the people, the jobs, and the operations that are under you.

MR. BOUVIER: All that I am expected to do is produce so much. If I do that, then everything is all right. They know I am doing a good job and they don't bother me at all. I like all the people in this company: Mr. Lincoln (vice-president), Mr. Welton (vice-president), Mr. Harvey (president). I like my superintendent, Mr. Mathenet, and the people in the engineering department, too. We get along fine, all of us together.

MR. WAUGH: Your principal interest is in keeping on top of the people and the jobs beneath you.

MR. BOUVIER: Yes. I have to keep on top of the jobs and the people.

Those are my responsibilities.

MR. WAUGH: If you didn't keep on top of them, you're afraid that maybe some of the people would take advantage of you, and things would get out of hand.

MR. BOUVIER: Yes, that's what would happen. I have to keep the people respecting me. People have to respect you if you are going to be a supervisor. That is very important. But if I know the jobs and the people, if I know how to handle the people, they will respect me and then everything will work fine.

MR. WAUGH: And you won't be taken advantage of.

MR. BOUVIER: No, that's all I have to look out for. (Pause) Well tell me a little about yourself. Are you going to some other companies?

Mr. Waugh told Mr. Bouvier something about himself and the nature of his research. Soon after that the two parted for lunch.

Before Mr. Waugh left Lincoln-Harvey at the end of his third day he had a short talk again with Mr. Hutton, production manager. During the conversation, Mr. Hutton said, "You should come back next Tuesday. Paul and Henri and I are getting together then to talk over the problems we see on the webbing line. I guess Paul has had to spend some time around the line lately because of some mechanical bugs we have had there, and he suggested that while the line is fresh in his mind, he and Henri and I sit down for a couple of hours and review the plans we have for the line and the steps we have taken. I don't know specifically what Paul plans to say or to suggest we talk about when we meet Tuesday. In fact, I don't know what I want to say then either. It might be an interesting meeting, though. As far as I know, we are in no crisis position on the line, and I don't think anybody feels like they have to put the heat on anyone. Yet I'm sure that we do have plenty of things to talk about. I mentioned some of them to you when we talked two days ago, before you went down to see the line. I may raise some of those questions Tuesday, but I'm not sure about that yet."

The Crandell Watch Company

THE Crandell Watch Company employed 1,000 people in manufacturing watches, compasses, and other precision instruments. One of the major departments of the company was devoted to repairing and adjusting. During the summer of 1952 the management of the company decided to introduce a system of standard times for the various job operations in the production and repair of their instruments. To carry out this program they hired Johnston Associates, a consulting firm, to work with them in developing and installing the standards and in training Crandell people to continue the work.

During the early stages of the introduction of time standards into the shops, Carl Conway, an interviewer from the Harvard Business School, visited the company. Mr. Conway talked with several people in various positions about their reactions to the time standards plan, including two foremen and a worker in the instrument repair shop, a foreman and a worker in the crystal and lens grinding shop, and the chief industrial engineer.

Mr. Conway had the following conversation with George Jackson, one of the foremen in the instrument repair shop, where a rough system of standards had been in operation for about six months:

MR. JACKSON: We had one big problem in this shop: how to rate the men in their work output. We had to find a way of determining who is doing his work and who is laying down. Before, we couldn't tell anything about how to rate the men. Mr. Brill, why don't you come over here and tell us what you know about this problem of rating workers?

Charles Brill, another foreman in the instrument repair shop, entered the conversation.

MR. BRILL: It's like George said. Before, we had nothing much to judge the men by. No criteria were spelled out. No facts. When we evaluated a man and his record it was always on the basis of our own subjective reactions, and can the fellows put up an argument with that method! But now we've got it licked. We got standards in this shop. Now we know without any argument if a guy comes up to them or not. We're getting better production too.

41

MR. CONWAY: You have standards working here?

MR. JACKSON: Yes, we've had them about six months. I guess we are the first shop to establish them in the plant. Charlie and I put them in ourselves and they are still on a rough estimate basis. The Johnston analyzers haven't clocked the operations yet. But even with this rough method, production has gone up some 30 per cent. Before we got standards, it was difficult to rate these workers. I found that if you watched them and saw how they worked and what they said about their work, you could make some sort of estimate. This, however, was very subjective. We had no criteria —now we know just how to look at the problem.

Let me show you. Look at this ledger. Here we have each worker's name in the left-hand column. Next to it we have the number of instruments he has worked on and the extensiveness of the repair, while on the right we have the standard for each instrument. You see on this page, we have 2.5 in the standard column. That means it should take a little over two hours to repair that type of instrument. Now you see this worker's record before me—he was 30 per cent below standard or below normal for last April. We had a talk and he said he'd get his production up. In May, he was 20 per cent below normal. A little better, but still not too good. In June, 19 per cent below normal; in July, 15 per cent—and so on. You see, he is consistently below normal. The trend is established. When his recommendation came up for a pay advancement last month, I had the facts to confront him with. So I didn't recommend him for production.

Now here is a man named Britten. His production is also low— just look. In April, 60 per cent below normal. May, 30 per cent below. He did a little better after he told us he would try harder. Here in June he was still 40 per cent below standard. Since he was ill, we accepted it as the same as the previous month. But in July and August no improvement. He says he's sick. Now for September, I just figured out his report and he is below normal again. I won't recommend him for any pay advancement. In fact, I dropped him back from the fourth pay step to the third. The fourth step calls for meritorious work. He doesn't deserve that status, since he isn't earning it according to the standards. He got up to that step mainly on the basis of seniority, not amount of work.

The next day Mr. Conway talked with Edgar Burkhart, one of the workers in the instrument repair shop. After a few comments, he asked Burkhart about his working conditions and if there were any problems.

MR. BURKHART: Problems, we got them! The problem of fixing watches is getting tougher everyday. You know you just can't decide what must be fixed in these instruments. You can't fix one part without checking and fixing other parts. You've got to spend time regulating these instruments. You can't do it in any set time limit. Now, when you make something new like this coffee lid [he picked up a lid lying on his bench], one worker can cut out the circular metal, another can mold it in the present shape, and another can paint the sides. You can do that with coffee lids, but you can't do that when repairing these instruments. When they build a new instrument, one guy puts this part in, another fellow puts another part in, and so on. It works pretty well, then, if you want to figure out motions and time. But even these new parts oftentimes don't work. They keep a troubleshooter around who does nothing but tear a watch down and look at all the parts and see why it won't run. How do you time his operations? Our work in repairing watches and compasses is something like the troubleshooter with the new instruments. You just can't fix up one part of the instrument like they think up there and assume the rest is all right. Just because it works fine here in the shop and through the preliminary tests doesn't mean it'll work all right. A week from now the thing will probably be back in the shop and it's all to do over again.

MR. CONWAY: You think that there will be trouble with the time standards they have in this shop?

MR. BURKHART: Will there be trouble? Why, there's plenty now. You ought to hear what the other workers are saying about it. Just talk with them. I wish you could go with me and listen to their gripes. None of them like it—least ways, not the ones I've talked with. Things have sure changed. This working under a time makes me nervous. You work under a strain anyway with these sets, and then you go and put these time standards on it. It's just too much for me. You know one of the best repairmen we have in this shop gave the foreman two weeks' notice that he was going to resign. He told me they kept asking him what he wanted to leave for and he just told them it was something "personal." But I know and so do the other workers that he is through with this standards stuff. You think things haven't changed—well, you just look around and talk with the fellows.

That afternoon Mr. Conway talked with James MacDuffy, a foreman in the shop where crystals and lenses were ground. They had met the previous day at a supervisory training session, which most of the workers in the crystal and lense grinding shop, as well as Mr. Conway, had attended. A film made by the Johnston Company to demonstrate the results of the time and methods studies in the shop had been shown at the meeting.

MR. MACDUFFY: The girls and I are enjoying your visit here. If you have any suggestions about the shop and its improvement, I would very much like to talk about them.

MR. CONWAY: I don't have anything to recommend, Jimmy. As I said yesterday, I'm here trying to learn from you people.

MR. MACDUFFY: Well, I guess you saw most of the operations the girls do here in the shop. You know, we try to keep everything going well here. I want the girls to be happy in the shop and I think they are. Just yesterday I was away about an hour in the morning returning the film projector, and in the afternoon I was away nearly 3 hours getting my picture taken for the plant paper, and the girls went right along with their work just as if I was here. I know that is true. Other people have told me how well they work when I'm away. I don't have to get after them. You saw the film we made in the shop with the Johnston Company?

MR. CONWAY: Yes, I did. Who was the girl doing the operations?

MR. MACDUFFY: That was Jane, our baby here. You know, the girls chose her to appear in the film. You saw how they all enjoyed the showing of the film yesterday? Well, they like to work here. The girls know what there is to do in the shop. If some girl lags on the job the others get after her for sure. Just the other day, one of the new girls was taking longer than she should at the morning coffee break. I was going to speak to her, but I didn't need to. Mary and a couple of the old-timers just got her in the corner and told her she had better straighten up and stop taking so much time, for it wasn't fair to the other girls. That's the last I heard of the coffee problem with the new girl.

You know sometimes we are under pressure to turn out a "hot" order for immediate delivery. Those orders have come down here as late as three o'clock in the afternoon. If we have work to do and we know that an order has to go out before we go home, all the girls really pull together. Joe usually runs the inspection set and the others trade off on various tasks to get the work done. I feel that they are fine and I think they like to work here. You know many suggestions come from the girls. Sometimes I think of the suggestions about the same time as they do, but I always let them tell me first. I don't say, "I've already thought of that." You know suggestions that are listened to make the girls feel they are a part of the operation here, and that is very important. A good attitude in the worker is what I work for.

MR. CONWAY: How do you get such an attitude?

MR. MACDUFFY: I take an interest in the girls and in their work. I know how well they are working. I think their attitude about accidents in the shop is important. Just this morning, Mary told me that a couple of shop chairs were about to fall apart. I consider that valuable. Charlie is fixing the chairs right now. Also I watch how they learn the job—if they make any notations when we explain the job to them and also how they perform the job. When a new girl comes in I watch how well the older employees explain the job to the new one. I think that is very important when it comes to determining if a girl is a good worker or not.

You know, people have different limitations. I don't think I could ever play the piano very well. Some of the girls have a good attitude about the shop, try hard, do a fairly good job. I think they deserve a bit of recognition. Now some of the girls, like Mary and Ann, have good attitudes and also are excellent workers. They're the best we have in the shop. Mary can do anything in here. You know, she's been here ten years. Her work is always high. There are others who don't do as well, but they try. I feel they ought to get raises, too, even though they don't turn out as much production. Some workers can do 30 units a day and others can only do 20. If the worker who turns out only 20 a day has a good attitude and works hard, I always try to help her up to a higher pay bracket.

Sometimes some of the girls get a little irritable, but we get along pretty well. You know some of that work is very intricate and tedious. I change the girls around when I see they are getting tired of one job. I don't want them to get too tired or too unhappy. So practically every girl in here can do more than one task. That way they keep interested, and such a procedure sure helps when a girl is sick or we have a rush order to get out. The girls change off on the various jobs until the order is filled.

MR. CONWAY: What do you think about the film we saw yesterday in the shop?

MR. MACDUFFY: Oh, that was quite an experience. The girls really enjoyed making that film. Like I said earlier, they all voted for Jane to appear in the picture. The ideas for the new unit came from this shop. It was quite a work improvement. It actually makes the operation easier and a worker can do far more than before.

MR. CONWAY: Do you look for any change in the shop with the introduction of the time standards?

MR. MACDUFFY: No, I don't think so.   You see, most of the work we
do in here is on an individual basis.   The gasket assembly and a
few other tasks can be improved by methods analysis, but you
saw that in the film.   The other tasks?   Well, I just don't know.
I don't think much will happen.   I'm sure we can keep our production up according to the standards they might set.   And, like
I said, I think the right attitude in the shop is very important when
it comes to work.

When Mr. Conway left Mr. MacDuffy's office, he talked with
Mary, one of the workers to whom MacDuffy had referred.

MARY: Where are you from?

MR. CONWAY: I'm from Boston.

MARY: I live just outside of West Branch.

MR. CONWAY: Isn't that quite a distance from here?

MARY: About 42 miles each way.   It takes me about an hour to come
and an hour to go home, sometimes longer when the traffic is
heavy in the evenings.   But I don't mind.   I've worked here for
ten years.   I came in 1942.

MR. CONWAY: How have things been in all that time working here?

MARY: You mean the people?   Well, during the war years everyone
pulled together.   But I've seen quite a few inhuman things since
the war.   A friend of mine who works for the Lintel Supply Company—you ever been there?   [Mr. Conway shook his head.]   Well,
they have certainly been making things rough since the war.   My
friend told me if you make one piece over what the groups want
you to do, no one will speak to you the next day.   The family
feeling is all gone.   Why, during the war, my friend said they
were so friendly there.

MR. CONWAY: What does your friend think brought about the change?

MARY: People are just different.   They are just more selfish than
they were during the war years.

MR. CONWAY: What do you think about it?

MARY: Well, they aren't that bad here.   We aren't pushed like my
friend is.   Why, at the Lintel Company she says people don't even
talk to each other, and they have to keep up all the time.   They're
on a standards system, you know.

MR. CONWAY: No, I didn't know.

MARY: Well, they are.

MR. CONWAY: What do you think the motion studies being done here will do, if anything?

MARY: I know what they tell us. They say it won't increase work and we'll be able to turn out more goods at the same rate of work as right now or even less.

MR. CONWAY: Do you think that is correct?

MARY: I don't know. I don't think much of anything will happen in here since there aren't too many operations they can time. Take the film on the gasket assembly, that's where the motion studies can be applied. I don't see how they can simplify the polishing process. They did have those analyzers in here with stopwatches. They timed the various motions. They may be able to set time standards on that operation. All I hope is that they don't start rushing us like they did where my friend works. I wouldn't want that.

Several of my friends in the other divisions of the plant are more worried than we are here. Down in the Repair Department some think they will lose their jobs because of this new standards stuff. Just the other day I heard that someone had thought of a new brainstorm whereby several men in one operation would lose out if they adopted the new method. Three men using the new method could do the work of some 20. That got several of the men scared about these new motion analyses. I got to thinking about it myself when I heard that.

Mr. Crosley, the chief industrial engineer, talked to Mr. Conway about the new program as follows.

MR. CROSLEY: In my estimation, this company has been working on an industrial setup as outdated as 1750, or maybe a little earlier. [He laughed.] All I know is that when I came to the company about three years ago, little had been done to improve production and cost conditions. You see, our costs are too high in comparison with our production and our repair output.

One of the basic reasons for this trouble stems from the fact that we had a very poor procedure for establishing work assignments and job responsibilities. With the old system, the one that the new time and motion studies are designed to replace, the workers were the ones who literally decided what was to be done in the manufacture and repair of our instruments. Well, the line supervisors helped some, of course, but in the main, the workers made the job decisions. Particularly was this true in the repair department, where the time standards were most needed.

How did things work in that department? Well, to begin with, it was the worker who surveyed a particular task, outlined the kinds of repair to be done, and requisitioned the necessary parts. In short, the company's authority to run the line was for all practical purposes in the hands of the workers. Oh, don't get me wrong, the supervisors were over the men on the job, but the actual work decisions were made more by the workers than by the supervisors. The supervisors had only a partial notion of what each job entailed. Problems and pressures arose in ordering parts and supplying them at the right time and place. Supervisors got tangled up in their orders; they didn't always keep enough of the right parts available, because they had no way of estimating requirements. They had no idea how long an operation should take. In short, the supervisors didn't have the authority to carry out the duties that management had assigned to them.

Before I arrived at the plant, the company had made some effort to correct this problem. They had set up a board to analyze our overall production methods at the plant. The job included manpower, equipment, tools, floor placement, but nothing on individual job operations. Working within the framework as outlined by the board, and drafting anyone with a set of brains who happened to be available, we did the best that could be expected in a short length of time.

The board, which is now dissolved, made a lot of fast decisions, some of them mistakes. Also, the board's recommendations were never very carefully checked in practice. They were forced through by the necessity of getting something done. But the standards plan which is almost ready to go into operation will correct these mistakes. A three-step operation is involved in the new plan. Let me show you what I mean. [Mr. Crosley produced pencil and paper and outlined the three steps as he talked.]

In the first place, an overall analysis of the plant's equipment, manpower, and layout had to be made. The board I mentioned sewed that up very fairly. With only a few changes here and there that work can be salvaged, so the Johnston Company assures me.

Now the second step involves an individual job analysis. This means that a careful study must be made of every operation in this plant. The various job operations in the manufacture and repair of our instruments must be analyzed in order to establish the most efficient methods of work. Methods of improvement must be found for literally hundreds of operations. These methods are to be devised during the intensive analysis period now nearly completed by the Johnston Company. Fact is, the Johnston Company has just made a film of the girls polishing the lenses, which demonstrates to the workers that by changing a few operations here and there, by introducing some new equipment in certain operations, the same worker can produce two to three times more than previously. This film clearly illustrates the possibility of doing similar studies and improving methods in practically every part of the plant. Now the third and final step in the new reorganization will be the establishment of time standards.

We have given extensive training to about ten analyzers chosen from the workers of various departments. They are to go into the shops with especially prepared charts and stopwatches to study and to clock each separate operation now being performed by the individual workers. The plan has been under way for about two months, and I look for another six to eight months before the time and motion studies have been completed, the workers familiarized with the new tasks, and the standard for each job established. This is no minor undertaking; but with time and patience we can put this company on the efficient production and cost basis which it badly needs.

MR. CONWAY: How do you think the program will be received by the supervisors and workers?

MR. CROSLEY: I'm glad you brought that up. Careful steps are being taken to prepare the way. The demonstration film I mentioned is just one of many techniques suggested and adopted by the Johnston Associates. We have made up right now some five such films. They are to be shown to the workers in all departments of the plant. Also, the first and second line supervisors have been exposed to a series of training sessions and lectures conducted by the Johnston Company. Each afternoon as many supervisors as can be spared have been going to these sessions, which illustrate, explain, and train them in the new program. In short, we are selling the supervisors right down the line on this program. We are showing them that the new standards will actually make their jobs easier. This new organization is designed to place responsibility in the hands of top management for planning the jobs, deciding about the parts for repair, supplying the materials, and determining the work schedule. All the first line supervisors will have to do is to sit back and see that the work is done. Actually, we here in the front offices will do the thinking for them; this is as it should be. We will ease their work load by taking this responsibility out of their hands, where it has no business being in the first place, and put it in top management. Furthermore, by passing the directions down the line, instead of the prevailing system of individuals going in several directions at the same time, we will place authority for decision making on the line in the hands of the line supervisors, as well as restoring responsibility for major changes to the hands of top management. As it is now, the supervisory staff hardly knows what's going on. As a consequence, we have conflicting ideas, wasted motion, responsibility where it doesn't belong, and directions coming from the bottom up when they should go from the top down.

MR. CONWAY: So far, what have the responses to the new program been in the plant?

MR. CROSLEY: Oh, we can't sell everybody. We'll get resistance. But the system will work, and once the workers get used to it, they will see how much better this system is in comparison with the old method. Like I said, we are selling the supervisors first. They in turn are going to sell the workers on the method. Why, I've got some supervisors really enthusiastic, so much so they are selling others. They think the ideas are great. The plan is all set. It is perfectly worked out on paper. We now only need to complete the mechanics of putting the system into operation. Like I said, that should be done in about six to eight months. Well, that's all ahead of us. I hope you've been able to talk to some of our foremen and employees, while you've been here. I'm sure you've found them enthusiastic.

The Eastern Electronic Company:
a Problem in Liaison

D R. Gordon Grandby, associate director of research for Eastern Electronic, strode energetically into the small conference room where seven of his top scientists were awaiting him. The eighth man in the room was Herb Grinnell, the young engineer who was chief liaison officer to Dr. Grandby's group for Cambridge Control Corporation, an affiliate of Eastern's. Dr. Grandby greeted the men quickly and nodded to his secretary to close the door.

"Gentlemen," he began, "you are all aware of the general purpose of this morning's meeting even though you have not been briefed on any of the particulars. I don't know all the particulars myself. The only essential fact to have in mind is that we're meeting at the request of Cambridge Control to discuss some possible changes in our liaison procedures."

Dr. Grandby then quickly reviewed the history and purpose of the liaison relationship. This relationship had grown out of the Research Laboratory's experimental ACS system. This promised to be a major breakthrough in the field, and Eastern's executive committee had decided to develop and market it. The Research Laboratory was responsible for the design of the system and Cambridge Control for its development and manufacture.

"As most of you know," Dr. Grandby said in concluding his opening remarks, "there have been a number of occasions recently in which Cambridge has challenged the effectiveness of our liaison. Consequently, I propose we begin this morning's session by letting Herb brief us on Cambridge's point of view. Then we can throw the meeting open for general discussion and analysis."

"Thank you very much, Dr. Grandby," Mr. Grinnell began. "I want to say that I appreciate the fact that all of you have been willing to take time out from busy schedules to discuss this matter. Quite frankly, Cambridge feels that it has assumed some urgency. We don't think for a minute that the difficulties have grown out of hand, but we do feel that they need earnest attention. As best I can, therefore, I will brief you on our point of view. At the same time, I hope you will feel free to interrupt as I go along. In this way we may have every chance to clarify issues and to resolve any differences of opinion we may hold."

"Fair enough, Herb," said Dr. Grandby, "and I'll take you at your word, if I may, to make a prefatory remark. It's quite likely Johnson will not be able to make this meeting, but I want you to know that I spoke with him late yesterday afternoon. He insisted I let you know that he doesn't want his absence to keep you from referring to the discussion that you, he, and I had on the phone last Thursday."

"I appreciate his courtesy, Dr. Grandby," said Mr. Grinnell, "and I think the discussion you refer to is an important illustration of the problems we at Cambridge are beginning to encounter. This is a good place to begin."

Mr. Grinnell summarized by recalling that Mr. Johnson had been at Cambridge Control the week before on a liaison mission from the Research Laboratory. At the time of his visit he had requested that one of the components he inspected be subjected to further testing under conditions he specified. He also requested that the component design be modified in certain ways and that this modified design be tested in a similar way. Mr. Johnson indicated that he would give his approval to the design that had the best test results.

"I'm going to interrupt again, Herb," said Dr. Grandby, "because, as you know, I was involved in the conclusion of this incident. It may make it easier for you and more meaningful for the rest of us to have me tell my side of it."

Dr. Grandby related that the chief engineer at Cambridge had called him on the phone soon after Mr. Johnson had left the plant. It seemed, Dr. Grandby explained, that Mr. Johnson had committed a procedural blunder by making his recommendations directly to a project engineer without going back through the project head. His action had apparently caused some ruffled feelings.

"Am I telling this right, Herb?" Dr. Grandby asked.

"Yes, you are," Mr. Grinnell replied, "but all of you will want to know that from our point of view there was much more to it than ruffled feelings. In fact, the chief was very concerned that no one here knew about the changes Johnson was suggesting. He expressed real concern about your system of authorization when you merely referred him back to Johnson as the authority on that part of the system."

"But all of us knew in a general way," broke in the physicist in the group, "what Johnson was about. We had discussed his line of attack in meetings many times. As a matter of fact, a number of us— and I was among them—had criticized Johnson's approach quite sharply in the beginning, but his logic withstood every attack."

"That's right," agreed Dr. Grandby, "and I said as much to the chief engineer."

"It seems to me," suggested the head mathematician, "that the quarrel here is really a very minor thing. You fellows at Cambridge, Herb, have a close system of control and a sharply defined chain of command. If we simply adopt a similar system—just as an *ad hoc* administrative convenience—I should think that would solve the basic difficulty."

Before Mr. Grinnell could answer, the physicist interrupted to deny that such a change was necessary. He argued that it would waste time and would place a burden of paper work on them that would be a substantial nuisance.

"I don't agree," the mathematician rejoined. "We should be willing to concoct a more formal administrative pattern—again, simply as an *ad hoc* measure—if it would enhance our relationships with the engineering groups."

"What's your feeling about this, Herb?" asked Dr. Grandby. "I think we need to get the full Cambridge point of view from you before we attempt any decision making, but we do want to be cooperative."

Dr. Grandby waited for Mr. Grinnell to go on. He began by stating that Cambridge Control was now in fairly broad agreement with the Laboratory on the system itself and that they were prepared to go ahead with the prototype device. Now that the broad outlines had been developed, the procedure at Cambridge was to break up the various parts of the development and to assign them to responsible project heads. These project heads had great authority to budget and develop.

"What you're saying," said Dr. Grandby, "is that now we're in close agreement on the system itself, you've thrown everything up to the project men. You give them responsibility for reaching the objectives and you'll hold them accountable right down the line."

"That's right," said Mr. Grinnell.

"This doesn't seem to be a good approach at all for the development of the ACS system," the physicist argued. "We've consistently taken a systems point of view in our design, and I think we need to keep a systems point of view now. No other approach makes sense to me.

We've got the men who know what they want and it seems to me they've got to have the responsibility for getting it."

"I don't think anyone at Cambridge is going to deny that the design responsibility is yours," Mr. Grinnell replied, "but I do want to stress that within our own organization we have an accountability, too."

"I think it would be helpful, Herb," said Dr. Grandby, "if you would spell out this point a little more fully."

Mr. Grinnell explained that each of the project heads had submitted preliminary plans for the prototype device. These plans had been approved at Cambridge Control. They were the same ones that had been sent to the Research Laboratory three months before and which had been returned to Cambridge with a series of criticisms and suggestions.

"As you know," said Mr. Grinnell, "all of your suggestions were thoroughly reviewed by the responsible project heads."

"But not all were tried," interrupted the physicist again. "As a matter of fact, Johnson's difficulty is a good case in point, for some of the tests he recommended last week were included in his comments of three months ago."

"That's true," replied Mr. Grinnell, "but our men felt that they were thoroughly checked out on that component. We've been using it for some time with excellent results and we thought Johnson was being overly cautious about it."

"But the component modifications he suggested last week," said the physicist, "were new to your people. It's quite possible they may make important differences in the reliability of that component.

"I can't testify to that," said Mr. Grinnell, "but I can testify to the planning difficulties involved."

Mr. Grinnell went on to explain that the approved preliminary plans had now become project plans. The engineers had begun to submit monthly reports covering costs and work on each project. These reports also covered estimates of future production costs and work load estimates. These reports went to divisional accounting.

"If Johnson's new component were installed," Mr. Grinnell went on, "it would add $10,000 to the cost of each production model. Naturally, the project head wasn't going to stick his neck out. He quite properly felt that he could do it only on the recommendation of some responsible research head. We all feel that the Laboratory ought to establish some clear-cut lines of authority in matters of this kind. We think also—and we offer this only as a friendly observation—that it would be helpful to all of us if you would delegate technical authority in a more systematic way."

At this suggestion, the research group broke into disordered discussion until the mathematician spoke up to summarize their feelings.

"The one thing we don't want to do, Herb," he said, "is to smother our attack on the ACS system under rules and regulations that will cut us off from one another. We have always felt that ideas can and should be generated by anyone in the Laboratory. We want the system to have the benefit of every technical competence we can bring to bear. We're afraid that if we fetter people with arbitrary procedures we're not going to achieve the breakthrough we're striving for."

"But there's a lot more to it than just rules and procedures," Mr. Grinnell continued. "At least, this is our feeling at the plant. We think we've progressed far enough in our work on the system so that we've got to ask for more responsibility in developing it."

"Well, we certainly want your people to have their share of the responsibility, Herb," said the mathematician, "but I think all of us here believe we've got to keep a steady eye on the system itself. This is the important thing—the *sine qua non*, if you will."

"But this is part of our argument," Mr. Grinnell countered. "We feel that we have kept the total system very much in mind during this long formative period. I think you'd agree that we've worked well together and in good harmony; but now the general feeling at Cambridge is that we must get on with it and that we must assume the responsibility for getting it done. This seems reasonable to us, and surely you will believe that we want the system to be the great success you all think it will be."

"But this doesn't affect our responsibility for the design of the system," said one of the research associates, "and we've still got to have the opportunity to say that everything is as well designed and as well planned as it could be."

"I can certainly understand your point of view," replied Mr. Grinnell, "but I must plead with you to understand ours. As much as you're responsible for the design, we're responsible for the execution. And as long as we're charged with completing the project and producing the system, we feel that we've got to have an area of judgment appropriate to determining what's to be done in our area of responsibility."

"And this is exactly our argument, too," said the physicist. "This is the very point of difference we've been debating. Now let us look at this point of difference in a *for instance*. Let us say, for instance, that Johnson hadn't suggested the component changes on his own initiative: would the project head then have sought him out for advice? I don't think so. Personally, Herb, I feel very strongly that your system of technical accountability stifles initiative. And I worry lest your production-centered philosophy sabotage our chances for success. No one at Cambridge wants to spend the time or money to try for something better than we've got."

"I agree with this, Herb," seconded the mathematician, "and this is important to us. Before we got into this development, we had to convince our executive committee that our concept of control promised to be a major breakthrough. We did this on the basis of our research here in the Lab. We're convinced that ACS system can become everything we've hoped for. However, it will fulfill its promise— and ours—only if we keep giving it everything we've got."

"All of this may sound somewhat selfishly defensive to you, Herb," added one of the research associates, "but you've worked with us long enough to know it's much more than that. You know that we very honestly believe we've got something big here. We know that we can build a reliability into this system that no one thought possible, but we can't cut corners. We've got to spend money and time to accomplish it."

The point, everyone seemed to agree, was that the research group was going to have to approve the final design. It was a matter both of professional pride and managerial responsibility.

"But you can't approve everything at every step of the way," Mr. Grinnell countered. He argued, courteously, that the Research Laboratory was not being reasonable about it. He implied that the whole question of approval seemed to be something of an obsession with the research group.

Mr. Grinnell also reviewed the history of Cambridge Control. They had been in the business—and very successful in the business—long before they had become an affiliate of Eastern's. Many of the components being used in the ACS system were originally developed and engineered by Cambridge men.

"Our whole experience in the field has been good," Mr. Grinnell argued. "The components which have been produced by our company are reliable, and all the data we get from the field bear this out."

Furthermore, he added, on top of their reliability record they had a rich pride in their ability to maintain schedules and cut costs. They had a reputation in industry for keeping two steady eyes on the economies of their systems.

"I certainly hope you understand," Mr. Grinnell concluded. "that I don't want to build an issue of this. None of us at Cambridge does. But I do want to stress that there is some feeling that the whole question of approval has become urgent now that the basic design is about complete."

"How do you feel about it, Herb?" asked Dr. Grandby.

"Do you mean how do I feel personally or do you mean what do I think is the consensus?" asked Mr. Grinnell.

"The latter," replied Dr. Grandby.

"Well," said Mr. Grinnell, "we respect the fact that the essential design is yours and we want to help you realize your objectives. But we also want you to be fair and helpful in turn. Look again, for instance, at this component modification of Johnson's. If we had made all the changes and run all the tests he wanted, it would have taken two to three weeks out of B project's schedule. Quite frankly, we can't go on this way much longer. We've got to find a means of bringing things to a head."

"But this is only one point of view," argued the physicist. "You should understand that both Johnson and I have grave doubts about the suitability of the component you are using. And it seems to me that we've got to have an opportunity of passing judgment on this kind of thing."

"But you've got to decide that somewhere, sometime, you're going to stop approving," rejoined Mr. Grinnell. "We feel very strongly that we've got to get a set of requirements and stick to them."

"But the system alone dictates the requirements," countered the physicist. "Johnson made the decision he did because the B project people hadn't done any more than adapt the old GBQ component to the new system. And our experience with the GBQ was essentially that it was no more than adequate. And we have some doubts that it will be as reliable as it should be for the ACS system."

"Well, I can only repeat again that we *are* concerned with reliability," replied Mr. Grinnell. "Perhaps it would be only fair, though, to add that there is a feeling at Cambridge that you fellows want extreme component and system reliabilities. We just can't take up every design idea that comes along. Why we'd be testing components and arguing theory from here to eternity. At some point you've got to have your project leader say: 'O.K., here's what we do.'"

"But, Herb," interrupted the mathematician, "it's very definitely our feeling that we are running some risk of getting inferior components into the system. After all, ACS will have to have better reliability than anything Cambridge has done before."

"But we have had the experience with the basic units," countered Mr. Grinnell, "and we feel that you've got to let us have the practical and basic engineering control over what we do. We know that we're already way ahead of anything that's now in production. But if we don't start moving soon, everybody else will be ahead of us—not on paper, nor in theory, but in real hardware out in the field."

"We sympathize with what you're saying, Herb," said Dr. Grandby, "but we're committed to producing a system that's not going to be one whit inferior to what we know it can be right now."

"Fair enough," agreed Mr. Grinnell, "but we've got to reach a point where we can be sure of going ahead. We feel that you've got to do this, for you can't possibly look at every drawing, at every detail. You've got to find some way of giving us final design approval. Believe me, gentlemen, we just want to get on with the job. And we want to do it in a friendly way and to have you make use of our experience and our judgment. Quite frankly, if you will permit me, your opinions have been too fragmented and divided. Somehow, you've got to find a method of arriving at a kind of group approval."

Mr. Grinnell leaned back into his chair, obviously finished.

"Herb," said Dr. Grandby in acceptance of his finishing, "we certainly want to thank you for making the Cambridge point of view so clear. Please accept my personal thanks for handling a difficult job as fairly and as honestly as you did."

"Gentlemen," Dr. Grandby added, turning to his associates, "let's take a coffee break. I would suggest we then reconvene here in about ten minutes to see if we can make a start at analyzing some of the problems Herb's presented. Perhaps we can even make a pass at finding some reasonable solutions."

Part Two

Group Processes

T HE cases in this section present data from several industrial work groups. In all of them, the task requirements imposed on the groups by the organizations are relatively unambiguous and stable. The formal authority structures in which they are imbedded are of conventional form, with a foreman or supervisor who is formally concerned with the group's productivity in charge of each. The productivity of the groups is clearly measurable. The group productivity of two of the groups—the Bank Wiring Room in the case entitled "Observations and Interviews on a Small Group of Workers" and the welders in the Agricultural Equipment Company—is measured as the aggregate of clearly identifiable and quantifiable *individual* outputs. The output of the crews in the Briggs Box Company, on the other hand, is clearly a cooperative, group product, which cannot be identified with particular individuals' efforts alone. There are also differences in the systems by which the members of the various groups are paid.

In all of these cases the nature of the particular technologies has important effects on the development of the groups. The technologies provide interaction patterns, prescribing sequences of activities and interactions as well as initiation-deference patterns. In addition, the jobs, tools, materials, working methods, and physical layouts provide routines, objects, and spaces which become laden with symbolic and affective meanings in the small cultures of the groups. In all of the cases, the groups' productivity is their major exchange with the external authorities, as well as an important basis for various demonstrations of internal cohesiveness. The Briggs Box case describes two different groups operating the same machine on different shifts, allowing a comparison of two groups holding technology and other organizational constraints constant, and bringing in the element of intergroup relations between two groups of "peers."

All the cases present some data on another major element of input, the social attributes of the individual members, including age, ethnic background, marital status, seniority, and education level. These data allow the comparison of external status factors with the status differentiations intrinsic to the technologies, as well as provide some indicators of the cultural and subcultural bases for the particular small groups such as their folklore, games, shared beliefs, and orientations toward authority.

The above kinds of data are nonbehavioral and may be treated as major determinants of the actual behaviors and sentiments, which are described in detail in the cases. Personality characteristics are not presented as such, but are abundantly manifested in the behavior patterns described. Although each group features a range of individual differences which cannot be explained solely by social determinants and group development, the differences tend to match closely the structural attributes of the groups. The personalities of the informal leaders and the isolates, to take examples of extreme structural positions, relate closely to their social positions in the groups. Hence, the behavioral data allow for an examination of the relationships between the individual and the group, as well as significant group attributes.

The groups' identities will be seen to emerge in the form of unique sets of values, norms, beliefs, and customs. These behavior and sentiment patterns accompany the groups' social structures. Within these structures informal social positions can be identified, including informal leaders, "lieutenants," regular members, deviant members, isolates, and specialized roles such as "jester." Subgroups are also major structural elements. Each group develops its unique system of social control, administering rewards and punishments to ensure conformance to its norms and social ranking; rewards take the general form of acceptance, maintenance of a higher rank, and the opportunity to influence the group. Punishments take the general forms of ostracism, ridicule, sarcasm, downgrading in rank, and kidding. In each case, the specific form of the group's social controls is part of its unique culture. "Binging" in the Bank Wiring Room is an example of such a practice which had a special social meaning in the group.

Most of the groups in these cases are relatively well developed, in that they feature relatively clear and strong norms that do, in fact, exert substantial control over the behavior of the members. These groups have been defined functionally in terms of technical and spatial proximity and organizational identity. Although they feature relatively high cohesiveness, the reader should try to understand why these particular groups are cohesive. It is quite possible to find industrial work groups that are not as cohesive and elaborate as those in the case studies presented here. In the Briggs Box case, #1 crew is an example of a less cohesive group, especially in comparison to #2 crew.

In addition to analyzing the relationships between the determinants and the actual behavior and sentiment patterns, the student has an opportunity to describe the consequence of the various groups' development for their organizations, for the individual members, and for the maintenance of the groups. These consequences include productivity, satisfaction, potential response to change, and general adaptability or learning.

The Observations and Interviews case was taken from one of the earliest explorations in industrial sociology, the Bank Wiring Room in the Hawthorne works of the Western Electric Company.[1] This study had an important influence in the development of research and training in human relations and organizational behavior. The observers and interviewers in this study were not members of the work group.

The Agricultural Equipment Company case material, in contrast, was gathered and written by a participant in the group. This report by an insider describes a group remote in time and space from the Bank Wiring Room of the Hawthorne Studies, but remarkably similar in attitudes, beliefs, and practices. Both of these cases highlight the workers' control of output through group processes, in marked contrast to the assumptions and intentions of the piece-rate payment schemes designed by the staff specialists. They also indicate the realities of the foreman's role, in contrast to the textbook prescriptions for correct supervisory behavior.

The technology in the Briggs Box Company is very much different from that in the first two case studies. The group members here are working together on a single, large, continuous-process machine, similar in certain respects to those used in papermaking. Although jobs are formally described individually, it is clear that quantity and quality of output are contingent upon group interaction. In this case, the groups'

[1] See references in Introduction.

social structures and processes of social control impinge directly on the operation of the machine. Technical control of the machine by the men is closely related to group processes, whereas in the other cases technical control is exercised by individuals over their own work, in which they act indirectly as representatives of group beliefs and attitudes.

The Briggs Box case compares the behavior patterns and underlying motivations of two crews operating on alternate shifts. The interpersonal relations and group development of the two crews are quite different, and the data challenge the student to discover the determinants of behavior in groups.

Observations and Interviews
with a Small Group of Workers

Over a period of six and one-half months a careful study was made of a group of workers in an industrial manufacturing plant. Fourteen male operators were segregated from a large assembly department and placed in a separate room. The room was equipped with standard work equipment and was made to correspond as closely as possible with the situation from which the men were removed. An observer was stationed in the room to observe behavior and to keep records of performance. Each man was interviewed to determine his attitudes toward work, co-workers, and supervisors, and to learn as much as possible about his personal history and current situation outside the factory. The following cases present data collected in the study. They are arranged so that Case A describes the work activities required of the men in the room. Case B presents excerpts from interview and observation records in respect to both nonwork and work activities. The case also includes charts based on the observer's records. Case C describes the problems existing between the workers and one of their inspectors. Case D describes some of the supervisors' problems.

CASE *A*: THE BANK WIRING ROOM

The 14 men worked in a room whose dimensions were about 40 by 20 feet. This room, the Bank Wiring Room, was equipped with standard work equipment and resembled the previous work environment as closely as possible.

Benches and Fixtures

The room's standard equipment included 19 metal workbenches, 3 feet high and 20 inches wide. Two heavy cast iron fixture supports were fastened on top of each bench, with a fixture placed upon them. Each fixture consisted of a wooden board about 6 feet long, 8 inches wide, and 1 inch thick. A row of 11 pairs of iron pins projected upward from the board, which was placed lengthwise on the workbench and upon the fixture supports so as to tilt toward the worker wiring the banks.

The "Equipment" and Banks

The finished product was called an "equipment." There were two kinds of "equipment," connector equipments and selector equipments. Connector equipments were usually 11 banks long; selector equipments, usually 10. Either could be 2 or 3 banks high. Each bank was about 4 inches long, $1\frac{1}{2}$ inches high, and convex in shape. Projecting fanwise from the face of each bank were the terminals and "points" which were to be connected by the wiremen.

The workers engaged in selector and connector bank assembly were concerned with two kinds of banks: those with 100 terminals and those with 200 terminals. The difference was in the spacing of the terminals, because the dimensions of the two types were the same. On a 100-terminal, or "point," bank there were 5 rows of 20 terminals. On a 200-point bank there were 10 rows of 20 terminals, spaced closer together. The wiremen preferred to work on 100-point banks because of the larger space around each terminal. Soldermen preferred the 200-point banks, because the terminals were all on the same level and could be soldered by sliding the soldering iron along the row, whereas the terminals on a 100-point bank were spaced so far apart that they had to be soldered separately. An "equipment" could be either 10 or 11 banks long and either 2 or 3 banks high. A 2-bank-high equipment could have either 2 rows of 200-point banks or 1 row of 200-point banks and 1 row of 100-point banks. When 100-point banks were used, they were always used on the top row only. The latter type was more common. A 3-bank-high equipment always had 3 rows of 200-point banks.

The wiremen sometimes used a small tool to spread the levels of the 200-point banks. In addition, a small pair of pliers was used occasionally to straighten bent terminals. A large spool was attached to a horizontal bar under the bench. The spool held a pair of colored wires which were twisted together and which unwound when pulled by the wireman. The wire had previously been run through a machine which stripped off portions of insulation at regular intervals. A small, clawlike tool was used to comb the attached wires out straight so that they would lie flat.

THE WORKERS AND THEIR JOBS

There were three groups of workmen in the Bank Wiring Room: nine wiremen, three soldermen, and two inspectors. Each of these groups performed a specific task and collaborated with the other two in the completion of each unit of equipment. Each solderman soldered for three wiremen, this group being referred to as a "soldering unit." The two inspectors in the room divided the work of the nine wiremen equally between them as shown in Figure 1. The nine wiremen are referred to as W_1 through W_9, the three soldermen as S_1, S_2, and S_4,[1] and the two inspectors as I_1 and I_3.[1]

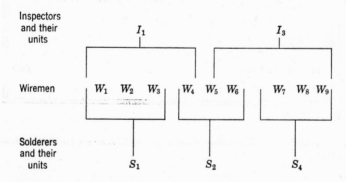

Figure 1. Division of workers into inspection and soldering units.

Figure 2 presents the layout of the Bank Wiring Room, in which the 14 operators worked. It shows the wiremen's bench positions, where each wireman alternated between two equipments. The second equipment was placed adjacent to the first on the same bench or on the bench immediately in front.

[1] S_3 and I_2 left during the study.

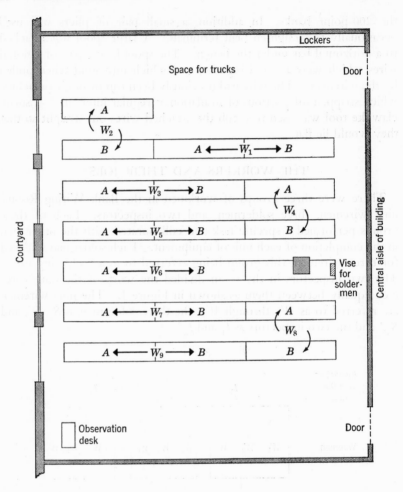

Figure 2. Diagram of observation room showing wiremen's positions (A and B). Not to scale.

After a wireman had wired the first level on one equipment, he shifted to the first level on the second equipment. Meanwhile the first equipment could be soldered and inspected. Six of the wiremen, W_1, W_2, W_3, W_4, W_5, and W_6, worked on connector equipments (11 banks long). The other three, W_7, W_8, and W_9, worked on selector equipments (10 banks long). Connector fixtures were about half as heavy as selector fixtures, although the technique of working was the same for both types. Table 1 presents some of the more important background facts about the 14 workers.

Table 1

Operator	Age	Education	Service Yrs.	Mos.	Nationality	Nativity	Marital Status
W_1	22	7 G.S.	3	2	Polish	U.S.	S
W_2	25	2 H.S.	5	5	German	U.S.	S
W_3	26	8 G.S.	2	5	American	U.S.	M
W_4	20	2 H.S.	3	7	Irish	U.S.	S
W_5	24	4 H.S.	2	8	Bohemian	U.S.	M
W_6	21	2 H.S.	3	1	Polish	U.S.	S
W_7	22	8 G.S.	3	2	Bohemian	U.S.	M
W_8	22	8 G.S.	3	8	German	U.S.	S
W_9	21	4 H.S.	2	10	American	U.S.	S
S_1	21	8 G.S.	5	4	German	U.S.	S
S_2	26	6 G.S.	9	8	Bohemian	Yugoslavia	S
S_4	20	8 G.S.	3	0	Bohemian	U.S.	S
I_1	23	4 H.S.	3	0	American	U.S.	S
I_3	40	3 Col.	7	0	Armenian	Turkey	M

In recording observations, the researchers used the following abbreviations:

W	Wireman
S	Solderman
I	Inspector
GC	Group chief
SC	Section chief
AF	Assistant foreman
F	Foreman
Int.	Interviewer
Obs.	Observer

Different wiremen, soldermen, and inspectors were designated by subscript numbers.

The Wiring Process

A fixture was taken from a nearby storage rack and placed in position on the support. Banks, wire, and fibre insulators were next obtained. Then a cable with a wired terminal strip was placed in position on one end of the wooden fixture, immediately behind the row of upright pins. Either ten or eleven 200-point banks were then slipped down over the upright pins, and the wiring task proper was begun.

First, certain colored wires in the cable with the wired terminal strip were attached to the bottom level of terminals of the end bank, immediately in front of the cable.   These were fastened in accordance with a color code.   Then, starting at one end of the equipment and using the pair of wires on the spool under the workbench, the wiremen attached the wires to the first two terminals in the lower level of an end bank.   He then attached the wire in sequence to the corresponding terminals of the other nine or ten banks.   This was accomplished by looping the bare wire, where the insulation had been removed, over the terminals and pulling it tight.   When the last bank had been connected, the operator broke the wire and, going back to the first bank, secured it to the second pair of terminals in the bottom level and proceeded as before.   This was repeated ten times, which completed the wiring of the first level.

The wireman then moved to his other work station and wired the first level of that equipment in the same manner.   While he was working on the second equipment, the solderman and inspector performed their respective functions on the completed level of the first equipment.   Before wiring the second level, fiber insulators were placed over the first level.   When the ten levels of the 200-point banks had been completed, a second row of banks was placed on top, and the operation was continued.

The wireman had to guard against two kinds of errors: reverses and wire breaks.   A reverse occurred when a wire was attached to other than the specified terminal.   Reverses might occur either in attaching the cable to the end bank or in connecting the terminals in sequence.   The wireman was solely responsible for reverses and partly responsible for broken wire.   Wire breaks which occurred where the wire was looped around a terminal might be caused either by the wireman or by the machine which stripped off the insulation.   The gauge on the stripping machine might be set so small that a portion of the wire was taken off with the insulation or, as was usually the case, the gauge might be set correctly but the diameter of the wire might vary slightly.   In either case, the wire would break easily when twisted.   Wire breaks within the insulated portion were usually the result of defects in the wire itself.

The Soldering Process

Each solderman soldered the work of three wiremen. Thus, S_1 soldered for W_1, W_2, and W_3; S_2 for W_4, W_5, and W_6; and S_4 for W_7, W_8 and W_9. The soldermen were equipped with electrically heated soldering irons and solder in the form of a wire, the center of which consisted of resin. The solder was melted by pressing it against the tip of the iron, from which it flowed onto the terminals. The soldering irons were equipped with detachable copper tips which had to be filed several times a day. Each solderman filed his own tips.

The Inspection Process

Each completed level of an equipment was thoroughly inspected. The inspector was equipped with a test set, with which he detected any serious defect in the equipment. The test set was attached to an equipment, and when a contact was made with a terminal, it made a buzzing sound. If the set failed to buzz when a terminal was touched, it meant that the circuit was not completed. The cause might be a cable reverse, a wiring reverse, a broken wire, or a cross-solder; the inspector determined which by visual inspection. Having tested for these four defects, he then examined the equipment visually for other defects.

The inspector filled out a quality form for each equipment inspected. An identification number stamped on the equipment was entered on the form. Each defect and the terminal upon which it occurred were entered on this record. The two inspectors in the observation room divided the work of the nine wiremen equally between them. Thus I_1 inspected the work of W_1, W_2, W_3, and W_4 and half that of W_5, and I_3 inspected the other half of W_5's work and that of W_6, W_7, W_8, and W_9.

THE WAGE INCENTIVE PLAN

The men worked under a system of group piecework; the entire department of which these men were a part was considered a unit for purposes of payment. For each unit of equipment the department assembled and shipped out, it was paid a fixed sum. The amount thus earned each week constituted the fund out of which all wages were paid. The greater the number of units completed each week by a given number of employees, the larger would be the sum to be distributed among them.

The allocation of the weekly departmental earnings to the individuals in the department was accomplished as follows. First, each employee was assigned an hourly rate, and that rate, multiplied by the number of hours worked during the week, was called the daywork value of the work done. By adding together the daywork value of the work of the whole department and subtracting the total thus obtained from the total earnings of the department, the excess of piece-rate earnings over daywork earnings was determined. The surplus, divided by the total daywork value, was called the "percentage." Each individual's hourly rate was then increased by this percentage; the resulting hourly earnings figure, multiplied by the hours worked during the week, constituted that person's weekly earnings.

Under this system, if hours of work remained the same, differences in the earnings of different people depended entirely upon differences in individual hourly rates. A uniform increase in the hourly rates of all the employees in the department, if output remained the same, would have resulted in no change in individual earnings. It would simply have lowered the "percentage," or the excess of piece-rate over daywork earnings. However, if output remained the same, an increase in hourly rates of a few people would have lowered the earnings of those employees whose hourly rates were not changed.

The only way in which the group as a whole could increase its earnings was by increasing its total output. Because of this fact, the department had established a "bogey" for each job done. The bogey was simply a standard in terms of which an individual's efficiency could be measured. It was something "to shoot at" and was intended to serve much the same purpose as a record does for an athlete. The closer to it the employees came, the greater was their personal benefit in terms of wages. The official bogey for the wiring job was 914 connections per hour, or about 7312 connections per day.

Inasmuch as the absolute amount of any individual's earnings was affected by the performance of every other person in the group, there could be only a rough relationship between his output and his wages. In general it can be said that a person who stood high in output received less than if he were on straight piecework, whereas a person whose output was low received more. In order to bring about a rough correspondence between individual earnings and output, increases in hourly rates were based largely upon performance. Records were kept of each person's efficiency for guidance in adjusting rates. These records were based on the individual's weekly average hourly output. At the close of each day the group chief in the room took individual output counts and obtained from each person a record of the amount of time lost because of stoppages. The time lost through stoppages beyond the worker's control was deducted from standard hours before his average hourly output was computed. If such time were not deducted, the efficiency ratings of those people who for some reason were delayed would suffer in comparison with those of people who had lost little time. The time thus deducted was called a "daywork allowance claim" and was used solely for computing efficiency records.

The successful operation of this payment plan demanded that all employees look constantly toward increasing or at least maintaining total output. It demanded that each employee should think not only of his personal interests, but also of the welfare of his fellow workmen. Thus if a worker, having achieved a high hourly rate, deliberately slowed up, he could receive in payment much more than he contributed to the earnings of the department. The chief thing which would prevent him from doing this was his concern for the well being of his co-workers and for their attitude toward him. Indeed, it can easily be understood that the employees might group together informally to bring pressure to bear upon the slower workers.

This was the wage incentive plan under which the group worked. Every aspect of it was based on some logical reason and could be defended on the grounds, first, that it should promote efficiency and, second, that it provided an equitable means of apportioning earnings among the employees.

CASE B: INTERPERSONAL RELATIONS AMONG THE WORKERS

The workers in the observation room participated in a number of social activities during lunch hours. They played games of chance, such as matching coins, and ran pools on horse racing, baseball, and quality records. Financial gain was not the main inducement, for most of the wagers were small, ranging from one to ten cents. Besides these games, there were other social activities—conversations, banter, arguments, and controversies—some of which were connected with their work and some of which were not. The material in Part I of this case, taken from observations and interviews, relates to many of these social activities, which expressed the relationships the workers had to one another. These observations have also been partially summarized in Figures 3, 4, 5, 6, 7, and 8. Charts which summarize the wiremen's output and material from interviews which show their attitudes toward the wage incentive system are given in Part II.

Part I: Games and Other Nonwork Activities

Figure 3 shows the people who joined in the games, such as matching coins, betting, "binging." The symbols indicating the different operators are enclosed in small circles. The operators are arranged roughly by soldering units, indicated by the spacing of the wiremen.

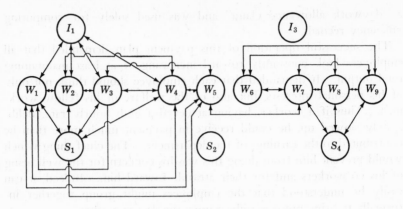

Figure 3. Games.

The inspectors are placed above the groups for which they inspected. (The same arrangement is used in subsequent diagrams.)   The arrows connecting the different circles indicate that the people thus connected participated in one or more games, either as pairs or as members of a larger group.

Figure 4 shows those men who joined in controversies over the windows and those with whom they participated. A person was judged to be involved in these disputes even though he participated only verbally.

Accurate records of job trading and helping were kept throughout the study and are summarized graphically in Figures 5 and 6.

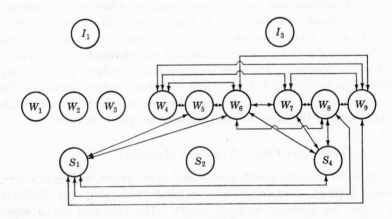

Figure 4. Windows.

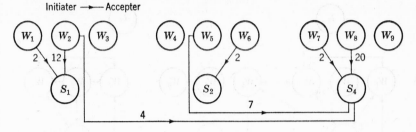

Figure 5.   Trading.

The inspectors are omitted from these diagrams because they did not participate.   In Figure 5 the arrows point from the person who initiated the request to trade to the person who accepted the request. The numbers alongside the arrows show the number of times the people so designated traded.   In Figure 6 the arrows point from helper to the person helped.

Figures 7 and 8 summarize the friendships and antagonisms which existed in the group.   In analyzing the observation data for evidence of these interpersonal relations, each occasion in which a person entered into association with another person was examined to see whether the relation expressed an antagonism or a friendship or was merely neutral.

12-17-31[2]

The section chief found S_1 soldering without any goggles.   He stopped S_1, who spent about five minutes hunting for a pair which he had mislaid. S_1 grumbled about wearing glasses as he hunted for them.

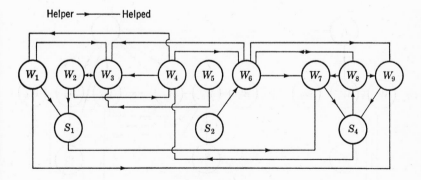

Figure 6.   Helping.

[2] The observations are organized by date.

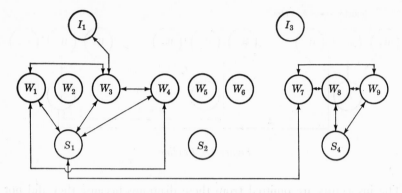

Figure 7. Friendships.

S_1: I don't know where the hell those glasses are. I suppose one of you guys hid 'em. There ain't no sense to wearing glasses anyway. I soldered for four years before they ever thought of glasses. Now you've gotta keep 'em on. There ain't no solder going to splash in a fellow's eye. That's just the damn' fool notion somebody's got. I've gotta go around here all day in a fog, just because some damn' fool wants us to wear goggles.

SC: Never mind why you've got to wear them, just get them and put them on.

W_2: I worked on a job for three years where I had to wear goggles and it didn't kill me.

S_1: Yes, and I suppose you wore them all the time.

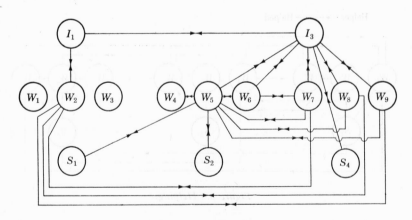

Figure 8. Antagonisms.

W_2: Well, maybe I didn't, but it didn't hurt me to wear them when I had to. There's one thing you've got to remember, S_1. Do you hear me? Don't do as I do—do as I say. Get that?

S_1: Why don't you guys wear glasses when you fix repairs?

W_3: We don't have to put them on for that little bit of soldering, but you're a solderman. You've got to wear them.

S_1: Aw, you guys are all a bunch of damn' fools.

2-1-32

W_8 (to observer): Oh, this is a rotten day! I feel terrible, but GC won't have any pity on me. He won't let me solder.

W_6 (to group chief): How about soldering today? I can't see a thing, I forgot my glasses.

GC: Nothing doing.

$Obs.$ (to S_4): These fellows are sure trying to get your job this morning.

S_4: I suppose I will have to wire.

$Obs.$: Don't you want to wire?

S_4: No, I don't like to be changing jobs all the time.

2-3-32

Just before S_2 went to the hospital.

W_6 (to GC): Hey, GC, how about a solderman here? This guy can't keep up.

GC: He's going to the hospital. You solder for him while he's gone.

W_6: Like hell I will. I won't solder for him. Get a solderman back here.

S_4: You're a good solderman.

W_6: I am not. I don't know a thing about it.

3-1-32

W_8 and W_9 were sitting near the observer's desk. Neither of them felt like working.

W_8 (to S_4): Go over and wire for me, will you?

S_4: Why should I? I'm a solderman.

W_8: Go on and wire them. There's only four rows to go. I'll never get four rows done today.

S_4: All right. I'll just do the four rows, though.

2-16-32

About 11 o'clock the group chief came in and called out, "Does anyone here want to get the lunches this noon?"

W_9: How much daywork do I get?

GC: Half an hour.

W_9: Is that a half-hour just for this room?

GC: No, for the whole department.

W_9: That isn't enough.

S_1: What's the matter with Red [solderman in other room]?   Why don't he get it?

GC: He don't want to anymore.   They cut his daywork down to a half-hour.   Well, if nobody wants to get it, I guess you'll all get your own lunches.

W_1: That isn't fair.   You can't do that to us.

S_1: We gotta have somebody get our lunch.   We'll waste 15 minutes of the noon hour getting it.

GC: All right, go out and get it then.

S_1: I'll get it for this room.   I won't get it for the rest of the department.

At 11:40 when S_1 started out for the lunch he got the group chief to help him.

2-17-32

Today when S_1 went for the lunch he called to the group chief, "Come on, help me carry it."

GC: Nothing doing.   If I'm gonna help you every noon I might as well get it myself.

W_6: Here, take my bucket for coffee.

S_1: I'm not going out there carrying a bucket.   I'll bring it in a cup.

When S_1 came back with the lunch, he said that was the last time he was going to get it.

GC: What's the matter?

S_1: Aw, they made me stand in line out there.

S_1 forgot to bring spoons and straws.   He also got the orders mixed up.   The group were all razzing him.   Some were asking for straws, others spoons, others wanted to know where their milk was. S_1 was disgusted.

S_1: There's your lunch.   I don't care whether you like it or not.   It's the last time I'll go out and get it anyway.

2-19-32

S_4 went for the lunch today.

3-22-32

I_1 (to group): Look who's getting the lunch today!

W_1 was going around taking the orders. After he had the orders written up and the money collected, he turned it over to S_1.

5-18-32

As S_1 was leaving the test room to return some irons, he said to W_1, "Solder for me while I'm gone."

W_1: You go to hell. Why should I solder for you?
S_1: All right, why should I get lunch for you?
W_1: I suppose you get lunch for me alone.
S_1: Well, mostly for you.

3-4-32

GC (to Obs.): I don't know that the fellows in here fool around any more, but they're more careless than the fellows out in the other room, and they make more noise. They get their work out just the same. That gang in the rear of the room is going bad. I used to think that S_4 was a good kid, but he is getting spoiled. If I had them out in the other room, I'd break them up.

Obs.: What do you mean?
GC: I'd put one in one gang and one in another—split them all up.
Obs.: Why don't you do it here?
GC: Do you mean put some of them up in the front gang?
Obs.: Yes, if that's what you think should be done.
GC: I don't know how that would work. I don't think those fellows in the front group would want to work any place else.

2-19-32

GC (to W_6): I'm going to give you selectors next.
W_6: No, you're not. I'm not going to take them.
GC: You've got to. I'm running short on connectors. I should have given W_8 selectors instead of that board he's got there now.
W_6: All right, but I'm going to work them on a connector board.

INTERVIEW WITH W_1, 9-11-31

Int.: Is it true that you fellows down there are arranged according to your efficiency? That is, are the fast workmen on one end and the slow workmen on the other?
W_1: Well, not that I know of. Come to think of it, though, there are

some pretty fast workers where I am, but I know there are some fast ones in the middle too. A lot of them could be a whole lot faster if they wanted to be. I don't know how they look at it in the office. Maybe they have something in mind the way they arrange us.

Int.: I just wondered. I thought maybe they thought that connector wiring was a little bit better than selector wiring because of that extra bank. I don't suppose it would be as difficult to make 6600 connections there as on selector wiring.

W_1: Oh, I don't know. I don't think there is so much difference there. The difference is in the boards. On selectors you have to carry one of those big boards on your back. I don't like that. I never did. You know, when I was wiring on selectors I always looked forward to getting on the connector wiring job. Now when I have it, well, it doesn't seem so much. But we have real light boards.

INTERVIEW WITH W_4, 10-20-31

Int: Aren't you new on connector wiring?

W_4: Yes, I've only been on connectors for a couple of weeks. I was on selectors before.

Int.: Which do you like better?

W_4: Oh, I think connectors is the better job. The boards aren't as heavy and you have an extra bank. It's easy to turn out more work. You see, the rate on connectors is around 6600 and on selectors it's only 6000. That's on account of that extra bank. As far as the job goes, there's no difference. You do the wiring just the same.

Int.: Would you say that connector wiring is quite generally looked upon as the better job?

W_4: Yes, I would. I always wanted to get on connectors when I was on selectors. I think that is pretty generally true.

INTERVIEW WITH W_4, 12-10-31

Int.: I was wondering if being put in a room by yourselves might not bring about changes. I wondered if it might not bring you closer together.

W_4: Oh, yes. We have sort of got together down there now. We're a group by ourselves. It seems like we are apart from the department now. It's too far for us to go, and we don't get to see the other people we used to know so very much.

Int.: You sort of feel you are apart from the department, do you?

You have made friends in the test room that you didn't have before, then?

W_4: Sure. You get to know everybody around. Everybody does a lot more talking. We're not all together, either. We're really two groups down there, the group up in front and the group in back.

Int.: Is that so? What do you think brought that about?

W_4: Well, the fellows up in front talk about one thing all the time and the fellows at the other end of the room talk about different things. It seems like most of us in front talk about the same thing all the time.

Int.: What do you talk about?

W_4: Well, we talk about different things, but they are of some importance. There's a whole lot of arguing. Gee, how we argue down there! Everybody gets in on it too.

Int.: What does the other group talk about.

W_4: I don't know just what—I don't talk to them very much. They mostly horse around. You see, right there are W_7, W_8, and W_9. They are the slowest workers in there. Not only in there, but they are the slowest workers in the department, too. The rest of us in front turn out all the way from 6000 to 7000, and those fellows up there never get up to 6000.

Int.: Would you say, then, that all the connector wiremen are in your group?

W_4: Oh, no. There's W_6. He's with the other bunch. He's wiring connectors. He's a good wireman too. Then there's W_5. He keeps pretty much to himself, though. About all he does is turn out the work.

Int.: Would you say that your group feels a little superior to this other group?

W_4: Well, we all turn out more work, that's true. I don't know. It seems like the fast workmen are always together. I think they have a tendency to do that anyway. Men who are fast can turn out a whole lot more work and they seem to get together easier.

12-16-31

W_7, W_8, W_9, and S_4 have been demonstrating a ritual which they call "binging." One of them walks up to another one and hits him as hard as he can on the arm. The one hit makes no protest, and it seems that it is his privilege to "bing" the one who hit him. The object of the game is to see who can hit the hardest. This "binging" is also used as a penalty. If one of them says something that one of the others doesn't like, the other one will walk up and say, "I'm going to bing you for that." The one who is getting "binged" usually complains about being hurt, and he says, "That one was too hard. I'm going to get you for that."

12-17-31

The gang in the rear of the room has been doing a lot of fooling this afternoon. They have been "binging" each other, and W_7 and W_8 have been boxing with the trucker. When W_8 and the trucker started boxing, W_7 noticed that the door to the room was open.

W_7: Hey, W_9, close that door.

W_9 ran over and held the door shut. When W_8 and the trucker finished, W_7 started to spar with the trucker.

W_7: I'll show you how to put over that one-two.
W_8: Look at him work! Come on! Get hot! Smother him! That's it. There's one that went home. [As they finished] Boy, you loosened up on him that time!

1-27-32

W_7 had his window open. W_6 walked over and opened his window wide. W_9 went over and closed W_6's window. W_6 ran over to grab the chain. He insisted upon the window's staying open. W_9 insisted that it was too drafty.

W_6: You run your own window. I'll take care of this one.
W_9: It's too drafty. You leave that window closed or I'll bing you.
W_6: Go ahead, start.

W_9 glanced up to see if he could take the chain off the top of the window. W_6 held the chain tight so that W_9 couldn't loosen it. They had quite an argument.

W_6 (to W_8): How about it? Is it too drafty over there?
W_8: No, it's all right.
W_6: There you are. Now leave the window alone.
S_4 (to W_8): What's the idea of lying?
W_8: I'm not.
S_4: You're lying if you say you don't feel the draft.
W_7: Why don't you bing each other and then shut up?

2-25-32

W_9 suddenly "binged" W_7.

Obs.: Why did you do that?

W_9: He swore. We got an agreement so that the one who swears gets binged. W_8 was in it for five minutes, but he got binged a couple of times and then quit.

Obs.: Why don't you want to swear?

W_9: It's just a bad habit. There's no sense to it and it doesn't sound good. I've been getting the habit lately, and sometimes I swear when I don't want to. I never used to swear until I got used to W_8, and now I find myself doing it all the time.

12-9-31

The Hawthorne Club representative came into the room to take orders for candy. W_1, W_2, W_3, and S_1 divided up the price of a box of candy. They had a few odd pennies and nickels left over. After the representative left, they lagged for a mark on the floor in the first aisle until someone won all of the coins.

12-11-31

W_9: Oh, am I sick! I feel terrible.

W_8: Well, you didn't have to eat all that candy, you know.

Obs.: You should have given some of it to W_6.

W_6: I wouldn't eat any of their damn' candy.

Obs.: Didn't you get your share?

W_6: I didn't get a piece of it, and I'm glad of it.

W_7: You could have had some of it if you hadn't been so bullheaded.

W_9: I wish I were home.

1-29-32

W_5 (to *Obs.*): Well, I just hit them. I got a dollar from the boys on my pay check.

S_1, W_1, W_3, W_4, and W_5 bet a quarter each week on the poker hand in the paycheck number. The highest hand took the pot.

W_5: I won a quarter in the card game this noon, and then I took the quarter and bet on the poker hand, so that now I have a dollar for nothing. Now I'm going to take that dollar outside and bet it on "Starch." If he wins, then I'll have four or five dollars.

2-4-32

I_1, W_1, and W_4 were trying to pick a winner from the paper. S_1 and W_3 kidded them when the observer asked if they had a "hot one."

1-27-32

I_1 (after finding a reverse on one of W_4's equipments): I'll bet on W_4 in today's race. He's coming strong in the stretch.

It seems that W_1, W_2, W_3, and W_4 keep track of one another's reverses, and whenever the inspector finds a reverse, he advertises it by offering to take bets.

2-11-32

W_5 was wiring in position 8, S_4 in position 5.

W_5 (to S_4): I'm coming back there tomorrow. I can't do anything back here. These guys monkey around all day. (To GC) I want to go back to my own position.
GC: What for?
W_5: Oh, too much monkeying around. First W_8, who is supposed to be soldering, went over to the hospital. He got lost and I had to solder. Then he went over to the service and got lost. Then he goes out for you and don't come back.
W_9: Shut up, you. You talk too much. You don't know when to keep your mouth shut.
W_5: Never mind about that.
GC: How about it, W_8?
W_8: I didn't waste any time I didn't have to.

12-8-31

W_7 and W_9 went out for a drink.

W_6: I don't think that guy W_9 will ever learn to wire.
W_8: He hasn't been here hardly long enough to be good yet.
W_6: Yeah, but he doesn't want to wire. I'll bet if they put him in my charge he'd learn to wire in a hurry.
W_8: Who are you, the boss?
W_6: I don't mean that. I mean if they give me all of the privileges, just put him under my control, he'd learn to wire. I'd get over him with a big club, and every time he'd stop wiring I'd sock him.
S_4: That would be no good. You would be a driver.

12-28-31

W_9 was called to the office by the assistant foreman. Shortly after he came back:
W_7: Well, did you get bawled out?

W_9: No. He just showed me how much money I was losing and then he told me to come back here and earn some.

A little later—W_5 had come back for more banks.

W_5: How many are you turning out now?
W_9: Oh, about 3000 or 4000.
W_5: Then you're losing $.09 an hour.
W_6: How do you figure that?
W_5: Well, his rate is $.37.
W_7: It is, like hell. It's $.39.
W_5: Well, then, he's losing $.11 an hour.
W_8: Watch him tear, now that he got bawled out.
W_9: Don't worry, I won't do any more.
W_6: He's got the same rate as I got. I'd just like to see what would happen to you, W_9, if they should ever make us a gang by ourselves. I'll bet you'd work. Just like I said the other day, we'd make you work.
W_9: I don't know whether you would or not.
W_6: Well, you wouldn't be turning in any 3000 connections.
W_9: Well, I suppose I'd get beat up a couple of times and then I'd quit.
W_6: You'd either work or quit, one or the other.

1-20-32

About 3:15, W_6 and the observer were standing at W_6's position.

W_8: Why don't you quit work, W_6? Let's see, this is your thirty-fifth row today. What are you going to do with them all?
W_6: What do you care what I do with them? It's to your advantage if I work, isn't it?
W_8: Yeah, but the way you're working you'll get stuck with them.
W_6: Don't worry about that. I'll take care of it. You're getting paid by the sets I turn out. That's all you should worry about.
W_8: If you don't quit work, I'll bing you.

They hit each other on the arm two or three times. Finally W_8 chased W_6 around the room.

Obs.: What's the matter, W_6, won't he let you work?
W_6: No, I'm all through, though. I've got enough done.

W_6 then went up and helped W_3 for a while.

W_8: Look at that hound. If he can't work on his own, he goes up there and helps somebody else. Can he go! He sure is a wireman. I sometimes think I can wire, but I can't keep up with that guy when he wants to work.

3-2-32

W_4 and W_6 were kidding each other about work this afternoon. W_6 was working very fast. W_4 was working faster than usual.

W_4 (to W_6): Go on, you slave, work! You're enough connections ahead now to take care of Friday.

Obs. (to W_4): Is W_6 going too fast to suit you?

W_4: He's nothing but a slave. A couple more rows and he'll have 8000.

W_6: No, I won't. I haven't got today's work out yet.

W_4: You should have quit when you finished that set.

W_6: I'm good for another 6000 connections. If they'd pay me for it, I'd turn them out.

3-16-32

W_2 (to S_1): Come on, get this set.

S_1: All right. (To *Obs.*) I want to introduce you to Lightning 2 and Cyclone 3. When those two get going, it's just like a whirlwind up here. Give W_2 a big chew of snuff and he just burns the solder right off the terminals.

W_3: You forgot the 4:15 Special over here.

S_1: Oh, yes, that's the 4:15 Special. He works until 4:15 every day.

5-12-32

W_1 (to W_2): Come on, Phar-Lap, quit. You wire just like that horse runs. You've got enough out for today.

W_2: I'm not done yet. Two more rows will make it.

5-19-32

GC_2 was taking the count.

W_4 (to W_6): How many are you going to turn in?

W_6: I've got to turn in 6800.

W_4: What's the matter? Are you crazy? You work all week and turn in 6600 for a full day, and now today you're gone an hour and a quarter and you turn in more than you do the other days.

W_6: I don't care. I'm going to finish these sets tomorrow.

W_4: You're screwy.

W_6: All right, I'll turn in 6400.

W_4: That's too much.

W_6: That don't make any difference. I've got to do something with them.

W_4: Well, give them to me.

W_6 did not answer.

Part II: Output and Attitudes Towards the Wage Incentive Plan

In Figure 9 the reported average hourly output per week is shown. The time period over which this record extends includes the observation period proper as well as a base period of 18 weeks just prior to the time the study began. This record is based on the output counts verbally reported to the group chief at the end of a day's work by each wireman.

Figure 10 compares the actual with the reported average hourly output. The reported output curves are the same as those shown in Figure 9. The actual output curves are based on the actual count of the number of terminals each wireman wired, taken at noon and at night by the observer. Both these curves should also be compared with the wiremen's concept of a day's work as expressed in the interviews: about two equipments, or 6600 connections, per day, or approximately 825 connections per hour.

Figure 11 shows, for each wireman during the entire period of the study, (1) average hourly output rate maintained throughout the day; (2) average hourly output rates maintained during the morning and during the afternoon; and (3) the percentage by which the morning hourly rate exceeded the afternoon hourly rate.

Figure 12 shows the average hourly output for each wireman during the period of study in relation to (1) his score in the Otis Intermediate or Higher Examination and (2) his score in a combined soldering and dexterity test. The wiremen are arranged in order of their rank in output, shown by the black portion of each column. Differences in the total heights of the columns represent differences in intelligence quotient or dexterity score.

In the excerpts from interviews with the wiremen following the charts, their understanding of and attitudes toward the wage incentive system are shown. Further illustrations from the observer's record will be found in Case D.

INTERVIEW WITH W_1, 9-11-31

Int.: What is the bogey?

W_1: On connectors, 6600. You see, that's two sets. There are 3300 connections on a set. Now on selectors the bogey is only 6000,

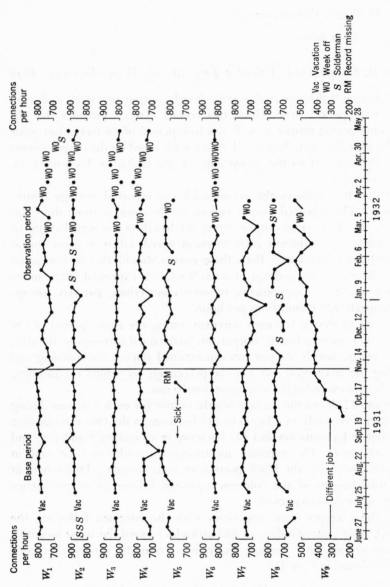

Figure 9

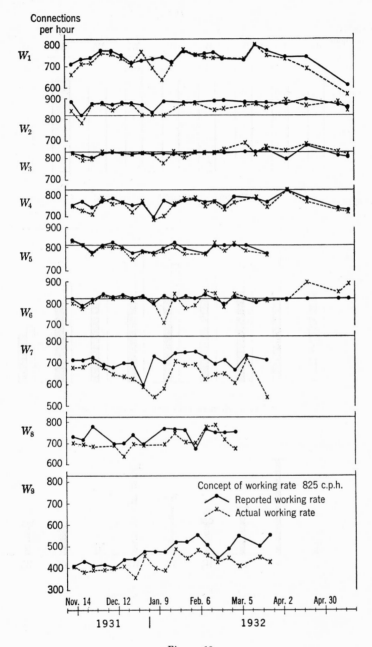

Figure 10

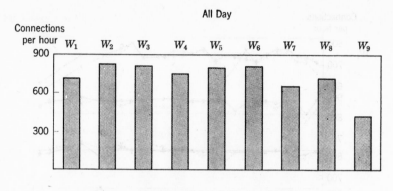

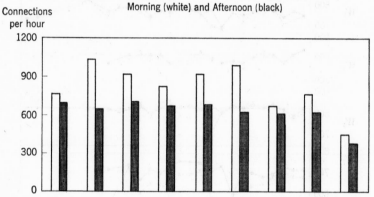

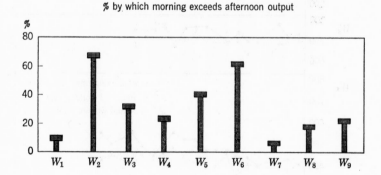

Figure 11. Average hourly output.

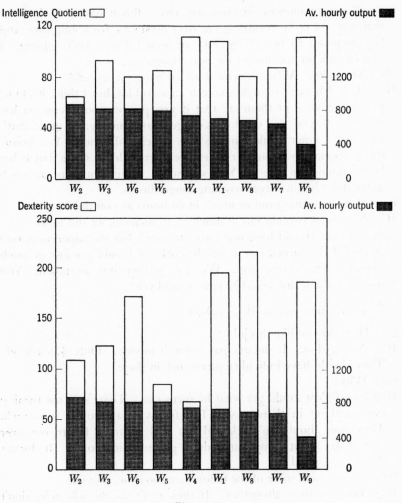

Figure 12

because there are only 3000 connections on a set. In order to turn
out 6600 there, you have to wire three levels on a third set.
Int.: And 6600 is your bogey then?
W_1: Yes, it's 6600. You see, they told us if we got out two sets a day
it would be all right. That's a pretty good day's work too. . . .
Int.: You are making $.39 now?
W_1: Yes. Of course, it's not according to the way they said it would
be when I started out. They said, "When you make so many, then

you'll get an increase in your day rate. But it hasn't worked out that way. I've been turning out over 6000 now for a long time, and I'm supposed to be getting $.41 an hour. But it isn't coming. I suppose it's on account of the way things are.

Int.: No doubt. What do you think of gang piecework?

W_1: Well, I haven't thought about it an awful lot, but I think it's O.K. I've heard some of them say that if you put out more, you get less money. If you put out less, you get more money. I guess that's true, but I don't think it makes very much difference. You know, the percentage was smaller when we started down there, but it has been coming up lately. You see, we're turning out just as much as we did when we were working longer hours.

Int.: You are turning out as much in 40 hours as you did in 48?

W_1: No, we're turning out as much in 40 hours as we did in 44. We thought we should have our rates increased, but the supervisors told us that if we turned out as much work we would get just as much money. That's true too. We are getting just as much. You wouldn't think that could be true, would you?

INTERVIEW WITH W_2, 9-9-31

Int.: How do you like this job?

W_2: Not so hot. It doesn't pay enough money. Only $26 a week. They should have individual piecework in there.

Int.: Why?

W_2: So a fellow could get what he turns out. There's no use turning out anything in there now. The fellows loaf around too much. They quit about 3 o'clock and just stall around. I turn out over 7000 a day right along, but I don't get anything for it. It doesn't do me any good.

Int.: So you think some of the fellows are too slow, do you?

W_2: Yes, too slow altogether. If they can't do the job, why don't they kick them out of there? They just hold the rest of us back.

Int.: Can you explain gang piecework to me?

W_2 (after a long pause): Well, now, I don't know. The fast one works fast, and the slow one works slow, I guess.

Int.: You mean the fast one makes up for the slow man?

W_2: Yeah.

Int.: I suppose it takes some time to learn the job.

W_2: I don't see why it should. I could turn out 6000 in three weeks. I think the rest of them could if they wanted to. They don't like to have me turn in so much, but I'll turn it in anyway.

Int.: Why do you turn out so much?

W_2 (after a moment's hesitation): Well, I want to get a good record. I want to get a good record so that when I go up and ask for a transfer there will be nothing to keep me from getting one.

INTERVIEW WITH W_3, 9-21-31

Int.: I wish you would tell me what you think of group piecework.
W_3: All in all, I think it's a good system. Everyone makes the same percentage and the variation in earnings depends on the day rate. As long as you can make a raise in your day rate occasionally, it works out all right.
Int.: How do you figure your percentage?
W_3: I really don't know just how it's figured. That's all done for us. The clerks figure it out and then post it so that we can see it.
Int.: Even though you don't know how to figure it, don't you have a pretty good idea of what it is?
W_3: No, I don't. You see, it varies quite a bit ordinarily, so I never do know just what it should be. I think it is based on the amount we turn out over our day rate. In addition to our regular percentage, we get a monthly bonus. Last month it was $5. That isn't very much. Sometimes it gets as low as $1 and sometimes it runs up to around $10.
Int.: I wonder how the monthly bonus is figured.
W_3: I don't know exactly, but I think it works like this. If we make 61 per cent in a week we are only paid 60 per cent and the 1 per cent is allowed to collect and go into a monthly bonus. It's the odd numbers over an even percentage.
Int.: I see. They must do that for convenience in calculation. And you turn out around 6000 a day now?
W_3: Oh, I turn out 6600 regularly. Sometimes I turn in 6800. I manage to average around 6600 every day though.
Int.: Is that what is expected of you?
W_3: Yes, they expect about that. Of course, you could make out less and get by, but it is safer to turn out about 6600. You see, that's two completed sets. There's 3300 connections on each set.
Int.: And is 6600 your bogey?
W_3: No, our bogey is higher than that. It is 914 an hour. No one can turn that out consistently. Well, occasionally some of them do. Now since this layoff started there's been a few fellows down there who have been turning out around 7300 a day. They've been working like hell. It's foolishness to do it, because I don't think it will do them any good and it is likely to do the rest of us a lot of harm.

Int.: How do you figure that?

W_3: Well, you see if they start turning out around 7300 a day over a period of weeks, and if three of them do it, then they can lay one of the men off, because three men working at that rate of speed can do as much as four men working at the present rate.

Int.: Do you think that's likely to happen?

W_3: Yes, I think it would. At present we are only scheduled for 40 sets ahead. In normal times we were scheduled for over 100 ahead. If they find out that fewer men can do the work, they're going to lay more of us off. When things pick up, they will expect us to do just as much as we are now. That means they will raise the bogey on us. You see how it works? Another thing about gang piece-work, there isn't much incentive to work faster. If you are not going to make any more than the men who work next to you, you don't feel like you should turn out any more work.

Int.: You say that there isn't an incentive to turn out more work. If all of you turned out more work, wouldn't you make more money?

W_3: No, we wouldn't. They told us that down there one time. The supervisors came around and told us that very thing, that if we would turn out more work we would make more money, but we can't see it that way. Probably what would happen is that our bogey would be raised and then we would just be turning out more work for the same money. I can't see that.

INTERVIEW WITH W_4, 10-20-31

Int.: You say the rate is 6600 on connectors and only 6000 on selectors?

W_4: Yeah, we figure that two sets a day is about a day's work.

Int.: By that you don't mean the bogey, do you?

W_4: No, I don't think that's the bogey. I think the bogey is quite a bit higher. Something like 900 an hour. I'd be in for more money if things were better. You see, 6000 pays $.41 an hour. Now that I'm turning out more than that I should be getting a raise, but I don't suppose it will be possible these times.

Int.: Do the other men around you make about that too?

W_4: I think they do. Nearly everyone in front makes about $.41. The slower men are in back there. They don't make so much money. Nearly all the new men are back there now.

INTERVIEW WITH W_5, 6-12-31

W_5: I like wiring. I don't care particularly whether I get another job or not, just so I make more money. About the only way I can see of making more money down there is by individual piecework. I had a plan that I worked out some time ago and told the boss about. It seems to me it should work pretty well. The idea is to adjust each man's day rate according to his efficiency. If a man was turning out, say, 5000 a day, he would get $.37 an hour. If a man was turning out 6000 a day, he would be given $.39 an hour. Then, if you turned out 6600 or over, you'd be given $.41 an hour. That way the faster workman would be given more than the slower workman. It would adjust the thing better. The way it is now, some of the fellows with a high day rate turn out about 5000, which is much slower than some of the faster workmen. There are a lot of fellows who lose money down there on that account.

Int.: You don't seem to think very much of the group piecework system.

W_5: No, I don't. About the only advantage of group piecework is that it is a little more economical. I think you save the time of a couple of clerks. But the fast workers produce for the slow workers. I hear that down there every day. There's always several fellows complaining about it. There is no excuse for their being slow either. The fellows just like to loaf around, I guess.

Int.: I should think the slower workers would be looked upon with disfavor by the group.

W_5: You know, that's what I always thought too, but I can't quite figure it out. It's just the opposite. The slow workers are looked upon as good fellows. You go down there and make a study of that department and you'll find out. You'll find that the fellows all like the slow workers. They don't seem to see that it is the slow worker who keeps their pay down.

There's another thing, you know, the fellows give the fast workers the raspberries all the time. Work hard and try to do your best and they don't appreciate it at all. They don't seem to figure that they are gaining any by it. It's not only the wiremen—the soldermen don't like it either. I think a lot of them have the idea that if they work fast the rate will be raised. That would mean that they would have to work faster for the same money. I've never seen our rate raised here yet, so I don't know whether it would happen or not. I have heard that it's been raised in some cases.

Int.: What is the bogey, 6600 a day?

W_5: No, that's not the bogey. The bogey is 7200, I think. It's pretty hard to make it working the hours we do.

Int.: What's the idea of having the bogey so high?

W_5: It makes you work faster. There's another thing I might as well tell you. Some of the fellows in the gang turn in more than they turn out.

Int.: Isn't that rather hard to do?

W_5: It's pretty hard to do if the gang boss is experienced, but every once in a while, as at present, when a new man comes in they can get away with it. This is the way they do it: You see, each man works on two sets at the same time so the solderman can finish up each level after it's wired. Well, suppose he had finished 5 levels on one set and 10 levels on the other. All he does is finish the two sets. He has to turn in 10 more levels on the one set and 5 on the other. Then he turns that in as two complete sets for the day. Unless the gang boss has kept pretty close check on him, he doesn't know the difference. That happens right along. The fellows think it's a pretty smart thing to do. They don't realize that it just works to the group's disadvantage. The gang boss is up a tree. He doesn't know how it happened. He finds that he's supposed to have had so many sets turned out and the actual count doesn't tally with it. He can't accuse anybody in the group because he doesn't know who did it. You see what that really does is to increase the individual percentage, but it lowers the group percentage—the individual gains at the expense of the group.

Int.: Doesn't the group resent that sort of thing?

W_5: No, not at all. They think it's a pretty clever thing to get away with.

INTERVIEW WITH W_6, 8-27-31

W_6: The bogey is pretty high. I turn out 6600 a day right along and that is pretty good, I think, for the average.

Int.: Is that the bogey?

W_6: I think it is.

Int.: Then you are turning out 100 per cent a day.

W_6: Well, I don't know about that. I don't think I am turning out 100 per cent. You see the bogey was 914 an hour for an eight-and-three-quarter-hour day, so I suppose it would be around 6600 for an eight-hour day.

INTERVIEW WITH W_7, 10-21-31

W_7: We should have straight piecework; that's what we should have. Then we could make more money. You don't have much reason for working down there. I got a raise last July, but I had to squawk to get it. I had it coming to me a long time. I was turning out pretty close to 6000 for a long time, and I never got it. You're supposed to get around $.39 for 6000. As soon as you make your rate, you're supposed to get a raise.

Int.: What is the rate on that job?

W_7: 6000 a day.   Oh, I guess there's another rate that is higher than that, but the bosses tell us that 6000 is a day's work.   They tell us that we should get a $.95 a thousand for wiring.   I can't figure that out because it doesn't make any difference how much you turn out, you don't get any more money.   That's the catch in the whole thing.   You see, if you were paid $.95 a thousand and were on straight piecework, you might turn out 6000 or 7000.   That would give you close to $6 a day, $30 a week.   That would be pretty good. But you'd never make it on the system they have now.

Int.: Why do you think you couldn't make any more?

W_7: I don't know.   That's where the company gyps us, I think.   You see, they take something out of it no matter how much we turn out.

Int.: Doesn't that include a charge for supervision and other expenses like that?

W_7: Maybe it does.   I hadn't thought of that.   If it does, that accounts for what we don't get.   But I think they should put us on straight piecework and let us do our own soldering.   The job gets so monotonous that it's good to have a change.   When you don't get to solder all you do is just wire, wire, wire.   That's all there is to it.   It gets awfully monotonous.   I can't keep my mind on my work.   Now some of those fellows down there can keep their mind on it pretty well.   They get a chew of tobacco and go right at it. I think you'll find that the best workmen all chew tobacco, and they're light.   A heavy person gets rather tired.   There's one little guy down there that turns out over 7000 a day.   I think there's a couple of them.   And we have to put up with it.

INTERVIEW WITH W_8, 6-10-31

W_8: I made up my mind I was going to turn out 6600 today.   I don't think I could have done it though.   When you came along I had only wired 9 levels.   Some of the fellows have turned out 12 levels by that time.

Int.: You have difficulty making your rate?

W_8: Yes, it is pretty hard to make the bogey.   In fact, I never have made it.   Some of the fellows do it every day.   Those are the speedy guys.   I make between 5500 and 6000.   On selector wiring they don't turn out as many.   I think they are supposed to turn out 6000 a day over there.   We have an extra bank on each set so that if we wire two sets we would be making 6600 connections a day.

Int.: Is that the bogey?

W_8: Yes, I think it is.

CASE C: THE CASE OF I_3

The following observations, arranged in chronological order, relate to the difficulties encountered by one of the inspectors in his daily work associations with other members of the group. It should be remembered that the inspectors belonged to a different organization from that of the wiremen and soldermen—the Inspection Branch. They reported to a different set of supervisors and were paid on an hourly basis. The symbol *IGC* stands for the inspection group chief, the supervisor to whom the inspectors reported. *IGC* is a different person from *GC*, the supervisor to whom the wiremen and soldermen reported, and who spent most of his time in the observation room.

12-15-31

The new inspector they brought in this morning is a short, heavy-set man between 40 and 45 years old. He seemed very slow, as though he did not understand the work. The 48-volt current was off, and he was just barely keeping up with the gang by giving the boards only a visual inspection. At 10 o'clock:

W_6 (to *GC*): How about some service?

GC (to *Obs.*): I've got to see this guy's boss. He's holding us back too much. He couldn't keep up with the fellows out in the other room. It costs us too much money to have a guy like that around.

About 11 o'clock I_3 was having some trouble on one of W_7's units. He didn't seem to know how to shoot the trouble. W_7 came over and tried to help him, and then W_9 played with it for a while. Neither of the wiremen knew what was wrong. Finally W_7 called I_1. He found a crossed solder very quickly. I_3 left the unit and was not watching I_1 shoot the trouble. He never did find out what was wrong. He did not seem particularly interested.

12-16-31

I_3 was trying to run a test set this afternoon. I_1 had explained it to him. His group chief had explained it twice, but he didn't seem to understand. W_6 was trying to help him hook up the set. W_6 didn't know much about it. They called I_1. He showed them how the set should be hooked up. I_3 went to the next set, and again he couldn't get the set hooked up. W_6 went over to help him, and they finally had to call I_1 again. On the next three or four sets W_6 was able to hook it up. I_3 still had the thing all mixed up.

12-22-31

The group in the rear of the room seemed to be working very fast this morning. I_3 couldn't keep up with them.

W_6 (to GC): How about getting a new inspector in here?   We can't turn out any work with this guy.

W_5: How about some service?   I've turned out five rows and I've had to wait five times.   If this guy can't do the work, why not get somebody that can?

GC (to Obs.): I'm gonna have to get that guy outta here.   We can't put up with that.   I'm gonna see the boss now.

At 11 o'clock I_3 was down again.

W_5: (to GC): I wired fifteen levels and I waited fifteen times.

W_6: I've got an hour and a half waiting time this morning.

W_9: I've got two hours coming.

GC: You guys all give me a pain with your daywork. It's always the bum workers that want all the daywork.

W_7: Well, how are you going to work when you've got a guy like this around?   You just get started and then you gotta go over and set down and wait.

GC: I know, but you don't have to turn in daywork for each minute you sit down.

W_8: You should try to get in here and make the bogey when you've gotta work like this.

Obs. (to I_3): The boys are making it kind of tough for you this morning, aren't they?

I_3: Yes, but I can't do anything.   I don't know what's the matter when that thing don't buzz.   Well, that's what they get when they put a man out here without any training.   I ran selectors in the other room, and when I come out here they put me on connectors.

After lunch I_3 ran into two more reverses that he couldn't find.   He was now so far behind that four wiremen were sitting along the radiator watching him.   He was standing by one of W_7's units waiting for I_1 to come back and find the trouble.

W_5 (to I_3): Come on down here and work my unit while you're waiting.

W_8: No, come on over and work mine.

I_3 unhooked the set and started back toward W_8's unit. W_5 and W_6 both called to him to come to their positions, and so he turned around and went down toward W_5's unit.

W_7: Hey, I_3, you can't walk off on me like that. That's no way to treat me.

I_3 continued down to W_5's unit. The group all thought this was an immense joke. I_3 was so befuddled that he didn't know what he was doing. I_1 came back to see what was the trouble with W_7's unit while I_3 was on W_5's. I_3 started to unhook his set in the middle of the test to come back. W_5 urged him to stay there, and the rest all called to him to come to their units. He finally finished W_5's unit.

W_7: That's the kind of a guy you are. Walk out on a fellow after you start his unit.

Everyone laughed.

W_6: (to GC): Well, I got four hours waiting time now.
W_5: Well, I did 25 rows and I waited 25 times.
GC (to Obs.): I can't do anything about this inspector. I talked to his gang boss and told him he'd have to get somebody else out here, and then I talked to the section chief. I suppose I better go and see the assistant foreman.
Obs.: The boys sure did have him all mixed up for a while there.
GC: Yes, if they'd kept quiet and left him alone, he'd a got along better.
I_1 (to Obs.): This fellow doesn't seem to catch on to this job at all.
Obs.: Is it a difficult job to learn?
I_1: No, it shouldn't take any time to learn it.
Obs.: I_3 was on selectors in the other room, wasn't he? Is there much difference between selectors and connectors?
I_1: The only difference is in hooking up the blocks. You shoot the trouble the same. If you can shoot trouble on selectors you sure ought to be able to do it on connectors. He was on selectors in the other room about two months. The fellows in there had him down most of the time. He's really been on the job long enough in this room to learn it. I don't know what makes him so slow.

12-23-31

I_3 was working hard this morning to keep up. At 9 o'clock he was just about keeping the wiremen going. They occasionally called for him to hurry.

At 10 o'clock W_5 and W_6 were calling for I_3. They were arguing between them as to who should get him first. While they were arguing an inspector came in. He asked the observer if he could talk to I_3. He showed I_3 a trouble sheet and they talked a few minutes and then he went out. About five minutes later he came back and called I_3 out of the room. I_1 came in and said that the inspector had found two crossed solders and three poor solders on one of the units I_3 had passed. Crossed solders are very serious defects.

I_1: They told this guy that if he got any more defects they'd give him the gate, so I suppose he's out there catching hell for it.

W_7: He's got a whole raft full of units that just were inspected by him visually. Wait till they get the trouble on those.

W_8: Well, that was when the test box wouldn't work.

I_1: Test box, hell. That test box would have run all the time if he'd known how to run it.

Just then I_3 came back into the room.

W_6: Well, did you catch hell?

I_3 had a sheepish smile on his face. He did not appear to answer.

12-28-31

I_3 seemed to have been doing better lately. He hasn't been holding up the job. Occasionally he has been able to shoot a case of trouble. He has not had many reverses during the last two days.

1-6-32

The gang in the rear of the room were having trouble with the inspector this morning. He seemed to be a little slow.

The check inspector found some trouble on one of I_3's boards. He called I_3 and showed him the defect, and then he told W_9 that he should not wire the next level until they got the inspection group chief. The inspection group chief came out and looked at the level and talked for a few minutes with I_3. Evidently I_3 told him that his test set was out of order. The test set has been out to the inspection group chief several times, and the group chief has found nothing the matter with it. Now he did not believe there was anything wrong, and he attempted to operate the set himself. He found that a minor adjustment was necessary in one set, but that the other one was O.K. While the inspection group chief was repairing the test set, I_3 sat down at the observer's desk.

Obs.: What was the fuss about?

I_3: Oh, that was a lot of foolishness. He found a little chip hanging on a terminal. It wasn't any more than a 32nd of an inch long. The inspection group chief himself told him that that was nothing. They have to find some kind of trouble or they wouldn't have a job.

Obs.: You seem to be having quite a bit of trouble this morning.

I_3: I can't keep up when I've got a bum test set. These boxes are nothing but junk. Then, too, the fellows themselves make it bad for me, especially that fellow W_5. He calls for me lots of times when he's just starting the other unit. I know where to go if they would only leave me alone. The solderman can make it bad for me too, if he wants to. Sometimes, you know, he will sit around and wait until he has three units to solder, and then he will solder the three of them as fast as he can. Then when the other solderman does the same thing I have to get behind. If they had given me some training before I came out here, I would know more about this job. I was in the other room about two weeks on selectors, and I just began to get on to them and then they brought me out here on connectors. The jigs out here are different, and I don't know anything about them. The fellows here treat me like I was an outsider. I am not one of them, and so they make it just as hard as they can for me.

The inspection group chief returned just then with I_3's test set.

IGC: Well, this box is O.K. now. Now you've got two good boxes.

I_3: Can I change the jigs that I am using over to this one now?

IGC: No. Use this as long as it will work, and then you will have a good one.

I_3: I'd like to use this one. It makes a louder buzz. When the buzz is loud I can tell when I get trouble; otherwise I have to listen real close.

The inspection group chief did not answer. I_3 started changing the jigs.

IGC: Wait a minute, now. See that you don't mix them up. Do you know which one goes on top?

I_3: Let's see. I don't remember. I guess it was this one.

The inspection group chief and I_3 tested the box and found that he had them right. The inspection group chief then came over and sat down with the observer.

Obs.: What was the trouble over there this morning?

IGC: Oh, they found a couple of loose solders on this fellow. It doesn't seem as though he can learn this job. I think that he don't want to learn. He wants to go back to the Cable Plant, and so I guess he thinks that if he does a bum job here he will go back.

Obs.: What kind of a worker was he over there?

IGC: I don't think he was much good. They were glad to get rid of him. That's just the trouble. Nobody wants him. I tried my best to get rid of him, but I can't. He's got somebody pushing him. When he was sent down here, the Inspection Personnel came down and told us to do the best we could for him. That makes it bad all the way round. Here he's getting $.72 an hour and can't do the job, and the rest of the men are between $.45 and $.50. I've been catching hell for all kinds of trouble. Last week they caught all kinds of reverses in the other room. The test box is always on the bum and he marks the tickets visual inspection whenever he gets a block reverse.

1-7-32

This group in the front of the room seemed to be having a lot of fun this afternoon. S_1 was telling them about a time when he used to weave rugs in Turkey. He told a very elaborate yarn. After this had been going on for a little while, he went back to I_3 and told him the story. They thought it was a great joke because I_3 listened to the entire story and believed it. The observer went over to I_3.

Obs.: What's the big joke?

I_3: Oh, this fellow is telling me that he used to weave rugs in Turkey. I guess some way or other they found out that I came from Constantinople and they are just trying to have a lot of fun with me.[3]

---

[3] Excerpt from interview with I_3, 3–10–32:

"Perhaps you know that I was not born in this country. I came here about 20 years ago. I was born in Turkey. Some people seem to think that because I was born in Turkey I am necessarily a Turk. That is not true. I am an Armenian. There is all the difference in the world between an Armenian and a Turk. Perhaps you know that the Armenians have been persecuted for centuries by the Turks. It's largely a religious difference. You see, I am a Christian. Armenians are Christians, but Turks are Mohammedans. There is a very bitter feeling between them. The Turks, of course, are the stronger people. They have subjected the Armenians for centuries. The reason I left Turkey was to escape the army. Everyone, when he reaches the age of about 20, has to serve in the Turkish army. To the Armenians it means almost certain death, because they are put in the most dangerous situations. On top of that, they are under Turkish officers who take every opportunity to humiliate them. The only way I could get out of that was to leave the country, so I decided to come here, to the United States. Three years after I came here my father was massacred. It was plain butchery. If I had been there, I would have been killed too."

Obs.: How did they find out?

I_3: That's what I would like to know.   If he comes back again, I'll ask him.

Obs. (to I_1): What is all this joke about?

S_1: Weaving rugs.

I_1: Oh, the boys are just having fun with this guy back here.

Obs.: Does he come from Turkey?

I_1: Yes, I guess he did.   It's no wonder that he can't run one of those things there.   A Turk could never run one.

Obs.: I wonder how the gang got hold of that.

I_1: I guess I told them.   I heard one of the bosses in the other room say it yesterday.   They were talking about his being a Turk.

1-28-32

I_3 kept W_8 waiting several times this morning. W_8 was again waiting for I_3.

W_8 (to *Obs.*): I'm going to have some fun.

W_8 walked over to I_3's test set and pulled the plug out far enough so that it did not make a contact.   It took I_3 some minutes to discover what was the matter.   As I_3 discovered the trouble, W_8 pulled the jig so that it caused a short.

A little later W_7 was waiting for I_3. W_8 was standing with him. When I_3 hooked up his set there was a cross-solder in the level solder some place, but I_3 thought that W_8 had fooled around.   He became so confused that he did not know where to look for the trouble. W_8 tried to help him locate the cross, but I_3 thought he was causing the trouble and so tried to get him away.   Finally, I_3 decided it was a block reverse and so called W_9 to fix it. W_9 decided that it wasn't a block reverse.

W_7: Why don't you fellows get away and let I_3 find the trouble?   I'd just as soon sit around here all morning.   If you stay there, maybe you'll find what's wrong.

Finally W_6 and W_7 tried to help and in the mix-up the set started to work. W_6 and W_8 each claimed that he had fixed it.

1-29-32

I_3 (to S_4): Go over and solder these two sets.   You are going to make me behind.

S_4: What are you trying to do, tell me what to do?

S_4 was sitting down.   He did not move. I_3 went over to the group chief and asked him to have S_4 solder the sets.

GC: What's the matter, S_4?   Have you got sets to solder?
S_4: Yes, there's two of them.
GC: Well, get over there and solder them.
S_4: You tell that inspector to mind his own business; not to be putting his nose in mine.   He can't tell me what to do.
I_3: You do your job the way you should.
S_4: Well, don't you be telling me what to do.

If S_4 had waited a few minutes longer, W_8 would have been forced to wait for the inspector. W_8 did not join in the argument when the group chief was in the room, but as soon as he left W_8 came over to the section chief, who was sitting at the observer's desk.

W_8: Say, how about a little service?
SC: What's the matter, are you short banks?
W_8: No, it's this inspector.   Aren't you anybody out in the other room?   Can't you get him out of here?
SC: I'll get him out of here before long.

A little later S_4 soldered three-fourths of one of W_7's equipments and then went over to one of W_9's equipments. I_3 thought S_4 had finished W_7's set and started to inspect it.

S_4: Get off of that set.   Wait till I get through with it.
I_3: You are supposed to be through with it.
S_4: Well, I'm not.

S_4 then came over and finished soldering the level. I_3 picked up a soldering iron to repair some defects.

S_4: Leave the soldering iron alone.   All you gotta do is pull up the connection.   I'll fix it.
I_3: If you were any kind of a solderman, I would do that, but I can't trust you.
S_4: Leave that soldering iron alone from now on or I'll hit you right between the eyes.
I_3: Go ahead, punch.
W_7: Poor I_3, he's getting it today.

2-11-32

I_3 was at position 8, near the door.

S_1: Hey, I_3, close the door.
I_3: I haven't got time.

He then walked away from position 8.

S_1: Why you god-damn' Turkish bastard!   You'd stand right there by the door and won't do a fellow a favor.

I_3: I'm not closing any doors for you.

S_1: You're a swell guy!

   He then got up and closed the door himself.

   2-17-32

S_4 and I_3 seemed to be having an argument this morning. I_3 was testing one of W_8's equipments and S_4 was touching up the solder connections on the same equipment.

I_3 (to GC): You've got to keep S_4 off these sets when I'm working on them.   He holds me back and then somebody else has to wait for me.

GC (to S_4): What are you doing over there?

S_4: I'm touching up the solder connections.

GC (to I_3): That's all right, he's just trying to do a good job.

I_3: Yes, but I can't do my work if he spends so much time touching them up.

GC: Well, you can't blame him if he wants to do a good job.

I_3: All right, then.   Don't say anything when these fellows have to wait.   I can only be one place, and if S_4 holds me up I can't help it.

Immediately after this argument the group in the rear of the room started to razz I_3.   They tried to confuse him by calling for him when he was working on another equipment.   Whenever he ran into trouble, they told him he was dumb.   They called him names.   Several of them suggested that he look at his jigs; others suggested a cable reverse; and still others told him that he had a cross-solder.   These suggestions confused I_3 until he could do nothing.   He finally gave up using the test set.   He inspected five or six equipments visually while W_9 fooled around with his test set. W_9 finally found the trouble.

W_8 (to $Obs.$): This guy I_3 will never be any good.   He don't take any interest in his work.   If he would study things out instead of sitting over there reading the paper, he probably would get along better.

   2-24-32

The observer noticed I_3 in the corner of the room, walking back and forth thinking about something.   Suddenly I_3 threw out his chest and strutted over to W_9's position.

I_3: W_9, I'm going to give you a test. You claim you've got an extensive vocabulary. I'm going to find out just how good you are.

W_9: I think my vocabulary is more extensive than the average.

I_3 wrote down a list of words.

W_9: What kind of test is this?

I_3: Oh, it's something like the Alpha test. It's a test for your intelligence.

W_9: I thought you said vocabulary.

I_3: That's what I mean, vocabulary. Now here it is. You write down the word opposite the word that I'm thinking of. It is a word that pertains to these words.

W_9: That's no test. How do I know what word you're thinking of?

I_3: If you know the word, you can write it.

W_9: That's no test. There are a lot of words that pertain to trees. How do I know what you're thinking of?

I_3: All right, then you get zero. You don't know.

W_9: Well, what word are you thinking of?

I_3: Arboreal.

3-3-32

I_3 was inspecting positions 9, 7, and 6 this afternoon. He could not get his test set to work. He didn't know where the trouble was. He fooled around on W_7's equipment until 4:15. The group kidded I_3 so much that he didn't know what he was doing. It appeared that the long and short cable wires were reversed. I_3 gave up in disgust, and W_8 and W_9 tried to locate the trouble. W_7 was sitting down. He did not appear to be interested. W_6 came back to W_7's position.

W_6: Do I have to come back here and show you fellows what's the matter?

W_6 played around with it for a while.

W_6: There, I told you. It's a long and short reverse.

GC (to I_1): Why didn't you come back and find it for him?

I_1: I told him what was the matter with it; if he don't want to pay any attention let him go.

A little later.

I_1 (to Obs.): It looks like everybody's disgusted with I_3. The inspection group chief told me a little while ago that he bawled him out because he mixed up no-solders and loose connections. I_3 answered, "How can I get them if the test set passes them up?" I guess he didn't even understand what the inspection group chief was talking about.

3-4-32

When the observer entered the test room this morning, the section chief and the group chief were standing near W_7's position talking earnestly.

W_9 (to *Obs.*): We caught hell this morning. The foreman came in and caught W_7 and S_4 sitting down, waiting for I_3. I guess he went out in the other room and raised hell too.

GC (to *Obs.*): That set of W_7's was all right last night. I_8 had his box all tangled up.

I_3 was not using a box this morning. He was inspecting visually.

GC (to *Obs.*): I wonder who jammed up that test box. I think W_8 did it. He's always doing something like that.

After 4:15:

Foreman (to *Obs.*): Say, did I_3 say anything to you about the fellows picking on him out there?
Obs.: No.
F: Well he went up to the Personnel with a long story. He said that they were calling him names and pushing him around when he tried to work. He said that the fellows were done at 2 o'clock out there and that they told the gang boss to go to hell. Did you see anything like that going on?
Obs.: No, I didn't.
F: They got me the first thing this morning and I went out there and saw W_7 and S_4 sitting down, waiting for that guy, and then we took his test box, and we found that the thing had been grounded with solder and screws. Some one of those fellows must have been monkeying around with it. I think it was W_8. I've had trouble with him that way before, but I think that guy lied about this other stuff. I checked up on the efficiency out there and they're turning out about as much stuff as they did in here, and I know that when a fellow is turning out between 6000 and 7000 connections he hasn't got much time to fool around. Those boys out there are a little noisy, but I don't expect a man to stand there and work all day without saying anything. Take W_6—it comes natural for him to be noisy. I used to come over to him once in a while when he was out here and say, "For God's sake, don't talk so loud." He'd tell

me that he couldn't help it. He talks the same way every place.
I know, I watched him play pool across the street, and I could hear
W_6 talk as soon as I come into the room. I don't mind that, but
I would like to find out who put solder in that test set. They had
the thing grounded so it couldn't work. Did you see anybody do
that?

Obs.: No, I'm not there all the time.

3-8-32

About quarter of four, I_1 came into the room. He seemed very
much excited. He came over to the observer's desk, where S_1, W_7,
and the group chief were gathered.

I_1: Oh, did I_3 fix you fellows up! He went up to the Personnel and
spilled the beans. He told them that you guys were through at
2:30, he said you swore at him, and that you told the gang boss
here to go to hell. Oh, he lined you fellows up right!

GC: I know, I heard about it. I was all ready to punch him in the
nose. Didn't you see how mad I was when I come in here one
time? Fellows telling me to go to hell! I didn't hear them if they
did.

S_1: Hey, you Turkish s.o.b.! Did you say that about us? You god-
damn' greaseball! You ought to have a punch right in the nose.
Hey, you Turkish bastard, did you say that about us?

I_3: What are you talking about?

S_1: Never mind what we're talking about. You know.

I_3: I don't know anything about it.

S_1: Don't try to lie to us now, we know what you said. You want
to look out or we'll take you for a ride. What we ought to do is
punch you right in the nose, and then take you for a ride.

W_1 went to the back of the room to get S_1 to solder a row.

S_1: I can't solder. I've got to tell I_3 what I think of him.

W_1: Come on and solder. Don't worry about him.

3-9-32

An inspection section chief came into the test room to collect the
inspector's donation for the unemployment relief.

W_5 (to group in the front of the room): Listen, fellows, shall I tell
I_3's boss what he did this morning?

S_1: Yeah, go ahead and tell him.

W_5: I_3 don't know how to find trouble. This morning he made me fix a reverse that wasn't there, and then I had to put the wires back again. The only trouble was a broken wire, and he made me fix two reverses. You better get somebody out here that knows how to shoot trouble. This guy don't know anything about the job.

The inspection section chief did not answer.
Later S_1 and W_5 were razzing I_3.

S_1: You'd make a fine dentist, you would! I'd like to have you fixing my teeth.[4]

W_5: If he fixes teeth like he found that broken wire, he'd have to pull them all out to find the one that was hurting you.
S_1: Maybe I_3 is good at driving camels. Why don't you go back to Turkey? That's where you belong.

3-10-32

The observer asked the inspection group chief to send I_3 up for an interview at 1:15.

IGC: All right, I'll see him right after lunch.

The section chief then joined the observer and the inspection group chief.

SC: It would be a good thing to get that guy out of there.
IGC: I think I'm going to take him out.
SC: Do you really mean that? That'll be the best thing you ever did.
IGC: Don't get excited, I'm going to put him out here inspecting wiring.
SC: Well, we can at least see what he's doing out here anyway. The trouble with him is that he's too old. Those kids are too fast for him. There couldn't any of us step in there and keep up with those kids.

[4] Excerpt from interview with I_3, 12–18–31:

I_3: I'm not in my line of work here. I am a dentist by profession.
Int.: Is that so? How in the world did you happen to get out here?
I_3: I got an infection in my finger and I had to have it taken off. You can't practice dentistry with your right index finger gone. I needed money badly, so I came out here and got a job, and I've been here ever since. I had a lot of trouble at that time. I just took the first thing that offered itself.
Int.: Where did you study?
I_3: At the _____ College of Dental Surgery. I took my degree in 1910.

3-11-32

I_1 (to *Obs.*): I hear I_3 isn't going to be here next week. I_4 is coming out and I_3 is going to go in the other room.

S_1: That'll be a happy day for us. The thing that made me sore about that guy squawking was that he got the group chief in bad, and the group chief is a hell of a swell boss. You'll never get anybody like him again. It makes me sore to see somebody get a fellow in bad just because he's a good fellow and tries to give the boys a break.

CASE *D*: PROBLEMS OF SUPERVISION

The chief function of the supervisory organization was to maintain order and control. The following observations show some of the problems with which the first-line supervisor was confronted in his daily supervision of the men. Some of these problems had to do with the question of daywork claims. Each time a wireman claimed daywork, he was supposed to give the group chief the reason for the delay, as well as the amount of time lost. Time lost by stoppages beyond the wireman's control was deducted from standard hours before his average hourly output was computed. Other problems the supervisor had to handle were related to the enforcement of housekeeping rules and rules relating to job trading and helping one another.[5] Formally, the employees were supposed to work only at the jobs assigned to them. They were not supposed to trade off or help one another unless it was absolutely necessary.

11-25-31

About 3:15 the group chief came over to the observer's desk.

GC: How did the room look to you last Saturday?
Obs.: I didn't notice.
GC: The foreman said that it looked like hell. I don't know what he wants. I thought it looked O.K.
Obs.: What did he say to you?
GC: Nothing to me. He told the other fellow. He never says anything to me. He always tells it to somebody else. (To S_3) Hey, you, S_3. Get that brush and clean up those benches.
(To group in general) Hey, you guys. Get those garboons put away.
(To *Obs.*) I don't know. Does this place look clean to you?
Obs.: I don't know. I don't see anything wrong.

[5] See also Case *B*, pp. 71–85.

GC: I guess it will have to do. If the old man gets up wrong in the morning, it will be no good. He used to be crabby as hell before vacation, but since then he doesn't seem to say much. I can't understand him. You never know what he thinks.

11-27-31

Another cleanup. The group chief did not seem to be so particular as he was last Wednesday. There was considerable resistance to his order. Several of the men almost refused. W_6 flatly refused. Finally, after some argument W_6 said that he would clean up after a while.

GC: Do it now.
W_6: I'll get it in a minute. I have something to do here. After a while I'll clean it up.
GC: How about your garboon?
W_6: That garboon is all right. It's clean. I just got it this morning.
GC: Never mind. Throw it away.

W_6 wouldn't throw it away, and the group chief took it over to the can himself.

12-4-31

W_6 (to *GC*): I can't wire today. I want to solder.
GC: Why do you want to do that?
W_6: Oh, I don't feel so good. I've got a stiff neck.
GC: No, you can't solder. We lose too much money.
W_6: W_8 can wire for me. We won't lose anything.
GC: I don't think we ought to let W_8 wire. He's under the hospital's care, and if he hurts himself, I'll catch hell.

Section chief came in.

GC (to *SC*): W_6 wants to solder and let W_8 wire for him.
SC: W_8's got a sore finger, hasn't he?
GC: I don't know. I guess his finger's all right.

Section chief walked away.

W_6: Well, I'm going to solder.

W_8 handed him his apron and walked over and started wiring. The section chief, who had walked up to the front of the room, came back.

SC (to *GC*): Are you going to let W_8 wire?
GC: I don't know whether we ought to or not.

As far as the observer could make out, the group chief never did make up his mind, but W_8 wired for the rest of the day. W_6 seemed to feel much better as soon as he started to solder.   His neck did not appear to be stiff.   He began to laugh and joke with the wiremen.

12-9-31

W_6: This wire's no good.

GC: Well, you've got to use it.   They won't let me bring any more back.   They tell me that you can get along with it all right.

W_6: That's the trouble around here.   There isn't any of you guys that know anything about wire, yet you try to tell us.

GC: The section chief is an old wireman.   He knows wiring.

W_6: Like hell he is!

W_8: He came from the plating department.

GC (to W_6): He was wiring when you were in short pants.

W_6: Well, maybe then.   But not since I've been here.

W_8 came over to the observer.   The group chief could not overhear what he said.

W_8: These guys here don't know anything about wiring, and yet the whole bunch criticizes us.   If they'd get in there once in a while and try to learn something about it, they'd find out that it's not so easy.   It's the same thing as when we go to a ball game.   We call a ball player a bum because he misses an infield grounder, but if we'd get out there and try it ourselves, we'd feel differently.   It's the same thing with these guys.   If they'd try to put on a few wires they'd know what we're up against.

12-10-31

The assistant foreman came out to the test room for the first time in three weeks with an announcement of a meeting of the Boys' Club. He distributed it to two or three of the boys in the group.   Then he came over and showed it to the observer.

AF: We're going to get that Mr. A to speak to the boys this next week. I'm tickled to death.   He's a mighty fine speaker.

The conversation about Mr. A and religion continued for some time.   The foreman suddenly opened the door.   The assistant foreman jumped.   He stopped his conversation in the middle of a sentence and pointed to the annoucement of the Boys' Club meeting, which was lying on the desk, and said, "Here, read this."   The foreman came over to the desk and picked up the announcement, and he, the assistant foreman, and the observer talked about that for a while. Then the foreman left.

Obs.: That's a clever piece of work. Did you do it?
AF: No, but that ought to get their interest.

The assistant foreman left the room. The group chief came in and started making out a report, sitting at the observer's desk. The assistant foreman came back.

GC: Well, I haven't seen you out here before.
AF: This is the second time today.
GC: What are you doing out here—looking for solder?
AF (laughing): No, but I guess the old man found a lot.
GC: I don't know where he found it all.
AF: He found it right here.
GC: I thought maybe he found some of it in the other room.
AF: No, I inspected the other room myself, and I didn't find hardly a scrap.
GC: I haven't been checking solder here. We've got doors on the room and I didn't think anybody'd steal it.
AF: Well, there's no locks on the doors. Anybody can come in that wants to. I should think you'd have a wireman checking the soldermen. Put somebody in charge of the room. You know, like we do in the other room.
GC: I guess one would be enough for the room. I'll probably have to do it. The old man won't find any more solder out here.

The assistant foreman left.

GC: I wonder what made the old man check the solder. (To W_6) I'm gonna give you a job tonight. You've got to see that all the solder is picked up.
W_6: You're gonna put me in charge? That's fine. Can I fire these guys if they don't have their solder picked up?

Toward the end of the afternoon the group chief started to look around for solder.

GC (to W_6): Come on, W_6, you follow me around and see that I don't miss any of this solder.
W_6: No, I'm not gonna do it. If I can't fire the guys that got solder laying around, I don't want to monkey with it.
GC: Come on, see that I don't miss any.
W_6: Nothing doing.

12-18-31

W_6 was soldering in S_4's place.

GC (to W_7): What's this daywork for?
W_7: Waiting for soldermen.
GC: You didn't wait that long.
W_7: Yes, I did too.   I was waiting three different times.
GC (to W_6): You see to it that these guys don't get any solder time today.   They've been getting away with murder lately.
W_6: Don't you worry.   They won't get any time on me.
GC: Well, if you don't do anything else all day, see that you keep these guys busy.
W_6: I'll keep 'em going.
GC (to $Obs.$): I hate to be putting so much soldering time on this sheet.   That reflects back on me.

(The group chief has been assisting the observer by giving him a list each morning of the daywork allowed for each operator in the group and the reason for the daywork allowance.)

$Obs.$: What do you mean, it reflects on you?
GC: Well, it's my job to see that each group has a solderman that will keep them busy, and if you should let the foremen see this list I've given you, he'd raise hell.

12-21-31

W_9 has had seven cable reverses to fix today.

W_9 (to GC after another wireman had called him to fix another reverse): What, another one?   This is the seventh one today. That's an hour and a half daywork.
GC: Where have you fixed seven reverses?
W_9: There were four on W_5's unit, two on W_4's unit, and one on W_2's unit.
GC: I'm going to see.
W_9: There they are marked on the sheet.
GC: Yes, there's seven all right, but you didn't take any hour and a half to fix them.
W_9: Yes I did.
GC: All you're looking for is daywork.
W_9: And then I've got daywork for waiting for the inspector.   You saw me when I was sitting down over there.

GC: Yes, I saw you sitting down a few minutes.

W_9: Well, I wasted at least a half-hour.

12-22-31

The section chief and GC_2 came into the room to inspect the wire. The men showed them a couple of rolls that were very bad. They argued about the quality of the wire for a few minutes. GC_2 told the men that they were being allowed 3 per cent for defective material in the rate, and that there was nothing he could do if the machine went wrong.

GC_2 (to *Obs.*): Gee, that guy W_6 is noisy. You can hear him above all the rest. You see, this is a pretty hard-boiled bunch of kids. You have a hell of a time doing anything with them. I remember back when we started this job. I had about 75 lads just like W_9. There wouldn't a one of them work. They were paying us 15 per cent that we weren't earning. Gee, that gang would do more things wrong. They reversed levels. They used the wrong banks. They kept me going from one to the other all day long, and then I didn't catch half the stuff they did wrong. This guy W_9 is about the only one we've got now that's no good. (To W_9) How much are you turning out now?

W_9: Oh, sometimes 3200, 3400, and if I really feel like working, 4000.

GC_2: You ought to be turning in your 6000 now.

W_9: Well, I'll never be able to do that.

GC_2: You're one of these guys that isn't smart. How do you think you're ever going to amount to anything?

W_9: Oh, I don't know. I don't know whether I want to amount to anything here. And besides that, I think I've got the average intelligence.

GC_2: Well, you haven't. If you were smart, you'd dig in there and turn out all the work you could. How do you think we're ever going to promote you? If they were looking for a man in another department for a good job, we could never give it to you. They'd run you back just as fast as you got in the new department. The way to get along is to work hard and get yourself a better job. The way you're working you'll never get anywhere.

W_9: I wouldn't take any other job around here. There isn't a job in this plant that I want.

GC_2: Well, don't worry, you'll never get any.

GC_2 left the room. W_8 came over to W_9.

W_8: What did he tell you—that the way to get ahead is to work?

W_9: Yeah.

W_8: Well, he sure must have been an awful loafer. He's been around here 20 years and he's still a group chief. If that's the way to advance around here, I don't want it.

W_9: I almost told him that. That would have shut him up.

W_8 (to *Obs.*): Gee, I love that guy!

W_9: So do I.

The test room group chief came back. The gang all started telling him how much daywork they were going to get. He didn't have any answer for them.

GC (to *Obs.*): The way banks are running and with this wire, I'll be crazy. This guy GC_2 gives me a pain. He's always butting his nose in some place where it don't belong. I was talking to him one day out in the other room and he went over and bawled one of my men out. If they got a bawling out coming, I think that should be my job. There isn't a job in this place but what he's got his nose into it. He can't be as good as all that or he wouldn't stay on the same job all the time. Maybe I'm a little too easy on my fellows, but I'd rather be that way than have them all down on me the way his men are.

1-8-32

When the observer entered the test room at about 8:30, he noticed that the group was very quiet.

GC (to *Obs.*): Well, the boys got hell this morning for making too much noise.

Obs.: Did they?

GC: Yes, don't you notice they're awfully quiet?

Obs.: I did notice that. What is it all about?

GC: Somebody from across the way kicked because they were making too much noise. Just wait until they start getting noisy again. I'll take the first one I catch into the office.

Obs.: Who bawled them out?

GC: I don't know just how it was. I wasn't in here. The old man got the section chief and the assistant foreman and told them plenty. They both came out here this morning and spread the news around.

Obs.: Oh, the assistant foreman talked to them? What did he say?

GC: I don't know. He went around to each one of them and then just as soon as he left, the old man came in and sat at your desk for about 15 minutes. He left just as you came in.

At about 10 o'clock there was just about the usual amount of noise, conversation, singing, and whistling in the group.

1-15-32

The section chief handed the paychecks around. W_6 and W_1 have the same day rate, but there was apparently a difference of a few cents in their checks. W_6 complained about this for some time, claiming that he got gypped a few cents every week. When the group chief came in, W_6 asked him to figure his pay. According to the group chief's figure, W_6 should have had about a dollar and a half more than he got.

GC: There must be something wrong here, but I don't know where it is. This is the way to figure it all right, but I don't come out the same as they do.

W_6: Well, I want this thing figured right. If I'm getting gypped I want some more dough.

The group chief finally gave up.

W_6: Well, you get the section chief out here. I want this thing figured right.

GC: All right, I'll get him.

W_6: I think that payroll is a lot of crap.

Just then the foreman entered the room. He hurried over to W_6 and said, "You've got to cut out that kind of language. Don't you know there are women working across the way?" W_6 did not answer. The foreman left the room.

GC (to W_6): You shouldn't talk like that. You talk so loud anybody can hear you a mile. It makes it bad for me when the old man catches something like that.

W_6: I know it. I didn't even see the old man come in.

GC: Well, you want to watch yourself.

2-4-32

W_7 was an hour late this morning. He same in about 8:20.

Obs. (to W_7): Did you get snowed in?

W_7: No, I overslept. I've got to get myself a new alarm clock. I can't hear this one.

W_9 (to W_7): The group chief took your count at 10 and 10 this morning.

W_7: Well, he's got to change that. I only wanted to turn in 9 and 9.

A little later the group chief came into the room.

W_7 (to GC): How did you take my count this morning?
GC: 9 and 9. Was that what you wanted?
W_7: Yes, that's all right. And I want an hour daywork. A half on bum wire, and a half on solderman and inspector.
W_9: That's right. I chiseled myself this morning. I've got a half-hour daywork coming. A quarter on W_5 in position S_4, and a quarter on the inspector.
GC: You haven't any daywork coming.
W_9: I have too.
GC: Aw, you were fooling around more than a half-hour yesterday. I don't know about W_7 here. Maybe he's got it coming, but you were fooling around.
W_9: I was not. I worked. I only had 11 rows in the morning because I had to wait every time. I worked every minute.

They argued back and forth for some time, but the group chief finally allowed W_9 the daywork. The group chief went around and talked to W_4 for a few minutes. They apparently were talking about daywork. The group chief appeared to be quite disgusted. He then walked past W_2's position.

W_2 (to GC): I want an hour's daywork.

The group chief announced that he was going to cut out all daywork.

3-16-32

$Obs.$ (to GC): Where are you going tonight?
GC: To another one of those safety meetings. They make me tired. I wish I didn't have to go.
$Obs.$: Do you really have to?
GC: Well, you pretty near have to.
I_1: How come nobody came out and told the rest of us about it? Don't they want us there any more?
GC: Didn't the section chief come out and tell you?
I_1: No, nobody has been out here.
GC: Wait till I go in and tell him. You fellows know that you're all invited to the meeting, don't you? You fellows better watch and see that you've got your goggles on tomorrow. After this safety meeting the old man will probably check up on them.

4-20-32

The group chief brought a truckload of empty boards down to the test room. As he entered the room he said to the group. "You're going to have a new boss next week."

S_1: How come?
GC: I'm going to have another job.
S_1: What are you going to do?
GC: I'll be adjusting relays.
S_1: Who's going to be the boss?
GC: GC_2.
W_6: Aw, hell, I'm going to quit.
S_1: Is that a fact? That's hell. Everything is going wrong today. Here we're losing the best boss we ever had.
W_6: He's not any better than the one who died.
S_1: Maybe not any better, but he's just as good, and the other fellow's dead.
W_4: It'll be hell working for that guy.
W_6: I don't like him at all.
S_1: I don't like him, and he don't like me, so that makes it worse.

Agricultural Equipment Company

THE material in these cases is based on the observations of Bob Thayer during the summer of 1947. Mr. Thayer had become interested in human relations in industry at college. He wanted to see for himself the extent to which some of the things he heard and read about actually occurred on the floor of a factory.

In the summer between his junior and senior years, Mr. Thayer went to an industrial city in the Midwest and roomed at the Y.M.C.A. He found a job in the welding department of Plant 3 of the Agricultural Equipment Company, one of the largest manufacturers of agricultural equipment in the country. He told the employment office and his fellow workers that he had been a self-employed radio repairman; that he had tired of the highly competitive, aggressive, and crowded East; and that, having no family attachments, he had decided to move.

Mr. Thayer told the same story about his background to the welders he worked with. He told them, "I never worked in a factory before, but I sorta thought I'd give it a try and see what it's like." Hence, he was able to ask many questions about what was happening. He found that it took about two weeks before he and the welders became familiar. During this period and the weeks that followed, he spent a good deal of the time when he was not working simply "hanging around" and participating in various activities, both inside and outside the plant. He ate with the welders whenever he could, arranged a "car pool" with some of them, played baseball, went swimming, played cards, and drank beer with them. He kept a log of his experiences and observations.

THE WELDING DEPARTMENT

At Plant 3 of the Agricultural Equipment Company, automatic agricultural equipment, such as haybaling machines, harvesters, and threshers, were manufactured. "Rough stock"—unfinished materials, angle irons, steel plates, and so on, which had been cut or molded to

119

a general standard size, but which had not been further finished—
arrived from a foundry some miles away and was sorted and delivered
to three departments in the plant. In the sheet metal department, the
stock was cut and formed to standard sizes for the different parts of
the frames. The material was then transported by overhead crane,
lift-truck, or "dolly" (a small rugged electric cart used to haul loads)
to the welding and machining departments. The machine shop
received both rough stock and material partly worked by the sheet
metal department. After being finished on lathes, grinders, screw
machines, and drill presses, these products were sent to either an
assembly line, a subassembly line, or the welding department for
further operations. The welding department received rough stock
from the foundry as well as parts from the machine and sheet metal
departments. The welders delivered the parts they worked on to
the assembly and subassembly lines.

LAYOUT AND JOBS: THE WELDERS

The welding department was made up of a line of eleven booths,
one for each worker, separated from one another by sheet metal walls
about six feet high (Exhibit 1). All except one were separated from
the central trucking lane by canvas curtains suspended on rods. These
curtains could be pushed aside when stock parts were delivered to
the booths and worked pieces removed from them. These arrangements virtually shut off each welder during the regular course of
work and also segregated the welding department from all others in
the plant. This was necessary because the bright flash accompanying
arc welding contained rays which irritated and burned unprotected
eyes. The welders wore specially prepared smoked goggles and hel-
mets which filtered out the rays. The walls and curtains of the booths
protected the eyes of nearby workers in other departments, as well as
the eyes of any welder who had removed his helmet to examine his
own work.

The booths, numbered 1 through 7, measured about 15 by 10 feet.
Each welder in these booths produced a single part of the whole
machine; this meant welding several component parts together. To
standardize the finished products, specially prepared "jigs" had been
made for each operation. These were heavy steel fixtures which
clamped the component parts together in fixed positions so that the
whole was securely held in place for welding and so that the heat of
the arc would not cause warping and variations from allowed tolerances. Some jobs required only one operation of this sort; others

EXHIBIT 1

AGRICULTURE EQUIPMENT COMPANY

Layout of Welding Department

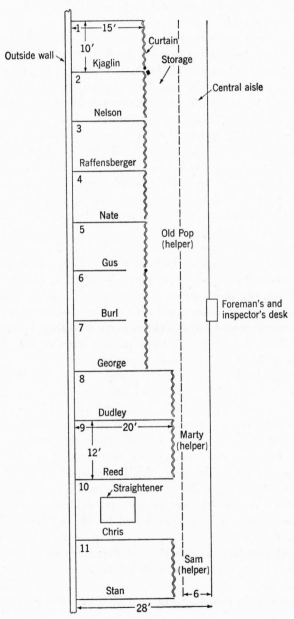

required the welders to produce more than one subassembly and then to weld the subassemblies together into the final part. The men in these booths were engaged primarily in one basic operation. They sat at steel tables and worked with easy-to-handle small parts which did not require many welds and tools and which took about one to five minutes to weld.

Booths 8 through 11 were about 20 by 12 feet. They were larger than the other booths because of the long frames and axles of the farm equipment that was made in them. The welder in booth 8 made axles and performed only one basic operation; but the welders in booths 9 and 11 worked on parts demanding three operations. These two men made 100-pound, 10-foot frames. The first two operations consisted of making up lots of right sides and left sides, each of which were composites of several pieces, and then combining the finished right and left sides and two base plates in a third operation to form the final frame. The operator in booth 9 made lower frames and the operator in booth 11 made upper ones. The order of these operations was left to the employee, as long as he met the overall requirements of the production schedule.

The operators in booths 8, 9, and 11 had the heaviest, largest, and most unwieldy parts upon which to work. Their operations required the greatest number of welds per unit (about 50) and hence the longest welding time per unit (20 to 30 minutes). In addition, because the work along 10-foot frames and 6-foot axles could not be done conveniently while seated, these welders performed their operations while walking along the length of their pieces. Furthermore, the frames had to be welded on both their upper and lower sides, and the axles had to be welded along their circumferences in several places. Because the welds could be made on only one side of a frame or an axle at a time, and because both frames and axles were too heavy to be turned by one man, these men had helpers to assist them.

Booth number 10 was not cut off from the trucking lane by a curtain. This was the station of the straightening-machine operator, who corrected defects in pieces that had warped while cooling at the foundry or following welding. He also used a variety of pneumatic hand grinders to remove "spatter" (excess welding) from the running surfaces of some of the parts finished by the welders. Most of his work was straightening the long angle irons used in the production of frames and grinding smooth their sliding surfaces. However, from time to time the operator was called on to correct faults in other materials.

Welders had to guard against two kinds of errors: poor or missed welding "spots" and failure to tighten all clamps before welding. Occasionally, a welder might fail to weld a spot that had been so designated by the engineering department's layout, or he might fail to set a clamp on the materials. Then the pieces would be finished without proper tolerances and clearances. The welder was solely responsible in either case.

THE HELPERS

There were three general assistants or helpers in the department. Although their work was not defined for them in a rigorous pattern, it centered about keeping the welders supplied with fresh parts and welding rods, removing finished products, and delivering them to the assembly line. One helper was assigned to help the first seven welders. One tray of the relatively small parts used by these operators was delivered to each of them in the early morning and would last for several hours. The other two helpers assisted the straightener in booth 10 and the welders in booths 8, 9, and 11. They worked together to get the grinding done and to deliver the finished frames to the assembly line. In addition, one of them helped the straightener with his work and did the grinding to remove the spatter on the parts he made. The other was usually kept busy servicing the three welders, assisting in turning over their pieces, and carrying the finished parts out of the booths. When these helpers were both busy, the first one sometimes worked for the welder in booth 8 and, in fact, usually did the grinding on his work. In addition, because the welder in booth 10 was responsible for seeing that the department floor was swept every Monday, Wednesday, and Friday morning, this task usually fell to his helper.

INSPECTION AND SUPERVISION

The inspection process was based on a "spot check" method. The inspector assigned to the welding department occasionally measured a piece for proper dimensions or scrutinized it for "missed welds." Furthermore, he could tell if the work was proceeding correctly by keeping in contact with the assembly line inspector, who reported to him if any defects appeared there.

The foreman, whose desk was centrally located to all the booths on the lane for carting materials, was responsible for scheduling the flow of work, for getting out the production, and for keeping production records for purposes of payment. He shared his desk with the inspector and apportioned his time between working with supervisors and staff men at the next higher level of the organization and checking with the operators to determine how their work was progressing.

THE WELDERS' PAY

The company operated on the so-called "straight line" principle of compensation, according to which pay was directly proportional to individual output. Under this plan the day rate or basic wage was guaranteed. Day rates were based on a labor grading system. This system covered all hourly rated operations performed in the plant. The lowest grade covered the simplest type of operations; the highest grades covered the operations requiring the greatest amount of skill or responsibility; all other operations were placed in intermediate grades according to the skill or responsibility involved. Ranges of pay for these basic labor grades were so established that they would be comparable to the rates of pay prevailing throughout the city for similar classes of work. The most recent union contract had resulted in an increase that raised rates somewhat above the average prevailing in the area. New employees were hired and assigned an hourly rate at the minimum rate of pay for the labor grade into which their work fell. They were advanced within the rate range or progressed to higher grade classifications as they became more skilled and proficient.

The labor grades supplied the base rates for the determination of incentive or piece rates. The straight piecework system by which the welders were paid involved production standards which were set in time studies of the operations. This in turn led to the establishment of a money rate per unit of output, which was easily applied to welding operations, since the latter were completely performed by individual employees and each welder's production was easily distinguishable.

An employee received the rate per unit multiplied by the number of units completed regardless of the time involved, except when the total piecework value of his work was less than the total daywork value of his time, in which case he received his guaranteed day rate. Idle time beyond the control of the welder fell into this category. The total daywork value for each worker was his hourly rate multiplied by the number of hours he worked.

Once a production standard had been set, it could not be changed unless there was a change in either the material, the equipment, or the method of processing. Furthermore, there could be no change in any piecework price except by mutual agreement of the company and the union's committee in the department, except as just noted. In addition, the union contract stated that no production ceilings would be established on any job. The contract read as follows:

a. When a normal qualified operator, efficient in the work he is doing, is not able, when working at piecework effort that can be maintained all day without excessive fatigue, to earn at least 20 per cent above the base rate for that job, after giving it a fair trial, it shall be evidence of the following:
   1. The production standard is incorrect.
   2. The method, material or process involved in doing the job has been changed since the standard was established.
   3. The operator is not doing one or more of the following:
      (a) producing at full piecework effort.
      (b) working efficiently.
      (c) following the established method for performing the job.
      (d) has not been properly instructed and/or trained.

b. This provision shall not be interpreted or applied as a guartee of the payment of the anticipated earning rate to the pieceworkers. Neither shall this clause be interpreted to mean that the pieceworker shall not be able to earn more than twenty per cent above the base rate. Instead, this provision means that if a normal, qualified operator, efficient in the work he is doing and working at piecework effort that can be maintained all day without excessive fatigue, cannot earn at least twenty per cent above the base rate for the job, he shall have cause for complaint under this provision.

c. During the life of this agreement there will be no change in any piecework price except by mutual agreement of the employer and the union's department committee except as otherwise provided in this agreement.

In another paragraph of the contract, management reserved the right to establish rates of any new job or on an old job in which there was a significant change in "either the material, the equipment, or the method of processing." Concerning idle time, the contract read:

Idle time beyond the control of the employee will be payed for at the employee's classified hourly base rate, provided the reason causing idle time is reported to the foreman when the idle time begins and the employee is required to remain in the plant.

The company's disciplinary policy was posted on the main bulletin boards. It stated:

1. All employees are expected to be at their work stations ready for work at the beginning of their shifts and to remain at work until the end of their shifts, unless other schedules apply.
2. Employees will not leave their assigned work station for other than personal reasons or in the performance of their job or for emergency treatment of injury or sickness, without first securing approval of their supervisor and a pass which will be issued for that purpose.

Exhibit 2 gives some personal information about the men who worked in the welding department.

THE WELDERS' BEHAVIOR AT WORK

Nonwork Activities and Conversations

FIRST DAY

"The welders of Plant 3 are Olsen's boys. He's the foreman; everybody calls him Gooba."

This was the brief picture of the welding department that the guard gave Bob Thayer and Marty, who was hired at the same time as Bob, as they followed him into the plant. During the previous week, Marty and Bob had filled out employment forms, had been examined by the company's doctor, had been instructed in safety precautions, and had received safety goggles. They were told to "report to work Monday morning at seven sharp."

The guard introduced Marty and Bob to Gooba, who chatted briefly about the department. He then took them to Chris' booth, explained to them what Chris was doing and told Chris to set them to work. Chris told Marty that he would find a broom in the closet behind the machine. He took Bob into the next booth and introduced him to Stan. The welder took off his helmet and assured Chris that he would set Bob to work.

After Chris left, Stan offered Bob a cigarette and proceeded to explain a little about the welding process, how a jig worked, and in what respects he needed help to perform his operation. After the smoke, he led Bob to a large pile of parts and demonstrated how to grind an angle iron, so that its welded spots were smooth enough to fit into the jig for the frame. Setting him to work on these, Stan returned to his own work. Bob worked steadily for half an hour,

EXHIBIT 2

AGRICULTURAL EQUIPMENT COMPANY

Personal Data about the Men in the Welding Department

		Age	Probable Ethnic Background	Education	Married or Single	Residence
Foreman						
	Gooba	45	Swedish	?	M	Suburbs
Welders						
1	Kjaglin	50	Swedish-Scandinavian	Grammar school	S	Had built own house in suburbs
2	Nelson	40	Swedish-Scandinavian	Grammar school	M	Suburbs
3	Raffens-berger[1]	41	Swedish-Scandinavian	Grammar school	M	Suburbs
4	Nate	39	American	2 yrs. high school	M	City
5	Gus[2]	37	Italian	2 yrs. high school	M	City
6	Burl	34	Part American Indian	High school	M	City
7	George	31	Anglo-Saxon-Yankee	High school	M	City
8	Dudley	28	Irish	High school	M (rec.)	City
9	Reed	28	Irish-Scandinavian-American	High school	M (rec.)	City
10	Chris	24	Irish-Scandinavian-American	High school	"Steady girl"	City
11	Stan	23	Irish-Scandinavian-American	High school	M	City
Helpers						
	Old Pop[3]	58	?	?	M	City
	Marty	22	German	Finished college	M	City
	Bob	23	American	In college	S	City

[1] Highest seniority among the welders.
[2] Union committeeman for the welders.
[3] About 5 years seniority.

at the end of which time Stan called him to help turn over a frame. Bob then returned to his grinding, facing the prospect of 500 more angle irons. After welding for about 15 more minutes, Stan again called Bob to help him remove a long bulky frame from the jig and thence from the booth.

After they returned to the booth, Stan muttered profanely about the heat and announced it was time for a drink and a smoke. Bob followed him to the water fountain and then back to the booth. Bob offered a cigarette, which Stan accepted. Just at this moment, a tall, strongly built man came into the booth. His name turned out to be Dudley. In a pseudocritical tone of voice, he directed his remarks to Stan:

DUDLEY: Goddammit, always goofin' off. Every time I come in here and visit you, you're settin' around. I haven't seen you strike an arc in the last three days.

STAN: Well, if you'd stop visiting me so often you'd get a little work done yourself, you toothless so-and-so. I know you never got permission from your folks to smoke, but have a cigarette anyway. Maybe you'll die on it.

DUDLEY: That'll be the day. What have we got here?

STAN: This is Bob Thayer, our new helper. Bob, this is Dudley, one of the best welders in the state; except for me, of course.

DUDLEY: Don't mind him. He'd probably still got a hangover from Saturday night.

STAN: Boy, you can say that again. I feel like hell this morning. I don't feel any more like working than I ever do. But, boy, what a weekend!

The two men proceeded to relate the social adventures of the weekend just passed. They leaned on the jig, assuming rather workmanlike positions as they talked. Bob followed suit and listened. It appeared that the wife of one of Stan's friends was rather fond of Stan and this had some disconcerting effects on her husband, especially in light of the fact that Stan had gone out with her Saturday night. Dudley's wife had gone to her parents' home in the country for the weekend, so he and Burl, a welder "down the line," had been "out on the town" for the weekend. They had been drinking their "whiskey-beers down around the Five Corners," that part of the town, Dudley pointed out, where "the bars served every fifth drink on the house."

The two men listened attentively to each other. About ten minutes later, Dudley casually said that he thought he might just as well go back to work and departed.

Later in the morning Reed came into the booth.

REED: I see we finally got some help.
STAN: Yeah, and it's about time.
  Bob was introduced.
REED: How many pieces have you got done?
STAN: Almost four.
REED: What! So soon?   Jes-us!
STAN: I won't have to turn them all in, though.
REED: No, I should say not.   If you work at this rate you'll be killing
  yourself after the time study men get around to us.
STAN: Well, how much have you done?
REED: Two.
STAN: Well, I guess I'll just goof off for a while.
REED: Yeah, hide those damn things or something.   Throw 'em out the
  window.   [Chuckle.]   Well, how was your weekend?

The two men proceeded to exchange details of their activities.
After about ten minutes more had elapsed, Reed left.

The first day on the job, Stan told Bob that he always ate lunch
in Reed's booth.   That day and for several weeks thereafter, Bob ate
his sandwiches there, along with Reed, Stan, Dudley, Chris, and Marty.
The conversation usually centered about social activities outside the
plant.   Plans were made for parties, get-togethers, and union affairs, and
previous social events were discussed.   Family or economic problems
often arose, and such topics as the best place in town to buy a cheap
secondhand car generally evoked a lively debate.

HORSEPLAY AMONG THE WELDERS

Reed, Stan, Dudley, Chris, and Marty spent a considerable portion
of their time visiting one another for a chat, a smoke, or occasionally
a discussion in regard to furthering the progress of their work.   Often
one would initiate a visit with the man in the next booth by throwing
a cigarette butt or a crumpled piece of paper over the wall separating the booths.   This kind of horseplay aroused the second to
retaliation and, finally, to conversation.   The offended welder might
jokingly threaten to report his antagonist to the president of the company or the president of the union, or might heap insult and derogation
on him for having obstructed the progress of the work.   At any rate,
the taunts seemed to have the effect of an invitation to converse, for
the two workers would soon get together and discuss the topic of the
moment.

On some occasions, a welder climbed on the tray of materials which stood near the wall separating his booth from the next, so that he could peer over the wall and shout to the man in the next booth. It was a great source of merriment and joking when one welder climbed on his tray, only to see several other welders doing the same thing. Then they would all "holler" at one another to get back to work and accuse one another of continually "goofing off"; or else one welder would holler to the others that if they could only see what little work his neighbor had done all day, they would not wish to be seen with him ever again. Then several would gather at the booth of the "lazy" one, and they would "kid around" some more.

One morning, Reed and Dudley dropped in to visit Stan, and they fell to telling Bob about the various tricks that they had played on each other.

DUDLEY: One morning Stan told me that he was feeling rough and that he didn't think that he could last out the day. So he left after lunch; but damn' fool that he was, he left a completed frame in his jig. Well, sir, Reed and I decided that we were going to straighten him out, by God. So after he'd been gone a while, we went into his booth and welded the under side of his frame to the jig. He came in the next morning, and you should have seen it; him and the helper grunting and trying to pull that damned thing out of the jig. They couldn't figure what had caused it to swell up, and they were hitting it with mallets and prying it with crowbars. Finally with enough swearing they got it out of the jig, and then they saw the little telltale welding spots on the under side where you couldn't notice it. Boy, was he mad!

STAN: I knew those two had done it, but they were keeping their eye out for me after that, and there wasn't much I could do. But if you don't think I had my day before too long, you're mistaken. First I drove these two guys crazy. I'd drop in when they were welding a long strip and "throw up the heat" so the damn stuff was running all over the place. Or else I'd drop in and reverse the polarity and throw down the heat, so the welding rod would stick to the frame. [Each welding machine had a variable amperage control for regulating the temperature at which the welding rod melts. Depending on its diameter, each rod had a standard operating "heat" at which the machine was set for maximum efficiency.] Every time they'd drop in to my booth, I'd watch 'em, and they didn't get away with a thing. But I was still waiting, and finally Dudley didn't come to work one day. Towards the end of the day, I went into his booth and got out all his tools, his hammers, clamps, mallets, and pliers. Then I went and got some real fine rods and welded every single tool of his to that steel welding table that's in his booth. When he came in the next day, he was very pleased to see all his tools laid out on his table for him, and he figured Old Pop was really looking after him. Then pretty soon he gets to work and goes for a mallet and finds that the whole set is stuck to his table. Boy, was *he* ever mad! He didn't hear the end of it for a couple of weeks!

The conversation continued for another five minutes, during which time they both lustily recounted the various ways that they had good-naturedly played practical jokes on one another. Once Reed had welded shut the door of Dudley's locker just before quitting time. "He was over an hour late getting out of there that night, getting the door open again so that he could get his clothes and go home." Another time, Dudley had welded a couple of long angle irons from Reed's jig across the booth to the girder running along the wall of the plant.

The welders occasionally dumped their trash in each other's booths and continually threw things at each other. It was a common form of greeting, when a welder from another booth arrived, for one welder to finish welding the rod at hand and then with a quick movement throw the hot stub of the rod at the visitor. They sometimes theatened to throw each other through the window into the power station just outside. Another favorite stunt was to turn off the ventilating fan in the booth or to direct it in such a way that the sparks from the welding process were blown back on the welder instead of away from him. Chris came in for his share of the horseplay, but more frequently seemed to be on the receiving end of the joke. On one occasion, Stan said to Bob:

STAN: I always make a point of seeing what is going on with all the boys in the department, but it's only with Reed and Dudley that I can really play hell. One time I left an old banana skin in Fatso's [booth 2] lunch box, and he was put out for days. Hellfire, something like that goes on between Reed and I or Dudley almost every day, and nothing ever happens. We just smile and take it, but not for long. For every trick that toothless guy has, I've got a million of 'em!

After sweeping the floor one morning, toward the end of summer, Bob went into Stan's booth. Stan turned to him immediately and said, "You go get a wet cloth and rub that sign off the wall. I just caught hell from Gooba on it, so get it off and now. MacFarlane [the plant manager] is on the way down." Reluctantly Bob did what Stan said.

Two days previously, Bob had written with chalk a large sign on the wall. To him it was a symbol of the cordial relationship that had developed between Stan and himself. The sign read:

ZADWORNY & THAYER
SUPER-DELUXE WELDING WHIZZARDS
OUR MOTTO:
"YOU WRECK IT, WE WELD IT"
LUXURY WELDING OUR SPECIALTY

The sign had been the subject of general amusement throughout the department. Everyone found some aspect of it to joke about. Stan and Bob countered by proclaiming that they were going into competition with the company by beginning the manufacture of fur-lined farm machinery for the cultivation and reaping of winter wheat. Workers from other departments had heard of the sign, and Stan's booth was a center of activity for two days.

While Bob washed away the sign, he asked Stan why they had to remove the announcement of their new-found "partnership." According to Stan, "The company doesn't like this sort of thing. We're supposed to be working, not kidding around."

Other Nonwork Conversations and Activities among the Welders

One day Reed asked Bob if he liked the work he was doing. Bob replied in the affirmative.

REED: Yes, we have a lot of fun in the welding department.
BOB: Yes, I can see that.
REED: Yuh. We raise a lot of hell in here but we get the right amount of work out, too.
BOB: That's right.
REED: What the hell! We gotta have some fun. After all, this job would drive ya nuts, if ya couldn't get together with the boys every now and then and raise a little hell or shoot the breeze with the other guys.

Stan elaborated on the point a few days later.

STAN: The way I feel, you have to work part of the time and you have to visit with the other guys part of the time. Now we can't work and talk at the same time. It's too noisy around here for one thing; and anyway it's just plain impossible to talk to a guy when you got your welding helmet pulled down over your face.

In fact the noise was so great in the plant that there was a regularly understood system of hand signals which the men preferred to use as a substitute for shouting when they were working together, even within a few feet of one another. In addition, the arrangement of the work prevented the welders from talking with their neighbors and attending to their work simultaneously. As Stan put it, "It's just plain impossible to talk to a guy when you got your welding helmet pulled down over your face."

As Bob came to know Dudley better, he noticed that each time after he had helped him remove an axle from the jig, Dudley always proceeded to engage him in conversation. Sometimes he would discuss his work and how it was progressing and sometimes the previous night's activities. On one occasion Bob happened to ask him what his daily rate was. Dudley told him that he had been timed at eight axles per day and freely admitted that it wasn't very much in light of the fact that he felt that he could produce twice that number if he were forced to.

DUDLEY: Sure, I suppose I could turn out an easy sixteen a day, but after all a guy's gotta have some fun at work. You couldn't expect him to get to work at seven in the morning and go straight through to lunch without taking a break and talking to somebody except for official business.

BOB: No, you're right.

DUDLEY: Hell, yes, I'm right. In fact, I know that I get more kick out of talking with the guys than I do out of anything else around here.

BOB: You do, huh?

DUDLEY: Sure, like you and me chewin' the rag after I finish each piece. Of course I don't get a helluva bang out of a child like you. Three whiskey-beers and you're not good for anything else. But with us men we like to raise a little hell with our work. Talking makes work more fun and more enjoyable. And then it breaks things up so you don't get bored. You wait till you've been working in a factory year in and year out, when you know just what to expect every day, you'll wanna break things up so you don't get bored.

BOB: Mm-hmm, you don't get so bored this way, eh?

DUDLEY: No, and in fact if I feel tired after I've been workin' a while, I find that if I take a break for a while then, I don't feel so tired and I don't mind going back to work. It ain't so tiresome then.
BOB: You like to take a break away now and then, huh?
DUDLEY: Sure, then you can get through the day easier, with the time passing faster; and you're doing something most of the time, either working, or talking with the guys.
BOB: You feel it's the best way to work.
DUDLEY: Sure, I don't mind working; but on the other hand, I don't like to work myself to death. What the hell, I'm gonna be working all my life, so if I didn't have some fun doing the work here, I'd uv quit long ago and gone out on a farm.

When someone dropped in Stan's booth for a visit, the two usually leaned on the jig and struck a pose that gave the appearance of two men discussing a method of overcoming the latest obstacle that had arisen in connection with their work. This kind of behavior was even more pronounced outside the booths than inside, where the curtains protected the men from being viewed by others.

Bob never heard any verbal agreements in regard to looking busy, but one time Dudley came into Stan's booth and forgot to close the curtain all the way. Stan hollered at him immediately in joking concern for the others, "Hey, shut that curtain! Do you want to burn the eyes of the others out there?" In general, when someone visited someone else, the two were always careful to pull the curtain shut. On the other hand, a report that a junior member of management was in the area usually broke up a conversation.

These social calls reached their height between nine-thirty and ten o'clock. By that time the men had an early start on the day's production, and by that time, as Reed put it, "It's callin' time."

Calls began in a variety of ways. Occasionally two men would happen to be reporting the day's output at the foreman's desk at the same time. One would say, "I guess I need a drink of water." The other would generally say, "Me, too," and they would walk to the drinking fountain together and then return. Or they might meet at the tool shed while drawing out a mallet; and while walking back to the welding department together, one would say, "Well, I gotta go to the can." Coincidentally enough, the other would feel the same urge, and the two would go to the men's room together and take seats side by side and talk for a few minutes.

It became a routine with Marty and Bob to clean the dirt from their safety-goggles together. Although it was commonly the practice to clean goggles at the start of a day's work, Marty and Bob preferred to wait to clean theirs until about an hour after work had started. Marty would pass Bob while helping another welder. On his return he would put his foot up on Bob's grinding bench, lean over, and say a few introductory words of greeting. Then he would say that his goggles were dirty, and Bob would walk along with him to the dispensary, where the cleaning fluid and tissues were provided. Though they seldom talked about work, they always found a topic for conversation.

After he had been in the city for several weeks, Bob made the acquaintance of a waitress at the restaurant where he regularly ate breakfast and supper and had his lunch made up to take to work. Eating there regularly saved Bob a dollar a week. One time during a "smoke break" with Stan, Bob told him about his girl and the problems accompanying the relationship. That day at lunch Stan told the rest of their eating group about the affair. Soon each member of the eating group inquired every day how Bob was getting along or if there were any new and interesting developments. Usually this occurred when Bob was helping a welder, but it was not rare for a welder to drop into a booth where Bob was working and to ask him about "the latest." Bob was encouraged to talk about his girl only if he wished to. The men never appeared to want to be prying into his private life. The welders enjoyed discussing the details of Bob's social life, and Bob related them as best he could. Much joking centered about his friend and himself, just as stories of all kinds centered about each man.

During the course of his work, Bob made the acquaintance of Mike, the disc-grinder in the machine department. He operated a huge grinding wheel about ten feet in diameter, which revolved on a horizontal plane. A small overhead crane lowered large heavy pieces on the wheel, which ground them smooth. These pieces were often ones that were made in the welding department, which Chris straightened and Bob then delivered to Mike. In this way, the two came to know each other, and Mike came to visit Bob at least once a day, generally not on business. Yet he seldom arrived without some tool or piece of metal in his hand. He would lean on Bob's grinding bench, and they would chat for some time.

One day Bob noticed that Mike liked to smoke cigars. He bought one for him and the following morning went to Mike's work station and presented the cigar to him. During the long and enjoyable conversation which followed, they both stood facing the machine, watching the material being ground, as if they were working out a new grinding technique.

One time during the summer Bob did not visit Mike for about three days. On the fourth day Bob visited him; in an offhand, joking manner, Mike queried, "What'sa matter? You're not dropping around to see me lately? Those welders keeping you too busy these days?" After that Bob visited Mike every day. He usually waited until the middle of the afternoon, when the work got boring and when he had heard everything that was new in the welding department.

FRIDAY: PAYDAY

Every Friday was payday, and the checks were generally delivered to Gooba about ten o'clock in the morning. On each check there was a five-figure number. Every week the welders—for that matter, almost every department in the plant—held what they called the departmental "poker pool"; the best "hand" according to the numbers on the check won the "kitty." One man was appointed banker; in the welding department it was Burl, in booth 7. Entrance to the pool was entirely voluntary; once having entered, though, each man was expected to "stay in." Every Friday morning each member delivered fifty cents to Burl before the checks arrived. Everyone speculated on the winner and accused the previous week's winner of collusion with management. Practically everyone boasted that he was certain to win the pool "this time." Sarcasm, ridicule, and coarse joking were rife on Friday mornings; it was surprising that any work was done at all.

When Bob came to work, Dudley had won the pool for three consecutive weeks. Thus, on Friday morning much activity centered in his booth. "Dumb luck" was attributed to him; he was jokingly accused of being such a drunkard that he needed the extra money for whiskey; others swore that they had been reading the tea leaves all week and that he did not stand a chance of winning for a fourth time; still others threatened to withdraw from the pool if he won, humorously urging him to confess his sinful collusion with the payment officer.

Finally, the foreman arrived with the checks and distributed them individually. Soon there was a great deal of talking again. Each man speculated on the quality of his hand. Everyone visited everyone else, checking to see how the others had fared. There was much horseplay and good-natured refusals to "show" on the part of those who considered that they held the winning hand. By eleven o'clock the field had narrowed itself down to two or three men; and to add to the spirit of things, Dudley refused to show his hand until all the others had been shown. He said nothing to all who questioned him; this in itself became a great opportunity for speculation and general joking. Finally, the man who proved to hold the best hand met Dudley in friendly rivalry in his booth. In the presence of four or five other workers and after lengthy verbal jockeying, Dudley finally showed his hand. He held one so poor that he did not even qualify. There was a great uproar, and the money was delivered to Gus, the winner. The jinx was broken, and Dudley was ridiculed for his crushing defeat. In mock pity, or expressing a "We told you so" attitude, the welders left the booth and settled down to work once more. At lunch the spectators at the "showdown" happily reported who had won to those who had missed the event. Every Friday morning something like this took place, much to the enjoyment of all concerned; for the rest of the day special plans were made and announced by everyone to help him win the pool "next week."

Work Activities and Conversations

A DAY'S WORK: "A DOLLAR-SIXTY-FOUR"

Bob participated in many conversations about output and pay. Almost every day in the early afternoon, for example, Dudley called on Stan. Either at once or in the course of the conversation, Dudley would announce with evident pride that he had made a "dollar-sixty-four." On other days Stan might drop into booth nine, where Bob was helping Reed, and ask him how much he had to go. Reed would answer that in half an hour he would have his "dollar-sixty-four." On one occasion Stan told Reed that he was not going to make his "dollar-sixty-four" that day.

One day Bob asked Stan what a "dollar-sixty-four" meant. Stan told him that the company had let it be known that they expected everyone to be able to "beat their rate" by about 20 per cent. That is, he thought that in an eight-hour shift he should turn out a number of pieces sufficient to give him a monetary return per day equal to 20 per cent more than he would have received had he been paid by the hour at his base rate. Since his day rate was $1.34 per hour, he thought he should turn out enough on piecework rates to make 20 per cent more than this, namely, $1.64.[1] Stan added that he never earned any

[1] The reader will note that 20 per cent of $1.34 is 26.8 cents, and this amount added to $1.34 makes a total of $1.608, not $1.64. Bob did not know how to

more than his $1.64 and that after he had turned out enough pieces to make the rate, it was useless to continue working, because the company didn't want him to earn any more. According to him, they would "only pay you so much no matter how many extra pieces you make."

A few days later, Bob asked Reed if he had "made his rate," and they fell to talking about the payment system. Bob asked about the 20 per cent and the $1.64. Reed told him that the union had decided that the men should be able to beat the rates by 20 per cent and that the company had come to expect it of the workers after that. He added that everybody in the plant was following this agreement and that for the welders $1.64 was the proper hourly piecework rate.

Bob realized that with each welder doing a variety of work with different rates per piece, their beliefs about a day's work had to be expressed in terms of earnings rather than in units of output. When their pay for an eight-hour shift amounted to $13.12, they stopped work and killed time, even thought it was not the official stopping time. They visited someone else or held over any additional output for the next day.

At one o'clock in the afternoon one day, Dudley told Bob that he had made his rate. He boasted that he never did much work after two-thirty in the afternoon, which left him an hour for his own free time. Bob inquired why the workers quit at $1.64. According to Dudley, it was sort of an agreement reached by all the men, and 20 per cent was the level above which they were "not supposed to do any more." He added, "If you don't believe me, just go around the plant and ask anyone else. They're all producing at 20 per cent. Our day rate is $1.34, so we're allowed a bonus to bring us to $1.64."

Bob once asked Dudley why he had decided to make eight axles a day, since he had told Bob that he felt he could have doubled his production if he wished. Dudley explained that George (at the time, in booth 8) had been asked by Gooba to work on axles. After a few weeks' trial, he claimed that he was too light and too short to be able to handle the unwieldy pieces and said that he was not going to take the work. Luckily, other work arrived, and Gooba put him on the smaller pieces. Dudley boasted that finally Gooba had come to him to perform the axle-welding operation because he was a "big boy." But, said Dudley, shortly after he had become accustomed to the job, the time-study men came around.

---

account for this discrepancy. It appeared likely to him that the "dollar-sixty-four" related to the "dollar-thirty-four," but he was not sure and did not think he could ask.

DUDLEY: Naturally, I couldn't make any more than George had made. He had been turning in eight a day on day work, so I had to do the same on piecework. After all, I couldn't make him look like a damn' fool by turning in ten or fifteen of the things.

Bob inquired what would happen if Dudley started to make more than his $1.64 a day. Dudley assured him that management would cut the rate and expect him to maintain the new level of production; that is, if he were to continue to take home the same paycheck. He also said that he had never experienced the cut in rate that he was guarding against, but he felt certain that it would happen.

According to Stan, it was "dangerous business fooling around very much with the rate." He asked Bob if he had ever heard the story of Joe, the sheet-metal cutter, at the company's Plant 4. The story went as follows.

> Joe was a family man who needed money badly. He was hired at Plant 4 and put on a huge hydraulic machine that cut a particular-shaped pattern from $\frac{1}{4}''$ thick iron plates. After Joe was timed, he realized that there was a one-inch clearance through which the steel blade descended upon the sheet of iron; and it occurred to him that if he inserted two plates at once, instead of one, under the cutter, he could produce twice as many finished pieces as he had been producing and in the same amount of time. Joe's production doubled in one day and remained at this high level for several days.
>
> In a short time, management became curious. The super-intendent was informed. He asked questions and looked on Joe's work with a critical eye; the rate-setters came down to look the job over; and the accounting department checked over the records. Everybody looked for something wrong, but they didn't have to look for very long. The time-study men soon saw what Joe had done to double his output and his paycheck; so they halved the piece rate and he was back where he started. The only difference was that he was putting out twice as much for the same amount of money.
>
> Well, poor old Joe wasn't too smart, and it was going to take him a while to learn from experience, because he knew that there was still sufficient clearance to cut three plates at a time instead of two. So he started inserting three plates under the cutter and pretty soon he was making the same pay that he had been making before they cut the rate. But again, after about a week, they came and cut his rate again, and he found that

he was producing three times as much as when he started the job, that he was working a great deal harder, and that he had received no monetary increase for the increased output.

Joe was now pretty discouraged, but he needed the money badly and he worked just as fast as he possibly could for a few days in order to make a little extra for the wife and kids; but it was too much strain to sustain a level like that for a very long time and from that time on he was just barely able to make the rate. He finally quit in disgust. He never realized the damage he had done to others as well as to himself. For ever after that, the men who took on Joe's cutting job always found that the rate was a very "lean" one.

Stan capped the story by telling Bob that it was absolutely true, that he had heard it from the man who had worked beside Joe, and that to verify it Bob had only to ask the others in the plant. At various times during the summer Bob mentioned the story to other workers and found that all the men who had worked in the plant for some time had heard the story and believed it. A few of them had heard it from the same man that had related it to Stan. No one, however, knew his name, and no date was ever mentioned. When Bob first heard the story, he asked Stan if he knew when Joe had had all his difficulties. Stan answered that he had failed to ask his informer. Several other men told Bob that they did not know; like Stan, though, they believed it had happened in the fairly recent past, within the past couple of years.

Later Bob made the acquaintance of the president of the union local at Plant 4. Bob asked him about Joe, and he assured Bob that though the story was a true one and generally known to the workers of Plant 4, Joe's misfortune had actually taken place at the company's Plant 10, located in another part of the city.

THE PACE OF WORK DURING THE DAY

The welders frequently expressed directly or indirectly the idea that they liked to plan their work so that they could finish between 2:30 and 3 o'clock in the afternoon. This permitted them a certain reserve in which to make their rate, if they had been delayed up to that time. They liked to feel that if they had trouble with the job or were not feeling well part of the day, they could speed up and make up losses later. They liked to have something in reserve for emergencies.

The welders had learned that their physical condition varied from day to day. Stan often came to work in a fatigued condition from lack of sleep the night before; yet he had merely spent the evening in what was to him normal social activity. Stan arose at 5:30 every morning in order to report to work at seven. Even what he considered a reasonable evening's activities the night before would not have allowed him eight hours of sleep, for he would have had to be home by nine-thirty. Occasionally, the welders came to work with upset stomachs or headaches. Chris once was emotionally upset over his sick wife's condition and said he just didn't feel like working that day.

Most of the welders told Bob that they preferred turning out the largest portion of their work in the earlier part of the day, and they did exactly that. However, they usually did not get down to work right away, because of visits from others and the preparation of materials. As the morning passed, they began to become anxious about their work and started turning it out at a high rate, which generally began to slope off about 11 o'clock. By this time they had assured themselves of a large part of the day's work; they therefore started calling on one another, but continued to do some work, at a decreasing rate of speed, as the noon hour approached.

After lunch they started again and speeded their work in order to assure the rest of the day's pay. Yet at the same time they did not wish to finish several hours before quitting time, because they felt that such loafing might be difficult to hide. Hence, they rapidly reached the point in their afternoon's labors where they subjectively estimated that it was time to begin extending the work in order not to have too much free time to conceal. Thus, they timed the work so that they slowly brought it to a close somewhere near the end of the working day. If they finished by 3:00 P.M., they could always find ways of spending the time until the day was over at 3:30 P.M.

Stan once said, "Making work is a pain in the neck. Here it is 1:30 and I've got my $1.64 made. Nothing else for me to do. Guess I worked too fast this morning." Bob watched him for the rest of the afternoon; he always seemed busy, though he did little welding.

Chris remarked to Bob one time that the day was passing at an uncomfortably slow rate. According to him, "The day is a lot more interesting, and the time passes much faster, if you can have something to do most of the time."

Dudley expressed his views on the best way to work as follows: "I don't mind working," he said, "but on the other hand, I don't like to work myself to death." He added that he found he could get through the day easier if he was doing something most of the time.

Stan once capped a conversation on the same topic: "I say, don't overwork, but don't underwork." The tone of voice with which he made this remark implied that he was quoting a time-honored maxim.

A few weeks after Bob started work at Plant 3, Reed quit his job. At that time, Burl was taken off his own operation and started producing frames. Bob then began to help Burl. Burl continued to eat with the welders from booths 1 through 7, however, and Bob ate with him. These men talked at length about their progress with the day's work and spent a great deal of time figuring out ways to finish it without either working too hard or attracting management's attention for loafing. They frequently consulted Gus, the union committee man for the department, asking him if a certain procedure was "safe" or permissible or what course should be followed. Though they asked him many such questions, Gus never referred to the contract. When the men asked if a certain action was "safe" he either said that it was or explained how it could better be done, but he never explained his answer in terms of the contract.

Toward the end of the summer, Bob decided to set down briefly but as accurately as he could how Stan spent his time.

Stan's Work Day
A.M.

6:58   Stan arrived at his booth and changed into his work clothes.

7:05   Turned on the welding machine; broke open a box of welding rods; distributed them in his favorite places on the jig; chatted with Bob.

7:10   Set up the jig and welded about five minutes.

7:15   Went into the next booth and talked with Reed.

7:25   Returned to booth and talked to Bob about his girl friend and the man he had socked on the previous Saturday night.

7:30   Worked for twenty minutes and finished the first piece.

7:50   Dudley came into the booth and talked about the fight Stan had been in.

7:55   Dudley left; Stan started to work steadily.

9:10   Pieces number 2, 3, and 4 finished. Average time per piece, 25 minutes. (Average time per piece in time study was 32 minutes.) Decided it was time to take a break. Leaned on jig, smoked, talked about his girl to Bob.

9:20   Back to work.

9:45   Piece number 5 turned out; started work on piece number 6.

9:50   Russ, the layout man, dropped in for a visit; complained about the engineers not knowing their job.

10:00 Russ left; Stan got sandwich from lunch box and ate it.

10:05 Got drink of water at fountain; then back to work.

10:35 Piece number 6 finished; started number 7.

10:45 Swore at heat; claimed it was time for a smoke. Again he talked to Bob about the fight he had had.

10:55 Back to work.

11:00 Milkman came around. Stan bought his regular bottle of chocolate milk. Got a drink of water. On way back from fountain went to timekeeper's office to pick up time card.

11:10 Back to work.

11:25 Finished piece number 7. Set up jig for piece number 8.

11:30 Reed arrived for a visit. Talked about freak rainstorm just passed.

11:35 Reed and Stan left to visit Dudley.

11:45 Stan returned and welded for about a minute. Looked up to clock to get the time. Took off helmet and gloves; lit cigarette.

11:50 Went for another drink of water; then to wash hands.

11:55 Returned to booth, waiting for noon whistle to blow.

12:00 Lunch whistle blew. Turned off machine and went to Reed's booth for lunch.

                              P.M.

12:30 Back-to-work whistle blew.

12:35 Stan went back to work.

2:35   With Bob's help, fast work done. Pieces 8 through 13 finished (six pieces in two hours; average time per piece, 20 minutes). They talked about how their work was coming along. Reed and Dudley had made their $1.64 and were all done. Burl said he had about fifteen more minutes' work before he would be finished. He jokingly remarked that he was slowing down in his old age.

2:40   Burl said he was going back to work. Reed and Dudley announced that they were going to see how George was coming along. As Reed left, he quietly turned up the heat on Stan's welding machine. Stan went back to work.

3:05   Stan finished his last piece, but left it in the jig. Went to lavatory and chatted with other men there; then washed hands and face.

3:15   Returned to booth; but left right away to visit inspector.

3:20   Returned to booth; changed back into street clothes, talked with Chris and Bob.

3:30   Final whistle blew. Stan dressed and cleaned and left the plant immediately.

Thus, Stan made 14 frames during the day. He had been timed at an average of 33 minutes per frame. In actual working time, though, Stan had worked 321 minutes to produce his 14 pieces, an average of 23 minutes per piece. Hence, in an eight-hour shift with a 20-minute allowance for personal time, Stan actually spent only five hours and twenty-one minutes directly on his work.

THE WELDERS' BEHAVIOR DURING A TIME STUDY

The welders knew that the company would not set production standards on a new job until they had become sufficiently familiar with the skills necessary to perform the operation. This was only to be expected. On a completely new job, especially one which required considerable dexterity, it was generally impossible to set the rate until the worker had developed the necessary skill. According to Stan and several others, the company waited for the men to develop a certain habitual method of working a new piece, on the assumption that this would mean a more unconsciously systematized working operation—more precise movements, less waste effort, and more speed, each in turn leading to leaner rates, greater production per hour, and greater profits for the company.

During the time that a welder was doing a job on day rate, he learned how long it took him to do one piece. He also learned how to do a thorough job, so that when he was timed, he could actually take more time to do one piece than he ordinarily required. Before the time-study man arrived, a few calculations would tell the welder how many pieces he would be expected to make. He could be timed at such a pace that he could easily make his 20 per cent "to satisfy the company" and thus his own desires would be taken care of too. For example, if the welder knew that he could finish three pieces in one hour, he would arrange the work in a time study so that he finished only two in one hour. Thus, his daily production rate would be 16 pieces per day, when he could actually produce 16 pieces in five hours and twenty minutes. This left him with two hours and forty minutes to spread out in the course of a day's work. This was actually the case with one of the welders.

During a time study a welder was very careful to follow every detail of the job instructions, avoiding all short cuts and putting in a few inconspicuous extras, if possible, to slow him down. At the same time he gave the impression that he was working steadily at an even pace, so that he would not be accused of stalling on the job.

A welder could "waste time" without seeming to do so during a time study in a variety of ways. First of all, during a time study a welder called for his helper only when there was a job that he physically could not do alone. The helper merely stood by the rest of the time and limited his help to assisting the welder in setting the long angle irons in the jig, in turning over the partly finished frame, and finally in removing the frame from the jig. In actual operation, after the rate had been set, the helper assisted the welder in other ways, including setting up the jig. For example, when Bob had been working for Stan for some time, he was able to set up the whole jig for him. In addition, Bob generally helped Stan set the plates in the jig and fasten the 20-odd clamps. Bob also helped Stan check his work for missed welds.

On the morning that he was to be time studied, however, Stan told Bob to help him only when he so ordered. Bob obeyed and watched or went about other business near at hand. Alone, Stan inserted the plates in the jig; he fastened all the clamps himself, and he also unfastened all the clamps after the first part of the operation. Only then did he call for Bob to help him turn over the half-completed frame. Once again he fastened all the clamps himself, another job that Bob generally helped him with. When the frame was finished, Stan unfastened all the clamps himself, pried loose the frame, checked it himself, and only then did he call Bob to help him remove the frame from the booth. In other words, during the time study Bob helped him only with the operations involving lifting; yet on other occasions, Bob had regularly been helping Stan in all but the actual welding itself. Needless to say, during the time study Stan was able to give the appearance of an operator "working efficiently at normal daywork speed," because that is precisely what he was doing. He did not slow down his rate of speed but rather arranged the work so that he had more things to do.

The reader may well ask why the helper was not included in the time study. There were some difficulties with this suggestion. If the time study of making a frame included one helper giving the maximum amount of assistance possible, the welders, and ultimately the union, would insist that the helper do no other work except to help that one welder in his whole operation. For example, Bob's work with Stan actually occurred at intervals of about fifteen minutes. During the intervals after Bob had set up a jig or helped remove a frame from the booth, he either helped Reed or Dudley or helped

Chris with the grinding. Had Bob been timed with Stan on making frames, Stan would have insisted that Bob be on hand at all times to help him. Then every welder would have requested a helper, and costs in the department would have increased considerably.

In the event that the helper had been included in the time study and had helped in all the ways possible, there were still other ways in which the job could be slowed down. For example, a welder could reduce the "heat" of his torch so that a standard welding rod would take a little longer to melt, with the result that each weld would take a little longer to make. Or the welder could use a rod that was a little thinner than the one prescribed for the job. Hence, it would take him longer for the job, because each weld required a specific quantity of welding steel to give the proper strength to the frame. In addition, if a thinner rod were used, the welder would need more rods. This meant that he could consume precious moments replacing rods in the insulated handle with which he welded.

The reader may again suggest that the time-study man should have with him a statement of the prescribed rod and "heat" to be used in the operation he was timing and that he should ascertain that these standards were met. But even if the time-study man insisted on the standard rods and amperage, he could not prevent the welder from using a larger rod and higher heat afterwards, so that his regular production could be done more quickly. It was impossible to prevent the welder from getting larger rods, because all diameters of rods were available at the stock room for various operations. If the stock room would not give a welder the size rod he wished without authorization, he could always "go down the line" and borrow the size he wanted from another welder who was using it.

Of course, some jobs were harder to "extend" than others. Bob understood from the helpers who worked in the machine department that it was much more difficult to "make a decent rate" on the lathes and drill presses than in the welding department. In fact, it was generally appreciated in the plant that the welders had the easiest time of all the workers in being able to get "fat rates."

MAINTAINING UNIFORM OUTPUT

The welders maintained uniformity in their output in a variety of ways. For example, each man recorded his own output on his time card, and the others appeared never to wish to question a man's integrity by asking him what he had recorded as the day's work. But they could always watch a man working. In the early days of his employment, even though he was not on piecework, Bob worked past

3:15 P.M. (Quitting time was 3:30.) Very soon he became the butt of inquiry and ridicule. "Getting started on tomorrow's work, are you, Bob?" Chris asked. Stan came up to him and gently kicked him in the rear and asked, "Hey, Bob, don't we give you enough work to do every day?" Dudley passed by and shouted to Stan that Bob was trying to make some "overtime," working after hours as he was. Bob understood and ceased working; but Reed commented to Stan early the next morning that they were going to work Bob "good and hard" that day, so that he'd feel like quitting when the rest of the men quit. And that is precisely what they did; for the rest of the day, in addition, Bob was the butt of some of the more ribald jokes of the day. The event passed over, however, and Bob felt no disfavor afterward; but he had learned his lesson.

Stan and Reed performed three separate operations, the order of which was left entirely to their discretion. Generally they produced a pile of left sides of the frames and then an approximately equal amount of right sides, before they proceeded to the final operation of making the complete frame. Each piece in each of their operations had a different price. Occasionally a delay in the regular routine of their work upset their schedule for making $1.64. If they continued making the same piece all day, they realized that at its end they might come out perhaps a dollar short or a dollar over the standard. Hence, they made calculations on the wall with their chalk to find out what combination of the differently priced pieces would permit them to come as close as possible to $1.64. They commonly juggled the combinations until they had contrived a work schedule for the day that brought them within a cent or two. A three-cent overage appeared to be forbidden, and they worked at the calculations until they found the "right" combination. Then they erased the figures and said to Bob something like, "Well, we'll make six more of these until 11:30, then we'll switch and make four complete frames for the rest of the day."

One day Reed arrived at the plant at about ten o'clock in the morning. His schedule called for him to make 17 frames a day, for he had been timed at 27 minutes per frame. Shortly after coming into the booth, he started making calculations on the wall with a piece of chalk. Bob noticed that he was dividing 120 by 33 (minutes absent divided by time per piece). After finishing, he erased the calculations from the wall, turned to Bob, and muttered that Bob would not have to work so hard for him that day, because he was only going to make 13 pieces (17 pieces minus the four pieces that he ordinarily made in two hours). He said that if he made his standard eight-hour production of 17 pieces in six hours, the company might have some embarrassing questions for him.

REED: First of all they'd want to know how come I could produce in six hours what normally took me eight. Then they'd figure that I was goofing off and that I could make the pieces faster than I have been, and they'd come to expect me to be able to do it all the time. So the first thing you know they'd be down here cutting the rate on me, and I'd be working harder than ever for the same pay. And they'd be patting themselves on the back for having cut the cost of making frames.

Bob asked him if he had ever exceeded the rate and the rate had been cut. Reed said that he never exceeded the rate anywhere he had worked, but that in one plant where his brother had worked, there was a worker no one liked who always produced more than he should have. This attracted undue attention from management, and it wasn't long before his job was retimed.

BOB: Well, on the other hand, what happens if you really can't make the rate that's set in the time study?
REED: That never happens in welding; you can always make it here. And what's more, you want to make it, if you've got any sense. You stop producing for very long, and they'll be down here to find out why. So you always want to make the rate. But at the same time you don't want to go over it by very much, or the rate will be cut on you surer'n hell. Of course, if by some chance you get a really "lean" rate that you can't make the twenty on, you want to kick like the very devil until they come down and change it.

In their attempts to maintain uniformity in their output, the welders resorted to two other practices. The first consisted of reporting sometimes more and sometimes less than they actually accomplished. The second, claiming idle-time or daywork allowances, operated as an excuse for the man who had made his rate and had nothing more to do.

Stan used to "save up pieces" when his output was high and report them when his output was low. On some days he said that he just did not feel like working fast. When he did not make his 14 pieces for the day, he nevertheless reported that he had made the requisite number. Toward the end of the day he would warn Bob that he would be working harder for him on the following day, because he was going to have to make 17 pieces to make up for the pieces that he had not made on that day. And the next day, Stan would turn out the production required to maintain his average. There was no way that management could have checked Stan's daily output, for Marty and

Bob always took each frame to the assembly line after it had been ground.

On other occasions Stan arrived late at work. He would figure out how many pieces he was expected to make in the time that he had been absent, subtract these from the day's work and turn in proportionately fewer pieces. Sometimes he would make a few more than he felt he could report, and these he would hold over for the next day.

One time Burl told Bob that George took an hour's time on daywork every day.

BURL: He always finds some excuse to get put on daywork. Something is always going wrong with the parts, the jig breaks down, or there's not enough material, or he's gotta go to the company hospital with that bad back of his.

BOB: Well, then he doesn't make so much money every week, does he?

BURL: No, he doesn't make as much as he would if he stayed on piecework all the time. But it only adds up to a little bit each week, so he says to hell with it.

Some time later Bob was helping to deliver several crates of material to George, and he took the occasion to ask him about it. George called Bob's attention to the fact that he was always working on small parts, whose production time was only a minute or so a piece. He explained that he had quite a bit of skill working these pieces and that he really could perform the operation very rapidly. He found that if he maintained that pace he would run through the day's supply long before the day was over. Yet he didn't like to work slowly, so what he did was to claim "off time" so that he could find something else to do or someone to visit without "letting 'em know" how fast he could work. Anyway, he added, the job got rather dull and boring; and if he changed over to daywork, he could pass the time a little faster. George was not going to show changes in his output, and so he went on "off time" to take up the slack. Of course, he turned in proportionately fewer pieces; but, as he said, this way it was "safer and easier going."

Another idea which the welders frequently expressed or implied was that their output should show little change from week to week, unless there were extenuating circumstances, such as delays beyond their control. This did not mean that all of them should achieve identical outputs expressed in earnings each week, but rather that each individual should be fairly consistent week after week. For the welders in booths 8 through 11, this meant making the $1.64 every day and every week. Their reasons for this were similar to those they advanced for neither exceeding nor falling for below the standard of a day's work. They felt that if their output showed much change either from day to day or from week to week, "something might happen." An unusually high output might henceforth become the standard which they would be expected to maintain. The men felt that it would be a way of confessing that they were capable of doing better. On the other hand, they felt that a low output would give management cause to investigate, and as Stan put it, "The farther they keep away from you, the better." According to Dudley, low output would afford management a chance to "bawl him out"; as far as he was concerned, "When they keep off my neck I know things are going all right."

THE WELDERS' ATTITUDES TOWARD MANAGEMENT

Bob's log of his observations contained several examples of the attitudes which the welders expressed toward the "front office," management, and, more especially, their foreman. One time Stan spoke as follows.

STAN: Listen, Buddy, you gotta remember that up in the front office, you're just a number to them. You know, I've been working here for three years, and I've yet to see a company man come around here and visit me when he's *not* on official business. Once Mac-Farlane [the plant manager] dropped into my booth with some engineers. He didn't even see me. All he knew was that he wanted to see the frame and figure out new ways to produce it.

Another time he spoke in a similar vein.

STAN: If they want to get rid of you, there are plenty of ways they can do it. Look at Ray Zupan, for example. They let him go for insubordination. Don't you worry about that. If they want to find a way of letting you go, they'll find it. Being in the union helps; but if they don't want you or don't need you, they can always find a way of letting you go.

Dudley made several comments along these lines.

DUDLEY: If the company's only interested in cost, profit, and efficiency, then they just ain't interested in us. There's always plenty more where we came from.

Over a beer one Friday afternoon, he spoke at more length.

DUDLEY: Bob, if the goddam' company don't give a damn about you, they might just as well come right out and say that they're out to screw you. Take an example. You're out swimmin' one warm sunny day, and you get cramps and start to drown. I'm walkin' by the swimmin' hole at just that minute and I see you there screamin' and hollerin', but I just keep on walking. What difference does it make whether I just keep on walking? What difference does it make whether I just don't care about you if you drown or not, or if I actually hate your guts? The result is the same. You drown in either case. Well, it's the same way with the company. The way they're always harping on getting out the work, they surer'n hell aren't for us. And I say that if they aren't for us, then you can bet your bottom dollar that they're against us.

Once Reed said to Bob, "We may need the company to pay us, but though the company needs workers, they don't necessarily need you and me." The day before Reed quit, Bob had the following conversation with him.

BOB: You know, with all the breaks we take, what would happen if a company man should come around and see you just sittin' here with no work to do? Ain't he gonna raise hell with your rate, so you'll be working harder?

REED: Hell, no. You tell him you've been workin' like a slave all day, and you figure it's about time you took a five minute break.

BOB: Mm-hmmm, but what if he sees that you're finished with your work. After all, you always finish the day's work around two o'clock.

REED: Yeah, but he don't see that I'm finished. If you ever get asked if your work is done, you tell him hell, no, you'll barely make your rate today.

BOB: Mm-hmmm.

REED: Sure. You see, you want to tell 'em what they like to hear, and the only thing that'll please 'em is to think that you're really getting out the production. What the hell do you think that they'd be down here for? To see if you went out last night? Or to ask you about the wife and kids? Or maybe they'd come down here to shoot the breeze with you for a while and see how things are going with you? There's only *one* thing that brings in the bacon for them and that's production. What do you think a time-study man is for, your health? Or for speeding up production?

BOB: They like to think that they're getting the most out of you that they can. Is that right?

REED: Sure, that's what keeps 'em happy—to think that they're making you work like a sonofabitch all day long for your pay; because if you are, you're really gettin' out the production.

The welders, though, thought that Gooba did what he could for them.

STAN: Gooba's a good guy and all that, but never a day goes by without him asking me how many pieces I've got done.

REED: Gooba knows just how many pieces I should have done at any time in the day, and whenever he asks me how I'm doing— and he always does—he looks just a bit worried if I'm a little behind in my work.   Maybe he's worried that I won't make the rate and take home what I want to, but I get the feeling that he gets a little concerned if I should drop my output.   I guess he's worried about what the company would think of him if he couldn't keep up the production every day.

DUDLEY: You see, the company has gotta know how the work is coming along, so that they can plan ahead and have the material here for us on time and so on.   So they want you to maintain the same output every day, so they can plan production way ahead of time.   That's one of the reasons that they want to time you, so that they can know how many pieces to expect from you every day. After all, if they didn't know how things were coming, the first thing they'd know, the assembly line would be held up because old Dudley here didn't get out enough frames one day.   So that's why Gooba is always hanging around asking the guys how they're coming along.   He's sorta nice about it, though, so we don't mind his asking.   But the other foremen around here really get scared if you can't make the same rate every day.   After all, the company didn't hire foremen because they like their looks.   They hire them to get out the pieces and to keep it up day after day.

The following is an example of what Gooba did for the welders that made a considerable difference to them:

One time Stan and Bob were kidding Reed about his never having won the "poker pool," and they had neglected to close the curtain. They had been making Reed the butt of their jokes for a few minutes when Gooba came along.   He glanced into the booth, quickly pulled the curtain shut, and continued on his way without a word.

In contrast, here is the way Bob heard that the foreman in the machine shop treated his men.   The conversation occurred one Friday afternoon after work, at the tavern where many of the men cashed their paychecks and had a glass of beer on their way home.   Mike, the disc grinder, had asked Bob to sit down with the group he was with.   A lathe operator from the machine shop spoke about his foreman.

LATHE OPERATOR: That sonofabitch, he's just like the company. He's trying to get in good with the guys on top, so he's trying to get as much work as possible out of us and that's all. Just so long as he keeps his departmental costs down. That's all he wants and he'll do everything to get 'em. So what does he do? First, he tries to arrange it so that when a new job needs to be timed, he gets one of his favorites to do it. And you know who his favorites are, the dumb guys that will work their heads off just to get in good with the likes of him. So he gets the job timed fast, and when one of us gets the job later on, ya gotta sweat like hell to make the rate; and the price per piece is cheap. Then the company thinks that he's a good foreman, and to hell with the guys. And then when we have to go fast, does he get sore if we waste material! That's all that counts with him, cost of material, gettin' out the pieces. All he wants is work. Good Christ, I work alone at the lathe all day, and if I go off seeing one of the boys for a little while, wham! He's right on my back in no time at all. He'll see me over talking with Carl or with this big lug here, and we'll get the dirty looks. Boy, I'm telling you, he just don't allow for nothing but production.

On another Friday afternoon over beer, a drill-press operator to whom Bob occasionally delivered parts talked about his foreman.

DRILL-PRESS OPERATOR: The goddamn' foreman doesn't realize that some pieces vary more than others, or that they come through to us defective. What happens? I get timed on a set of pieces that come from the foundry, and I can drill 'em each in one minute. They're soft. Then, when I'm on the job, I suddenly get a set of hard pieces. Then I find myself having to take longer to drill 'em, or I start breaking drills and wasting time going to the stockroom to get new ones. So that day, I either have to move at breakneck speed to get out enough pieces to earn my day's pay, or else I just don't make it and take home less at the end of the week. And, then what about pieces that break? I only get paid the piece rate for finished pieces. But sometimes they break when I'm half way through 'em, and all this through no fault of my own. The pieces just can't stand the strain. Sometimes I have to work on one hundred and ten pieces to get out one hundred good ones that I can get paid piece rate for. Aww, it's hell in the machine shop, I tell you. You guys in welding don't know how lucky you are.

Stan once told Bob, "Those poor guys in the machine shop. I feel sorry for those poor guys, working their heads off like they have to some days. We're lucky."

The Briggs Box Company

David Roberts, a student of the dynamics of small-group behavior, started his field research work at the Briggs Box Company with keen interest in the opportunity it afforded to study the responses of two crews in identical external circumstances.

He discovered quite early in the seven-month observation period that the patterns of personal relationships and work routines differed markedly between the two crews, but that in spite of this fact there was little difference in their productivity. Probing the reasons for these seemingly contradictory responses became the focus of Mr. Robert's personal attention and of his conversations with the two crews and others in the plant associated with them.

The observations and conversations that constitute the larger part of the following material are preceded by a description of the plant organization, work process, and physical equipment, constituting the external environment, and a brief description of the two crews with an account of certain changes in crew membership during the research period. Following this background information are excerpts from Mr. Roberts' experiences which he considered significant both in illustrating the types of behaviors and in providing clues as to why they occurred.

The behavioral material is organized, without regard to chronological sequence and with some unavoidable overlapping of content, to depict: the prevailing pattern in each crew; the attitudes of those who worked on both crews; the response of each crew to changes and to crises; intercrew relations; the relations of the crews to management; comparisons in their work records; and management's views of the crews.

BACKGROUND INFORMATION

The laminating section, where Mr. Roberts conducted his study, was a strategic part of the Briggs Box Company's operations; it manufactured the fiberboard for many of the company's boxes. Workers

154

in other sections of the fiberboard department printed and folded the fiberboard sheets and assembled them into boxes which were usually shipped flat, or "knocked down." In the rest of the plant other kinds of packages, cartons, and crates were produced. Briggs was an old company which manufactured a wide variety of boxes and packing crates and employed about 300 workers, most of whom lived within three or four miles of the plant.

Organizational Setting

The laminating and the printing sections were under a supervisor who reported to the superintendent of fiberboard production, Fred Dorn (see Exhibit 1). Ed Dyer was the supervisor of the two sections on the day shift; Tom Lewis had the night shift. Mr. Dorn was also in charge of a finishing and cellophane section, located on another floor. The workers in the latter section made and inserted the cellophane windows which a few customers specified for their boxes. All sections were visited from time to time by representatives of the planning, waste, and quality control departments. Servicing the laminating crews were truckers and stock and glue men.

Physical Settings

The laminating section occupied about one-third of the first floor of the plant. This space was separated from other sections by large storage areas and was dominated by the noisy laminating machine, which stretched for over 150 feet along one wall. An elevator shaft at one end of the machine led to the basement stock room. Near the same end of the machine was a smoking area encircled by a rail and furnished with a bench, a drinking fountain, a pedestal desk, and a bulletin board where notices about output and bonuses were regularly posted. The laminating area also contained a wash basin and three lockers.

THE LAMINATING MACHINE AND ITS OPERATION

The operations of the laminating machine were similar to those of a papermaking machine, although its raw material was heavy paper, not pulp. Laminated fiberboard was usually made of three layers of paper. The two outer layers were strong, tough material; the center was weak, inexpensive paper, much like the filler in corrugated paper. The paper came in large rolls of several hundred pounds apiece and up

EXHIBIT 1

THE BRIGGS BOX COMPANY

Partial Organization Chart as of January 1954

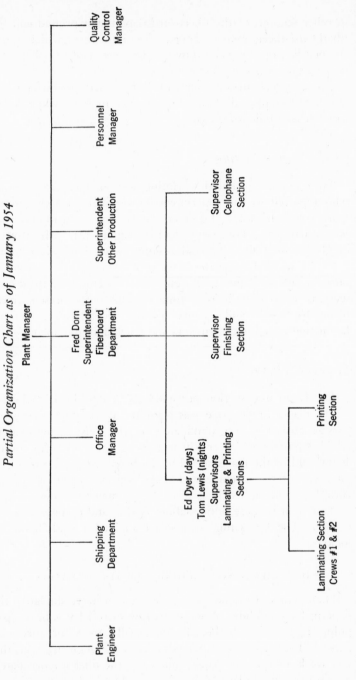

to 60 inches in width.   The rolls were stored on the floor below the laminator and sent up on the elevator when requested.

At the "front," or "wet," end of the machine the paper for the three layers of finished sheet were wound off the rolls on which they came. The paper for one of the outer layers and for the center layer fed into the laminating stand from different sides (see Exhibit 2).   After being heated and dampened under pressure, the paper for both layers passed up into and through the storage bin and down into the glue station. After the other outer layer had been heated and dampened, the three layers were glued together by the machine.   At the bottom of the machine was a wax pan containing the adhesive wax in which the cylinders which applied the wax and rolled the paper along its way were partially immersed.   The glue station was equipped with valves controlling the inflow of the waxes and an outflow trough to carry excess wax back into the tanks located on the floor below.

From the glue station the sheet passed in a continuous operation into the pressure section of the machine, where it was dried and pressed together as it passed between heated pressure cylinders.   As the sheet came out of the pressure section into the "dry end," it was cut by rotary knives, first into the widths and then into the lengths required by customers' orders.   Finally, it was removed from the receiving table and stacked, ready to be taken to the printing section.

Many and frequent variations in speed, heat, pressure, and wetness were required to meet different operating conditions, as well as the specifications of individual customer orders.   The controls for these adjustments were located at several places along the machine.   At the laminating stand, for example, the whole machine could be started and stopped, as well as adjusted for speed, heat, pressure, and wetness of the cylinders.   Similar adjustments could be made at the glue station, the pressure section, and at the "dry" or "receiving end" of the machine.   All these controls were necessary, since a slight variation in speed or pressure at any part of the process resulted in tearing the sheet or web, which when wet was extremely fragile.   A tear usually led to a shutdown of the whole machine and required the rethreading of the paper through the machine.

For customers who needed boxes of extra strength, an additional layer of tough paper was added to each side of the fiberboard for a total of five layers in the finished sheet.   Making sheet of the usual weight was called "normal laminating"; the other process was known as "triplex laminating."   Another variation in customers' orders called for two rolls of approximately half the width instead of one full-width roll.   This operation was called running "split rolls."   Both triplex

EXHIBIT 2

THE BRIGGS BOX COMPANY

Schematic Diagram of Laminating Machine

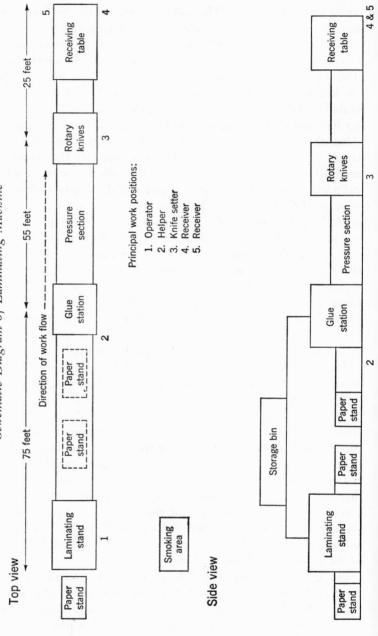

Top view

Principal work positions:

1. Operator
2. Helper
3. Knife setter
4. Receiver
5. Receiver

Side view

laminating and split rolls required extra work to set up the additional rolls and to run them. For example, in the event of a tear, rethreading the paper through the machine was more difficult.

THE JOBS OF A LAMINATOR CREW

The laminator was operated by a crew of five men. The jobs in the order of their responsibility were known as operator, knife setter, helper, and receiver; there were two receivers in each crew. Descriptions of the individual jobs are given in Exhibit 3. Because of the nature of the process, all the jobs were highly interdependent. The members of a crew signalled one another by blowing a horn controlled by buttons located at each man's usual work position. The crews also employed a hand signal code.

EXHIBIT 3

THE BRIGGS BOX COMPANY

Job Descriptions, Laminating Department

JOB NAME: *Operator*
FUNCTION: Responsible for the operation of the machine and the direction of its personnel.
DUTIES: Responsible for the entire wet-end operation, involving the personal operation of laminating stand and glue station, which involves:
Have stock shafted ahead at all times.
Maintain proper spread of wax adhesive by transfer roll adjustment.
Maintain proper speed ratio between laminator stand and glue station.
Maintain proper pressure between various rolls.
Maintain proper balance between speed over heating units and quality of finished sheet. Maintain proper level of wax adhesive in pans.
Turn in daily time work and keeping work sheets.
Assist in the performance of general departmental duties.
Learn and observe safety rules.
Perform such other duties as may from time to time be assigned.

JOB NAME: *Knife setter*
FUNCTION: Set up knives and maintain their proper operation.
DUTIES: Set up knives.
Check quality and specifications.
Change knives as required.

Check sheet widths and lengths; check for clean edges; check knives for square breaks and cuts.

Cut out excess sheet and turn knives when changing orders.

Assist receivers.

Watch side trim to keep sheet lined up.

Keep spare knives in orderly fashion.

Assist operator with grade or size changes.

Maintain cutting list.

Keep dry-end equipment and work area clean at all times.

Assist in the performance of general departmental duties.

Learn and observe safety rules.

From time to time perform such other duties as may be assigned.

JOB NAME: *Helper*

FUNCTION: Operate glue station, maintaining proper lineup of outside lines and webs.

DUTIES: Set guides for width changes and maintain proper wax spread.

Start new rolls of paper on glue station.

Assist operator with the operation of the laminating machine.

Assist operator in the setup of rolls.

Notify receivers of bad sheets coming through the machine.

Keep equipment and work area clean at all times.

Assist in the performance of general departmental duties.

Learn and observe safety rules.

Perform such other duties as may from time to time be assigned.

JOB NAME: *Receiver* (2)

FUNCTION: Take off sheets cut on the main laminator and pile them evenly on skids and conveyors.

DUTIES: Grasp and bundle sheets; jog and transfer to skid in orderly pile.

Pile loads to heights which can be efficiently handled at the next operation.

Push loads aside and position empty skids or boards.

Inspect sheets for inferior quality and notify knife setter of imperfections.

Discard imperfect sheets and keep count of same.

Set cutoff knife for length of cut.

Notify knife setter when to break off and change stock, and keep equipment and work area clean at all times.

Assist in the performance of general departmental duties.

Learn and observe safety rules.

Perform such other duties as may from time to time be assigned.

The operator and helper worked at the wet end of the machine. At the beginning of each shift the operator checked with the foreman the sequence in which orders were to be run. The orders were listed on a clipboard kept near the operator's position. He arranged the orders, whose sequence had been tentatively established in the production planning department, to minimize the number of changes that would have to be made in the width of the rolls of paper being run. When a change of this sort occurred, the whole machine had to be shut down and the rolls, whether used up or not, changed on all the stands. Unfinished, or butt, rolls were sent back to the basement to be run the next time that width of sheet was called for. It was advantageous when either triplex laminating or split rolls were required to schedule and run as much as possible, once the machine was set up for the extra rolls.

With the helper, the operator prepared the heavy rolls of paper for the machine when they came up from the floor below. The men moved the rolls from the elevator and placed them where they would be easily accessible. When one was needed, the operator and helper replaced the wooden blocks around which the paper was wound with a heavy iron pipe, to serve as an axle for the roll to turn on after it was placed in position on a paper stand. This operation was called "shafting." They then hoisted the shafted roll into place at a paper stand and secured it with a clamp, or paper brake. If the paper on the outside of the roll was dirty or torn, they cut off the soiled part.

To start making sheet, the operator threaded the paper from the first two rolls through the cylinders of the laminating stand, up into the storage bin, and down to the helper at the glue station. The latter then threaded these layers of paper, as well as the one from the third stand, through the cylinders of the glue station and into the pressure section that carried the sheet, as it dried, to the receiving end. The two men made adjustments in the setup of the laminator and glue station required by the size and thickness of the paper about to be run and by the quality of the finished sheets specified in the customers' orders. The helper operated the controls of the glue station.

Operating the laminating stand and glue station efficiently called for experienced judgment. For example, before a roll supplying paper for the first outer layer was exhausted, the operator was supposed to run the laminating stand faster than the glue station. In this way he could build up enough extra paper in the storage bin to keep the rest of the machine running while the first roll was being changed. Similarly, whenever the roll for the second outer layer had to be changed, the laminating stand could be kept running by letting paper from the first roll accumulate in the bin. Both machines had to be stopped whenever the roll supplying the central layer was replaced. Making roll changes correctly was also important because only a limited amount of extra paper could be stored in or made available from the bin.   Consequently, anything more than a slight delay usually led to a complete machine shutdown and wasted paper and time while the sheet was being rethreaded, possibly through the whole machine.

The knife setter and receivers worked at the dry end of the machine. The former was responsible for adjusting the rotary knives that cut the sheet lengthwise as it came out of the pressure section. He was also responsible for seeing that customers' orders were correctly filled as the cut sheets came off the machine. He could make certain adjustments of the knives while the machine was running; for others the machine had to be stopped. An important aspect of his job was to arrange the sequence of orders being run from the same width of paper so that these stoppages were made during a change of rolls at the front end of the machine. Finally, the two receivers operated the back, or side, knife, which cut across the sheet; they removed the cut sheets from the laminator and stacked them to be taken by a trucker to the printing section. The receivers also cleaned the cylinders at the glue station.

The nature of the work did not require the continuous activity of all members of the crew at all times. When the machine was operating smoothly on a long run, perhaps only the receivers would be busy. When roll changes were being made by the operator and helper, the others could relax. On a shutdown for knife change, the knife setter might be the only one whose attention was required. Although parts of the various jobs could be dovetailed to speed production, there were many intervals in which individual members of the crew had opportunity for purely social activity. Smoking, though not permitted on the job, was allowed in the smoking area. Neither the truckers nor the stock and glue men were thought of as members of the laminator crew. The truckers worked in all sections of the fiberboard department. They also removed waste paper which the crews had piled in hand trucks kept near the laminator.

Up to about six years prior to Mr. Roberts' study, a sixth man had worked on each crew. His task had been to assist the operator and helper, particularly in connection with preparing and shafting the heavy paper rolls and swinging them into place at the paper stands.

HOURS AND PAY

At the time of Mr. Roberts' study, the laminator was operated by two crews, known as the #1 and #2 crews. Though the supervisors and service men always worked the same hours, the two crews alternated day and night shifts each week. A laminator shift usually ran for eight hours, with the men eating informally on the job as the work allowed.

Under the union contract each job carried its own rate of pay, with a lower rate for a learning period. An individual's earnings, however, might be higher than the job rate for two reasons. The Briggs Company, like many others, granted some "red circle," or special, rates, whereby an individual who was transferred through no fault of his own to a lower-rated job continued to receive the rate for his old job. A second reason for earnings higher than the job rate was a man's share in the group bonus which the company had instituted for a crew's production in excess of a standard amount. The expected standard was adjusted for down time not due to faulty operation, and the measure of the amount produced was adjusted for the amount of waste. A man's share in the crew bonus was in proportion to his base rate. It was not uncommon for the bonus for a shift to be 20 to 25 per cent of take-home pay. Though the truckers received a small share in the bonus, the stock and glue men did not; neither did a trainee, until he had completed his training period.

THE CREWS

Although there were occasional shifts in personnel to replace those absent because of illness or vacations, each man was thought of as a member of the crew with which he normally worked. Some data on the normal personnel of the crews, including name, age, years with plant and on laminator, and wages are given in Exhibit 4. It also includes the names and positions of others closely associated with the crews.

An unusual number of crew changes was occasioned during Mr. Roberts' field work by the illness of George Hart, operator of the #1 crew. He developed a back condition which required him to undergo surgery. For several weeks before he was hospitalized, and also after his return, a series of assistants were assigned to Mr. Hart to perform his heavier duties. The major personnel shifts follow. During Mr. Hart's absence his helper, Leo LeBouef, acted as operator of the #1 crew, and Al Brogan, helper of the #2 crew, filled Mr. LeBouef's regular job. Mr. Brogan's regular position was filled by Billy Mellon, who became assistant to Mr. Hart on his return.

THE RESEARCH

Mr. Roberts' intense interest in small work groups led him to center his attention on the laminator crews themselves. He concerned him-

EXHIBIT 4

THE BRIGGS BOX COMPANY

Personnel—Laminating Section

Line and Staff Supervision	
Fred Dorn	Superintendent
Ed Dyer	Foreman (day shift)
Tom Lewis	Foreman (night shift)
Jack Zolbe	Quality and Waste Control (day shift)
Hal Anderson	Production Planning

#1 Crew

			Service in Years		
			With	On	
Name	Position	Age	Company	Laminator	Base Pay
George Hart	Operator	47	20	7	$1.45*
Leo LeBouef	Helper	53	34	10	1.32†
Joe Kern	Knife setter	36	7	7	1.39
Ralph Langley	Receiver	32	2	2	1.39‡
Don Halligan	Receiver	28	3	$1\frac{1}{2}$	1.24

#2 Crew

			Service in Years		
			With	On	
Name	Position	Age	Company	Laminator	Base Pay
Charlie Cappielo	Operator	33	5	$2\frac{1}{2}$	$1.32
Al Brogan	Helper	28	3	1 mo.	1.29
Nick Jones	Knife setter	44	8	8	1.39
Bill Evans	Receiver	38	6	6	1.39‡
Jim Carson	Receiver	28	$1\frac{1}{2}$	$1\frac{1}{2}$	1.24
Billy Mellon	Temporary helper; later asst. to operator on #1 crew	24	4	1 mo.	1.32‖

Service Men

Sam Lynch	Trucker (day shift)
Mel Freeman	Trucker (night shift)
Claude Schlick	Stock and glue man (day shift)
Frank Stephenson	Stock and glue man (night shift)

* Previously laminator foreman; after illness worked as operator.
† Was operator on third shift during World War II.
‡ Previously a knife setter.
‖ Had been assistant foreman in another department.

self with other persons in the Briggs Box Company only insofar as they were related to these men.

In his visits to the laminator, Mr. Roberts spent his time observing and talking with the members of the two crews. He stood by their sides and walked along with them as they went about their jobs. When he had the opportunity, he asked questions about what they were doing and about their reactions to their work and to one another. Sometimes he sat with the men in the smoking area and participated in their conversations. His observations of and interactions with them were thus closely connected with their job activities.

Over a period of time, Mr. Roberts came to feel that the men on both crews had confidence in him and would talk with him freely. His primary reason for this feeling was that most of the men had little or no hesitation in discussing with him their separate, and occasionally opposing, accounts of the same incidents. He knew that the men talked to him as an outsider, differently from the way they talked to their superiors or even to their companions. But this was not his primary concern, as long as he felt that what they were telling him was helping him to understand their point of view. He behaved, of course, in such a way as to maintain any personal confidences which he received. He tried to take the same attitude in his conversation with their supervisors.

PREVAILING CREW PATTERNS

The behaviors and attitudes of the two crews, within the context of identical job definitions and working environment, revealed strikingly different patterns when Mr. Roberts examined, for each crew, interaction involving workers at the front end, at the receiving end, and at both front and receiving ends.

The #1 Crew

THE FRONT END

One of George Hart's jobs as operator was to arrange the orders at the beginning of a shift so that paper widths and knife settings would have to be changed as few times as possible. A change had to be approved by the foreman at the beginning of each shift, but within limits Mr. Hart could make changes himself. Occasionally the sequence of orders had to be changed to meet unexpected customer demands; in this case, Hal Anderson, from the production department, contacted Mr. Hart directly.

Mr. Roberts was talking with Mr. Hart and Mr. LeBouef, the helper, one morning, when Mr. Anderson walked into the area. He glanced at the orders on Mr. Hart's clipboard, thumbed through the daily paper runs, and then turned to Mr. Hart.

MR. ANDERSON: Say, George, I'm going to put 16,000 feet of triplex laminating on here. The boss wants it out in the next few hours. They've got a special order to fill.

MR. HART: Sixteen thousand feet of triplex laminating? Well, now, I don't know about that.

MR. LEBOUEF: What did I tell you, George? Every time we get a good run this happens.

MR. HART: I know that's true. Sixteen thousand feet, O.K., O.K. (He made a characteristic "hands in the air" gesture and laughed.)

MR. ANDERSON: I see on the sheet here that you've got down below this 55,000 foot order another 19,000 feet of triplex laminating. You can run the two together.

MR. HART: I want to run the 55,000 after the 16,000, as I planned.

MR. ANDERSON: But, George, you'll have the machines all set up for triplex laminating when you do the 16,000; just run the 19,000 at the same time.

MR. HART: Now I don't want to do that. I want to do it the way I planned. I'll run your new 16,000 feet, but I'm going to run the 55,000 normal laminating after it. Then, if I get to it on this shift, I'll run the 19,000 as the order sequence shows.

MR. ANDERSON: Well, we'll see about that.

Mr. Anderson walked out of the area and toward Superintendent Dorn's office. Mr. Hart watched him go, and in a few minutes turned to Mr. Roberts.

MR. HART: Happens every time like this. Whenever they've got something hard to do they look up George and the #1 crew to do it. They're the ones who can get them out of trouble. It's the #1 crew and George Hart that are really important when it comes right down to the tough jobs. I've seen it happen time and time again.

MR. ROBERTS: You get the tough runs in here.

MR. HART: Yeah. I can't figure it out, but I'm telling you, every time there's triplex laminating or a tough job to do, they let George do it.

MR. ROBERTS: This isn't very fair.

MR. HART: It isn't fair at all. Say, what time is it?

MR. ROBERTS: About 10:30 A.M.

MR. HART: Well, I guess it doesn't matter a lot, if I run all this triplex laminating off at the same time. I'll have time to do the big order anyway. And I'll have to do both triplex laminating orders anyway, so I might as well do it all together.

Mr. Roberts believed that the following conversation with Mr. Hart expressed in more detail the attitude he had toward his job.

When the #2 crew came on duty one afternoon, Mr. Hart picked up his tools, tipped his cap to the operator and helper of the #2 crew, and started for the lockers behind the glue station. Mr. Roberts went with him.

MR. ROBERTS: Say, what are these here, George?

MR. HART: Oh, these are the lockers for the operators.

MR. ROBERTS: These are different from the lockers you have in the washrooms?

MR. HART: Yes. These lockers here are only for the laminator operators. You see, there are three of them, and this meant a locker for each operator on each of the three shifts. Of course, when the company did away with the third shift, that left a locker vacant. And then Charlie Cappielo, the new #2 crew operator, never uses the second locker here. He doesn't give a damn about his tools. He says he doesn't have to worry about them. For my part, I keep clean rags here, my scraping tools, light bulbs, a couple of wrenches, and an extension cord. You never know when something is going to happen on the laminator or glue station and you're going to need a spare wrench to straighten things out. Also, we have two or three drop cords around the laminator and glue station, and the bulbs are always burning out in those sockets. So when that happens I don't have to call a maintenance man; I just screw a bulb in and go right on. Same way, when something gets loose on the machines, I just take my wrenches and tighten things up.

MR. ROBERTS: What does Charlie on the #2 crew do about such problems?

MR. HART: Oh, I guess he doesn't worry about things like that. When he has troubles, I guess he calls up the maintenance boys and just sits tight until they come. But I don't. I can get around most of them.

MR. ROBERTS: So Charlie doesn't need a locker back here?

MR. HART: It's here if he wants it, but he doesn't bother. I keep mine locked. Every day I lock my tools up. I don't want them to get in the shape these other guys keep theirs.

MR. ROBERTS: They don't take care of their tools like you?

MR. HART: They don't take care of them at all. When they come to work they just throw their jackets over there in the smoking area. They leave their scrapers out, never put them away, as far as I know. They bring their paper knives and small wrenches with them to use on the cylinders. But I certainly wouldn't treat my tools the way they do theirs.

It's just like I said, we get all the rough work given to us. Like last Saturday I was home ill. I wasn't feeling so well, and I was vomiting a little. So the #2 crew came in and had to do the rough orders for a change. Well, they had a lot of trouble. I don't know, something was wrong with the brushes and the valves, they said, and they never got anywhere at all. That crew is always getting upset and excited, and can't work much at all. Every time a real rough order comes along, George Hart gets that one; the #2 crew just can't do it. Well, what happened? They didn't get the orders out last Saturday. So came Monday morning I had to do it for them. They had all sorts of excuses. They called in the planner, they called in the maintenance men, they called in the man who mixes the wax downstairs. They blamed the machinery.

When I got here Monday morning, I just looked things over. It was a simple problem. All I did was to go downstairs and turn a couple of valves here and there; just give them a slight twist with my hand. There wasn't any trouble with the cylinders; there wasn't any trouble with the wax; they just don't know how to run these machines in here.

But, of course, they won't listen to me; they don't want to learn anything. They're just not interested. They go blindly along, getting excited, running here and there. They never will learn anything, as far as I can tell.

MR. ROBERTS: They don't see all your experiences and training as important?

MR. HART: I guess that's it. I can't figure it out, but that whole #2 crew is one big problem.

Mr. LeBouef, the "helper" who ran the glue station, also had definite ideas about what was important in his job. On another occasion, Mr. Roberts talked with him about them.

MR. LEBOUEF: You've got to be careful on this job in here. The most important thing you've got to watch is not getting burned, not getting hurt. You know these cylinders, they're very, very hot.

MR. ROBERTS: The job's pretty hard here?

MR. LEBOUEF: No. No, it isn't that. You just got to know what you're doing, take your time, and be careful. You've got to take care of the machines down here. You gotta watch them very closely.

MR. ROBERTS: You mean you've got to keep them in good running condition?

MR. LEBOUEF: Yeah, that's right. You know, when it comes time to quit here, I'll hang on a while longer and oil all these machines up. You got to keep them going just right. Why, if you let any part go—bang! Out it goes, and before you know, you've got to replace the machine.

MR. ROBERTS: That takes a lot of know-how, a lot of knowledge to do that?

MR. LEBOUEF: You bet it does. It takes a lot of knowledge to know all these little parts that've got to be oiled. You know, some parts of these machines you only oil about once a month, and other parts you've got to oil every day or you'll burn something out. I've worked with them for years. I don't know how it got around that I knew about these things, but I guess my many years here count. It got around that I was the only one here who knew enough about them, so they let me oil the machines.

MR. ROBERTS: Well, I guess that's pretty important, right?

MR. LEBOUEF: Yeah, it's important all right. You know when George and I work together here we often come in on Saturdays and check over the equipment. The company wants us to. They pay us for the time we check the machines and report any worn parts so they can be replaced. When George and I work the night shift, we stay after quitting time for a couple of hours just cleaning up the machines and oiling them for the next day's run. Well, it's just about quitting time. I'm going to get my oil cans. See you later.

THE RECEIVING END

In time, Mr. Roberts became better acquainted with Ralph Langley and Don Halligan, the two receivers of the #1 crew. He learned that Mr. Halligan was 28 and had worked for Briggs for three years. He had known Mr. Langley since he started working at Briggs, and the two men were good friends.

One afternoon, Mr. Roberts joined Mr. Langley and Mr. Halligan for a smoke at a time when the machines were stopped for a paper change.

MR. HALLIGAN: We're just going to wait here until George blows his horn to call us, that is, if he ever pulls himself together up there.

Mr. Langley propped his right knee against the railing which encircled the rear smoking area. He stared at the ceiling.

MR. LANGLEY: If he'd only learn that you dont change rolls the way he insists on changing them. He knows how, but he always makes such a big mess of it. He won't let Leo help him so they can do it properly. I've talked to Leo about it and he says the same thing. Of course, he's always trying to cover up for George.

Mr. Halligan nodded agreement and changed the subject.

MR. HALLIGAN: Coming to the Christmas party next month, Ralph?
MR. LANGLEY: I guess so.
MR. HALLIGAN: That party should be something. I've spent enough time on the arrangements. (He got up and stretched.)

They continued talking about the coming party, occasionally including Mr. Roberts in their conversation. In the middle of their chat, the laminator horn sounded.

MR. LANGLEY: There goes that horn again. (He remained seated.) Let it blow.
MR. HALLIGAN: (Grinding his cigarette under his heal.) Blowing that horn is the one thing George does a good job of.
MR. LANGLEY: We'd better get back, Don, before George starts up the machines and spills sheet all over our work area. He'll do that if he sees we aren't there. You know George, he gets mad when he's ready to go and we aren't around.

Mr. Halligan nodded. Both men took a drink at the fountain and then moved briskly back to the receiving end, where Joe Kern, the knife setter, was waiting. Seeing them, he breathed deeply and began looking over the orders. Mr. Langley and Mr. Halligan took up their positions behind the receiving tables.

MR. KERN: Let's see. The next change will be to a 53-inch, then comes two nice long runs of 61 inches. (He looked up and grinned at Mr. Roberts, who was leaning on the high pedestal desk.) Those long runs won't be hard to take.

After the men had been working awhile, Mr. Langley yelled to Mr. Halligan from his position at the back knife.

MR. LANGLEY: Boy, am I glad it's your turn to work this torture rack tomorrow. Say, Don, can't you stir the boys upstairs into doing something about this knife?

MR. HALLIGAN (laughing): Sure, I'll see about it right away. Anything else I can do for you?

Mr. Roberts walked over to the back knife. While he worked, Mr. Langley spoke as follows:

MR. LANGLEY: We have to break our backs just because we can't get this back knife fixed the way it ought to be. And that isn't the half of it. You can't get the maintenance department to tighten the belts of the conveyor system for love or money. Then, too, most of the time the orders they send down from planning are all fouled up. If I were Joe, I wouldn't put up with the guff he takes. But Joe, he's just too much for the company. You know, I used to work the knife setter's job on the third shift. But for some time now, I've been working here as a receiver. But I still get knife setter's pay and take over that job whenever Joe isn't around. You've got to know what you're doing when you work that job. It's the best job at this end. You don't get anywhere being a receiver.

Later, Mr. Roberts asked Mr. Kern about the job on the back knife.

MR. KERN: It's the toughest job in the department. No one could work that knife everyday. I know. I worked it off and on for a couple of years before making knife setter. I still get a taste of it whenever I relieve Don and Ralph so they can have a smoke and rest their arms and backs. We have our difficulties with that job. Nobody wants to work it for long.

THE FRONT END AND THE RECEIVING END

One afternoon, while Mr. Roberts was in the take-off area, Mr. Le-Bouef motioned for the receivers to come to the glue station. Mr. Langley interpreted his gesture to Mr. Halligan who was some distance away.

MR. LANGLEY: George wants the glue rollers cleaned.

MR. HALLIGAN: Not again! We just cleaned those damn things, didn't we?

MR. KERN (interrupting): It was close to two hours ago. (He motioned to Mr. LeBouef that Mr. Halligan and Mr. Langley were coming.)

Mr. Hart was waiting when the two men arrived at the glue station.

MR. HART: You fellows know these rollers have to be cleaned every so often. The paper just won't stick properly otherwise.

Without a word, they picked up long, hoelike poles and started to scrape the rollers. Mr. Hart stood back and watched them.

MR. HART (pointing): Get those big chunks along the side there.

After the scraping was completed, Mr. Langley laid down his hoe and reached for an automatic air hose. Glue cinders and paper splinter filled the air. After the air cleared, the rollers appeared shiny.

MR. HART: That's more like it. The paper will stick properly now.

He spoke only to himself, for the receivers had already turned and started back to the take-off area.

MR. HALLIGAN: That damn paper sure bothers me a lot. (He mimicked Mr. Hart's voice and gestures.) "The paper isn't sticking properly."

They both broke into laughter.

MR. LANGLEY: Yeah, but who cares but old George?

The machines were going again, and the receivers started picking up the boards in unison. During the next few hours, the boards flopped off the knives rhythmically. The three men in the receiving area began joking back and forth. In particular, they kidded Sam Lynch, the serviceman, who frequently came into the work area to load the stacks of boards onto a little railway truck and take them to the printer. They usually played on Mr. Lynch's gullibility by telling him elaborate stories, and then they laughed about their joke after he left the area.

When the machines ran smoothly, the workers at the front end also moved around and talked more freely. Mr. Hart usually stood or sat next to the laminator when he wasn't working. Occasionally, however, he would get a drink of water at the fountain and then stand for some moments eyeing the bonus chart. He kept track of his daily bonuses by writing them down on a piece of paper. He and Mr. LeBouef frequently discussed their bonuses and the amount of footage they had completed in each shift. Mr. LeBouef also spent much of his free time keeping track of his bonus money.

Occasionally, Mr. Kern and the two receivers came up to the front end to watch a paper change. Mr. Kern often lent a hand, while the others observed from the smoking area and talked together.

MR. HALLIGAN: Say, Ralph, now that the machines are down, wouldn't it be a good time for George to clean the wax pan on the laminator?

MR. LANGLEY: Yeah, but try to get him to do it. He'll clean that wax pan when he feels like it and not a minute before. We'll be right in the middle of an order, and then he'll decide to clean that pan.

MR. HALLIGAN: Well, why doesn't he do it now while the laminator is stopped and Blackie (Mr. Hart's temporary assistant) and Leo are finishing the paper change?

MR. LANGLEY: Go over and ask him.

MR. HALLIGAN (shrugging his shoulders): Oh, that wouldn't get us anywhere, I guess.

MR. LANGLEY: Sometimes, I think you're afraid of George. (He laughed.)

MR. HALLIGAN: Oh, he runs his end. He's an old woman, all right, but he's smart all the same. (He tapped his forehead with his index finger.) He knows his stuff.

Some months later Mr. Hart's doctor gave him medical clearance to perform all the jobs he had before his operation. He took his release up to Mr. Dyer's and Mr. Dorn's offices and told them that even though he was completely fit, the job required a permanent assistant to the operator on both crews. As he told it to Mr. Roberts some days later, they refused his request.

MR. HART: I went up there and told them we needed another man down here on the crews, because the operator was just too busy. You need someone down here to shaft the paper rolls and look after the waste scraps of paper. The operator has his own job to do.

As it is now, Leo has to come over here sometimes and help me on the laminator. Well, that's not right. The helper's job is over there on the glue station, not here on the laminator. That's my job, and I've got to look after that. So I try to tell them what the operator's job is and that he really needs an assistant all the time.

But the guys down here wouldn't stand behind me. It used to be that we stood together, but not any more. Joe and Leo are fine fellows and all of that, but when they get up to Dorn's office, they just shut up. They won't say anything. If I ever had to leave this company, I could go somewhere else to work. I try to do my work down here and try to do my job, and I don't think they appreciate it very much. Well, they said that they couldn't afford to put another man on the crews because cost is too high already, waste is high, and paper quality is pretty low. I asked them if I was responsible for that. I asked them how is the waste figure on my crew. Oh, they tell me, of course, the waste on my laminator is low, which it is. You know, I can't be responsible for waste figures in the whole department. I can only do what I can. I want to get the fellows on the #2 crew an assistant as well. But like I said, none of the guys here would stand up for me. They won't say a word while they are in the office. They just stand there with their hats in their hands while I tell them. (Mr. Hart laughed at this point and shrugged his shoulders characteristically.)

You can't buck city hall! You can try, but it doesn't get you too far. I knew I was licked before I started, but anyway I told them. So when I took the doctor's certificate up to them I said, "Well, I'm as good as new. I can go back to work and won't need the assistant any more." They told me, "We will leave the assistant down there for a while, George. You may need him for a time yet." I said to them, "If you do that, you do it on your own because I'm ready to go back to work just as I was before the back injury. If you want to leave that assistant down there, you take responsibility for doing it." They smiled and said, "O.K."

So I don't know what they'll do now. The guy is still working here, but any day they might need him someplace else. They will take him away one of these days, and that will be the end of that. The two of us, Leo and myself, will have to do the work. But, you understand, this is a three-man job here. It's true that the third man when he isn't busy sometimes goes over and sits in the smoking area. Then Ed or Fred come by and see that, and, well, they don't like it. But you can't do all the work yourself.

MR. ROBERTS: You'd still like a third man even though he isn't always busy.

MR HART: Sure, I would. But they come back with the same old story. They say there's not another laminator the size of ours on the East Coast that has three men on the job. But they forget one thing, Dave, there's no other company that does the type of work we do here with the type of paper and orders we get. It may be a two-man job in other companies, but this is a three-man job here.

One evening soon after this conversation with Mr. Hart, Mr. Roberts asked Mr. Kern about the assistant problem.

MR. KERN: I suppose George told you he was trying to get another permanent worker on this operation. He's been talking to Leo and me about that for quite a while. I don't know exactly how Leo feels about it, but at first, I thought it was a pretty good idea. A permanent helper might take some of the pressure off of George. But I asked Don and Ralph how they felt, and they turned thumbs down. You see, if we got another worker in here on a permanent basis, the bonus would have to be split six ways instead of five. They didn't want that, and I can see why. And, after all, the #2 crew manages with five guys.

So, I told George he'd have to talk to Dyer and Dorn by himself about this one. You know, a few months back, when George talked to me about splitting his bonus with the assistant, I went up to Dyer's office for him. George wanted the bonus split six ways, but Ralph and Don wouldn't hear of it. Well, Dyer asked George and Don to come to his office to talk it all over, and George wanted me to go in his place. I think he didn't want to get involved with Don or Ralph. At any rate, Don was really mad about this bonus thing; he and George weren't even on speaking terms. I went up to the office with Don and Ralph, but we couldn't work it out. Later, Ed spoke to George and George said that he didn't want a big fuss, that he would be willing to split his bonus with the helper. The issue had no sooner been settled when George cornered me at the laminator and told me how unfair he thought the whole thing was. He said he got this back condition working with these fellows, and they ought to stand behind him. I could understand how he felt, but when he suggested that I was siding with Don and Ralph, I just walked away.

Personally, I thought the fair thing would be to split the bonus six ways. But Don and Ralph—and I guess Leo, too—were against the idea. So what could I do? I tried, but when George wouldn't even come to the meeting himself, how could anyone think he was seriously interested in the matter? So it was dropped. Anyway, George didn't have to share his bonus with his last assistants. But, now with his request for a permanent helper, the bonus would have to be shared to get any decent worker interested in the job. George asked me to stand up for him with Ed and Fred about a permanent helper, and frankly, I told him no. I can understand how he feels, but he's got to speak up for himself about these things. Besides, Don and Ralph are so strong against the idea that I thought it would stir up more trouble on the crew. We don't want any more trouble on this crew than we have now. The best thing for George to do is drop the whole idea and get back to work. Maybe Don and Ralph are right—he's been on the gravy train too long. (Pause.) I don't know.

One evening shortly afterward a long triplex job was scheduled for the #1 crew after completion of a run which was on the machine when they reported for duty. For the first 15 or 20 minutes, Mr. Roberts noticed that Mr. Hart and Mr. LeBouef said little to each other. They went about their work quietly. After a while Mr. Roberts got up from his seat on the bench and went over to the laminator where Mr. Hart was working.

MR. ROBERTS: How are you doing, George?

MR. HART: Oh, not so good. It's going to be a rough one tonight.

MR. ROBERTS: You got a lot of hard runs?

MR. HART: Well, we got 60,000 feet of triplex laminating, and that's not good. (He laughed, raised his hands in his characteristic gesture of resignation, and shook his head.)

MR. ROBERTS: What does that mean?

MR. HART: It means that there's a lot of work down here tonight. But I'm not going to be in any hurry shafting the rolls and getting the sheet out. I'm going to run the machines slowly and take it easy.

MR. ROBERTS: Where's your assistant?

MR. HART: I don't know quite what that story is. He's got to go to some sort of Navy meeting on Monday nights. He's working with the #2 on that day, so he won't be around tonight. I sure need him, too, but my assistant days are about over. He's going to work over on the printers starting next Monday, so that's the end of that.

MR. ROBERTS: You'll miss him?

MR. HART: Oh, I suppose so. Sometimes he gets in the way, of course. But lifting these shafts is pretty heavy work. You take that one on the far end. That one weighs about 160 pounds.

MR. ROBERTS: You lift that?

MR. HART: I used to, but I'm not going to any more. I'm going to take my time down here; and if we get behind, well, we just get behind.

Just then Frank Stephenson, the night shift stock and glue man, came up from the basement and walked over and sat down in the smoking area. He lit a cigarette, while Mr. LeBouef talked with him.

MR. LEBOUEF: We've got no assistant tonight. That means George is going to have to go to work for a change.

MR. STEPHENSON: It's about time.

MR. LEBOUEF: You know George; he's not too easy to get along with when he hasn't got an assistant, particularly when we have a lot of triplex laminating; and we've got 60,000 feet this evening.

MR. HART: (Calling to Frank Stephenson.) Frank, I want you

to get some more Grade *B* wax mixed. We're going to use about twice the normal amount tonight doing this triplex laminating.

MR. STEPHENSON: Why don't you use the Grade *A* wax? It's all mixed and ready to go.

MR. HART: Because I said we're using Grade *B* wax. I'll need about 200 more gallons than usual.

He turned back to the laminator. Mr. Stephenson spoke to Mr. LeBouef.

MR. STEPHENSON: I don't see why he doesn't use Grade *A* instead of Grade *B* wax. Always making more work for me, that's what he's doing.

A yell from Mr. Hart interrupted him.

MR. HART: And, Frank, tell Tom Lewis (the night shift foreman) to come over here. We need a new battery in the lift truck. This one just gave out.

Tom Lewis arrived shortly and took the lift truck to the maintenance department for the new battery. About 20 minutes later, Mr. Hart shut down the laminator and signaled to Joe Kern to hold things up. Mr. LeBouef took this opportunity to walk down to see Mr. Kern and the other workers on the receiving end. Mr. Kern walked up to the front end with Mr. LeBouef, went over to the smoking area, lit a cigarette, and watched Mr. Hart and Mr. LeBouef prepare the machines for triplex laminating. Then Don Halligan and Ralph Langley walked up and joined him in the smoking area. Mr. LeBouef walked over, and the four men stood in the area smoking cigarettes and talking to each other.

MR. LANGLEY: What in the hell is he doing down there? What's the holdup anyway?

MR. LEBOUEF: We're ready for the triplex laminating; but the battery on the automatic lift truck is out, and Tom Lewis took it downstairs to get a new one.

MR. LANGLEY: Leo, you are to do only your work down here tonight. Meathead is going to hold his end of the load up for a change.

MR. HALLIGAN: That's right, Leo. You're to work on the glue station and shaft only the paper rolls that you are supposed to. George's going to work tonight. He's going to have to get used to it sooner or later. This assistant thing is all over.

MR. KERN: I can see it all now. I know exactly what I'll be doing the rest of the night. I'm going to sit right here on this bench and see to it that George shafts his own paper rolls. Also—well—I can see that I'm going to have to help shaft rolls, too. If that paper breaks while we've got that triplex laminating on, we'll have paper all over the floor. What a mess that will be, besides all the work involved in rethreading it! We'll never get that run out, if we have many breaks. (To Mr. Halligan) What are you and Ralph going to do if we have a break?

MR. LANGLEY: Do our own work.

MR. KERN: That's what I thought.

During this conversation between the four workers, Mr. Hart did not look in their direction. He stood next to the laminator, tinkering with the steam valves and looking at the paper. He finally sat down next to the laminator with his back to the four men.

MR. HALLIGAN: Now why in the hell doesn't he clean out his wax pan, now that he's shut down?

MR. LANGLEY: Why don't you ask him?

MR. HALLIGAN: By God, I think I will. Say, Leo, why don't you stand up to George anyway? Are you afraid of him or something? Boy, I'd stand up to him. Why do you let him push you around the way he does? I don't want to see you do any more work tonight than you're supposed to do on the glue station. He's going to buckle down for a change.

Mr. Hart got up and started to shaft a paper roll. Mr. LeBouef went over to help him. They did the job together; while one worked the automatic hoist controls, the other guided the paper roll into place and tightened the paper brakes. Mr. LeBouef then returned to the smoking area.

MR. LEBOUEF: You see, I can shaft a roll faster than he can anyway. It doesn't hurt me like it does him. He's the boss. I might as well do them tonight.

MR. HALLIGAN: Aw, now listen, Leo. You're going to do your own work up here and that's all. It's about time he realized he's no privileged character like he assumes half the time.

MR. LANGLEY: Hell, yes. I don't know who in the devil he thinks he is. Meathead, meathead, that's what he is, and he's going to work tonight or I'm going to know the reason why.

MR. HALLIGAN: Why don't you stand up to him, Leo? If you let him push you around that way, sure he'll take advantage of you.

But I'm not that way and I want to know why he hasn't cleaned out that wax pan. We'll just have to stop later on for him to do it, if he doesn't do it now.

MR. KERN (interrupting): Leave Leo alone, Don. He didn't make George. If you don't like the way George does his job, why don't you tell him so? He's right over there.

MR. HALLIGAN: Aw, it wouldn't do a bit of good, except get him madder than hell. That's his machine and it's his headache.

MR. LANGLEY: Yeah, but when he doesn't clean it, that means we all have to wait. (He started for the receiving end.) Come on, Don, I want to look at the side knife. It isn't working right.

MR. KERN (rising and stepping on his cigarette): Let me know when I can do something, Leo.

MR. LEBOUEF: Okay.

A short time later, Tom Lewis returned the lift truck with a new battery. Mr. Roberts watched Mr. LeBouef and Mr. Hart prepare the paper stands and machines for the triplex laminating. After they had loaded all the stands, Mr. Hart operated the machines while Mr. LeBouef climbed the ladder and pulled the paper down the overhead racks to the laminator. When the paper had been threaded through the laminators and glue station, Mr. LeBouef signaled, and Mr. Kern and Mr. Hart started the machines. Mr. Roberts stood next to George Hart, and both watched the paper go through the machines.

MR. ROBERTS: A little trouble, George?

MR. HART: Aw, not much. The battery on the automatic truck here went out and Tom Lewis took it down in the basement to get a new one.

He picked up a metal shaft and carried it over to a new paper roll. He inserted the shaft in the roll and looked at his hands.

MR. HART: Look, grease.

He took a rag out of his pocket and wiped his hands clean; then he carefully wrapped two rags around the shaft where he had to touch it when lowering it on the paper stand. He looked at Mr. Roberts.

MR. HART: Grease and dirt. That's not right for an operator to have grease and dirt on his hands.

Mr. Roberts nodded, then returned to the bench and watched the crew work through the triplex laminating. Mr. Hart and Mr. LeBouef said very little during the operation. On several occasions, Mr. Kern came to the front end to help with a paper change. At these times, he joked briefly with Mr. LeBouef and Mr. Hart, and the three men worked together on the operation while the receivers waited at the receiving end. The triplex laminating was completed in time for the #1 crew to make a bonus; however, the crew members seemed very tired at the end of the run. When the shift ended, Mr. Kern and the two receivers left almost immediately. Mr. Hart and Leo LeBouef remained to clean and oil the machines. Later, Mr. Hart and Mr. Roberts walked to the locker room together.

MR. HART: I guess I'm getting old. That laminator is getting harder to manage. It's not as easy as it once was. Sometimes I'm so tired at night that I just sit in front of the TV and never move. There was a time when I could put in a full day's work, go home and help the wife with the housework, and then spend half the night square dancing. But not anymore. Also, I can't seem to sing like I use to, either. Just can't seem to hit those high notes. I've been thinking about dropping out of the church choir.

The #2 Crew

THE FRONT END

When Mr. Roberts reviewed his field notes about the #2 crew, he found that frequent interactions between the men were characteristic. More than once, for example, he saw Al Brogan, the helper, operate the controls of the laminator and Charlie Cappielo adjust the controls of the glue station with apparent spontaneity. Their conversations were filled with talk about home, children, after-hours activities, betting, sports, and so forth. Often when they were together they laughed and joked and slapped each other on the back. Now and then Mr. Brogan rode up and down the aisle between the machinery and the smoking area on a dollie as if it were a scooter.

Most of the time Mr. Roberts found it difficult to overhear the men's conversations because of the noise of the machines. When the machines stopped, though, he could hear them clearly. This happened one day when Mr. Cappielo spoke to Mr. Brogan.

MR. CAPPIELO: Say, Al, we've got to make a full paper change. That's the end of that order. Signal Nick down there we are going to stop the machines.

Mr. Brogan nodded and blew the horn. Nick Jones, the knife setter, and Jim Carson and Bill Evans, the two receivers, all came up to the front end. Mr. Evans told Mr. Roberts that they were going to change all the paper rolls because a different width was coming next.

MR. ROBERTS: Do you fellows usually come up for the change, Bill?
MR. EVANS: Whenever we aren't too busy down at the other end. The company allows us about 10 minutes for the paper change, and so we all want to pitch in and get the job done. By doing that, we save time, make it easier for everyone and make a bonus. You see, when Charlie and Al see us pitch in and work, then they really get in and pitch, too. In that way we keep things coming all the time. Well, here's where I go aloft. See you in a few minutes.

He climbed up on the storage bin between the laminator and glue station, grasped the paper coming out of the laminator, pulled it along the storage bin, and handed it down to where Mr. Brogan was waiting to thread it through the glue station. While this was being done, Mr. Cappielo found a long scraping hoe and leaned it against the glue station. Jim Carson was already at work with a similar tool, cleaning the cylinders where the wax had stuck and made it difficult for the paper to pass over them. When Mr. Evans got through on the storage bin, he came down and picked up a hoe and joined Mr. Carson at the scraping job. Nick Jones assisted Mr. Cappielo and Mr. Brogan in shafting the new paper rolls and preparing them for the paper stands. Mr. Carson finished his scraping and then assisted with the paper brake adjustments. Mr. Brogan grabbed the air hose and blew the loose wax out from under the hot cylinders. In a few minutes the paper was threaded and the machines were running.

As Mr. Jones, Mr. Evans, and Mr. Carson returned to their positions on the receiving end, something went wrong with the paper from one of the rolls as it went through the glue station.

MR. CAPPIELO: Did you readjust the paper after we put it through, Al?
MR. BROGAN: Oh, God. I forgot. (Laughter.)
MR. CAPPIELO: Let's get with it. (He shook his fist at Mr. Brogan.)

They both ran down to the glue station. Mr. Cappielo went around to the far side of the stand, while Mr. Brogan got on the other side to adjust the paper brakes and straighten the paper. He twisted hard on the paper brakes with a small tool.

MR. CAPPIELO: What you need is a pipe wrench, and you wouldn't strain so damn' much.

MR. BROGAN: O.K., I know I'm out of shape; but who cares? (They both laughed and finished the work.)

A short time later Mr. Cappielo speeded up the machines; Mr. Brogan smiled, turned back to his work, and started whistling.

Occasionally, Mr. Cappielo and Mr. Brogan came over and sat on the bench in the smoking area next to Mr. Roberts. Once, when they were near the bench:

MR. BROGAN: Say, Charlie, do you hear what I hear? I think the paper is tugging on the laminator.

MR. CAPPIELO: Yeah, I'll catch it in a minute.

MR. BROGAN: Never mind, I'll get it.

He walked over to the laminator and made some changes in the speed of the machine. As he finished, Mr. Cappielo called to him, "Say, Al, let's eat." Mr. Brogan nodded. They both got their lunches out.

The laminator crews ate right on the job; they never shut down the machines during lunch or supper periods. The other sections of the department shut down for 30 minutes for each of these periods, but the workers were not paid for the time. The members of the laminator crews usually worked it out among themselves so that each individual could rest for a few minutes during the eight-hour shift.

MR. BROGAN: I'm going to the cafeteria. Want some coffee and pie, Charlie?

MR. CAPPIELO: Sure.

MR. BROGAN: O.K., be back in a few minutes.

He returned shortly, carrying two paper containers of coffee and two pieces of pie. He put them down on the desk in the smoking area and started to eat a sandwich. Looking up, he saw something on the machines, called to Mr. Cappielo and pointed to the paper stand on the far side of the laminator. Mr. Cappielo laughed and walked over to it. The brakes that held the shafts securely in place were smoking. He stood looking at them for a few moments and then made an adjustment. The smoke died away; but as it did, he cupped his hands over one of the smoking brakes and rubbed them vigorously several times as if to warm them. Both he and Mr. Brogan broke out laughing. Mr. Brogan turned to Mr. Roberts.

MR. BROGAN: You see, I heard that noise on the laminator—that uh, uh sound—and I knew the paper was tugging. It was pulling a little too tightly. Then I looked down there and I saw that smoking set of brakes. That's when I knew something needed adjusting. Of course, we are supposed to make the brake adjustments before they start smoking; but when they do, we know we have to make it or no more bearings.

MR. CAPPIELO (to Mr. Brogan): Say, what do I do with this wax bucket of yours?   I don't want it around here.

MR. BROGAN: Put it over by the sink where it belongs.

As he said this, he laughed again, slapped Mr. Cappielo on the shoulder, and ran down to the glue station.

MR. CAPPIELO: Oh, yeah, the sink.

He picked up the bucket used for excess wax and tossed it several feet in the general vicinity of the sink, where it landed with a clatter. The two men laughed at this and returned to work.

Another time, Mr. Roberts was standing near Mr. Cappielo when the machines were running along smoothly and Mr. Cappielo had little to do.   Mr. Brogan was about to be transferred temporarily to the #1 crew as helper, and Mr. Roberts and Mr. Cappielo were talk-ing about the general subject of breaking in on jobs around the laminator.

MR. CAPPIELO: You see, I used to work on the third shift with Gus. You never knew Gus, did you?   He's not here anymore.   Well, I first started to work on this machine with Gus on the third shift. You know what he told me the first night I came to work here?

MR. ROBERTS: No.

MR. CAPPIELO: He said, "You shaft the rolls and I push the buttons and that's the way we work on this shift."   Well, I hadn't done that, but a couple days when I began to catch on that that wasn't right—me doing the shafting of the rolls and he doing the pushing of buttons.   So I backed him into a corner about the third day and really laid into him.   I told him this is no way to treat me and I wasn't going to stand for any more of it.   He got real smart and said, "Oh, yeah, well, we'll see about that."   I let him have it. I hauled off and hit him right in the face.   After that, things got better on that crew.   No more pushing buttons and shafting rolls. He started to shaft some rolls and I did too, and we both pushed a few buttons, too.   He turned out to be a pretty good guy after that.

MR. ROBERTS: What happened after that?

MR. CAPPIELO: Oh, I came to work on the #2 crew with Sam Barnett. You remember Sam, the fellow they transferred?

MR. ROBERTS: Yes.

MR. CAPPIELO: Well, Sam was operator and I was the helper and we got along O.K.

MR. ROBERTS: You liked him a lot.

MR. CAPPIELO: I sure did. He used to come over and say, "O.K., Charlie, you're the operator for the night. I'll be the helper." That's the way I learned to be an operator. I don't guess I'd have learned otherwise. Gus wouldn't let me touch a button on his laminator. But when I got into trouble on the #2 crew, Sam would give me a hand. That's how I learned the laminator racket. When Sam went to the hospital with that bad burn, I came over to the operator's job and Al became the helper.

THE RECEIVING END

Once when Mr. Roberts and Jim Carson were talking together at the receiving end, Mr. Carson called over to Bill Evans:

MR. CARSON: Say, Bill, tell Nick this sheet isn't cutting properly. It's all wiggly on the edges here.

MR. EVANS: O.K., Jim. (Calling over the noise of the machines.) Say, Nick, Jim says the sheet isn't cutting properly.

NICK JONES: I'll look at it.

He went down to check the cutting blades, and Mr. Carson explained the trouble to Mr. Roberts.

MR. CARSON: You see here, Dave. See that edge there? It's all wiggly, though the sheet is all right otherwise.

MR. ROBERTS: What does this mean, Jim?

MR. CARSON: Oh, it doesn't mean an awful lot. Fact is, it's quite passable sheet. It'll go through the printers without any trouble. (He took one of the sheets and folded it.) See, it folds all right. But I just don't like it that way. It just doesn't look very good.

MR. ROBERTS: What do you think Nick will do about it?

MR. CARSON: Oh, I don't know. He's coming back now and it's still going bad. I guess he didn't do anything about it.

MR. ROBERTS: Maybe Nick doesn't know what the trouble is.

MR. CARSON: Well, he's the knife setter. He ought to know. All he has to do is ask me. (In a few moments, he called to Mr. Jones again.) Say, Nick, this sheet still isn't cutting right.

Mr. Jones came over to where Mr. Carson was working and looked at the sheet.

MR. JONES: Yeah. Looks like it's got arthritis, doesn't it? (All three laughed.)
MR. CARSON: It sure does, Nick.
MR. JONES: Well, I guess there's something wrong with that one cutting blade. Just a minute, Jim, I'll check it again.
MR. CARSON: O.K.

Mr. Jones checked the cutting knife again. He signalled to Mr. Cappielo at the front end that he wanted the machines stopped for a few moments. He spent about four minutes removing the old blade and putting on a new one and signalled that things were ready to roll again. The machines started. As the sheet came off, Mr. Carson smiled.

MR. CARSON: That's more like it. You see—that's cut straight now.

Another time when sheet had stopped coming through the back and side knives, Mr. Carson called to Bill Evans.

MR. CARSON: Say, Bill, I'm going down to the sandwich counter for some coffee. You want anything? (To Mr. Roberts.) That Bill eats all the time. I've never seen anyone eat so much, but I guess he's a good worker, though. (Winks.)
MR. EVANS: Aw, I don't think I do, Jim. Wait a minute. I guess— I guess I'll have a coke. Get me a coke, but get me a glass with some ice in it, too. The cokes are never cold enough without ice.
MR. CARSON: O.K. We'll see what can be done to fix you up.
MR. EVANS: Here's the money for it.
MR. CARSON: Fine; get someone to wait on my position while I'm gone. (He left the area and Mr. Jones took over.)
MR. EVANS (turning to Mr. Roberts): You know I do kinda like to eat. You don't have too many pleasures in life and one of mine is eating. I guess I do make a pig of myself now and then. I eat a little too much.
MR. ROBERTS: You don't look overweight, Bill.
MR. EVANS: No, I work most of it off here. Most of the guys working on this job lose weight, but I can hold my own or even gain a little now and then. My kids, they sure take after their pop when it comes to eating. Nick over there has got a couple of kids, too. You know, Nick's a very active member of his community. He helped establish a boys' and girls' club and works with a couple

of boys' basketball teams when he has a chance. In a way, it's too bad he has to work so much and he can't spend more time in the community. You ought to see him play basketball!

MR. ROBERTS: Pretty good?

MR. EVANS: The best in the plant. He's one of the best players we've got on our team.

MR. ROBERTS: He looks easy to work with.

MR. EVANS: Yeah, you tell it. We all pull together down here. We pulled together that time we broke the record.

MR. ROBERTS: I heard about the record.

MR. EVANS: We work just as hard on any other day, you understand. But things just got clicking that record night. Machines ran well, signals back and forth between the two ends went swell. We started out with a lot of short runs and that's always slow, but we just went on.

Once Mr. Jones talked to Mr. Roberts about his job and the #2 crew.

MR. JONES: You see, when I took over this job a couple of years ago, I was pretty green about the work. I was pretty nervous.

MR. ROBERTS: You were afraid you couldn't do the job?

MR. JONES: No, it wasn't that exactly. I knew I could catch on to making these knife changes. I had watched the other setter well enough for that. I also knew that we could get out production O.K. But that wasn't quite it.

MR. ROBERTS: Something bothered you?

MR. JONES: You know, that first week that I worked as the knife setter, I didn't hardly sleep at all. My wife would say to me, "What's the matter Nick; why don't you go to sleep?" I used to lie awake worried if I could make the knife changes fast enough for the rest of the fellows on the crew. I was afraid if I lagged behind too much, the other fellows would suffer. They would lose bonuses because I wasn't holding up my end of the load. This job here isn't one where everyone goes his own way. This job demands that fellows all work together. If one guy lays down on the job, doesn't hold his end up, then the rest of the fellows suffer.

MR. ROBERTS: That doesn't happen here?

MR. JONES: We all get along on this crew without any trouble.

MR. ROBERTS: How do you mean?

MR. JONES: Well, everyone kinda pulls together here. That makes the load easier. For instance, this morning I've been up at the front end helping shaft paper rolls. We're short a couple of shafts, so we have to jump to keep ahead of the orders. Besides, Charlie needs a little help since he's breaking in Billy Mellon. Al's over on the #1 crew for a while.

This job is a five-man crew and every one of them have got to work together or it just throws extra work on someone else. This isn't the type of job where if one man lays down the other four go on doing their own work, and only that one man suffers as a consequence. That's just not true on this job. When one man lays down, then one of the other four has to do his work for him or all the rest don't make a bonus. We are paid on how much sheet we turn out, so if we want a bonus, we have to pull together. And like I said, it's easier that way, too.

Another time Jim Carson, one of the receivers, spoke about Mr. Jones.

MR. CARSON: It used to be before he came on this job you couldn't keep anyone working here. It was terrible. Just ask anyone on the floor here. Ask anyone who's worked with Nick Jones. They'll tell you what a swell guy he is.

MR. ROBERTS: He makes the job pretty easy for you?

MR. CARSON: Yeah. You see all this waste paper coming off the machine here? (Mr. Roberts nodded.) Well, he'll come around and help you carry it over to the carts when he gets a free moment. He does things for me all the time. Like take these breaks, for instance. He comes over here and relieves me quite often. I can go over and take a rest. I really appreciate that.

MR. RORERTS: It's not always been that way, Jim?

MR. CARSON: Good God, no. Used to be when the last setter on this job was here, before Nick, you had a hell of a time working. He'd never do anything for you. Take, for instance, split rolls, when we have two sheets coming off the machine at the same time. That's really rough. The knife setter doesn't have to help you. That last one never did. Just do it yourself. Break your own back at it. Why, he would go over in the smoking area and prop his feet up and just enjoy his sweet time about things. And here I would be breaking my back, catching both sheets as they came off the machine and stacking them up. He'd never do a thing for you.

MR. ROBERTS: You never brought this up with him?

MR. CARSON: What was the use? He'd always say that's your job. That's what they're paying you for. I guess he was right about the pay stuff; it wasn't his job. But it doesn't make it any easier.

You take Nick, here though, when we have two sheets coming off, he always comes back here and takes part of the load. He'll stack up one side and I'll stack up the other one. But that other guy, when I worked for him, he didn't do a damned thing that he didn't have to. But things have changed since then.

THE FRONT END AND THE RECEIVING END

At the beginning of their shift one day, Mr. Brogan and Mr. Jones came into the receiving area together. The two men went over to the desk to look at the order sheet for the day's run. After studying the sheet, Mr. Brogan spoke.

MR. BROGAN: Say, Nick, I've been figuring up these order sheets here. Look on the clipboard—we've got about 18,000 feet of sheet to run for the next two orders. That's not bad, is it?

MR. JONES: No, that's O.K. You say about 18,000?

MR. BROGAN: I guess so. I added them up. You look at it here— what do you think?

MR. JONES: Yeah—that's about 17,000 or 18,000. A thousand feet one way or the other. Say, you wanta buy a thousand feet of sheet? I'll sell it to you, Al.

MR. BROGAN (laughing): No, thanks. Don't want any. Say, Nick, with the orders lined up this way, I can bring up some wide paper for the last part of that run, can't I?

MR. JONES: Sure, go ahead. That's the way we'll run them, if it's O.K. with you and Charlie at the front end?

MR. BROGAN: Oh, sure, that makes it easy for us, too. I wanted to make sure so we could get our paper rolls set up. I'll see you later.

As he started to leave the area, he stopped by and talked a few moments with Jim Carson and Bill Evans. The three of them joked about the work. Mr. Roberts watched Mr. Jones arrange the orders for the runs.

MR. JONES: Oh, I'm setting up these orders for the knife changes. I do this before we run the orders. I always like to stay ahead. I try to keep the setups at least one or two ahead. This makes the work here for the crew much easier all the way around. When I do that they don't have to wait at the front end of the laminator for me to set up the orders. All I have to do is push the button here and the rotary blades turn around and bingo, the next order is ready to go. That way, Charlie and Al don't have to stop the laminator or glue station but for a second or so. They like that, because when they stop the machines, it can be a lot of work getting them going again, particularly since the paper sticks to the cylinders when the machines are stopped. The paper can break when that happens, and that means more work for all of us.

MR. ROBERTS: You do that yourself, Nick? You figure out the way the orders are to go?

MR. JONES: Well, the planners upstairs send down the approximate ways the orders are to go when it comes to changing the paper size. But within each paper size, I can make changes so that I can give myself enough time to get ahead on knife setups. You see here on the order sheet: the first order calls for 250 boxes and the order following that one calls for 300 boxes. Well, the way these machines run, it would only take a matter of a couple of minutes to run off 250 boxes and then if I ran the 300 box order in another couple of minutes, I wouldn't have the knives set up for the next order. That would mean that Charlie and Al would have to shut down the machines and we'd lose time and bonus pay. So what I do when something like that comes along is to put a longer order, but with the same paper size, between the 250 and 300 orders. That way I have plenty of time, and the crew doesn't have to stop for me.

One evening, while Billy Mellon was working as helper, Mr. Cappielo held his hand up with his five fingers extended for Mr. Mellon to see. He shook his fist and blew the horn and Mr. Jones looked up. He extended his five fingers again. Mr. Jones nodded, and he sped up the machines. Mr. Roberts then spoke to Mr. Mellon.

MR. ROBERTS: What does that mean?

MR. MELLON: Oh, that means we're five minutes behind on this order. That doesn't mean this five minutes has anything to do with the order sheets. We are way ahead on that. But, you see, Charlie told me about a half hour ago that at a quarter of four we'd be through with this order that's on the machines. Now he tells me we're not quite through with it; we're five minutes behind, so he's going to make up the five minutes. Look, he's speeding up the machine right now, and I bet we make it, too.

MR. ROBERTS: Doesn't this complicate things for the other end?

MR. MELLON: Oh, a little bit. They have to work a little faster when he speeds the machines up, but they know what Charlie is doing. They know he wants to get to the next order before 4 o'clock, and it's O.K. with them.

MR. ROBERTS: Doesn't this make the work harder?

MR. MELLON: Naw. We have all sorts of games like this. Now and then Charlie leaves the machines and he lets me play operator. He goes down and kids with the guys at the other end and helps them. You know, Nick Jones is always coming up here and helping Charlie and me out. This makes the day go much faster. You know, things aren't so dull that way.

MR. ROBERTS: You like working here?

MR. MELLON: Well, I didn't much at first. But now I do. You see these guys all pitch in and show you what to do. Gee, I got to go help Charlie. See you later.

He ran across the floor to where Mr. Cappielo was working. The two made a paper change. Mr. Cappielo pointed to the paper in the storage bin overhead and as he left the work area, spoke to Mr. Mellon.

MR. CAPPIELO: Watch the paper, Billy.

MR. ROBERTS: What'd he say?

MR. MELLON: Oh, he is going down to see Nick and the others and he wants me to keep an eye on the paper up there in the storage bin between the laminator and glue station. If an excess of paper isn't kept in that storage bin at all times, the glue station might make a big pull and snap the paper. If that happens, then we have to rethread the whole machine. That's a big headache. So I'm watching it. (He smiled and looked at Mr. Roberts.) I don't have to stand here like this, but I like to; beside there's nothing else much to do right now.

MR. ROBERTS: You like to do these things.

MR. MELLON: Sure, sure. I like to watch. (He pushed the button on the laminator and the machine ran a little faster.) Charlie thinks it's important, so I like to help.

MR. ROBERTS: You like Charlie a lot?

MR. MELLON: I sure do. He's swell. This whole bunch is swell. You see, these two machines aren't synchronized. They don't run at the same speed, so you've got to slow down or speed up the laminator a little bit now and then to keep enough paper in the storage bin. The fellows at the other end can speed up or slow down the glue station, but not the laminator.

Mr. Cappielo came back into the area. He picked up one of the small wooden blocks that came stuffed in the paper roll and tossed it at Mr. Mellon, who caught it and tossed it back at him. They both picked up a few of the blocks and, standing back a few feet from the barrel they were kept in, tried to hit the barrel. Everytime one of them succeeded, they both laughed.

Another time, Mr. Roberts was at the receiving end when Billy Mellon came down to speak to Nick Jones.

MR. MELLON: Say, Nick, Charlie wants to know what's going on down here? (He laughed.)

MR. JONES: Looks like I'm going to have to give both Charlie and you a talking to.

They walked up to the laminator. When Mr. Cappielo saw them coming, he made a couple of gestures. Mr. Jones gestured back.

MR. ROBERTS: What does that mean?

MR. JONES: Oh, he's telling me to get the hell back down to the other end where I belong. I motioned back for him to get to work.

Mr. Cappielo grabbed Mr. Jones and started pushing him back in the direction of the receiving end.

Another time, Mr. Cappielo was down at the receiving end helping Mr. Jones take sheets off. Mr. Jones was busy stacking up the sheets, when Mr. Brogan signalled from the front end that he was ready for a knife change. Mr. Cappielo walked down to the knife controls and pushed the switch that swung the knives into position for the next order. He was clearing the waste paper away from the blades when Mr. Jones came down.

MR. JONES: How's it coming, Charlie? Say, if you worked hard at it, you might make a knife setter some day. Here, fellow, take this waste up to your cart; ours is practically full.

MR. CAPPIELO: So is ours. What do you want me to do with it, throw it under the laminator?

They both laughed at this, and Mr. Jones helped Mr. Cappielo gather up the waste paper. Mr. Cappielo could hardly see over the armloads of waste as he carried it up to the front end. After the two men dumped their paper, Mr. Jones started to make a new order setup.

MR. CAPPIELO: Just what do you think you're doing? Back to your own end, bud; you're messing up the whole works. (To Mr. Roberts.) I try to get these fellows to work right and they don't. (He laughed.) Look, I even drew a chalk line down between the laminator and the glue station, when Al went over to the #1 crew and Billy here came to work with us. I'm doing it just like the rules say. What'd I tell you, Billy, when you came to work here?

MR. MELLON: (Smiling): That all the area on that side of the chalk line was your job and everything on this side was my job.

MR. CAPPIELO: Right. So, Nick, get the hell out of here. (Pause.) Well, O.K., what do you want, now that you're here?

MR. JONES: I saw that the sheet was just creeping along, so I figured you needed some help. I thought probably you were kinda getting tired. You know, this is a young man's game.

MR. CAPPIELO: Get outta here, you!

ATTITUDES OF THOSE WHO WORKED ON BOTH CREWS

In the course of his study, Mr. Roberts had opportunities to talk at some length with several people who had worked on both the #1 and the #2 crews. He recorded some of their impressions and the ways in which they described the differences between the two crews. Some of these conversations follow.

AL BROGAN, HELPER

When George Hart was in the hospital and Mr. Brogan was shifted from the #2 crew to work as Leo LeBouef's helper, he talked with Mr. Roberts about the two crews as follows:

MR. BROGAN: I don't like working on the #1 crew much. Oh, I can get along with Leo. For that matter, I can get along with George, too. But this crew is different. I guess I like to work more with younger guys. I like to work with fellows about my own age.

MR. ROBERTS: You like to work with Charlie?

MR. BROGAN: Yeah, I like to work with Charlie a lot. I like to work with the whole gang of them. We do things differently than they do on this crew.

MR. ROBERTS: What do you mean, Al?

MR. BROGAN: Well, we just do. You know, everyone on this crew here don't work together at all. They all do their own separate jobs. They don't pay much attention to anyone else. I think they're kind of catching on, however. Now and then I see Leo trying to and I pitch in and help him.

MR. ROBERTS: This crew doesn't work too well together, is that it?

MR. BROGAN: Something that way. Look here, for instance. You see those big paper rolls coming off the elevator there? (He pointed to the elevator.) Well, hell, you can break your back trying to get one of those things off yourself, pushing and pulling it around. But once someone gives you a hand, gets behind that truck and gives

it a push, you can go right along with it. If you try to pull and
tug that thing yourself, you're all out of wind. You're tired out
in an hour or two. You never do get much done if that happens.
But when I work with Charlie, the two of us pull together. We
don't have any special job. If Nick wants something done on the
other end of the laminator, I go down and help him. If I want
something done down here, he comes down and helps me. We
don't worry about who does what job. Well, I got to go back to
the glue station.

Later, when he walked over to the bench in the smoking area, Mr.
Roberts followed him.

MR. BROGAN: I'll be very glad when I can go back to my own crew.
They have all sorts of troubles working on this crew.
MR. ROBERTS: How's that?
MR. BROGAN: They just do. Nobody cares about anyone else. When
the machines stop, the fellows at the other end go off and grab a
smoke. Look down there. See, the machine's stopped. They've
got to make a knife change. Look at that setter; he's just taking
his time. And the other guys aren't doing much of anything. I
don't do that with Charlie. That fellow, Nick Jones, you know,
the knife setter on the other screw, he's really good when it comes
to his job. He knows all the things ahead of time. It only takes
him a minute or so to make a change. Why, if the knife man
doesn't set up the orders ahead of time, you lose plenty. Not so
much in bonus; you lose that, too; but when these machines stop
for any length of time, the paper up in the storage bin gets cold and
the steam causes the paper to stick on the cylinders. Then when
you start up the glue station and laminator, "Bang!" goes the paper,
and what a mess!

But that isn't the half of it. Almost every time we change over
on a new paper, the cylinders beyond the glue station have got to
be cleaned. Keeping those cylinders clean is the job of the two
fellows on the other end. Well, on our crew they know that, and
they don't even wait to be called. Sometimes they are so fast, we
don't have to stop the machines but for a few seconds. They
jump right in and get the job done. One gets on one side and
another on the other side and those cylinders are cleaned in a hurry.
Not only do they clean the cylinders, but they usually pitch in
and help Charlie and me. And a lot of times Bill Evans or Jim
Carson will climb up on the storage bin and pull the paper down

for us, while Charlie and I rethread the operation. Nick and I see they want to work, so we do, too. We pitch in with them. We get those paper rolls on the paper stands and hooked to the machines in no time flat.

Look there, Dave. See, the machines have been stopped too long, and that's why Leo has to pour oil on the paper while he waits for them to finish the knife change. But on our crew, we make that change in a hurry, and we don't have to put up with that kind of trouble. (Pause.)

I don't know what it is, but the guys on the #2 crew talk with each other. The day doesn't seem so long then. You know, they kid with each other. Charlie and I go down and talk with the fellows at the receiving end, and they come up and see us. But on this crew everyone's so glum; always complaining, or watching out for troubles, or something like that. I don't know. Like I said, I'll be damn' glad when I go back with my old gang. The foreman told me I could go back, if I'd come over here and work with Leo for a while.

BILLY MELLON, GEORGE HART'S ASSISTANT ON THE #1 CREW

One evening after Mr. Hart came back from the hospital, Mr. Roberts was talking with Mr. Mellon, who had temporarily taken Mr. Brogan's place in the #2 crew and was currently Mr. Hart's assistant. After they had talked a while, Mr. Roberts asked how he was getting along.

MR. MELLON: I get along all right with George. (Pause.) Leo has some trouble with him, however.

MR. ROBERTS: You mean Leo doesn't get along too well?

MR. MELLON: I don't know what it is. There's a lot of ill feeling on this crew. It's hard to put your finger on it. Leo tells me he hardly ever speaks to George, particularly when George is in one of his moods. That's how he gets along with him. And I talked to some of the other fellows and none of them like George too much. I can get along with him all right, don't get me wrong. But I just don't feel good working with him.

MR. ROBERTS: He's not like Charlie?

MR. MELLON (smiling): Oh, say, that Charlie, he's one swell guy, you know. The #2 crew is a wonderful bunch of guys to work with. I've never seen anything like it. It's really something.

MR. ROBERTS: You like them very much?

MR. MELLON: Sure, I do. I came down here and I didn't know anything much about the helper's job, so what happens? Charlie takes
me over and he takes his hand and makes a line between the glue
station and the laminator. He said: "This is your side of the machine,
and all of that is your work. On this side of the line, that's my
side of the machine and that's my work." (He broke out laughing.) But he didn't mean a word of it, of course. It wasn't three
minutes after I'd gone to work that I got in some sort of trouble
over on my machine and he was over there helping me get it fixed.
A few minutes later I saw he needed some help on his machine, so I
went over there to help him out and he said, "Get back over on your
side where you belong." I laughed and went right on working
with him. He's quite a guy, you know.

MR. ROBERTS: You see something of a difference, then?

MR. MELLON: I can't put my finger on it; I don't know. Age, I
thought that was part of the reason. They're much older on this
crew; but you take the guys down at the receiving end on this
crew, they're all pretty young. Fact is, some of them are younger
than the #2 crew. I don't know what it is, but I sure feel
differently. Things just aren't the same.

MR. ROBERTS: You can talk with Charlie?

MR. MELLON: That is a big part of it. When I came down here to
work, I tried my damnedest to work, to get along with everyone.
I'll do all that's expected of me, but I gotta have some help. Well,
I came down here and I was trying. I was new and I didn't know
the job, even though I have worked down here off and on as a
roll shafter. I was trying to work out on the job, so Charlie and I
got along pretty well at first, but then he clammed up, didn't say a
word for an hour or two. I couldn't figure it out, so I went up to
him, "What's the matter, Charlie? Have I done something wrong?"
Charlie kinda laughed and said, "Naw, naw, I'm just teed off with
these damn' machines here. I'm O.K." And what happened?
Everything went swell from then on. But up to that time, boy, I
didn't feel so good.

MR. ROBERTS: But you wouldn't go up to George with something like
that?

MR. MELLON: To George? Huh! I wouldn't tell him anything.
I wouldn't ask him anything. I just can't. When something goes
wrong on the #2 crew, no one gets excited. They don't blow up
and get mad. So they know they're losing money on the bonus.
But the bonus isn't everything to them. In fact, I think the bonus
comes second in many ways. Don't get me wrong; they want to

make a bonus as much as anyone. But they don't stand around stewing and worrying about it. Here on the #1 crew, every time the machines stop or something happens, always in the back of their heads is the idea, "I'm losing my bonus. You've got to get the work out. You've got to get things done." Aaah! And so they're always on and at each other. Always working against each other.

MR. ROBERTS: On the #2 crew they offer to help you?

MR. MELLON: Yeah. They really do help you. You don't have to ask for help. They come and help you. You ask a question on the #2 crew and you don't get your ear chewed off. You make a mistake and they say, "Everybody makes mistakes." But make a mistake on this crew and George crawls up one side of you and down the other. Oh, he may not say anything, but he doesn't have to say anything. It's the way he acts, just the way he looks at you. There's a big difference between George and Charlie. You don't realize that until you work with both of them. Take for instance this making a bonus. Now there's some days when Charlie only makes $5 in bonus, and George makes $10 in bonus. So what does Charlie say? "Good for you, George. I'm glad you made a good bonus!" But let the thing be the other way around; let Charlie make the $10 and George make the $5, and George just bristles and gets mad. I'm telling you, George is a jealous man. Oh, don't get me wrong. I like George. I can work with him, but I just don't like to be around him.

MR. ROBERTS: He makes a day very hard for you?

MR. MELLON: You said it. Long and hard, and nothing else to it. Now you take, for instance, when I used to work with Charlie. I'd be sitting there on the bench and he'd come by and flip a piece of wood at me and say, "Snap out of it kid, what's eatin' you?" We'd joke about the way the machines were going. We'd talk about our families and what we'd do after hours when the work was over. Or we'd whistle or run up and down. But none of that here. It's just work all day long. Like I said, they want me back upstairs in the cellophane department. I don't mind going back one bit. I'm really tired of things down here.

MR. ROBERTS: I guess you'd like to be back with the #2 crew?

MR. MELLON: Well, I don't know. I'm going back to my old department Monday, and then I'm leaving the plant completely next month. You see, my folks are living upstate on their farm. They're kind of old, and I go up and see them whenever I can, once or twice a month. When I was working on the #2 crew,

Al Brogan swapped jobs with me, so I could spend a few extra hours with them. He'd take my place that day, which meant he had to work almost 17 hours without any break. I put in the same routine Monday to repay him; and, boy, was I tired. The #2 crew is O.K.; and from what I hear, Al's pretty glad to be back on it.

HERBERT ORR, ANOTHER OF HART'S ASSISTANTS

A few weeks later, Mr. Roberts met Herbert Orr, a new man, working on the #2 crew. Mr. Orr told him that this was his last week on the laminator.

MR. ORR: Ed Dyer told me that I was to go over to the printers next Monday.

MR. ROBERTS: Have you been working with the #2 crew?

MR. ORR: No, just Monday. Usually I'm George's assistant. But you see on Monday evenings I have to go over and serve with the Navy Reserve Corps, and I'm away from the job from about 6:00 P.M. on. So on Monday I've been working with the #2 crew when they have the day shift. Of course this is only my third week here in the plant, so I haven't had many Monday's with the #2 crew; and like I said, I'm practically through on the laminator anyway. Dyer is putting me over on the printers next Monday.

MR. ROBERTS: You'll miss the laminator?

MR. ORR: Oh, I suppose.

MR. ROBERTS: You like working with the fellows here?

MR. ORR: Some I do; others I don't. (Pause.) You take Charlie and Al here; they're swell guys. I'm not so tired when I work with them. They help me shaft the rolls and get the paper on the stands.

MR. ROBERTS: That's different?

MR. ORR: Well, George and Leo are much older on the #1 crew; and then again, George has that bad condition in his back.

MR. ROBERTS: I see.

MR. ORR: But it still is pretty lonely with that bunch. No one helps you much. Oh, now and then Leo will help me, but I don't have a lot to do with his machine. I work mainly around the laminator. But as far as shafting rolls for the laminator is concerned, I do most of that myself.

MR. ROBERTS: George isn't too helpful.

MR. ORR: I think he means well, at times. He's kind of old, you know, and gets pretty excited about little things. But you're right, he doesn't help much. Of course, shafting the paper rolls is my job since he has had that operation. But that's all over now. The fellows around here say that George is going to have to go to work now that his assistant is leaving.

RESPONSE TO CHANGE AND CRISES

As time went on, Mr. Roberts became interested in further exploring crew differences by examining specifically the way the crews reacted to changes in their membership, or job assignments, or unusual working conditions.

The #1 Crew

GEORGE HART AND HIS ASSISTANTS

A short time before he went into the hospital, Mr. Hart was discussing the new assistant with Mr. Roberts.

MR. HART: See that fellow over there? He's my new assistant they gave me about a week ago, when my doctor told me I couldn't pull or haul or lift anything until I got an operation.

MR. ROBERTS: How's he working out?

MR. HART: I doubt if he makes it. Doesn't catch on too fast. Doesn't show much initiative. That work's too rough for him; that's what I think. (He laughed.) It takes a long time to learn the tricks of this trade. You don't pick these things up all at once. I've been working on laminators for over 20 years and I don't know all there is to know even yet.

A few days later. Mr. Hart abruptly broke off a conversation with Mr. Roberts and hurried toward Henry Black (Blackie), his young assistant, who was engaged in shafting one of the big paper rolls.

MR. HART: That's not the best way to shaft the roll. Here, let me show you. (Mr. Black's face became sullen as he stepped back and watched Mr. Hart screw the shaft into place.) Isn't that more like it?

Mr. Black nodded, and Mr. Hart immediately returned to the laminator. When his back was turned, Mr. Black lifted a wrench in the air and shook it in his direction. Then Mr. Black turned to Mr. Roberts.

MR. BLACK: I don't know who he thinks he is. He's always complaining about something. Nobody ever does anything to suit him.

Even old Leo there never pleases him, and they've worked together for years. (He continued as he screwed a shaft into another paper roll.) I'm no rookie, even if I have worked this job only for a couple of weeks. I've been with the company for seven years, working all over the plant. I was on the printer operation when they transferred me over here. (He put down his wrench and with Mr. Roberts following walked over to the bench in the smoking area. As he lighted a cigarette, he pointed to several paper rolls near the laminator.) You see, I'm way ahead in my work. I've got all those rolls ready to go. I'm just waiting on the next paper change, so I have nothing to do right now. But it sure burns George up to see me sitting here smoking. He wants me busy all the time.

Mr. Black leaned over to drink at the fountain next to the bench and then glanced up at the bonus chart which hung above. This chart listed each worker's name and indicated the bonus he earned on each shift. Frowning, Mr. Black continued.

MR. BLACK: And another thing, he never stops harping about how he's got to split his bonus with me. I didn't ask him to do that. He decided that for himself. But he's always making such a big fuss that I wish he'd keep the whole bonus and shut up. (Pause.) No, on second thought, I don't. I deserve the money for all the work I do. (He put on his work gloves and got up.) I do just what I'm told to do and nothing more. He thinks he's working me on this job. He's crazy. I'm working him. (Mr. Black grinned broadly and returned to work.)

Several weeks later when Mr. Hart returned to work, Mr. Roberts walked over to the laminator to see the #1 crew. Mr. Hart saw him coming and came over to shake hands with him. After talking about his recent operation and other personal matters, he pointed to Billy Mellon.

MR. HART: Well, he's my assistant. He's worked down here before as a helper on the other crew. We used to have him every so often when we had split rolls. He's from upstairs in the cellophane department. Well, frankly speaking, he's not much good.
MR. ROBERTS: How's that?
MR. HART: He doesn't show any interest in the job. He's got no initiative. Doesn't ask any questions, doesn't do anything unless you tell him. He wanders off on the job here, goes over and visits with the girls over in assembly, goes wandering off to the

receiving end, or goes over and sits down on the bench—he's never where you want him. You've got to tell him to get up and do something. Goes downstairs and messes around with paper and talks to the man who makes the wax. When you want him, he's never around—never attending to business. You've got to do the work yourself or look him up—all that sort of thing.

Now that isn't right. He doesn't know what the job is down here. He's new. He's not going to last. He's going back upstairs next week. You know what they're paying that boy?

MR. ROBERTS: No, I don't George.

MR. HART: They are paying him laminator operator's pay. The same pay I'm getting! That young kid there! He doesn't know anything about the machinery. He could no more operate that laminator than fly. I can't figure out what this company's trying to do. Twenty years I've worked on this job, twenty years of experience. It took me all that time to become a good operator. Now they bring this young kid in here and give him a job that pays the same as mine. Doesn't experience count any more about here?

MR. ROBERTS: Seniority doesn't count like it should when they do this?

MR. HART: Does it, when they do a thing like this? Twenty years on the laminator, and I've done all sorts of favors for this company. Many's the night I'd barely get home after putting in eight or nine hours and my phone would be ringing. I'd pick it up. "Oh, George," Ed or Fred will say, "We're in trouble. Can you come down and help us out? We can't get things running right." So I'd drop everything, put on my hat and coat and come back to the plant.

MR. ROBERTS: They appreciate that?

MR. HART: I don't know. I wonder, when they put a young kid like this on the machines and pay him operator's pay. But you wait and see. One of these days I'm going to walk up to the office and say, "I want a special rate. I deserve a special rate." (He laughed.) I don't suppose I'll ever do that, but this does bother me.

Look at that guy. That's the fastest I've seen that kid move in three days. Just indifferent, that's what he is. Doesn't care. Doesn't ask any questions, doesn't show any initiative. Like I said, at the end of this week he's going back upstairs to cellophane.

MR. ROBERTS: What will you do then?

MR. HART: Oh, we got a new man we're breaking in on the #2 crew. He'll be over to help me, I guess, for two or three months. (He picked up some tools and started working on the laminator.)

Mr. Roberts asked Fred Dorn, the superintendent, about Billy

Mellon, since Roberts had met Mr. Mellon when he was filling in on the #2 crew.

MR. DORN: Yeah, he's a damn' good worker. One of the most flexible men in the whole company. He can and will do most anything on the jobs around here. He's worked in many capacities; on the laminator, on the printers, in assembly, and he was upstairs in the cellophane department before he came down here to work on the laminator. He shows great promise. He's making as much as a head operator on the laminator right now. He was assistant foreman upstairs.

MR. ROBERTS: He's going to be promoted?

MR. DORN: Fact is, I'd make him a supervisor in a short time if he wanted to stay here. But his heart is elsewhere. You see, Billy and his wife want to open up a little business of their own, so in about a month he's leaving. Like I told him, if he wants to come back if it ever gets too rough, we'll find a place here for him.

About a week later Mr. Roberts greeted Leo LeBouef at the glue station. Mr. LeBouef nodded toward the new assistant at the laminator.

MR. LEBOUEF: That's our third assistant for the week down there working with George. We really go through 'em. (He laughed.) It's pretty tough down there.

A little later Mr. Roberts spoke with Mr. Hart about his assistants.

MR. HART: I sure go through the assistants. They come down here for a day or two, and I'm a little too tough on them, I guess, because they don't stay long. (He laughed.)

MR. ROBERTS: I guess this breaking in a new assistant presents problems.

MR. HART: It sure does. When a new guy comes down here to work, you've got to start him from the beginning by taking him around and showing him everything to do. Of course, I get all sorts of guys down here as assistants, some who want to learn and some who don't. I've had quite a group of bad ones. Many of them don't care about the machinery and don't realize the importance of the job.

MR. ROBERTS: They don't have much respect for the work?

MR. HART: Something like that. Many of them get pretty damn' smart-alecky, and they start telling me within 30 minutes after they get here how I should run my machinery. I've been around these laminators for over 20 years, and *I* don't even know all the things about them. Then those smart kids come down here and in a matter of minutes they start telling me how I ought to run the job!

MR. ROBERTS: This makes you damn' mad?

MR. HART: It sure does. I wonder who they think they are anyway. The main thing wrong with most of them is they don't really want to work. I usually find out in the locker room who the next assistant is. The first thing I tell him before he ever comes out on the machines is that he's coming to a man's job. We don't play around. "If you don't want to work," I tell him, "then you might as well go some place else in this plant. If you come on the laminator you've got to be ready to get your hands dirty."

MR. ROBERTS: You prepare them for what is to come.

MR. HART: When they come down here they find out what's in store for them. Usually when a new guy comes to work I play pretty dumb. I try to help him all I can to get started, but then pretty soon I kind of watch him to see how he acts. I want to see if he takes any interest in the work, whether he shows any initiative or not. Or whether he just wants to goof off on the job.

MR. ROBERTS: Most of those who leave show little interest in the work.

MR. HART: They don't show any interest in the work at all. Tney think it's just a job. They don't see the importance of making paper. I remember a character who worked here a year or so back. He was a big husky guy. He used to pick up those shafts for the paper rolls and walk around with them half way up in the air something like this. (He walked around pretending that he was carrying a metal shaft.) Boy, he really thought he was something. Well, he wasn't here but a couple of hours when I saw he wasn't going to make it. Never would get this job done right.

MR. ROBERTS: He was showing off?

MR. HART: He acted like Tarzan or someone like that. I knew right then and there when he started acting up that he'd never be any good working here.

I sized him up pretty fast. He got real smart and started talking to me. You know what I mean, telling me how I ought to run the job. I just took so much of that and I told him where to go. He said, "If you want to settle this, we'll just step outside and see about that." So I said if he wanted it that way, I was willing. So I was just about ready to hit him when Ed Dyer came by and asked what was going on. He took us both up to the office and we had it out. I told Ed that it was either me or this Tarzan character. He was either going to leave or I was going to leave. There wasn't room enough on that laminator for the both of us. So this Tarzan character said, "Never mind, foreman, I'll quit. You keep this fellow. He knows his business." So he left, and I never saw him again.

MR. ROBERTS: Ed knows you're a very valuable worker?

MR. HART: Well, I think so. Then sometimes I don't know. Just a few days before I went to the hospital, Ed and Fred had some trouble with the machines down here, and they called me to come back after I had already put in a full day.

MR. ROBERTS: Did they appreciate that?

MR. HART: I wonder, when they pull something like this—this kid down here making operator's pay. I have to break him in to the job and share my bonus with him. I don't think they really appreciate age and experience when they do that.

You remember that Benson boy that came here last week to replace Billy Mellon? He came down from the same department Billy was in, too, but he was a trainee so he didn't share in my bonus. He wanted to learn the assistant's job and to be my assistant for about three months. He wasn't a bad worker. He got around and did everything I told him. But the second day he worked down here his neck started to bother him. I guess he had some sort of neck injury from some years back and the work bothered it quite a bit. He told Ed Dyer that he couldn't do the work. So they sent him back upstairs.

MR. ROBERTS: Wasn't he working down here before?

MR. HART: Yeah, that's true. He worked on the #2 crew for about a week, but he just stood around and watched them, I guess. He wasn't really working. When he came over on my shift last Monday, he started to complain about his neck hurting him and the next day he said he wanted to go back upstairs. After he left, they sent me another guy. I think he was new in the plant. I don't know whether he quit or was sent to some other part of the plant, but he only lasted one day down here. His second day, he didn't show up at all. He was really a card. You couldn't teach him anything. He'd never worked around a machine in his life, and he hadn't been here but a couple of hours before he started telling me how we should run the job. I could see right then and there we weren't going to get along. I told Leo and Ed that. I'm pretty tough on them. (He laughed.)

All I know is last Thursday this fellow came to work. (He pointed toward the new assistant a few yards away.) I've forgotten his name. (Calling.) Say, fellow, what's your name?

ASSISTANT: Bob. (He went back to his work.)

MR. HART: Bob. Yeah, I remember now. He's going to be all right. He's been around machines before. He's worked over in another box outfit before he came here. He's new and inexperienced, of course; but with training and time he should be pretty good, and he doesn't share in my bonus because he's a trainee. He catches on pretty fast. He asks me questions and does what I say without a lot of back talk.

MR. ROBERTS: He has respect for experience and age?

MR. HART: Yeah, I think so.

MR. ROBERTS: But not the other fellows?

MR. HART: Something like that. Some of these young fellows have had it pretty easy, you see. They haven't really worked in their whole life. So they come in here and in a couple of hours decide to tell me what to do. You take that fellow who works over on the printers who came over here a few months back to work on the laminator with me. He hadn't been here but an hour or two and he decided the work was too tough for him. So he went back to the printers. So you see what the whole thing is. These guys don't really want to work. They don't know what a hard job is.

MR. ROBERTS: They don't see why it's worth all the effort?

MR. HART: If it weren't for me on this laminator and Leo on the glue station, the rest of this department wouldn't have any work to do.

MR. ROBERTS: You run the show when you are on duty?

MR. HART: That's just about the size of it. It's right here and here only that the sheet is made, not over at the printers or the assembly area. We do the big, important job. If this machine doesn't run, no other machine in the whole department will run for long.

MR. ROBERTS: Your work is really important?

MR. HART: That's what I think, but you know sometimes you can't tell people around here what you're doing for them. They all think you're just running a machine.

MR. ROBERTS: Not much of anyone sees how important this job it?

MR. HART: I don't think the foremen see it half the time, either. Sometimes I don't see them but once or twice in a full eight-hour run. They may drop around for a minute or so in the afternoon, and then I'll go home without seeing them again. In many ways I like that. It's my responsibility down here.

MR. ROBERTS: You make many of the decisions?

MR. HART: A great many of them. There's the paper to work with, there's the tools, the machinery, and so on to clean, and there's the parts to inspect and oil and order replacements for. Well, I got to get back to work. See you again, Dave.

Two weeks later Bob Billington, Mr. Hart's sixth assistant in two months, quit. Mr. Roberts later learned from Ed Dyer that Mr. Billington quit because he said he could not work on Saturdays. In the four weeks Mr. Billington had been at the plant, he had had to work two of the four Saturdays and he said that was too much. When Mr. Roberts went around to see Mr. Hart that afternoon, Mr. Hart described how Mr. Billington had come to leave.

MR. HART: I thought he was going to make the job without too many hitches. We were getting along right well, but then he ups and quits. He told me that he couldn't make enough money working here on the job, so he had to go out to the race track on Saturday and win enough to support his family. (He laughed.) Isn't that the darndest thing you ever heard? Why, I bet he loses far more money than he ever wins. Can't work Saturdays, got to bet on the horses to make a living! I never heard anything like that before in my life.

OTHER CREW MEMBERS

Two incidents involving job or personnel shifts pointed up characteristics of other members of the #1 crew. The first incident occurred while Leo LeBouef was acting as operator with Al Brogan as his helper. Mr. Roberts was talking with Mr. Brogan in the smoking area when Mr. LeBouef ran past them calling out something about the glue station. Mr. Brogan hurried down. When the two workers got there, wax was spurting out of both sides of the machine and dripping on the paper and the floor. At about this time, Ralph Langley came walking up to the machine. He held in his hand a piece of sheet saturated with wax. He waved it in the air and said, "Just what the hell is this?"

By then Mr. Brogan has stopped the glue station and broken the paper going through the pressure section. He ran to the other side of the machine and began to dig around in the trough that carried excess wax back to the tank. He pulled out a large piece of laminated sheet which evidently was acting as a stopper and had blocked the wax from flowing properly.

At this moment, Ed Dyer, the foreman, came up and inquired why the machines were stopped. Joe Kern walked up to see what the trouble was. Mr. Langley turned to Leo LeBouef.

MR. LANGLEY: Say, Leo, won't that wax dry in the pressure section there and get all sticky and clog up the knives at our end?
MR. LEBOUEF: Yeah, I guess it will.

MR. LANGLEY: Well, let's do something about that.

MR. BROGAN: It's all right. I broke the paper shortly after the machine stopped, and it passed through the pressure section carrying most of the wax with it.

MR. LANGLEY: Good.

He walked over to the smoking area, where Mr. Kern was standing. Mr. Roberts stood watching Mr. Brogan and Mr. LeBouef work on the glue station, trying to get it ready to run again. The cylinders inside were covered with a hard coating of wax. Mr. Brogan got out his tools and tried to scrape the cylinders clean. Mr. LeBouef helped a little and then stood back and shook his head. He removed his glasses and got up on the glue station and leaned over into the machinery. Heavy gurgling, popping sounds were coming from the pipes on the machine. Mr. LeBouef turned to Mr. Dyer.

MR. LEBOUEF: We've got air in the pipes now.

MR. DYER: Well, maybe when we get the wax circulating, that will stop.

MR. LEBOUEF: We're going to have trouble just the same.

MR. DYER: How did it happen?

MR. LEBOUEF: Some board got in the trough and clogged up the wax circulation. I guess Al wasn't watching it too carefully.

Joe Kern heard this and walked over.

MR. KERN (Half jokingly and half seriously): Now, look, Frenchy, let's not give Al too rough a time. We'll get this thing going. (He smiled at them and started to help them investigate.) Leo, you're acting something like George.

MR. LEBOUEF: Yeah. (He laughed.)

Mr. Kern and Ralph Langley returned to the receiving area. Mr. LeBouef went back to the laminator to check something. By then Mr. Brogan had gotten the wax line cleared and had rethreaded the paper through the glue station and into the pressure section. He started the machine up, and it ran for about 30 seconds; then there was a loud snapping sound from overhead. The extra supply of paper in the storage bin was gone and the paper broke. Mr. Brogan made a laughing remark about how that wasn't his fault anyway. Mr. LeBouef hurried down to the laminator and started it up, but the paper had become stuck to the hot cylinders and it broke again. By this time, Mr. Brogan was perspiring quite freely. Sweat was running down his brow and the sides of his head and the back of his shirt were saturated. He ran down to where Mr. LeBouef was and said, "Okay, fella, let's get it rethreaded." Mr. LeBouef tapered the end of the paper and Mr. Brogan handed it to him to thread through the laminator. Then Mr. Brogan got hold of the large roll of paper in back, and when Mr. LeBouef said, "Okay, let her go," he flipped the roll in order to absorb the shock as the machine started to pull the paper through. The paper tugged and strained but went through. Mr. Brogan went up the ladder and dragged the paper over the storage bin and down to the glue station. Mr. LeBouef was there to help him thread it through the machine. With this operation accomplished, production got under way again.

MR. ROBERTS: What happened, Leo?

MR. LEBOUEF: The wax got stopped up by a piece of sheet in the return drain. The wax must keep circulating or else the sheet won't stick properly.

MR. ROBERTS: It was just an accident?

MR. LEBOUEF: Naw, not quite an accident. Sure, that paper fell down there in the drain and clogged up the wax; but Al should have watched the glue station closer. I always watch to make sure that never happens. You see, the paper sometimes gets stuck on the cylinders and a piece will break off and float down the trough. It's happened before.

Mr. Roberts walked past the glue station as he prepared to leave the plant for the day.

MR. ROBERTS: Just an accident, I guess, huh, Al?

MR. BROGAN: Yeah, that's what it was. You can't ever tell about things like this at all. They just happen on these machines. Charlie has told me about several things that have happened to him while he worked on the glue station. Come to think of it, I believe he mentioned something like this once happened to him. You see, the chunk of sheet I fished out of the trough stopped up the return drain line and "boom!"—we had wax everywhere.

The second incident concerned Ralph Langley in particular. It was related to Mr. Roberts by Mr. Black, who had been Mr. Hart's first assistant and was currently temporary knife setter on the #2 crew.

MR. BLACK: Hi ya. I guess you're kinda surprised to see me working on the laminator?

MR. ROBERTS: Yeah, I am.

MR. BLACK: Well, I guess I've worked on every job in this department
by now. I'm over here working on the #2 crew because Bill Evans
had to go be the knife setter on the #1 crew. The acting knife
setter there, Ralph Langley, broke his big toe yesterday. Ralph
was taking Joe Kern's place, because Joe was out. Now Ralph
will be out for three or four weeks, I guess. Those fractures don't
mend overnight. He can hardly stand on his foot for any length
of time, and he certainly can't move around like he has to when
he works here.

MR. ROBERTS: He took it pretty hard?

MR. BLACK: I doubt it. I think he was pretty damn' glad to be away
from here for a time. You see, I was working with him on the #1
crew the day before his toe got broken. I was working his position
while he worked as knife setter. We had some troubles with the
runs that day.

MR. ROBERTS: Troubles?

MR. BLACK: Yeah, on Ralph's third day there his first run got all messed
up. The sheets for that order were all cut wrong, and no one on
the crew discovered it.

MR. ROBERTS: Ralph was pretty new on the job?

MR. BLACK: He's been a knife setter before. When we had three shifts
in here, he was the knife setter for that crew, but that was about
three years ago.

MR. ROBERTS: How did the order get messed up?

MR. BLACK: When a crew quits at night, the knife setter on the crew
sets up the first order for the next day. In that way, the knife
setter has time to straighten up his day's run and can start the first
run through without bothering about setting it up. Well, Nick
Jones here set the order up for Ralph, but I guess he didn't tighten
one of the knife blades right, because the order came off wrong.
I heard Joe Kern say once that when it gets around 11:00 or 12:00
at night, the knife man is pretty tired and he wants to go home.
Sometimes he isn't as careful as he might be. That's why I think
both Joe and Nick always check the first run in the morning, to
make sure no mistakes were made, when one of them sets the run
up for the other the night before.

But I don't think Ralph looked at the order. He turned on the
machine and ran the order. The mistake wasn't caught until about
noon, when the printers tried to run the boxes through. Ed Dyer
came over here looking for Ralph. He wanted to know what had
happened. Ralph told him he didn't know anything about it. But
you know Ralph; he gets real excited about things like that. Dyer

said that the order wasn't set up right and Ralph was responsible for the bad run.   Ralph said it wasn't his fault, that Nick Jones on the #2 crew had set up the run, not him.

MR. ROBERTS: I see.

MR. BLACK: So Dyer told Ralph that he was responsible for any orders that came off the laminator during his shift.   Ralph got pretty mad; so when Dyer left the area, he started bawling us out for not check-ing the mistake.   You know, when I worked over on the printers and when the foreman came around and bawled out an operator, the operator always bawled out the rest of us.   Ralph was damn' mad the rest of the shift.   He didn't say an awful lot, but he thought it wasn't his fault at all.   When Nick and the #2 crew came on duty, he told them what had happened.   Of course, they all felt pretty badly about it; but what can you do?

The #2 Crew

There were fewer personnel shifts in the #2 crew than in the #1 crew.   But such temporary workers as they had were immediately in-corporated into their joking give-and-take relationships, as illustrated by Billy Mellon's experience, cited earlier.   Furthermore, Charlie Cappielo's comments to Mr. Roberts about some of the temporary workers arose incidentally when he and Mr. Brogan were discussing summer vacation plans.   Mr. Brogan was scheduled to work on the #1 crew for most of the summer.

MR. CAPPIELO: Who's going to work for you this summer while you go on vacation, Al?

MR. BROGAN: I guess Biff Hendricks.

MR. CAPPIELO: Oh, hell no, he isn't.   He told me definitely he wouldn't work for George again.   He's through with the laminator.

MR. BROGAN: Someone's got to work down here during the vacation.

MR. CAPPIELO: Yeh.   (Speaking to Mr. Roberts directly.)   When Al leaves, its going to be rough on me.   Don't think it wasn't rough down here, Al, when you worked with Leo on the #1 crew and I had that young kid, Billy Mellon.   Of course, Billy tried and worked hard, but I had to lift a heavier load than usual.

MR. ROBERTS: You'd miss an experienced man like Al.

MR. CAPPIELO: I miss Al plenty when he has to work with someone else.   He's really a go-getter down here, and we work swell to-gether.   That young kid, Tommy, would have worked out too, in time, but I hate to break them in on my time.   I guess I told you that the other kid—Keith Benson—wanted to work down here for the summer. He'd have worked out very well, I think, and we need someone experienced to work the reliefs, not just a new guy you have to break in. That's too tough on the regular workers when that happens. Keith wanted to stay on the job. He'd have been damn' good by now. He wanted to work the vacation shift and get that extra pay with the bonus. He would have gotten about ten weeks work. But it didn't work out at all. I understand his neck was bothering him that week he worked with Al and I, but he was catching on and he said he'd put up with the pain. He really wanted the job.

MR. ROBERTS: Then what happened?

MR. CAPPIELO (throwing his hands in the air): Who knows what happens when you work for George? Keith quit the second day on the job. He said his neck got to hurting him too much.

MR. ROBERTS: I see.

MR. CAPPIELO: Well, you know George. The kid only worked a couple of days and quit. He had his troubles with George.

MR. ROBERTS: It's hard to work for George.

MR. CAPPIELO: I don't know anyone around here who can get along with George too well, except perhaps Leo. But Leo just lets George push him around. Whoops, there goes the machine. I'd better get back and straighten it out, because old crybaby George will be here in a few minutes to go to work.

The above reference to Billy Mellon reminded Mr. Roberts of a crisis which involved both crews and which became known as the "wax mix-up."

The Wax Mix-Up

One afternoon when Mr. Roberts came in, he saw Ed Dyer down in the receiving area looking over a large stack of sheets that had just come off the laminator.

MR. ROBERTS: Hi, Ed.

MR. DYER (looking up from his examination of the sheets): Oh, hello, Dave. We've had our headaches today.

MR. ROBERTS: Oh?

MR. DYER: I've worried over that damn' glue station and laminator all day long. I've stood over those two machines thinking that something must be wrong with the cylinders, or that the steam wasn't feeding through them properly We're behind in production by three or four hours. We can't get the sheet to stick properly. You see, it's all loosely waxed together, and the moment they try to put it through the printers, probably the stuff will come apart. To make matters worse, we're under pressure to get the orders out. The customers want their boxes.

MR. ROBERTS: You don't know what the trouble is, Ed?

MR. DYER: Well, after standing over those machines all morning long, we finally discovered that the *A* wax had been mixed with the *B* wax. It must have happened sometime last night on the #2 crew. I'm not sure why something wasn't said about it, when we came to work this morning. I don't know why a message wasn't left explaining the trouble.

Just then Fred Dorn came by to see Mr. Dyer. They were talking about the orders, when the machines at the front end stopped. All three walked up to see what the trouble was. In a few minutes, all the workers from the receiving end came up. Leo LeBouef and Al Brogan were busy working on the glue station. Mr. Roberts spoke to Ralph Langley, who was standing next to Joe Kern in the smoking area. Mr. Dorn and Mr. Dyer were a few feet further away talking to each other.

MR. ROBERTS: Say, what's the trouble here?

MR LANGLEY: Looks as though Leo let the paper on the left side of the laminator run out. It went through the laminator, over the storage bin, through the glue station and the pressure section and out. That means they have to rethread the whole machine.

MR. ROBERTS: A lot of work?

MR. LANGLEY: Yeah, and time and bonus lost, too.

He and Mr. Kern put their cigarettes out and left the area. Mr. LeBouef and Mr. Brogan worked to get the paper rethreaded and the machines back in operation. Mr. Roberts walked over to listen to Mr. Dorn and Mr. Dyer.

MR. DYER: Well, what do you think about it?

MR. DORN: I don't know. We're behind in orders, that's true. I think if we change some of the orders around, we'll be able to get some of them out before this shift is over. Why don't we go through the orders and see if we can mark the more urgent ones?

MR. DYER: I've never before seen anything quite like the way this *A* and *B* wax got mixed up. I wish someone had told me about it. I spent almost the whole day trying to figure out what in hell the trouble was. All the time I thought it was the machines, only to find out that someone on the #2 crew had dumped the *A* wax back into the *B* wax. That paper down there, Fred, it's—well, I guess it will be all right.

MR. DORN (rubbing his hand over his forehead): Yeah, I suppose so. I hope it doesn't wrinkle too much when it goes through the printers. Maybe the #2 crew will do a little better—I don't know. They'll come on duty in a couple of hours.

Later, toward the end of the shift, Tom Lewis, the night foreman, walked up to Mr. Dyer and Mr. Dorn.

MR. LEWIS: I just heard about the trouble. We had the same trouble last night, but I thought things were working all right when we left. I knew the *A* wax got dumped into the *B* wax; fact is, the new kid at the glue station, Billy Mellon, made the mistake.

MR. DYER: Why didn't you leave a note or something?

MR. LEWIS: Well, I thought the whole matter was cleaned up. The #2 crew kept up production all right. We did shut down for a few minutes every so often to clean off the cylinder, but things were going fine near the end of the shift. I thought the trouble was all past.

MR. DORN: Ed's had trouble with it all day long. Fact is, he just found out a couple of hours ago what the trouble was. He thought it was the machines.

MR. LEWIS: I'm sorry. I would have left a message, if I thought they weren't running properly. But the #2 crew kept them going very well.

MR. DYER: Maybe having the machines sit overnight caused us the trouble. You know, the wax probably got worse just setting between shifts.

MR. LEWIS: I bet that is what happened.

A few minutes later, members of #2 crew began to report for duty, and Joe Kern explained to Nick Jones the several order changes. Mr. Jones nodded and Mr. Kern left the area. Mr. Dorn and Mr. Dyer stood some distance away from the work area watching the men at work and talking about the orders. Finally, Mr. Dyer said he was calling it a day and Mr. Dorn nodded. He remained to watch the workers at the receiving end, and Mr. Roberts decided he would go back up to the front end and talk with Leo LeBouef and Al Brogan.

MR. LEBOUEF: This has been one hell of a day!

MR. ROBERTS: Everything seems to go wrong today, Leo?

MR. LEBOUEF: Boy, you're telling me. I have never seen anything quite like it before in my life. This has been a mess.

MR. ROBERTS: What's been wrong, Leo?

MR. LEBOUEF: What hasn't been wrong! The big trouble is that the #2 crew screwed up.

MR. ROBERTS: What do you mean?

MR. LEBOUEF: Well, that young kid they put on as helper on the #2 crew doesn't know what he's doing. He turned the wrong valve, I guess, and drained the *A* wax back into the *B* wax. Then it got all messed up. The wax got hard, and we couldn't work with it at all today. Time and time again the sheet wouldn't stick together right.

MR. ROBERTS: That seems to be it?

MR. LEBOUEF: Sure it is. I don't see why I didn't figure that out before now. I should have known what the trouble was, but it's been so many years since anything like it happened. Of course, I don't know what I could have done, even when and if I had figured it out. When you get *A* wax mixed in the *B* wax, about the only thing to do is to drain the whole batch out of the tanks and start again. They must have messed up 300 gallons. We've run the stuff all day and still have some left. (He examined the wax in the pan and dug out several large lumps.) When that stuff gets tangled like that, the mixture just hardens into tiny little balls, and it'll play hell with the sheet. The lumps allow air to get between the layers of the sheet; as soon as the sheet begins to dry, it pops right open. That kid didn't know what he was doing. They should have watched him. They shouldn't have let a new kid do something like that. He doesn't have enough experience to run a machine like the glue station. (Pause.) You don't get anything but headaches on this operator's job. There's just one big headache after another. There is too much responsibility. I'll be glad when I go back to the glue station.

Mr. Roberts talked a little longer with Mr. LeBouef and then went over and sat down on the bench in the smoking area. Billy Mellon, the new helper, came in and looked around. Charlie Cappielo also came on the floor; he saw Mr. Brogan working on the glue station and went over to him.

MR. CAPPIELO: I heard about it in the locker room.

MR. BROGAN: It's been one big mess. I don't think Leo knows what in the hell to do when the laminator gets into trouble.

MR. CAPPIELO: We had plenty of trouble with the wax last night, but we finally got the stuff to stick pretty well. The new kid turned the wrong valve and dumped that *A* wax into the *B* wax when we started to change over. It was a damn' fool thing to do, but he didn't know any better. I bet we were a full 20 minutes trying to figure out what was wrong. Finally, Nick Jones saw the trouble. He saw the *A* wax valve wide open and still feeding into the machines, while we were using the *B* wax. I don't see why the company doesn't use *B* wax all the time and be done with it instead of changing back and forth. I know they say that the *A* wax makes a stiffer sheet and some customers want just that, but certainly it wasn't worth all the trouble it's caused us the last two shifts.

MR. BROGAN: I bet Leo spent five hours trying to figure out what was wrong with the machines; and after he did, he didn't know what to do to get the sheet out.

MR. CAPPIELO: I finally decided to dump more *B* wax in the mix and keep the pipes hotter. That way, the *A* wax wasn't quite so pronounced in the glue and the hot steam kept the stuff from forming too many lumps.

MR. BROGAN: I heard Leo and Dyer talking. They think that maybe when the machines set overnight the mix got worse.

MR. CAPPIELO: That might be right, Al. I never thought of that.

MR. BROGAN: Well, probably there's something to that; but still I think if Leo had done something to the mix early, we wouldn't have had all this trouble. I'm telling you, Charlie, we haven't stopped all day, and we have practically nothing to show for it.

Mr. LeBouef came over and spoke to Billy Mellon.

MR. LEBOUEF: Boy, I'm telling you, I've been coming and going all day long.

MR. MELLON: I'm sorry, Leo, about what happened. I didn't mean to—

MR. LEBOUEF: Yes, yes, I know. Well, there's been one big mess. That *A* wax spilled in the *B* wax: that was something, don't think it wasn't.

He walked back to the laminator. Mr. Mellon and Mr. Roberts sat down on the bench in the smoking area.

MR. ROBERTS: Leo's pretty sore, isn't he, Billy?

MR. MELLON: Yeah, it looks that way. What could I do? I'm new down here. I don't know what the deal is yet. I didn't know about that damn' valve. I heard all the troubles the #1 crew had with the *B* wax and *A* wax down in the locker room.   The fellows were talking about it.   I didn't mean to do it.

He did not say anything more about the incident at the time.   Mr. LeBouef came over to the bench a few minutes later and again spoke to Mr. Mellon.

MR. LEBOUEF: You see that order sheet over there?   You see how they got all the orders set up?   You guys on the #2 crew have had all the long runs, and we get all the rough ones.   This is the third time this week we've had triplex laminating, and you fellows haven't had it once.

Mr. Mellon didn't answer him.   He got his equipment and relieved Mr. Brogan on the glue station.   Mr. Brogan went over to the smoking area to get his lunch pail off the desk.   He stopped for a moment.

MR. BROGAN (to Mr. Roberts): What Leo says about the triplex laminating is right.   We have been getting the worst of the work this week.   We have had triplex laminating three times already. Well, I better go cheer up the old fellow before I leave today.   I see he's getting out his oil cans, and I think he's pretty down in the dumps.   See you, Dave.

About halfway through the #2 crew's shift that evening, Nick Jones, the knife setter on the crew, noticed that the sheet was not sticking as well as it should.   He walked up to the front end to see Mr. Cappielo and Mr. Mellon.

MR. JONES: I don't think all that bum wax is used up yet, Charlie. (They looked at the piece of sheet Mr. Jones had with him.)
MR. CAPPIELO: I can dump a little more *B* wax in the mix like we did last night.   I'll feed it in gradually.
MR. JONES: The boys on the other shift must have had a rough time. The orders were pretty mixed up when we came on duty.   I think most of it's getting straightened out, however.
MR. CAPPIELO: All they need around here is the #2 crew.   (He reached his hand in the wax pan.)   There's a little left.   I'm going to shut the machines down in a few minutes and clean the whole mess out.   I'm sure that will help.   Then I'll run the *B* wax a little heavier.   That should fix things up.
MR. JONES: Clean out the pan now, too, if you want, Charlie.
MR. CAPPIELO: That isn't a bad idea.   While you're up here, we can look at the machines together.

He signaled Bill Evans and Jim Carson at the receiving end that he was shutting down, then threw the main switch and stopped the machines.   Mr. Jones and Mr. Mellon stood around the laminator while he worked.   He gave the wax pan cover a jerk and lowered the bottom to expose the cylinders that spread the wax.

MR. CAPPIELO: Hand me that bucket over there, Billy.

Mr. Jones crouched next to Mr. Cappielo and watching him clean the cylinders with his hands and scraping tools.   Mr. Mellon stood next to them and listened.

MR. CAPPIELO: Here are some of the *A* wax lumps.   I think if Leo had kept this pan clean as he worked, he'd have had less trouble getting the sheets to stick.   He should know that, considering how long he's worked on these machines.   (He looked about and pointed to a large, hoelike scraper.)   Hand me that, will you, Nick?

Mr. Jones handed it to him and steadied the pan while he cleaned the cylinders.   Several minutes elapsed.   Mr. Mellon decided to line up some paper rolls for later use.   Bill Evans and Jim Carson had cleaned their work area and were resting on the work tables.   Mr. Capiello and Mr. Jones went on talking.

MR. CAPPIELO: There, that does it, Nick.   (He reached for the large metal cover and the two men put it back on together.)   Now I'll mix in a little more *B* wax and see how the sheet comes out.   I'll check all the rest of the machine while it's running.   If things don't improve at the receiving end, give me a signal.

Mr. Roberts wanted to talk more to the men on the #2 crew about the mix-up in the wax.   A few days later he came in one afternoon while they were working.   He talked first to Nick Jones.

MR. ROBERTS: Hello, Nick.
MR. JONES: Hi, there, Dave.   What's new?
MR. ROBERTS: Not much, Nick.   Where've you been?
MR. JONES: Oh, I've been up at the front end helping out Charlie and the new kid, Billy.
MR. ROBERTS: I understand you had a little trouble in here the other day?
MR. JONES: What about?
MR. ROBERTS: Oh, I meant about the mix-up in waxes.
MR. JONES: Oh, that.   Yeah, that was something of a mess.
MR. ROBERTS: What was that all about, Nick?

MR. JONES: Oh, last Thursday evening we had something of a mix-up on the glue station here. The *A* wax got mixed in with the *B* wax, and we had trouble getting the sheet to stick properly.

MR. ROBERTS: How did it all happen, Nick?

MR. JONES: Oh, Billy, the new kid, turned the wrong valve when we were preparing to change over from *A* wax to *B* wax at the glue station. You see, when we change waxes, you have to drain the machinery at the glue station of one wax, like *A* wax, before using another, like *B* wax. Billy thought he was draining the *A* wax back into its tank, but instead he drained the stuff into the *B* tank. No one discovered the mistake until the sheet started coming off at the receiving end. Then we saw the wax wasn't sticking the sheet together properly. The wax was all lumpy and hard. I guess when the *A* wax hit that hot *B* wax, it just crystallized, and we were trying to wax the sheet together with hard little rocks. When it happened, I went down and saw Charlie, and we experimented around a little bit to try to solve the problem. We found that if we'd dump more *B* wax in at the glue station, it would absorb the *A* wax. So we did that. Every time the paper refused to stick, we'd just dump some more *B* wax. But when the bosses came around and saw we were using too much *B* wax, we'd lay off of it for awhile. But the moment we got a chance, we'd dump some more *B* wax into the machine. We kept that up for about five hours. We got the sheet out all right, but at times we had our doubts.

MR. ROBERTS: You mean you kept production up with all that trouble?

MR. JONES (Laughing): Oh, sure, we didn't get behind much. The sheet was a little wet, but you would be too if you were bathed in that much *B* wax. We just slowed down the pressure section a little and turned up the heat and ran the sheet a little slower, so it would dry out before coming off at the receiving end. It wasn't the best sheet we ever made, but it went through the printers in the next section.

MR. ROBERTS: When the #1 crew came on the next morning, they had considerable trouble with the *A* and *B* stuff, didn't they?

MR. JONES: Yes, they did.

MR. ROBERTS: I wonder why they had so much trouble?

MR. JONES: I don't know. I guess they didn't do what we did. I suspect they tried to run the *A* wax and *B* wax just as it was. It wouldn't work that way. We found that out but for sure.

MR. ROBERTS: The kid felt pretty badly about the mix-up, I guess?

MR. JONES: Oh sure, but no one chewed his ear off. It wasn't completely his fault. Like I told him when we were trying to find out what the trouble was, I've worked on these machines about eight years, and I don't know which valve turns which way half the time. He just made a mistake; we all do that. He didn't know the score yet, so he turned the wrong valve.

The following week, Mr. Hart returned to work following his stay in the hospital. Leo LeBouef went back to his regular job as helper on the #1 crew; Al Brogan became helper on the #2 crew. Billy Mellon went to the #1 crew to assist Mr. Hart with the heavy work. During the week, Mr. Roberts talked with Mr. Mellon about the two crews and the mix-up with the wax.

MR. MELLON: The #1 crew sure had a lot of trouble with that wax the other day. When we came to work the next day after the trouble started, we also had a hard time getting the paper to stock properly. But what happened? Charlie shut down the whole laminator and took a look. He went all over the machines, checking everything. He checked the cylinders, the wax pipes, the spacers, the paper, and so on. He cleaned the cylinders and wax pan thoroughly and the paper started to stick much better. Oh, I guess we were done in half an hour or longer. The other fellows, Nick, Bill, and Jim, all came up and helped. Now Leo had that same trouble over an eight-hour shift, but he never figured out what to do. They never stop the machines at all on the #1 crew, if they can avoid it. In the back of Leo's head is that idea, "I gotta make the bonus. Every time the machines stop, well, that means money out of my pocket. I've gotta keep rolling." George's the same way.

MR. ROBERTS: How did the problem arise, Billy?

MR. MELLON: I can tell you exactly what happened. I turned the wrong valve at the glue station and the A wax drained into the B wax tank. The trouble was discovered some time later, when the sheet wouldn't stick together correctly. The man down in the basement who mixes the wax came up and had some white stuff on his hands. He came over to me and said, "Look at this." I looked at it and said, "So what?" Then he took the wax sample over to Charlie and he looked at it. I heard Charlie say, "So what?" (He laughed.) He didn't know what it was either. Well, about that time Nick Jones signalled to us that something wasn't right with the sheet coming off the receiving end. He came down, and we started looking around and then we found that the A wax was draining into the B wax tank. I found out I had turned the wrong valve. Finally, we figured out if we dumped a little more B wax mixture and ran the sheet very slowly so it could dry properly in the heated pressure section before it was cut into boxes, it would stick good enough to get by.

MR. ROBERTS: So it worked out pretty well?

MR. MELLON: Yeah.

MR. ROBERTS: I understand the #1 crew had considerable trouble the next day with the mixture.

MR. MELLON: They did. I don't think they ever figured out what to do. It was something of a mess, but you can make all sorts of adjustments here if you want to. Charlie does that all the time on the laminator. Oh, don't get me wrong, George and Leo know more about these machines than anyone else around here, but they go about it differently.

MR. ROBERTS: How do you mean, Billy?

MR. MELLON: The #1 crew are always working at odds with each other. When that accident happened, no one got too excited on the #2 crew. Sure, we all wanted to get the trouble corrected, but no one got on to me. But here on the #1 crew, they really get on you when you make a mistake.

MR. ROBERTS: You like to work with the other crew better?

MR. MELLON: Yes, I do. They—I don't know what it is. Now you take Nick Jones. He may not know as much about the job as Joe Kern, but he knows just exactly what is to come next and how to ease the strain for us here at the glue station and on the laminating stand. He knows just what to do to keep the others moving and the machines rolling.

INTERCREW RELATIONS

After noting the differences between the crews, Mr. Roberts became interested in the way in which these might be reflected in intercrew relations. For instance, what attitudes did each crew have toward the other? Did they differentiate between individuals of the other crew? To what extent were the crews competitive? What did they have in common? Mr. Roberts thought that insights into such questions might be gained from the following episodes.

THE RECORD RUN

The day before George Hart left for the hospital, the #2 crew set a new plant record for the production of laminated sheet. Mr. Roberts arrived one evening a week or so after the event to talk to the members of the #2 crew. Just as Mr. Roberts was hanging up his overcoat in the foreman's locker, Tom Lewis, the night foreman of the laminator and printers, walked in.

MR. LEWIS: You should have been here a week ago last Friday night. We really had some excitement.

MR. ROBERTS: Really? What happened?

MR. LEWIS: The #2 crew broke the plant record on production. They set a new record on the laminator—146,000 linear feet of laminated sheet in one eight-hour shift. That's the best that's been done since the plant started some years back.

MR. ROBERTS: Is that right! I guess you are pretty pleased?

MR. LEWIS: To tell you the truth, I am. That #2 crew really went to town. Of course, they kinda got lucky, you understand. They had a long run, so they could keep the machines running without making too many stops and starts. I was sure happy, but it can't happen every night.

Mr. Roberts next went upstairs to the laminating section to see what the #2 crew had to say about the new record. Jim Carson, Bill Evans, and Nick Jones were at work on the receiving end. He spoke briefly to Mr. Evans and Mr. Jones and then stopped to talk with Mr. Carson.

MR. ROBERTS: Hi, Jim, what's new?

MR. CARSON: Nothing—same old stuff. Oh, I got me some snow chains for my car, and I got me some sand, too, for my driveway. But you know, it isn't snowing any more. (They both laughed.) Oh, say, Dave, something has happened since you were here. We broke the production record.

MR. ROBERTS: Yeah—I heard about that. That was something.

MR. CARSON: I suppose so, but now the #1 crew's mad at us. They wouldn't even talk to us afterwards. I came to work the next day and all the #1 crew had for us were daggers. I stepped onto the floor the day after it happened; and when Don Halligan and Ralph Langley saw me coming, they just turned and walked off in the other direction without saying a word.

MR. ROBERTS: They didn't like what you fellows did?

MR. CARSON: You said it. I think they are just laying for us. They're gonna wait until we get off guard and then they will snow us here. They told us all sorts of things a couple of days later, when they had cooled off a little. They said we just got lucky and we had easy runs to handle. But that's not true; we worked with split rolls practically half the evening. But we're having our troubles this morning with the machines. Charlie's been working with the wax and the paper; the two don't seem to want to stick. This is a $1 day, not like a few days ago.

MR. ROBERTS: Not like when you set the record?

MR. CARSON: Yeah—that was the day I had in mind. That was no $1 night. You know we made a great deal in bonus that night.

MR. ROBERTS: You'd like that kind of bonus more often. What do you think was the difference, Jim?

MR. CARSON: Oh, I don't know. The record day started out like any other day. We had some good orders to work with; but hell, we've had good orders to work with for a long time, but we have never been able to put out the kind of footage we did that record day. You know, we put out a little over 146,000 linear feet of sheet. But I don't know what it was, Dave. At first it seemed like any other day. We just came in here and started to work. We had all those split rolls to work with, but things seemed to go off very smoothly. The machines ran perfectly and we started to work together—well, by—I don't know—but by 7:30 or 8:00 in the evening, we had gone way over the usual run of that kind. We had over 80,000 feet and we had nearly 5½ hours yet to go. Well, then we really began to push to break the record. We saw we had a possibility of really setting something and all of us buckled down and pulled together. You know it happened at night, too, between 5:00 P.M. and 1:00 A.M. Anyone would think that it would probably happen during the day, when people usually feel better. But there it is; it happened at night.

MR. ROBERTS: Well, how did everyone take it all—take this record?

MR. CARSON: Poor Leo, you know, the helper on the #1 crew, he took it pretty badly along with the rest of that crew. He had a photograph down here of the time his bunch set the plant record a few years back. The damnedest thing was he took that home just the day before it happened. He used to say, "You'll never break that record. They don't make men like that any more." Aw, he really took it hard. He's just now getting over it.

MR. ROBERTS: I guess you felt pretty badly about Leo?

MR. CARSON: Yes, I did. But we've taken one hell of a riding from them also. Jeez, they're all mad at us. But screw 'em. I don't care. I heard Charlie Cappielo, the operator, say that they were all mad at us. But he said, "Screw 'em," he didn't care either. They really gave us the razz-razz stuff. Got our autographs, you know, and photographs, and oh boy. The whole thing was just so much hogwash to them. Like I said, by God, they're just now getting over it. And they aren't over it by no means yet. I still think they're going to try to break the record against us one of these days. It's really got their goat. I mean it got them down.

A week later, on the #1 crew, Don Halligan, Ralph Langley, and Joe Kern were working their regular jobs at the receiving end when Mr. Roberts joined them. He spoke to Mr. Kern, who was checking the order sheet.

MR. ROBERTS: Hi, Joe, how have you been?

MR. KERN: Well, hello. Where have you been keeping yourself?

MR. ROBERTS: Oh, the usual. What's news with you?

MR. KERN: Well, I guess you've heard by now about the excitement a couple of Fridays ago?

MR. ROBERTS: About the #2 crew setting the record?

MR. KERN: That's it. Well, like I told the boys, you can't eat the laurel wreath they hang around your head. They can hang it there, and you can be the champs, and all that; but like I told them, they can't eat it.

MR. ROBERTS: Yeah, I guess you're right.

Just then Don Halligan came over.

MR. HALLIGAN: What are you two talking about? How the #2 crew beat the record?

MR. KERN: Yes, we were, Don.

MR. HALLIGAN: Sure. See that sign above the desk. You see what the #2 crew wrote after we kidded them so much: "No more autographs, fellows, please. Signed—The Champs." The boys sure took a ribbing about setting the record. We rode them pretty hard about being the "hungry crew." They even drew a laurel wreath in green crayon on the sign. (He laughed.) I guess we kinda got under their skin.

MR. ROBERTS: I guess they won't do that again very soon?

MR. HALLIGAN: I don't suppose so.

He went back to work. During the rest of Mr. Roberts' visit that day, neither worker said anything more about the record run.

GEORGE HART'S RETURN

Because Mr. Roberts was observing the #2 crew when George Hart returned to work, it was not until several days later that he spoke with Mr. Hart.

MR. ROBERTS: Hi, George. You're back.

MR. HART: Yes, Dave. I've been out quite long enough. I've been out of bed nearly two weeks. But I wasn't allowed to move very much, just sit or lie down. If there hadn't been a television set in my room, I think I'd have gone nuts. I'd sit there and watch the programs, and then when the commercials would come on, I'd get up and walk around the room. Gained a little weight, though. My friends all sent me wine, beer, candy, flowers, and so on. Oh, I really was treated like a king.

MR. ROBERTS: How did the operation go?

MR. HART: Oh, it went pretty well. Had some complications at first. The doctor tells me I can't lift, pull, or push anything heavy for maybe three or four months. He's warned me very closely about that. He said, "Now, George, you may think I'm joking with you, but I'm not. You've got to be careful. You've got a potentially serious back condition there, and it would be dangerous if it returned." So I'm going to take it easy for some time.

MR. ROBERTS: How are things going on the job now that you're back?

MR. HART: Oh, first couple of days I was really tired. I'd keep going pretty good until about 12 o'clock, but I didn't think I could make it the rest of the day. Boy, when I got home, I would lie down and go right off to sleep. The afternoons still get awfully long. But I guess they did miss me around here.

MR. ROBERTS: You think they did, George?

MR. HART: I'm sure Leo's glad I'm back to take over the responsibility.

A few evenings later, as the #2 crew was about to start its shift, Nick Jones, the knife setter, came into the laminator area looking for Mr. Hart. He was carrying the clipboard that held the work orders his crew was to run.

MR. JONES: Say, George, weren't you supposed to do that last order with split rolls?

MR. HART: Yeah, yeah, that's right, but the guy down in the basement sent up 42-inch rolls. He didn't send up any split rolls, so I put them on the machine and ran them. (He laughed.) What else could I do?

MR. JONES: I guess you're right. I was just checking.

MR. HART: O.K.

Mr. Hart finished washing his hands and left the work area for the day. Shortly after he left, Charlie Cappielo caught Mr. LeBouef's attention, as he oiled the laminator.

MR. CAPPIELO (screwing up his face and rubbing both of his hands in his eyes): Poor, poor Leo. (He "cried" some more.)

MR. LEBOUEF: Don't give me that. I can't get along with him any more than the rest of you. What's wrong with you guys?

MR. BROGAN: What do you want, Leo, the purple heart? Go on and oil your machines. That's what he wants, Charlie, the purple heart.

They went back to work, while Mr. Roberts spoke to Mr. LeBouef.

MR. ROBERTS: They're mad at you, Leo?

MR. LEBOUEF: Naw. They're just mad at George. They'll get over it in a minute.

Mr. Cappielo stopped the laminator and glue station. He loosened the wax pan under the glue station and started to clean it. Mr. Brogan came back with the wax bucket for him. Mr. Roberts stood watching the work.

MR. CAPPIELO: If I left this machine in this condition, George would be up in the office in two minutes flat raising hell.

MR. ROBERTS: It's a mess?

MR. CAPPIELO: He's pulled this stunt three times this week, and I've come to take the very last of it. Just look at this laminator. He hasn't cleaned this wax pan out all day.

MR. ROBERTS: He doesn't care what he does to you?

MR. CAPPIELO: He's just a big crybaby, that's all. No one, I don't care who they are, can get along with him. See that wax here, it's all lumpy. Look at those cylinders there, you see that? That wax has been caked on those cylinders for hours. He hasn't cleaned this machine all day long. So what does he do? He just picks up his cap and scoots out. Well, if that's the way he wants to play the game, I know that way, too. This is the last week I'll clean this laminator for him.

MR. ROBERTS: You have to clean the laminator at night when you get off duty here?

MR. CAPPIELO: Oh sure, you have to clean it then, because if it lays over for a few hours, the machine would be terrible to clean and try to run. But don't worry, next week I'm on days, and he'll be on nights. He gets a dirty machine every day, and we'll see how he likes it.

Nick Jones came up from the receiving end of the laminator.

MR. CAPPIELO: Nick, I'm going to be delayed about 20 minutes getting this machine clean. George left it dirty again.

MR. JONES: O.K., Charlie. Can I help? (He bent over the machine and helped remove some of the lumpy wax.)

MR. BROGAN: Say, Charlie, did you see what they wrote on that roll of paper that we left on the paper stand last night?

MR. CAPPIELO: Yeah, I saw it.

MR. JONES: What was that, Al?

MR. BROGAN: Last night Charlie and I left a paper roll beside the laminator. So this morning when George came to work he went down there with his black crayon and wrote on the paper, "This paper roll was left by the #2 crew." (All three laughed at this.)

MR. CAPPIELO: What a cry baby!

Mr. LeBouef heard the conversation and spoke to Mr. Cappielo.

MR. LEBOUEF: Now look you fellows, don't be mad at me. I didn't do anything down here to bring on this trouble.

MR. CAPPIELO and MR. BROGAN (together): Oh, go away, old man, don't give us a hard time. You're one of George's boys, we know that. You stick with him.

MR. LEBOUEF: That's not true, but you know George.

Mr. Brogan, in a good natured gesture, picked up a rag and tossed it at Mr. LeBouef, who threw it back, and they all started to laugh.

MR. LEBOUEF: Well, I'll see you guys tomorrow.

The next day Mr. Roberts began his observations at about the same time that the #2 crew came on duty in the afternoon. Mr. Cappielo had already arrived and was talking with Mr. Hart. Just before the #2 crew took over, Mr. Roberts saw Joe Kern signal Mr. Hart about the work which the #1 crew was running. Mr. Cappielo spoke to Mr. Hart about the signal.

MR. CAPPIELO: Is that guy going crazy down there or something?

MR. HART: What do you mean?

MR. CAPPIELO: Well, that's the signal to straighten out the edges of the sheet, when you're running split rolls. You're not doing that here now. What's this edging stuff got to do with it?

MR. HART: I don't know a thing about it.

He made his familiar gesture of shrugging his shoulders and raising his hands, put on his cap, picked up his tools, and started for his locker. He tipped his hat to Mr. Cappielo and Mr. Brogan and left. The #2 crew started to work. Mr. LeBouef stayed around to oil the machine.

In a few moments a butt roll came up on the elevator. Mr. Cappielo took one look at it and went over and checked the clipboard, where the sequence in which the orders were to be run was listed. He walked over to the elevator and pushed the roll off the platform. He pushed the elevator switch. When the elevator got halfway down, where he could see between the basement and his floor, he yelled to Claude Schlick, the stock and glue man in the basement.

MR. CAPPIELO: You trying to screw me or something Claude?

MR. SCHLICK: What do mean, Charlie?

MR. CAPPIELO: I come on duty up here and I find one, two, two butt rolls on the floor and split rolls over in the corner. Now I see down there you are going to send up some more split rolls. There are three full rolls of 42 inch paper on the machines. Aren't you supposed to send the butt rolls up before the full ones?

MR. SCHLICK: It says on my order sheet that the runs call for 4000 feet of split rolls and then 21,000 feet of 42 inch rolls.

MR. CAPPIELO: Yeah, that's what it says here, but that isn't what's on the machines up here. Why did you send up 42 inch rolls, anyway? For George?

MR. SCHLICK: What do you mean? I sent up some split rolls, but I also sent up some 42 inch paper, too, because he wasn't through with the previous run.

MR. CAPPIELO: Not according to George. I just talked with him. He said you sent the 42 inch rolls up first; and he said you didn't know what you were doing, so what could he do. So he put the 42 inch paper on the stands and started the 21,000 foot run.

MR. SCHLICK: I did exactly what George said. What do you mean I sent up the 42 inch for the 21,000 foot order! He's not on that one, yet. The 4000 feet of split rolls have to come first. In fact, I sent up the first set of them a while back, and the rest are lined up down here ready to come up.

MR. CAPPIELO: That isn't what George said. (Both men got their respective clipboards.) Now look on your order sheet. It should read just like mine. Mine says that the order for 4000 feet of split rolls is to come before the 21,000 foot run of 42 inch paper. But George told me that you sent up the 42 inch rolls first. So he went on and did that order.

MR. SCHLICK: I'm coming up there. I've got my order sheet here. What he told you isn't right at all. He's not going to blame me for this. I'm not the fall guy for him. I don't know who he thinks he is, but if he told you I sent up the 42 inch rolls and skipped the split roll order of 4000 feet, well he's lying. I'm coming right up.

MR. CAPPIELO: O.K. (He smiled, walked back to the laminator, and spoke to Mr. Roberts.) I don't know what's gotten into George. This is the third or fourth day straight he's pulled something like this. He hasn't been cleaning up his machine before he leaves, and now he's messing up the runs. I know what he's done. He's run the 21,000 foot run first because he didn't want to mess with the split rolls. Oh, he's a cagey fellow. You've really got to watch him.

MR. ROBERTS: I don't think I understand, Charlie. What's happened?

MR. CAPPIELO: Well, you see he was supposed to go on split rolls an hour ago for this order of 4000 feet here, but he told me when I came on duty that Claude had sent up full rolls of 42 inch paper instead of the smaller split rolls. So he slapped them on the machines and started the 21,000 foot run. Now I know why Joe Kern signaled down here to straighten up the edges. He thought George was on the splits rolls, as his order sheet showed. But George didn't even start that split roll run at all.

MR. ROBERTS: What does this mean?

MR. CAPPIELO: It means simply that George has been screwing the whole damn' thing up, and he's been telling me that Claude in the basement is responsible for it. The same thing happened the other day, when Nick Jones asked him about a split roll run. He said Claude sent up the paper for the next order that day, too. He thinks I'm a greenhorn around here, but he can't pull something like this on me and think he's going to get away with it.

Mr. Schlick walked into the area carrying his clipboard.

MR. SCHLICK: Now here's the order sheet, Charlie. You can see right here on this side that he was to go on split rolls after he finished this 9000 foot run. I didn't know he had finished that run. So I sent one more series of 42 inch rolls, thinking he'd need them to complete the 9000 feet before going on the 26 inch split rolls. I thought I was doing him a favor. But the split rolls came right after the three full 42 inch rolls. Now, he didn't signal me at all that he didn't want those three rolls. I didn't know he was so near the end of the 9000 foot order. Fact is, I rang the bell and tried to talk to him on the intercom system, but he never answered. Isn't that right, Leo? I called at the same time I sent the three 42 inch rolls up.

MR. LEBOUEF: I don't remember anything about it, Claude.

MR. SCHLICK: Sure you do. Remember when I sent the full rolls up about an hour ago, I rang the bell, but I didn't get any answer from George. I thought, naturally, when he was through with the 9000 foot order he'd go on the split rolls. That's why I sent them right up. I never dreamed he'd take those three 42 inch rolls and start the 21,000 foot run.

MR. CAPPIELO: Well, he did, and he parked the split rolls over there in the corner. That accounts for the butt you sent up. You thought they came before the full 42 inch rolls for the 21,000 foot run. Well, Claude, George already began the 21,000 foot run and skipped the split roll run altogether. Pretty slick, isn't he?

MR. SCHLICK: You might have known what he did, Leo. Why didn't you say something?

MR. LEBOUEF: Now, Claude, you know George. You know how he is. He does what he wants to. I can't tell him anything. That's between the two of you.

MR. SCHLICK: Well, that's not right. He's got no right to behave that way. If that's the way he wants to work around here, I can do that, too. Now we got all those split rolls in the basement lined up to come up next, and he's off on the 42 inch 21,000 foot run. We'll need some more full rolls before we can go back and pick up that run, won't we, Charlie?

MR. CAPPIELO: That's the way I figure it.

MR. SCHLICK: And we get all those butts that haven't been used. They'll have to go back downstairs now. He didn't use those up either, did he?

MR. CAPPIELO: I don't know what's gotten into him; but like I said, just because I'm a greenhorn is no sign he can treat me this way.

MR. SCHLICK: I've taken all I'm going to take out of him, too. From now on he gets the butt rolls, he gets the telescope shaped rolls, he gets all the twisted, warped, dirty stock. Two can play this game. He's got no right to blame me for this, telling you I got the orders mixed up. Hell, he knows me better than that. I know what's up around this place.

MR. LEBOUEF: You can't do that to us, Claude. You'll hurt me just as much as George.

MR. SCHLICK: I hate to do it to you, Leo. I like you. I really hate to do it, but that's no way for him to act. He's got no right to make me a fall guy.

MR. CAPPIELO (laughing): It isn't that serious, Claude. He doesn't care about anyone, including his own crew. I've seen this coming on for some time.

MR. SCHLICK: I'm sorry this happened, Charlie. You guys here treat me decent, and he pulls something like that. I think it's terrible.

MR. CAPPIELO: I don't think he appreciates anything we do around here to help him. You take last night, we left all the stock lined up and left the machines full of paper for him. But when Al came on today, he was burning mad that there was no paper on the stands and no stock up. Just butts all over the floor. We try to help you out down there, by finding out what we have up here in stock. But George doesn't appreciate that. Well, send up the rest of the 42 inch, now that he's started it. I'll send the butts back down to you.

MR. SCHLICK: Okay, Charlie. But it isn't right and that's all there is to it.

In a few moments, Mr. Jones signaled to shut down the laminator. There was no more room at the receiving end to stack sheets until they cleared some space. Mr. Cappielo signaled back that he would clean out the wax pan at the same time. Mr. Roberts went over and watched him work.

MR. CAPPIELO: That George is a jealous man. Now we've just a bunch of greenhorns on this #2 crew, but we've really made him mad recently. George, this big crybaby, really has been mad ever since this crew has kept up with him on production or gone ahead of him; ever since a greenhorn like me has come up to his production and has been turning out as much sheet as he has. We're doing a good job, don't think we aren't. That's what's burning George up and the whole #1 crew. We've got them all riled up. We're the greenhorns, we're the guys that don't know anything. When I worked with Sam Barnett and Gus on the other shifts, they never could get near George's record. I don't know what it was, but he sure had them buffaloed.

MR. ROBERTS: You're the first that's ever kept up with George or gotten above him?

MR. CAPPIELO: That's about the size of it.

Mr. Brogan came over to the laminator where Mr. Cappielo was cleaning the wax pan.

MR. BROGAN: Say, Charlie, I just found out that they only did 98,000 feet in nine hours of work.

MR. CAPPIELO: (laughing): Yeah, I heard about that myself.

MR. BROGAN: No wonder the old man was touchy. Huh. I'd be touchy too. Ninety-eight thousand feet in nine hours! Wheeew! We can beat that with one arm tied behind us.

MR. CAPPIELO: I was just telling Dave about the #1 crew and how jealous they are, particularly George.

MR. BROGAN: You tell him that ever since we beat the record a couple of months ago, they haven't really gotten over it?

MR. CAPPIELO: Yeah. About three weeks back they tried to beat our record for eight hours.

MR. BROGAN: (laughing): They came within 5000 feet of doing it, too, but they like to kill themselves doing it.

MR. ROBERTS: What do you mean?

MR. BROGAN: Well, the next day the guys on the receiving end of the operation could hardly come to work, they were so beat. It was all they could do to drag themselves up to their jobs, and that day they did very little work.

MR. ROBERTS: They blew a fuse trying to beat you.

MR. BROGAN: They came pretty close, too. Like I said, within 5000 feet, but hell, I thought they were going to have to get some new men for the receiving end. I'm telling you, they were really tired. They were dead on their feet.

MR. CAPPIELO: I thought so too; they were really broken down.

MR. ROBERTS: But they still didn't beat your record.

MR. CAPPIELO: No, and I don't think they ever will, because those guys don't work together. This isn't an everyone-for-himself job and the other guy can go to hell. It won't work that way. You've got to pull together or you're through. If you don't, you never turn much paper out, and you'll get tired, too.

MR. ROBERTS: You like the guys on this crew?

MR. CAPPIELO: We're here to make a buck and the way to do that is get in there and pitch.

MR. ROBERTS: How do you do that?

MR. CAPPIELO: Nobody's a special character. We all work any and all jobs when they come along. It's for all of us, the bonus, that is. One guy makes a buck and we all make a buck.

MR. ROBERTS: And George?

MR. CAPPIELO: He's all out for George and no one else. He's just that way, a mean character, and that's all there is to it. I can't figure it out, except he's just plenty mad about us guys on the #2 crew showing him up. He's got all the experience, but here we are, a bunch of greenhorns, showing him how to work on this job. It's gotten to be too much for him. So he pulls these stunts like today. He's pretty cagey, but he's going to get in trouble. He knows his business down here, though. He knows more about that laminator than I probably ever will, but he can't make it with his fellows. They just don't click.

MR. ROBERTS: I see.

MR. CAPPIELO: I got on to him about leaving this wax pan dirty, and he cleaned it today, but that's the first time in three days running. I guess he thought I didn't know the difference, but he found out he can't get away with something like that. He'll hear about this paper deal he pulled, tomorrow, when he comes to work. As if he didn't know already what he did. The machine is still kinda messy, but he did clean it out once today.

MR. ROBERTS: He tries now and then?

MR. CAPPIELO: Sure. But he stands over this laminator and watches everything. He's been stepping it up now and then, because we're hot on his trail. He's got him an assistant, so that's really three against two. But in spite of the third man, Al and I are keeping up with him, and sometimes we're in the lead. But the assistant is going pretty soon now, and then we'll see what he does.

MR. ROBERTS: I hear he wants to keep his assistant on the crew.

Al Brogan spoke up.

MR. BROGAN: If he does, we're going to get one, too, that's for damn' sure.

MR. CAPPIELO: He isn't going to keep his assistant, Al. It's time he went back to work for a change. When he gets back to work, we won't have to worry much then. He'll be kept pretty busy running around shafting rolls, and he won't have time to stand over the laminator.

MR. BROGAN: If he gets an assistant, we're going to have one, too.

MR. CAPPIELO: Well, maybe so, I don't know.

Nick Jones came up to see Mr. Cappielo.

MR. CAPPIELO: I guess you heard about the stunt George pulled.

MR. JONES: Yeah, Al, came down and told us.

MR. CAPPIELO: I tell you, Nick, I'm getting pretty fed up with that guy. I don't know who he thinks he is, but that's the third time he pulled something this week. First he didn't clean out the wax pan, and the other day he didn't do the split rolls like the order sheet said, and today he pulls this.

MR. JONES: Come on, Charlie, you can cry on my shoulder right here if you want to. (He indicated his shoulder with his hand.) I know it's been a little tough, but we'll get along all right, Charlie.

MR. CAPPIELO: I suppose so.   (He laughed.)

MR. ROBERTS: It's a pretty raw deal, Nick?

MR. JONES: When you pull something like this, you only hurt yourself. You cause a bunch of hard feelings from everyone. It all averages out in a month's run. So he pulls something like the split rolls and gets a few more thousand feet today, but in a month's run it's six one way and a half dozen another.

MR. ROBERTS: You wouldn't want to do the same thing?

MR. JONES: It wouldn't be any good. George will be sorry about it. He's been doing something like that for two or three days now, and it isn't right. He knows it isn't right, and we know it, too. I'd much rather get to work and do what we have to do. Hey, Charlie, I think the area's pretty clear down there, so if you've got the paper up and the machine cleaned, we'll start whenever you say.

MR. CAPPIELO: I'll give you the horn signal in a minute, Nick.

THE NINE-HOUR RECORD RUN

For months after the record run Mr. Roberts was still hearing about the competition between the two crews. For example, Fred Dorn told him late in April that the #1 crew had set a new nine-hour record in production.

MR. ROBERTS: I see. Does that mean that the #1 crew now holds the plant record?

MR. DORN: Yes and no. The #2 crew still holds the record for the regular eight-hour shift, but the #1 crew set a new production record for a nine-hour run.

Mr. Roberts spoke to Leo LeBouef a little later that day.

MR. LEBOUEF: We set a new record the other day here on the laminator—150,000 feet in nine hours.

MR. ROBERTS: That makes you feel pretty good, I guess, Leo?

MR. LEBOUEF: Well, the #2 crew still holds the eight-hour record. I would have done better than what the figures show if that damn' glue station hadn't given me trouble.

MR. ROBERTS: How was that, Leo?

MR. LEBOUEF: It's pretty old, you know, but I know how to handle it. I was operating the laminator, so I couldn't watch the glue station too closely. But it acted up a lot. So I couldn't run the machine as fast as I would have liked. So the production wasn't quite as high as it might have been. But if you look at the bonus sheet over in the smoking area there, you'll see we didn't do bad that day at all.

Mr. Roberts looked at the chart in the smoking area. Joe Kern, the knife setter, was standing there smoking a cigarette. Up above the bonus chart was a picture of the #2 crew and the words: "Picture of the #2 crew after they set a new production record in the department."

MR. ROBERTS: I see they took a picture of the #2 crew.

MR. KERN: Yeah. (He looked up at it.) Not a very good picture, is it?

MR. ROBERTS: No, it is a little blurred.

Mr. Kern smiled and walked off towards the receiving area.

RELATIONS OF THE CREWS TO MANAGEMENT

With the thought that the attitudes of the crews toward management might throw additional light on the interrelations of the crews and on their production records, Mr. Roberts turned again to his notes. Both crews seemed to have accepted the idea that they should make an effort to produce the amount of work assigned. But their acceptance of the company's efforts to reduce waste was quite different.

CONTROLLING WASTE ON THE LAMINATOR

At the beginning of 1949 the management of the Briggs Box Company began a drive to cut down the amount of waste production. During the war, substitute materials had resulted in a reduction in the quality of the boxes the company manufactured. In 1953, customers were again becoming particular about the precision with which their specifications were met in respect to exact sizes and quality as well as dates of delivery. Supervisors heard rumors of a reorganization and restaffing of the company's quality and waste control system. Meanwhile, all levels of the production organization were urged to tighten up the controls they were already using and to communicate this spirit to the workers in their departments.

On one occasion, when the #2 crew was working on the day shift, Ed Dyer came into the area. After checking the order sheet, he picked up one of the orders and came over to Nick Jones.

MR. DYER: What happened here, Nick? I see on the order that you've got over 100 more boxes than the order calls for.

MR. JONES: Where's that, Ed?

MR. DYER: Down here. (He pointed to the bottom of the order sheet.)

MR. JONES: Oh, yes. Well, Ed, you see we had some trouble with that order. At first we were told that the order called for 1000 boxes. We ran those off and we changed paper and went on to another order. Then, Hal Anderson (from production planning) came down and added another 300 more boxes to the first order. I went up and talked with Charlie Cappielo, and we decided to run the rest of the order we had in the machine; because if we hadn't, we would have had to make three paper changes to get the necessary 300 boxes. As it was, we had to make one extra paper change, anyway. When we got the 300 boxes completed, Charlie wanted to use the remainder of the roll. There was such a little, so we ran off some extra boxes.

MR. DYER: That doesn't do our waste figures any good.

MR. JONES: I know you're right, Ed.

MR. DYER: I wish you'd tell me these things before you do them. I don't see how—this isn't the way to run things.

MR. JONES: It's only a few boxes, and Charlie wanted to run off that little butt roll he had. It would have been an awful lot of trouble if we hadn't done it. Why don't we stock the leftovers and use them for the next order that comes along?

MR. DYER: We may make a million boxes before we get that size again. We used to save leftovers some years back, even the little extra sheets. We had so many sheets stacked around here we couldn't get around in the department. So we had to throw them all away. (Pause.) Well, I guess it was all right. But try to watch that, Nick. The waste figure is pretty high.

MR. JONES: I will, Ed.

As Mr. Dyer left the area, Mr. Roberts turned to Mr. Jones.

MR. ROBERTS: What was that all about?

MR. JONES: Oh, he was a little hot and bothered because we ran a few extra sheets on that order he had in his hand. Charlie didn't want to send the butt roll back downstairs. Like I told Dyer, we had already done the order the way production planning had originally sent it down. We had already made a complete paper change. If we had done it the way Hal was telling us to do, Charlie would have had to make three paper changes. As it was, we made only one paper change to get the extra 300 boxes.

MR. ROBERTS: This waste thing is getting to be quite a problem?

MR. JONES: They blow hot and cold on it. One month the big push is to get waste down, particularly when we have a slack period in orders. But the next month, the orders pile up and production is everything. Waste could be cut down, I believe, but not so long as production is the most important thing. To get a better sheet you have to slow the machines down and let it stay longer in the pressure section. Doing that means that production will be slowed down. So if we slow down production during a busy month, the foremen want to know why we aren't getting the sheet out. So we speed up production and the quality of the sheet suffers and waste goes up. Besides, sometimes the foremen get pretty excited over little things.

MR. ROBERTS: The 100 extra boxes isn't much?

MR. JONES: Sure. The time we would waste stopping the machines and changing paper rolls would amount to more actual money than running off the old roll and starting with a clean one. That's what we did. Besides, Charlie doesn't like a lot of butt rolls around. It means extra work when that paper size comes up again, for he'll have to put the small butt on the machine first before using a full paper roll. You would think that the 100 boxes added up to a lot of money to hear Dyer talk.

MR. ROBERTS: It isn't much in the long run?

MR. JONES: Practically nothing. Also, sometimes I can't understand all this talk about waste. You would think that the customers never paid for a bit of it. They pay for all the trimming and design cutting that is done. Besides, the other waste isn't a total loss. The company bales it up and either has it reprocessed or sells it to scrap dealers.

MR. ROBERTS: They're making a pretty big issue of this?

MR. JONES: Well, they think that all mistakes can be caught and waste cut to almost nothing. You take the other day. There was a mistake on the job. A big stink was raised over it and made everyone feel terrible. That didn't do any good at all. Everyone makes mistakes on this job. I remember about three years ago, when Bill Evans, Jim Carson, and I were working on this job, an order involving nearly $1500 was ruined. I was the knife man at the time. I set the knives to cut the sheet at 61.8 inches. It looked like 61.8 to me. When those sheets got over to printing, the mistake was discovered. We brought the order slip back and found the mistake. Instead of the order sheet reading 61.8, it should have read 67.8. But somewhere along the line the top of the "7" had gotten covered by a drop of ink and you couldn't read it, and it looked just like a "1."

MR. ROBERTS: What happened?

MR. JONES: We were pretty much on the spot. I thought for a time I would be fired. But Bill and Jim both said they had looked at the order sheet and it looked like a "1" to them. Fact is, the foreman working down here on the laminator at that time said it looked like 61.8 to him, too. That made four of us; but when things got hot, the foreman wasn't sure. But Bill, Jim, and I stuck together. Dyer came around a couple of times and said something about the mistake, but we didn't know how we stood with the company. We didn't know whether we'd be fired or not.   And then one afternoon, we were all called up to Fred Dorn's office.   So Bill, Jim, and I went up.   We thought we might be fired, but that meant firing three workers at one time.   Don't get me wrong; we were all damn' sorry it happened, and we don't want it to happen again, but there it was.   The sheets were already ruined.

When we got up to the office, both Dyer and Dorn were there. Well, Dorn started to say something, but then he got so mad he gave Dyer the order sheet and walked out of the office.   Well, Dyer told us that there are two places to check the measurements on the order sheet, and the second place, up in the top right-hand corner, clearly indicated that the sheets were to be cut for 67.8.   Up to that time we had always taken the measurements from the center of the page. Dyer said we should have looked at the second measurement, and we would have seen the error.   He was correct.   There wasn't any smudge mark over the figures up in the right-top corner.   It was very clearly 67.8.   Of course, from then on, we check both figures. We haven't pulled a Herbert Anderson since.

MR. ROBERTS: A Herbert Anderson?

MR. JONES: Yeah, that was the name of the order we ruined.   Herbert Anderson & Company.   Ever since then we refer to a boner as a "Herbert Anderson."   If you want to get the fellows excited, just say, "Better watch out—or you'll pull a Herbert Anderson."   Just a few weeks back we were joking about the Herbert Anderson order when Fred Dorn came by and we made some remark that we hadn't pulled any Herbert Andersons for a long time.   "You'd better not do it, either," Dorn said and laughed.   That's the first time I've seen him laugh about the waste problem.

On February 1, 1953, a reorganization of the company's quality and waste control system went into effect.   The former head of the department was transferred to other work, and a waste and quality inspector, reporting directly to the plant manager, was assigned to each department.   Jack Zolbe was transferred from sales and service to head the waste and quality control system in the fiberboard department.   Mr. Zolbe had been working in the sales office and was told that if he succeeded in reducing waste in the department, he would receive a promotion to a position as salesman.   He had been on the job about three weeks, when Mr. Roberts met him checking the quality chart near the receiving end of the laminator.

MR. ZOLBE: I've been trying to go around and just watch the workers at their various jobs.   You know, get acquainted and see where the major problems are in this waste thing. I wanted to work on the various jobs down here so I would really know the problem, but the plant manager didn't think that would be necessary. He told me when he put me on this job that the waste figure down here is far too high—something like 12.6 per cent for the past few months. He wants that dropped considerably. Too much money is being swept out the door.

MR. ROBERTS: I guess the job is still pretty new to you?

MR. ZOLBE: Well, yes, but it's coming. In these three weeks I've been here we have dropped the waste figure to around 10.8. That's not bad for a start, but the plant manager says we must get it lower, to around 8.2. That would be nice, but I don't know.

MR. ROBERTS: You don't know whether you can do that or not?

MR. ZOLBE: That 8.2 figure is pretty idealistic when you get down here on the floor and look things over. You take today, for instance. This is going to be a bad day for my waste figures. The fellows on the laminator have worked all day with split rolls. It's difficult to cut waste down when you work with stuff like that. But I think if the fellows help me some, I can get the waste figure down.

MR. ROBERTS: They have got to get behind it too?

MR. ZOLBE: You know, a fellow can't be here all the time watching them. The workers have to help me. That's the most important thing. If I can get the fellows to like me, if I can convince them I'm not trying to make things tough on them, then they can make a go of it here with the waste problem and the plant manager will give me a crack at selling.

MR. ROBERTS: You'd like that?

MR. ZOLBE: Plenty. That's where my heart really lies. The plant manager suggested if we can clean this problem up pretty well down here, I'll go up to sales. That's where the money is and where you meet the people. Sales is the department where you meet customers and display the products and take their orders. Boy, would I like that job! That's what I'm shooting for.

MR. ROBERTS: Have you worked in the plant very long?

MR. ZOLBE: I came up from the bench. I want to move up, of course, if I can. I believe I can lick this waste problem down here, but there's a lot of bugs to take out. I've got me a poster and chart up on the bulletin board. It shows the workers the daily waste record and also indicates graphically the average waste for the month. Fact is, I've got the waste figures for the past three years charted up there on the poster.

MR. ROBERTS: This helps to get the workers interested?

MR. ZOLBE: I hope so. My most important job is still to win the workers' confidence. Sam Lynch, the trucker on the day shift, who takes the laminated sheets over to the presses, and Mel Freeman, the night worker on the same job, weigh the waste for the crews and report those figures to the office upstairs where they figure the workers' bonuses. Sam and Mel also give me the daily waste figures so I can chart my averages. That way, we see how we are doing in getting waste down. I've gotten these men to like me, so that helps plenty.

MR. ROBERTS: They are getting behind it?

MR. ZOLBE: Yeah, and getting the other workers interested is about the size of licking this problem. I go around and talk to all of them on their jobs. I think that's coming along pretty well.

MR. ROBERTS: The workers like you quite a bit?

MR. ZOLBE: I think so. When they see you are a pretty decent Joe, they don't give you too much trouble. The big trouble starts right there on the laminator. If the sheet is bad there, then it's going to be bad all over the department; the printers will have to throw the sheets away, and the assembly workers will have to do likewise. Well, I've got to be looking around and checking my waste.

About three weeks elapsed before Mr. Roberts and Mr. Zolbe had another extended conversation. Mr. Zolbe chatted with Mr. Roberts now and then, but only to say "Hello" and to indicate that he was pretty busy. One afternoon Mr. Roberts ran into him up at the front end of the laminator. He was sitting on the bench in the smoking area.

MR. ZOLBE: Today's a bad one. We've worked all day long on split rolls. Besides having production way down, split rolls means that the waste will be terrible. Every time they have to make a paper change, of course, they have two rolls from which to cut paper instead of one.

MR. ROBERTS: It's not going so good, your waste control?

MR. ZOLBE: Well, it varies from week to week, Dave. Now I think a pretty good waste figure would be around 9.2 per cent. It's a lot better than when I took over back in February. It was up around 12.8 then. But the plant manager upstairs thinks a very good waste figure would be around 8.2 or something like that. I think he's right. I'd like to see that, too, but I don't think we'll ever make it. We'll never make it when we have orders like the ones we have to put up with today.

MR. ROBERTS: This waste picture is a pretty big headache for you, Jack?

MR. ZOLBE: Yeah, it's a headache all right. You see, we've got all sorts of waste around here. We've got what we call customer's waste and what we call worker's waste. There's also a certain amount of waste that accumulates when the man down in the basement trims the paper prior to sending it up the elevator to the laminator. I've really brought that figure down. That used to run from 200 to 400 pounds a day. I've gotten it down to about 60 pounds. I've gotten the man down there to watch it very closely and he's doing a fine job.

But then when the paper gets up here on the laminator, they've always got a few sheets to cut off here and there before they start using it. But if you watch the workers and kinda sell them on the idea, then the waste comes down quite a bit. It's gotten much better since I've taken over. You see, if you don't watch the workers pretty closely, they may be a little careless. For instance, sometimes the operator or helper here nick the paper too deeply with their paper knives and that means three or four more layers on the roll are wasted. I've asked them to watch that. They dump the waste over in that cart. We have a cart here by the laminator, one down at the receiving area, two over by the printers, and one in the assembly area.

MR. ROBERTS: What happens to the paper when it goes to the carts?

MR. ZOLBE: It's weighed in. We have a scale out on the loading platform behind the work area here. Sam Lynch usually weighs the waste. You have got to watch him pretty closely.

You see, when it's cold, Sam sometimes won't go out there to weigh it. I've caught him just making a rough estimate. But he's weighing it now. I got on to him and tried to help him do his job. Sam weighs the cart here by the laminator, the one in the receiving area, and the first of the two that are over by the printers. Anything that won't go through the presses over there is counted as laminator waste. So those three carts are weighed pretty carefully, for I believe if I can stop the waste here on the laminator, I'll lick the problem. If we get good sheet to start with, it remains good in almost all the rest of the operations.

The biggest percentage of the total waste, though, still comes from the category of customer's waste. That waste is unavoidable. Punching out the designs and trimming the sheet is all customer waste, and you'll never be able to avoid that. The only point is, when you look at the monthly figure, the customer's waste is always in the total figure with the waste in the entire department. Now when one reads that figure, he is supposed to deduct the unavoidable customer's waste percentage. The customer pays for that waste when he contracts for the boxes, so the company is losing nothing there.

MR. ROBERTS: The plant manager sometimes forgets that a large percentage of the figure at the end of the month is customer's waste, which you can't avoid too much?

MR. ZOLBE: That's a big part of it. Now you take George Hart here. He's very conscientious about this waste thing. He tries very hard to keep the waste down. He's got several methods of doing that, and they work. I've won his confidence, and he helps me a lot. That's the biggest problem you have, Dave, showing the workers you're really interested in keeping waste down and finding ways and means of getting them interested in doing it.

MR. ROBERTS: But you have trouble doing that?

MR. ZOLBE: Oh, sure. You see, they don't see the over-all picture like some of us do. They don't see the importance of waste. They don't see the reasons why they should always look at it so closely, as long as they get production out. Getting production out and making a bonus is the most important thing to them. Waste makes them lose a certain amount on their bonus; but I think they believe that by putting out more production, they compensate for that waste loss. Probably they do to a large degree, but that doesn't help me much with my waste percentage.

The months of February and March went by, and Mr. Zolbe expressed to Mr. Roberts his confidence that waste was getting lower. His figures for both February and March had dropped to around 9.4 per cent. Early in April, Mr. Roberts talked with him again at some length. They were sitting on the bench in the smoking area.

MR. ZOLBE: I don't guess we're going to be able to get this waste down at all, unless we get some long runs again like we used to have a couple of weeks ago. Boy, this place has been like a graveyard this week.

MR. ROBERTS: Business is slow, Jack?

MR. ZOLBE: You tell it. Things are really buzzing up in some of the other departments; but down here in laminating, there hasn't been a lot to do. It's been short, choppy orders and plenty of waste. I've decided to clamp down right here on this waste problem. It's not getting any better. I'm afraid it's worse than before I took over.

You know, I thought I was doing a pretty good job on this waste problem. When I took over officially, the first of February, the figures were pretty high. About 12.4 or 5, and then I got it down to around 9.4, at least I thought I had. Remember some time ago when I told you the plant manager wanted the figures to be dropped to around 8.2? Well, I don't know how that can ever be done, particularly with this last month just behind us. Let me show you what I mean.

He took a small notebook out of his pocket and pointed to some figures.

MR. ZOLBE: You see here. These are the daily input records for last month, and in the next column is the waste for each day expressed in pounds for the laminator operation. Look here, waste reads: 250 pounds for March 1; 320 pounds for March 2; 270 pounds for March 3; and so on. Looks pretty, doesn't it? Well, these figures don't tell the whole story at all. Come the end of March, the balers reported the monthly total waste figure for this department. Take a guess what the difference was between what I had on my records and what they reported after they had baled the waste?

MR. ROBERTS: I'm afraid I have no idea, Jack.

MR. ZOLBE: Thirty thousand pounds! That's how big the discrepancy really was.

MR. ROBERTS: I don't think I understand.

MR. ZOLBE: I mean that the figures here for the daily reports of 250 pounds, 320 pounds, and 270 pounds, and so on are just not accurate. If you break down the 30,000 pounds that was not reported on the daily weight for the month of March, you'll find that for the laminator alone all these figures are just about half of the actual waste for each day.

Now I know it's hard for those fellows, Sam Lynch and Mel Freeman, to report the actual weight, particularly since they are also on the laminator bonus list. They didn't report the right weights once last month. What did they do? I guess they took the carts out on the scales and when it read 550 pounds, they called it 250 pounds for the day and reported that to the office that figures the bonuses. So at the end of the month we were 30,000 pounds short on my books, but we had the waste all baled and weighed.

Now we had the same trouble in February, but I thought it was because we had gotten off to a bad start and I was new on the job and had plenty to learn. I knew we weren't doing so well as the figures kept saying we were; I suspected we were riding for a fall. Down inside I knew those fellows weren't reporting every pound of waste, but I never dreamed that they would do this to me. Thirty thousand pounds is an enormous figure, and I had no record at all about it. I didn't learn about it until the figures were recorded upstairs in the office and the plant manager called me in.

We've had several meetings about this problem since. We had a big meeting just the other day and out of it some decisions for changes were made. First of all, it was decided that Sam and Mel would not weigh the waste any more. We decided that two of the workers over in the assembly area of this department would be assigned the job. And have these first three days for this month made a difference! The waste figure is getting worse instead of better.

For the 1st, 2nd, and 3rd of April, the waste figures have been awful. Just look; for April 1, 1000 pounds; for April 2, no input in the laminator at all, and we still had over 1000 pounds of waste. Of course that was waste from the printers, and we have no input, because the laminator didn't run that day, and there isn't any production figure to help soften the blow.

And I have a hard time trying to tie down where the waste comes from. Sometimes you have a cart down in assembly that has several hundred pounds of waste, but actually the sheet was ruined up on the printers or over on the laminator. So you can't blame assembly for that. They just tell you that the sheets came down to them that way. So you go up to the printers, and you've got to be careful there, because the sheet might have been ruined over on the laminator.

You see, oftentimes the sheet is no good when it comes off the laminator, but the workers there send it over to the printers anyway. When it gets there the printers just have to dump it there or try to push it through. Then it gets all mixed up when they try to use it, for the assembly department has to throw it out. All I know is that we are getting this huge waste figure at the end of each day and it has got to stop.

Don't get me wrong, we got all sorts of other reasons for this. A large percentage of all the waste that comes through here is customer's waste. You know, that's the waste caused by stamping out designs and trimming off sides and edges. This the customer pays for. That's a large percentage of the whole figure, but sometimes they don't look at that too closely up in the front office. They always look at the grand total, and it nearly always looks bad.

MR. ROBERTS: How do you see your problem, Jack?

MR. ZOLBE: Well, that's why I'm camped right here on this bench. I know if I'm going to cut down waste anywhere in this department, it's got to be done right here on the laminator.   But I'm not quite sure what can be done.

You see, every time we have a nice long run we usually have a low waste figure.   But every time we get a bunch of short, choppy runs like we've been having the last couple of weeks, what happens?   Every roll that comes up here we've got to take a lot of waste paper off of it.   Every time an order is changed, paper is wasted.   You just can't avoid it.   Every time you make a paper change or a knife or wax change you're going to ruin a certain amount of the paper.

MR. ROBERTS: Then much of your problem has to do with the kinds of orders you get and the nature of the paper used?

MR. ZOLBE: Yeah, that's what I think one of the main problems is; you can see along the columns in this book that when we have a long run, we have little waste; and every time we have a short run, the waste figures jump right up.   We're going to have another meeting in the plant manager's office tomorrow.   I don't know if the foremen of this department will be there or not.   Also, Dave, one of the big problems is getting the workers to cooperate.   You see, the two men under me, who go around to the three work areas here in the department to check the quality of the sheet, can only ask the workers to make the corrections.   They can't force them.   That's within the jurisdiction of the foremen here, and at times we have trouble finding them.   It's only possible to check the work areas once every 30 minutes or so, and in that space of time the workers can ruin a lot of sheets.

Just take the other evening.   Pete Hunter, the quality inspector in the evening, checked a large order of sheets.   He thought something was wrong with them, but he wasn't sure.   He thought the printing was a little off center, which it was, but that wasn't the real difficulty.   The next day the real error was found; the boxes had been run through the printers in reverse, so when they tried to fold the boxes over in the assembly section, one side of the box hung over the edge of the fold about a $\frac{1}{4}$ inch and the other side was that much shorter.

MR. ROBERTS: What happened?

MR. ZOLBE: Well, that was a big customer.   Six thousand boxes were involved, and they were bad.   About midway through the morning, the plant manager called Ed Dyer and myself up to his office, and he was pretty sore.   I can still remember what he said: "Are you proud of that?   Well, Ed and Jack, what do you plan to do about it?"   What could we do?   Three operators on the printers were involved in the mistake, and we couldn't fire all three of them.   I talked to the fellows myself, and they felt awful about it, but the mistake was done. We worked around and finally salvaged a goodly number of them, but they are seconds and this customer is pretty cranky; only the best for him. Also, I think the company is trying to woo him for more of his business, and this bum shipment of boxes won't help matters at all.

MR. ROBERTS: Are things looking up at all?

MR. ZOLBE: This is a thankless job I've got, Dave. Now the other day, we did pretty well on waste. I went around and congratulated the workers; they did it, not I. I told them that. I was happy for them. That helped a little, after we had changed the men who weighed the waste for them.

MR. ROBERTS: They didn't like your swapping men to weigh the waste?

MR. ZOLBE: Well, what can you expect? Sam and Mel share slightly in the laminator crews' bonuses. Besides that, they like the fellows who work on the laminator operation. So after we made the change, they didn't like it at all. Fact is, I had trouble getting them to speak to me for a few days.

The crews raised quite a stink with Dyer and Dorn about this waste thing. They said that if we are going to be so careful about weighing the sheets, then they want to trim their own paper before it goes on the laminator. Dyer and Dorn couldn't see anything wrong with that, and I couldn't either. The old practice was to take the initial rough sheets off the paper rolls in the basement before sending them up the elevator to the laminator and glue station. But the workers wanted to trim their own rolls, for they said that they could save paper that way. Even when the paper rolls were trimmed in the basement before being sent up, they said that they had to retrim them because the outside of the paper got dirty, and sometimes several sheets were ruined in getting the paper from the basement to the machines. So we decided to make the change. The paper rolls are now sent up from the basement untrimmed, and the workers do the trimming themselves. But as far as the waste picture goes, we are right back where we started about two and a half months ago.

MR. ROBERTS: How's that, Jack?

MR. ZOLBE: When the men in the assembly section started weighing the waste more accurately, the workers' bonus on the laminator dropped a little, and that's when I started getting the dirty looks. Well, now that the workers are trimming their own paper rolls, the bonus has gone back up, but the waste is still just as high as before.

MR. ROBERTS: I don't get it.

MR. ZOLBE: You see, when the workers started trimming their own rolls, we got them another cart to throw that waste in. That waste is not counted against the laminator crews. So what happened? You can probably guess. They are throwing nearly all the laminator waste in the cart marked for paper trim. Just go down and take a look at the two carts. The trim cart is stacked up as high as it will go every day, and the laminator waste cart is just about two-thirds full.

I know what they are doing, and I think the foremen and Dorn know, too. I can almost check the figures against my book. I predict that today the trim cart will weigh about 420 pounds and the laminator waste cart will weigh about 400 pounds. To make the figures right for the laminator waste, about 250 pounds of the trim cart's waste should be put in the laminator's waste cart. I know that, but what can I do? As far as I'm concerned, the whole waste system in here stinks.

The plant manager knows the problem down here. He knows that as long as the company is stressing production and more production, I can't do anything much with quality and waste. I've told him more than once that as long as the machines have long, uninterrupted runs and we have good paper and good wax, the waste will be low. I've shown him that waste has never been below 10.4 in most of the past years. But he says, "How about 1944, when it was 7.5?" Now he knows and I know and everyone in this department knows why the waste for that year was so low. We had an extra knife setter working right over there on the receiving end of the laminator and one upstairs in the cellophane department who did nothing but take misshaped, short sheets and partly damaged stock and recut them for second quality products. That's why the waste was down to 7.5 for that year. He knows that. But to emphasize that the sheet should be made right the first time, they cut that out.

MR. ROBERTS: It doesn't do much good to say this to the plant manager?

MR. ZOLBE: He's convinced that waste can come down, and he believes that just by saying it over and over again, it will. I try to tell him that as long as input is low and we are working with split rolls, the waste is never going to come down. Like I said before, Dave, this is a thankless job. I've thought about quitting, but I don't know. When I first came to Briggs, before the war, I worked on the bench with the rest of the workers. I got in a fight with one of them once and was fired because of it.

During the war years, I was in the Navy and worked with the fellows. They liked me and we got along fine. Take in here, I know these workers. They tell me what they think about this company. They won't tell anyone else around here in the management bunch what they think, but they'll tell me.

Well, you had better untwist your ear. I haven't blown off like this in a long time, but now and then I just get fed up. Well, I'll see you later.

WORK RECORDS

As part of his study, Mr. Roberts was interested in further exploring the extent to which differences between the crews correlated with their work records, particularly with the amounts of production, wastage, and downtime. Realizing that, quite apart from the crews' actions, these data might be affected by the number and types of runs assigned, Mr. Roberts first examined the actual assignments to see whether the work given to the two crews appeared to be approximately the same.

WORK ASSIGNMENTS

Mr. Roberts collected data for a 75-day sample period on order setups and knife changes, which were a measure of the number of orders handled by the crews, and on roll-change setups, which indicated changes in paper size, type of run (such as split rolls on triplex laminating), or both. When he examined the assignments, Mr. Roberts found only small differences in the number and types of orders distributed to the #1 and #2 crews. These data are presented in Table 1.

Table 1

Compared Work Assignments
(75-Day Period)

	Order Setups & Knife Changes	Roll Change Setups
Crew #1	1,509	227
Crew #2	1,484	210
Difference (approximate % #1 > #2)	25 (1.7%)	17 (8%)

A mathematical interpretation of the differences in Table 1 is as follows:

If the orders had been assigned without regard for which crew was to handle them, the probability is approximately 0.65 of obtaining differences, through random fluctuation, at least as large as the observed difference in the order setups and knife changes. A corresponding statement holds for the roll change setups, with the probability in that case of approximately 0.40.

OUTPUT, WASTE, AND DOWNTIME

Turning to the work records of the two crews, Mr. Roberts obtained detailed production figures (see Table 2) for the full seven months of his study. He obtained daily output and waste control data and monthly totals on downtime. Downtime was reported by each crew to indicate the amount of time spent in resolving machine difficulties not "directly attributable to their error." This system had been started so that the crews would not be penalized for production time lost for reasons beyond their control.

Summary figures from these data are presented in Table 2, followed by a mathematical interpretation. Graphic presentations of output, waste, and downtime data for the period including the seven months of the study and the ten months preceding the study are given in Exhibits 5, 6, and 7, respectively.

Table 2

Production Data
(7 Months, November 1952 through May 1953)

	Output (Ave. daily linear footage)	Waste (Ave. daily weight in lbs.)	Downtime (7-month totals in hours)
Crew #1	92,567	615	61.7
Crew #2	93,575	667	35.4
Difference (& approx. %) {#1 > #2 / #2 > #1}	1,008 (1.1%)	52 (8%)	26.3 (74%)

The following mathematical statements can be made, based upon the data Roberts collected:

Output. If the true long-run output rates of the two crews had been the same, the probability is about 0.64 of observing differences, arising from random fluctuation, at least as large as the observed value, 1,008.

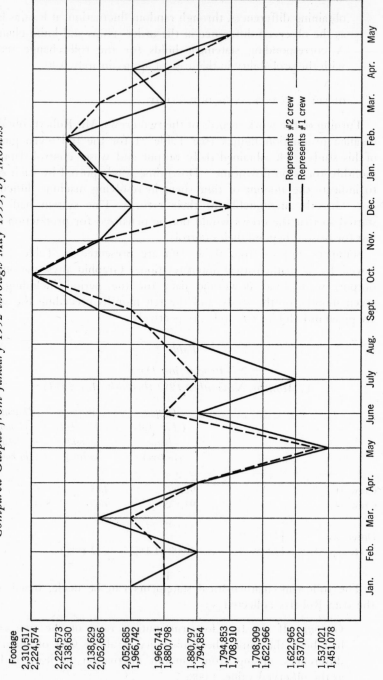

EXHIBIT 5

THE BRIGGS BOX COMPANY

Compared Output from January 1952 through May 1953, by Months

EXHIBIT 6

THE BRIGGS BOX COMPANY

Compared Downtime from January 1952 through May 1953, by Months

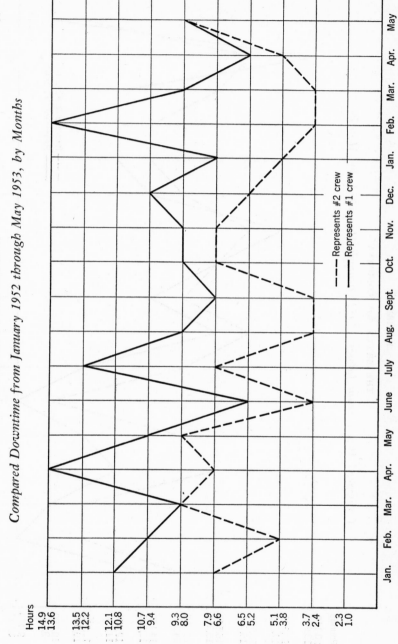

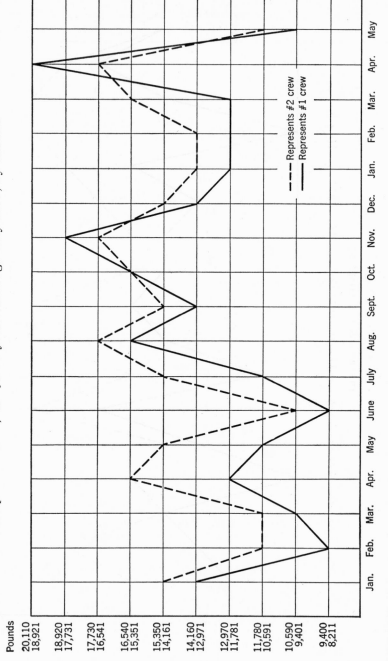

EXHIBIT 7

THE BRIGGS BOX COMPANY

Compared Waste from January 1952 through May 1953, by Months

Waste. If the true long-run waste rates of the two crews had been the same, the probability is less than 0.05 of observing a difference, arising from random fluctuation, as large as the observed value, 52.

Downtime. If the true long-run downtime rates of the two crews had been the same, the probability is less than 0.01 of observing a difference, arising from random fluctuation, as large as the observed value, 26.3.

MANAGEMENT'S VIEWS OF THE CREWS

To round out his study, Mr. Roberts reviewed his conversations with members of management concerning the crews. Two of these conversations seemed typical of the management's approach.

FRED DORN'S VIEWS

One day not long after Mr. Roberts had begun his observations in the plant, Fred Dorn, the superintendent, inquired how he was getting along.

MR. ROBERTS: Fine. I am beginning to get a picture of both crews. There is one impression that I would like to check with you, though. Am I right in thinking that there are quite a few differences between the #1 crew and the #2 crew?

MR. DORN: Yes, I guess so. What sort do you have in mind?

MR. ROBERTS: When I speak of differences, Fred, I don't necessarily mean that one is better than the other. I don't know quite how to put it, but I've noticed that the #2 crew seems to work pretty well together. They're always helping one another.

MR. DORN: Well, if you want to talk about the two crews that way, #1 crew versus #2 crew, I guess there are some differences. I think the two crews complement one another very well. With the #1 crew you have the experience, the skill and the maturity. With the #2 crew you have a hard-working, rough, young outfit. You know, Charlie Cappielo runs the machines at top speed whenever he can, but then he has to slow them down quite frequently. He doesn't keep the steady pace that George Hart and Leo LeBouef do. Furthermore, the workers on the #1 crew look after the machinery, and that's very important. If it wasn't for the care and experience of George Hart, Leo LeBouef, and Joe Kern, those machines would give us no end of trouble. They are constantly checking them and reporting needed repairs. If they weren't cared for, the #2 crew would get into trouble.

I'd say that there is something of a difference between the two crews; but like I said earlier, they complement one another. Charlie would run into a lot of trouble, if George and Leo didn't look after the laminator and glue station the way they do.

Also, if you look at the production figures over a long period of time, say three years, you'll find that the #1 crew are the more stable workers. They can be counted on in a pinch to come through. Joe Kern, the knife setter on the #1 crew, has more technical skill and experience than Nick Jones, who has the same position on the #2 crew.

MR. ROBERTS: You're pretty happy with the crews the way they are?

MR. DORN: Well, yes. Like I said, I would like to improve them, but they do complement one another beautifully.

ED DYER'S VIEWS

Mr. Roberts talked with Ed Dyer, supervisor of the crews, in Mr. Dyer's office late in April. On the wall above his desk was a photograph of the #2 crew, with the inscription "The #2 crew broke the production record, January 14, 1949." Mr. Roberts looked at the picture.

MR. ROBERTS: I see you've got a photograph of the #2 crew.

MR. DYER: Yes. You know both of those crews have been doing a wonderful job the last few months. Let me show you what I mean. (He took two folders from his desk drawer. He opened the top folder, took out some papers, and pointed to some figures.) You see here, for January the average production per hour was 51.4; for February it was 52.5; for March it was 54.3; and this month—April—I think it's going to be around 56.8. That's all right.

MR. ROBERTS: You sound pleased.

MR. DYER: It's wonderful, particularly when you consider that the runs haven't been so hot this new year. Actually, many of them have been short, and the paper hasn't been so good either, and yet they have kept this production pretty consistently.

They haven't done work like this since the war years. During the war years, of course, we had all the work we could possibly do. We had a four or five month backlog of work. Then the stress was entirely on production. The customers would buy all the boxes we could make, but now, of course, it's gotten much tighter. Production has slacked off considerably, and the quality of the box has become primary. We are putting out more boxes and better boxes per hour than ever before, except perhaps during the war years.

MR. ROBERTS: I see.   How do you account for this, Ed?

MR. DYER: Frankly, I can't very well.   Except I think, of course, the bonus is helping an awful lot.   Naturally we have our troubles with the workers.   We have some trouble with the #1 crew.   They fight among themselves quite a bit.   You know, they're always complaining about the orders.   They want to know why they get all the short, choppy runs and the triplex laminating.

They've got some funny idea that the #2 crew gets all the long, gravy runs.   Of course, it isn't true; but some of the guys on the #1 crew think so.   I've looked over the order sheets very carefully to see if their complaints have any basis in fact.   I even went up to the planning department a few times to see Hal Anderson and talk to him about this condition.   He's been hearing about it, too.   The #1 crew thinks he's been giving all the good runs to the #2 crew. We both went over the order sheets for both crews, and we could see no difference.   One day the #2 crew had triplex laminating and a lot of short orders with a great many knife changes, and the next day the #1 crew might have the triplex laminating and short, choppy orders.   As far as we could see, all the long runs and the short, rough runs were equally distributed between the crews.   I even took the order sheets down to the #1 crew and showed them that what they said just wasn't true.   I used to get alarmed about their complaints, but when I looked over the order sheets carefully with Hal, I realized there wasn't much to them.

MR. ROBERTS: You don't see anything too serious in what they say.

MR. DYER: No.   How can I, when they turn out work like this? Just look at this month's orders.   The #1 crew is about 9000 feet ahead per week in production over the #2 crew.   Now you know, if they were really mad at each other and were doing a bad job, well, I'd be worried; but as it is, and like I tell 'em: "Look, you fellows complain a lot; but do you want me to bust you up, when you put out sheet like this?"   They're doing swell, when it comes to work.   Oh, sure, they argue and fight among themselves.   You take George—I don't want to mention any personal names or single out anyone—we have two or three who don't get along too well on the #1 crew.   But like I said to them, "You want me to break it up, when you're doing so well?"

MR. ROBERTS: You think they quarrel to be quarreling, more or less.

MR. DYER: I know they have their problems and fight and scrap quite a bit among themselves, but I can't take it too seriously as long as they work like they do.   I sure don't want to take anyone off that crew, because I might do damage to the rest, when I put someone else on it.

MR. ROBERTS: It's just the ups and downs of working together.

MR. DYER: I guess that's it. It just comes and goes in streaks. It's like this three-month high-production period I just showed you. It's the big feast. Come July, the middle of the summer, you'll have a big famine; it'll bobble all up and down. We seldom have such a thing around here as an average production month. It's always real high or real low. There's nothing in between. I can't figure it out, either. Of course, without the bonus system we'd have trouble getting out production. I'd sure hate to see it taken away, but now the talk around the supervisors is that the company wants to take the bonus system out, if possible. When the time and motion people came in here to set up the standards on the laminator, they were set pretty low. The workers can always make a bonus on the laminator; and if they work pretty hard, they can make a big one.

MR. ROBERTS: Then you think work and production down here is closely tied up with the bonus system. If you lose the bonus as an incentive, you'd be up the creek in getting production out.

MR. DYER: Well, maybe not quite that. But we'd be in trouble. I'd be in favor of a bonus system throughout the whole department, instead of just in the laminating and printing sections. But, like I said, the company now wants to cut out all bonus work, if they can. That's going to be a tough one.

Part Three

Interpersonal Dynamics

THE five cases in this section concentrate on individuals in work settings. In the first three, the individuals' membership in small, face-to-face work groups is a relevant part of the data. In the fourth case, Grosvenor House, the central figure is a manager-entrepreneur whose work setting involves him in relationships with several groups and individuals. The fifth case concerns the relationship between a senior and junior minister in a church. This "pair" relationship re-enacts many of the dilemmas of authority experienced throughout the life cycle.

In each case, descriptions of the individuals' interpersonal relations with others, in and around their work settings, are presented along with their personal interpretations of these events. Each individual's "world view," in terms of values, motives, and the emotional meanings attached to external things, ideas, and people, is described by himself in the interview, or conversational setting, and is, at the same time, reflected in his characteristic behavior patterns with others.

In addition to the person and his behavior toward others, the cases include indications of others' characteristic behaviors toward the person. A secondary pattern becomes evident: the manners in which one person's characteristic behavior tends to evoke patterned behavior from others. Margaret Mahoney, for example, seeks and gets caring from others, while Richard Carleton rejects and is rejected by others. Joseph Wexler's behavior causes him to be fired. Josef Belair, in

255

Grosvenor House, is suspicious, competitive, and critical toward his customers and subordinates; this attitude is seen to cause their dissatisfied response. In each case, the consequences, in terms of the others' behaviors, reinforce the person's initial attitude; they "prove" his personal theory, or, more accurately, his behavior toward them causes his theory to be proved. This effect has been called the "self-fulfilling prophecy" by some, "the interpersonal reflex" by others, and is a well-documented pattern described in the literature of psychotherapy.[1]

The Howard Atkins and Joseph Wexler case confines itself to "here-and-now" data—the individuals' behaviors and verbalized attitudes during a relatively short time period. The interpersonal behavior patterns and their consequences may be analyzed in relation to each other, but leave open the question, "Why do these people behave in these ways?" The individual's relationships to the work group, the foreman, the company, and nonwork activities and ideas are evident, and make up a consistent pattern. To pursue the question, "What gives rise to these events?" we need more data on the history of events in the individual's life.

The Margaret Mahoney and Richard Carleton cases present historical data on the lives of the individuals, as well as describe their current work and social worlds. These two people actually encounter one another in their work group, but their roles in the group and the emotional tone of their interpersonal relations are distinctively different. Here another kind of consistency appears; the individuals' here-and-now interpersonal involvements appear to be continuations of earlier patterns. They are behaving "now" in terms of the rewards and deprivations experienced by them in distantly past situations in their early families and adult life on their own. From these data, chains of historical causes may begin to be traced. In addition to an examination of here-and-now consequences, these data allow for the assessment of the causal chain of behaviors and consequences over the two individuals' lifetimes.

In all three of these cases—Atkins and Wexler, Mahoney, and Carleton—the meanings of work and people within the lives of the individual are central. The organization, as represented by managers' values and goals, is so remote as to be almost indistinguishable as an important element in the individual's work-life. As in the earlier sections of this book, these situations again allow a comparison of individual motivations with the traditional purposes of the organiza-

[1] See reference in Introduction.

tions in which individuals work. The student has an opportunity to reflect upon the significance of these "worlds apart," while attempting to understand the problems and processes in which these workers are involved.

The Grosvenor House case belongs in an entirely different world from that of the workers in the other cases. Here, a son of a self-made man finds himself serving the needs of high society in an Eastern city. A lady public relations counselor and other individuals try to help him become a business success. Throughout the case, Josef Belair, the manager-entrepreneur, indicates that what he is trying to do in this business venture is not strictly "business"; rather, it contains strong indications of his endeavoring to prove something to someone and "using" the business—a high society restaurant and ballroom—as well as his interpersonal relationships around his work as a means of expressing and satisfying strong personal needs. His very naïveté in the high society business allows his personal problems to float visibly on the surface of his interpersonal situations.

In this case, Josef's references to his father, his brothers, and his minority group ethnic background come out in spontaneous conversations with the public relations counselor. The entire sequence of events takes place under the conventional guise of "business" proceedings, yet their content, dynamics, and consequences bear unmistakable similarity to the proceedings described in clinical accounts of psychotherapy or group therapy. The roles into which Josef forces his interpersonal contacts are of interest. Almost without exception, he forces them to "help" him in one way or another. They either accommodate personally, by resigning themselves to letting him act out his episodes while they remain passive and accepting, or mediate as "shock absorbers" between him and third parties, or both. Thus, though Josef Belair is the central character, in the literary sense, in the Grosvenor House study, his effects on others are documented in sufficient detail for the student to change focus, putting others at the center. Treating Theresa Blake, the public relations counselor, as a central figure for analysis, with Josef and others as peripheral characters, opens up some interesting questions as to her interpersonal modes, motivations, and life-work patterns, and how these intersect with those of Josef Belair.

The Community Church case focuses attention on conflicts in authority relations. The organizational context, a church, differs from the work settings of business but nevertheless brings into sharp relief how organization design and procedures may provide a collective means for defense against anxiety. The sources of anxiety are within the individual, yet are stimulated by the acting out of the authority dilemma whose roots lie in the individual's developmental experience.

The analytical frameworks suggested above are based on the individual person, and his relationships with other persons in his environment, as the unit of analysis. Once the student has gained some competence with this kind of analysis, and greater understanding of interpersonal processes, it will be appropriate for him to reflect on the cases included in the section on group processes, where the group was the unit of analysis. The challenge is to connect the two frameworks by investigating the ways in which the group social structure and processes of social control express shared aspects of the dynamics of individual personalities and interpersonal relations. An understanding of group processes alone is no more adequate for understanding human behavior than is an understanding of individual personality processes alone. Both are necessary. But even this combination leaves out important determinants of human behavior which are "located" in the larger context of social institutions and culture. The influence of these environmental constraints is most evident in the series of cases which follow this set of cases on interpersonal dynamics. At this point it is of some importance to anticipate the cumulative nature of the ideas which can come from studying the cases in the sequence presented in this book.

Howard Atkins and Joseph Wexler

THE Brainerd Instrument Company manufactured instruments for the aircraft and electronic industries. The company had several large contracts, but it had grown, during its ten-year existence, primarily because of its ability to handle small orders for products adapted to meet new and often unique conditions. Indeed, one of the executives said that the company's success was due to its personnel's ability to meet new situations "with flexible thinking from the top down." It had recently moved to a new building with room for future expansion.

The company was equally progressive in its attitude toward management-worker relationships. It conducted a training program for its supervisors, in which they read about and discussed words like "leadership," "human relations," and "understanding the worker." Furthermore, the request of a university human relations researcher that he be permitted to use the company as a field setting for the study of social organization of work groups was warmly received, and the company suggested that the researcher select the particular group he would like to observe.

The group selected consisted of the workers in the small machine shop where many of the heavier parts needed in some of the instruments were made. Although the company subcontracted more than half this kind of work, the management was considering enlarging its own production. Currently fourteen men worked there under the direction of a foreman, Howard Atkins. Eight of the men were skilled machinists and six unskilled. None were college graduates, but all except one had completed high school, and four had had one or more years of college work. Only one or two of the older workers had the traditional machinist's apprenticeship training. Most of the younger workers were "graduates of the school of hard knocks," including semislum areas, racial discrimination, military service, and a miscellaneous assortment of jobs.

In the machine shop, work lots as a rule were small, and the processing steps for the different parts varied considerably in sequence and required skills. Therefore, after job orders and parts were delivered to Mr. Atkins, he assigned jobs to individual men according to their ability and the completion dates scheduled on the orders. Any worker who needed help could call on Mr. Atkins, but usually the men turned to some other worker, especially Bill, a skilled machinist. When a worker finished a job, he went to Mr. Atkins for another.

Mr. Atkins had had little formal education. This made him both proud and resentful: proud because he had achieved some position and standing in life despite this handicap, and resentful because considerable social recognition seemed to go to "college men." He divided his world between the "practical men" and the "theoretical." Practical men included those who had "come up the hard way." Theoretical men included the engineers with whom he dealt in his present job and in previous ones. He delighted in relating incidents in which theoretical men made mistakes practical men would not have made.

Mr. Atkins spoke of himself as an "oldtimer" machinist. He had completed an apprenticeship with a large manufacturing company in the early 1930's. Apparently his apprenticeship had been a choice one, and he pointed with pride to the rising careers of many men in the informal alumni group which still existed. The apprentice program, besides encompassing technical training, also provided a well-understood framework for such relationships as apprentice-journeyman and apprentice-supervisor. An apprentice was expected to act as a learner at all times, to treat his superiors with respect, to take periodic criticism, and never to talk back. Journeymen and supervisors were expected to be gruff, hard-boiled individuals, to teach the apprentices well, to treat them as socially subordinate, but not to abuse them. In reminiscing about his experiences with older journeymen or supervisors, Mr. Atkins would say they "taught me a lesson I'll never forget as long as I live."

During prewar days Mr. Atkins worked as a machinist at a Navy Yard which followed the traditions of the machine shop, shipbuilding, and the Civil Service. Later, as a supervisor at the Navy Yard, he was beset with the wartime influx of new workers, most of whom were unskilled, unschooled in the old traditions, and prone to utilize the Civil Service grievance procedures and boards of appeal.

In his work at Brainerd as foreman of the machine shop, Mr. Atkins seldom asked his superiors for equipment for the shop, even when it would not have been expensive. He knew that the company's special advantage in its field lay in the cost-conscious, but imaginative, contributions made by management in the design and assembly of the delicate instruments manufactured. Consequently, he preferred to work out problems which arose in the shop by using his own ingenuity and existing equipment rather than by making what he considered costly or unreasonable demands upon the company's resources.

Except for the contacts required by his job, Mr. Atkins did not spend much time with his men. Neither did he associate with the other supervisors, most of whom were younger and all of whom had more formal education and were more familiar with the jargon of electronics. During breaks he usually sat alone at his desk, drinking coffee or checking orders, blueprints, and time tickets. He left the shop only occasionally to attend foreman meetings and to talk with the superintendent to whom he reported. When outsiders came to the shop, usually staff engineers or accountants, he took care of them.

At his first meeting with the research observer, Mr. Atkins talked about one of the skilled machinists, Joseph Wexler. Mr. Wexler was single and about 40 years old. In mentioning him, Mr. Atkins called the observer's attention to several notices pinned on the wall near the entrance to the shop. Some of them described chess problems and their solution; two quoted material from a textbook on machine shop practice. The latter emphasized that carboloy cutting tools should be used for machining heat-treated and hard metals. At the bottom of these notices, printed in large letters, was the following:

WHY DON'T WE HAVE CARBOLOY TOOLS IN THIS SHOP?

In referring to Mr. Wexler, Mr. Atkins said, "There is one fellow around here who is a problem to me. That's Joe. He won the city chess championship. You may have noticed the wall with all those chess notices. Well, they were put up by Joe. He's even got some of the men around here playing the game. He may be surly or rude to you when you speak to him. If he is, just walk away and forget about it. You may go up to him on another day and he'll be all right. You just can't tell about Joe, so don't let him bother you."

Actually, the observer found Mr. Wexler friendly and eager to talk about himself. After they had been introduced and the observer had answered a few questions about the study, Mr. Wexler said, "Let me give you a problem and see if you can answer it. Perhaps you've noticed the things I put up on the bulletin board. Now, those things go up for a purpose. Right now I'm writing a paper on inventory. Here, let me show it to you." He stepped over to a stand near his lathe and extracted from the middle of a folded newspaper a few sheets of paper. "Here, read these and tell me what you think."

The paper was entitled, "What Is An Inventory? Part I." It posed the question: To whom does an inventory belong—the management, the stockholders, or the workers who use the inventory?

He then continued, "Let me explain what I'm trying to get at. Under the present scheme of things, with the existing hierarchy, things have to fall into designated places, little boxes in the organization chart, or management is unhappy and becomes suspicious. Things are ordered. This person is in charge of costs, or that person is in charge of inventory. That's the way things are set up. But here I am, a worker, who works with the machine or the materials. When I go over to a machine, I should see near it all the equipment that goes with this machine. Why should I be kept in the dark? After all, to whom is this information more important than to the person who has to work at the machine?

"Or take the stockroom. In drawing out supplies, why should I be kept in the dark as to what is available? After all, I'm the one who has to use the supplies. But no, this inverts the hierarchy, it destroys the order that has been established. Even the very act of bringing the ideas which I have up to my supervisor or someone else in management can be taken only as a criticism of the way in which they introduce the ideas. If I do so, then it implies they are not carrying out their function. Do you see you are stuck?

"That's why I take the trouble to write out these papers and post them on the bulletin board. Because once the idea is publicized, it becomes generally known, and it can't be ignored. But even then, you see, this goes counter to the system, and it must be taken as an implied criticism of management and the supervision. But because it has been publicized, the idea cannot be ignored. That's the one thing that must be maintained, publicity.

"Here, let me show you other things that I'm going to post on the bulletin board." Joe reached into his newspaper and pulled out several sheets of paper. One quoted from a poem by Yeats and another from a poem by Ogden Nash. "They're beautiful, aren't they? I also put up chess problems. I put these up in the interests of giving people something to think about and appreciate. There's more to life than what we see here, and anything I can do to broaden horizons helps.

"As you can probably see, I'm somewhat of a maverick. I'll be leaving this job pretty soon. It's bound to happen. Just like at the _____ Company, my last job, and others. Because

I introduce ideas that go counter to the expectations of the hierarchy on what a worker should be doing, I can't last long here."

A few days later the observer saw that the notices had been removed from the wall. When he had an opportunity to talk with Mr. Wexler, Bill Tompkins joined them and spoke first.

MR. TOMPKINS: Howard called me over and told me that he didn't have anything to do with the removal of your things from the bulletin board. He said the superintendent took them down, and he (Mr. Atkins) wanted me to tell you that he didn't do it. (Mr. Wexler shrugged and smiled.) Why don't you go over to the superintendent and ask him why he took them down?

MR. WEXLER: What good would that do?

MR. TOMPKINS: Well, go on over anyway and ask him.

Later Mr. Wexler went to see the superintendent; he described the conversation to the observer as follows:

MR. WEXLER: I asked the superintendent why he had taken the notices from the wall. He said to me, "We can't have the walls getting cluttered up. The next thing you know, we'll be having pictures of naked women on the wall." Can you imagine that? Well, so what I've done is make my own bulletin board that I've put right next to my machine. So I'll put my notices up here and get them publicized that way.

He showed the observer a crude bulletin board on a stand which he had built and placed next to the lathe on which he worked. No notices had been posted as yet.

On the observer's following visit to the plant, a few days later, Mr. Wexler spoke to him again.

MR WEXLER: Say, let me ask you something. What do you think? Do you think this bulletin board of mine is going to drive management nuts? (Laughter.) . . . The management believes that it has the ideas and that a person who is in a worker's position shouldn't be expected to have ideas. That's not his job. It's just like this business with the inventory. That's supposed to be none of my business. All I'm supposed to do is just stick to my job.

That's what's wrong with this new merit rating thing they just put in. It's based on the assumption that the worker is responsible for the output. After all, output is based on a lot of things and largely on supervision. It is based on the condition of the machine, the material, and the kind of supervisor you have, but the supervisors here aren't being rated. I wonder what the management would think if we turned it around and rated them. I'll bet they wouldn't like that one bit. You'll probably disagree with my ideas, but I think things should be just the reverse of the way they are. The saying goes that workers should be paid a standard rate and that management should get the results of output. I think that's just the reverse of the way things should be. What we should have is the workers getting the results of output, a continually increasing wage, and management getting a going rate or a standard pay. That's a different idea, I know, but it's what I believe.

As Mr. Wexler predicted, he did not stay around the shop very long. He had a "run-in" with Mr. Atkins, who described the incident as follows.

MR. ATKINS: You know, I had to let Joe go. It was just one of those things. I've run into situations like this before and you can't help yourself. It all began with the notice he put up on the bulletin board. Some people get the idea that they know how things should be run and that they have a lot of hot ideas, but as you know, if they come over and tell you about it, you can explain why it is not practical for this shop, and then they usually understand. In this case, though, he put the notice up on the bulletin board where everybody could see it. It said something like, "Carbide tools are better for certain kinds of metal and what's wrong with the management here that we don't have carbide tools?" Well, I saw the notice, and after all, it made me look bad. It's supposed to be my job to get the proper tools in here, and if people don't think that the proper tools are here, then it is a reflection on me. I took the notice down and I gave it to the superintendent. Then I came back in the shop and I called Joe over and I asked him to sit down. I explained to him why he couldn't put notices like that up on the bulletin board and he got up and said to me, "Is that all you want to see me about?" and I said to him, "No, as a matter of fact, there's a little business I want to talk to you about." Well, he turned around and walked away toward his machine. I followed him to the machine and I said to him, "Joe, there was something else I wanted to talk to you about," and he replied to me, "Look, I'm getting paid to work, not to talk to you, so get the hell out of here." Now, when Joe said that to me, I could just feel my blood pressure going up, but I didn't say anything. You know you have to learn to control yourself in this business. I took a walk around the shop and I came back and I said then,

"Now look, Joe, there's something wrong with your attitude."
And he said to me again, "Get the hell out of here." And I said a
second time, "Now, look, Joe, this attitude of yours is no good. I
suggest that since you feel this way about it, you'd better collect
your pay at 4:00 o'clock and call it quits." And he said, "You
mean you want me to finish up, is that it?" And I said, "I guess it
has to be that way." And he said, "That's all right with me, but
get the hell out of here now." Well, after a third time, I said to
him, "Well, Joe, I guess maybe it would be a better idea if you
collected your pay at 12:00. You don't have to work straight
through." Well, I didn't know if my boss would back me up, but
the superintendent called me in later on and asked me what the
story was. I explained it to him and he said that I was perfectly
right in what I had done.

Margaret Mahoney and
Richard Carleton

Among the many workers observed at the Miller Hawkes Company, Margaret Mahoney and Richard Carleton presented the most interesting contrast. They both worked in the department which was being studied in a research project designed to investigate the relationships among worker motivation, group membership, productivity, and satisfaction.

The research project included an intensive period of field observation and interviewing. Each worker met privately with an observer for two interviews. During the first, the worker was asked to describe his personal history and social background; during the second, which was conducted at the conclusion of the field observation, the worker was asked to talk about his feelings with respect to the job, supervision, associates, the company, and the union. The researchers listened for the worker's beliefs and values in each of these areas, as well as for the basic facts.

Since there was such a marked difference in the attitudes expressed by Mrs. Mahoney and Mr. Carleton, and in their roles in the social structure of the group, the researchers became interested in why these contrasting patterns evolved. They believed that the answers might lie in the following material, which they prepared from the field observation and interview data.

MARGARET MAHONEY

Mrs. Mahoney was 50 years old and had worked at the Miller Hawkes Company for 11 years. She was the youngest of the six children of an Irish Catholic family. She had attended high school for two years before taking her first job. Below are some comments Mrs. Mahoney made about her personal history.

> My mother died when I was three years old. My oldest sister looked after me. I guess I was the spoiled one. My brothers

and sisters catered to me a lot. I would go into tantrums if I didn't get what I wanted. My sister was strict with me. I had to be in by a certain time and all that. I wanted to be on my own. They screamed and hollered when I wanted to get married when I was 18, but I wanted to get on my own.

When I got married, I didn't know how to even cook because everybody had done things for me. I wanted to get on my own. But I learned it wasn't so nice. After I was separated my brothers and sisters helped me out, so it worked out okay. My brother down South used to send me a check for $50 every now and then. I guess they felt sorry for me and the kids.

Mrs. Mahoney had been married for 14 years before her separation. Three of her five children were married, and one daughter lived in an apartment "to be near friends." Another daughter had been killed in an accident. Mrs. Mahoney had recently moved to suburban community to live with a brother. Of her new home, she had this to say:

I just love my house in the country. Everybody said I'd be scared living way out in the woods, but I'm not. I always wanted to live in the country, because I love gardening and hiking. Everybody says I have a green thumb, just like my father. I keep looking at the calendar to see when spring comes. I can hardly wait.

Everything in my house is so nice and new. I just love it. I've never been so contented in my life.

I see my children and my grandchildren. I just love them, and they're crazy about me, too. I'm happy and contented.

I would like to stay home and putter around. People tell me I wouldn't know what to do with my time, but I could find plenty to do. But I couldn't afford to stop work.

For most of her 11 years at Miller Hawkes, Mrs. Mahoney worked in one department, at a job which was rated as a skilled job for female workers. Her production rate was "on the line," meaning that it conformed to the production percentage of the majority of the workers in the department. Compared with the department as a whole, she interacted at a high rate with co-workers. She was chosen many times as a "friend" by fellow workers, and was herself a "high chooser" of friends. She was a member of a subgroup made up of older women who were Irish-Catholic, long-service employees. The members of this subgroup had been widowed or separated, and they saw each other frequently outside the plant on social occasions. Most of them chose Mrs. Mahoney as a friend and looked to her to initiate social activities in and outside the plant.

During the final interview, Mrs. Mahoney made these statements about her job:

> I love my work. It's a funny thing, it's a messy job, but I'm not happy when I'm not doing it. A carpenter came to my house to fix my kitchen cabinets. He got a big kick out of it when I told him I was a finisher on an assembly job. Imagine a woman finisher! I guess he thought I worked on big assemblies, but they're only little ones. But I do love my job, I don't know why, but I do.
>
> I've always enjoyed working here. I never worked in a factory before. I thought it was dirty work and a tough class of people. I thought it was terrible. But I got a rude awakening. My brother used to say "Don't become a factory girl." But the majority of the girls were very nice. Sue (who worked with Margaret) used to be a stenographer. She makes more money here.
>
> I hate machines. I never worked in a factory before. I guess I'm just afraid of machines. I don't want to do it. I guess I'm just tense when I work on machines. You get to like your own work. It's all right to go down one day, but when I'm on machines, I rush back here and look for assemblies to do. I guess I just like to work with my hands. I like anything that's fast and with your hands. Then, I'm not confined. I can stand or sit. If you're confined, like on machines, it's boring. I had a chance to go on grinders at 10 cents an hour more, but it's too confining. The 10 cents doesn't mean that much. I had seniority, too, for the grinders, so I wouldn't have been on the bottom of the list. So it wasn't losing seniority that I didn't go on grinders.

She also made statements about her boss, the company, the union, and the department in which she worked.

> You couldn't find a better boss in the United States. I couldn't pick any one thing out that makes him so good. He's fair, good and he's not a slave driver. He gives you help when you ask for it. You can go up to George (the foreman of the department) with any problem. If you ask for time off, he

doesn't go into it, asking questions. He just lets you. He trusts you. Other bosses, they work for the company, but George works for his people. You give him a fair day's work and he's fair.

A fair day's work is 200 assemblies a day. He comes over and asks, and if it's 200, he says it's wonderful. Yesterday, we only did 166. He said it was wonderful, because he knew that was all the motors we had. He understood and he didn't take us off the bench. He knows that when they come through he gets a fair day's work. George relies on me. The work is like second nature to me. I used to do everything at the bench. I guess the job goes with me.

The company is very, very fair. I've enjoyed working here because they've treated me good. Once a foreman we used to have here tried to get someone else in my job. It was a friend of his, and he had more seniority, and he tried to get me out. The union and the company straightened it out. They said there was nothing to worry about. This company knows who puts out work and who doesn't.

The people should stand in back of the union. Some people are afraid of their job. They agree with the company and then with the union. A good union gets their demands, but they give and take. The union works for its people, but we have some morons here. Some people want their dollar. If you cut their pay, then they become good union members.

We have a good department as departments go. We have some insincere people—they're nice to your face but are insincere. When we didn't have all these girls (in the department) it was nice—like one big happy family. A good department means having sincere people.

Mary (a co-worker) and I were the first women in the department. Crazy Joe (a co-worker) was here, and he used to stand in the aisle and look us up and down and whistle. But they couldn't do enough for you. They would swear and then excuse themselves. After awhile, we took it for granted, but they were never obscene. If they'd swear, they'd say "I'm sorry." We were like two queens for awhile. I would prefer working with men. There's no petty gossip, and men are more sincere. I like a little bit of gossip, but I wouldn't spread it. The foreman used to say we were better than six men, we worked so fast. We kept going like two Trojans. The group leader used to send us out to the ladies' room because we worked so fast.

The researchers had noted that about half the members of the department were Irish in ethnic background and asked Mrs. Mahoney to comment on how the workers got along. She said:

> Nationality doesn't mean a thing here. Oh, I might say to Al (the mail boy, who was Armenian), "Hey, you little rug merchant." And then he says something about the Irish. But it's in fun, and nobody brings up nationality or religion.

The researchers also asked Mrs. Mahoney to comment on the pools and collections which were common in the department.

> The (savings) pools have dropped off. We had a ten-week $2.00 pool. I was in all of them. (Another worker) and I used to run a $1.00 pool. But we stopped it. I put my money in the bank now. It's taken out of my pay.
>
> In the savings pool, we first pooled by name, then by number. We used to use the money for maybe a dress sale or something. The $2.00 pool stopped at the layoff. I used to run it, but I got tired and turned it over to (another worker). The boys were in the $1.00 pool. They didn't have it to spend and had a few dollars when they got the money.
>
> You take up collections for sicknesses or a death. I took it up for (another worker). There are a few people that give you a story, "I'll give it to you later." So I put it in for them and got the money later. But I have somebody watch me put it in for them. Some people give more in a collection than others. A lot of people just throw in change. I always feel as though I should give a dollar. When I was sick, they gave me a brand new fifty-dollar bill, and they sent me flowers besides. I got the highest amount of any collection. They cut down on those who don't give too much. We usually give money rather than flowers, because the money comes in handy.

An incident occurred during the field observation period which interested the researchers, especially since it involved Mrs. Mahoney. One morning a male co-worker approached Mrs. Mahoney and began to joke with her. He put his arms around her exclaiming that he was about to give her a "bear hug." She laughed, but then cried out in pain. The worker released her, but the pain persisted, and she experienced considerable discomfort. She consulted a close friend, who accompanied her to the plant nurse. Mrs. Mahoney reported that she had hurt her side when she slipped on some grease and had fallen against a work bench. The nurse examined her and suggested that she report to a nearby hospital for X-ray examination. Accompanied by her friend, Mrs. Mahoney left work for the hospital. Her friend returned to the plant alone later in the day and reported that the X-ray showed a fractured rib. Mrs. Mahoney had to be taped and was ordered to bed for several days' rest.

The next day, a safety inspector arrived in the department and examined the floor for grease spots. The incident had been recorded by the foreman and plant nurse as an accident. Mrs. Mahoney returned to work a few days later and learned that she would receive sick pay under the company's accident compensation rules.

In commenting to the researchers about the incident, she said:

> I couldn't get mad at him (the worker who had "bear hugged" her). He didn't mean it, or do it intentionally. I have to laugh, I can't stay mad at him. I call him a big fat slob and he doesn't get mad. He never says anything smutty—just good clean fun. Smutty stuff doesn't go. They're a clean, decent bunch of boys here.

RICHARD CARLETON

Richard Carleton was 57 years old and of Yankee-Protestant ethnic origin. He was a high school graduate and had worked at Miller Hawkes for 11 years. The following excerpts from the initial interview with him reveal some facts about his personal background.

> I started out in life at a disadvantage. My father died before I was born. (His father and grandfather were lawyers.) Mother, to earn a living, went away to learn how to become a chiropodist. My sister and I were placed in a children's home in the town where we lived, in New York State. After she learned the business, we came home again.
>
> After I got out of the service (1919), I met a girl and married her. I went into business with her father. I got my basic training in business administration.
>
> I worked in this business until the early '30's, when the company went into bankruptcy. I was too young and couldn't get credit. There was no work for a long time. I finally got into the city chorus and my wife into another WPA choir. Finally, I got a job singing part time for WXYZ's early-morning religious program. That's where I became interested in ministers.
>
> After we lost our business, my health went. I'm supposed to be psychosomatic. All my money goes to doctors' wallets.
>
> During the war I worked for a company in Philadelphia.

When work let up (a few months earlier), I was let out. (During a production downturn at Miller Hawkes prior to the research study, Mr. Carleton was laid off.)   I walked the streets for nine months. I don't want to do it again. It burned me up. I was over 50, and I couldn't even get a laborer's job; of course, the insurance people are to blame for that. It's age that licked me. I'm just too old, and it used to drive me crazy. I'd go into a place and ask for a job, and they would tell me I was too old and they couldn't hire me. It just used to make me boil inside, and it's still just as bad on the outside, from what I hear. Now it's only worse. If you're over 35 years old you can't get a job. I could have had a beautiful job with the Old Gold people. They would have given me a car. I had a friend who tried to get me in, but I couldn't get a job on account of age. When you get to be my age you don't give a damn. You lose your initiative. Finally, I got a job at the public library. They dressed me up like a stuffed monkey; they wouldn't even let me talk to the other guard when there wasn't a soul in the building. All of that time I lived on $25 a week. I was one of the last to be called up. If it hadn't been for the union, I'd never have been called up.

I have always been musically inclined, as was Dad. It always got me all wrought up. I used to write a lot. At 19 I won a prize for writing the most dramatic poem entered in the contest.

My wife is wrapped up in her work. We handle the choir for our church. I don't pretend to be a noble religious fellow, but I enjoy the association with the church. I live in a triangle— here, church, and the chair at home. I don't go to the movies or anything. I've got my chair, and I did buy a television set.

I lived in one place 18 years and just moved to another house in the same block two years ago. We always lived with my in-laws. They lived upstairs. Never had a harsh word with them in all the years before they died.

My wife never could have children. The only child I have is a four-legged mongrel dog. A Congregational minister gave it to us. It is getting old and sick. I bought a $300 Simmons Hide-A-Bed so I could sleep on it and the dog could sleep on my wife's bed. I built special steps for him to climb up to the bed.

I think my wife and I have only four people we can call our friends. In the old days, when I ran the business, we had lots of friends.

With me it's like with everyone else. There are no two people alike. No two peas in a pod. Maybe some people do things because of their own liking or because of things they can't control. With me, my whole reason for being here is because of things I can't control. I'm an individual doing things I shouldn't be doing. All of my life I've been doing things I shouldn't have been doing.

Now I am not in good health. My stomach is kicking up and I can't start out afresh. At night I go home and fall into a chair just so I can get enough strength to come in the next day. I force myself to like this job, but the job doesn't like me. I'm not a mechanical man, I'm a musical man. I wanted to stick with music, but I couldn't. The position I'm in you've got to like your job to make money to exist. I know I shouldn't feel this way, and it's not doing my health any good. I lost my business during the depression. The doctor keeps putting me down as a neurotic. Psychosomatic, he tells me. I tell the doc it isn't so, but deep down I know it's true. Way down in the unconscious it bothers me. After I lost my business in the depression I said it wouldn't bother me, but way deep down it did. I know it did.

I've been living with this for 18 years. I was 40 years old when I went broke. They say life begins at 40. Do you remember a book by that title? Well, it just isn't true, and nothing can be done about it. I had three major operations in that period, and I can't do anything. But getting back to this place and hearing about other places, I think this is a fine place. If I was mechanically inclined I could have gone ahead, but I lost my vision in one eye. I used to have my own business, and then I supervised other people. I was good with that. The way I feel mentally, I can't do anything. Whenever I get ready to turn over a new leaf, I get physically exhausted. I just go home and rest and wake up in the morning totally exhausted. You know it's nerves, of course. Now take singing. Every Thursday night we have a rehearsal, that's tonight. When I get home I have to do a few chores, and then all I want to do is go to bed, yet I have to go to a rehearsal, but I'm too tried and I can't sing. I'm just too tired. I just don't have any pep. The little organist, she's got a lot of pep. She gets $30 for playing on a Sunday, and she wants us to keep singing and to get peppy too, but I'm just too tired, and when Sunday comes I get a couple of days' rest and I'm all fired up for singing, but without a rehearsal I can't keep up. I've lost my breath control on account of my poor health, but I know if I could get started again it wouldn't take too long.

I'm 57 and my wife is 60 years old. We're not kids, and we can't do things any more, not without our health. Our landlord upstairs, he's 77 years old, and he can run rings around me. He had a virus last week, and that was the first time I ever knew him sick. Imagine that, a 77-year old man running rings around me. If I had my health I would be doing something about this. I would go into the musical game. My wife and I were both in it. We both loved it and wished we didn't have to leave it, but the depression wiped us out overnight. We had our own business, a summer place on the Cape. It took us just like that. We haven't been off our street since 1932. No vacations, no trips, or anything. We just sit at home.

If I had $25,000 I would start my own business. But maybe— you'd hire those Italians and Polacks, and they'd be in your office telling you how to run your business.

I'd like to go South and get away from the Roman Catholics.

I'm at $1.58. For a while, when overtime was around, I thought I could get a car. We keep up our license renewed in hopes of getting a car again.

The good Lord meant me to be an outdoor man. I would give anything if I could get away from it and into some quiet town, but what few friends we have are still here, and my wife wouldn't want to go. Age has just got me licked.

On his job, Mr. Carleton's output percentage ranked him as a low producer. He interacted infrequently with his fellow workers and chose no one in the department as a friend, nor was he chosen by anyone. He was not a member of any social group, and he sat alone during coffee and lunch breaks.

While discussing his job in the second interview, he made the following comments about the company, his work, supervision, his associates, and the union:

Considering all, this isn't a bad place to work. People have gone to other places and said they would never come back here, but once they leave they're awfully anxious to get back. The company as a whole is a decent place to work, but there are other types of people around here who are trying to do management out. They know it's the best place around here, but you know, it's not a healthy place to work. I have never known if I would have my job from month to month. (The president) wrote an article in the last issue of (the company newspaper). He just laid it on the line and told us how bad off the company was, that we were losing orders and that we were being underbid by competitors. I read that article and I asked several of the fellows if they had read it, and they said "No."

There's no job here that I'd prefer, none whatsoever. The only job that's available for me is Joe's (the group leader's job), but I couldn't handle it. I just couldn't handle it. I can run a lathe all day as far as operating it goes, but I can't tear it down and set it up, and then I can't grind. I can't work on the grinders because I lost my eyesight. You know, I originally came here as an inspector. I got my basic inspection training in Philadelphia. For three years I did nothing but inspect (at Miller Hawkes), and I really liked it. After V-J Day the axe started to fall, and out on the street I went. By luck I got called back, and shortly after that the axe began to fall again, and rather than go out I decided to go into production. They came over to me two or three times and asked me to go back into inspection, but you know as well as I do that the first people that get laid off are the inspectors, so I stayed where I am.

They're got me on edge on this job all the time. I try to give them what they want. I sit at the bench when the bell rings, and I give them what they want, and I don't know how the others do it. I don't know how they turn their count in unless they lie. I'm just too tired.

George (the foreman) is tops. I like him very much. He's a thorough mechanic, and he's tops in every way. He's been around and knows his machines. You can go to him with any problem, and he'll be able to answer it.

Now, when it comes to Joe, (the group leader), there's a fellow. He's so exasperating. He's the most exasperating fellow I ever met. I like him, mind you, and he's smart as a whip, but when it comes to supervision I just don't know. Now take for example what happened the other day. He put a wrench there, but then a few minutes later he was walking around all over the place looking for his wrench, and I heard that when he goes home at night he turns on the television and lays down on the couch and goes to sleep and wakes up at 12 or 1 o'clock with the television still going. No matter what he wants he just comes over and takes it. Like, the other day I got up from my chair to go out to the men's room. He knew I was sitting there, but he came over and he took my chair without even asking. I came back and I didn't have a chair to sit down on. I often say to him, "I don't know how you keep your job. Other places wouldn't stand for it." Now he's a good-hearted guy, but there's just this one thing.

As I told you earlier, I was brought up by my mother. My father died when I was very young. She was a business woman, and we had to do everything just right. She gave us a lot of training that's still with me today. If I were to go into your house and saw some magazines criss-cross, I would just walk over and straighten them out. I can't stand confusion. The doctor has a name for it. He calls it something, I've forgotten what it was. Some fellows are pretty messy and others are neat. Joe is the messy kind. I like things neat and clean. It's the training I had all my life. I wish I wasn't that way. I can't imagine how his home life is. It must be all confusion with two daughters and all that.

Now take Gus (another worker). He didn't even look at the article (the one the president wrote concerning the company) and I walked over and got a copy of it and gave it to him. Now that fellow, he comes in late every morning. He could walk here in five minutes if he wanted to, and he has a car, too, a great, big Buick car, and he even admitted that when he gets to work the engine hasn't even warmed up. And then he goes back and forth to the men's room. The company is full of those people, and nobody seems to do anything about it. When I had my own business I used to be able to tell how things were going by the noises in the shop. It seems to me they ought to be able to do that around here.

In my mind, unions are a necessary evil. It's the threat value if management takes out their whip. You know, there just isn't private enterprise around here any more. The union runs things. All that the girls have to do is just shed a few tears, and they get what they want. I can see management's side of things because I had my own business. The union helps to a certain extent. I saw the day when (the general superintendent) wanted to put a man on the job which was out of his classification. The union steward got after him and fought about classification and seniority. (The general superintendent) had to go along, even though the man who was on the job wasn't fit for it. Nowadays you have to go to the union for everything. You see, I can see management's side. How many people around here think about man-hours? The company gives them coffee breaks, they used to give it to them in the afternoon as well as in the morning. Do you know how many man-hours are involved in that? The help as a whole don't look at it that way. They'd like to take three coffee breaks if they could get away with it, and then five minutes before the bell rings you see them standing around waiting with their boxes to get some coffee. This all costs management money. Management has tried to be decent around here. If everybody would buckle down we wouldn't be behind in our bids. Now down there in the shipping room, take that for example. They are three months behind in their schedule, and the customers won't wait. I was talking to (someone outside the department) just the other day. He told me that they spent $100,000 on a machine loading system and now we're not using it any more. I noticed that because there are no dates on orders any more. Imagine, $100,000 experimenting, and yet it had to go out the window. They are always trying things around here. You see, we have a job shop here. We make maybe four or five things at a time. That stuff costs like the devil. It would be different if we made standard articles. I feel sorry for management. Lord knows they're trying. They've changed top personnel around here so many times I can't count it. They sure are trying.

You know, I don't have a car. I haven't owned a car since 1926. I just can't afford one. I would be paying the bank if I bought a car, and then what would happen if I lost my job? This is the kind of place I'm working in, I never feel sure of my job.

You know we have an Irish city here. I guess eight out of ten people are Irish. There are only a half a dozen Protestants here, and I don't think there are even a half a dozen Jewish people. We have to stick together against the Romans. It's a ticklish subject to talk about. I try to be tolerant, and I pray to God I can be tolerant, but sometimes it's hard. Why, their moral laws are of no significance compared to us. We had a Catholic priest at our church. He believed anything was all right as long as deep down in your heart you want to do right. Next door to me there is a hall. They have weddings there. You should see all the whiskey they bring in and the drinking that goes on. We think our weddings are serious and more sacred. These other people I'm talking about, they're always going to the men's room. How they account for their pieces I don't know. How they are able to do a day's work when they are always going to the men's room I'll never figure out. All they do is stand around and gab, and they are late, and they are always sitting around playing cards or gambling. They are not supposed to do it, but there's a central clique of fellows around here, and all they do is gamble. They'll beat us to go to church all right, but once out they don't give it a thought. They don't think about it at all until next week.

I wouldn't say I have any friends around here. I couldn't say that I dislike anybody; I suppose it's more that I pity them, but I don't have any friends here. We have a young fellow there in our section, five times every morning and five times every afternoon he goes out to the men's room. I don't check him or anything like that, but I've observed him a few times, and that's what he averages going to the men's room. The only thing he ever did for me was to break my glasses, and it cost me $6.00 to fix them, but I have pity for him.

I don't dislike the girls, but we have a wrong situation here. Management should do something, but I think they're stuck by the union. We still have married women up here, yet we haven't received any overtime work this year. That's what comes of the union saying they are equal with us. They ought to keep the married women in one department all by themselves and lay them off and consider them as one department, and they shouldn't be allowed to bump a married man the way they do here. Management can't do anything. There is work around here that women shouldn't do. Now take Betty (a fellow worker). She's working on cams. That's the work I do. She shouldn't be doing that. You have to tighten up the vise, and it takes a lot of pressure, but I've got to hand it to her, she doesn't squawk, but it certainly is man's work. All the jobs in the department except the light machine work is men's work. The women came in during the war. I realize they were patriotic, that they made sacrifices and wanted to help out during the war; but after the war was over, they should have been put on a separate classification and in one department all of their own. Do you know that there are veterans still walking the streets while these married women work? The only way to change things around here is for a general vote in the union meeting, but the women outnumber us, so where would it get us? Now take the assembly room. I heard they wanted to make a department of their own out of it, but the girls yelled and squawked. If they made a department of their own out of it, those girls would have got laid off first instead of bumping men.

I just rest my eyes during lunch. I have never played a game of cards in all my life. Lord knows I've gambled, but not in pool. I gave all that up several years ago anyway. I still have a hobby, though, of charting the dogs and the horses, but I have given up on gambling. I only do that as a hobby. When I made overtime I used to make about $100 a week, and I gambled then because that's the only way to get ahead with all the money worries I had and the mental trouble. When I go home I give my wife my check. I'd go crazy if I had to run the house. Then my wife gives me my weekly allowance, just enough to get me here and back. That's about $4.50 a week, and she handles everything else. I don't understand how other people do it, the way they buy these big cars. All I have is my wife, myself, and a dog. We pay $40 a month rent, and that isn't too bad, but by the time we pay the bills there is nothing left. The only luxury I have ever bought myself in the last 20 years is television. I have had three sets, and I have had to pay out on them. I have just made my last payment. All I am able to do is just make my bills.

Carleton said this about collections:

These collections are all right if you're one of the gang. I've never gotten one red penny out of it. I had three major operations, my wife was sick, I lost my mother and my father-in-law, and I had to borrow money to meet the bills. I had to go to the doctor twice a week for treatments. That cost me $5.00 a week, and I lost my overtime, and all during that time I never got one red penny. When I had my major operation, it just happened that Margaret Mahoney was out sick, too. They took up a collection for her. In fact, they canvassed the whole building for her, not just the department, so you see it makes a difference who you are and who you travel with. Maybe it's individual favoritism. Maybe it's because I don't go out bowling. If I went bowling maybe I could get in with them. That might make a difference. Now take (another worker). She's on our side of the fence. No one has ever made a collection for her, and I don't know whether (the other worker) ever got anything. Maybe he did, but I never saw a box go around for him even when he was out sick. It seems like you have to be in with the crowd to get something on these collections.

During the research period, methods men were retiming some of the jobs in the department. Mr. Carleton made these statements about these men and his job.

You've seen that heavy-set guy who's been around here? Well, he's been timing us. He's retiming the job. He wants to get all the data on perforated cards. He's retiming them now so that they will be able to figure out their costs better. He's hit me two or three times, and that's why I started to keep my little book with the record of my time. George has a book, and Joe has a book too, and they can tell you how many pieces you're supposed to do. One time George came to me on a job and said why did I only put out a hundred pieces in eight hours instead of a hundred in one hour. I was taking all the rough edges off, and it didn't call for that on the operation sheet. The reason I did it was because the inspector told me to. When George came over to me, I was doing that very same job. He said to me, "What's the story, Dick?" He said I was spending too much time, and I told him I couldn't help it that the inspectors wanted the rough edges taken off. Well, he did something about it. He sent the work downstairs to be tumbled. That's the way they get these rough edges off now, and it does a beautiful job.

Everybody knows how much they are supposed to do, but they never know whether a fellow is telling the truth when he turns in his count. Nobody ever checks up on him. They just go over to (the timekeeper) and tell her how many they did, but no one ever knows if that's true, because no one checks. But that's all they talk about in our section, how many you can do an hour and how fast you can get your day's work done. Yesterday one of the fellows said he was through at 2 o'clock. I said to him he shouldn't do that. He comes in in the morning and tears through to get his day's work done and then all he does is slow down. I produce more than I'm supposed to. I'm one of those fellows who do. It's just my natural quirk. I can't go slow. Like when I'm working on a milling machine, I just can't turn those handles slow. I have to do it fast because it's my natural pace. The other fellows can get away with it. They can go slow, but it's just my nature to work fast. Just because I've made my count, I just can't sit back and take it easy, but an awful lot of the fellows can. If you produce more in our section, they just kick to you. They make out as though some-

thing awful will happen, but nothing does.   Like yesterday, I was
doing those wheels.   You're supposed to do 11 an hour, though
that's ridiculous.   I can do 10 of those in 15 minutes.   Why,
I turned in both days over 200.   I called Joe and told him it
was ridiculous to make the count so low.   George (the foreman)
admitted it even himself.   I think the company would go out of
business if things keep up like this.   I have my regular speed
and I keep working most of the time, even though I have pains
in my groin, stomach, and bladder.   I just get used to it.   I just
keep plowing along.   Like I had terrible pains today.   It was
pain in my stomach, but I guess I'm getting immune to it.   I've
had gall bladder operations.   They took out six stones.   I guess
I don't have much of a gall bladder left, but I just keep plugging
along.

   If I knew I wouldn't get laid off, things would be a lot better.
I would get a car and go out on weekends and get some relax-
ation.   My friends tell me I'm weak.   They say to me, "Go
ahead and take a chance."   Maybe I should have taken a chance.
After all, I have been here 11 years and nothing awful has
happened to me yet.   Sure, I got laid off a few times, but I
always came back, so maybe I really should have taken a chance.

Grosvenor House

THERESA Blake often felt during the summer of 1947 that the sale of the Wainwright mansion to Josef Belair was fast becoming a *cause célèbre*. All her friends and associates were concerned about it. She heard that the sale had occurred largely because maintaining a staff big enough to take care of the 30-room house had proved too difficult for the Wainwright daughter and her husband. Early in the spring, they had moved to their country house, and before most people had known the house was on the market, notice of its purchase appeared in the newspapers.

The Wainwright mansion had been a showplace for more than 50 years. In Philadelphia, where it was located, it had been the setting for the most important social entertainment of three generations. At the turn of the century all society had coveted invitations to the brilliant balls held there. The Wainwright library was well known, and many people hoped that the city's museum would some day house the Wainwright art collection.

Thomas Wainwright had built it for a town house in the late 1890's, and after his death in 1910, his married daughters and their children had continued to occupy it. In later years, particularly during the two World Wars, the mansion had opened its doors for international benefits, which both the European and American press had reported.

The mansion, located at 27 Bond Street, stood in the heart of the city's oldest residential section. In this small area were the few remaining blocks of brownstone houses in which the city's wealthiest and most socially prominent families lived. In recent years, many of them had moved to the suburbs, and the fact that some of them had sold their property to "newcomers" was bitterly resented by those who still carried on the old in-town traditions.

In the early summer of 1947, the front page of the local morning newspapers carried the annoucement of the sale of the Wainwright mansion to Josef Belair of the nearby industrial city of Coatesville. The papers stated that the mansion would be open to the public in the fall as a residential hotel with drinking, dining, and party facilities.

They reported that Mr. Belair had operated a commercial hotel in his home town and in Florida and that this purchase marked his first venture in the metropolitan area.

The evening papers carried a story on protests by several leading citizens against granting a hotel, victualer, and liquor license in what they termed "their city's most exclusive neighborhood." They began legal action, which continued for several weeks and only terminated when it became evident that there was no way to prevent the granting of this license. No one had foreseen the possibility of such a development on Bond Street.

Theresa Blake was frequently asked what she thought could be done about Mr. Belair's coming into the neighborhood. She found that even after accepting a commercial enterprise of this sort on Bond Street, many people felt that Mr. Belair was "completely unsuitable" as its owner. As a "foreigner" with no connections in the city, how, they wondered, could he be prevented from "ruining the neighborhood?"

Theresa was a woman in her middle thirties. Originally, she had been a reporter on one of the city's leading morning newspapers and had become the only woman feature writer on its editorial staff. Shortly after her marriage, some ten years ago, she had resigned from the paper to open the public relations agency of Blake Associates with her husband, Tom.

Although they had a small staff and represented only a few clients each year, the firm had been highly successful. While they dealt in all types of advertising media, the Blakes attributed much of their success to continued close association with the press. They continued to feel their responsibility as "good reporters," often calling attention to newsworthy stories that otherwise would have escaped attention and frequently submitting releases which appeared without revision in the papers.

Blake Associates expressed particular interest in clients "who needed a reformulation of their operating policy in relation to specific groups of the public." Tom specialized in industrial accounts, while Theresa handled principally what she liked to call "cause" accounts. They always started by carefully scrutinizing the client's objectives in relation to the public with which he dealt and helped him define his policy in respect to the needs or requirements of that public. They then implemented this policy through action taken by the client that would indicate to the public his acceptance of those requirements. This often meant working with those members of the client's organization who dealt with the public to see that they understood the implications of such a policy for their behavior. These activities so varied from client to client that the Blakes had no precise way of describing them, but they often resulted in favorable press attention and in improving relations between the client and the public with which he was dealing.

"Sure, I take only 'cause' accounts," Theresa often said. "And if I don't believe in them, I can't handle them. And I don't mean just the relief drives I handle. Lots of times business deserves a hearing it can't get through advertising alone. The harder the problem, the more it interests me." In the course of the years, she had built what she considered a unique position for herself and one which she attributed largely to her successful work with civic and relief organizations.

Most of her clients lived during the winter within a ten-block radius of 27 Bond Street and maintained summer homes in various fashionable resorts. She often went to committee meetings in their homes—formal, late morning, or late afternoon affairs—which set the tone and established the policy of the various charities in which they were interested. Theresa said she had always found them kindly men and women, easy to deal with if one conformed to their pattern. She respected the fact that the leaders of the city's banking and industrial circles were willing to give several hours each week to discussing the most minute details of the operation of these institutions and "causes." The women, for their part, she found tireless in their efforts to raise funds through whatever means they deemed fitting. Theresa had worked with them on the details of promotion by setting up the broad plans which she knew only they could implement; she enjoyed working with them.

One of her colleagues who specialized in radio had said, after putting a client of Theresa's on the air, "Good Lord, Theresa, how can you work with women like Mrs. Martin? She absolutely terrified me. I've had enough people on my program, goodness knows, but there was something about her that had me almost tongue-tied. She was so darn sure of herself that she made me feel like an impertinent schoolgirl. Why, I've had nightmares about it since. How you work with them day in and day out is beyond me."

Theresa had replied with surprise, saying that she felt occasional stiffness of manner merely cloaked a fudamental shyness and that in her long experience with them she had never found them difficult.

"This isn't like any other city in the country," she would say. "When you know half a dozen boards of directors, you know them all. And once those people know you, there's nothing they won't trust you with."

In view of the amount of talk created by the sale of the Wainwright mansion and the number of times the problem of what was to be done had been brought to her by her friends, Theresa had rather expected to hear from Josef Belair; she was not surprised, therefore, when he telephoned her early in September and asked her to come to see him "right away." She made an appointment for the following day.

Telling her husband that Mr. Belair had called, Theresa said, "I think it's something we'd better take on, Tom; there's Belair with a mansion he wants to make a go of, and he doesn't know how to begin; and there's the whole neighborhood up in arms. I'm just idiot enough to think I can get them together. It's another of my 'causes'!"

The following morning, Theresa walked into the marble entrance hall at 27 Bond Street, gave her name to a woman seated behind a long mahogany table, and was ushered into an adjacent room. Looking around her, Theresa noted that the large, high-studded room, paneled in fine-grained oak, still retained the atmosphere which the Wainwrights had created. Only the number of small tables, chairs, and divans indicated that is was to be used as a cocktail room. Through the arched doorway, she saw another large room similarly decorated.

After about twenty minutes Mr. Belair walked quickly into the room and seating himself said, "Well, well, well! I've heard a lot about you. Everyone has said to me, 'You want to get hold of Theresa Blake.' That's why I called you." He offered her a cigarette but did not light it for her, and as she fumbled in her purse for a match she felt his scrutiny and supposed he was deciding whether he had been correctly informed about her.

"They tell me you absolutely made Ed Stevens," he continued, referring to an uptown hotel manager for whom Theresa had acted as public relations counsel for several years. "Yes, everyone says that he never would have made the success he did if it hadn't been for you. That's why I want to talk to you."

Theresa told Mr. Belair that she was glad to meet him and that she had heard a good deal about the purchase of the Wainwright mansion.

Mr. Belair continued with his explanation. "They say you know people, the right people. Well, I want them in here. I want them fighting to get in. This is a beautiful house, and I think it's a gold mine."

Josef Belair sat forward on the edge of his chair, talking rapidly and using his hands for emphasis. He was of less than medium height, dark complexioned, and was dressed in a light brown suit, with a colored handkerchief in the breast pocket of his coat.

"But there are troubles," he continued. "In the first place, what are we going to call it? In New York, maybe 27 Bond Street would be enough—you know, like the '21 Club and all those places. But, even if it were enough here, I want a name for it."

Theresa asked Belair if he had considered a promotional budget, and he replied, "Oh, the main thing I want is what they say you can do. Like you did for Ed Stevens. You just figure out how much you're going to charge for putting this place over, and it will be all right with me." Theresa replied that she would talk it over with her associates and let him know in a day or two.

"Now don't you change your mind," he said, as if the matter had already been settled. "Funny thing," he concluded, "never did have much use for women except in the home. But everyone says you know your stuff, and I think we could get along all right. So you just let me know how much it's going to cost me, and let's get going. Yes, let's hurry up. Once I start something, I like to get it settled."

During the next two days Theresa considered the problems of 27 Bond Street at some length. Because of the degree of alarm expressed by the protests of the immediate neighborhood and because of the important civic positions of the people who lived there, she felt that Mr. Belair's project had no chance of survival unless these people were interested in it. Her first step, therefore, was to try to develop in her mind advertising copy that would describe a character and policy for the enterprise with which they could not quarrel. Although she was occupied with other matters during the day, she wrote the copy, which was later used with only minor changes in the opening advertisement, just before she went to sleep on the day she first met Mr. Belair. In this copy she "typed the house." She suggested an atmosphere and a kind of operation that she felt would be pleasing to the people of the immediate neighborhood and, at the same time, indicate to the wider public a quality not readily available. She knew that if this were translated into terms of good food and service, the house would fast become a popular meeting place.

During the next day she studied with Tom and her staff the various steps that could be taken to ensure that such an enterprise would get off to a good start. They considered that the naming of the property would greatly affect its future. Because of the strong ties that had always existed between the social group of this city and England, Theresa felt that such names as Barclay, Cornwall, Dorset, and Grosvenor would have a familiar "ring" to the neighborhood, as well as suggest "quality" to the wider group that it was necessary to attract.

In view of Josef Belair's lack of connections in the city, they felt it was essential to his success that he get off to a good start with the press, the one group within direct reach which could help make or break him, depending on how he handled himself. Newspapermen were the people who would fill the columns of their papers with copy about 27 Bond Street or toss it into their wastebaskets; they were the people who would "front page" or "bury" a scandal that might develop once operation started. Although press parties had become familiar procedure in launching ventures of this sort, several of Theresa's staff thought it was an unnecessary risk to take with Mr. Belair. The usual invitation from him might produce only a small attendance, and they were doubtful as to what sort of an impression he would make. Nevertheless, both Theresa and Tom considered that the desired result could be accomplished in no other way and decided that with the backing of the firm a successful party could be developed.

They then considered the social calendar and habits of the city and wondered what type of notable event could be brought to 27 Bond Street which would set the tone for the place. It must, they felt, be an event that would automatically receive good notice by the press. With sufficient publicity from such events, Theresa knew that there was a good chance of attracting the wider public which tended to follow the lead of the socially prominent.

When these conferences were completed, Theresa felt sure that this venture could be successfully promoted and felt no hesitancy in undertaking it. Although she had not yet told Mr. Belair that she would handle his account, she spent many hours developing details for an adequately broad opening program.

A few days later she called Mr. Belair and made an appointment to see him. As she waited for him, she looked over her notes. She had outlined this conference carefully, and the notes indicated each step in her reasoning. She felt that they did justice to the development of this new venture.

She heard him approach with a cheerful, "Well, Mrs. Blake! I was glad to get your phone call this morning. I knew you'd do this job for me. Now tell me how much you're going to charge me."

Theresa named the figure she considered reasonable and Mr. Belair said, "Fine! Fine!"

Theresa responded with, "I'll have my lawyers draw up a contract for you to look over."

"All right," he replied. "Fine. Just have it drawn up and I'll sign it. Now let's get to the point. How are you going to put this place over? Thought of a name? Well, I have. I was thinking last night how there are a lot of Norton College men, men who ought to be glad to come in here, and I thought, 'Why not call it the Norton?' What do you think of that Mrs. Blake?"

Theresa noted the eagerness in his voice and asked, "You liked Norton College?"

"Well, it's like this," Mr. Belair replied. "Norton was all right. I got out of there when I was only sixteen, did I tell you? I used to box up there, made quite a name for myself boxing. And so I thought lots of the Norton men might recognize the name Belair; or I could write them a letter, you know, telling them that an old Norton man was running this place and how about dropping in."

Theresa told him she thought it would be a good idea to let the Norton men know he was in town. Mr. Belair interrupted with, "Well, what thoughts have you got? Norton was just an idea, probably not much good, but I thought I'd mention it."

Theresa told him that she thought well of his idea. Still, Norton was the name of a well-known square in the night club district of the city, and people might be more apt to identify it with the square than with the college.

"Why, of course," Mr. Belair said. "Never thought of that. Well, that's out then. Let's hear your ideas."

Theresa reviewed with him the various names that she felt might produce the desired results. She suggested first that she thought the word house should be included in the name, so that she could develop her promotional ideas around the fact that one of the finest private town houses was now open to the public.

"Fine, fine," Mr. Belair said. "Good idea. Specially now when everybody's cooped up in small quarters like I am. I'll bet they all wish they had a great big town house, like you say. Well, they ought to. It's a wonderful house. I never thought I'd own one like it."

"Yes, it's lovely," Theresa agreed, looking about her. "They really built this one to last. You know, Thomas Wainwright was Anglo-Saxon. That is, he was of English descent."

"Yeah!" Mr. Belair responded excitedly. "Wouldn't it be wonderful if we could call it the Wainwright House!"

Theresa immediately thought of how upset the Wainwrights and their friends would be if any such attempt were made and said, "That might just confuse it with the Wainwright mansion. We have a new venture here. It's a good idea, though, to get the Anglo-

Saxon flavor into the name. I think that Grosvenor House sounds just right."

"Hm, Grosvenor House," Mr. Belair said. "Grosvenor. I kind of like that. English, eh? I think my father would like that. Did I tell you that he was in England before he came over here? All right, Grosvenor House it is. Now, what do you do next?"

Theresa started to outline some promotional ideas from her notes when Belair interrupted. "Now, the other trouble is these rumors about my buying into this neighborhood. I suppose you've heard them?"

Theresa noted that his tone was defiant. "Well, yes, I have Mr. Belair," she replied quietly. "But I am sure that's only because people don't know you and don't know what plans you have for the house."

"Oh," Mr. Belair exclaimed. "So they want my pedigree now! Well, let me tell you, the Belairs didn't have their money handed to them. No sir! They worked for it. Why, my father is a wonderful man. Made every penny himself. Why, the papers said he owns a hotel in Coatesville and one in Florida, didn't they? What more do these people want to know?"

Giving Theresa no chance to answer, he continued, "And my father did all right by me. Why, he sent me to Norton College along with the best of them. Yes, and I was only sixteen when I got through, too. So, I must have a brain or two. Now, what else do these people want to know?"

"Oh, this is a funny city, Mr. Belair, but it's really very friendly once people get to know you. They're always suspicious of outsiders at first. But if you could plan to be around yourself, and let them see you and know you, you'll find them friendly in no time at all. Naturally, they're worried now about what kind of a house you're going to run. Once they see good standards, they'll start to relax."

"Oh, they'll see fast enough," Mr. Belair retorted. "Nothing but the best. That's why I called you up. This is a beautiful house and I want to run it right. I want to run it so that all the people who turned up their noses will be fighting to get in. That's your job."

Without further discussion he approved the advertisement for the opening of Grosvenor House which Theresa had drafted and the cock-tail party she suggested for the press on the evening before its official opening.

"He was a pushover," she said later to Tom in commenting on the interview. "I only had to suggest something to have him agree to it. He seemed to think before I even got there that if we handle the promotion everything is all right with the world. I could hardly get a word in edgewise. He didn't want to know about any long-range program, only how fast we're going to start."

In planning the press party, Theresa counted heavily on her long and close association with the press. Both she and Tom invited publishers, editorial writers, and many of the working press by phone and through personal visits. More than 300 invitations in the form of memoranda on Blake Associates' letterhead were sent individually to the newspapermen on the papers in the city.

On the afternoon of the party, Theresa found Mr. Belair obviously excited. As she arrived, she saw him giving the rooms a last-minute inspection, and approving large trays of hors d'oeuvres, cocktail glasses, bottles ready to be uncorked, and waiters in their immaculate uniforms.

"Is everything all right?" he asked her at least a dozen times before the first guests arrived. She assured him that it "looked in good shape" to her, and as the first few guests began to trickle in, she went with Mr. Belair to his office on the third floor. She had told him to have someone keep track of the guests for him and not to appear until they had started to form into small groups—until at least two dozen guests had arrived. As she left he began poring over the galley proofs of the advertisement which was to announce the opening of Grosvenor House in the following morning's newspapers.

An hour later, the Adam Ballroom, named for the unusually hand-some Adam fireplace which Mr. Wainwright had installed at great expense, was well filled. Adjacent to the restaurant, it was here that the Wainwright balls had been given and here that the private social functions at Grosvenor House were to be held. Theresa saw Mr. Belair come through the doors across the room. She walked over to him and brought him up to the group with which James Wickersham, managing editor of the leading newspaper, was standing. Wickersham briefly complimented Mr. Belair on the party, then turned to Theresa and said, "Now, tell me, Theresa, just what are you going to do with this place? It's beautiful, but how are you going to sell it? It's not a private residence any more, not the Wainwright mansion; it's not a hotel, I gather, since you have only five apartments, and they're for permanent residents; it's not just a restaurant, because you have the whole house; it's not just 'cocktail lounges,' because those rooms still look like someone's drawing rooms. You call it Grosvenor House, nice name. But what is it going to stand for in this town?"

Before Theresa could reply, Belair gave her a look which seemed to say, "See, I'm all ready for that one," and drew from his inside pocket a galley proof. Handing it to Wickersham, he said, "This is the page one ad which we're running in your paper tomorrow morning."

For the advertisement, the display lines had been set in Barnum, an Old English type face, and the body of the text ran two columns on six inches in a deckle-edge frame, which gave it the appearance of a letter on Grosvenor House letterhead.   It read:

September 17, 1947

GROSVENOR HOUSE
27 Bond Street

Carriages with fine prancing horses and liveried coachmen no longer pull up before the arched, canopied doorway of 27 Bond Street.

Yet Grosvenor House is strongly reminiscent of carriage days, when Bond Street families began that tradition of graceful living for which they became renowned.

Grosvenor House recaptures the easy tempo of yesterday.

Once the setting for the loveliest parties that the city knew, when invitation lists were carefully scrutinized, Grosvenor House now is open to everyone who appreciates beauty of surroundings.

To the oak-panelled, high-studded, imposing rooms of the city's finest town house has been added perfection of service.   Overlooking the Mall, the restaurant and cocktail drawing rooms achieve a quiet charm heretofore unknown in today's generation.

Grosvenor House bows to yesterday as it salutes tomorrow.

Theresa noted Mr. Belair's pleasure at his guests' favorable comments on the advertising copy.   It seemed to answer fully the question that Mr. Wickersham had posed.

Shortly thereafter Theresa led Mr. Belair from one small cluster of people to another, introducing him to them all: publishers, who stayed only long enough to be courteous; managing and city editors; drama critics; columnists; night club and society editors; and members of the working press, more than 200 of whom drifted in and out—many of them staying late into the evening.

Theresa was acutely aware of Mr. Belair's every action and word and felt that he acquainted himself creditably.   He answered the questions asked of him carefully and without elaboration.   Yes, he was from Coatesville; he was born there.   Yes, his father was the Belair who owned real estate and operated a hotel in Coatesville.   No, the hotel was nothing like this; it was just a small hotel in an industrial town, but it was a money-maker.   Yes, his father had done very well with his Florida real estate and hotel, too.

"As a matter of fact," Mr. Belair said, and Theresa noted later that this was his only unsolicited remark that day, "I'm sorry my father isn't here today. I wanted him to come, but he said, 'No, Joe, this is your party; I'll come by and take you to dinner later.' "

One of the sports writers with whom Mr. Belair had been discussing his boxing days at Norton College asked, "And how do you like the tossing around you're getting in this neighborhood?"

"Oh, that!" Mr. Belair exploded, "you'd think I was going to turn the place into a honky tonk! Now, what would I want to buy this kind of place for if I were going to do that? No, I want to keep it just like it was. Impressive. The name is that, don't you think? Grosvenor House. Rich sounding. My father thought of that name; he was in London once and remembers the square there. Yes, it's a rich-sounding name."

Yes, he was married, he told one of the society editors in answer to her query. Theresa noted he offered no information about his wife's absence. Yes, they had one child, a little girl almost two years old. Yes, he planned to spend most of his time at Grosvenor House. Yes, he had been in the war, two years in the Pacific. Yes, he told another sports reporter with evident pleasure, he was the Belair of the Norton College boxing team. "Those were the days."

He passed from one group to another, signaling to the waiters as he saw empty glasses or the need for hors d'oeuvre trays. "Nice little character," several of the reporters remarked to Theresa during the evening as they watched Mr. Belair.

Theresa began to feel that Grosvenor House was off to an auspicious start. Confirmation of this came a few minutes later, when Mr. Darrin, the advertising manager of the newspaper which Mr. Wickersham served as managing editor, approached Theresa as she stood looking over the party with Mr. Belair.

Mr. Darrin had a galley proof of the advertisement in his hand and said, "Theresa, I wondered how you'd handle this one as soon as I heard that you had taken it on. When this came to my desk a few minutes ago, I picked up my hat and walked uptown for the first time in a long while just to tell you that I rarely have the privilege of reading copy like this."

As the guests started to leave, Theresa found herself alone with Mr. Belair for a few minutes, and turning to him she said, "I think things are coming along. We'll be ready to open. We need some big social function, and I've been checking with the society editors this evening. They can give me the picture layout a week from Sunday. I'm going to call James Appleby. He's the head of the Anglo-American Society, and I know they expect Lord Hayes to open their season for them. I thought it would be a good idea for you to offer them a fairly good price on their opening tea. If it's held here you're made."

Watching her intently, Mr. Belair replied, "That's it. That's it exactly. Just the kind of thing I want. You tell Mr. Appleby to come on in to see me. I'll give him a good price all right."

Theresa explained that Miss Butler, the executive director, would probably be sent over, and Mr. Belair said, "Women again! Well, you be here when she comes, eh? I don't believe in wasting money on advertising, but you fix up things like this tea party, and we'll be all set. Let me know when Miss what's-her-name is coming over, but please, you be sure to come. I don't know how to talk to people like that."

"The Howard Blunts have said that they are going to bring out their daughter here early in November," continued Theresa.

"A coming-out party!" interrupted Mr. Belair. "Well, isn't that something! Now tell me confidentially, Mrs. Blake, why do they have coming-out parties for daughters? My little girl is only two. Suppose I'll be doing that for her some day? Oh, what am I saying? A coming-out party for Corrie! What am I saying?"

"Those two events will do a lot for us," Theresa said. "The Anglo-American Society has among its members many of the people who worried most about the sale of the Wainwright mansion. I handled the Society's public relations during the war years, and Jim Appleby seems to like me. I think I can swing its opening meeting into Grosvenor House. I'll see to it that there are important stories about Lord Hayes which all the papers will be glad to take. That will follow up our initial advertising to perfection."

"Will a thing like that actually do us any good?" asked Mr. Belair. "There must be a lot of people that don't know anything about this Anglo-American Society."

"That's true," Theresa agreed, "but theatres, hotels, even shops in this town, depend very much on the approval of the inner circle. Most people watch the society columns and follow the lead given them by the prominent families.

"What I expect," she continued, "is that people will respond to something *different* from the hotels they usually frequent, that they'll find here at Grosvenor House an atmosphere duplicated only by the clubs whose membership is limited to these same prominent and wealthy families."

Mr. Belair, whose eyes narrowed as he talked, said when she had finished, "That's exactly it, Mrs. Blake. I want this whole place to be perfect, just perfect, and I think it's a gold mine! I don't like the china we're using in the restaurant. I want something much better than that. Like the slipcovers downstairs. They were made in just one week for me. Measured, ordered, put together, and delivered all in a week. I move fast when I want something. Got a discount on those slipcovers, because they didn't fit just right. I've called up some china people, and they're coming in to see me. I'm going to get something good. Something rich, you know, like the house.

"Well," he broke off, as some guests started over to say good-bye, "how did we do? Was the party all right?"

* * *

As she had promised, Theresa came over to meet Miss Butler, executive secretary of the Anglo-American Society, when she came to Grosvenor House to see Mr. Belair. Theresa thought that he did well with Miss Butler, and she was glad that she had urged him to be around and to let people know him. He was very quiet when Miss Butler explained that their members liked "just thin bread-and-butter sandwiches," and it was very good indeed of Mr. Belair to give them "such a good price." He smiled and expressed delight that the Anglo-American Society was going to hold its opening tea there. Only later, when Miss Butler left, did he say to Theresa, "Now, can you imagine that? Those rich people, and all they want is 'thin bread and butter and no cake, thank you!' And getting a special price, too, when they could all afford the best!"

Then, after a pause he added, "What am I going to do about a head-waiter? You know the fellow I have now just won't do."

"I know a good man," Theresa replied. "John Coris, who used to be with Ed Stevens. He has quite a following and knows his stuff. I hear that he has left Ed. I'll tell him to come see you."

During the next two weeks, Theresa was in constant touch with the board of governors of the Anglo-American Society, as well as with the society and news editors of all the newspapers. Lord Hayes' imminent arrival, frequent meetings of the most prominent members of the organization, and items of news interest were the basis of a daily publicity campaign of stories and pictures released through Theresa's office. She also had numerous pictures taken in the various rooms at Grosvenor House, giving newspaper readers their first glimpse into what was described as the "finest the city had to offer." Theresa knew that hard work had provided the working press with endless details that had saved their time and held their interest, and she began to think that things were running smoothly until she received a frantic telephone call from Miss Butler two days before the reception, asking Theresa to meet her at Grosvenor House.

Theresa found John Coris, the headwaiter, with Miss Butler and Mr. Belair as she arrived. They were in the formal, second-floor dining room, where the reception was to be held. "I'm sorry to have brought you all the way up here, Mrs. Blake," Miss Butler said, "but there seems to be some difficulty about the tea urns. I thought of course Mr. Belair was supplying them, and I find that there aren't any in the house."

John made the suggestion that tea services could be rented from Mr. Grigsby, the caterer, and Theresa noted that Mr. Belair made no response to this practical solution. "The thought has just occurred to me, Miss Butler," Theresa said, "that one of the ladies on your board would be willing to bring over her own silver tea service. As a matter of fact, Mrs. Baker often does that for the church library. Don't you worry about it, I'll call her."

Reassured, Miss Butler left, and as she disappeared Mr. Belair exploded with, "Tea urns! What's the matter with the waiters coming around and pouring the tea?"

"But Mr. Belair," John interjected, "we haven't even a linen cloth for the tea table."

"Tea table?" Belair shouted. "What are you going to do with that?"

Together, Theresa and John explained to Mr. Belair that the room would have to be set up for the reception "with a long table across from the doorway through which people will enter. Women pourers will sit at each end and pour tea and coffee for the guests once they pass through the reception line, which will form at the left directly in front of the fireplace."

Theresa met Jim Appleby on the street a few days after the Anglo-American Society's reception. As they stood chatting, Mr. Appleby said, "Theresa, you were an angel to get all that publicity for us. You know how much we appreciate it. But honestly, did you ever see anything like that cold cinnamon toast? Mountains of it, literally, with Lord Hayes talking about the lack of food in England. And thick! And cold! Can't you do something about it? Grosvenor House is lovely, of course. Although what old Tom Wainwright would say if he could see the changes, goodness knows. I knew that house when I was a boy, and there was nothing like it this side of Europe."

On her next visit to Grosvenor House, Theresa noticed several pages of recent newspapers on the marble table in the entrance hall.

Glancing over them, she saw that they were all pictures and stories on Grosvenor House, particularly those relating to the reception for Lord Hayes.

Mr. Belair joined her as she stood there and, smiling broadly, said, "Boy, we're sure getting a play in the papers!"

"Yes," she replied, "this is what I was counting on. This will start filling your house. They'll start coming because they think it's the place to go. But remember, we have to keep this inner circle happy. And they're a funny crowd. When they say 'bread-and-butter sandwiches,' they mean just that."

"Who told you that? Appleby? Well, let me tell you something, Mrs. Blake," he said. "I've been watching Appleby. He comes in here often for lunch. If you ask me, he doesn't know a good thing when he sees it. Why, he never orders anything but the cheapest luncheon. That's right, he never spends any money in here.

"Besides," he added, "he wears the funniest neckties. Ever notice? Very full bow ties, green sometimes. And he always needs a haircut."

People, indeed, had begun to come to Grosvenor House. The dining room was usually filled at the luncheon and dinner hours, and the cocktail rooms were doing a brisk business. Reservations had been made for several large private parties in the Adam Ballroom, and after Dorothea Blunt's coming-out party there was a marked increase in party reservations. As with the Anglo-American Society's reception, the Sunday papers had devoted the first page of their society sections to the Blunt party. Repeatedly in the following weeks the papers were filled with pictures and stories of the gay afternoon and evening affairs that were being held there. Events of sufficient importance to ensure coverage by the society editors were being held frequently. When the camera men were there for their editors, Theresa was on sufficiently friendly terms from her long association with them that they were glad to give her the "breaks" and went out of their way to show every attractive nook and cranny in the house.

In going over the clipping book with Mr. Belair, Theresa called his attention to the amount of publicity the house was getting and he said, "Sure, I know. It was a wonderful party and I admit it got a lot of publicity. But how about all the kids that were here? Do you see them coming back to eat? Are they spending their money here? Oh, no. I suppose they spend their money in those snooty clubs of theirs. Grosvenor House isn't good enough for them, I suppose."

Theresa pointed out that most of the young people were still in college and that, except for parties, they were probably not going out much. Apparently not satisfied, Mr. Belair continued, "Another thing.

I never got any thanks from Blunt. Not him. He comes in before the party, though, and chisels me down on the price of champagne, but I don't hear him thanking me afterwards. Oh, no!"

Theresa told him that in her opinion the publicity space he was getting was invaluable and that paid advertising could not begin to compete with it.

As the fall progressed, business increased sharply, and scarcely a day passed without a party in the ballroom. At the same time, the dining room was serving a capacity crowd. Since the ballroom and dining room were adjacent and were reached by the same circular staircase, there was often a bottleneck at the head of the stairs. This was upsetting to the guests and made good service difficult.

During this period, Mr. Belair and Theresa had first laughed together about the "traffic jam." "I'm sure getting a full house," Belair would boast.

"That's right," Theresa would retort, "and we've got to give them their money's worth."

Later, however, she suggested, first jokingly and then seriously, "Why not a special traffic cop at the foot of the stairs? Would that help the service? You know a lot of people get upset when they have to wait. Why is it always so bad when they have parties in the ballroom?"

"Listen, Mrs. Blake, do you realize that we have to serve 200 dinners in that ballroom! We get to the regular customers as fast as we can. Why, I took on two extra waiters tonight! Good ones, none of those union waiters who know everything and won't work. Say, listen, don't you worry, they'll keep coming."

"I hope so," Theresa told him, "but I hear a lot of complaints. It's particularly difficult on Thursday noon. That's the day of the Philadelphia Orchestra, and you've probably noticed that the restaurant is always packed with women. Ormandy doesn't like people to be late. They make a point of getting to the concert punctually at two-thirty, and they tell me it's difficult to get served in time."

"So now it's the concert they have to get to!" Mr. Belair exploded. "This isn't a quick-lunch counter, and I don't see why they expect to get served in a hurry!"

"Oh, not in a hurry, Mr. Belair," Theresa replied, "but they shouldn't have to leave without their dessert and coffee. That doesn't make a particularly good impression on them."

"Well, why don't they get here earlier?" Mr. Belair said. After a pause, he continued, "You know those savings bank women who had their meeting here the other day? Well, Mrs. Walsh, who was in charge of the luncheon, came up to me on her way downstairs and said 'Everything was wonderful, Mr. Belair. Just wonderful!' That's what I hear on all sides. Same thing with those editors that are coming in here regularly now for their monthly dinner. They think the house is terrific! Why, they told me there isn't another place like it in the country."

During the Christmas season, Theresa spent an hour with Mr. Belair one late afternoon. The preceding week had been unusually busy at Grosvenor House, with most of the large tables reserved for groups of young people home for the holidays. Theresa had noted that they had often waited almost an hour for their dinner and that their mood had been far less cheerful than when they had arrived. Consequently, that afternoon she came to Grosvenor House concerned about this problem and determined to speak to Mr. Belair about it, but he greeted her with, "Those morons! Morons, I tell you!" and she knew that she would have to "listen him out" first. "I've just been up talking to John," he continued. "I like him, you know. I agree he's a good headwaiter, and people seem to like having him here, but I just told him plenty. 'John,' I said, 'You're spoiling those waiters. Just spoiling them!' You know John works hard, just like I do, but what do those boys of his do? Let him work. That's the way help is today! I've been watching John. He takes the orders from the customers himself. Now, why can't those lazy waiters do that? Not them. They just stand around taking it easy." He went on in this vein for some time and concluded with, "Believe me, I told John he'd better work those waiters harder before he ruins them altogether."

"I was thinking about the restaurant too," Theresa said. "Pretty busy lately, and honestly, Mr. Belair, I don't think people will stand waiting for their dinner as long as they have to. Last night there were lots of young people in, young people home for the holidays and out for a good time. They were going on to the theater, and they all must have gotten there late and disgruntled."

"Aha, those kids!" Mr. Belair exclaimed. "Who wants them in here anyway? Just cluttering up the place. And most of them don't drink, under twenty-one, so they just fill up the tables, and I don't make a nickel on them. Had to wait, did they? Well, it won't hurt them any."

Theresa pointed out to him then, as she had often done before, that Grosvenor House had achieved wide publicity and the reputation of being "the place to go."

"The trouble is, Mr. Belair," she said, "I can bring these people in, but I can't make them come back. That's up to you. And I don't think that making them put up with slow service is the way to do it. After all," she continued, "we've said that Grosvenor House 'recaptures the easy tempo of yesterday.' Sounds good in print, but people don't like to find that it means poor service."

"Sure, sure, I know," Mr. Belair said. "I don't know what's the matter with those morons. After all, I work hard, harder than any of them. Why, do you know, I heard the other day that one of the hotels in town has no dumbwaiter, makes its waiters run up and down 52 steps? Maybe that's what I'd better try around here. Make them work harder, that's the system. Well," he said, terminating the meeting as he looked at his watch, "I've got to go down and see the cooks. See you soon!"

A few days later at a political meeting, the governor of the state cornered Theresa to ask, "What's John's last name? I want to see that he gets something for Christmas. He's a good man. Takes good care of me when I come down to Grosvenor House for lunch."

Thinking it might please Mr. Belair, Theresa told him just after Christmas that the governor thought well of John Coris and had sent him a Christmas present.

"Why, I sent one to the governor myself," Belair replied, "and I haven't even heard from him. Yes, I sent a personalized bottle of whiskey, with their names engraved on it, to each man living in an apartment here and to twelve of my best customers. Haven't heard from any of them. I sent a poinsettia to each of the ladies in the house, twelve of them. Cost me ten dollars apiece."

Theresa knew that the people who received these presents would feel only embarrassment; that if they thought of Mr. Belair at all, it was simply as the owner of Grosvenor House. She felt they did not know how to deal with such a personal gesture on his part. She told Mr. Belair, however, how nice she thought it had been of him and that she was sure that the gifts had been appreciated.

Later, she commented to Tom, "The poor little fellah! Do you suppose I'll ever be able to teach him?"

"Have you tried everything you can think of?" Tom queried.

"Well," she said after a pause, "I haven't shown him Gaston's. Of course it's small, but the service is perfect and the food is out of this world. You know how exquisitely it's decorated."

Early in January, Theresa asked Mr. Belair to lunch with her at Gaston's. It was the first time that they had ever met outside of Grosvenor House. She had reserved a quiet table in the corner where they could see what was going on. Mr. Belair showed her an almost continental attentiveness, seating her with courtesy, snapping his fingers for the waiter to bring the menu, ordering, and later insisting on paying the check, although Theresa had expected him to be her guest.

The food and service were all that Theresa had learned to expect at Gaston's; the menu, written in French, listed only a few luncheon dishes particularly suited to the "social" crowd who lunched there frequently. The food was hot and solicitously served. From time to time during the meal, Theresa mentioned to Mr. Belair a few things that appealed to her at Gaston's, but she felt that he only compared them adversely with Grosvenor House.

As they left the restaurant, Mr. Belair said, "So that's Gaston's! Now what do people see in that little place? Crowded, hot, small, noisy! I can't imagine why they come here when they could come to Grosvenor House."

* * *

Originally, Theresa had thought that she would not have to spend much time in Grosvenor House itself, although she had recognized that special events would require considerable effort from her. However, she felt that public relations was not simply a matter of placing newspaper publicity for a client, but that every impression a client made on the public was an integral part of a sound program. She felt considerable responsibility for the success of Grosvenor House. She found that whatever time she had away from other business she spent in the house. Often her visits coincided with the luncheon and dinner hours, when she could watch the trend of business and determine the kind of people who were coming in. She saw many familiar faces in the restaurant during the winter months, and frequently acquaintances stopped to speak to her about the house. She felt that she still had ample reason to be proud both of the increase in the volume of business and in the type of people who were coming in.

The newsclip book was now a thick volume. In 14 weeks she had accomplished more than she had imagined possible in the fall. In this period eight "spreads," the front picture page of the society sections, had been devoted to Grosvenor House. This was indicative of a wider social acceptance for the house than she could have "imagined in her wildest dreams." The momentum would carry over well into the spring. Mr. Belair always showed the bulky volume proudly to the people who came in to discuss debutante parties, dances, weddings, and other functions. It was producing results. She knew that she would occasionally have to put her weight behind some social function in order "to bring it in," but she felt that, for the most part, the developmental work had been completed.

One evening early in January she said to Tom, "Well, kid, I guess I've made the grade. I stopped in at Sweet's today to check the social calendar. You know, that's where all the invitations are printed, and they've become the final court of appeals on who can have a party when. Anyway, Mrs. Sweet told me we're getting so good at Grosvenor House that we're taking business away from the Chase Club. Seems that Mrs. Marlin and Mrs. Hobson wanted to bring out their granddaughters at the club where, of course, they had come out themselves, and the kids said, 'No.' Darned if they didn't actually insist on coming out at Grosvenor House. How's that for news?"

In spite of these developments Theresa became increasingly discouraged during these winter months about the possibility of Mr. Belair's running an establishment that would continue to appeal to the type of people she was attracting. People had been willing to forget their original worries about the Wainwright sale and were accepting Grosvenor House as the place to go. Yet she knew that the operating standard was far below that which this same public would accept for long. Poor service, she felt, might be excused once or twice but would not be tolerated for long. She noticed, too, that Mr. Belair seemed increasingly agitated over the internal problems of the house.

When she met Georges Milan in the cocktail room of Grosvenor House early in January, she was reminded that he had once had to find a way of getting along with this same inner circle. Years ago, when she had first known him, he had started with a small dance orchestra and had aspired to become the band leader for the society crowd. Today he had more than 20 orchestras playing only for debutante and society parties throughout the East. Now he led his orchestra only on special occasions, and she knew he had agreed to play for the Dance Evenings at Grosvenor House early in the spring.

The Dance Evenings were a series of three parties, held a month apart during the spring, and were the most exclusive affairs of the social season. Only 40 engraved invitations were sent, and each new name on the list had to be sponsored by two people who had attended the previous year. These were the only parties of the year that could not be "crashed," since the invitations were carefully checked at the door. Previously, these dances had been held at the Chase Club; this year, however, Mrs. John Duke had said, "Grosvenor House is *just* as suitable and the ballroom is better."

Theresa had always liked Georges Milan, and through the years they had been of considerable help to each other. She was partic-

ularly interested in the concern that the young Frenchman was showing about Grosvenor House as he talked.

"Gee, Theresa," he began, "I've been talking to Joe about the
Dance Evenings, and he doesn't seem to know what he's got. This
place has got everything and Joe doesn't seem to know it. I never
thought they would let him open up on Bond Street, but they did,
right in the heart of the best residential section in town. Then, he
has a ballroom here that no hotel can compete with—no hotel started
out as the Wainwright mansion. It really has everything, and the
whole town's talking.

"Believe me, I know." He went on, "The hotel men are green
with envy. They see all their best people coming over here. But
I was talking to Joe Belair the other day and he doesn't know what
he's got! He seems to take it for granted that this just happens. You
open and, bingo! Everyone comes running through the door. You
and I know that things don't happen that way."

"He's a peculiar fellah, all right, Georges," she replied. "I'm
having my own troubles with him. I try to make him see my point
of view on this, but I don't get very far."

"Well, how about the three of us sitting down to lunch together
some day?" he asked. "Maybe I can help him. I was new in this
game once myself."

"But you knew how to handle yourself," she said. "It certainly
would be a help to me if someone like you could talk to Belair and
make him see that in dealing with this crowd there are some things
that you can do and some things you can't."

A few days later, as the restaurant was emptying itself of its
noonday crowd, Theresa, Mr. Milan, and Mr. Belair sat at luncheon
together. Mr. Belair and Mr. Milan had met only casually before, and
after the first cocktail they were talking easily together, almost for-
getting Theresa. Of the same nationality, they occasionally lapsed
into their native tongue, joshing each other good-humoredly. When
the second round of cocktails was ordered, Belair said jokingly,
"Don't worry, Georges. You're not paying for them!"

The conversation then became general and Mr. Milan and Theresa
recalled together many episodes from Milan's early days. Mr. Milan
recounted in some detail how his business had grown. He frequently
spoke of how Theresa had helped him.

After the dessert and coffee had been served, he turned to Mr.
Belair and said, "Look, Joe. You've got a wonderful chance here.
Wonderful! Everyone in town is talking about Grosvenor House.
But, good Lord, Joe, I figure I'd better come over and wise you up.

"Take your clothes!" he said, and Theresa watched him lean over and flick the hankerchief that Belair wore in the breast pocket of his coat. "No handkerchief after this. Ix-nay. Isn't done. And look at that suit. Too loud. Now, I know, Joe, you like loud clothes. So do I. But I don't wear them. Used to. But, see this suit," he continued, pointing to his own navy-blue, well-cut clothes. "I always wear a dark suit. When I get home, that's different. But, now, look Joe, you've got to dress like them."

Milan pointed to the few remaining men in the restaurant. "You and I may not like them, but jeez, Joe, we're doing business with them. We've got to look the way they want us to.

"Another thing," Mr. Milan continued, "watch your house! First place, there's the traffic problem. One of the mothers told me the other day that she liked the place all right when her daughter came out here. Except for one thing. Seems there was a Greek wedding party waiting to come in as they left. Now, you can't do that, Joe. It's all right to have the Greeks in here, but for Pete's sake, don't have them meet the social crowd on the stairs. Better to lose the booking than to mess up your traffic. That's what it is, a traffic problem. Don't have the society crowd and the other crowd on the same day. It just won't work!"

He looked around the restaurant, then at their own table as the waiter brought the food. "Now look at this, Joe. The china doesn't match. White dinner plate. Blue cup and white saucer. How can you do it, Joe? You've got a wonderful chance here, Joe. Don't lose it through slipping up on the little things.

"And did you notice," Mr. Milan concluded, "how long it took our lunch to get here, Joe? Thirty minutes. Too long, I tell you."

"Oh, all right," Mr. Belair returned good-naturedly. "You're not paying for it. But seriously, I know what you mean, Georges. And I appreciate your coming over and telling me."

*   *   *

A few days later on the phone to Theresa, Mr. Belair said, "Sure, sure, I'll be here all day. No, I don't know what time. Just come on over. I'll be around."

Theresa often casually dropped in on Mr. Belair. This day she was particularly interested to see what impression Mr. Milan had made on him. As she walked up to Grosvenor House that morning, she recollected that, although Mr. Belair would never make a definite appointment to see her, she never had any difficulty in making an appointment for him to see someone else at a time that she decided.

She also reflected that Mr. Belair had not asked her to come to see him since their first appointment. It was almost as if, in some way, he was working for her.

As she came into the entrance hall, she saw Mr. Belair disappearing through the far door and called him. He hurried towards her and said, as he led her into one of the cocktail rooms, "Come on in here! I want to show you something. This ought to keep them from thinking they can put one over on me." He drew from his pocket a mimeographed sheet which he handed to Theresa. It read:

NOTICE TO ALL EMPLOYEES OF GROSVENOR HOUSE
from JOSEPH BELAIR, OWNER

Beginning immediately, all employees will leave through the front lobby on Bond Street. All parcels or packages that they carry will be examined by me. *Under no circumstances* shall employees leave Grosvenor House through the rear door. Any employee found leaving through or loitering near the rear door will have violated this notice and will be dismissed immediately.

"This will show them who runs this show," Mr. Belair said as Theresa finished reading the memorandum. "These no-good scum," he went on without pause. "Why the union won't even take 'em. They think they can get away with murder. The way the food disappears around this place, you'd think I was running a charity. It's bad enough feeding them without them expecting me to feed their relatives, too."

Theresa settled back in her chair, knowing that once Mr. Belair started off this way, all he wanted was a quiet audience. She reminded herself that on occasion Mr. Belair could adopt a suave, quiet manner with customers very different from the excited behavior he was now demonstrating.

"I said to my cooks last week," Mr. Belair continued, 'How do you think I'm going to make a penny if you don't watch the supplies better than this?' Of course they came up with the same old answer about how there had to be a certain amount of waste to serve quality food. They forget who they're talking to. Why, when I was in the Navy the men tried the same trick, but we found out soon enough that they were holding out extra rations for themselves and charging it up to 'necessary' waste.

"You remember last Tuesday?" he queried, scarcely waiting for Theresa's nod of assent. "Light crowd for lunch, light crowd for dinner; tenderloin of beef on the special and a great big side of beef in the kitchen. All right. You know how much of that was left yesterday, Wednesday? Nothing. Not one, single shred of beef."

"Do you know how many orders were served?" Theresa asked.

"Why should I have to know that?" Mr. Belair exploded. "Dogs they must have, I tell you. Nice little dogs that love nice tenderloin steak. Or ailing mothers, maybe. Or fifteen children, maybe. I'll bet they all went out with a nice big package under their arms. Sure, out the back way and laughing to themselves about what a good one they'd put over. Well, I'll show them."

Taking back the notice from Theresa, he scanned it again with obvious pleasure and said, "I sent it to all of them, every last one. The housekeeper, the maids, the waiters—oh, I know John is all right, but I wasn't making any exception—the checkroom girls, the cooks, all of them. How do I know who takes the food? Might be any of 'em. I tell you they're just scum, taking good wages from me and good tips from the customers, and then sneaking out the back door with food to take home.

"And the airs they put on," he continued. "As if they didn't know who is boss around here. It's 'Yes, sir' and 'Good day, Madame' to the customers; but never mind about Mr. Belair. Why, I run my legs off every day in this place and nobody pays *me*. Do they ever stop to think about that? No. Oh, no. 'Mr. Belair can pay us,' they think. 'That's his worry. He owns this place.' As if I was some kind of a millionaire. Do they ever stop to think what it costs me to run this place? No, they do not. All they think about is how much they can make out of it. Why, I work twice as hard as they do. Running the stairs all day, in the kitchen trying to show the cooks how to cook a meal, keeping after that lazy housekeeper, turning out the lights. Do you think they would ever turn them out?

"You know what she does, that Mrs. Barnes, the housekeeper? Just stands around and bosses the maids. Thinks she's a lady! The other day Norma was sick and didn't show up. Do you think Mrs. Barnes pitched in to do the Rocks' apartment? Oh, no, not Mrs. Barnes. 'I'm an executive housekeeper, Mr. Belair,' she says. Why don't I 'call up the agency and get a replacement maid for the day?'

"It would kill her, I suppose, to push a carpet sweeper around herself," Belair went on. "Just one little carpet sweeper to pick up some of that dust that Mrs. Barnes just can't bear. Now, I ask you, does she ever stop to think of what *I* do in a day? Not her. Not any of them. Just take my money and then steal my food besides."

He stopped to light one of the small cigars which he permitted himself when Grosvenor House was fairly quiet. He took a long draw on it, blew out the thick smoke, then motioned with the cigar to indicate the scope of the house. "This is a big house," he continued. "But do I ever stop to think how many steps I take running around it all day? No. Well, would it hurt the help to think about me once in a while? Why, I put in sixteen hours every day, yes sir, from nine in the morning until one o'clock closing time. No eight-hour shifts for me. Oh, no. I just own the place, I'm just the boss. So I can kill myself working just to make it easy for the help. Why, when I think of the soft job they have—and then they go steal food on top of everything else."

Mr. Belair paused a minute as the customers from the adjacent cocktail room came to the threshold and looked into the room. A fashionably dressed woman, accompanied by a middle-aged man, they admired the oak paneling and the fine oils on the wall. They muttered something scarcely intelligible about the Wainwrights, then left.

"Wainwright!" Mr. Belair continued, apparently having caught something of the couple's comment. "I'll bet those Wainwrights would be plenty surprised if they knew what I had to put up with in help. You know the daughter closed up the place because she couldn't get any decent help. She was right. But at least her old man ran this place without any trouble. Those were the days, I guess. You just hired some good Irish girls green from the hills of Ireland, paid them nothing, and kept them where they belonged. Not this trash today!

"Why, do you know," he added in a lower voice, leaning towards Theresa confidentially, "one of my cooks came in drunk the other day. I showed him, though. He was due in at three, but he didn't get here until four. I was waiting for him. All the help in the kitchen were standing around watching when he came staggering in. He was dead drunk and came weaving over towards me. I was so blind mad at the nerve of that dirty scum coming in here drunk that I don't even remember what I said. I just picked him up by the back of his neck, carried him up the stairs to the back door and booted him out into the street. I tell you, it did me good to get my hands on him. Lucky for him that I didn't beat him up. I just left him out there on the street and walked back down into the kitchen. No one said anything, but I'll bet it taught them a lesson about who was running this place.

"Well," Mr. Belair concluded as he looked at his watch. "I'm glad to have had this talk with you."

He smiled genially at Theresa, obviously more relaxed than at the beginning of the meeting. "It's just a question of showing them who's boss," he said as he folded the memorandum and tucked it away in his pocket.

Although it was just twelve o'clock when Belair terminated their meeting, Theresa went up to the dining room. On the preceding evening she and Tom had dined there, and they had noticed that John had avoided his usual light talk with them. After he had taken their order, they had not seen him again. Knowing about Mr. Belair's memorandum, she now thought it likely that John had been upset, and she hoped that he would not be too busy to talk to her.

As she had expected, none of the tables were occupied as John led her to her usual window table in the far corner, and he bantered with her when he took her order, pretending to disapprove of her request for coffee before, during, and after lunch. "Keep you awake," he admonished.

He returned to her table after he had given her order to a nearby waiter and stood talking to her, keeping one eye on the door. "Maybe you noticed," he said, "I didn't come over last evening. I wanted a little time to think. You know, like I've said to you, Mrs. Blake, I like Mr. Belair all right. But, yesterday, when I got a notice from him I thought maybe he'd gone too far. Do you know about it? Of course, he's pretty excitable, but I never thought he'd send out such a notice, acting as if all my waiters were theives. They're good boys, most of them, and they didn't like it. I didn't know what I was going to say to them, but finally I said, 'Boys, don't you mind, that's just the way Mr. Belair is. He doesn't mean anything by it.' They asked if they really had to go out the front lobby way and have Mr. Belair check them out, but I said, 'No, you just go on doing the way you always have.' So, they left out the back door the same as usual last night, and nothing happened. Mr. Belair, he came in a few minutes ago to talk to me, and he acted like he'd never sent the notice. He's a funny man."

John left her abruptly to seat a group of men and women who had arrived at the door. Coming back to her table, he began immediately with, "You know, it's kind of like my waiter, Dick. Did I tell you about him? You remember how Mr. Belair told my waiters about a month ago that the laundry bill was too high and how they shouldn't change their coats every time they just happened to feel like it."

Theresa remembered Mr. Belair's complaints to her a few weeks ago about the way the "waiters changed their coats five times a day if it suited them and let me worry about the laundry bill." She knew that Dick was one of his best waiters and listened with interest as John continued. "Well, one noon Dick was serving lunch and his jacket was dirty. I know it was dirty because I saw it myself, but the room was crowded, and before I could say anything to him Mr. Belair saw him. 'John,' he said to me, calling me over to the door, 'don't let me see that moron Dick around here again. Fire him. You'd think he'd have sense enough to wear a clean coat!' He spoke to Dick, too. He was pretty excited, but I just said to Dick that night, 'Don't worry. Come on in to work tomorrow. The boss will get over it.' Well, you know he's still here, and Mr. Belair never did ask me why I didn't fire him."

During February and early March, the nature of social entertaining was somewhat modified by Lent. The parties were for the most part small luncheons and dinners. There were no debutante parties. Mr. Belair seemed to be increasingly worried about the operations of the house, and one day when Theresa came in to see him he told her that he was going to fly down to Florida to see his father, who was spending the winter there. He was absent for two weeks, and during this period Theresa observed little change in the operations of the house. The dining room seemed to run smoothly, although the food and service did not improve. John said to her once, "Gee, why doesn't he go away more often! When he's not around, everyone feels better."

When Mr. Belair returned early in March, he began to complain to Theresa about his health. "My father is worried about me," he said many times during their meetings in the succeeding weeks. "He thinks I'm carrying too much responsibility and working too hard. My doctor, too. He says I've got to take it easier. You know, get out and play golf. As if I could ever get away from here!"

As the date for the first Dance Evening drew near, Theresa became increasingly anxious. She knew that, while the pleasure of that particular group would greatly enhance the prestige of Grosvenor House, its displeasure could do immeasurable harm.

She was not at all surprised when Mrs. Duke came into her office one afternoon and said, "My committee wants to go over to Grosvenor House. They think it's charming, and, of course, it is, but I stopped in to make arrangements last week and, really, Theresa, I found your Mr. Belair very difficult. I had to wait for him for almost an hour, although I had an appointment. He was very flustered when he came to talk to me. Told me about the troubles he's having with his help and how hard he has to work. I'm sure I'm sorry, Theresa, and I suppose it's hard on him that he can't sleep at night and that he is very nervous, as he says. But, really, he scarcely listened to me when I told him how the rooms had to be arranged for our Dance Evening.

I just wonder if everything will be all right. You know how important details are. Still, I must confess that the Wainwright house will be a perfect place for the party."

Theresa replied, "I am sorry. I know how difficult Mr. Belair is lately. He's been worrying me, too. I'll do everything I can to make sure that things will be as you want them."

When Mrs. Duke left, Theresa dictated a lengthy memorandum on the Dance Evening, outlining all the details that would have to be watched. She included instructions for the setting up of the tables, for the flower arrangements, for the special champagne bar that was to be opened in the dining room, for the amount of floor space that would have to be cleared for the dance itself. When she had finished, she decided that she must go over these notes carefully with Mr. Belair.

According, the next day she went to Grosvenor House and told Mr. Belair that she had come up to discuss the Dance Evenings with him. He said, "Sit down, I'll be with you in a few minutes." Then he walked quickly into the bar, and Theresa overheard him talking to Jimmy, the head bar man. Theresa settled herself, and some 20 minutes later Mr. Belair joined her. "What a day!" he began. "I wonder what these morons would do around here without me. Just now, I was finishing stocktaking with Jimmy. I swear, I don't know what happens to the liquor around this place. I say to Jimmy: 'Look, our customers pay for one drink at a time; you needn't be so generous with my liquor.' Still, the liquor disappears. You should see the jiggers they use. Plenty big to measure with. But no, they have to put a little extra in always!"

Theresa knew that Jimmy was considered one of the best bar men in town and that he had a large following of customers.

"Now, those Dance Evenings!" Mr. Belair exclaimed. "And that Mrs. Duke! She's just like all the rest of these rich people. I tell you, they want everything, everything! Why, she came in to see me yesterday morning just to ask me what kind of flowers we were going to use to decorate the tables. Said the committee wanted to know. Now, I ask you! I suppose they expect orchids, too, for that price. I gave them a good price on their party, but believe me, I never would have if I'd thought they'd bother me like this. Do they ever worry about me? Not them. Oh, no, it's 'give us this and give us that' and never mind how Joe Belair is going to make a nickel.

"I tell you," he continued vehemently, "these people are just cheap-skates! Why, not one of them made any money, ever; they just inherit it from their folks and then they hang onto it as tight as they can. And the manners they have! They come sailing in here as if they owned the place. Cold fish, they are. Hardly time to bow to me. Do they ever stop to think that I own this place?"

He took a small cigar from his pocket, snapped off the end, lighted it, and then pointing it towards Theresa continued, "You know my father! Now, there's a real man. Smart? Why, my father's smarter than all these people put together." He sat back in his chair, and his eyes lighted with warmth. "My father is really a remarkable man," he said. "I've never met anyone like him. Why, do you know, he came over here without a penny to his name? Not one cent. And today he's a rich man. Nobody gave him a nickel; he made every cent for himself. Do you know, he started out with a little vegetable cart in Coatesville, just peddling vegetables on the street. And two years later he'd bought himself a grocery store. Not much of a place. But he was from the old country and he knew good vegetables and meat; and he saved his money, and a few years later he bought the lot the store was on. That was before I was born, but my folks lived up over the store with my two brothers and two sisters. They're all older than I am. I'm what you'd call the baby of the family."

He was obviously enjoying himself, and Theresa listened quietly. "Well, just twelve years later, when I was ten, my father owned the whole square block around the store, and he kept right on buying real estate. There was a hotel on his property that burned down, so he took that over. Gee, what a gold mine it has been for him! He took it over and rebuilt it in my sophomore year at Norton. During summer vacation, I came home and carried bricks. Most fun I ever had! I often think when I see the people around here about how much I liked being a bricklayer. Good clean work, and I sure had the muscles for it. I was the best boxer at Norton, you know."

He smiled and flexed his muscles, taking hold of his left upper-arm and saying, "Still in pretty good shape for a man of 38! Well, as I was saying, I laid bricks when I was in my sophomore year. I went to college young, you know. Only 16 when I got through Norton. My father was proud of me, too, thought I was pretty bright. But then, my father has always been good to me.

"Look at this place," he said, looking around the room. "Beautiful, just beautiful. My father came in to look at it with me when we were thinking of buying it, you remember. But once he'd bought it for me, he said, 'You leave me in the background now. This is your place.' You remember, he wouldn't even come to the press party before we opened up.

"My brothers are green with envy. There they are just plugging away in the Coatesville hotel, and every time they pick up a paper they read about Grosvenor House! 'Quite a place Joe is running,' they say." After a pause he said, "They haven't been in here yet.

"Really," he said, warming up to his subject again, "my father is a wonderful man. Wonderful! By the time I was through college, he had bought up real estate down in Florida. He isn't as well as he was, and I worry about him. Well, anyway, he bought all this real estate down there and he just hung on. World War II came along, and he made plenty of money when the government took over. He owned a hotel down there by that time, and the government took it over for the WACS. I renegotiated the contract with the government for him later. He made plenty out of it. That's the thing. Nobody ever gave him a cent. He's not like these rich people that come in here, but he made a fortune for himself. He knew how to make money. Everything he touched turned to money. Both my brothers work down at the Coatesville hotel, you know, but I never had anything to do with it—except laying bricks, that is.

"I lost a lot of years in the war," Belair continued. "Five years in the Pacific! But before that, I worked at this and that. I was a liquor salesman for a while. That's why these morons in the bar drive me crazy. Acting as if they knew more than I do about liquor.

"But anyway, when I got through the war, my father asked me what I wanted to do. I'd gotten married, my little girl is almost two now, and he wanted me to get settled. He's a wonderful family man himself. People are always coming to him asking his advice; really, everyone thinks my father is a wonderful man." He smiled again warmly and continued, "He would have given me the money to go into the personal loan business, where I had a good opportunity, but that didn't appeal to me. I heard this place was for sale, and you know that once I saw it I knew I had to have it. Beautiful, isn't it? Just beautiful! These brothers of mine plugging away down at the hotel in Coatesville, but look what I've got here. Nothing like it! Well, my father said all right, if that was what I wanted. Of course, that's why I've got to make a go of it. Once in a while my wife will say to me, 'Why aren't you ever home any more?' But how can I be home when I need to keep my eye on this place every minute?

"Women!" he said. "Always complaining! 'Why don't you take me to the show?' my wife asks. Or, 'Don't you want to play bridge?' Bridge! Can't she realize that if I didn't stay in here all the time, these morons would ruin it for me? Why, they'd steal the food and liquor right away from me. Remember that notice I sent around? Well, I notice the food isn't disappearing so fast. Oh, no. They know I'm watching them."

Theresa asked if the help were checking out through the front lobby, and he shrugged, "Of course not! I can't have those scum bumping into the guests, can I? But they know they can't get away with anything." A bar waiter came over to tell Mr. Belair that a Mr. Kelly wanted to see him, and he sent word that he'd be right out. "Have him wait in the lobby."

"Now that's an example of how things are around here. You remember I told you how I'd bring the cost down on food when I took over the buying. I said to the cooks, 'If you won't save any money for me, I'll show you how it can be done.' This Kelly that wants to see me, he's a salesman for a wholesale company. I'll be right back."

Returning some ten minutes later, he reseated himself and said enthusiastically, "Now that proves it! Kelly told me just now that I could save three cents a pound on fowl. Can you imagine those cooks, the morons, buying down at the market and paying any prices they feel like? Wait till I tell them they could have gotten fowl three cents a pound cheaper!"

Theresa realized that the cooks must still be doing the food buying, in spite of many threats that Mr. Belair had made to take it out of their hands. Only occasionally, when salesmen like Mr. Kelly came to call, did Mr. Belair repeat his threat to take over the purchase of the food.

"Now, about this Dance Evening, Joe," Theresa said, thumbing through her notes.

"That Duke woman!" he exploded. "Her and her kind! She drives me crazy. No, don't bother me about that. You just work it out with John, will you?

"Well," he said, rising, "it was mighty nice seeing you. I've got to go now. I'm going down to tell that fool cook what I found out about the price of fowl."

He walked away quickly, and as Theresa started up the stairs to see John, she heard Mr. Belair running down the marble stairs towards the kitchen.

From then on Theresa worked closely with John on the details of all three Dance Evenings. Preparations for each party were so hectic that Theresa and Mrs. Duke both felt the rooms would never be ready in time. When the time came, however, the parties seemed to go reasonably smoothly. The change in locale from the Chase Club to Grosvenor House was an event which Theresa was able to build into an unusual amount of space in the press. Pictures and stories appeared almost weekly on these Dance Evenings and other events during these months.

Mr. Belair was not at Grosvenor House on the night of the first Dance Evening. Georges Milan came on from New York to lead his special string orchestra and expressed to Theresa his concern at Mr. Belair's absence on such an important occasion.

"He'll be sorry to have missed you." Theresa said. "He must have been detained by something important."

Actually, she had expected him to be there. This was the first time that he had not been present when an important event was taking place at Grosvenor House.

* * *

At the conclusion of the Dance Evenings late in April, Mr. Belair informed Theresa that he had been able to have Bill Quigley's orchestra engaged for the dances that had been booked later in the spring. Because he was a nonunion musician, Quigley was banned from the hotels in town.

"Milan never brought me a nickle's worth of business," Mr. Belair told her. "Quigley says he'll bring some real business in here next year. He's had a tough break, and I think he ought to be given a chance."

Community Church (A)

"GENTLEMEN, I'm through," Reverend Richard Whyte stated one spring evening in 1946. "From this point on, I'll do anything that Dr. Emory says. Whatever he wants me to do, I will do it."

The small unofficial gathering of Community Church trustees had been conferring with Reverend Whyte all evening. The trustees were unanimously in favor of dissuading the 23-year-old minister from resigning his position as "associate" to Dr. Clyde Emory, the pastor of the church.

"Surely there ought to be something that we can work out," said one of the old trustees, when the clamor which had followed the associate minister's announcement subsided.

"I must do as he says because I'm afraid of him. I'm afraid of what he can do to me personally and professionally. Please excuse me now." Reverend Whyte left.

Dr. Emory, who had been the subject of much of the evening's conversation, was not present at the meeting. Although he was nearing 70, the pastor was still a man of force and vigor. He had come to Community Church 36 years before the associate minister, and despite the younger man's popularity, Dr. Emory retained a great deal of prestige among his congregation. When he had taken the pastorate of Community Church almost forty years earlier, there were only two hundred in the congregation. By 1945, the congregation had grown to more than one thousand members. Dr. Emory was characterized by some of his congregation as "aggressive but with great qualities of personal charm" and as "a man who dominated every situation he was in."

His title of "Doctor" was an honorary one. He held a Master of Divinity degree from a large Midwestern university. He was the father of two grown sons, both of whom were in the armed service. Seven years after the death of his wife, he had remarried. His second wife was a woman of independent wealth. Chiefly because of his religious writings, in which he had always been interested, Dr. Emory was well-known in ecclesiastical circles throughout the United States.

His position in Community Church was, in many ways, unique, partly because of the peculiarly loose-knit organization of the church and partly because of his own dominant personality. Community Church, located in one of the suburbs of a large industrial city in the Midwest, was one of the many independent churches in America. Although it was affiliated with a brotherhood of similarly independent or "free" churches in a national association, each church had final authority over its own local problems. The pulpit of the church was also "free"; the Board of Elders (the ranking unit in the hierarchy of the church) did not presume to question the minister's theology. Everything which occurred in Community Church was initiated locally—primarily through the leadership of Dr. Emory. It was said that "he represented the masterpiece of authority."

The power of the church was supposedly invested in a Board of Elders, a Board of Trustees, and a Board of Deacons. These three groups plus the president of the congregation constituted the "Official Board" of the church. The Board of Elders was made up of ten men: three schoolteachers, a doctor, a lawyer, an engineer, and four businessmen. The Board of Trustees consisted of twelve members, including business and professional men. Some of them were prominent in the industrial life of the city in which the church was located, and a few were extremely wealthy. The Board of Deacons was composed of seven younger men, a good many of whom had been in the armed services. Most of the Deacons were businessmen. The chairmen of each of these three Boards and the president of the congregation were elected to their positions by the congregation as a whole.

There were few, if any, of the congregation who knew all the men who were on the Official Board, which met only when the pastor called a meeting. Although the by-laws of the church originally called for a three-man Board of Trustees, its size had been gradually increased to the present twelve; Dr. Emory had seen to it that prominent men (doctors of philosophy, wealthy businessmen, and well-known professional men) were appointed to this Board from time to time. When he desired to get something done quickly, the pastor called together only those members of the Official Board whom he thought favorable to his ideas.

Although many men on the various boards were well-to-do, the congregation was made up of many people in ordinary circumstances. Contributions ranged from 50 cents to $200 per month. The congregation was characterized by the president of the congregation (a YMCA secretary) as "a healthy lot—not too religious, with a high sense of values, a broad sense of humor, and a healthy outlook."

Final authority lay in the hands of the congregation, which had the power to hire and fire the minister. Every January an annual election of officers was held. The greater part of the congregation participated in the election, and at that time the minister was also elected—in the case of Dr. Emory, re-elected.

There was no written outline of duties for Dr. Emory, and as one member of the church stated, "he dominated the entire congregation." The congregation elected its own president, however, and this man had power to call meetings of the congregation without contacting the Official Board.

The church had ordained Dr. Emory as its minister, and "after that," said a member, "it was a one-man show."

The sequence of events which resulted in the unofficial meeting at which Reverend Whyte announced his decision to do as Dr. Emory told him began when Dr. Emory told the Board of Elders that because of his age (he was 69), he could no longer carry on his former duties without the aid of an assistant. Four years previously he had been advised by the Board of Elders to retire because of his age, and, in fact, he had said that he would do so. When the years had passed and he had done nothing definite about retiring, his more intimate associates on the Official Board of the church concluded that he would not retire until he died.

In 1941 when war was declared, Dr. Emory decided to remain active "for the duration." During the following years, the possibility of hiring someone to assist him in his duties was discussed with him numerous times. Mrs. Arthur Bates, whose husband was one of the largest contributors to the church, urged him to engage Reverend Richard Whyte, a young man whom she had heard preach while on her vacation. Dr. Emory, when this was first suggested, rejected this particular man because he felt an older man would be more suitable. He did eventually, however, accept the idea that an assistant would be helpful to him.

In September 1945, Dr. Emory told the Board of Elders that he needed a man to help him in administrative matters. The Board of Elders recommended to the Board of Trustees that an assistant minister be employed. In turn, the Board of Trustees authorized the raising of funds to engage a man. The members of the Official Board, having had some previous experience in matters of this sort, lost no time in taking the necessary steps to help their pastor, for whom all the members had a high regard.

Everyone was in complete agreement as to the type of man needed. Since Mrs. Bates strongly recommended that Reverend Whyte could "fill the bill," and since there were not very many men available (the war in the Pacific had hardly ended), Dr. Emory made up his mind that young Reverend Whyte was "the man for the job" even before he invited him to meet the Official Board. The Board of Trustees raised $1000 to help defray the expense of employing an assistant minister.

Reverend Whyte was hired through a committee of the Official Board, with the approval of the entire Board. Although Mrs. Bates's son was instrumental in taking the direct action which brought him under contract, young Whyte was the final choice of Dr. Emory.

Before he was hired Reverend Whyte had numerous conferences with Dr. Emory. Broad objectives of their work together were discussed fully. They concluded that they were to be "comin?isters," that the young minister had certain responsibilities, that Reverend Whyte was not to be the errand-boy of the older man, and that Reverend Whyte was to preach at least once a month. This latter agreement was surprising, since Dr. Emory, from the beginning, had not been at all interested in getting an assistant who could preach. The two men also made a gentlemen's agreement not to limit one another's duties to an arbitrarily prescribed schedule. That one man would carry on the service whenever the other man preached was, however, implicit in their agreement.

Richard Whyte had spent a year and a half studying at two divinity schools of well-known interdenominational colleges, in addition to being a graduate of a metropolitan college. He had volunteered for service in the Navy but had been rejected because of a physical disability. At Clearwood, the summer resort at which Mrs. Bates had met and heard him preach, the young minister had been pastor for more than a year. His congregation there was small in the winter but comparatively large during the summer.

When he came to Community Church in October 1945, Reverend Whyte was well received immediately. Said a member of the Board of Trustees, "God blessed him with good looks, a good mind, and a good voice." He was married to an attractive woman who had been a Phi Beta Kappa student at college. Both were invited to dinner parties frequently—sometimes alone, often with the older minister. At first the two men sat down together from week to week and worked out their plans cooperatively. Although the older minister had never spent time calling on members of his church (except when someone was ill), young Whyte habitually visited various members of the congregation. Before very long Dr. Emory, too, began calling upon members of the congregation, many of whom had been previously visited by the younger man. "Associate" Minister Whyte knew of these visits but he said nothing about them.

The congregation of Community Church, many of whose members were from distant parts of the city, had been decreased during the war because of the curtailed transportation facilities. It began to increase steadily after Reverend Whyte's arrival at the church. The congregation was noticeably larger when he spoke than when Dr. Emory spoke. After a sermon by the young minister, the congregation flocked about him. Contributions grew larger. The work of young people in the church began to expand. Even the budget was increased. Everywhere, Dr. Emory began to hear "how nice that new young man was."

It soon became evident to Reverend Whyte, however, that Dr. Emory and he were not getting along. The young minister confided in a friend: "Our personalities clash; our methods are different; even our goals aren't the same." The two men found they could not talk together with any great degree of understanding. Mrs. Bates's son was one of the first to notice the widening gulf between the old pastor and his associate. Although he had never been a "church" man before, young Bates had joined the church because he liked Reverend Whyte. Meeting the two men together one day, Bates sat down with them and asked: "What's the matter with this team? It doesn't seem to be clicking." At this point the old minister lost his temper and angrily accused his young associate of attempting to undermine him.

As a result of this outbreak Reverend Whyte realized that there was more than a personality conflict between Dr. Emory and himself. The young minister had believed up to this time that the older man would soon retire. However, Reverend Whyte concluded that Dr. Emory would not retire if he thought that he (Reverend Whyte) were to become his successor. Young Reverend Whyte believed that Dr. Emory should have retired because, he said, of "his age, his mental inflexibility, and his hyper-excitability."

Sometime later the old minister left Community Church for a two-month vacation. Before he went away, he urged the young minister not to work too hard and not to be too concerned about his sermons. While on vacation, Dr. Emory met an old, retired minister with whom he discussed his worries and fears. The retired minister warned him to be careful of the young associate minister because he might "stab you in the back."

Meanwhile Reverend Whyte assumed full responsibility in Community Church during his colleague's absence. The congregation became increasingly larger as the weeks passed and the young man filled the pulpit. Young Whyte was very pleased, and, when Dr. Emory returned, the young minister waxed enthusiastic. "There's one thing I learned while you were away," he casually boasted to his superior, "I can run this church."

Soon after he returned, Dr. Emory began to talk in a derogatory way about Reverend Whyte. He said, even from the pulpit, that "certain young men should have been in the armed services during the war" and implied that Reverend Whyte had been a slacker. He talked about the young minister more and more to various members of the congregation. He implied on more than one occasion that the young associate minister needed more education. For three weeks after his return he preached a series of "Judas" sermons from the pulpit.

On Easter weekend, 1946, Dr. Emory went to the office of Reverend Whyte and asked him some pointed questions about his future plans and intimated that the young man should by all means continue his education. Reverend Whyte, who had never deliberately crossed Dr. Emory before, became thoroughly incensed at this point and asked bluntly: "Why don't you retire?"

Dr. Emory "hedged" at first, and then he began to argue with the young minister about a number of things. For the first time Reverend Whyte "talked back" to his superior. Reverend Whyte told Dr. Emory that he was his own worst enemy and that he had an uncanny faculty for "hurting people." The young minister cited examples of persons who had fallen away from Community Church after arguments or misunderstandings with the pastor. Their altercation continued for about three hours, during which time they were not interrupted once. Finally young Whyte said: "I'll tell you what I'll do, Dr. Emory. I'll resign my position if you will resign yours."

This decision was apparently satisfactory to the old minister. He said if Reverend Whyte would resign, he would retire, effective the following annual meeting in January 1947. The next week Dr. Emory made known his plans to several members of the Board of Trustees. He also asked Reverend Whyte to write out his resignation. Dr. Emory dictated certain statements to be included, which would protect him from any possible accusation that he was turning the young minister out. Reverend Whyte gave as his reason for resigning the desire to continue his education. After signing the resignation, which was to be read to the congregation by its president the following Sunday morning, Reverend Whyte submitted the resignation to Dr. Emory. (The practice of reading resignations and other official documents to the congregation was in keeping with an unwritten law of the church.) Before the following Sunday Dr.

Emory took Reverend Whyte's resignation to some of the trustees. All were bewildered by it, so they invited Reverend Whyte to confer with them. The upshot of their conference was that the trustees advised the young minister not to resign, even though he had presented his signed resignation to Dr. Emory.

By this time news of the impending resignation began to leak out to the congregation. The telephones of many church members rang constantly, and members of the congregation began to discuss the situation in Community Church. Gossip increased. For a few days there were unofficial meetings among the more interested members of the church. They talked and argued about the possibilities of losing the young minister. Young Reverend Whyte was called into many of these meetings. He stated his side of the case clearly and gained considerable support. It was at one of these meetings that he said, "I must do as he says because I'm afraid of him. I'm afraid of what he can do to me personally and professionally." The entire Board of Trustees, which had been very close to the old minister for more than thirty years, now took the side of the young man. When it was found, however, that nothing could be decided at the many unofficial meetings, which Reverend Whyte and members of the Board of Trustees had attended, Reverend Whyte refused to have anything more to do with working out a solution.

Discussions among members of the congregation and the Board of Trustees continued—in the streets, over telephones, and in small gatherings at the homes of church members. Soon persons who had no affiliation with Community Church learned of the impasse. One member of the congregation who had followed developments carefully estimated that more than 75 per cent of the congregation was in full sympathy with the young minister. Approximately 100 young, college-age students of the church school, all of whom had been friendly with Reverend Whyte, threatened to leave the church. Many of these students had joined the church since the young minister's association with the school.

The Official Board—with notably few exceptions—was also in sympathy with the young minister. Most of the blame for the situation which had been precipitated was accorded to Dr. Emory. It was generally conceded that Reverend Whyte had done nothing to undermine his older colleague.

On the Friday night preceding the Sunday on which the young minister's resignation was to be read, the president of the congregation announced that he would not read it in church on Sunday. On Saturday morning Dr. Emory announced that Reverend Whyte would read his own resignation. Later that day the old minister said that no one would read the resignation. An official meeting of the Board of Trustees and the Board of Deacons took place on Saturday night. At the meeting Dr. Emory tore up both his statement of retirement and Reverend Whyte's resignation.

On Sunday morning nothing unusual occurred: the old minister preached the sermon; Reverend Whyte carried on the service and sat on the platform with Dr. Emory.

The congregation of Community Church was in a turmoil. Dissatisfaction was mounting when the church service was over.

Part Four

Environmental Constraints

THE cases in the previous sections of this book provided opportunities for analyzing the nature and some of the determinants of group and interpersonal processes. Environmental determinants—influences "outside" the group or the interpersonal relationship—were present in all of these cases, but in most of them some important aspects of the environment were at least one step removed from the group. The groups of industrial workers, for example, did not deal directly with customers or suppliers, and had little to do with the design of their work technologies. Group boundaries were permeated mainly by relationships with authority figures within the organizations and by the individual workers' lives outside of working hours, in their families and subcultures.

In contrast, both studies in this section involve groups whose members are in more intimate contact with relevant environments while on the job. In the Watkins and Worster advertising agency, the account executives and creative and technical personnel interact daily with their various clients and suppliers, as well as with each other. Their statuses within the organization may be related to the social classes and statuses of the particular outsiders with whom they, as individuals, interact in the performance of their work. Furthermore, cultural effects attach differential value, or prestige, to kinds of clients (compare banks with food products and industrial products) and kinds of advertising media (compare television, radio, national magazines, and local newspapers with each other). Thus, the values and meanings attributed in the wider culture to the various objects, symbols, and activities involved in the agency's work are encountered continually by the members on their jobs and with each other. In addition, the individual's salary and job title in the organization, educational background, "cosmopolitan" or "local" type of experience, and whether male or female, all come to bear in the work situation, with consequences which may be investigated through analysis of the case data.

In addition to presenting the usual kind of case data, the Watkins and Worster Agency material includes an interpretive analysis which spells out in detail the influences of environmental constraints. It is important for the student to separate the data from the interpretation in his mind, and to attempt to offer different or additional interpretations on his own. At the same time, he has the opportunity to study one model of interpretation which may be of help in analyzing other cases, and to study the implications which the case analyst discusses.

The New England Markets, Inc. study takes place around a research investigation into causes of differences in the profit performance of individual stores in a supermarket chain. It describes the research strategy and presents the data uncovered in the study. In this case, interpretation is left to the student. As in Watkins and Worster, the personnel in the grocery stores interact daily with outsiders as well as insiders. For some of the workers, their customers may be their neighbors. Furthermore, there are significant differences between part-timers, mostly young high school or college students, and regular, full-time workers. The study focuses attention on the movement, or lack of movement, of various kinds of workers from one part of the store to another. Technically, such movement is necessary to meet fluctuations in the hourly and day-to-day flow of customers and merchandise in and out of the store. However, this mobility, and especially the lack of it in some instances, has a social and emotional meaning to the individual workers and groups involved which has little to do with the technical requirements of managing the flows of groceries and customers, but which bears a significant relationship to the profitability of the store. An understanding of the cultures, both within and outside the store, can lead to a deeper understanding of what it is, socially and interpersonally, that the individuals move toward or away from while working in the store.

The Watkins and
Worster Agency (B)

*A Study of Interpersonal Relations
in an Advertising Agency*

Watkins and Worster: What Is It?

The Watkins and Worster advertising agency was a large, well-established company with headquarters in New York and regional offices in several other cities. A case researcher from the Harvard Business School studied the W & W Northwest City Regional Office in the spring of 1958. This office had been in existence about a year, employed 26 persons, and served four W & W clients in the area.

Watkins and Worster: What Does It Represent?

The case material represents two main foci of interest. First, it provides the opportunity to examine the environmental constraints surrounding the 26 agency employees and the manner in which these constraints influenced their group formation, interpersonal relations, and problem-solving capacities. Second, it provides the opportunity to see how these issues were worked out in a largely middle-class milieu of salaried, "white collar" personnel whose skills were professional or semiprofessional and whose approach to work and to life in general closely approximated that of members of the more established professions.

Life in the advertising industry may be permeated with "Madison Avenue" connotations of glamour and controversy. The public reads of particularly fascinating personalities working in this modern and dynamic industry or hears arguments between those who believe that advertising agencies perform a useful function in society and those who contend that advertising does a disservice to society. The arguments on both sides range from the purely economic to the purely moralistic. The agency itself is the "arena" in which such controversies are acted out.

What Is Meant by "Environmental Constraints"?

Environmental constraints are the physical, technological, and social characteristics that impinge upon the members of a group from the world around them. The members' responses influence the structure of the group and the interpersonal dynamics.[1]

ANALYSIS OF THE REGIONAL OFFICE ENVIRONMENT

The environment of W & W's Northwest City Regional Office can be analyzed along several different dimensions, each of which had certain influential or constraining characteristics. The dimensions to be used in this analysis will be: (a) the advertising *industry* as a whole; (b) the *technology* of advertising and marketing services; (c) the *geographical proximity* of the Regional Office to the Head Office and to the client organizations; (d) the *functional proximity* of the office to these other organizations; (e) the *formal organization* of the office; and (f) the *status attributes* and *value systems* of the employees. Sections I, II, and III of this paper will describe and analyze the environmental constraints impinging upon the personnel of the Regional Office.

THE INFLUENCE OF ENVIRONMENTAL PROPERTIES ON GROUP PROCESSES

Defining the concept of "constraint" is one starting point for an analysis of the influence of environmental constraints on group processes. To constrain is "to compel, to force; to secure by bonds, to confine; to bring into narrow compass; to hold back by force, to restrain."[2] Hence, a constraint is that which compels, holds back by force, or restrains. How do environmental factors hold back or restrain group processes? What sort of a group is it? How do

---

[1] In analyzing W & W's Northwest City Regional Office, the term "group" will refer only to the persons working in the office. It will not refer to the office itself, since its formal organization was one of the important environmental constraints impinging upon the group.

[2] *Webster's New Collegiate Dictionary,* Second Edition, 1959.

members define their group situation? We shall try to determine how constraints of the Regional Office environment "bring into narrow compass" the answers that actually apply to the group. In Section IV of this analysis, case material pertaining to the social structure of the regional office group will be presented.

INFLUENCE OF ENVIRONMENTAL PROPERTIES ON THE INDIVIDUAL

During the research, several officewide account group meetings were recorded in the Northwest City Regional Office. Section V will examine the influence of environmental constraints upon several agency personnel, as manifested in the interpersonal relations that are portrayed in the transcripts of some of these meetings. The analysis will highlight the relationship between external environmental characteristics and such internal phenomena as self-concepts, feelings of competence, feelings of dependence or independence, role types, manifest and latent role relationships, and relationships with authority.

THE INFLUENCE OF ENVIRONMENTAL PROPERTIES ON PROBLEM SOLVING AND THE ACHIEVEMENT OF ORGANIZATIONAL OBJECTIVES

In the final section of this analysis, Section VI, we shall examine the management implications arising from the social organization of W & W's Northwest City Regional Office. We shall review our analysis primarily from the point of view of John Goode, the regional manager and vice president of W & W, and examine the issues facing him as he sought to direct the group to work together toward the achievement of the organizational objectives of the regional office and the agency as a whole.

I. THE FORMAL ORGANIZATION AS AN ENVIRONMENTAL CONSTRAINT

Not all organizations are equally influenced by all the environmental constraints outlined in the introduction. The most important environmental characteristics for the W & W Northwest City Regional Office were: (a) the formal organization of the office; and (b) the status and value "givens" that the office personnel had brought with them into the agency. Other characteristics of the regional office had less constraining or controlling influence on group processes, interpersonal relations, and problem solving in the organization. These characteristics will also be discussed briefly.

The Division of Labor

Exhibit 1 presents the formal organization of the Northwest City Regional Office. It shows the formal relationships of the 26 individual employees of the agency in performing the agency's tasks. This organization of personnel represents two differentiations that were formally drawn between the members of the office group: one was type of work and the other was amount of authority.

The specialization of function portrayed in Exhibit 1 was clearly set forth in the W & W Operations Manual. Account management served as the main contact between the clients and the agency, and saw "that the clients they service receive the best possible work from each department and from the agency as a whole."

A client's account was normally served by at least an account supervisor and an account executive. The Operations Manual stated that the account supervisor was expected to "maintain client control through high-level contact, . . . attend important meetings with the clients but train his account executives to handle day-to-day contacts, . . . be responsible for overall marketing plans and all major advertising plans, . . . be a marketing expert in the fields of his clients, . . . and be responsible for the quality of work done for the clients." In W & W's larger offices, the account supervisor reported to the regional manager.

Reporting to the account supervisor were the account executives assigned to several different accounts. According to the Operations Manual, the account executive was expected "to do a majority of contact work with his client, . . . to communicate on all account matters to his account group, . . . to assist the account supervisor in preparation of marketing plans, . . . to write advertising plans based on work prepared under his direction by his account group, . . . to delegate detail work but not responsibility to the account coordinator, . . . to respect client's wishes but not accede to unreasonable demands for waste work, impossible due dates, or special services without proper remuneration, . . . to assume responsibility for keeping cost on his account within the client-approved budget."

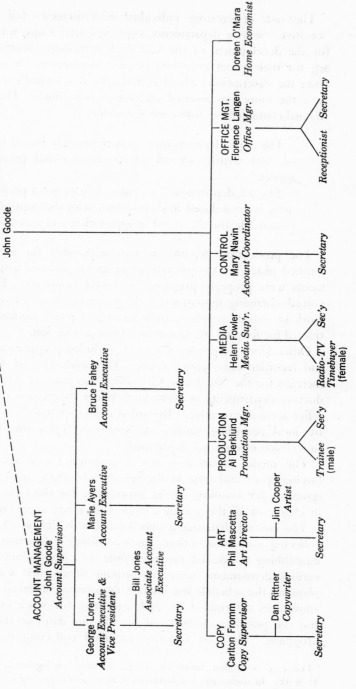

EXHIBIT 1

THE WATKINS AND WORSTER AGENCY (B)

Organization of the Northwest City Office

--- Regional Manager and Vice President
John Goode

ACCOUNT MANAGEMENT
John Goode
Account Supervisor

George Lorenz
*Account Executive &
Vice President*

— Bill Jones
*Associate Account
Executive*

Secretary

Marie Ayers
Account Executive

Secretary

Bruce Fahey
Account Executive

Secretary

COPY
Carlton Fromm
Copy Supervisor

— Dan Rittner
Copywriter

Secretary

ART
Phil Mascetta
Art Director

— Jim Cooper
Artist

Secretary

PRODUCTION
Al Berklund
Production Mgr.

Trainee   Sec'y
(male)

MEDIA
Helen Fowler
Media Sup'r.

Radio-TV   Sec'y
Timebuyer
(female)

CONTROL
Mary Navin
Account Coordinator

Secretary

OFFICE MGT.
Florence Langen
Office Mgr.

Receptionist   Secretary

329

The task of creating individual advertisements fell to the two "creative"[3] service departments, copy and art. Copy was responsible for the development of the verbal ideas used in advertisements, and art, for their visual interpretation and appearance. It was not clear from the descriptions which department was formally considered to have the more fundamental creative responsibility. The Operations Manual contained the following statements:

> The copy department . . . is responsible for all creative work on, and writing of, all advertising material prepared by the agency.
>
> The art department . . . once an idea for a printed advertisement is crystallized in conjunction with the copy department, is responsible for the visual interpretation and execution of the ad.

The production department was responsible for seeing that the finished plates for the printing of magazine and newspaper advertisements were properly prepared by outside suppliers. This work involved obtaining quotations, making agreements, and overseeing the work of outside suppliers, such as art and photo studios, which contracted for finished art, layout, and plate production.

Other kinds of production work included preparation of TV film and recorded radio commercials. The production of TV film commercials for the Northwest City office was done by the W & W production departments in New York under supervision of the regional office account executive. Recorded radio commercials were produced by local recording studios in Northwest City, usually under the supervision of the copy department.

The media department was responsible for recommending and buying space and time in the several advertising media. It was responsible for choosing media appropriate for the campaign and was in charge of all the agency's work with media representatives.

The control department coordinated activities on all accounts and collected cost information. Its coordinating function consisted of establishing a detailed time schedule and determining whether the various departments were performing their work accordingly. In planning the schedule the control department observed both the time allowances determined by each executive for work on his accounts and the priorities necessitated by the due dates of the promotional programs. The cost function included collecting cost data while

---

[3] The case researcher heard the word "creative" being used in two ways at W & W. In some cases it referred to both art and copy, and even certain aspects of production. In other cases, it appeared to apply only to copy.

work was in progress and forwarding the raw data to the New York office. For work performed within the office, the control department collected time allocation sheets from each person; for outside work, it collected invoices according to the job order. The New York office performed final accounting work for the Northwest City office. According to the Operations Manual, however, responsibility for the expenditures and profits of an account rested with the account executive.

The office manager supervised the office, including payroll, personnel, and supplies. She was directly in charge of the receptionist and of one secretary, who acted as replacement receptionist and performed secretarial work for the associate account executive. The office manager also kept time and attendance records for the weekly-salaried employees, who were the only staff members eligible for overtime pay: secretaries, receptionist, trainees, radio-TV timebuyer, account coordinator, home economist.

The only person in the office not specifically assigned to a department was the home economist, who normally worked in the promotion department; the Northwest City office home economist prepared recipes for use in the promotion of food products.

For specialized promotion work, market research, and certain minor functions, the Northwest City office relied on the appropriate New York departments.

This specialization of function clearly differentiated the office into two main subgroups: account executives and creative-service personnel. The account executives' work took them outside the regional office. They established and maintained close working relationships with the agency's clients. Thus, they were the source of the agency's business and its revenue. The creative-service personnel, on the other hand, were not in contact with client organizations, and were not the direct source of any business or revenue for the agency.

Since the account executives were the source of revenue, the creative-service personnel depended indirectly on them for their salaries. Thus, account executives might be considered more worthy of esteem and high status than creative-service personnel. The data presented in Sections IV and V will indicate the status actually accorded members of the two subgroups.

The Structure of Authority

In addition to the specialization of function the organization chart (Exhibit 1) indicates four levels of authority within the regional office. The top level of this hierarchy was occupied by John Goode, the regional manager and vice president, who was also the account supervisor for the region; the bottom level was occupied predominantly by female secretaries. The intervening two levels were occupied by persons with varying degrees of professional and technical competence, the more competent occupying the second level and the less competent, the third level of authority.

More interesting, however, is the existence of two different channels of authority within the formal organization of the regional office. One channel of authority extended from the secretarial level up to Mr. Goode in his capacity as regional manager and vice president; the other from the secretarial level again up to Mr. Goode, in his capacity as account supervisor. The two channels correspond to the primary division of labor—those who worked "inside" the office, and those who worked "outside."

The two channels also roughly correspond to the types of authority that Mr. Goode was called upon to exercise in his dual role as regional manager and account supervisor. As account supervisor the appropriate type of authority was predominantly professional. Such authority, based on the account executives' acceptance of Mr. Goode's superior knowledge and wisdom in the field of advertising, was derived from his experience. As regional manager, Mr. Goode was required to direct the activities of people such as the art director and the account coordinator, whose backgrounds and training in the advertising industry were much different from his. Within this channel, his authority was primarily organizational. It was based on his formally prescribed power as regional manager to direct and control the work lives of his subordinates and to hire, fire, demote, and "blacklist" personnel.

Mr. Goode's dual function in the regional office was an interesting one. His was the position that formally integrated the two major subgroups of the office. He had separate and distinct responsibilities to each subgroup. The problems of role conflict and of administration that this separation created will be examined in Section VI.

Formal Patterns of Influence

The prescribed flow of work in the Northwest City Regional Office illustrates which members of the group initiated the work of the group, and which members carried it out.

The regular flow of account work began with a "marketing plan"[4] which was prepared for each client's account. It established, for each

---

[4] As commonly used in the advertising industry, the term "marketing plan" included the activities here described.

of the client's products, a general outline of the kind of advertising campaigns that would be run, the media that would be used, promotion efforts that were appropriate, and the budget for such advertising and promotion efforts. It also reviewed the past year's efforts, including sales volume of the product, and estimated future sales volume.

The marketing plan was produced largely by the account executive, with assistance from the media supervisor and representatives from the New York market research and promotion departments as needed. The creative people also sometimes assisted him, but usually the plans were not so detailed as to require specific "creative" ideas. The account group met during the development of the marketing plan and to make final decisions on it. The plan then went to W & W's New York office for approval, after which it was submitted to the client. The modified marketing plan served as a basic outline for the year's advertising and promotion efforts.

As the time approached for a specific advertising campaign to get under way, the account executive called an account group meeting. At such a meeting the tasks to be done were discussed and assigned to the appropriate departments.

After the initial account group meeting, the account coordinator wrote job orders for the specific tasks and assigned appropriate deadlines. The copy department then started to work on the specific advertisement. At the scheduled time, the account coordinator transferred copy from the copy department to the art department. For printed advertisements, the art department produced a rough copy; for television commercials, it produced a "story-board," which was a series of panels showing the visual action in one box with the aural script written below each panel. When the art and copy departments had agreed upon an advertisement in either of these "rough rough" forms, it was presented to an account group meeting. If they approved it, it was then made into a finished "rough" and taken by the account executive to the client for approval.

Once the client had approved the "rough," the account coordinator gave it to the production department with the necessary work orders. The production manager selected an appropriate supplier and worked with the supplier in producing the advertising materials.

When the finished materials were completed and approved by the account executives, the media department delivered them to the proper media. A large part of the media supervisor's time was spent in talking with representatives of newspapers, magazines, and radio and TV stations. Many of these representatives called upon the media supervisor to solicit business. The media department also inspected the media for proper usage of the advertisements.

Throughout the process of producing an advertisement, the account coordinator checked with individual departments to maintain the work schedules. Frequently, he carried the roughs and the relevant papers and work orders from one department to another. He also worked with the appropriate account executives as problems in account work developed.

Thus, the account executives supplied the creative-service people with work. They acted as liaison men between the clients and the creative-service personnel within the office. In this way, the creative-service personnel came to work "for" the account executive on material for "his" client. We will examine the formal organization of this account group system in the following section. The point of interest here is in the "pipeline" of work. The account executive, initiating the flow of work, was the most active, most independent member of the executive-service system. The creative-service personnel were formally required to be more passive and more dependent in relation to the account executive and the work he brought to them. The formal arrangement of work flow placed the account executive in a more masculine role, and "his" creative-service personnel in a more feminine role. Since the executive's work took him outside the agency, and the work of the creative-service personnel required them to help and support him, the formal structure of the regional office was much like the model of a middle-class home. The male leaves the home to earn a living for the family and to "bring home the bacon"; the female remains in the home to provide backstage support and assistance to the more assertive partner.

Another aspect which indicates an analogy between the Northwest City Regional Office and a home arises from specialization of function. Creative-service personnel had specialized skills in art and literature, both requiring a highly developed aesthetic sense, and perhaps "artistic" temperaments. Research has demonstrated that, in the American culture, these attributes fall close to the feminine end of a masculinity-femininity scale. Thus, the femininity accompanies competence in artistically creative activities; this characteristic was part of the role demands that were placed on the creative-service personnel by the formal organization. Many of the noncreative service personnel were women; they possessed an even greater degree of natural congruence between themselves and the organizationally defined demands of their roles.

The account executives were the "outgoing" members of this system. There were individual differences, however, in the extent to which each account executive played the role of the vigorous, economically-oriented, self-assertive and dynamic advertising man pictured in the Madison Avenue mythology of advertising. For instance, one account executive, Marie Ayers, was a woman; her assumption of the stereotyped executive role would have been most incongruent and likely to net her more punishment than praise. At the other end of the scale, George Lorenz, another account executive, acted the role stereotype almost to perfection, as will become apparent in the analysis of the recorded account group meetings. Despite individual differences, there was a general dominance exhibited by the account executives.

Although the flow of influence in the regional office was unidirectional, moving from the account executive group to the creative-service group, the account executives nonetheless depended on the creative-service personnel for producing advertising ideas, messages, and material suitable for their clients. The account executives were formally in a position to initiate work for the creative-service personnel, but they had to depend on these personnel to satisfy clients. Conversely, the creative-service personnel were formally required to remain in a passive position in relation to the account executives, but they must have realized that without their best efforts the executives would probably lose their clients.

The creative-service personnel perhaps viewed themselves as the only creative link in an otherwise noncreative chain. Both groups must have been aware of the position of the other in this situation. Such a reciprocal but ambiguous power situation would be a potentially tense one in any organizational setting, and there are data to indicate the existence of tension between the account executives and the creative-service group in the Northwest City Regional Office. These data describe an informal system of *fines* administered by the creative-service group, levied on any person arriving at an account group meeting after it had started or leaving the meeting for any reason before it had formally adjourned. Since it was usually the account executives who were called away from these meetings, the fining system provided the creative-service personnel with a way of asserting authority over them. This fining ritual had considerable significance for all office personnel and will be dealt with more fully in the analysis of the informal organization of the office.

Managing Work and Controlling Feelings

The formal organization of the Northwest City Regional Office included a system of account groups and account group meetings.

The coordinated planning of marketing and advertising campaigns for a client was the responsibility of the account group. The account group for each client was formally composed of the account supervisor, the account executive, a supervisor from each of the service departments (copy, art, media, and production) and the account coordinator. Members of certain of the W & W headquarters office departments, such as market research and promotion, were nominally members of Northwest City account groups, but attended work meetings infrequently, typically when the annual market plans were being developed.

The W & W Operations Manual stated that "account group meetings should be called whenever *combined thinking* is likely to contribute constructive ideas." The manual stated that account executives were responsible for calling the meetings and that supervisors of each of the service departments "attended primarily as specialists in their own fields but should participate in the general discussion of account strategy." The manual did not give detailed information on the conduct or function of the meetings.

According to Mr. Lorenz, account group meetings in the Northwest City offices were held with wider participation than in the New York office. Account group meetings in the Northwest City office usually included, in addition to the required people listed above, the following: other account executives if they were not busy with work on their own accounts; the copywriter, if he was working on the campaign being discussed; the home economist (at Fisher account group meetings); and the secretary of the account executive who was holding the meeting.

The researcher did not learn of any formal rules or universal customs regulating what should and should not be discussed during the account group meeting. Rather it appeared that the account executive could determine the agenda as well as the degree to which an idea should be worked out in the meeting or left to the discretion of the responsible individuals. The frequency of meetings varied greatly according to the needs of the account, but a rough average for the Conn and Fisher accounts appeared to be about once a week; the Durifilm account group met less frequently; and the First National Bank account group met infrequently.

Mr. Goode stated that his original decision to have frequent meetings with broad participation was based on a desire to inform the personnel in the office about the various phases of each account. He said, "The important thing is that these people feel they are a part of this group, that they see where they fit in, and that they see their work as important."

Just as the account executive had the initiative in the flow of work, so he had the initiative in calling meetings of his account groups. The creative-service personnel were to participate as "specialists in their own fields," which from our analysis so far would indicate that their participation was of a lower status, more passive, and perhaps more suportive than that of the executives. This supposition will be tested in the analysis of the meeting data.

This lower-status participation probably made the meetings less meaningful to creative-service personnel than to account executives. Mr. Goode evidently believed this to be the case, since he instituted more frequent meetings to prompt the creative-service personnel to feel they were "a part of this group," and to show them that their work was important. He evidently thought it necessary to exert this extra effort in frequent meetings in order to ensure that the creative-service subgroup's organizationally defined passivity would not be taken as disintegration and disinterest.

Account executives did not need frequent meetings and communications from Mr. Goode to show them that their work was important. Moreover, they were also interested in getting good work from the creative-service personnel. But they adopted the more direct method of competing with each other for the attentions of the creative-service personnel. Each executive had his own way of inducing the creative-service personnel to expend more effort on the material for his accounts. They tended either to "fight" or to "make love," each executive being particularly adept at one or the other form of behavior, as will be seen in the meeting transcripts.

II. STATUS CHARACTERISTICS AND VALUE SYSTEMS: CULTURAL INFLUENCES WITHIN THE AGENCY

Status is the position occupied by an individual within the organization of a group, society, or other social system. The principal property of status is its hierarchical nature, which always places some persons above certain positions and others below. Status characteristics such as style or opulence of dress, manner of speech, or grey hair all indicate position—whether the person is superior, equal, or inferior to others.

People tend to categorize others according to status wherever they go. Status characteristics are therefore of interest within a business

338   ENVIRONMENTAL CONSTRAINTS

group such as the W & W Northwest City Regional Office. In some cases such characteristics supported and in others they tended to weaken the formal organization of the group. If the members of a work group occupied the same positions relative to one another both in the formal organization of authority and in the commonly accepted hierarchy of their culture, then the influence of the status system would reinforce that of the formal organization. If the positioning of people relative to one another is radically different along these two dimensions, then the influence of the more widely held status system will weaken the structure of the formal organization. Extremes of congruence and incongruence between the culturally determined status hierarchy and the organizationally determined hierarchy of authority entail dysfunctional consequences for a purposive organization.

Status ranking of individuals in relation to one another is not done directly, but through the use of characteristics commonly associated with given status positions. However, such status characteristics cannot be meaningfully separated from the value systems that provide the basic legitimization of the status hierarchy itself. When Veblen[5] expounded his notion of "conspicuous consumption," he was not merely describing the attributes by which people in society's upper-status positions seek to be recognized. He was also inveighing against the legitimacy of the social system that placed such people at the top. Veblen's thesis was, in other words, based on a value system different from that which supported the status hierarchy whose characteristics he described.

If age is used as a status characteristic, there must be general consensus within the social environment that age, or experience, or wisdom is a valuable thing. If marital status is used in this way, and married persons are generally considered better or more worthy of respect than unmarried persons, then the supporting value system must say, in effect, that marriage is a more esteemed estate than that of celibacy. Every status characteristic must have value criteria.

This section will pay more attention to status characteristics than to value systems. However, all the status characteristics to be listed below imply a system of shared values within the office, arising largely from the employees' social backgrounds and experiences outside. A description of this system of shared values would necessarily approximate a general cultural analysis of the predominantly middle-class "American Way of Life," and is far beyond the scope of this case study. To legitimize each of the status characteristics outlined, the

[5] Veblen, T., *The Theory of the Leisure Class: An Economic Study of Institutions.* New York: B. W. Huebsch, 1919.

reader should address this problem by establishing in his own mind the likelihood that values or precepts exist.

Classification of Status Characteristics

The status characteristics of the 26 employees of the Northwest City office can be classified according to the generality or specificity of their origin in the cultural surroundings of the group. For purposes of the present analysis, we have used status factors that are present (*a*) throughout the nation, (*b*) in business organizations generally, (*c*) in advertising agencies, and (*d*) specifically in the W & W Northwest City Regional Office. The status factors present in the office during the period of the case research were:

(*a*) Status factors of nationwide significance: age, sex, education, marital status, ethnicity.

(*b*) Status factors pertaining to business organizations: position in the formal organization, title, salary, worth to the organization, seniority.

(*c*) Status factors in the advertising industry:

1. Closeness to client operations (For instance, the account executives were closer to client operations than the creative-service personnel.)

2. Level of contact within the client organization (For instance, high-level contact within client organizations was formally the prerogative of the account supervisor, not the account executive.)

3. Type and size of client account (For instance, one account executive handled the business of a commercial banking organization, while another handled a company canning crabs and other seafoods. Also, another executive handled a volume of business from two to five times as large as that handled by the above two executives. See Exhibit 2.)

4. Closeness to a certain medium (For instance, the nature of a client's product might permit one executive to advertise in prestige magazines such as "Life" or "Fortune," whereas another would advertise in less prestigious journals, like "Materials Handling" or other trade journals and papers.)

5. Extensiveness of clients' markets (For instance, the executive with the seafood account was involved in a nationwide marketing arrangement, whereas the executive handling the commercial bank dealt only with the Northwest City metropolitan area.)

EXHIBIT 2

THE WATKINS AND WORSTER AGENCY (B)

Accounts in the Northwest City Office, February 1958*

Name of Account	Product	Market Area	Relative Volume of Billing**	Account Executive
Conn Milk Company	Full line of dairy products and miscellaneous food products	3 states around Northwest City	11	George Lorenz, account executive Bill Jones, associate account executive
John Fisher Company	Fisher Devilled Crab and other canned sea food	National	5	Marie Ayers, account executive
The Durifilm Company	Plastic packaging films	National	2	Bruce Fahey, account executive
First National Bank	Commercial banking	Metropolitan City area	1	Bruce Fahey, account executive

* Mr. Goode was account supervisor of all Northwest City accounts. Until the end of 1957, he was also account executive of the First National Bank account. The Conn Milk Company account, supervised by Mr. Lorenz with Bill Jones as associate account executive, was one of the largest supported by any company located in the Northwest City area. The advertising media were regional newspapers, TV, and radio. The Fisher account, with Miss Ayers as account executive, advertised mainly in national women's magazines. The Durifilm account, supervised by Bruce Fahey, placed advertisements mainly in packaging and food trade journals. The First National Bank account, also supervised by Mr. Fahey, advertised in Northwest City newspapers.
** These volume figures give relative size of billings and not absolute dollar amounts. Illustrative in interpreting the volume figures, the Conn account was 11 times larger in dollar billing than the First National Bank account.
Source: Interview data.

> 6. Size of the client within its industry (For instance, was the client the biggest company in that industry, regardless of the overall size of the account, or the industry?)
>
> (d) Status factors in the Northwest City Regional Office
>> 1. A person's point of origin (For instance, was the individual from the New York office, or was he a "local boy," completely unknown to those in New York?)

2. A person's ethnicity (Although listed at the top level of status generality, this factor assumes specific importance in situations where congruence is required between the ethnicity of an executive and that of a client, or the client's organization.)

This list merely presents the status factors that existed in the regional office at the time of the research. It does not describe the particular constellation of status attributes that existed for each person in the office. It does show, however, the complexity of the constraints brought to bear on a single group of 26 persons by their cultural environment. Status factors toward the specific end of the list are only of concern within the office group. These range from status criteria that find their meaning in the cultural environment of the group, to the more informal criteria that are developed internally and are applicable specifically within the group. The informal criteria also constrain group development, interpersonal relations, and problem solving. Thus a group is constrained from within as well as from outside. However, the internal constraints are beyond the scope of this study, which will attempt to demonstrate that there is no sharp and clearly distinguishable break between environmental and internal constraints.

Status Congruence and Incongruence

Exhibit 3 presents some selected status data on personnel in the Northwest City office. These data do not cover all the people in the office, so that we cannot examine completely the extent to which the status hierarchy of office personnel reinforced or weakened the hierarchy of formal authority. It will be noted, however, that Mr. Goode was the oldest man in the group, earned the largest salary, was married, and had a college education. In addition, he had originally worked in the New York office and had been transferred to Northwest City to handle the Conn account about six months before the Northwest City Regional Office was opened. In these respects at least, Mr. Goode's status reinforced his position as formal leader of the group.

Although we cannot examine fully the extent to which the status hierarchy within the office followed the hierarchy of authority, we can examine the extent to which several of the major dimensions of status were in line with each other. The following diagram represents the ranking of the office personnel who attended group meetings most

EXHIBIT 3

THE WATKINS AND WORSTER AGENCY (B)

Selected Data on Personnel in the Office, as of February 1958

Name	Position	Salary	Service with W & W	Marital Status	Age	Education (Beyond High School)
Account Management						
John Goode	Regional mgr., v.p., & acct. supervisor	$30,000	1 yr. 8 mo.	M	52	College
Marie Ayers	Account executive	$20,000	1 yr. 8 mo.	S	46	Secretarial school
George Lorenz	Account executive & vice president	$18,500	3 yrs. 4 mo.	M	34	College
Bruce Fahey	Account executive	$12,500	1 yr. 2 mo.	M	37	College
Bill Jones	Associate account executive	$10,000	1 yr. 7 mo.	M	30	College
Copy						
Carlton Fromm	Copy supervisor	$12,500	1 mo.	M	38	College
Dan Rittner	Copywriter	$10,000	1 yr. 10 mo.	Divorced	30	College
Art						
Phil Mascetta	Art director	$14,500	1 yr. 10 mo.	M	41	Art school
Jim Cooper	Artist	$ 7,800	1 yr. 6 mo.	M	32	College
Media						
Helen Fowler	Media supervisor	$ 8,250	1 yr. 6 mo.	S	35	Secretarial school
Corporate Services—General						
Florence Langen	Office manager	$ 4,940	1 yr. 11 mo.	Widow	49	Secretarial school
Corporate Services—Control						
Mary Navin	Account coordinator	$ 4,420	1 yr. 8 mo.	S	31	Secretarial school
Print Production						
Al Berklund	Production manager	$ 8,500	3 yrs. 10 mo.	M	30	College
(Promotion)						
Doreen O'Mara	Home economist	$ 3,900	6 mo.	M	28	College

Source: Company records, plus salary information given by John Goode.

frequently according to their salaries, as shown in Exhibit 3, and according to their function in the office.

	Executive-Administrative	Creative-Service
High Salary	John Marie George Bruce	Phil Carlton
Low Salary	Bill Mary	Dan Al Helen Jim

This diagram shows that the high salary group in the office consisted primarily of those in executive and administrative jobs. These jobs were higher in status than the creative and service jobs because of their closeness to the client organizations. The account executives were the ones who obtained the business and the revenue for the Northwest City Regional Office. They initiated the work flow within the office, were the heads of the various account groups, and were the chairmen of the account group meetings. Their role in the work of the office was generally dominant and masculine.

The low salary group consisted mainly of creative and service personnel; theirs were the lower status positions in the organization. The creative and service personnel were not in direct contact with the client organizations. They did not obtain revenue for the agency. In fact, they were the ones who ran the costs up. They received work in the office and helped and supported the account executives by conceiving of ideas and bringing these ideas up to acceptable advertising standards. Theirs was a generally supportive and feminine role.

The high salary group was older than the low salary group, respectively 41.3 and 31.3 years on the average. Five of the high salary group were married; in the low salary group, only three were married.

On all these status dimensions, the ordering of the personnel was approximately the same. Not only were the status dimensions congruent with each other; they also were in line with the ordering of the personnel according to the formal organization of the office.

Not all status characteristics, however, manifested this degree of

order.   A number were not in line with the formal organization, nor
with the above-mentioned characteristics.   The high salary group
contained four persons with college educations, but the low salary
group contained an equal number.   Also, the average seniority of the
high salary group was less than that of the low salary group: about 1
year and 6 months against 2 years, respectively.

There was also considerable status incongruence surrounding the
positions of Miss Ayers and Mr. Lorenz.   Miss Ayers was the only
female account executive in the office.   Her salary was second only to
Mr. Goode's.   She earned more than Mr. Lorenz, who had been with
W & W twice as long as she had, and who was bringing in twice as
much business as she.   She was the only account executive who did
not have a college degree.

Mr. Lorenz was the youngest account executive in the office, yet
he was the only person besides Mr. Goode who had the title of vice
president.   Despite his age, he had served the longest as account executive and had more seniority than Mr. Goode.   As has been mentioned,
he was bringing in the most business—in fact, more than both the other
account executives combined.

Some of the status characteristics of group members placed them in
relation to one another as required by the formal organization of
authority and the formal division of labor within the office.   In this
way the cultural environment reinforced the influence of the formal
organization upon members of the group.   The status characteristics
of some individuals, however, neither corresponded to their positions
in the office nor supported the formal organization of the group.

This study will not comment on the merits of in-lineness or out-of-
lineness except to say that extremes of either would probably be dysfunctional for the organization.   Complete in-lineness of all status
characteristics among personnel and with the formal organization
would have promoted "frozen" conditions within the group, so that
persons such as Miss Ayers and Mr. Lorenz could not have assumed
positions as account executives, regardless of their talents or capabilities.
Complete out-of-lineness of such characteristics would have made the
social organization of the group around the agency's work very difficult.   It would have required the employees to develop and learn
a new set of responses to a new social situation for which their
previous social experience had left them unprepared.   For example, in
such a situation of complete out-of-lineness, it would have been the
"pip-squeaks" who ordered the "big shots" around, something that common experience teaches most people to resent and resist.   However, the
particular balance of environmental constraints that acted on the

regional office appears, on the one hand, to have permitted a socially integrated work effort to be carried out; on the other, it permitted such persons as Mr. Lorenz and Miss Ayers to enter somewhat incongruous positions in the organization.

This does not imply that this balance eradicated all tensions and hostilities within the group. On the contrary, the balance that kept the group from being "neither fish nor fowl" was a constant source of friction. The sacrifice of clearly defined lines of influence and authority was one of the costs of the situation. Mr. Goode's dual authority role has already been examined. He could invoke neither professional nor organizational authority unequivocally in the face of the status incongruities that existed below him in the organization. His administrative resolution of this problem was frequent meetings and increased communication within the group. His interpersonal resolution of the problem resulted in a mild and gently persuasive presentation of himself to others in the office. This will be observed in the transcripts of the recorded account group meetings. These transcripts will also show that, under the compulsion of status incongruities, the behavior of Miss Ayers and Mr. Lorenz differed markedly. Miss Ayers adopted an interpersonal style of consideration and kindness, somewhat similar to Mr. Goode's, whereas Mr. Lorenz seemed to prefer a good fight.

OTHER ENVIRONMENTAL CHARACTERISTICS AND THEIR CONSTRAINING INFLUENCE WITHIN THE AGENCY: A BRIEF OVERVIEW

The Industry

The fast-moving and controversial advertising industry is a particularly salient focus of hostilities and enthusiasms in modern America. It embodies forces that are making themselves felt in the stirrings and aspirations of nations less economically developed than the United States, yet it provides a model of how life should be lived that disturbs some and horrifies others. Fromm[6] describes the "marketing man" as a type which he believed would become the distinguishing character of our civilization: the man who views everything, including himself and his personality, as a commodity to be bought and sold, packaged, promoted, and advertised. W. H. Whyte[7] believes this phenomenon

[6] Fromm, E., *Man for Himself*, an Inquiry into the Psychology of Ethics. New York: Rinehart, 1947.
[7] Whyte, W. H., *The Organization Man*. New York: Simon and Schuster, 1956.

is caused by the declining strength of the Protestant ethic of individualism and self-respect.

The advertising industry today is also the vortex of conflict between systems of values of a more socio-economic nature. There are those who believe that the function of the advertising industry is both constructive and worthwhile; that advertising agencies facilitate the flow of goods and services to the consuming public, and thereby help to maintain the economic development and high living standards that have become such an important part of the American way of life. On the other hand, those who consider the function of the advertising industry pernicious and immoral believe that advertising adds needless amounts to the cost of goods, stimulates false demands, creates wants and desires where none existed, and fosters perpetual material discontent, which leads to a collapse of the traditional spiritual values of American civilization.

These issues have an impact within the advertising industry which will probably increase as the growth of consumer organizations and government controls force the industry to do more public relations work for itself and its clients. Another influence is the popular conception of what the advertising industry is, and what sort of people are to be found in it. This affects those going into advertising and those already in it, since to a certain extent, they want to "give the customer what he wants." The advertising industry thus tends to create its own "personality." Although there are common elements of this "personality" among agencies, each agency has a specific image.[8] This determines what type of person will make a successful account executive or copy writer in a particular firm such as Watkins and Worster.

Technology

Technology refers here to the science of an industry, rather than the specific instruments or tools used. The wide variety of skills and knowledge constituting the technology of advertising falls roughly into three categories: (1) theoretical and practical knowledge of marketing and distribution; (2) skills as a consultant; and (3) the artistic and creative talent required to produce effective advertising materials. A fourth category, not represented in the Northwest City Regional Office, is ability to conduct research to determine the effectiveness of marketing strategies and advertising materials.

[8] Mayer, M., *Madison Avenue USA*. New York: Harper, 1958.

The importance of making these divisions within the technology is to point up the subgroups formed on the basis of specialization of skill and knowledge. In the Northwest City Regional Office the first two types of knowledge and skill were combined in the "outside" subgroup of account executives; the third existed in the "inside" subgroup of creative-service personnel. Thus, effective cooperation around a task became something that had to be consciously planned and coordinated. Such a condition in the technology of advertising involves a definite risk. If, in order to obtain effective cooperation around a task, the management of an agency decides to organize its agency personnel formally into task groups rather than into specialist groups, the personnel becomes relatively incompetent in their own spheres of specialization, and thus less valuable to the agency.

Geographical Proximity

The W & W Head Office was located in New York. The clients served by the Northwest City Regional Office were all in the immediate vicinity. In a geographic sense, the regional office was more a part of the client organizations than it was a part of W & W. The result was that the account executives would strive to please their clients who were close by and to increase their volume of billings, while the head office would try through their official representative, the regional manager, to maintain profits by refusing unreasonable deadlines and by holding down "needless" costs of overtime pay and wastage.

Functional Proximity

Functional proximity refers to the flow of work from one operating unit to the next. If one operating unit is immediately adjacent to another in the flow of work, these two units have the highest possible degree of functional proximity. If one is separated from another by several steps in the flow of work, however, the functional proximity is not considered as great. In its everyday line operations, the Northwest City Regional Office was functionally closer to its clients' organizations than it was to the W & W Head Office. However, in accounting matters, and in certain staff operations such as special promotions and market research, the regional office was functionally closer to its head office than to its clients. The consequences of the dual nature of the flow of work were similar to those arising from technological constraints, and tended to divide the group within the regional office.

IV. SOCIAL STRUCTURE WITHIN THE AGENCY,
AND ITS RELATIONSHIP TO
ENVIRONMENTAL CONSTRAINTS

The formal organization of the W & W Northwest City Regional Office defined its constituent groups as formal work units. But the socio-psychological characteristics of these groups—the resultant activities, interactions, and sentiments—are matters for empirical investigation. During the research, interviews were conducted with the people listed by name on Exhibit 1, except Florence Langen, the office manager, and Doreen O'Mara, the home economist. The people interviewed were those in most frequent attendance at the account group meetings, although Miss O'Mara and some of the secretaries attended some of the meetings.

In the course of these interviews, the researcher asked each person questions concerning whom in the office he liked most, with whom he ate lunch, and with whom he worked closely. The responses to these questions are summarized in Exhibits 4, 5, and 6, respectively. Below each of the matrices are diagrams which show the mutual choices.

In accordance with the diagram on page 343, the twelve persons interviewed were divided into two groups of six: the executive-administrative group and the creative-service group. Using this dichotomy, a 2 x 2 table of "choosers" and "chosen" was then constructed for each of the three sets of sociometric data: Liked Most, Luncheon Partners, and Worked with Closely. These three tables are Exhibits 7, 8, and 9, respectively.

These tables indicate that underlying the sociometric choices of the regional office group was a dynamic similar to the one discovered by R. F. Bales during his experimental studies of problem-solving groups.[9] Based on this research, Bales proposed an interpretive scheme that viewed the behavior of problem-solving groups as a Hegelian dialectical interchange between two opposing modes of behavior: the task-oriented or external-adaptive mode and the socially oriented or internal-cohesive mode. A group faced with problems presented by its environment mobilizes its members to work on these problems; the dominant mode of behavior is external-adaptive. Sustained external-adaptive behavior, however, creates tensions that must

[9] Bales, R. F., "The Equilibrium Problem in Small Groups," in P. Hare, E. F. Borgatta, and R. F. Bales (eds.), *Small Groups*. New York: Alfred A. Knopf, 1955, pp. 424–456.

EXHIBIT 4

THE WATKINS AND WORSTER AGENCY (B)

Personal Choices for "Liked Most"

Chooser \ Chosen	John	Marie	George	Bruce	Bill	Mary	Phil	Jim	Carlton	Dan	Al	Helen	Others*	TOTAL
John		1	1		1		1		1		1	1		7
Marie					1		1							2
George					1		1		1			1		4
Bruce														0
Bill	1		1	1			1	1	1		1	1		8
Mary					1		1				1		1	4
Phil								1	1					2
Jim							1		1					2
Carlton	1				1		1							3
Dan					1		1	1	1		1		4	9
Al							1							1
Helen		1	1											2
TOTAL	2	2	3	1	6	0	9	3	6	0	4	3	5	44

*"Others" mentioned were all secretaries in the office.

Mutual Expressions of Liking

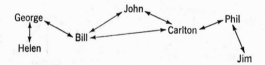

be released before the group explodes. Therefore, at some point in the process the dominant mode switches from external-adaptive, problem-solving behavior to internal-cohesive behavior that re-establishes interpersonal solidarity in the group. The group is then able to get back to work on its externally imposed problems. Groups must establish a balance between these two modes of behavior or cease to exist. Bales referred to this as the equilibrium problem of small groups:

> As we think of the matter, the instrumental-adaptive activity of the preceding participant tends to build up tensions in the present participant to some point where he enters the process

EXHIBIT 5

THE WATKINS AND WORSTER AGENCY (B)

Personal Choices for Luncheon Partners

Chooser \ Chosen	John	Marie	George	Bruce	Bill	Mary	Phil	Jim	Carlton	Dan	Al	Helen	Other*	TOTAL
John	╳	1	1	1										3
Marie	1	╳		1										2
George	1		╳		1							1		3
Bruce	1			╳			1		1			1		4
Bill					╳		1		1		1	1		4
Mary						╳							3	3
Phil							╳	1	1	1	1			4
Jim							1	╳						1
Carlton							1		╳					1
Dan							1			╳				1
Al			1				1				╳			2
Helen		1	1		1				1			╳		4
TOTAL	3	2	3	2	2	0	6	1	4	1	2	3	3	32

*"Others" mentioned by Mary were two secretaries and Doreen.

Mutual Designations of Luncheon Partners

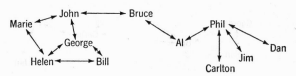

and changes to activity of an expressive-integrative relevance, which tends to "bleed off" the tension to some point at which he changes the focus himself and continues again with the instrumental-adaptive activity. *The problem of equilibrium is essentially the problem of establishing arrangements (or an "orbit of activity") whereby the system goes through a repetitive cycle, within which all of the disturbances created in one phase are reduced in another.* The dilemma of all action systems is that no one disturbance can be reduced without creating another.[10]

[10] *Ibid.*, p. 433.

Bales also found a tendency for the members of his experimental groups to specialize in certain styles of behavior. He interpreted the results of this specialization as follows:

> Movement in the instrumental-adaptive direction tends to upset the equilibrium of the system, and recovery mechanisms must be worked out if the system is to turn full cycle and regain equilibrium. The more "directive" and constricting" the quality of the activity, the more likely it is to arouse negative reactions. If a man begins to specialize noticeably in this direction, the negative reactions tend to be centered on him. . . . The center-

EXHIBIT 6

THE WATKINS AND WORSTER AGENCY (B)

Personal Choices for "Worked with Closely"

Chooser \ Chosen	John	Marie	George	Bruce	Bill	Mary	Phil	Jim	Carlton	Dan	Al	Helen	Others*	TOTAL
John	X	1	1		1		1		1		1			6
Marie		X				1	1		1		1	1		5
George	1		X		1		1		1					4
Bruce	1			X									1	2
Bill			1		X	1						1		3
Mary		1	1	1	1	X	1	1	1	1				8
Phil							X	1	1		1			3
Jim						1	1	X						2
Carlton			1				1		X					2
Dan		1	1	1	1	1	1	1	1	X				8
Al		1	1	1	1	1	1		1		X			7
Helen			1		1							X		2
TOTAL	2	4	7	3	6	5	8	3	7	1	3	2	1	52

*"Other" named by Bruce was his secretary.

Mutual Naming of "Worked with Closely"

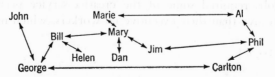

EXHIBIT 7

THE WATKINS AND WORSTER AGENCY (B)

Group Choices for "Liked Most"*

	Chosen		
Choosers	Executive-administrative	Creative-service	Total
Executive-administrative	9	15	24 (62%)
Creative-service	5	10	15 (38%)
Total	14 (36%)	25 (64%)	39 (100%)

* "Others" shown in Exhibit 4 are not included.

ing of positive affect on a secondary man is another mechanism by which the solidarity of the group—its integration as a collectivity of persons—can be re-established. Such a man can be warm, receptive, responsive, and rewarding, can "conciliate" and "bind up wounds," without diverting the movement of the system too far from the kind of movement in the instrumental-adaptive direction which is also felt to be necessary. He can do this because he does not assume the "responsibility" for the movement of the system in these directions, but leaves this to the technical or executive specialist.[11]

There is a striking similarity between the formal organization of the regional office and the structural characteristics of the Bales model. The account executives were formally charged with the responsibility of coping with the problems and demands of the agency's clients, which is an excellent example of behavior in the external-adaptive mode. The creative-service personnel were formally required to work in the office, in account groups led by the executives, and on material requested by the executives. The supportive nature of this relationship has been described. Whether the relationship was also emotionally expressive remains to be tested. Certainly, the very nature of their jobs required some of the creative-service personnel to be more expressive than their executive co-workers, which means that to

[11] *Ibid.*, pp. 453–454.

a certain extent the expressive potential of internal-cohesive behavior was present in the creative-service subgroup.

Love Flees Authority

Bales described the antithetical nature of the external-adaptive and internal-integrative modes of behavior. The two occur cyclically in group processes, but never simultaneously. In other words, the love of warmth and interpersonal cohesiveness in a group flees the authority issues pressing in on the group from its environment. Similarly, the authority of externally oriented realities takes flight in the face of enthusiastic expressions and acting out of warmth and love within a group.

Exhibits 7, 8, and 9 indicate that this dynamic underlay the sociometric choice patterns of the members of the regional office group. These exhibits indicate that (1) the executive-administrative group was the more actively choosing group in the office; (2) the balance of sociometric relations between the two groups varied in the three types of social phenomena studied; and (3) consonant with Bales' model, as the groups moved away from the external-adaptive aspects of the office's operations, the creative-service group became increasingly most liked. In other words, the regional office group was dynamically as well as structurally a representative of Bales' model.

The data in Exhibits 7, 8, and 9 fall at three different points on a continuum from internal-cohesive to external-adaptive behavior. The

EXHIBIT 8

THE WATKINS AND WORSTER AGENCY (B)

*Group Choices for "Luncheon Partners"**

	Chosen		
Choosers	Executive-administrative	Creative-service	Total
Executive-administrative	8	8	16 (55%)
Creative-service	4	9	13 (45%)
Total	12 (41%)	17 (59%)	29 (100%)

* "Others" shown in Exhibit 5 are not included.

EXHIBIT 9

THE WATKINS AND WORSTER AGENCY (B)

*Group Choices for "Worked with Closely"**

	Chosen		
Choosers	*Executive-administrative*	*Creative-service*	*Total*
Executive-administrative	13	14	27 (53%)
Creative service	14	10	24 (47%)
Total	27 (53%)	24 (47%)	51 (100%)

* "Others" shown in Exhibit 6 are not included.

sociometric choice data on "Liked Most" (Exhibit 7) fall closest to the expressive, internal-cohesive end of this continuum. The socio-metric choice data on "Worked with Closely" (Exhibit 9) fall nearest the external-adaptive end of the continuum. "Luncheon Partners" data (Exhibit 8) fall between these two extremes. The shifting choice patterns at these three points along the continuum demonstrate that the "love flees authority" phenomenon was operating in the group.

Exhibit 9 indicates that the amount of sociometric choice *between* the executive and creative groups was relatively well balanced in comparison with the choice patterns shown in Exhibits 7 and 8. Of the total number of choices, 53 per cent were made by executive-administrative personnel, and 47 per cent by creative-service personnel. Executive-administrative personnel were chosen 53 per cent of the time, and creative-service personnel were chosen 47 per cent of the time. It will be noticed that the percentage differences in socio-metric choice levels between the two subgroups, both for choosing and for chosen, are greater in Exhibit 8 than in Exhibit 9, and are still greater in Exhibit 7. The evenness of choice between the two sub-groups on the topic of "work with closely" probably reflects the formal requirements placed on the employees for the accomplishment of the agency's work. Although the members of one subgroup were required to work closely with members of the other subgroup, they were not required to like one another, and the data seem to indicate that greater freedom and specificity of choice operated around matters of friendship than around matters of work.

The data in Exhibit 9 indicate that the executive group was more active in choosing than was the creative group, and was chosen slightly more than the creative group. This stems from the fact that the creative-service personnel chose the higher status executives more frequently than they chose members of their own group. The executive group distributed its choices almost equally between the two groups.

Moving closer to an internal-cohesive type of activity, we find the beginnings of an interesting shift in choice patterns. Exhibit 8 shows that, in choosing luncheon partners, the executive group was again more active than the creative-service group—in this case, relatively more active than in the choosing of work partners. Despite the fact that the executive group was the more actively choosing group, the creative-service group had now become the more chosen group, a reversal of Exhibit 9. This popularity resulted from the relative preponderance of own-group choice by members of the creative-service group. Evidently, they liked to eat lunch with one another. Again, the executive group distributed its choices about equally between the two groups. It appears that lunching, falling in an intermediate position between task and nontask activities, had no particular influence on the choice pattern of the executives. However, once the activity had changed from a purely external-adaptive nature, the creative-service personnel seem to have preferred the pleasure of their own company. A decrease in the number of over-all choices would indicate that lunching was a less important activity in the office than was working closely with others.

The choices of whom one liked most, as shown in Exhibit 7, are the closest of the three sets of data to the internal-cohesive end of the continuum. The importance to the office personnel of "liking most" certain others in the office is illustrated by the resurgence of the level of over-all choosing from the low point established in the "luncheon partners" data. There was also an upswing in the relative activity of choosing on the part of the executives over the creative-service personnel and an increased popularity of the creative-service group. The popularity of the creative-service subgroup was a result of that group's preference for its own members and of the executive group's distinct preference for creative-service personnel. This last finding is in marked contrast to the apparent impartiality of the executive group's choice patterns in Exhibits 8 and 9.

Two factors probably accounted for the marked preference of members of the executive group for members of the creative-service group. The account executives sought the cooperation of the creative-service personnel. They did not compete with them. Therefore, it was easy and probably expedient for the account executives to like the creative-service personnel. The account executives were, however, more directly in competition with each other, both outside the office for larger and more prestigeful accounts and inside the office for the assistance and support of creative-service personnel. Therefore, it was easy for the account executives to dislike each other and to transfer feelings of friendship to the creative-service personnel, who represented a scarce, valuable, and noncompetitive commodity in the life of the office. It would appear that, for several reasons, the creative-service personnel were the friendship favorites, the specialists in the internal-cohesive phases of group life in the regional office.

In summary, Exhibits 7, 8, and 9 seem to indicate the presence of the following dynamics:

(1) The members of the executive-administrative subgroup were more active in their relations with others in the office than were the creative-service personnel. As the intimacy of issues increased, the executive-administrative group became proportionately more forward (active) and the creative service group more coy (passive).

(2) Different constellations of choice existed around the external-adaptive and the internal-cohesive phases of the group's operation. When the agency's work was relevant, choosing between the two groups was relatively well balanced, with evidence of some choosing up on the part of creative-service personnel into the higher status executive subgroup. Where questions of friendship were concerned, creative-service personnel were by far more liked, both by members of their own group and by executive-administrative personnel. Thus, the evidence indicates that the interpersonal dynamics of the group reflected the active-passive, masculine-feminine, task-social dimensional constraints of the group's environment.

(3) Task and socio-emotional activities (work and friendship) appear to have been more important to the group than activities in which both task and social aspects were mixed (lunch). This finding supports Bales' contention that problem-solving and tension-releasing activities cannot be both simultaneous and satisfying, but must occur cyclically if the ongoing process of a group's existence is to be sustained.

The general sociometric atmosphere in which the members of the two subgroups worked in the office can be illustrated by the following summary exhibit. Exhibit 10 presents the data pertaining to the extent to which each subgroup chose and was chosen. The "deficit"

EXHIBIT 10

THE WATKINS AND WORSTER AGENCY (B)

*Surpluses and Deficits in Group Choices**

	Liked Most		Luncheon Partners		Worked with Closely	
	Executive-administrative	Creative-service	Executive-administrative	Creative-service	Executive-administrative	Creative-service
Chose	24	15	16	13	27	24
Chosen	14	25	12	17	27	24
Surplus	—	10	—	4	—	—
Deficit	10	—	4	—	—	—

* "Others" shown in Exhibits 4, 5, and 6 are not included.

category in the exhibit indicates those occasions when a subgroup was chosen less often than it chose. The "surplus" category indicates those occasions when a subgroup was chosen more often than it chose. These data illustrate clearly some of the costs of membership in the higher status executive subgroup, and some of the payoffs for the lower status creative-service subgroup. There were neither deficits nor surpluses in choices involving "work closely with." (The balanced sociometric choice around task issues has already been described.) However, in shared lunchtime activities and in friendship choices, the higher status executive group operated at a deficit, and the lower status creative-service group had a surplus of interpersonal choice. Members of the higher status subgroup were relatively friendless within the office, while lower status personnel seemed to have more friends. The account executives probably had well-established friendships with clients and with executives from other agencies, but it seems plausible that these people must have felt some degree of loneliness within the office. In other words, the higher status Account Executives paid for their position by having to sustain and tolerate certain feelings of loneliness in the office. Each executive probably mobilized his energies in his own way to overcome these feelings. As we shall see, Mr. Lorenz behaved in an overtly aggressive manner toward others in the office, whereas Miss Ayers was exceedingly friendly and supportive. Each of these styles of behavior can be viewed as a possible defense against unpleasant feelings of anxiety.

The creative-service personnel, on the other hand, received more friendships than they offered. This situation may have more than adequately rewarded them for the lower status positions they held in the office. Having a surplus of friendships, they were free to indulge themselves in many small ways, and short of destroying the friendships that were directed toward them, they were able to violate many of the forms of behavior that the higher status personnel might traditionally have expected of subordinates. A good example of violation of traditional expectations was the informal system of fines that the creative-service personnel imposed on members of the executive group during account group meetings. This fining ritual is described in the next section.

V. INTERPERSONAL RELATIONS WITHIN THE NORTHWEST CITY REGIONAL OFFICE

This section will continue the examination of the interpersonal dynamics that existed within the regional office. The fining ritual which the researcher observed is an example of how environmental constraints influenced interpersonal relations, particularly as the persons belonged to one or the other subgroup in the office.

Environment also bore upon each person as an individual and affected those behaviors which were related to his particular problem. Each member of the office faced worries about his identity and personal behavior. The transcripts of actual account group meetings will be used to study interpersonal behavior related to these worries. The analysis of the data will be more illustrative than definitive, since the nature and extent of the data do not permit the rejection of invalid hypotheses about behavioral constraints at ascertainable levels of statistical significance.

The Final Ritual

Before the researcher went to his first account group meeting, Mary Navin, account coordinator, described a custom of levying fines for the infringement of "ground rules."

MISS NAVIN: Be sure to have your money if you disagree with the account executive.

RESEARCHER: How so?

MISS NAVIN: Oh, there is a system of fines. It's 50¢ if you come late, 25¢ if you interrupt the meeting by taking a phone call there, or 25¢ if you're excused. And it's one cent if you disagree with the account executive.

The researcher observed that the levying of fines was accompanied by considerable joking. He also noted that Phil Mascetta, the art director, was in charge of the fine "kitty" and was the arbiter of whether a fine was owed and of the appropriate amount. The researcher observed fines being levied for lateness, telephone interruptions, and for early departures from the meeting, but not for disagreement with the account executive. He also noticed that the rules did not seem to be applied consistently. Mr. Goode, who arrived late for most of the meetings which the researcher attended, never escaped being fined for lateness. The account executives were usually fined for lateness but only occasionally for telephone interruptions. The researcher noticed that when other account group members arrived late, the fine rules were less consistently applied.

Mr. Mascetta, talking about the system of fines, said:

It started a while back. They had it in another agency I worked at. Everyone seemed to be scrambling around at the meetings here. John or maybe George or myself might be late, held up by a phone call, perhaps. That would mean a few people would be sitting 20 minutes waiting. So we started the fine system, and it worked. Then we added to it for interrupting, contradicting, and so forth. Of course, we're not very consistent; we sometimes forget. But I really have to jump to it; since I started it, they jump on me if I'm late. I'd say all have contributed about equally to the kitty.

At a meeting of the Fisher account group on April 1, Miss Ayers asked what was going to be done with the fine money. After Mr. Mascetta had stated that there was $50 in the kitty, including $2 of IOU's and a streetcar token, Bill Jones stated that he thought he had found a good lodge they could rent with the money for a spring skiing weekend. The group expressed interest in this and Mr. Jones said he would check further.

After this particular meeting, the researcher asked Mr. Jones about the fine system and his part in it.

MR. JONES: We started it last summer so the meetings wouldn't be chaotic. By the fall we had $12 in the kitty. I was appointed chairman of the committee to decide what to do with it by a bunch who were relaxing after work late one night. I think the rest of the committee was Helen, Phil, Al, and one of the secretaries —the idea being one from each department. We haven't met since that time, but I started looking into this skiing weekend idea a few weeks ago. This deal may fall through. You can't tell really how many in the whole office like to ski. Most of us did who were in the original discussion. We might try a beach party in the summer if we can fit it in between people's vacations.

This informal system of fines was used by the creative-service personnel in a conscious or unconscious attempt to establish conditions of equality and justice in the office. The unsystematic manner in which the fines were imposed also indicated that the system was used as a vehicle for the indirect expression of hostility that the creative-service personnel felt toward members of the executive-administrative group, principally toward the account executives.

There are three important aspects of the fining ritual: (1) who was in charge of the ritual and whose attentions kept it alive; (2) what was the code of the ritual, and what was the meaning of its rules for those who adhered to it; and (3) how were the rules applied, and what meaning underlay the apparently inconsistent manner in which the rules were applied?

Mr. Mascetta, the art director, was in charge of the fine "kitty" and was the judge of who should be fined and how much. His position in the formal organization, his age, his seniority, and his salary all contributed to making him the highest status member of the creative-service group. As such, it was the "head man" of the creative-service subgroup who levied fines against members of the executive-administrative subgroup. There was much joking about the imposition of these fines, but on the whole it was through the insistence of the creative-service personnel that the system was maintained, and it was the senior men in the executive-administrative group who bore the brunt of the fines.

The code of the ritual set forth three degrees of "badness" of certain activities. The most highly penalized activity was coming late to meetings. Interrupting meetings by taking phone calls was only half as bad. In both instances the "badness" originated in the account executive's proximity to clients, whose demands often caused the executives to leave the creative-service personnel sitting idly by, waiting for them to show up or to return to the meeting.

The third penalty set by the code of the ritual expressed the disregard of the creative-service personnel for the subordinate position in which the formal organization of the office had placed them in relation to the account executives. Disagreeing with an account executive was worth only one cent, one-fiftieth of the punishment usually imposed on executives for coming late to meetings. In other words, a creative-service person was considered able to disagree with an account executive at will, and the code of the fining ritual set forth the service personnel's conception of their freedom to upset one of the formally defined hierarchies of authority.

This informal negation of formal authority was reinforced by Mr. Mascetta's unwillingness to impose fines for disagreements with account executives. Other inconsistencies in the application of the fining code indicated how this system was used by creative-service personnel as a means of "getting back" at members of the executive group. Mr. Goode, the "boss" of the office, was always fined for lateness. The account executives, somewhat lower in the formal hierarchy of authority, were usually fined for lateness, although less consistently than was Mr. Goode. The apparent reasonableness of their answering a telephone call caused the executives to be fined only infrequently. Finally, the lateness of creative-service personnel to meetings was often unnoticed, and usually not fined. As Mr. Mascetta stated, "We sometimes forget."

As interesting aspect of the fining ritual was that the creative-service personnel could enforce it, could make it "stick." If they had been unable to enforce it, it would have died a quick death. The data from the meetings will indicate that the fining system was an important matter for everybody in the office. Members of the executive group were annoyed and harassed by it and in some instances expressed resentment about it, but they accepted its imposition. This was where the passivity and subordination of the creative-service personnel were redressed, and where the dependence of the account executives on the talents and good will of the creative-service personnel came to the fore. The account executives needed the creative-service personnel. Therefore they capitulated, however, grudgingly, to certain demands of the creative-service group. The fining ritual provided the "arena" in which both the dependence of the executive group on the creative group and the power of the creative group over the executive group could be acted out for all to see.

A final aspect of the fining ritual is seen in the disposition of funds collected by the imposition of fines. Mr. Jones, a low status member of the executive group, was "appointed chairman" to carry out the difficult and menial job of planning a *social* activity to be financed by the funds in the "kitty." Thus, the funds collected by the social specialists were to be used for a social activity, but the "dog work" or arranging that activity was left to a relatively low status task specialist, who unenthusiastically predicted a low probability of success for the venture.

Analysis of the Meetings on the Morning of March 12

On the morning of March 12, Mr. Goode scheduled a short talk to the entire office staff, immediately prior to a Conn account group meeting scheduled for 10:00 A.M. As people crowded into the room, the following conversation took place.

MR. LORENZ (to an unidentified person): Keep your fingers off the walls. (Women's voices heard saying: ". . . Look at those walls. . . . Oh, aren't they terrible! . . . How did they get that way?)

MR. LORENZ: Because nobody like Fran Parsons volunteered to come in and wash them.

MISS PARSONS: I cleaned the mail room last. I'm through with my good deeds for this month.

MR. LORENZ: We'll take volunteers. You, you, and you.

The aggressive and dominating way in which Mr. Lorenz presented himself in the group becomes immediately apparent in the first few seconds of the meeting, with his flat statement, "Keep your fingers off the walls." In saying, We'll take volunteers. You, you, and you," he immediately voiced his assumption of being second in command of the office.

MR. GOODE: I've got two or three things I want to talk about this morning. (Mr. Lorenz's voice in background saying, "Quiet.")

Here again he played the role of "the enforcer," or second in command to Mr. Goode.

MR. GOODE (continuing): I'll give you the good news first. A year ago you may remember that we were beaten out by Smith & Company for the publicity and public relations part of the John Fisher account. They were hired and didn't deliver. Fisher examined their work side by side with our advertising contributions and last week they fired Smith & Company and hired us. Well, this is the first break in 1958 in a new piece of business. This will increase the size of our Fisher account by 50 per cent. (Miss Ayers, account executive of the Fisher account, was out of town and absent during this meeting.) We're very happy to be able to make this announcement right on the heels of having gotten Supermobile (an automobile account) at our New York office. This is our Supermobile.

Mr. Goode's opening statement to the group, "I'll give you the good news first," reflects the considerate and comradely style of behavior he had developed to cope with the role conflict involved in being both regional manager and account supervisor. This conflict can best be illustrated by using Max Weber's concepts of "legalistic" and "charismatic" types of authority.[12] In his organizational capacity as regional manager, Mr. Goode was required to exercise a rational, "legalistic" form of authority over his subordinates. In his more professional capacity as account supervisor, he was more in the position of a "charismatic" leader, guiding and controlling the behavior of his followers by manifestations of superior knowledge, skill, and insight. However, in account group meetings he was required to be simultaneously "legalistic" and "charismatic," to be bureaucratic and rational on the one hand and individualistic and emotional on the other. As Weber himself pointed out, these two types of authority are opposed to each other, and the presence of one tends to drive out the other. Mr. Goode appears to have attempted to solve the problem by stepping somewhat away from both authority positions, acting instead in a more "peerlike" or brotherly fashion. For instance, one significant aspect of a superior-subordinate relationship is that the superior has access to valuable information not available to the subordinate. By maintaining a fairly complete flow of information, Mr. Goode minimized his authority over the group by establishing a "band of brothers" atmosphere in which each "brother" would determine and control his own behavior. In this way, Mr. Goode was able to move a certain distance away from the ambiguous authority position he occupied in the office. Nonetheless, he had to control behavior and proceeded to do so, even though for him the matter of coffee money was "really important business."

MR. GOODE (continuing): Now for the really important business. Doreen is getting more and more angry at everybody here because they don't put their nickels in the coffee . . . er . . . pot.

MR. LORENZ: Would you straighten that one out? (General laughter.)

Mr. Goode had no sooner begun to assert his authority than Mr. Lorenz rose to the bait. We see him not only asserting his right to a position of second in command, but also flirting with the possibility of upsetting Mr. Goode and assuming the topmost power position himself. Mr. Goode refused, however, to recognize the challenge.

[12] Bendix, R., *Max Weber: An Intellectual Portrait.* Garden City, New York: Doubleday & Company, Inc., 1960, Part III.

MR. GOODE: Instead of breaking even on it, Doreen's running in the hole. We want to bail her out and have her on the right side of the ledger; we can't have red figures even in Doreen's figures. (General laughter.) That's about all I had to say, with one exception. We gave our Fisher presentation to the plans board in New York; our Conn plans too, but that didn't include the creative work, while the Fisher included both the marketing and the creative plans. The kudos which were sung down there have now made it necessary for us to produce this thing on a little more polished basis. It's to be circulated to all offices of W & W as an example of an excellent handling of an account, creatively and in the use of research in the development of the creative work. So everybody that had a part in it, meaning everyone here, can be very proud of the fact that this is going across the country as a representation of W & W's best. And it comes from Northwest City, of which we are very proud. (Mr. Goode then talked for a few minutes of his plans to give a series of presentations to the whole office staff.) Well, that's all I had this morning. I thought you'd want to hear the good news about our new piece of business. It should bring smiles to some faces around here.

MR. LORENZ: How much do you want to fine him, Phil? He ran over two minutes. (Some laughter among general conversation.)

MR. GOODE: Everybody's here . . . .

MR. LORENZ (interrupting): No, the thing is, I'm fining you, John, for delaying the meeting.

MR. GOODE: There's going to be an account group meeting, so those scheduled for the Conn account can just stay where they are.

It can be seen from the above that Mr. Goode continued his control-through-information policy while Mr. Lorenz continued to obstruct and challenge him in a "humorous" manner.

As the main group of people broke up, there was general talk in the room. Mr. Lorenz asked Miss O'Mara, the home economist, to stay for the meeting, although she ordinarily did not attend Conn account group meetings. After about two or three minutes, he started to open the Conn meeting. A notice had been circulated to account group members concerning the agenda for the meeting. The agenda read: "Discussion of promotion campaign for Conn's Flavored Drink."

MR. LORENZ (loudly): I'm not excusing anybody after the meeting starts. (Commotion still going on.) Can I have your attention? Can I have the attention of the few of us who are here? (The

researcher is trying to take a tape of this.)   I can't imagine that anyone in the group would be nervous because the tape recorder is
running, but try and talk up enough to this mike to give (the
researcher) half a chance of getting it.

RESEARCHER: I tested it and it picks up even murmurs. Please just
go ahead and do what you would ordinarily do.

MR. LORENZ (interrupting): Now if anybody has to say anything
real nasty, reach out and cover the mike.   (He laughs.)

MISS FOWLER (to Mr. Lorenz): You sit close to it, then.   (Some
laughter.)

Mr. Lorenz's specific and revealing reference to nasty remarks
pointed to a highly visible characteristic of his own interpersonal
style of behavior. Miss Fowler's response, and the laughter that
followed it, indicate that this characteristic was indeed an integral part
of the group's perception of Mr. Lorenz.

MR. GOODE: How long do you intend to take for this meeting?

MR. LORENZ: We have a half-hour time limit.

MR. GOODE: O.K.   Fine, because I have a luncheon date.

MR. LORENZ: You're welcome to leave any time.

MR. GOODE: Yeah, I know, but I don't want to have to pay for it.
(Several laugh.)

Mr. Mascetta came in after the meeting had started, as did Ginnie
Hodges, a secretary, who squeezed in between Miss Navin and Miss
O'Mara. Mr. Goode's statement indicates that the fining ritual was
on people's minds and that it had a significant controlling influence
over the behavior even of the regional manager. Notice, however,
that when Mr. Mascetta and Miss Hodges entered the meeting late,
no mention was made of fines.

MR. LORENZ: To begin very quickly, yesterday, at the Fisher account
group meeting, we discussed having a cross-ruff[13] promotion between Conn and Fisher in which we would band small cans of
Fisher to half-pints of sour cream, and large cans to pints, to offer
a combination for a dip. Fisher was quite interested in it, but
in talking with the Conn sour cream product manager, he gave
every indication that somewhere between 70 per cent and 80 per
cent of their sour cream sales are to Jewish people—not necessarily
Orthodox Jews, but the feeling was that banding shellfish and sour
cream together would be an insult to some people.

[13] Word used in the advertising trade to mean an effort wherein two products
are being used to help sell each other.

Now, Conn felt that because of Fisher's domination of its particular market and good distribution, this would be advantageous
to them, so they asked us to work up a cottage cheese-Fisher
Devilled Crab promotion. That is, Conn has. This might very
well be the fall cottage cheese promotion campaign. This would
be very advantageous for Fisher. And I think it would be advantageous for Conn, because if it *wouldn't* be advantageous for
Conn, we aren't going to do it. But I'd like to request you,
Doreen—and I don't know how to handle this billing-wise, where
to charge the time to, and frankly I don't care, because it all goes
into the same pot on this, so you can charge it to Conn I guess—
I'd like a half-dozen variations on dips involving cottage cheese
and devilled crab.

MR. GOODE: Do you want to stick to just the two ingredients?

MR. LORENZ: Well, no. I want those to be the base ingredients.
And what I'm after is "devilish dips" or something of that sort,
and from that we should work up later, after we've had the base,
and make up the recipes and have both Conn and Fisher try them,
then we should work up a "Devilish Dip Booklet," banding methods, and pricing with Fisher. Now, Marie isn't here, so it's hard to
discuss this. But this would mean support of this thing including
a TV commercial somewhat on the Kraft style, showing dips being
made, point-of-sale, the works. In other words, this could very
well be our consumer plan for the fall of 1958. And Conn seemed
to think this was a wonderful idea.

MR. GOODE: On cottage cheese?

MR. LORENZ: Yeah.

MR. MASCETTA (just arrived): No sour cream in this at all, just cottage
cheese?

MR. LORENZ: No.

MR. GOODE: No, before you came in, George explained that this was
a conflict between ethnic use of sour cream and shellfish.

Mr. Mascetta, by his question, called specific attention to the fact
that he had arrived late to the meeting. Mr. Goode's statement indicates that his lateness had not been overlooked; yet still no attempts
were made to fine him. It appears that the fining ritual was considered to be so much the property of the creative-service group in
general, and Mr. Mascetta in particular, that it was inconceivable that
its laws should be applied to him, the "high priest."

MR. LORENZ: They are not worried about cottage cheese because they
don't feel they sell that high a percentage of their cottage cheese

to Jewish people who would be bothered. But they know that 70 or 80 per cent of their sour cream customers are Jewish people. Even though these people don't necessarily follow dietary laws strictly, banding shellfish on the packages would be like waving a red flag in their faces.

MR. MASCETTA: Yeah.

MR. LORENZ: So that is an assignment, Doreen, if you will take it. This is a kind of problem as far as charging time is concerned. (To Miss Navin) Would you issue a job order, a Conn job order for this. It's all speculative and her time is actually going to be charged against commissionable time and space anyway, so it's not a question of who pays for it. But from the standpoint of getting Mr. Goode off my back on whether or not we can make the Conn account profitable, some portion of that might well be charged to Fisher either under their new public relations budget or something; we'll find a way of squeezing it into Marie's pocket too.

MR. JONES (aside): Inequitable split. (Several laugh.)

All the agency's revenue was obtained outside the office by the account executives. All the costs were incurred inside the office by the creative-service personnel. The profitability of an executive's accounts was thus in part determined by the amount of creative and service work that was done for him. In this way the account executives "paid for" the assistance and support they received from the creative-service personnel. In other words, there were two sides to the executives' competition among themselves for the attentions of the creative-service personnel. The more an executive was "lucky in love" the more he had to "pay the piper." The allocation of costs was always a tense issue, particularly on cross-ruffs.

MR. LORENZ: The main thing is to get a taste test on a bunch of dips. I think six to eight dips would be adequate. And it might be more than dips, incidentally. You might have a cottage cheese, devilled crab, and egg omelet sort of deal—I don't know—but we can start with "devilish dips" and go on from there. *The key is cottage cheese.* This means that if it goes, it would mean a hell of a sales jump for Fisher. It would be a good deal, because a banded combination of this sort with the price-off deal, the way Conn sells cottage cheese . . . .

MR. JONES: Well, it would actually be better than the sour cream, as far as distribution goes, because it's much better . . . .

MR. GOODE: Yeah, that's too spotty to do a job on.

According to Mr. Lorenz, "The key is cottage cheese." He then admitted that his client was also hoping to increase sales by cross-ruffing. However, it is obvious which of the two account executives —he or Miss Ayers—he considered to be the dominant and more independent one. This, in part, might have accounted for Miss Ayer's absence from a meeting concerned in such a vital way with one of her clients.

MR. LORENZ: Yeah, they were hoping that with Fisher, there might be a possibility of increasing sales.

MR. GOODE: You want . . .

MR. FAHEY: Do we get a hitchhike on this thing for sour cream by making some sour cream recipes ride on those?

MR. LORENZ: We could. We could have a sour cream recipe in there, Bruce. I don't think . . . . I think the key, though, is to have half a dozen good recipes involving a combination of devilled crab and cottage cheese and then anything else we can throw into a booklet.

MR. MASCETTA: Well, as I understand it, is that going to be in the package, that little recipe book?

MR. LORENZ: I think it should be, yes. I think we need some real clever art and production technique that will make this thing a real deal for . . . .

MR. BERKLUND: The same basic treatment we had before? A round booklet that fits the top of the package . . . ?

MR. JONES: John, do you know if Fisher would be approachable about printing the inside of their label, of their overwrap, I mean?

MR. GOODE: I doubt that, because that involves a complete . . . .

MR. JONES: Plate change.

MR. GOODE: Separate plate change, the whole thing . . . .

MISS FOWLER: I don't think that would be a very good effect. You tear so much when you rip it off.

MR. GOODE: I think they have outserts that they now put on their can of devilled crab, which is much more effective than printing the inside anyway. I think they would be approachable very definitely, where they share in this thing. But what their share will be in the price concession and the printing, we haven't any idea at this point. We have to explore what the sales possibilities are, and then we have to examine the profit structure to see that there's something desirable in it for both Conn and Fisher, and when we get to that stage, I think we can take it from there.

MR. JONES: Yeah.

MR. LORENZ: We can pretty well block out where the money'll be spent.

MR. GOODE: I want to put in just one request, George. If Mary will, in all her assignments, indicate that "rough roughs" are to be done copywise and artwise for examination before we go any further . . . .

MR. LORENZ: Oh yeah. We can.

MR. GOODE: Then we can discuss it with both Conn and Fisher so they can see we're not putting a lot of unnecessary detailed hourly development work on this beyond the basic thought that will go into . . . .

MR. LORENZ: The basic plan exists.

MR. GOODE: Now what you want. . . .

MR. LORENZ: All I'm looking for, John, is . . . . We have been talking about a premium or a consumer purchasing inducement to go with cottage cheese. This is Fisher Devilled Crab. This is wonderful from our standpoint as an agency and from Fisher's standpoint, while Conn gets the benefit. The only contribution we would want is in the form of a price concession on the devilled crab.

Mr. Lorenz was highly committed to his concept of himself as a competent marketing man, as noted in his reactions to Mr. Goode. He further indicated his unwillingness to be counselled about the marketing arrangements for the cross-ruff below. It turned out, however, that Mr. Goode was talking not about marketing matters, but about administrative matters.

MR. GOODE: I'm not talking about . . . .

MR. LORENZ: Now as far as the other piece is concerned . . . .

MR. GOODE: You've given Doreen an assignment; you've asked for recipes and so forth. (Conversations continue indistinctly for a few sentences between Mr. Lorenz and Mr. Goode.)

MR. LORENZ: Well, that's all. All Doreen has to do is come up with a half-dozen recipes that we can use . . . .

MR. GOODE: Art and copy aren't doing anything?

MR. LORENZ: Nothing yet. We're too far ahead; it's a fall campaign.

MR. GOODE: O.K.

MR. LORENZ: Later, we'll come up with TV commercials, the works. But that will be when we get to the fall plan. We have too many that are coming up before the fall plan. After all, that runs in September. We don't want to start it until the 15th of August, do we?

MR. JONES: We still have the same relationship? It's perfect, the small and the eight-ounce, and the large and the sixteen-ounce?

MR. LORENZ: Yeah. Keep it in that proportion, Doreen.

MISS O'MARA: All right.

MR. LORENZ: (Picking up a piece of paper that indicated he was turning to a new subject): Now, I want to run through this flavored drink promotion just once and see where we stand on this thing.

Mr. Lorenz then spoke for about four minutes, explaining the issues involved in this campaign. The product was skimmed milk with any of several different flavorings added. The product's appeal was primarily to children. This was to be the second promotion. The first one, conducted the previous year, had been unsuccessful. He stated that the main reason for this failure was the client's decision to override W & W's proposal to use newspaper advertising.

The 1958 campaign was to be based on advertising on the Conn-sponsored TV show, "Mounties on the Trail," and on newspaper and point-of-sale advertising. Mr. Lorenz indicated that it was essential to prove the effectiveness of the TV show. The promotion was to be three-pronged: it would include giveaways, self-liquidating premiums, and store prizes. The giveaway, probably a plastic belt-buckle with a "Mounties on the Trail" motif, would be attached to every unit of the flavored drinks bought during a certain period. The self-liquidating premium, which Mr. Lorenz did not specify, would require proof of purchase.[14] The store prize, an item such as a barbecue set, would be won in a drawing at each store by the person who held the lucky entry blank. Entry blanks would not require proof of purchase. Mr. Lorenz also mentioned that the pricing structure on the flavored drinks would make this item more profitable for the home route delivery salesmen than it had been.

MR. FAHEY: Are you going to have a breakage problem with store sales?

MR. LORENZ: I don't think so, particularly with Pure-Pak (a cardboard container), where we can duck any problem. The product is handled fairly carefully, Bruce. I'm not terribly worried. We're not sure that this is the final strap on it. But where they've used a strap on it they've had minimum breakage.

---

[14] "Self-liquidating premium" meant that the purchaser would be charged enough for the item to cover the cost of it to Conn and the mailing expenses. "Proof of purchase" meant the sending of some specified object, such as the package top, indicating the customer had bought the item.

MR. GOODE: The store gives it fairly careful handling, anyway, because those cartons are subject to having seams opened if they're dropped and that sort of thing.

MR. FAHEY: Well, the cartons, yes . . . . I was thinking about the bottles.

MR. LORENZ: On the bottle this would be a giveaway at the home, Bruce . . . .

MR. FAHEY: O.K.

MR. LORENZ: . . . in which case the route man will actually use these things indiscriminately. I mean, he will deliver six of them to a house with six kids for one quart of strawberry or chocolate drink. Now, the self-liquidating premium—we have not yet received a final selection recommendation from New York. They've been extremely busy on something back there; I haven't figured out what and they haven't come up with it yet. The belt buckle was our suggestion, and we have a couple of alternatives which we will not work up in art work but which we will give the client as alternatives.

MR. MASCETTA: For the bottle hanger, you've got a holster.

MR. LORENZ: Now that's the self-liquidator, Phil, remember?

Mr. Mascetta seemed to forget the arrangements surrounding Mr. Lorenz's account. There is also a hint of derision directed by Mr. Mascetta toward Mr. Lorenz's ideas. Either of these tendencies, if carried further, would have made it difficult for Mr. Lorenz to get good work out of the creative-service personnel. He took this risk by behaving toward others in the office as he did. His behavior, and the reactions it prompted, will be clearly illustrated in the data from Miss Ayers' meeting.

MR. MASCETTA: Yeah.

(Mr. Lorenz then again describes aspects of the selling campaign, including the self-liquidating premiums and the store contest.)

MR. LORENZ (continuing): . . . We supply the store with pads of entry blanks and the consumer is not required to purchase anything in order to enter this thing. But we have learned through experience that about four out of five people who wish to enter feel that they can win only if they purchase, and will purchase the product involved. The primary reason for this is to take these metal ice tables on which to display the product, build a western corral, "Mounties on the Trail" atmosphere stuff, and . . . (Telephone rings. Miss Navin answers.)

MISS NAVIN: George. George, it's for you.

MR. LORENZ: Who is it?

MISS NAVIN: I don't know.

MR. LORENZ: Excuse me just a second.   (His voice heard indistinctly in background for a while.)

MR. GOODE: Incidentally, on this purchase ratio for the store deal that George is working on, on the Super Tea test we've had better than 2500 entrants which we checked through . . . (Mr. Lorenz can be heard in background saying, "I'll be right out." He hangs up and waits as if to say something.) . . . er, from the time they entered until the time they left the store. We checked at the checkout counter and they averaged 17 out of 20 purchases.

The stage was now set for the imposition of a fine on Mr. Lorenz. We shall see the ritual played out in its customary fashion: insiders against outsiders, with Mr. Goode giving an assist to both sides.

MR. JONES: Is that right?   That many?

MR. LORENZ: Bill, would you pick this one up?   I gotta take a call from New York. I'm going to excuse myself so there'll be no fine.

MR. BERKLUND, with a few others: Ohhhh-hhh.

MR. GOODE: You're outvoted.   Sorry.

MR. BERKLUND: Getting pretty dramatic around here.

MISS FOWLER: In fact, there was an interruption *and* leaving . . . .

MR. GOODE: Yeah, *that's true.*

MR. BERKLUND: Helen, thank you.   Two!

MR. MASCETTA: A phone call's an interruption and leaving is another one.

MR. GOODE: O.K.   Go ahead.

(Mr. Lorenz leaves.)

In the following portion of the meeting transcript, a startling difference can be seen in the behaviors of Mr. Jones and Mr. Goode after Mr. Lorenz had left. Mr. Jones immediately moved up from having said relatively little, and even that mostly in the form of questions, to the position of dominant talker in the group. It will be noticed, however, that his concept of the role of the account executive, that is, how an account executive should behave, was different from Mr. Lorenz's. Mr. Jones' verbal behavior points up this difference.

Mr. Goode changed also. It will be noticed that his interference with and control over Mr. Jones was much more direct than was the case when he was dealing with Mr. Lorenz. It becomes obvious that Mr. Lorenz's interpersonal style was not only partially successful in controlling the behavior of his peers and subordinates in the office, it was also partially successful in controlling the behavior of his boss, Mr. Goode. Once he was no longer present, Mr. Goode's own aggressiveness became noticeably less restrained.

MR. JONES: Well, we promised that this would only be a 30-minute meeting. So why don't we get through this thing. We've gone . . . George has gone through the giveaway, the self-liquidating aspects of it, and the raffle. Why don't we go right into the creative? The only thing . . . this starts the first of June, so we haven't got the gun right on top of us on this one, so we should . . . .

MISS NAVIN: Well, you do according to the schedule. Tomorrow . . . .

MR. JONES: You can't get ahead of it. You really can't beat it. (Laughter.) So we're right under the gun (more laughter) and away we go.

Miss Navin tried to move in on Mr. Jones, but he demonstrated that he did not intend to let go of the meeting. He did this through a humorous jibe at Miss Navin's department, which aligned the sentiments of the others in his favor. The laughter indicated his success.

MR. JONES (continuing): Uh, but . . . I think with the group here we should look at this thing very carefully. (Most of the people are looking at a "rough" of a newspaper ad which was tacked up on the bulletin board. The ad showed a young boy in cowboy outfit drawing two six-shooters, with a headline concerning, "the fastest growing guns in the Northwest.") My comments on this one . . . I don't know . . . I scratched that gun, the "fastest-growing gun" thing once, but it's gotten back in there. I don't know why. But I think it is in very poor taste.

Dan, why don't you read what you have written? All this material's due tomorrow, and this is what has come out of the art department so far. The rest of the copy is there, as I understand it now.

DAN RITTNER: Yeah, it's there.

MR. JONES: How did this "fastest-growing guns" thing get back in there?

MR. RITTNER: I never knew it was taken out.

MR. JONES: Well, then does anyone else feel that this is distasteful? I do.

MR. RITTNER: Why?

It can be seen in the next few minutes of this meeting that Mr. Jones was "after" Mr. Rittner, and Mr. Goode "after" Mr. Jones. The harder Mr. Goode attacked Mr. Jones, the harder Mr. Jones attacked Mr. Rittner. At one point, this underlying process became particularly clear when Mr. Rittner said, in a somewhat plaintive voice, "Well, yeah. I didn't intend it to be taken as seriously as everybody has taken it." The meeting continued.

MR. JONES: Well, I know Conn wouldn't buy it, in the first place; I don't think we should, in the second place. This "fastest-growing guns in town"—people don't want their kids to be associated with being . . .

MR. MASCETTA: I think it's a guy being . . .

MR. JONES: . . . quick on the draw. This is a bad relationship for Conn to be in with parents, I'm sure.

MR. GOODE: You're appealing not to the youngsters but to the kids, uh, I mean . . .

MR. JONES: To the parents.

MR. GOODE: Parents.

MR. GOODE: This is for parents, a printed ad; and the kids come into the TV more heavily. I have a basic question before we start in on the headline, Bill. With the premium ad in the newspapers, the major thing we're selling is the premium. At least we should be, if we utilize it the way our experience has shown over and over again that you must do to make it a success. This thing, the premium doesn't come in until down at the bottom; it isn't played up in the headline; there isn't anything that says there's something that is a free premium on here unless you read the whole ad.

MR. JONES: Yeah. Sorry, I got sidetracked on that.

Mr. Goode's observations hit home, which was probably their latent intent, as Mr. Jones' response indicated. However, at the manifest level, Mr. Goode only complicated the issue by introducing another consideration into the meeting. It will be seen that from this point the meeting vacillated between a discussion of the copy, where Mr. Jones could take it out on Mr. Rittner, and a discussion of premiums versus product, where Mr. Goode had it over Mr. Jones.

MR. GOODE: So that the ad in itself, for the purposes that we decided and that George reviewed for us again this morning before, uh, it doesn't come off at all, it's completely . . . .

MR. JONES: I think, Phil, we'll have to get away from . . . .

MR. MASCETTA: Yeah, I agree, but why was this asked to be played down?

MR. RITTNER: Yeah, George just said that they intended to subordinate it and that the job the ad was to do was to sell the Conn flavored drinks to adults on a copy platform which I have here, which is embodied in this copy, uh . . . .

It is interesting that it was to Mr. Mascetta, whom we have already identified as a dominant figure among the socio-emotional specialists of the creative-service subgroup, that Mr. Jones turned at the particularly stressful moment.   Also, it was to Mr. Mascetta that Mr. Rittner responded in pointing the finger at the now absent Mr. Lorenz. This in turn prompted Mr. Jones to defend his boss and to reactivate the discussion that would allow him to fight with Mr. Rittner.

MR. JONES: This is absolutely true, but . . . .

MR. RITTNER: Now . . . .

MR. JONES: We're trying to illustrate the ad somehow.   We're going to have an illustration in the ad . . . .

MR. RITTNER: It was my thought to have the belt buckle shown but not big, down at the bottom, and maybe have it shown on the figure of the boy.

(Miss Navin heard indistinctly saying something about a holster.)

MR. JONES: Why don't you go ahead and read your copy platform?

What Mr. Jones was saying in effect was, "Dan, why don't you go ahead and make a fool of yourself, out loud, so everyone can hear you."

MR. RITTNER: Here, this is the actual copy for that ad which embodies the points.   (Reads ad copy, which stresses health, flavor, and convenience.)   Then we go into this little box . . . which I won't read . . . .

MISS FOWLER: Why does the milk ad have to be appealing to adults mainly?   Why couldn't we shoot for the kids in that, too?   Instead of using a child, what about using Cap'n Jim (A TV character)?

MR. JONES: Well, I think the child is somewhat wasted.   I think we're devoting an awful lot of space to something that doesn't mean a a darn' thing as far as selling flavored drinks goes.   I think John's point about . . . .

Mr. Jones was now in the area he controlled, and Miss Fowler's question allowed him to express, indirectly, sentiments that might well have been too strong to be expressed directly toward Mr. Rittner. At this point, Mr. Goode moved in to take another whack at Mr. Jones.

MR. GOODE (interrupting): To go back to the basic objective, George has stated, apparently after the fact, of the objective of the whole thing that our newspaper ad must be directed toward selling chocolate drink, or flavored drinks. If we're going to put money into a premium, and we're going to use the premium as a means of moving chocolate milk, we know perfectly well that to try to straddle a fence like this isn't going to do either job any good. We either go out and sell chocolate milk with the bare mention of the fact that there's a premium there and knowing beforehand that we don't expect the premium to move the product; or if we're going to use the premium as a lever to move the product, then we've got to sell the premium. We know that is so; this is a basic fact that we proved so many times; we don't even have to give it a second thought. Now, which is our objective? This is a promotion built around a premium. We're going to put point-of-sales effort on it. The Conn organization is going to sell this premium. Therefore, I feel that this advertising direction that is taken in this newspaper ad, Bill, is completely off base.

Mr. Jones protested at a manifestly none-too-relevant level.

MR. JONES: Well, the only way that they could be criticized, John, would be with exclusive distribution in stores and at retail. If they're going to buy a flavored drink, they're going to buy the one that's in the store. With the strap on the package . . .
MR. GOODE (while Mr. Jones is speaking): Why have a premium?
MR. JONES: To tie in with the Mounties show. I mean this is a good, legitimate way of selling.
MR. GOODE: . . . selling the Mounties?
MR. JONES: That's right.
MR. GOODE: O.K.
MR. JONES: But we haven't been able to sell it any other way.
MR. GOODE: Let's come back to this other fact, that if they're gonna buy a flavored milk, they're gonna buy Conn's, according to distribution and availability.
MR. JONES: (simultaneous with Mr. Goode's last phrase): . . . at the point of sale. That's right.

MR. GOODE: Now, if that's the case, then let's leave the whole premium deal out of this thing, and go after selling chocolate milk.

MR. JONES: Well, to get them interested in buying chocolate milk, we're shooting for the people that are now using either a mix or are not using flavored drink at all—are using white milk or not drinking milk because they don't like it.

MR. GOODE: All right, the way we would sell chocolate milk would not be to sell it for gunmen; we'd sell it for . . .

MR. JONES: For health, or . . .

MR. GOODE: For health, for flavor, for ease and convenience because the kids love it, because it has soda-fountain flavor and that sort of thing. And not because he's drawing guns.

MR. JONES: Well I don't think anyone disagrees with that.

MR. GOODE: So far as . . .

MR. JONES (over some words of Mr. Goode): . . . on the wrong track.

MR. GOODE: . . . either ought to go one direction or the other. We know darn' well that if we concentrate our effort toward one thing, we'll do it better; we'll get better results . . . .

MR. JONES (simultaneous with Mr. Goode's last phrase): Well, the way I think it should be concentrated is in selling flavored drinks, selling the product and bringing the premium in as an additional plus. But not selling it through the showing of a kid with two guns on him. I don't know where this got into the thing. Dan, was this your illustration suggestion?

Again Mr. Jones turned away from his area of disadvantage with Mr. Goode toward his area of advantage over Mr. Rittner. It would appear from the ease and rapidity with which both men were switching the conversation to suit their needs that very little work was being done at the level of the group's manifest reason for meeting, namely, the formulation of an effective marketing strategy. The meeting, was, in effect, an aggregate of collective monologues. It would appear that, for a variety of reasons, the meeting had become more closely involved in the latently aggressive-defensive behavior of attack and counterattack than in accomplishing the work for which the account group had met.

MR. RITTNER: Yes. It was the idea of tying the show to the product and utilizing . . . .

MR. JONES: With that we've gone overboard. We're promoting the Mounties and . . .

MR. RITTNER: Yeah.

MR. JONES: Subordinately selling flavored drink.

MR. RITTNER: Well, yeah. *I didn't intend it to be taken as seriously as everybody has taken it.* (Emphasis added.) We have some awfully cute illustrations of kids in cowboy outfits and guns and the idea was to show this little kid—who obviously is not going to grow up to be a gangster—having fun with a cowboy suit on. And the headline was intended to be light, not heavy. It was taken wrong, so obviously it is wrong and should be changed. I . . . .

At this point, perhaps as the result of Mr. Rittner's plea, the group members evidently realized that they had departed from the purpose of the meeting. Miss Navin laughed and chatted on the side with Miss Hodges. Mr. Jones and Mr. Goode joked about young Gary Cooper about to plug his mother—an aggressive fantasy, to say the least, but acted out in such a way as to re-establish solidarity. Attempts were then made to reach an agreement.

MR. GOODE: I would say that the illustration here looks as if he is kind of . . . . (Miss Navin laughs.)

MR. RITTNER: That looks pretty grim, I admit.

Mr. Mascetta says a few words indistinctly and Miss Navin and Miss Hodges whisper to each other.

MR. JONES: This is the young Gary Cooper.

MR. RITTNER: Yeah.

MR. GOODE: (Few words indistinct) . . . plug his mother any minute. (Several laugh.)

MR. RITTNER: But we do have all those points that John mentioned in the copy.

MR. JONES: I think what we have to do . . . .

MR. MASCETTA (simultaneously with Mr. Jones' sentence): . . . decide what is most important.

MR. JONES: . . . is we have to sell flavored drinks on its own qualities.

MR. RITTNER: Exactly.

Finally, one agreement was reached. The next discussion was in a different mood. Mr. Goode and Mr. Jones agreed to have children depicted in the selling messages. Mr. Jones even pointed out favorably the presence of something in Mr. Rittner's ad that the others had overlooked.

MR. JONES: And as an illustrative device build it around kids with western outfits on or whatever . . . .

MR. RITTNER: . . . doesn't have to be . . . .

MR. JONES: But not, not a gunslinger.

MR. MASCETTA: We've got some of the kids drinking milk in that other series, Dan, with cowboy costumes on.

MR. JONES: It's got to done very genuinely, very lightly, very nicely.

MR. RITTNER: Yeah.

MISS FOWLER: There were plenty of kids on the other series on the quality milk.   Why go on it again on this?

MR. JONES: I don't know; there were only two kids on the quality milk . . . .

MISS FOWLER: Well, I think we're going overboard on kids.

MR. GOODE: Can we start with something that is important to the quality of the product we're trying to put over, so that their attitude toward that product will rise and be reinforced with the illustration? Could you . . . .

MR. JONES: You mean take it out of the soft drink . . . .

MR. GOODE: Well, let's say you had three kids in cowboy outfits sitting at the counter in the kitchen and your headline is sort of a "fountain at home—no fuss, no bother, always so good" or something—"Conn flavored milk."

MR. JONES: Yeah.   Or you could have three kids western style at a bar thing with their feet up on a rail with the guns hanging up, you know, just back views of them in the soda-fountain-at-home idea. I think the product advantages here are two, primarily.   One, help, and second, convenience.   I mean, if parents have trouble getting the kids to drink milk, this is an easy way of doing it.   It's already in the carton; there's no mixing.

MR. MASCETTA: Shouldn't we say somethin' like that, then?

MR. JONES: Well, I think Dan has it in the copy.

MR. RITTNER: It's all in the copy.

In the rest of the meeting, disagreements continued to occur, but in a comparatively neutral group atmosphere.   It can be seen that the meeting turned to its task at hand, and worked on it.   Alternatives were suggested and were developed or rejected.   Questions were raised.   Information was communicated.   With feelings more under control, members were able to persevere at the task level without regressing to hostility and defensiveness.

(Mr. Mascetta's voice discussing the headline and Mr. Goode's voice discussing reasons for buying are heard simultaneously.)

MR. GOODE: One other thing, Bill.   Is the "soda fountain at home" going to be in conflict with Conn's objectives of selling soda fountain

ice cream and all the rest of their things? Will the soda fountain
. . . ?

MR. JONES: I don't think so.

MR. GOODE: You don't think so.

MISS NAVIN: Is it possible to do comic strips on a regular page? In
other words, just the style, not necessarily . . . .

MR. JONES: It's a 13-week commitment.

MISS NAVIN: I don't mean on a comic-strip page. I mean on any page
. . . .

MISS FOWLER: It doesn't matter where you use it. They vary the
requirement by all papers. We went through all this last year.

MISS NAVIN: You can't buy a single line at the bottom?

MR. JONES: We . . . without any more discussion, we have to rule
that one out.

MR. MASCETTA: Do we have to stick to straight flavored drinks? Can
we mix 'em with ice cream for sodas?

MR. JONES: I think you dissipate your . . . . (Voice becomes indistinct behind Mr. Goode's voice.)

MR. GOODE: I think so, too. You can do a pretty good job . . . .

MR. JONES: People know. I think people know what they can do with
it. It isn't something that's foreign to people. You mean "brown
cows" and that kind of thing.

MR. GOODE: Well, you can have the mother being the soda fountain
attendant or something of this sort. And one of them saying,
"Make mine strawberry." The other one saying "Chocolate." So
forth—so you can get the flavors in there and then play up the
headline, the advantages of buying the prepared flavored milk.
Something along that line. But you're sure how you want to pitch
this and not go out for the premiums? You don't think the
premium's strong enough?

MR. JONES: No. My feeling on the premium is that the premium is a
good secondary device to interest kids in buying flavored drinks.
But if we're shooting primarily for adults in this thing, they aren't
particularly interested in getting the kid a belt buckle. So to me,
the prime advantage in the ad should be definitely on the product
itself.

MR. RITTNER: Well, let me add a little bit longer view. I think that
George said this may be our last opportunity to promote the
product. I think one of the things we should do is to promote the
product. We do have a good start . . . . (Voice becomes indistinct.)

MR. FAHEY: Which raises the point which has been bothering me for last five minutes or so. Maybe I didn't hear it when it was stated, but what is the marketing problem here and what are the marketing objectives?

Finally the question had been raised that might well have been asked at the very outset of the meeting, if feelings of the group members had not prohibited such rational inquisitiveness.

MR. JONES: The marketing problem is . . . . it has changed within the last 12 months. This product returns as much margin to Conn as does white fluid milk. This product has been limited to about six or seven weeks in the summertime where the sales go crazy and then right back down again to a level even below what it started out at. I mean, because of the seasonal aspect of the product, it tapers off very quickly going into the holiday season and it's really not much more than a nuisance item for the rest of the year. We've been trying to broaden that a little bit to increase the usage of the product in the home as a replacement for milk. Now we were always squashed on this idea before because it didn't return the margin that fluid milk did . . . . So now that it does, there's no reason not to promote it. And this is strictly on increased consumption. We find . . . I think we can accept what Politz (a marketing research company) has found out that this is not sold, nationwide, anyway, as a replacement. I think it's only a two or three per cent replacement product, which is very surprising and which was something that we didn't know previously.

Mr. Jones stated part of the problem, but none of the solutions. He and Mr. Fahey then chatted in a desultory fashion, while the other members probably rested. Mr. Lorenz returned to find the meeting no further advanced than when he had left it.

MR. FAHEY: Why is it only a six- or seven-week seasonal product? It's not like bock beer, is it?
MR. JONES: No. Oh no.
MR. FAHEY: You can have it all year long?

The meeting continued for about 30 minutes longer.

Summary of Frequency and Amount of Participation in the Conn Account Group Meeting

Exhibit 11 presents a summary of participation in the Conn account group meeting of March 12. This summary is based on the number of times members spoke and the number of lines that their talk covered

EXHIBIT 11

THE WATKINS AND WORSTER AGENCY (B)

Frequency and Approximate Amount of Speaking in Conn Account Group Meeting*

First Part of Meeting, Chaired by George Lorenz

Name	Number of times person spoke	%	Number of lines in original typescript	%
George Lorenz	33	40.2	201	72.3
John Goode	23	28.1	44	15.8
Bruce Fahey	4	4.9	5	1.8
Bill Jones	7	8.5	10	3.6
Mary Navin	2	2.4	2	0.7
Phil Mascetta	5	6.1	6	2.2
Dan Rittner	—	—	—	—
Al Berklund	4	4.9	5	1.8
Helen Fowler	3	3.7	4	1.4
Doreen O'Mara	1	1.2	1	0.4
Ginnie Hodges	—	—	—	—
	82	100.0	278	100.0

Second Part of Meeting, Chaired by Bill Jones

Name	Number of times person spoke	%	Number of lines in original typescript	%
Bill Jones	46	43.4	108	43.2
John Goode	23	21.7	73	29.2
Bruce Fahey	3	2.8	8	3.2
Mary Navin	5	4.7	6	2.4
Phil Mascetta	7	6.6	9	3.6
Dan Rittner	18	17.0	37	14.8
Al Berklund	—	—	—	—
Helen Fowler	4	3.8	9	3.6
Doreen O'Mara	—	—	—	—
Ginnie Hodges	—	—	—	—
	82	100.0	250	100.0

* Those participants who are also shown in Exhibits 4 to 6 are here listed in the same order, except that the chairman and John Goode appear first and second, respectively.

in the original typescript and pertains to the sections of the meeting presented in the preceding section.

Analysis of the Fisher Account Group Meeting of April 1

The following material is from the tape recording and the researcher's observations of the meeting of the Fisher Account Group on April 1. Fining was still very much alive in the minds of the group members and influential in directing the course of at least the initial phases of the meeting. As before, Mr. Mascetta assumed the initiative in activating the ritual, although it is interesting to note that in this instance he deferred to Miss Ayers by asking her permission to start the fines. This behavior indicates that the relationship that Miss Ayers had developed with the creative-service personnel was different from that which Mr. Lorenz had developed with the same group. This difference underlies much of the behavior manifested in the meeting. The suitability of Miss Ayer's approach was finally explicity attacked by Mr. Lorenz, whose inability to equal her deftness in an interpersonal setting led him into occasional difficulty during the meeting. This was perhaps generally indicative of his work life within the regional office.

MR. MASCETTA: About time to start collecting fines?

MISS AYERS: Yes, it is.

MR. MASCETTA: What's the right time?

MISS AYERS: Ten o'clock.

MR. MASCETTA: (to Mr. Fahey): You just made it under the wire.

MR. FAHEY: May I be excused? I have got to get some stuff together for the First National Bank book, which closes on the nineteenth.

MR. MASCETTA: (to Mr. Jones): You're about one second late.

MISS AYERS: (to Mr. Fahey): The meeting won't be complete without you, but go.

MR. JONES: Huh? Say, I was going by my clock. Who has the official time?

MISS AYERS: It's thirty seconds past ten.

MR. MASCETTA: You owe half a buck.

Miss Ayers' statement to Mr. Fahey indicates the general style of the approach which she used in relations with the people around her. One way of describing it would be the phrase "enhancing the other." As we shall see, this approach could easily be contrasted with Mr. Lorenz's style of "deprecating the other." Another aspect of Miss

Ayers' behavior is that she sided neither with the executive group nor with the creative-service personnel, at least not in the informal bickering that went on between the two mutually dependent but unequally powerful groups. In saying, "It's 30 seconds past ten," she gave Mr. Mascetta the opening to fine Mr. Jones. However, she then suspended Mr. Mascetta's rule and Mr. Jones got off without a fine, but not without protest from the service personnel.

MISS AYERS: No, he doesn't.   Sit down, Bill.

MR. MASCETTA: Well, I have about five minutes after.

MISS AYERS: You're not late.

VOICES: Don't let him get out of it . . . Come on, pay up. . . .

MR. MASCETTA: Don't act like that, Marie.   We can't make any money if you let these characters get out of it.

MISS AYERS: We need his creative thinking at this meeting today.   We have to have them in a good mood.

The last statement indicates Miss Ayers' way of enhancing the other—in this case, Mr. Jones—while at the same time indicating a real appreciation of the value of creativity and the need for supporting creativity.   This appeal could hardly be unwelcome to the creative-service personnel.   The meeting continued.   Mr. Jones' clowning led the group out of the field of work, and Miss Ayers followed with a statement that took the group even further away from the work waiting to be done, which everyone was too tense to begin.

MR. JONES: (with different vocal mannerisms than usual, as if imitating or mocking someone else): I'm willing to pay my share of the load here.

MISS AYERS: When are we going to have that weekend?

MR. JONES: Spring skiing.   (General laughter.)

MR. MASCETTA: Suppose I collect all the IOU's.

MISS AYERS: How much do we have?   Do I owe you anything?

MR. MASCETTA: Berklund owes a fortune.

MISS AYERS: We better plan it before spring really arrives.   (To Mr. Lorenz.)   Good morning.

At this point, the fining ritual was acted out again, but in a different mood than in the first instance.   Miss Ayers did not mediate, as she had before.   Also, Mr. Lorenz gave evidence that he refused to play the game, thus threatening to upset the tenuous informal balance of influence that the creative-service personnel had established through the fining ritual.

MR. BERKLUND: Here's a guy here.

MR. MASCETTA: A half dollar.

MR. LORENZ: Go to hell!   (Several laugh.)

MR. MASCETTA: Come on, it's after ten.

MR. LORENZ: It's not after ten; I just called the time signal.

MISS AYER: Here we go again.

MR. LORENZ: Pick up the phone.

MR. MASCETTA: Sneaky.

MR. LORENZ: Damn right I'm sneaky.   (Mr. Mascetta in background repeating: "Sneaky.")   I can't afford you and your bad habits. Dial the time number.

Mr. Lorenz was at the point of invoking incontrovertible evidence, and even before this evidence had been obtained, Mr. Mascetta was reduced to the childish level of name-calling.   To a certain extent, Mr. Mascetta's action must have reflected resentment toward Mr. Lorenz for placing him in such an awkward position.   He could not have enforced the norms of the fining ritual in any explicit way, since the fining ritual was part of the informal system of the office, and was considered "illegitimate" within the context of the formal rules and regulations of the organization.   At this point, the meeting fragmented into several small subgroups, each discussing a different topic.

MR. JONES: (to Mr. Berklund): How did you make out on the train Friday night?

MR. BERKLUND: All right.

MR. JONES: Real late?

MR. BERKLUND: Kind of a chug-a-chug job.

MR. JONES: Did you catch a three o'clock train?

MR. BERKLUND: Yeah.   (Several voices are indistinct as several conversations go on.   Mr. Lorenz dials the telephone number that gives a time signal.   Several others discuss a premium idea for the Conn account while he dials.)

MR. LORENZ: It is now 30 seconds after 10 o'clock.

MR. MASCETTA: So?   You haven't been here 30 seconds.   (Miss Navin and Mr. Jones continue discussion concerning Conn premium.) Now here's someone, right here.   (Mr. Goode enters.   Conversations continue as Mr. Lorenz hands the telephone handset to him.)

Mr. Goode's entry provided a convenient focus and resolution of the troublesome issue that centered around Mr. Lorenz.   Fortunately, Mr. Goode behaved in such a way as to fulfill the informal expectations that were directed toward him.   With a final discharge of nonwork energy, the group settled down to work.

MR. LORENZ: Someone wants to talk to you.
MR. GOODE: Hello.   (Long pause.   A smile appears on his face.   Mr. Lorenz laughs loudly and long.)
MR. LORENZ: That's what I call living proof that the fine is owed. (Laughs again.   Several talk at once, including remarks about the fines.)
MISS AYERS: The main purpose of this meeting is to discuss the commercials for the Northwest area, radio commercials.[15]   But before we start on that, I have a nice little letter to start the morning with, from Fred Mays (a Fisher executive): He says, "Having in mind the discussion we had last year about the preparation expenses for Fisher Devilled Crab magazine advertising,"—Mr. Berklund—"I'm delighted to see that you got under the estimate by nearly $3000. Please express my thanks and congratulations to all your associates for such a fine job."   (Applause.)
MR. LORENZ: Does that go in the kitty?

Miss Ayers' opening remarks were very much in keeping with her manner of enhancing others.   In the instance above, she acknowledged before the group that the satisfaction of a client, and the work of an account executive, both depended on the contribution of creative-service personnel.   One would predict that this approach would not be consonant with that of Mr. Lorenz, and that he would be very skeptical of it.   This apparently was the case, if his statement, "Does that go in the kitty?" can be taken to mean, "What good is what you have just said?" or "How much is it worth?"   Regardless of how much it was worth for getting work accomplished, good feelings were flowing between Miss Ayers and the creative-service group.   The somewhat aggrieved jokes made by Mr. Jones and Mr. Lorenz in the script below indicate that they felt threatened by the harmonious relations from which they were being excluded.

MR. BERKLUND: Can I get more money for the juice then?[16]
MISS AYERS: Please don't spend any more than $2000 now; but you've achieved such a fine record.
MR. MASCETTA: You can spend a hundred eighty for that poster now, Al.

[15] This was a campaign just being initiated on the Fisher account.
[16] Another Fisher product on which the office was preparing advertisements.

MR. JONES: This'll mean they'll cut your salary by seventy-five per cent if you go over that.

MR. BERKLUND: How about that! Isn't he a nice man!

MR. LORENZ: It's easy to see now, Bill. Ours has been running so high because he's been charging the time on our account.

Miss Ayers was having none of it, however, and with a reproving statement directed at Mr. Lorenz, turned the meeting back to the work at hand.

MISS AYERS: Never mind how he does it; he saved $3000. Carlton, you have some material, I believe, on radio commercials.

MR. FROMM: Well, I have the . . . .

MISS AYERS: We checked with the radio stations first on whether there would be any objection to starting off by saying something about "go to the devil," or "my wife gave me the devil," and there's no objection if it's used in good taste. So . . .

MR. FROMM: I have the estimates here on these jingles if you'd like to hear those, if you want to. The cost is . . . .

MISS AYERS: Well, let's hear the commercials first.

MR. FROMM: Well, I did three on "She gave me the devil," and Dan has some on "The devil with cooking," right, Dan?

MR. RITTNER: Yes.

MR. FROMM: I assumed and maybe wrongly, I don't know, but I assumed last week that you objected, Marie, primarily to the fact that we did not get to the sales story fast enough in the other commercials I presented.

MISS AYERS: Yes.

MR. FROMM: So these go into the sales story a lot faster. Takes you about . . . .

MISS AYERS: These are twenty seconds?

MR. FROMM: No, no. These are minute spots, but they go into the sales story in perhaps fifteen seconds at the outside. This first one is about two little boys. (He reads the following, imitating different boys' voices for the opening lines.) "Mummy just give me the devil." "Your mummy just give you the devil?" "Sure—I asked her to give me the Devil." "You diiidd?" "Yeah. Fisher Devilled Crab." (He then reads, in his normal voice, the announcer's part of the commercial, which emphasized the flavor and convenience of Fisher Devilled Crab. He goes through the same routine for a second commercial, involving two women, one of whom had given her husband "the devil." The announcer makes the point that more women would be wearing minks if, when they give their husbands the devil, it was Fisher Devilled Crab. He finishes): . . . And it goes on with the . . . .

MISS AYERS: Um-hum.

MR. FROMM: The selling copy.

MISS AYERS: Yes, I . . . .

MR. FROMM: The other one is two men, fundamentally the same thing, about how one's wife gave him the Devil, and why did she give him the devil, and so forth.

MISS AYERS: Um-hum.

MR. FROMM: But it's a little play back and forth, and it only takes about 10 or 15 seconds to establish that, and then you go right into the selling . . . .

MISS AYERS: Um . . . what . . . um. I'd like an opinion on that. Let's go around the room. Mary, how does it appeal to you?

In the last statement above, Miss Ayers again demonstrated the difference in interpersonal style of behavior and problem-solving that existed between herself and Mr. Lorenz. Where he probably would have stated his own opinion directly and somewhat antagonistically, Miss Ayers proceeded to survey the opinions of others before stating her own decision. The reader will notice that she had reached an opinion before she surveyed the opinion of others, since the results of the "voting" that followed were specious. But her manner of operating in the group prompted her to use what, at first glance, appeared to be genuine group decision-making techniques. The members of the group were not hesitant in expressing their opinions to her.

MISS NAVIN: I don't think that if I were just listening to the radio, I'd hear them. I mean they'd be on, but they wouldn't impress me so that I'd listen.

MISS AYERS: Um, hum. Phil?

MR. MASCETTA: I think they're all right. There's one thing that confused me there on that mink . . . how it tied in.

MISS AYERS: Well, that's a detail. I don't . . . I'd like to discuss just the basic, general idea.

MR. MASCETTA: Generally, I think they're all right.

MISS AYERS: Helen?

MISS FOWLER: I may be terribly old-fashioned, but I object to this Devil business.

MISS AYERS: You do?

MISS FOWLER: Ummm.

MISS AYERS: John?

MR. GOODE: Oh, I liked the last one, including the mink, but I didn't care about having the kids doing it.

MISS AYERS: But do you think the basic idea, using . . .

MR. GOODE: I think it's in poor taste to have the children doing it.

MISS AYERS: Yes. But do you think the basic idea of using the Devil as an attention-getter at the opening and then going into "sell" is right?

MR. GOODE: Yeah, I think that's all right, the way it's used in the second one, but I don't care about the first one.

MISS AYERS: George?

Given the relationship that existed between Mr. Lorenz and Miss Ayers, any reply by Mr. Lorenz was bound to be an interesting and revealing one. Part of his reply was, ". . . but I think you are fighting something here." This statement points accurately in a direction not intended by Mr. Lorenz, namely toward himself. The reader might care to describe his position in the social structure of this meeting, and how he felt about it, and then check this description against his behavior in the remaining portion of the meeting. What was it that he was fighting?

MR. LORENZ: (starting very quietly): I don't like them at all. I don't think they make a memorable point for Fisher Devilled Crab at all. They give good name identification for the Devil, but I think you're fighting something here, Marie, where you're going too much against a lot of other devilled products—devilled eggs, for example—and I think just the Devil association is not enough. We've gone, in my opinion, a little too far.

MISS AYERS: Um, hum.

MR. LORENZ: (to Mr. Fromm): I don't think your sale . . . your selling power carries through after that intro, old friend.

MISS AYERS: Dan?

MR. RITTNER: I think that the Devil, gave me the Devil, is a memorable phrase. It's a phrase in the popular idiom. Uh, I think, I don't agree with George's point. I don't think we're selling this against any branded devilled products at all.

MISS AYERS: Um, hum.

MR. RITTNER: And I think we can stand alone with the devilled crab idea. On the other hand, we could probably use a little bit more reinforcement of the selling points of the use idea.

MISS AYERS: Um hum . . . . You think it's a . . . .

MR. RITTNER: But, I think it's a valid, a valid idea for radio.

MR. GOODE: May I add to mine one thing that occurred to me. When we use the Devil we use it as the Black Devil. So that on the second time around we might say Black Devil.

MISS AYERS: Um, hum.

MR. RITTNER: The Fisher Black Devil?

MR. GOODE: Because we found that in the research, if you remember, on name brand identification that Black Devil is known almost better than the word Fisher.

MISS AYERS: Um, hum.

MR. GOODE: And it's a well-known brand identifying . . . it's commonly . . . .

MISS AYERS: Yes. Al? (Mr. Lorenz talks with Mr. Goode in lowered tones as Mr. Berklund speaks.)

MR. BERKLUND: I like the first one. The two kids, which could be done in a pretty off-beat voice, I think. And I think it had a lot of sell, George, that commercial, the meat of it. Geez, Fisher pounded home like Lucky Strike does. Fisher, Fisher, Fisher. But that Black Devil idea is just a Devil to stop. As you said just the other day, George, you hear one piece of profanity on the radio and it stops you dead. And then after that, maybe you can say Black Devil. After the initial stop is there.

MR. RITTNER: Well, it isn't really profanity.

MR. BERKLUND: No, but it's . . . .

MR. MASCETTA: You're not a Southern Baptist?

MR. RITTNER: No. I'm not. (Quiet laughter.) I admit.

MISS AYERS: Bill?

MR. JONES: Are your requirements for the Northwest the same as nationally? I mean you'd have to build usage, variety of usage for the product?

MISS AYERS: Increase . . . . We need to increase purchases and then increase consumption.

MR. JONES: As I remember your problems you have trouble with recognition of the uses of the product, not of the name. I'm thinking of 20 seconds versus a minute. I think the first 20 seconds is strong and then I think it just goes into general copy points that aren't too memorable. I wonder if you couldn't avoid this, "the Devil with . . . ," which I think may be a little bit objectionable to a lot of people, by using the "Devilishly good, Devil of a good, . . . dish" or something like that instead of "Go to the Devil," which is I think the strong . . . .

MISS AYERS: The shocker.

MR. JONES: . . . part of this . . . for no particular purpose.

MISS AYERS: Well, how do you feel about that as a basic idea that perhaps could be refined?

MR. JONES: The go-to-the-Devil part of it I don't like, but I like the Devil association; I think that's a good one. I think you've built it, so why not use it?

MISS AYERS: Um. If . . . .

MR. GOODE: Could we, could we take a series of incidents in the early colonial days when the witchcraft business was going. Uh, there is many, there are many tales of burning at the stake and so forth, and could we start off with a factual, "In 1665, Mary Hutchinson was burned at the stake, to shake the Devil out of her (several murmum "Wow!"), but when they have the Devil in them today," or something, I don't know . . . .

MR. RITTNER: Oh, what the Devil, I burned the steak!

MR. LORENZ: Would you really like one of those geniusly creative ideas that I give you every once in, say, once in two years?

MISS AYERS: Yes, surely.

MR. LORENZ: If you're going to play the Devil, play it big. Have two people. For instance, two men talking. And you open up with a man saying, "My wife told me to get the Devil." Then the other fella says, "The Devil you say?" "No, she said, 'The Devil with cooking!'" "What the Devil do you mean?" "She told me to get Fisher's Devilled Crab. She doesn't want to cook."

Mr. Lorenz was now objecting to the objections. The message he was thereby communicating to the group was his refusal to be aligned with *any* of them. He, the "loner," was telling those present that he would not be in a group with anybody, no matter what opinions or sentiments the group had united around.

Miss Ayers' response to his "geniusly creative ideas" indicated that her evaluation of his contribution was significantly lower than his own evaluation of the same.

MISS AYERS: Well, George . . . .

MR. LORENZ: And then, I mean if you're gonna stress the Devil, bring him in in several different ways and come off it, into your straight "sell."

MISS AYERS: Well, George, basically this is the same idea, basically, that, uh, that is what Carlton is giving us . . . .

MR. LORENZ: Use "the Devil" as if he were mad at him; just once.

MISS AYERS: Yes; but this is—we're discussing a basic concept, not the refinements; this is the first rough. We're discussing whether to use

the Devil as a shocker at the opening to get attention and then go into
sell.   Now how it's done . . . .

MR. LORENZ: Well, I think if you're going to shock with him, really
shock with him, bring him in in several connotations, not just one.

Notice, in this last remark, the emphasis Mr. Lorenz placed on the
value of shock in interpersonal settings, where one person is seeking to
influence the behavior of others.   This fits with much of his own behavior in the two meetings recorded, and adds another dimension to an
understanding of how he perceived himself as an extremely talented,
competent, and independent individual—a "loner"—whose considerable
effectiveness in working with and through people was based on the
essential validity of his ideas, and on the dramatic forcefulness of his
presentation of himself, which "shocked" others into taking full notice
of him and of his worth.   Our data indicate that his behavior had been
successful along certain dimensions of status, and less successful on
interpersonal dimensions.   It would also appear that his concept of himself was simultaneously related both to this status success and to this
relative lack of interpersonal success.

MISS AYERS: Well, that is a refinement of how this basic idea might be
done.   Irene, do you have, have you summarized how many are for
and how many are against on this?
IRENE SMITH[17]: Uh, well actually some of them said yes and then
modified . . . there are really five for it and two definitely against.
MISS AYERS: Five for and two against.   Now I'd like to add mine.
Mine is for, too.   I think basically the idea would accomplish what
we're trying to accomplish, and that is to get that Devil image
planted in the person's mind.   And in the opening, with somewhat
of a shock treatment.   If we did that, then went into our "sell,"
and all that of course would have to be worked over.   But if we're
in agreement that the basic idea is right, or if the majority are at
least, I suggest that we get together with the creative people.
Carlton, if you and Dan and I can get together and work up a list of
the objectives, of the specific objectives we want to accomplish and
then perhaps you can do some more refined commercials and then
let's discuss them again.

The reader may want to check the validity of the vote count.   The
principal function of the "ballot" was to permit Miss Ayers to convey
to the group her own decision on the matter in a way in which she
felt comfortable.   As a woman and a relative newcomer to the group,
she probably felt the necessity of operating in a relatively accom-

[17] Miss Ayers' secretary.

modative fashion to those in the office upon whom she was dependent. The deference of her behavior makes it more difficult to infer the way in which she viewed herself, but one thing is obvious, namely that she viewed herself as much less independent than Mr. Lorenz. She, too, was both successful and unsuccessful in relation to others in the office. She had not achieved a position on the status dimensions equal to that of certain others, which to a certain extent must have been a result of her being a woman. However, it would appear from the data of this meeting that she was more successful along interpersonal dimensions than was Mr. Lorenz and that he felt her to be so. (This will be demonstrated below in his remarks, culminating in his statement, "You're being much too kind to the copy people, Marie. It leads to biting the hand that feeds. . . .") Thus, it can be said that Miss Ayers' concept of herself as a dependent or interdependent person prompted her to behave in such a way that, in certain areas of life, she avoided many of the difficulties that Mr. Lorenz was busy creating for himself.

MR. GOODE: I think one thing, one thing I would like to add in qualifying my being for it. I would like it better if it was used in some such way as Bill mentioned, or George mentioned, or woven into an incident, rather than "Go to the Devil," or something of this kind.

MISS AYERS: I don't think . . . .

MR. GOODE: . . . because while it's a shocker, I think, . . . maybe it's maybe it's . . . .

MISS AYERS: A pleasant shocker we need. Not an objectionable one.

MR. GOODE: Yeah. I don't think when it gets to be . . . it's not on the pleasant side. I think you can use the Devil without . . . .

MISS AYERS: Being offensive.

MR. GOODE: . . . telling somebody to go the Devil.

MR. LORENZ: May I make another suggestion.

MISS AYERS: Um, hum.

MR. LORENZ: I think these are extremely flat commercials. I'd suggest that before you even attempt to refine this technique you take these sample commercials and make a tape of them with half-a-dozen off-the-air commercials exactly like it, showing no particular creative brilliance. Just another group of commercials that'll fill a minute at the end of a program or somewhere else. Put these up against them and see just how really terrible they can be.

MR. GOODE: I'd suggest we get the Conn commercials. (Miss Ayers and several others laugh, drowning Mr. Lorenz's words.)

MR. LORENZ: . . . but this is another example of the same thing.

"Extremely flat commercials" that are "really terrible" represent what must have been a hostile statement for the sender, and a threatening remark for the receiver of that particular message in that particular setting, despite the fact that the intent of the message was clothed in the apperent logic of a suggested experimental design. Mr. Goode obviously felt that Mr. Lorenz had exceeded acceptable limits in his expression of hostility toward Miss Ayers. His formal position was such that he could hardly let one of his account executives debilitate another, and his method of enforcing his control was through the use of a joke that left Mr. Lorenz with little ground to stand on. The only thing left for Mr. Lorenz to do was to protest to Miss Ayers about her behavior, which he could not emulate, and which was bringing her a whole range of rewards that were closed to him.

MISS AYERS: Well, this is a rough draft, and as I said, we're discussing a basic treatment.

MR. LORENZ: You're being much too kind to the copy people, Marie. It leads to biting the hand that feeds . . . .

MISS AYERS: But we don't want to cut off something that isn't finished, when it's just in its . . . .

From Mr. Lorenz's point of view, Miss Ayers was too kind. She loved, praised, and otherwise verbally caressed other people with whom she interacted more than he could. He viewed the relationship with creative-service personnel as potentially a biting one, one in which the creative-service personnel would hate, fight, and do damage to an account executive if given the opportunity to do so. He viewed the account executives as feeding the creative-service personnel, directly with work and indirectly with salaries drawn from the revenues that the executives brought in from clients. In this relationship, Mr. Lorenz probably expected that gratitude *should* be shown him rather than the hate and destruction he anticipated he *would* receive should he permit himself to be open to the creative-service personnel's expressions of feeling toward him. This inconsistency probably increased the distrustful and controlling attitudes expressed in his complaint to Miss Ayers about her behavior.

Miss Ayers' response to Mr. Lorenz indicates her much greater appreciation of the supportive atmosphere that must surround a creative endeavor. This in itself probably further endeared her to the creative personnel. (Mr. Mascetta asked her if it were okay for him to start the fines.) At the same time, in line with the concept of limited affectional resources, it further alienated Mr. Lorenz from the people upon whom he, too, depended for work.

At this point in the meeting, it was Mr. Lorenz who moved the group from affective issues back to the level of work.

MR. LORENZ: What did you do with the musical treatment business?
MISS AYERS: Well, we have that for consideration too.   We're trying to bring out all the ideas we can, and then choose which is the best. Now in addition to this treatment, Dan Rittner, I believe, has another one.

Mr. Rittner then read another copy idea for the Fisher Product. The meeting ended after another 20 minutes.

Despite the affect communicated in this meeting, principally between Mr. Lorenz and Miss Ayers, the meeting stayed at the work level for a proportionately greater time than had Mr. Lorenz's meeting.   This single bit of evidence would lead us to investigate further, either as a researcher or as an active member of the social system, whether Miss Ayers' or Mr. Lorenz's style of interpersonal behavior was the more effective for organizing and administering the work of the office.

Exhibit 12 presents a statistic summary of the Fisher Account Group meeting, similar to that shown in Exhibit 11 for the Conn Group meeting.

VI. IMPLICATIONS FOR MANAGEMENT PRACTICE

The foregoing analysis has suggested a number of questions of significance for management practice.   Although the information available is not sufficiently extensive to provide definite answers to the management problems that the analysis indicated were important, the issues involved appear to have sufficiently widespread applicability to other business situations to permit presentation here as a starting point to further thought and discussion.

We shall consider briefly three of these areas of potential concern to executives:

1. The management of role conflicts
2. The management of cooperation and competition
3. The development of subordinates

The Management of Role Conflicts

Any executive seeking to work in an organized and purposive social setting soon finds himself faced with problems of conflicting demands.

EXHIBIT 12

THE WATKINS AND WORSTER AGENCY (B)

Frequency and Approximate Amount of Speaking in Fisher Account Group Meeting*

Name	Number of times Person Spoke	%	Number of Lines in Original Typescript	%
Marie Ayers	55	37.9	97	34.0
John Goode	11	7.6	30	10.5
George Lorenz	20	13.8	44	15.4
Bruce Fahey	2	1.4	2	0.7
Bill Jones	11	7.6	25	8.8
Mary Navin	1	0.7	3	0.8
Phil Mascetta	18	12.4	21	7.4
Carlton Fromm	9	6.2	31	10.9
Dan Rittner	7	4.8	13	4.6
Al Berklund	8	5.5	15	5.3
Helen Fowler	2	1.4	2	0.7
Irene Smith	1	0.7	2	0.7
	145	100.0	285	100.0

* Those participants who are also shown in Exhibits 4 to 6 are here listed in the same order, except that the chairman and John Goode appear first and second, respectively.

These demands can arise from within himself, according to the way he believes he should behave, or they can be placed on him by persons and groups around him, according to the way they believe he should behave. Conflicts can arise because (a) the demands the executive places on himself may not coincide with those placed on him by others; and (b) the demands placed on an executive from one point in his environment may not be compatible with those placed on him from another. For instance, some of an executive's subordinates may expect him to give them direction, to make decisions for them, and to behave toward them in ways that are compatible with their expectations of "authority." Other subordinates, or the same subordinates at different times, may expect the same man to behave warmly, understandingly, and helpfully toward them, more suggestive of a "peer-like" relationship than of one of authority. The conflict may be heightened further by the executive's difficulty in recognizing who wants what and by his difficulty in supplying the type of behavior his subordinates want. He may also have conflicting beliefs about the appropriateness of giving what is wanted, considering that his principal executive responsibilities are usually thought of as being of a different nature. He may experience some genuine confusion as to whether he, himself, wants to be primarily as "authoritarian" or a "peer-like" superior to those working under his direction. On the one hand, the executive may have personal needs to assert himself, to exercise authority, and to control the behavior of others. On the other, it would not be unusual for him to need to be liked by others on a personal and equalitarian basis. Should he act in a "brotherly" fashion toward his subordinates, he might be treated warmly by them, but he would also run the risk of not being respected and obeyed.

As an added complexity to the resolution of conflict inherent in the executive role, the executive function requires both understanding and control. To be in a position to take responsible action, an executive must gain an understanding of the social system he is administering. He must also exercise control over that system, since he has a unique responsibility for its output. That is, he must influence the direction in which the system is moving.

Understanding is facilitated when the executive behaves as a peer toward his subordinates. For instance, this style of administrative behavior would facilitate the flow of information upon which to base his understanding. But control might not be facilitated by this type of behavior; it may require more direct and aggressive behavior. Switching from one style of behavior to the other would also involve a cost. The executive might be perceived, both by himself and by his subordinates, as "hypocritical."

Turning to the concrete situation in the W & W Regional Office, we found at least three executives potentially in the midst of role conflict: Mr. Goode as the head of the office and Mr. Lorenz and Miss Ayers as the two highest status account executives. We saw in Mr. Goode's behavior strong elements of warmth, permissiveness, and equality. Aggressiveness and directiveness appeared most frequently when he was evaluating a marketing proposal, as in the second part of the Conn account group meeting described in the case. Whether, on balance, he was successful in resolving this role conflict can only be a matter of the reader's judgment, based on an evaluation of Mr. Goode's behavior in the meetings recorded.

In the case of Mr. Lorenz, we noticed a strong and consistent trend toward aggressive behavior. It might well be that his "need to be liked" was relatively low, and therefore he experienced little internal conflict as a result of his behavior. On the other hand, we should not ignore the fact that he made a number of "humorous" remarks that can be viewed as an attempt on his part to discharge internal tensions generated by his own aggressiveness.

Finally, Miss Ayers presented a very different picture from that of Mr. Lorenz. Consistent with her being a woman, she appeared to behave in a warm, supportive, and permissive manner. This behavior would seem to have assured her of being liked and accepted as a person by the others in the group. However, a careful analysis of the meeting indicates the presence of a controlling undertone or objective in her behavior, if we examine the way in which the "voting" decision was reached, and if we note her role in directing the group toward that particular decision. Her behavior suggests a subtle combination of warmth and control that appeared to be well received by some in her group, but not by others—certainly not by Mr. Lorenz. Again, we leave the judgment of the over-all effectiveness of this style of behavior, and its consequences, to the reader.

The Management of Cooperation and Competition

In any group of persons working toward a common goal in an organized social setting, one would expect to find elements of both cooperation and competition. Cooperation is generally considered to grow out of (a) a common acceptance of the group's goals; and (b) the division or specialization of function which impels cooperation if group goals are to be obtained. Competition within the group grows out of members' desires for the rewards possible in group interaction and the limited number of each type of reward available. The rewards we have in mind are those of status, power, esteem, friendship, and intrinsic job satisfactions.

There were various indications of both the cooperative and the competitive elements in the Watkins and Worster group. There were, for example, indications of cooperation and support among the creative-service personnel in the Fisher account group meeting. For instance, the "yes" votes tended largely to come from the creative-service members. Indications of competition were also available. The competitive elements appeared most strongly in the relationships among the account executives. Specifically, Mr. Goode and Mr. Lorenz appeared to be competing at times, as did Mr. Lorenz and Miss Ayers. Competition among the account executive subgroup could have been the result of two forces: (1) the desire of the persons concerned to achieve prestige within the agency and among clients and prospective clients; and (2) the desire on the part of account executives to secure favored attention for their clients from the creative-service subgroup. The management of these competitive forces appears relevant to the job of the agency manager. Mr. Goode attempted to deal with the competition among account executives by taking the side of the person who appeared to be on the defensive, as in the case of his responses when Mr. Lorenz attacked the ideas presented during the Fisher account group meeting.

Was this allocation of cooperation and competition completely functional in achieving optimum results for the agency? Both the caliber of the creative work and the coordination of marketing programs would suffer in a social system in which cooperative feelings and acts were confined to the creative-service subgroup, and in which competitive feelings and acts were the only currency of exchange in the interpersonal economy of the account management personnel.

The Development of Subordinates

A third issue of management significance arising from the case analysis is that of the role of the executive in the development of his subordinates. One can identify, in this case, particular behavior patterns manifested by Mr. Goode's subordinates that must have been of actual or potential concern to him for the achievement of organizational purpose, the maintenance of group cohesion, and the career development of the individual subordinates involved. For example, we saw that Mr. Goode could become concerned if a subordinate of his behaved too aggressively in meeting his responsibilities, and thereby stifled the contributions of other subordinates. Or one could detect, as in the case of Mr. Rittner in the W & W creative-service subgroup, a person who was essentially under-rewarded. He was easily put on the defensive when he attempted to contribute and may even have become a scapegoat for the group's aggressions.

An executive who heads such a group must frequently have cause to seek change in the behavior of his subordinates, if the group is to remain effectively oriented to the work it has to accomplish. If the executive seeks to alter his subordinates' behavior, then he must direct his attention to the conditions within the social system of his group that facilitate or prevent individuals from changing. At the same time, he must direct his attention toward the forces within each individual which that individual uses in maintaining or changing this existing pattern of behavior.

This dual challenge is complicated further by the question of who, in a work group, perceives the need for change. The executive is faced with a difficult situation if, for some reason, it is only he who perceives such needs. Evidence is available to suggest that unless a person perceives the need for change in his own behavior, he will strongly resist any proposed change that will affect him in any real way. The data and analysis of this case permit the reader to identify areas in which changes may have been needed within the W & W Regional Office. Once these areas of needed change have been established, the paramount concern becomes the problem of how Mr. Goode might have instituted the change process.

New England Markets, Inc.

T HE chief executives of New England Markets had just received copies of a memorandum together with the request that they study it in preparation for a conference to discuss its implications. The memorandum was an interim working paper prepared by a group of researchers in human relations who had been invited to make a study which might be helpful to the management of the supermarket chain in dealing with the problem of labor efficiency. The president requested specifically that the executives evaluate the concepts of the research and the significance of the data, make any further correlations that might throw additional light on the problem, and be prepared to suggest what further data might be desirable and ways in which the implications of the research could be applied in managing the stores.

The Origin of the Research Project

In the spring of 1957, the executives of New England Markets were seeking an explanation of the differences in labor efficiency among their many supermarkets. They were aware that the higher profits of some stores were associated with lower payroll costs, as compared with other stores which were similar in sales volume, number of customers, store size and design, managerial ability, and surrounding market characteristics.

In discussing the profit differences with the human relations research group of a large eastern university, the executives found that the two groups had a common interest in determining the human factors which affected labor efficiency. They therefore agreed to explore the question by cooperating in a short-term research project to be designed by the research group.

The researchers planned a study consisting of five steps:

1. Select for study two comparable stores, between which the only important difference would be in profit and payroll percentages.
2. Gather data on store employees from the company's personnel files.

401

3. First week of field work: meet with store managements and become acquainted with store employees and procedures.
4. Second week of field work: observe the behavior of store employees
during working hours.
5. Third week of field work: interview employees and managers.

Stores 5 and 6

After examining data on almost fifty New England Markets stores,
the researchers and the management selected two, called Stores 5 and
6 in the study. Company research had indicated that the stores

EXHIBIT 1

NEW ENGLAND MARKETS, INC.

Comparisons of Stores 5 and 6 as of March 1957

	Store 5	Store 6
General Data		
Location	Winston*	Marshton*
In operation as of March 1957	1 year	3 months
Source of labor	Winston, Mansfield, Lintown, Somerville	Marshton
Age of manager	45 years	62 years
Experience of manager with NEM	25 years	33 years
February Operating Figures		
Store operating gain, % of sales	4.12%	1.87%
Average grocery sales per customer	$6.86	$7.56
Grocery department sales	$164,000.00	$156,000.00
Grocery department payroll % of sales	4.49%	5.69%
Grocery department man-hours per $100 sales	3.18 hours	4.03 hours
March Weekly Figures		
Grocery department man-hours per $100 sales:		
Week ending March 2	3.25 hours	4.38 hours
Week ending March 9	3.10	4.27
Week ending March 16	3.14	4.13

* Both towns were suburbs of comparable economic level near a large New England
city.

EXHIBIT 2

NEW ENGLAND MARKETS, INC.

Operating Percentages for a Recent Year

Sales		100.00%
Cost of goods sold		81.72
Gross		18.28%
Controllable expenses at store level:		
Wage expense	7.38%	
Supplies	.83	
Cash over or short	.04	
Repairs	.31	
Sundry	.19	
Hired service	.28	
Utilities	.53	
Stamps and direct advertising	2.24	
Check cashing	.03	
Total		11.83%
Store operating gain after controllable expenses		6.45
Chain overhead (not controllable at store level)		3.33
Operating profit before tax		3.12%

were in comparable market areas. The size and layout of the stores were almost identical mirror images of each other, with the exception that Store 5 had a cellar storage area and Store 6 had a backroom storage area. Some comparisons of the two stores appear in Exhibit 1. Exhibit 2 shows some operating percentages for the entire chain.

General Organization of Activities

The "front-end" operations of the supermarkets included handling the customer check-out area, front window displays, shopping carts, parcel pickup activities, and the parking lot, all under the supervision of the Cash Department Head (CDH).

The grocery department, which accounted for 65 per cent of the supermarkets' sales, was managed by the Grocery Department Head (GDH) and two Assistant Heads (AGDH). Grocery clerks primarily performed "back-end" activities, including receiving merchandise, storing it, marking prices, and stacking the goods on the selling shelves or tables. The merchandise of the grocery department included all store items except meats, fresh fruits, and vegetables. Much of the responsibility for a few grocery lines—frozen foods, dairy, and bakery goods—was borne by the full-time personnel assigned to those counters.

Exhibit 3 is an organization chart which applied to both stores.

The Personnel and Their Activities

Management explained to the researchers that a supermarket's work force consisted of both full-time and part-time employees. In addition to the store manager, the department heads, and their assistants, the grocery department full-timers were male grocery clerks (FGC's)* and female cashiers (FCa(f)'s). Full-timers worked a 40-hour week. Full-time grocery clerks (FGC's) were assigned to back-end operations, and their work week included some evenings. FGC's were called up to the front-end check-out areas only when there were not enough front-end employees to handle the customer traffic.

Full-time female cashiers (FCa(f)'s), according to management, handled the cashiering and bundling operations during Monday through Friday daytime hours. In addition to their cashiering duties, a few FCa(f)'s were assigned to service particular aisles such as candy, cigarettes, and drugs. During the Thursday and Friday heavy traffic periods, the cashiers received bundling help from FGC's in the morning rushes and from part-time front-end employees in the afternoons.

In addition to the full-timers previously mentioned, each supermarket employed other full-time employees. A male clerk and a female cashier (FOf and FOf(f)) were assigned to Store 5's office. Store 6 had one male office clerk (FOf). These office employees kept store records on purchases, receipts, and payroll and also handled customer check cashing. The other full-timer in each grocery department was a female cashier assigned to bakery goods (FBa(f)).

Each store employed part-time workers in both the back and the front ends. Part-time grocery clerks (PGC's) worked in the back end and their duties included all its activities. At the front end were part-time male and female cashiers (PCa's and PCa(f)'s), part-time male front clerks (PFC's), whose primary duty was bundling, and part-time page boys (PPa's) in Store 5 and part-time pickup clerks (PPC's) in Store 6. The PPa's chiefly assisted customers with their bundles and the PPC's worked primarily at the outside parcel pickup station of Store 6.

* Codes are explained on page 408.

EXHIBIT 5

NEW ENGLAND MARKETS, INC.

Organization Chart for Both Stores

(District Manager)

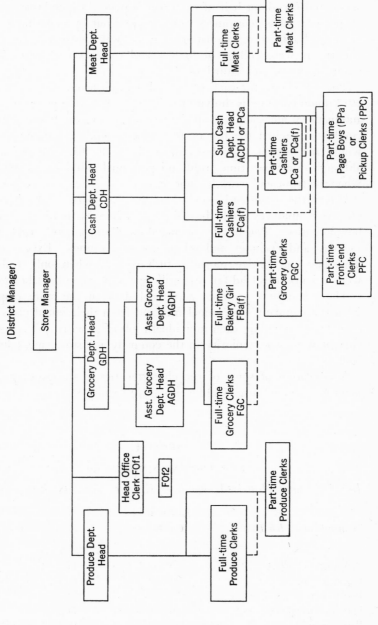

Part-timers worked less than 30 hours a week individually, but they accounted for about half of each store's payroll expenditures. About 80 per cent of all customers were checked out by part-timers, whose working hours were regulated to meet peak customer loads. Most part-timers were college or high school students who worked afternoons, evenings, and Saturdays.

The wage rate for each of the job classifications under the March 1957 union contract is shown in Exhibit 4. Each job position received automatic wage increases approximately every six months until the employee reached the top of his classification. The union contract would not permit page boys to work in the back end of a store, although other part-time front-end personnel could be assigned there when the front-end work became light.

When the front-end work load became particularly heavy, all grocery employees could be called to help with bundling and page boy activities. This usually occurred on Thursday and Friday during the day and evenings and on Saturday mornings. Except for the Thursday and Friday morning rush periods when only full-timers were at work, this load fell primarily upon the part-time labor force.

The researchers acquired additional data on the store employees from the company's personnel files and from their initial visits to the two stores, including each individual's job title, actual job assignment, current wage rate, seniority in the company and store, age, education, and sex.

A tabulation of some of the characteristics of the grocery department workers in Stores 5 and 6 appears in Exhibit 5.

EXHIBIT 4

NEW ENGLAND MARKETS, INC.

Job Titles and Hourly Wage Rate Ranges within Each Classification

Union Contract Job Title	Hourly Wage Rate Range	Job Codes
Full-time male clerks	$1.25–$1.82	FGC, FOf
Full-time female clerks	$1.07–$1.47	FCa(f), FOf(f), FBa(f)
Part-time male cashiers	$1.25–$1.82	PCa
Part-time female cashiers	$1.07–$1.47	PCa(f)
Part-time male clerks	$ .90–$1.30	PGC, PFC, PPC
Part-time male page boys	$ .90–$1.10	PPa

EXHIBIT 5

NEW ENGLAND MARKETS, INC.

*Some Characteristics of the Work Forces in Stores 5 and 6
as of March, 1957*

	Store 5	Store 6
Total number of grocery employees (excluding department heads and assistant heads)	47	49
Number of part-timers	35	37
Part-timers who were college students	13	4

Subsequent Developments

The president of the company had occasional informal contact with the research group during their field work. Shortly afterwards, when the researchers mentioned that they were keeping current a memorandum for their own use while still in the process of exploring the data, the president asked to see it. Since he considered that the memorandum might prove useful in the further development of his executives, he persuaded the research group to make it available.

THE MEMORANDUM

Working Hypotheses

1. The front of the store is the crucial area, since its labor requirements fluctuate widely, and it must be adequately manned at all times to maintain customer good will.

2. The produce and meat departments do not need to be considered, since their personnel are not involved in front-end work.

3. The study should be focused primarily on the part-timers, since they check out 80 per cent of the customers and are called on to move between the front and rear areas much more frequently than are the full-timers.

4. The employees in the stores with higher productivity records are more willing to work in the cash register check-out area than are employees in the stores with lower productivity records. If reluctance to move is widespread among workers in grocery supermarkets, then management is required either to increase the size of their labor force in order to accommodate peak loads or to attempt

to force the workers to move. Either of these alternatives will yield lower labor efficiency compared with situations where the employees move willingly between the front and the rear of the store. Accordingly, there will be more willingness to move from the back to the front end in Store 5 than in Store 6.

5. The pattern of the willingness of individuals to move between jobs in the check-out area and in the rear of a store will reflect the informal social organization of the work groups in the store.

6. The interviews will reveal that there is an "internal system," which emerges from the workers' social processes, and which may be at variance with the "external system" as determined by management. The internal system of Store 5 is probably more congruent with the external system than is that of Store 6.

Codes for Individuals

Each individual is identified by his or her full (F) or part (P) time job as a grocery clerk (GC), cashier (Ca), office clerk (Of), bakery clerk (Ba), front-end clerk (FC), pick-up clerk (PC), or page boy (Pa). In addition, for each store, individuals in each assignment are ranked by numbers according to pay and company seniority. The symbol (f) following the rank number indicates a female employee.

The codes for individuals in each store are:

FOf 1	Full-time office employee, first office employee in seniority and pay, male.
2(f)	Full-time office employee, second in seniority and pay, female.
FGC 1	Full-time grocery clerks etcetera
FCa 1(f)	Full-time cashiers, female
FBa 1(f)	Full-time bakery, female
PCa 1 or PCa 1(f)	Part-time cashiers, male or female etcetera
PGC 1	Part-time grocery clerks etcetera
PFC 1	Part-time front-end clerks etcetera
PPC 1	Part-time pick-up clerks etcetera
PPa 1	Part-time page boys etcetera

Observations on Movement

Purpose: To discover any differences between the two stores in the relationship between the employees' regular job assignments and where they actually worked.

Method: At half-hour intervals, a record ("count") was made of who was in the stores and whether they were working in the check-out area. The counts were made during the rush hours and were comparable in the two stores in number and timing. For each job assignment, the percentage of those present in the store who were working in the check-out area was tabulated for each store. See Exhibit A.

EXHIBIT A

Relation between Job Assignments and Actual Location of Workers in the Stores*

	Store 5			Store 6		
Job Assignment	Counts in Store	Counts in Check-out Area	% of Counts in Check-out Area	Counts in Store	Counts in Check-out Area	% of Counts in Check-out Area
Office	77	3	4%	35	0	0%
Front end						
FCa(f)	131	106	81	71	58	82
PCa	342	213	62	295	177	60
PCa(f)	70	59	84	198	121	61
PFC	155	63	41	224	117	53
PPa	120	64	54			
PPC				105	1	1
Total, front end	818	505	62%	893	474	53%
Back end						
FGC	183	18	10%	137	9	7%
FBa(f)	36	5	14	29	0	0
PGC	244	20	8	275	0	0
Total, back end	463	43	9%	441	9	2%
Total, store	1,358	551	41%	1,369	483	35%

* See Exhibit M for absences during the observation period.

EXHIBIT B

STORE 5

Pattern of Friendship Choices

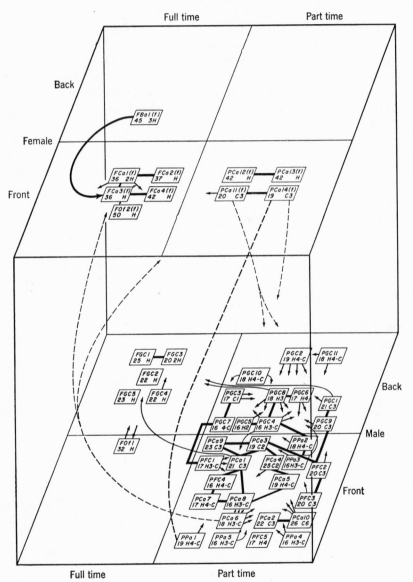

(*See legend, p. 411.*)

Pattern of Friendship Choices

Purpose: To ascertain differences between the two stores in the pattern of friendship choices plotted against those differences between individual workers which they used to identify themselves and others (status factors).

Method: Tabulation of the friendship choices designated by each worker in the interviews plus screening of the interviews for those differences between individual workers which were found to differentiate choice groups. The interviews showed that both the employees and management commonly used as identification: sex, part-time or full-time employee, and front-end or back-end regular assignment. For each store these features were mapped as areas on the upper and lower surfaces of a transparent cube, and within the appropriate area, sociograms were drawn. Each individual was represented by his or her full job identification together with a codification of the individual's educational status, since these two factors had also been revealed as points of differentiation. See Exhibits B and C.

Exhibits B and C show a greater number of PCA(f)'s than were present during the field work. In order to present complete sociograms the positions of these individuals were based on information given by others. Not represented in the statistical data are 2 PCa(f)'s H—12 and 13—in Store 5, and 1 PCa(f) H—14—in Store 6.

Status Factors and Friendship Choice Patterns

Purpose: To discover any significance the status factors had for social structure and how this might differ between the two stores.

Method: Tabulations were made of the friendship choices, by the

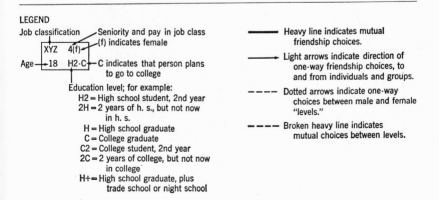

LEGEND

Job classification — Seniority and pay in job class
XYZ 4(f) — (f) indicates female

Age — 18   H2-C — C indicates that person plans to go to college

Education level; for example:
H2 = High school student, 2nd year
2H = 2 years of h. s., but not now in h. s.
H = High school graduate
C = College graduate
C2 = College student, 2nd year
2C = 2 years of college, but not now in college
H+ = High school graduate, plus trade school or night school

——— Heavy line indicates mutual friendship choices.

——→ Light arrows indicate direction of one-way friendship choices, to and from individuals and groups.

– – –→ Dotted arrows indicate one-way choices between male and female "levels."

– – – Broken heavy line indicates mutual choices between levels.

EXHIBIT C

STORE 6

Pattern of Friendship Choices

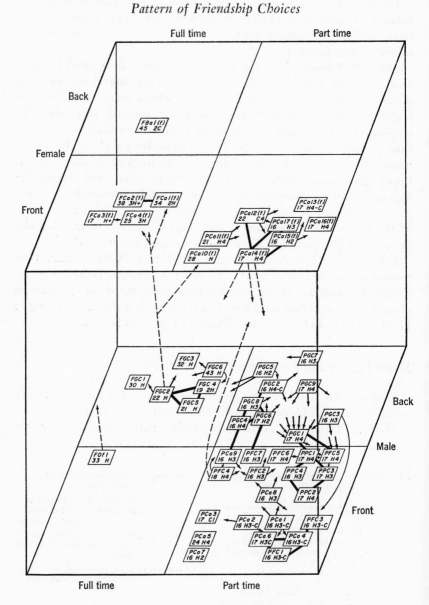

(*See legend, p. 413.*)

status factors of the choosers and those chosen, together with "no effect" models.

Exhibit D includes all employees present during the field work and uses the status of part-time versus full-time worker. Exhibits E through K include only part-timers and relate each of the other status factors to the friendship choices made within the part-time work group. Exhibit L compares, for the two stores, some indices obtained from data in the friendship exhibits.

The status factor of education was originally subdivided into three parts: college students (C), high school students aspiring to go to college (H-C), and high school students or graduates who did not aspire to go to college (H). Examination of the number in each educational classification and the sociograms in Exhibits B and C, as well as the data of Exhibit E, showed that the number of subdivisions could be reduced to two for each store without serious distortion of the data. Therefore in subsequent exhibits "college" and "high school" were used for Store 5, since the choice patterns of high school students aspiring to go to college could "absorb" those of high schoolers not aspiring to go to college. For Store 6, "college aspirant" and "non-college aspirant" were used, as the college aspirants could suitably "contain" the college students.

Status Factors Related to Movement

Purpose: To see if movement behavior indicated that status factors were important to the part-timers.

Method: Status factors were related to movement by coding and retabulating the data on part-timers summarized in Exhibit A. See Exhibit M.

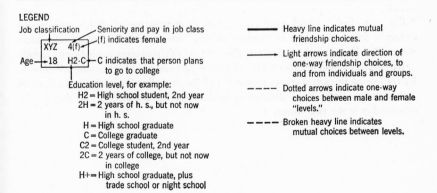

LEGEND

Job classification — Seniority and pay in job class
                                    (f) indicates female

Age — 18   H2-C — C indicates that person plans
                                    to go to college

Education level, for example:
H2 = High school student, 2nd year
2H = 2 years of h. s., but not now
        in h. s.
H = High school graduate
C = College graduate
C2 = College student, 2nd year
2C = 2 years of college, but not now
        in college
H+ = High school graduate, plus
        trade school or night school

——— Heavy line indicates mutual
            friendship choices.

———→ Light arrows indicate direction of
            one-way friendship choices, to
            and from individuals and groups.

– – – → Dotted arrows indicate one-way
            choices between male and female
            "levels."

– – – – Broken heavy line indicates
            mutual choices between levels.

EXHIBIT D

Friendship Choices: Full-Timers vs. Part-Timers

Store 5

Actual Choices   "No Effect" Model*

Chooser \ Chosen	33 Part-timers		12 Full-timers		45 Total	
	No.	%	No.	%	No.	%
33 Part-timers	107	91	11	9	118	100
12 Full-timers	0	0	18	100	18	100
45 Total	107	79	29	21	136	100

Chooser \ Chosen	33 Part-timers	12 Full-timers	45 Total
	%	%	%
33 P.-t.	73	27	100
12 F.-t.	73	27	100
45 Total	73	27	100

Store 6

Actual Choices   "No Effect" Model

Chooser \ Chosen	36 Part-timers		12 Full-timers		48 Total	
	No.	%	No.	%	No.	%
36 Part-timers	114	95	6	5	120	100
12 Full-timers	0	0	20	100	20	100
48 Total	114	81	26	19	140	100

Chooser \ Chosen	36 Part-timers	12 Full-timers	48 Total
	%	%	%
36 P.-t.	75	25	100
12 F.-t.	75	25	100
48 Total	75	25	100

* The "no effect" model represents the mean distribution of choices one would expect to find if there were no "social structure" among the collection of individuals observed.   For example, in Store 5, about 33/45 of the choices made by either full- or part-timers would be expected to fall among part-timers, 12/45 among full-timers. By comparing the actual choice patterns with the "no effect" models, the reader can make inferences about any differences in the direction and intensity of the specific relationship in the two stores.

EXHIBIT E

Friendship Choices between College Students, High School Students Aspiring to College, and High School Students or Graduates Not Aspiring to College, Part-Timers Only

Store 5

Actual Choices							"No Effect" Model			

*

Chosen	13 Col.		16 H-C		4 High		33 Total	13 Col.	16 H-C	4 H	33 Total
Chooser	No.	%	No.	%	No.	%	No.	%	%	%	%
13 College	28	67	11	26	3	7	42	13 Col. 39	49	12	100
*{ 16 High-Col.	22	42	23	43	8	15	53	16 H-C 39	49	12	100
{ 4 High Sch.	4	34	4	33	4	33	12	4 H 39	49	12	100
33 Total	54	50	38	36	15	14	107	33 T 39	49	12	100

Store 6

Actual Choices							"No Effect" Model			

*

Chosen	4 Col.		8 H-C		24 High		36 Total	4 Col.	8 H-C	24 H	36 Total
Chooser	No.	%	No.	%	No.	%	No.	%	%	%	%
*{ 4 College	2	25	2	25	4	50	8	4 Col. 11	22	67	100
{ 8 High-Col.	1	5	13	65	6	30	20	8 H-C 11	22	67	100
24 High Sch.	5	6	10	12	71	82	86	24 High 11	22	67	100
36 Total	8	7	25	22	81	71	114	36 T 11	22	67	100

* See explanation on p. 413.

EXHIBIT F

Friendship Choices by Status Factors, Part-Timers Only Store 5

Store 5

Chosen

Chooser — Location in store	Educational level	Job title	Sex	No. in class	Front end — College PCa F	College PCa M	College PFC M	High school PCa M	High school PFC M	High school PPa M	Back end Col. PGC M	Back end H.S. PGC M	Total
Front end	College	PCa	F	2	2*	1	2					2	7
	College	PCa	M	6		12	1	4		1		3	21
	College	PFC	M	2		2	2				2		6
	High school	PCa	M	4		5		6	1			2	14
	High school	PFC	M	3		3			1			2	6
	High school	PPa	M	5	1	4	1			2		7	15
Back end	Col.	PGC	M	3			2	1			3	2	8
	H.S.	PGC	M	8		4		4	2	5	7	8	30
	Total			33	3	31	8	15	4	8	12	26	107

Store 6

Chosen

Location in store	Educational aspiration	Job title	Sex	No. in class	Front end — College PCa (F)	Front end — College PCa (M)	Front end — College PFC (M)	Front end — Non-college PCa (F)	Front end — Non-college PCa (M)	Front end — Non-college PFC (M)	Front end — Non-college PPC (M)	Back end — C PGC (M)	Back end — N.C. PGC (M)	Total
Front end	College	PCa	F	3	3	1		3	1					8
	College	PCa	M	6		6	3			1				10
	College	PFC	M	2		3	1							4
	Non-college	PCa	F	4	4	2	1	7		1			2	17
	Non-college	PCa	M	3	2			1	1				1	5
	Non-college	PFC	M	5		1	1			5	1		6	14
	Non-college	PPC	M	4						1	10		5	16
Back end	Col.	PGC	M	1								2	4	6
	Non-college	PGC	M	8		1	2			10	3		18	34
		Total		36	9	14	8	11	2	18	14	2	36	114

*Underlined figures in diagonals indicate the number of choices made by people in a classification to other people in the same classification.

417

EXHIBIT G

Friendship Choices: Males vs. Females, Part-Timers Only

Store 5

Actual Choices

Chooser \ Chosen	2 Females No.	%	31 Males No.	%	33 Total No.	%
2 Females	2	29	5	71	7	100
31 Males	1	1	99	99	100	100
33 Total	3	3	103	97	107	100

"No Effect" Model

Chooser \ Chosen	2 F %	31 M %	33 Total %
2 Females	6	94	100
31 Males	6	94	100
33 Total	6	94	100

Store 6

Actual Choices

Chooser \ Chosen	7 Females No.	%	29 Males No.	%	36 Total No.	%
7 Females	17	68	8	32	25	100
29 Males	3	3	86	97	89	100
36 Total	20	18	94	82	114	100

"No Effect" Model

Chooser \ Chosen	7 F %	29 M %	36 Total %
7 Females	19	81	100
29 Males	19	81	100
36 Total	19	81	100

EXHIBIT H

Friendship Choices: Front End vs. Back End, Part-Timers Only

Store 5

Actual Choices

Chooser \ Chosen	22 Front End No.	%	11 Back End No.	%	33 Total No.	%
22 Front end	58	84	11	16	69	100
11 Back end	11	29	27	71	38	100
33 Total	69	64	38	36	107	100

"No Effect" Model

Chooser \ Chosen	22 F.E. %	11 B.E. %	33 Total %
22 Front end	67	33	100
11 Back end	67	33	100
33 Total	67	33	100

EXHIBIT H (*Continued*)

Store 6

Actual Choices							"No Effect" Model			

Chosen / Chooser	27 Front End		9 Back-End		36 Total			Chosen / Chooser	27 F.E.	9 B.E.	36 Total
	No.	%	No.	%	No.	%		%	%	%
27 Front end	60	81	14	19	74	100	27 Front end	75	25	100
9 Back end	16	40	24	60	40	100	9 Back end	75	25	100
36 Total	76	67	38	33	114	100	36 Total	75	25	100

EXHIBIT I

Friendship Choices: Cashiers vs. All Others, Part-Timers Only

Store 5

Actual Choices							"No Effect" Model			

Chosen / Choosers	12 Cashiers		21 Others		33 Total			Chosen / Choosers	12 C.	21 O.	33 Total
	No.	%	No.	%	No.	%		%	%	%
12 Cashiers	30	73	11	27	41	100	12 Cashiers	36	64	100
21 Others	19	29	47	71	66	100	21 Others	36	64	100
33 Total	49	46	58	54	107	100	33 Total	36	64	100

Store 6

Actual Choices							"No Effect" Model			

Chosen / Choosers	16 Cashiers		20 Others		36 Total			Chosen / Choosers	16 C.	20 O.	36 Total
	No.	%	No.	%	No.	%		%	%	%
16 Cashiers	28	70	12	30	40	100	16 Cashiers	44	56	100
20 Others	8	11	66	89	74	100	20 Others	44	56	100
36 Total	36	32	78	68	114	100	36 Total	44	56	100

EXHIBIT J

Friendship Choices: College Students vs. High School Students, Part-Timers Only

Store 5

Actual Choices							"No Effect" Model			
Chosen	13 College		20 H.S.		33 Total		Chosen	13 Col.	20 H.S.	33 Total
Chooser	No.	%	No.	%	No.	%	Chooser	%	%	%
13 College	28	67	14	33	42	100	13 College	39	61	100
20 High Sch.	26	40	39	60	65	100	20 High Sch.	39	61	100
33 Total	54	50	53	50	107	100	33 Total	39	61	100

Store 6

Actual Choices							"No Effect" Model			
Chosen	12 Col. Asp.		24 N.C.A.		36 Total		Chosen	12 C.A.	24 N.C.A.	36 Total
Chooser	No.	%	No.	%	No.	%	Chooser	%	%	%
12 Col. Asp	18	64	10	36	28	100	12 Col. Asp.	33	67	100
24 Non-C.A.	15	17	71	83	86	100	24 Non-C.A.	33	67	100
36 Total	33	29	81	71	114	100	36 Total	33	67	100

EXHIBIT K

Friendship Choices: Cashiers, Other Front-End Workers, and Back-End Workers, Part-Timers Only

Store 5

Actual Choices								"No Effect" Model				
Chosen	12 PCa & PCa(f)		10 PFC & PPa		11 PGC		33 Total	Chosen	12 PCa & PCa(f)	10 PFC & PPa	11 PGC	33 Total
Chooser	No.	%	No.	%	No.	%	No.	Chooser	%	%	%	%
12 PCa & PCa(f)	30	71	9	22	3	7	42	12 PCa & PCa(f)	37	30	33	100
10 PFC & PPa	14	52	5	18	8	30	27	10 PFC & PPa	37	30	33	100
11 PGC	5	13	6	16	27	71	38	11 PGC	37	30	33	100
33 Total	49	46	20	19	38	35	107	33 Total	37	30	33	100

EXHIBIT K (Continued)

Store 6

Actual Choices							"No Effect Model"			

Chooser	16 PCa & PCa(f) No.	%	11 PFC & PPC No.	%	9 PGC No.	%	36 Total No.				

Actual Choices

Chooser	16 PCa & PCa(f) No.	%	11 PFC & PPC No.	%	9 PGC No.	%	36 Total No.
16 PCa & PCa(f)	28	70	9	23	3	7	40
11 PFC & PPC	6	18	17	50	11	32	34
9 PGC	2	5	14	35	24	60	40
36 Total	36	32	40	35	38	33	114

"No Effect Model"

Chooser	16 PCa & PCa(f) %	11 PFC & PPC %	9 PGC %	36 Total %
16 PCa & PCa(f)	44	31	25	100
11 PFC & PPC	44	31	25	100
9 PGC	44	31	25	100
36 Total	44	31	25	100

EXHIBIT L

Some Comparisons of Friendship Choice Patterns
among Part-Timers

	Store 5	Store 6
Average choices made per person		
All part-timers	$\frac{107}{33} = 3.24$	$\frac{114}{36} = 3.17$
Front end	$\frac{69}{22} = 3.13$	$\frac{74}{27} = 2.74$
Back end	$\frac{38}{11} = 3.45$	$\frac{40}{9} = 4.45$
Cashiers	$\frac{41}{12} = 3.41$	$\frac{40}{16} = 2.50$
Non-cashiers	$\frac{66}{21} = 3.14$	$\frac{74}{20} = 3.70$
College students	$\frac{42}{13} = 3.23$	
High school students	$\frac{65}{20} = 3.25$	
College aspirants		$\frac{28}{12} = 2.34$
Non-col. aspirants		$\frac{86}{24} = 3.59$
Males	$\frac{100}{31} = 3.23$	$\frac{89}{29} = 3.07$
Females	$\frac{7}{2} = 3.50$	$\frac{25}{7} = 3.57$
$\frac{\text{"Others" choice to cashiers,}}{\text{\% of "others" total choices}}$	$\frac{19}{66} = 28.8\%$	$\frac{8}{74} = 10.8\%$
$\frac{\text{Back end choice to front end}}{\text{Back end total choices}}$	$\frac{11}{38} = 29\%$	$\frac{16}{40} = 40\%$
$\frac{\text{Cashiers' choices to cashiers only}}{\text{Cashiers' total choices}}$	$\frac{31}{41} = 75.7\%$	$\frac{18}{40} = 70\%$

EXHIBIT M

Status Factors and Movement: Counts in Check-Out Area as Per Cent of Total Counts in Stores for Part-Timers, by Status Factors

	Store 5			Store 6		
	College	High School	Total	College aspirant	Non-college aspirant	Total
Front end,	2*	—	2	2	3	6
Cashiers,	59–70	—	59–70	73–102	48–96	121–198
Female	84%	—	84%	72%	50%	61%
Front end,	6	4	10	5	3	8
Cashiers,	119–198	94–144	213–342	137–204	40–91	177–295
Male	60%	65%	62%	67%	44%	60%
Front end,	2	8	10	2	8	10
Clerks, Male	26–69	101–206	127–275	41–70	77–259	118–329
inc. PPa & PPc	38%	49%	46%	59%	30%	36%
Back end,	3	6	9	1	8	9
Clerks,	7–79	13–165	20–244	0–34	0–241	0–275
Male	9%	8%	8%	0%	0%	0%
	13	18	31	11	22	33
Total	211–416	208–515	419–931	251–410	165–687	416–1097
	51%	40%	45%	61%	24%	38%

* Code example.

2   ← Number of people in classification

Counts in check-out area → 59–70 ← Counts in store

$$84\% \leftarrow \left\{ \frac{\text{Counts in checkout area}}{\text{Counts in store}} \right.$$

NOTE: Absent at time of observations were: in store 5, 2 High School PGC's; in Store 6, 1 PCa(f) N.C.A., 1 Ca C.A., and 1 Clerk N.C.A. in the front end.   All 5 are included in the other statistical data.

Status Factors Related to Job Preferences

Purpose: To determine the relationship between status factors and part-timers' sentiments about activities and locations in the stores.

Method: Tabulated for each store, by key status factors, the responses of the part-timers when asked which nonsupervisory job they would most like to have permanently and which they would like the least.   There was no limitation on the number of choices an individual might make in either category.   See Exhibit N and O.

Selected Interviews

The following extracts from employee interviews have been selected on the basis of an expression of values which the individuals attached to work in the store.

Purpose: To see what significance these values may have in explaining the stores' differences in labor efficiency, when the sentiments expressed are viewed in the context of the work and social roles of the speakers.

Method: The interviews have been arranged by job classification in each store, and the friendship choices of the speakers have been indicated; CR means choices received from others, and MC indicates mutual choices.

INTERVIEWS

| | Quotations on page numbers | |
Job Classification	Store 5	Store 6
Front end		
Full-time Cashier (f)	423–427	442
Part-time Cashier	427–430	443–445
Part-time Cashier (f)	430–431	446–447
Part-time Front Clerk	432	447–448
Part-time Page boy	433	
Part-time Pickup Clerk		448
Back end		
Full-time Grocery Clerk	434–437	448–450
Part-time Grocery Clerk	437–442	451–452

1. STORE 5 FCa(f) CHOICES RECEIVED (CR) 4 MUTUAL CHOICES (MC) 1

You know, this store isn't as friendly as the old store was. I guess it's because it's a lot bigger. One of the things that burns me up is that when you get started on a floor job you always have to stop in the middle. It seems to me that part-time cashiers should be made to cashier until we get our floor jobs finished. And I think that the men ought to bring things up from the basement for us so that we can get our floor jobs finished more quickly. It's this getting started on something and then not being able to finish that upsets you. I don't think that management is aware of this problem.

Job Preferences of Part-Timers Classified by Key Status Factors—
Store 5

				Office M	Office L	Cashier M	Cashier L	Bundler M	Bundler L	Page boy M	Page boy L	Miscel. f. end M	Miscel. f. end L	Cellar M	Cellar L	Gen'l tables M	Gen'l tables L	Dairy or froz. fd. M	Dairy or froz. fd. L	Recvg. room M	Recvg. room L	Miscel. b. end M	Miscel. b. end L	Other depts. M	Other depts. L	Total M	Total L
Front end	College	Cashier	Female n=2	1		2		1	1																	4	1
	College	Cashier	Male n=6			6		2	2	1	1	1			1		4	2	1							12	9
	College	Clerk (inc. pa.)	Male n=2	1		1			1		2					1	1									3	4
	High school	Cashier	Male n=4			3									1	1	2	1	2							5	5
	High school	Clerk (inc. pa.)	Male n=8			2		1	2				1	2	1	7			1		1		1			12	7
Back end	College	Clerk	Male n=3			1			2						2	3		1								5	4
	High school	Clerk	Male n=8			5		1	3			1		2		2	1	2	2	1	1		1			14	8
Total M's				2		20		5		1		2		4		14		6		1		0		0		55	
Total L's					0		0		11		3		1		5		8		6		2		2		0		38

Legend: M = Number of choices as a "most liked" job.
L = Number of choices as a "least liked" job.

Job Preferences of Part-Timers Classified by Key Status Factors—

Store 6

				Office M	Office L	Cashier M	Cashier L	Bundler M	Bundler L	Pick-up M	Pick-up L	Misc. f. end M	Misc. f. end L	Back room M	Back room L	Gen'l tables M	Gen'l tables L	Dairy or froz. fd. M	Dairy or froz. fd. L	Rec'ng room M	Rec'ng room L	Misc. M	Misc. L	Other depts. M	Other depts. L	Total M	Total L
Front end	College aspirants	Cashier	Female n=3	1		2	1										2									3	3
			Male n=5	3		2			1										1		1				1	5	4
		Clerk	Male n=4	1		1			1																1	2	2
	Non-college aspirants	Cashier	Female n=4	2	1	2						1			1			1					1		1	6	4
		Cashier	Male n=4			2									1			1			3			1		4	4
		Clerk	Male n=9				2		5	2				2		1		2	1		1			2		9	9
Back end	College	Clerk	Male n=1						1					1						1						2	1
	Non-college	Clerk	Male n=8			1	1		6					3						1				2	1	7	8
			Total M's	7		10		0		2		1		6		1		4		2		0		5		38	
			Total L's		1		4		14		0		0		2		2		2		5		1		4		35

Legend: M = Number of choices as a "most liked" job.
L = Number of choices as a "least liked" job.

You know, though, this job is a lot more fun than just being at home, and I've got an important reason for working, too. My husband is ill and I need the money to make sure that we can get along.

(When asked what jobs she might like to do she said:) I'd rather not say anything about that. I'd just rather not talk about it.

(In relationship to the office job:) You know, seniority is needed for that job. FOF2(f) shouldn't have had it. She doesn't have that much seniority. And I think you should work on a job for a while in order to get promoted to it permanently.

2. STORE 5 FCa(f) CHOICES RECEIVED (CR) 4 MUTUAL CHOICES (MC) 2

I don't think I could ever work in an old store again. There stores have better hours and you don't have to work Saturdays or nights. The cashier systems are better. I worked in the old Lintown store. This is a very beautiful store, we work harder but you don't go out any evening with that old tired feeling. On the other hand, we remarked to our ourselves that this store is one where the customers are hardest to handle. I don't know, it's something funny about them in this place; you get a certain amount of phonies. They feel above you; they think we're working for peanuts, and they're actually pretty surprised if we ever tell them how much we get with our benefits and everything. But I prefer this to an office job. I used to work in a doctor's office. Here I can meet people, and you don't have to have as close contact with the other people who work here if you don't want to; that is, you don't have to have close contact with other people who work here. While you're working you have the customer in between you, but you can associate with those you choose who work here if you want.

My preference has always been working on the cash register; in fact, I'm transferring to one of the other new markets at the end of the month, and I turned down the bakery job there in order to work on the register. The new store is closer to my home.

I guess the secret to success around here is for you to do everything willingly, keep your cash straight so you don't have shortages, show some initiative, and do the little things like scrub up and other things you're not expected to do.

The part-time help annoy me because they don't exert themselves. PCA1 is tops, and PCA5 and PCA8 are good too, but the girls who came in as part-timers just don't exert themselves; I did double the work they did on Friday even though they were here all day, but I guess that's just a part-timer attitude.

3. STORE 5 FCa(f) CR3 MC 1

You know, I'm very happy working in this store, even being as busy as we are. I wouldn't leave here for anything. I'd quit the company first.
One of the things that I don't like very well is that I don't get enough help from the part-timers, especially in the later hours when things are so busy. There just aren't enough people here. You know, the front end is the most important part of the store. We ought to have more people up here to get things done when the rush is on. Only the slow girls get bundlers. There's just too much transferring around to really do the job right, but I like the company fine and I like a busy store. I couldn't go back to a small store if I had to. I like the variety and the customers. The people here are really swell. It's just the system of running things isn't so good.
There's a lot of future here for men, but not so much for women.
Sometimes the job gets a little boring, but then I can go out and straighten up my cigarettes and so on. Mostly, though, I like to stay behind the machine and just talk to the customers. They're all really very wonderful people. I was very surprised the other day when one of my customers turned up working in one of the other stores. I'm hoping that she can transfer over here. She's a lovely person; I'd like to work with her.

4. STORE 5 PCa CR11 MC4

You see, some of the cashiers and bundlers liking to work together, for example PCa7 and PFC4, but one of the unwritten laws of the store is that girls have to have bundle boys before anybody else does. The girls usually work on machines number 7 and 8. The girls seem to be satisfied with the slower machines but the guys don't like them. Over-all I like working here because I know this business and I've been at it for some six years. I'm confident that I can do almost anything well in the store. Regardless of what they tell me to do or which particular job they want me

to work on, I'm willing to do almost any of them; I get paid
the same regardless of what I do.

As far as the fellows whe really knock themselves out, I guess
PGC3 and PGC7 are the real hustlers. The goof-offs around
here are PFC1 and PPa1, but they're both stuck up in the front
end.

5. STORE 5 PCa CR2 MC1

I like the work here. I like the variety, the moving around.
There are some personal clashes that I get into, and I see inconsistencies in management once in a while. I just don't think
they're using their talent efficiently. They ought to put cashiers
out on the floor instead of having them bag.

I'll tell you one guy I don't like. That's the district manager.
Boy, he's a cold fish. You know, I got to meet him a while
back and since then he's never remembered me. He's just an
impersonal guy.

I'll tell you, I've got a philosophy about being a leader. You
can only expect what you yourself are willing to do, so you got
to be able to work everywhere. One thing I've got to learn
to do is to control my temper toward people that I don't like.
What I'm doing now is I just stay away from them. There's a
lot of irresponsible guys around, and I've just got to learn to
stay away from them.

One of the things that I've tried to do when I've been in charge
here is to challenge some of the fellows by criticizing them.
Sometimes it works, but I think it's not too good an idea to be
too strict. All I do is to let them know that I know that
they're doing something wrong or trying to get away with something. That's all.

6. STORE 5 PCa CR9 MC5

The thing I don't like here is there's too many bosses telling
you what to do all the time. All the mechanical kinds of things,
though—the conditions of work, the coffee breaks, and the
union and everything—that's all good, but why do they have to
protect the women so much? It seems to me that the guy who's
busiest, he's the one that ought to get the bundler. It doesn't
matter whether he's a man or a woman.

I don't like being given such general assignments when they put
me out on stocking shelves. I can't get to know any one job

well enough. Working around where the customers are climb-
ing all over you all the time. Boy, that's not for me.
What I really like to do is to move around once in a while, but
have a specific responsibility—sort of alternate between things.
I wouldn't even mind bundling once in a while as long as I
didn't get too much of it.

7. STORE 5 PCa CR3 MC2

I don't have anything to complain about. The money is good;
the work isn't too hard. You know, I like seeing people, but you
can get too much of it. It's when these people come through
at the end of the day, and they start adding up their bills, and
I have to stand there and wait for them—the women especially.
They really get me. As far as being a full-time job, there's just
too much worry to it. All these customers at you all the time.
I couldn't take it.
There's a pay differential between working back on the floor
and up here on the registers, so that must be a promotion, mustn't
it?
I like to move around once in a while. My left leg goes to
sleep if I don't, and I bake from the sun coming in the windows.
The darn thing needs some shades on it.

8. STORE 5 PCa CR7 MC2

I wish the heck they'd move the bundlers around more or have
fewer registers so we could have bundlers on each station. Boy,
it's rough trying to do this all by yourself when the rush is on.
I like working on the register, though. You're your own boss
there, you know. They're a friendly bunch of guys to work for,
especially the head cashier. They don't push you around.

9. STORE 5 PCa CR1 MC0

The part-timers rate working on the registers highest. The
full-timers rate being in the back end highest. They'd rather
work on the stock. As for myself I just don't care for being
shut off from the customer. Nevertheless, the customers in this
store are different, they're funny people. They're quite wealthy,
and they expect too much service; others who have worked in
other markets here seem to feel the same way as I do on this.
Management in the front end is good, but we didn't like the old
cash department head; he didn't treat us as if we were human,
he changed the entire system of lunch and rest periods and fixed

it up so we couldn't get ten-minute breaks in the afternoon. He didn't use the right way of telling us to do things; it used to be a pleasure to work up front before he came, and they used to get a lot of cooperation, but he was just trying to push himself up in the organization. Management doesn't distribute the help right. They don't switch bundle boys around to different cashiers. Bundle boys are inclined to stick on one register even though another cashier may need one more. The bundle boys ought to divide their time.

The customers are always waiting for us to make a mistake, and that wasn't true in some of the other stores where I worked. Some of the gray coats[1] just like to start using their influence and show people that they're important. In this store they can make it unpleasant for some of the rest of the help.

I don't like to work with PCa2. The old cash department head appointed him as his assistant, and PCa2 has been using too much influence on us. I don't feel that we should have to take orders from him.

10. STORE 5 PCa CR4 MC3

I like this job as a whole; the people here are nice to work with. Sometimes, though, the customers really get your goat. I spend quite a bit of time moving around on different jobs, and I like that; it makes the time go faster and doesn't make the job as monotonous. Usually they have me working either on the registers or on dairy or frozen foods in the back end.

11. STORE 5 PCa(f) CR1 MC1

One of the things that I like about this job is that every so often you can get time off for social things. It's not too often, but once in a while.

That PCa2—I sure don't like him very much. You know, I tried to get some time off one time, and he was just as nasty as could be, making all kinds of cracks about what I wanted to do with the time off. PCa1 is a lot different. He's more understanding. A lot of fellows swear an awful lot, and I don't care for that, but not PCa1.

I like the customers and I like the people that I work with here, though, a good deal. You know, I really think that the fellows that bundle for us girls really are awfully nice. They protect us

[1] "Gray coats" refers to assistant department heads and above.

when anything happens that, you know, might be embarrassing
or a customer gets rough about something.

Poor PPa6,[2] you know, he really wasn't at fault.   He was just
trying to protect me.   The customer started making some cracks
about the way I was ringing up the merchandise and then he
started getting after PPa6 for not packing his bag properly.
When someone is like that you just can't hold back your temper
all the time.   I felt awfully sorry for him.

I wish I could get more hours here.   I really need the money.
I'm afraid I'm going to have to quit for the summer because
I won't be able to save enough to get through school next year.

I wouldn't want to have to do any bundling work.   You know,
you have to take orders from the cashiers, and it's hard work.

You know, if someone gets moved from the front end of the
store back to stocking or doing some work in the back end,
you can tell that's a promotion.

The main reason I'm here is just to make some money.   At times
it gets pretty tedious, but at times it's nice for a change, too.
I guess I describe myself as being medium satisfied.   I love running
the register, and I don't mind giving change and stamps, but
when I have to bundle it kills me.   I don't like doing things I
don't do well.   I'd say the hardest worker in the place is PGC1.
Up front there aren't really any hard workers.

12. STORE 5 PCa(f) CR1 MC1

I like the people in the store well enough.   It's the customers I
don't like so well.

Where would I like to be promoted to?   The question doesn't
mean very much, because getting promoted around here just
isn't in the realm of possibility.

13. STORE 5 PCa(f) CR2 MC1

Oh, I like this job all right; I wouldn't want too much of it.
You know, my husband is in this business.   Lots of places people
don't mind their own business, but here they do.   I wouldn't
say this was a very friendly store, and the people here are pretty
strict.   You've got to be on the job or you get bawled out.
But I enjoy it.   I could use more help I guess—bundling particularly.   The girls don't always get bundlers when the men already
have them.   I don't think that's fair.

[2] PPa6 was allowed to resign after an alleged altercation with a customer.

You know, they send a couple of us out together. PCA12(f) and I get sent out to eat together all the time. I don't know why they send us out together. Maybe it's just because we have the same hours together.

14. STORE 5 PFC CR4 MC3

The thing I'd like to be doing really is stacking the shelves, there's not as much pressure on you in that job, but they've got me working up here in front. I don't really like working in the store, it's just a means to an end. A few bucks for gas in the car. I don't like either the customers or the job, which has too many chiefs or managers and not enough indians. My friends here are the college fellows but not the high school fellows, they all act pretty much like kids. Still, most of the part-timers feel the same as I do, this is just a job for pin money, you do what you have to do, take care of the customers, sweep floors, and that's about it.

15. STORE 5 PFC CR1 MC1

I don't expect too much from this job. The money is pretty good and it's not too hard. It does get a little monotonous once in a while, and the hours are kind of late, but I enjoy it well enough. They look out for you pretty well here.
I like to do work downstairs—any old work—just enough to get away from the crowd.
If I really wanted to stay in this company, boy, I'd show a lot more interest than I do.
I don't think they use a person's potential around here. Both PFC2 and I have had math and accounting experience, and we've told them about it, but they just put us up here in the front end on the bundling jobs. People want service too fast out here on the front end. We have to work too long at night after the store closes due to the customers staying around too. I don't see why they don't make PFC2 and me cashiers, I don't think it's because we don't work hard enough.

16. STORE 5 PFC CR3 MC2

I can't say I care very much for the customers, but I do like the people pretty well that run this place. They don't push you around. They're a nice bunch of guys and you get some freedom. These bosses, you know, you can talk back to a little bit. They don't hold any grudges against you. I've gotten to know them all pretty well.

The boss I like best, PCa1, he really breaks the job up for you so that you don't get lousy jobs all the time.

17. STORE 5 PPa CR3 MC2

I'd rather be a cashier than a page boy. You get more money as a cashier; you also have a bundle boy to handle the bagging, and all you have to do is press buttons. As far as the job is concerned, I like the pay, it's the best part-time job around. I don't like so many bosses. There are too many bosses and too few brains. Some of them lord it over you, like PCa2; he gets some sort of delight out of pushing people around. The customers sometimes really make it difficult too, some of them are really mean. I'd rather bundle for the part-timers who are cashiers; they have more fun, and they're my age.

18. STORE 5 PPa CR0 MC0

This job sure has got me confused. I came in here to work as a bundler. I was there for a month, and then they sent me over to the fruit department, and then I worked there for a month. Now they're bringing me back to the front end again. I don't know why. Maybe it had something to do with the fact that I went out for spring football. I sure don't like being moved around that way, though. I'd rather stay in one place. Now I'd rather stay in the fruit department. Frankly, I don't like the fruit manager very well, and I kind of think he was at the bottom of having me moved back again.

Whatever I'm going to do with my life, I'll tell you it isn't going to be in the grocery business.

19. STORE 5 PPa CR1 MC0

There are too many bosses around here. They're good guys, and they do things for you, and they don't jump on you, and they don't really need to. But there's too many of them. This bundling, boy, is that boring. I'd like to move around more.

You know, one thing I don't understand is here we've got a union and I never seen the representative. Why not? I don't have anybody to tell my problems to. Why should I pay union dues? I get nothing for it.

I like to do most anything if I can be myself and be my own boss.

20. STORE 5 FGC CR2 MC1

You know, I sure worry about having to work on the dairy. You have to be so careful that you don't spoil things there. In fact, I wish I didn't have to move around from job to job at all. This is kind of a new thing here, and it's a pain in the neck. Nobody likes it. I can see where getting broad experience is necessary, but I sure don't like it. After all, a guy may not be able to do everything well. It seems to me that a man should be given credit for doing one thing very well. After all, it may foul up your chances for promotion. Maybe a guy just likes to do one job.

It all boils down to one thing: I plan to go to school nights again under the GI bill and major in marketing and to come back to work for this company. I like working with customers, and I've had experience in a smaller store in another chain. I like the facilities here, but there's not enough help, and sometimes I feel as though I have so much to do and not possibly enough time to do it. This company is moving, and the chances for advancement are good here. I'm doing exactly what I'd like to be doing, because I'd rather be on either the frozen foods or the dairy, where it's your responsibility. That's what I did in the other store.

If you want to get ahead in this store I guess a fellow can't afford to dislike a certain job too much. You also really have to have a liking for the business. Schooling isn't necessary, but it helps. You have to take what you don't like as well as what you do like. Sometimes it's sort of frustrating to be called up to the front end when you're behind on a place like dairy or frozen foods. However, if you can see the reason for it, it's not so bad. Sometimes they have to pull the full-time clerks up to the front to move the people through.

The thing I like about our people here is that they don't bother you. Nobody ever holds any grudges against you—no hard feelings.

I really like working in the cellar best, right here where I am now. Nobody bothers you down here.

You know, one thing that bothers me is that they don't really show a difference between the different full-time clerks' jobs. Some require less responsibility, and some more. Take frozen foods, for instance. Now that's a very important job. It seems to me that a guy who works on that ought to be recognized more by getting more pay. After all, he has to work on his own time and do a lot of extra things that some of the other guys don't. After all, working in a cellar is a lot more important than just stocking shelves, and it's a lot harder too.

21. STORE 5 FGC CR2 MC0

When I first started this job I looked at it as a career, but now I'm looking around for an opening somewhere else. If the breaks fall in this field I'll stay, but now I'm looking around. Part of the problem is that now in these newer stores they have a rotation system.

It's a brainstorm of theirs. You leave one department and you rotate, so that the new department is a completely new animal as far as you're concerned. It's pretty rough when a full-timer has to turn around and ask a part-timer things about the department he's supposed to be working in, but that happens when you keep rotating every so often. You're just in one job long enough to learn it, but then they yank you off into another area. Rotation doesn't benefit the customer, either. A fellow has got to learn all the customer's gripes and problems each time he switches to a new area.

One thing lacking in the new stores is that people are only interested in the job they are doing themselves, because they don't have time to help anybody else. Everybody is only concerned with his own job and they're all involved in making it better. In the larger stores everybody is self-ambitious, trying to move ahead; they're all trying to do more than they're supposed to do. That's one reason why the full-time clerks prefer the dairy and frozen foods counters; there you at least know how much you're supposed to do. For example, the dairy man looks to the Jewish line, which is on the adjoining counter, as being an outside concern, and he won't touch it until somebody comes and tells him to. It's the same on the frozen food line; you have the potato chips and things like that on the counter you're supposed to handle, but you don't do anything with those until you have to. The grocery department has no limits like dairy and frozen foods. A guy working in the grocery department just has the limits of the store. When you're classified as a dairy or frozen food man, right then and there you draw your limits. The same is true with the cashiers on the candy or the bakery girl. You can draw your limits then. I used to work on dairy, but this week I've been put in the cellar, and I understand I'm being transferred to the grocery department. That means I'll be doing anything from the register to bagging, to unloading the trailers. My next logical step after dairy would have been to be head clerk or head cashier, but they've taken me off the dairy and put me on grocery, and that's a big let-down. I don't know who will get an opening now. The roulette system really keeps you guessing. Another problem is the part-timers. When you get behind they'll send anyone who is available, not a specialist who knows the ropes but some ignorant part-timer who's likely to be more hindrance than help. You've got to teach him as well as do your own work then. If it were an experienced part-timer you could get some work done.

The full-time help here is getting the feeling that they've cut this too far to the bone.

The full-time grocery clerks don't mind being called up to the front end, except where they have their own department like dairy or frozen foods; then they don't want to move front for anything, it's just an outside aggravation.

When I was on the dairy counter I didn't get a chance to intermingle with the fellows in the grocery department or the frozen food man, but based on previous relationships I've worked with all the full-timers in the store, particularly when the store was new and the entire crew was brought in to clean up and get the store on its feet. Then we were all one big happy family, but it's all begun to split up, and there's been an unconscious separation of the help. Each one now works in his own department. The customers have noticed it. It leads to the question can we be big and small at the same time.

22. STORE 5 FGC CR4 MC1

I'll tell you that this is a lot better than working in a clothing company or a factory somewhere. The management here is really good. Best management I've seen anywhere, and it's a nice clean job. It's a job where you can wear a white shirt. It's the kind of job I like. The thing I like about management is you can really talk to them.

But I want to move up in this company. I'm giving myself a year, and if I don't move up by then, then I'm going to quit.

Nobody really bothers me in this store. That's what I like about it most, I guess.

If I have to move and go on some other job away from frozen

foods, which I like a lot, why I'll do it. If I have to get promoted, that's what I'll do.
The only thing I don't like about this job is every Friday I have
to go up on cashiering and get thrown into those customers.
That's not for me.
I'm going to night school starting in the fall. I'll be going for
three years. I want something to fall back on just in case this
job doesn't work out.

23. STORE 5 FGC CR1 MC0

I want to go to the very top of this organization. I was with
another chain for three years, but they want all part-timers, and
they lose in the end. I made up my mind when I was a kid that
I would get into this business. I want to get a gray coat before
the draft gets hold of me.
This is the best outfit I've ever seen. The store manager introduced me to every single full-timer when I first came here, and
I think that's pretty darned considerate. I guess in terms of the
jobs to be done here you can separate them and describe them in
terms of whether or not they're challenging or fun. I'd say the
most challenging job as far as getting ahead is concerned is
dairy, then frozen foods, then receiving, then cellar, then working
on the floor, and finally working in fruits and vegetables. Dairy
is the most challenging because you've got to do a lot more
thinking. The most fun job is receiving, because it's easier and
you meet a lot of people. And working on the floor, on the
tables, is simple, and the cellar isn't hard either. Those are the
fun jobs. I don't mind working in the front end either, but it
kind of knocks down the amount of work I can get done in the
back end. A full-timer has got to show the part-timers that he
can work faster than they can. It's better to work with them
than against them, but you've got to show that you're a better
man. If I were the manager, I would only hire fellows who are
interested in becoming grocery managers. You've really got to
like the grocery business. You can never refuse to do what one
of the head men wants you to do; if that means to move from one
job to another, you do it.

24. STORE 5 PGC CR4 MC1

The thing that gets me, boy, is having all those customers get in
your way all the time. That's why I like it down here in the

cellar where it's nice and quiet. I like to pass the time anyway, and you can work pretty hard down here. I like moving around once in a while so it doesn't get monotonous, so long as I can stay away from the customers. My father liked the grocery business too.

You know, I've learned one thing. The more you can learn about this company, the more valuable you are to them.

25. STORE 5 PGC CR4 MC1

One of the things I don't like about this place is the union. It stops your progress going up. It seems to me all that counts is seniority. Things are too standardized here. I like to work hard. After all, all I do all day is sit in school, but sometimes you can't work hard because things get so rigid. I like being independent too.

I don't mind working out in front of the store, except for the customers. They get on your nerves.

I like GDH. He's a hustler. AGDH1 is a real swell guy. He treats everybody well. It's too bad he probably won't go very far because he is such a good guy. CDH is too easy-going too. My best friends are the hard workers. I like people who work hard and who know what they're doing.

I have four bosses, in other words all the graycoats. That makes me low man on the totem pole. I guess they all want to boss you around at the same time. The cellar is dreary downstairs, but sometimes it gets a little hectic up here, especially when the customers start pouring in. In the beginning GDH was a real pusher, he wants to make store manager. When he first came he didn't know how to handle the part-timers. For the most part, though, he's gotten a lot better now. They'll take the goof-offs and stick them up on the front end. You'll find most of the goof-offs are page boys up there. Anyway, I could be a part-timer cashier if I wanted to. They offered me the job, but I wouldn't want to take the guff from the customers. I'd rather work back here.

Most of the fellows back here in the back end are in high school in Winston, I guess. I go to City College and I just come to work on weekends I don't see any of the other fellows outside of work.

Whenever any of the part-time cashiers come off the front end and work back here they tend to goof off. They come to work on the aisles during the lulls up front when the pressure is off up there.

26. STORE 5 PGC CR4 MC2

The bosses around here really know what they're doing, and they'll listen to you. Sometimes I think there are too many of them, though. But I like having people that know what they're doing even though it means they get quite strict.

I would like a little bit of more leeway though. I think the schedule here is too rigid. I'd rather have a chance to get different hours once in a while. Another thing I like, though, here is the variety of work you get doing different jobs. But I don't like to have to quit a job before I've finished it. You sort of get a feeling that you're doing something and then all at once they stop you and you go somewhere else and you never have a chance to really do it up the way you'd like to. There's one job I really like to do, but now I'm getting to think that maybe I don't want to have it after all, because they keep taking me off it before I can finish it.

I'd like to get more responsibility. Boy, I could really know that something was mine to do and I was completely responsible for it.

Working this way, though, you know, is a kind of a waste of time. You don't get enough experience if this is just for spending money.

Of course, you know, there are good opportunities here if you get to know how to do a lot of things. You have to know how to do everything. You have to be able to fill in for people. Of course, though, this takes time.

I've often thought that they ought to assign everybody to a specific aisle. I guess I can see why this isn't possible, but I wish they could. And I wish they could give you an idea of whether you're doing things right or not and how is the store doing. I'd like to know about that too, but they don't tell us. They don't tell us why things happen. You kind of get the feeling that you're not too important. You know, if you work hard at something, you like to know if you're doing all right.

27. STORE 5 PGC CR1 MC0

You know, a lot of the guys said they would like to work down here in the basement. They think it is a lot easier because there isn't so much pressure down here. But you have to work just

as hard or harder than you do upstairs. GDH doesn't think we
have to work very hard down here but, boy, we do work hard.
You know, I don't mind having to work real hard when the
pressure is on, but when the pressure is off, and we still have to
work just as hard as before, I don't see any sense in it. I don't
think there's enough people around here. That's the trouble. I
get along pretty well with these guys. There're a pretty good
bunch of guys. The pay is pretty good and the work isn't too
hard. Frankly, though, this is strictly a temporary job for me.
The pay is too low and the hours are too long. Two more
months and I'm through with it.
I'll tell you one thing, boy, when you work here, you get away
from the customers just as far as you can.
You know, I've got a lot of respect for GDH. He does his own
dirty work at least. He's a real good worker himself. He's
awfully hard on people, but he's okay. Quite often I think there's
too much pressure—that his expectations are too great—but at
least I've got to hand it to him. He doesn't make anybody do
anything that he wouldn't do himself.

28. STORE 5 PGC CR6 MC4

This is the best job I can get around here. It's got a nice
atmosphere, and the pay is good. It's a lot neater than some of
the other jobs I've had. I do get annoyed, though, when I'm
doing a job and one of the graycoats rushes up and switches you
to something else. Then while you're doing that second job
they'll rush up and call you to still something else. It makes you
feel kind of useless sometimes. The other thing is that whatever
you're doing at any particular time is going to be taken apart right
away by the customers. You realize that there is nothing
permanent about anything you're doing, and you'd rather do
something that would last, I think.
You have to keep plugging all the time here as a part-timer.
They really do watch you, some of the fellows like PGC3 really
knock themselves out. He's the hardest working kid here. The
rest of them I guess are pretty much like I am. You do your
work, but you don't really knock yourself out. But they keep an
eye on you anyway. PGC6 is another fellow who really knocks
himself out and all of a sudden PGC7 is working hard, I guess he's
bucking for promotion or something. He's pretty outspoken,
and they moved him out of the front end because I guess he sassed
one of the customers.

As far as the fellows who goof off, FGC3 is one of them, but he can really put it on when he has to. PFC1 is probably the worst goof-off in the store, and PFC2 and PFC3 are being punished up in the front end because they goofed off while they were grocery clerks back here. I guess I'm not at either extreme; most of the others feel the same way. They're not going to kill themselves. They just keep an even steady pace, but it's hard to gauge it, really.

I don't mind moving up front. I even like to bundle for PCa3, he's a comedian with me and always good for a lot of laughs. I like to bundle for PCa1 too; he's a fast checker, but it's a nice atmosphere up there working with him. Management likes to have us bundle for the girls, and I don't mind bundling for PCa11(f) and PCa14(f).

PCa4 doesn't seem to get bundlers much, but he's a nice guy. Maybe it's because he's quiet or something.

In the summertime the whole atmosphere is different. Last year a couple of guys from high schools always used to be on the last register, but it's too busy now, if there were more spare time we'd get more of a chance to see our friends than we do now. But now there isn't enough time for talking because the store is so busy.

As far as working in the back end is concerned, the favorite stacking item of everybody is the cereals, they're easiest to stack, then I guess the baking stuff, and the least popular are the soups and the pickles and aisles where there are lots of things to put up. Generally the smaller the item, the less it's liked by the fellows. Management wants the fellows to move from aisle to aisle in the back end, and I guess if I had my choice I'd want the same thing. For a while I though I'd like to have one aisle for myself, but I guess then that some fellows would be unhappy because others didn't have as much to do so I guess all in all I'd just as soon move around.

29. STORE 5 PGC CR4 MC1

This job has good pay, the bosses are fair, and most of the kids who work here are pretty good. I don't like the hours and I don't like the kids fooling around in the back room when I'm trying to get some work done. One fellow I've got a lot of respect for is PGC3. He really knocks himself out at his work. They like to have us keep moving up to the front end when they need us, but it's really a pain in the neck. It prevents us from getting our own work done in back.

30. STORE 5 PGC CR7 MC1

I'll be frank with you. I don't like this job. I'd rather work outside somewhere. The hours are too late. You never catch up on anything. I don't like working nights—that's no good. The pay is good; I'll admit that, and the work isn't too hard. But I'm against it. It's just too boring. I've got to move around. If I stay in one place, I can't stand it.

31. STORE 5 PCG CR2 MC0

This kind of a job is okay for part-time work but, boy, I sure don't like the late hours. They do take care of you pretty well. I like this a lot more than other jobs I've had.

I like jobs where you can see that you've accomplished something. Other jobs are okay just for a change, but you wouldn't want them very long, things like bundling. I'd hate to get on any job where I'd have to be confined to doing it all the time.

I like guys who are hustlers.

Store 6

1. STORE 6 FCa(f) CR2 MC1

This job is nice. I like it very much. This company is very understanding when you have personal trouble. You get to meet a lot of customers and nice employees and you get to move around. But the day drags if you stand behind an empty register. I even cleaned up the ladies room the other day with FGC2 just to keep us from getting bored.

We're as high as we can go. The head checker, office, and bakery jobs have too much responsibility and they're not really promotions.

Customers talk to you a lot, and it's important for them to confide their problems. They'll tell you that they're pregnant again and don't know how they're going to pay for it.

2. STORE 6 FCa(f) CR2 MC1

I like my combination of jobs as a whole, but I wouldn't care to do any one of them all the time.

I like everybody—get along with everybody. This is a very friendly place to work. Bosses are pleasant, clerks help me with the drugs, and the part-time girls are very nice and very conscientious. I have a teenage daughter, you know.

3. STORE 6 PCa CR4 MC0

I came here because I thought I could get a part-time job where the hours would fit in well with my college work. I thought I would be a grocery clerk, but they put me in as a cashier. I really like cashiering. I like people. You get to meet the public. It pays well and it's a pleasant environment. ACDH used to be a cashier before they made him ACDH. Before that we used to have a college boy who was really a great guy, but ACDH orders us around and is really rude to us. CDH, on the other hand, is a great guy.

I like to keep busy. When there's not much doing up front, I don't mind stocking shelves. I even volunteer to clean the lunch room just so I won't be standing around. I do that pretty often now.

I have no real friends here. My friends are the kids I grew up with or those I know from school (City College).

You noticed my honor roll badge. Well, that badge is too conspicuous, I think. People are always interrupting my ringing to ask what it means. But it's important to be on the honor roll, because it lets you know you are appreciated and that you are doing a good job.

4. STORE 6 PCa CR6 MC3

I really like it here. The money is good. It's close to home, and the hours are good, so I can get my homework done. I like the people I work with, and I like the customers. Stocking shelves is all right, but you don't get to meet people.

Best thing about cashiering is the money. I would prefer to stock shelves if the money was the same. Stocking is good because it keeps you busy, and it's a haven. You like it. But I couldn't stand it permanently. I prefer to move around. I like change-making[3] because you can run so many customers through so fast. Having a bundle boy makes a big difference in your speed.

[3] Under some conditions three people were assigned to work at each check-out station: a cashier, a change-maker, and a bundler. Under other conditions there could be either a cashier only or a cashier and a bundler.

5. STORE 6 PCa CR0 MC0

I like it here. If you don't cross the bosses they can't cross you too much. The atmosphere is good. It's a bright store, also a good class of people. There are pretty good pay and hours for the part-time work.

I don't like being switched around all the time. I would like to be on one or the other, register or floor, but switching is no good. I don't like working without a bundle boy, either. The cashier is the head of the team. You have to see the group as a whole and know what each guy's doing.

I am going to be a pastor, and what I would like to do most is to go around opening up closed churches.

I guess that most of my friends are on the front end, but I am sort of an individualist. PCa12(f) and PCa11(f) are at the same college, but I don't see them much on campus.

This has been a good job for me, because I have learned how to talk with people. I have come out of my shell. And another thing, when you are ringing, you have got to think fast.

6. STORE 6 PCa CR3 MC2

I like it very much here. You've got something to do with yourself. Money actually is sort of a side product. The main thing is that you have a sense of belonging, a camaraderie. It's like another school activity, but you're doing something that is important. The feeling of togetherness, I would say, occurs in two places, up front and in the aisles. Up front when you're bundling or change-making, and everything is going along well, you feel that you belong to a group that includes the ringer, the change-maker, the bundler, and the customer. Back in the aisles you have the same feeling, but it is a little bit less, because you have to be more conscious of what you are doing in the aisles and attend to that. Up front you only have to devote your attention about 40 per cent to what you're doing, and that leaves about 60 per cent left over to be aware of your surroundings. In the aisles it is about the reverse of that. Of course, if you yourself are ringing, then you have to be quite conscious of your work and you really can't participate in that group feeling. But, now, why do I like to check when I just said the camaraderie opportunity is least there? (Pause) Well, I think there is probably the least amount of physical work in checking, and the time goes very fast there. (Pause) Actually, there is something else, too, I guess, and I feel sort of silly saying it, but in the scheme of things here in this store, when you are checking you feel superior to the people who are bundling and to the stock boys, and this superiority is because of the responsibility of the job—not simply because it pays more.   Actually, a poor ringer could always feel superior to a good bundler or a good clerk, and it doesn't really have anything to do with the individual.   It's the job.

But we would never feel superior to a full-timer.   Every part-timer feels inferior to full-timers.   You obey a full-timer.   Even though they have no official status, they have the ability to know what needs to be done, and so you obey them, and so you feel inferior to them.   Actually, though, I feel on a par with the full-time checkers but not the full-time grocery people.

7. STORE 6 PCa CR0 MC0

I like this job very much—it's the highest paying job around. Boy, the pay is great for high school kids.   I get $1.47 per hour, and most high school kids only get $1.00.

8. STORE 6 PCa CR0 MC0

I like it a lot on this job.   It helps me out on my finances, and it's a white collar job.   Being a cashier is the best job a kid can have in the store.   Being a cashier is a big responsibility.   It's hard for me to think of anything I dislike.

I don't get along with the kids because I am too cooperative and don't fool around like they do.   I can't stand the kids.   They always seem to rib me.

I think maybe I will go into commercial art.   I like singing, too. I am in the glee club choir.

9. STORE 6 PCa CR1 MC0

I sure don't like changing around all the time.   I hate to be ordered over the loud speaker.   In other stores you are on the register or on the floor, one or the other.   But here you are always being shifted around.

I don't mind being on frozen foods.   You are more or less your own boss, and you are confined to a certain part of the store with certain duties.

10. STORE 6 PCa CR1 MC1

In this store you get the feeling that they really care about you. They care what we get for hours and allow for our own activities.

It's clean work, and cashiering is a transferable skill. This is one store where all the bosses are pretty good. They don't rush you. I don't like the funny lunch hours, like today, when I had to go at two o'clock. I was the only one, and I had to eat alone.

Cashiering is monotonous, but I like the pay. I like to keep busy. I don't like watching the clock. I like to ring quick and then help my bundler. I guess I like cashiering because I am not on it all day.

I like moving around, it breaks the monotony. Last summer I worked in a factory and couldn't stand it because it was so monotonous.

11. STORE 6 PCa(f) CR1 MC0

I *love* ringing! The best of anything I've ever done. There's no frustration. Whenever you need something—change, or a bundle boy—it's right there when you call for it. Only once in four months have I not had a bundler when I needed one.

With CDH, as long as you don't move in a bizarre way, its okay with him, and you can help whoever you want and go wherever you want. But ACDH keeps moving you around all the time. And it makes a real difference in our relationships among each other which manager we have. I'd rather have someone make change out of my cash drawer than ring on my register. No reason, just psychological. There's nothing anyone can do to my register to hurt it. I just love to ring. It gives me a sense of pride to ring more, harder, and faster—and to have two or three people working for me.

12. STORE 6 PCa(f) CR3 MC1

I like working here very much, as a means to an end, of course. I am a senior in college, and I will be going into nursing, I hope in a foreign mission. This has been a new way to meeting people for me. I used to be much more shy, but having to work with the customers and the kids has helped me a lot.

There are good kids to work with here. We all believe in helping one another. But you can't always work with the people you would like to.

The trouble with change-making is that you often get a ringer and a bagger who works at very different speeds.

I don't move much, but I don't think it's bad to move. It might be a variation.

13. STORE 6 PCa(f) CR1 MC0

I like this job real good. *Much* better than the department store I was in. Ringing is a job with a lot of responsibility, all the cash and stamps and everything. We handle thousands of dollars a week. I like meeting people and handling money. I like a nice, clean store, and the music. And I like the hours—perfect for me. I do get tired, though.

14. STORE 6 PCa(f) CR2 MC0

The things I like best about this job are the friendly people. We've got nice bosses and good kids to work with. But sometimes you get bad customers, and that's the worst thing about this job.
Some days you feel like you can't face the customers, and those days I like to dust or mark prices.
My best friends in the store are the cashiers, but my real friends are not here in the store.
I would rather mark prices in the stockroom than anything else here. It's so easy and relaxing. I hate it when I have to stop and scrub floors, and I would quit if they ever put me in the meat department. My father is a wholesale meat dealer, and I have had enough of that.

15. STORE 6 PCa(f) CR3 MC2

The thing I like best is seeing other people. I like other people. They interest me. I don't like the back room, though! That's where all the men are.

16. STORE 6 PFC CR4 MC2

When I came here I thought I deserved a job as a ringer, but they already hired the ringers before they hired anybody else. I really don't mind bundling, and I would just as soon bundle as stock shelves, depending on the mood I am in. My best friends are cashiers, but sometimes the customers can bother you so you would like to go back and stock. Anyway, it breaks the monotony. I would least like to work in the back room dragging and stamping.
I don't know what to think about moving back and forth from bundling to stocking. Usually it's a mad rush. I don't want to move if I like the job I am doing, but if I don't, I would just as soon go some place else.

17. STORE 6 PFC CR4 MC1

I like to move around. It's good variety and it's a relief to get away from bundling.
There's really nothing I don't like, although I don't really like bundling. I like to be busy, and it would be good to work in the courtesy booth. There's nobody to boss you around there and plenty to do. People here are easy to get along with. All the ringers and checkers and the cashiers and bundle boys are my friends.

18. STORE 6 PFC CR4 MC2

This job's okay. You have to go along with it.

19. STORE 6 PFC CR7 MC1

It's a good part-time job while you're going to school.

20. STORE 6 PFC CR6 MC0

I don't see any point in bundling. You can't ever see what you are accomplishing.

21. STORE 6 PFC CR2 MC1

It's all right. It gets pretty boring, though.

22. STORE 6 PPC CR7 MC3

It's all right. I like working outside.

23. STORE 6 PPC CR2 MC2

I like working outside. This business is no good if you got any brains, though.

24. STORE 6 PPC CR3 MC2

I like working outside.

25. STORE 6 FGC CR2 MC0

It's a good job—it's not monotonous—you're free to do things on your own initiative. You have a chance to learn the best way to do things, because they're looking for new ideas; if theirs is best, you do it that way, and if yours is best, you do it your way. It's clean work. You get a chance to contact people and say "hi" once in a while.   And this company isn't on your back; other chains are always pushing you.

If I were a part-timer, I'd like cashiering best because of the pay, but actually floor work is better because you are on your own and get to talk to people.

But as a full-timer, the back room is ordinarily the best; but in this store, it's too small, so the work is to hard because of the high piles of merchandise.

I consider my time on the floor as supervising part-timers.   Full-timers aren't supposed to, but actually they do.

This store's manager is famous for keeping a low payroll.   Store 6 is very low in payroll.   In fact, it's the lowest in the whole chain for new stores and the highest for profit.   That's because they move us around all the time—wherever they need us.   The shelves aren't quite so neat that way, because the men don't have individual pride in particular shelves.   But you got to have one thing or the other.

26. STORE 6 FGC CR2 MC0

I don't like to be on any one thing too long.   I like to move around. You can learn more that way and get more experience.   I used to be a cellar man, but then you don't know what's going on. You don't get to see anything or anybody.   I used to work in the fruit department, but I didn't like that.   It's the same thing all the time, really tiresome.

I would like to get ahead around here, but it takes 30 years to be a store manager.   I know anything that AGDH knows, but I would have to know how to order in order to be more than that.   The company sends many store employees on training programs where they learn how to keep books.

I think the best way to run a store is to have a man assigned to every aisle and keep the shelves neater.   There would be less shorts and could be more accurate prices.   If I had one table, I could do it all in three hours.   But I guess the bosses are afraid I would stretch it out to seven.   I would personally prefer moving around, but if I were store manager, I would put men on individual aisles and switch them every three months.   When I was at my last store I had my own aisles, and I did my work and did it perfect, but I didn't go looking for no more.   If they had shifted me around every three months I would have learned more and probably would have done more.   I could help the order fillers in my spare time.   Here I don't get no chance.

27. STORE 6 FGC CR6 MC2

Moving around is a pain in the neck. I would rather work in one place, and I would prefer to work on particular aisles.

What I like best about this store is I know what I am going to do when I come in in the morning. I do not have too many jobs. Everybody is friendly here. They are all my friends.

I like a big store because everybody is not always in a hurry like they are in little ones.

28. STORE 6 FGC CR5 MC2

I'm the boss of the back room. Nobody else's rank means anything there. I'm the boss.

This is not a bad place to work. The pay increases are slow. but you keep busy and move around. The nicest thing is that if you don't like a job, you can transfer out of that store. This is the fourth I have been in since I have been in the chain.

I can usually get anything I want without the union's help just by moving. But if I don't get to be AGDH in the next couple of years, I will get all the way out of the company.

The nice thing about the back room is you can see the end product of your work. Where on the shelves, just as soon as you get them filled up they are empty again. We never get a chance to see the job all the way done.

The head meat-cutter and I used to be great friends, but now I never see anybody in the meat department. The only people I see are grocery people and sometimes the front enders. I used to work in a small store. It was just one big happy family. I knew everybody in the store, even a lot of the customers. Here, it is a lot different. You don't know so many of the people, but because there's more of them, there's always somebody that you can go to lunch with or to coffee with. In a small store, you had to go out one at a time.

Moving around inside the store is an awful nuisance. When I have to do it, it keeps me from getting my work done in the back room. If the girls worked hard, I would not have to go up there, but when the girls talk and horse around with one another, that means the guys in the back room have to come forward to help out.

29. STORE 6 FGC CR0 MC0

Now I've got a job as a night chef in addition to this job here at the store. I've got to keep occupied. I don't sleep much, and if I had to be around the house all the time, I would go out of my head. My wife's always saying, "Why don't you relax and take it easy," but I'm not like that. I got to be doing something all the time.

I like meeting the people. It's a relief to go to the front end and see the public and see what's being sold.

30. STORE 6 PGC CR2 MC2

The kids out back like the back of the store best. They don't like being called to the front part. I guess this is something you just have to live with.

All the part-time clerks started as bundle boys. The best workers are now in the back room. Most part-timers in the back room have regular assignments. They do mostly the same thing every day. Like me, I'm the only part-timer who ever puts up displays. It's good to be in the back room because it's so informal. The boys I know best in the store are ones I know from playing sports before I came here or who used to live near me.

31. STORE 6 PGC CR11 MC2

Good thing about this job is that there's no interference from the bosses. They do not watch you, and you feel trusted. I like the way things are run. Everything is on a system.

I have only been up front three times since the store opened. It's a good thing, because I can't stand bundling.

It would be good to have a shelf of your own. I like putting up tonic and sugar or being in the back room. Being in the meat room would really be tremendous.

I like to move around in the back. It makes for variety.

32. STORE 6 PGC CR1 MC0

The trouble with this job is there's so many bosses, so many people telling you what to do. There's so much to do we can't get it done. You don't have anything to work to. You can't ever fill the counters 'cause we're so short handed. One full-timer and me working 20 hours used to do the frozen foods. Now they have "canned" the full-timer, and they gave me 23½ hours and things are supposed to be the same. Well, it doesn't work out that way. I never get to catch up.

The best time of the week is when I clean out the freezer. Nobody ever finds you in the freezer.

I don't think I am smart enough to cashier. If I had my choice,

I would like to stamp and cut in the back room.   Moving around is okay, but the customers get in your way.

33. STORE 6 PGC CR2 MC2

I love it here.   It's a clean job.   Other jobs I have been on, when you wear a white shirt, it gets dirty.   It's close to home, the hours are good, and it's easy work.
I guess I am sort of in charge of the bottle and cardboard room. I would rather be there than any place.   There's nobody watching over me, and since I am on my own I get a chance to straighten the place out and make it really look nice.   I am a senior in high school now and the youngest fellow in my class.   When I have to move around in back I like it 'cause I get to learn everything, but I would hate to have to go up front.

34. STORE 6 PGC CR7 MC3

The work here is not very interesting, but it's not very hard. They give you the breaks and they trust you.   You get a chance to meet people and to improve your work.   Lots of times, though, we wait around for work and then have to rush at the end of the night to get it done.
I like stocking shelves better than stamping.   It's better out on the aisles than in the back room.   I would like to be in charge of a couple of aisles, and I understand that pretty soon each kid will have an aisle of his own.
Whenever I have time I try to put boxes on the wagons and help the other kids out.

35. STORE 6 PGC CR3 MC0

They're good guys here; they'll stick up for you and lend you money if you need it.
I don't know why everyone says cardboard is the worst job. I guess it is the worst job because everybody says it's the worst job.   You're usually alone on it, but not always.
I bundled last night for the third time in six weeks.
I like the glass aisle the least.   They're hard to stack.   I don't like bagging because I don't know how to do it.   I always have a soft, round bag when I'm through, while those other guys have a straight, hard one.

Part Five

Leadership and Change

This final group of cases affords an opportunity for analyzing processes of leadership and change. In the first two, The Lightner Company and Cold-Air Corporation, technical changes are imposed upon work groups by staff specialists. The Tremont Hotel and Allmetal Steel Corporation cases involve discussions of needed, or suggested, changes involving higher levels in the organizations. In the Allmetal case, which concerns a sales organization, problems of formal leadership are not involved directly, although influence is an important element. In the other three cases, leader behavior is described and is a major element in the change processes.

The Lightner cases describe events within two different groups: the management group which plans and initiates the change and the worker group whose behavior is affected by the change. In addition, these cases report interactions between members of the two groups during the changes. Unplanned changes take place within each of the groups and in their relationships to each other, as an outcome of group, interpersonal, technical, and organizational factors. Another focus, sharpened by the change itself, is on the disintegration of group relationships and the rebuilding of group cohesion, cooperation, and productiveness. Within the history of changes, certain key events and crucial individual role performances stand out. The roles of formal and informal leaders, and the courses open to them, may be examined against the context of the change process.

453

Tony Mastico, a new foreman on a new assembly line, is the central person in the Cold-Air cases. Technical changes and problems beset him through the channels of interpersonal and group processes in a manner that makes it difficult for Tony and the reader to separate one kind of problem from another. Superimposed on this complex of problems are various attempts at getting and giving "help." The supervisory training session with which these cases end was supposedly designed to help resolve these problems. The content of the day's lesson in the course relates logically to the real events taking place in and around the group session. The lack of any valid connection between the two at the time leaves the participants, and the reader, wondering about the utility of conventional educational techniques for helping persons involved in change. The data in the case represent unanticipated consequences of a technical change, and pose some questions as to adequate methods for dealing with the social and interpersonal aspects of technical problems.

The use of a supposedly educational group discussion setting as a device for stimulating and implementing change is also involved in the Tremont Hotel case. In this situation, the principals, including outside professional consultants, are attempting to communicate with each other about solutions to communications problems existing outside the meeting. The problems about which they talk are vividly demonstrated as real within their discussion—questions of decision making, evaluation, influence, allowing people to make suggestions, and responding to suggestions. Both the roles of the consultants and the hotel staff's response to them are of interest. The paradox and challenge represented in the case is a universal one: if "communications" inside the meeting were effective, many of the external, organizational problems would not exist. How, then, can more communication solve communication problems? At what points in the discussion could suitable interventions on the part of the consultants or the other participants help the group deal more effectively with their problems "here and now" in the meeting, and thus contribute toward resolution of some of their "out-there" problems?

The final case, the Allmetal Steel Corporation, consists of a consultant's report on a sales group, including observations, analysis, and recommendations for change through the use of training programs. The diagnosis of the existing situation is of interest in itself, in light of the processes and problems involved in all of the previous cases. In addition, the analysis implies need for changes which may increase the effectiveness of the sales group and the organization. Using the previous two cases, Cold-Air and Tremont Hotel, as illustrations, the reader is in a position to evaluate the consultants' training recommendations, and to suggest modifications and additions.

In all of these cases, leaders at various levels are caught in situations where they are supposed to be agents of change, but at the same time must change their own behavior in significant ways in order to effect the change. Changes in technology and organizational procedures are seen here as deceptively simple, but superficial, approaches to increasing work effectiveness. At the same time, educational programs and pseudodemocratic discussion methods tend to be ineffective when used at the service of the existing sets of social and interpersonal relations. The entry point into these self-reinforcing cycles is difficult to locate: where does one start to effect successful programs of change? Concrete action ultimately is taken by the individual, not by the abstract "group" or "organization." The object of change is the behavior of individuals. It would appear that the most promising steps toward increased individual, group, and organizational competence involve processes of personal and interpersonal inquiry, experimentation, evaluation, and self-directed change. In these cases relevant questions are raised by certain persons at certain times. Many of the following events feature defensive avoidances of inquiry. It is at these key points that the student can analyze how alternative responses on the part of certain individuals could have led to more effective consequences.

The Lightner Company (A)

T HE Albany plant was one of seven large manufacturing units in the Lightner Company. During the fall and winter of 1953–1954, Herbert Lockwood, a case writer from Northwestern University, made an intensive study of a small work group on blower 16 in the core room of the Albany plant. This is a distillation of his observations, impressions, and interviews with supervisors, staff personnel, and workers, all of whom were involved in one way or another with blower 16.

THE FOUNDRY DIVISION

The Albany plant produced machine parts and grey iron castings for gasoline and diesel engines. The largest division in the plant was the foundry, where some 900 workers and supervisors were employed in manufacturing grey iron castings for large commercial power units.[1] The foundry division consisted of several departments, each representing a major work operation in the sequence of production.

The initial operation in the manufacture of castings was in the core room of the foundry. There workers rammed specially prepared sand into core boxes, either by hand or with the use of large machines which were referred to as blowers. After the sand cores were formed and removed from the boxes, they underwent a baking and dipping process which hardened and prepared them for the molding department.

In the molding department the cores were encased in steel forms, additional sand was packed around them, and molten iron was poured around the cores to produce the many varieties of castings. Following a cooling and "shake out" process, the rough castings were transported on a large conveyor to the chipping and finishing department. There, workers using heavy grinders and air-powered chipping hammers cut the excessive fins from the casting and then smoothed all rough edges

[1] See Exhibit 1, page 458, for an organizational chart for the Albany plant.

with circular grinding disks. In the final stage of manufacture, the castings were carefully inspected for flaws, given a coat of paint, and marked for shipment to other Lightner Company plants for use in the assembly of gasoline and diesel engines. The sequence of manufacture in the foundry division can be outlined as follows:

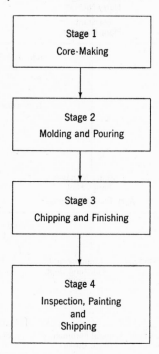

The Core Room and Blower 16

The core room where the sand cores were produced was divided into several small work sections: core-making, baking and dipping, and finishing and inspecting. The work was done in two- or four-man operations. Work on smaller machines and at hand packing tables was performed by one or two workers; the larger blower machines required groups of three or four men who shared equally in the piecework rate prices. The core room covered an area approximately the size of a city block and employed 150 workers and supervisors. Management personnel included a superintendent, an assistant superintendent, three general foremen, and nine foremen (Exhibit 1).

Blower 16 was one of the largest core-making machines in the department. It was vital in the work flow of engine blocks from the

EXHIBIT 1

THE LIGHTNER COMPANY

Albany Plant (Partial Organization Chart as of August 1, 1953)

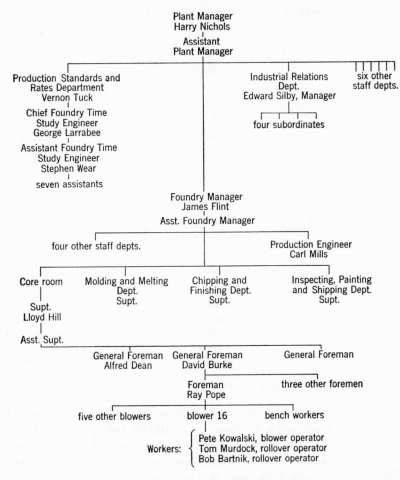

core room to the molding department. The work operations on the unit were as follows: three workers, a blower operator, and two rollover operators performed their jobs outside of a large circular conveyor system referred to as a "merry-go-round."[2] A dozen large core boxes on casters revolved around the "merry-go-round" to the blower and rollover machines. The 12 core boxes were pushed

[2] See Exhibit 2 for a diagram of the layout of blower 16 and auxiliary equipment.

EXHIBIT 2

THE LIGHTNER COMPANY

Blower 16

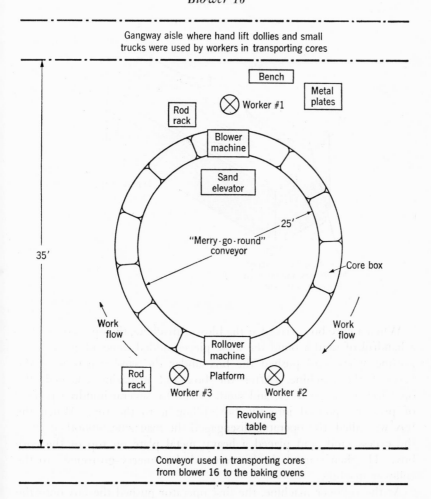

Gangway aisle where hand lift dollies and small
trucks were used by workers in transporting cores

Conveyor used in transporting cores
from blower 16 to the baking ovens

around the "merry-go-round" by the crew.   Each core box contained
a number of small metal loose pieces and rods which served to shape
the core while it was in the box and to support it after it had been
removed from the box.[3]   Rollover operators removed and cleaned
the loose pieces and inserted new rods.

[3] See Exhibit 3 for a diagram of a core box.

EXHIBIT 3

THE LIGHTNER COMPANY

Core Box

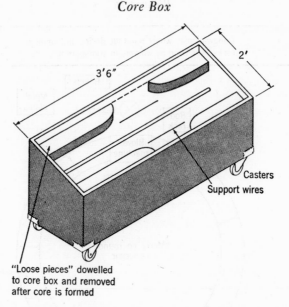

Casters

Support wires

"Loose pieces" dowelled
to core box and removed
after core is formed

When a core box arrived at the blower machine, the operator packed a handful of sand around the loose pieces, added some additional supporting wires, and pushed the box under the sand magazine at the base of the machine. After the box and magazine engaged, the operator pressed a lever, and sand, driven by several hundred pounds of pressure, poured into the box, filling it to the top. When the box was filled, the operator disengaged the magazine, smoothed away the excess sand, and placed a heavy metal plate on top of the core box. He then started the box around the "merry-go-round" to the rollover machine.

At the rollover machine, the first operator pushed the box onto the machine and clamped it into place. Then the second operator engaged a number of levers on the machine and the core box rotated upward and swung over, dropping gently in an inverted position onto the machine platform. The next operation consisted of drawing (removing) the core from the box. The two operators worked together in freeing the core using an air vibrator and a wooden mallet. One worker operated the air vibrator while the other struck the corners of the box with the mallet to shake the core loose.

When the core was freed, it was placed on the small revolving take-off table until the core box, which was still in an inverted position, could be swung back to its original position and engaged once again on the "merry-go-round" conveyor. After this operation was completed, both rollover operators worked together removing the loose metal pieces from around the sand core. These metal pieces, as well as the core box, had to be cleaned of all adhering sand before they could be used again. As the process of drawing cores continued, those cores previously placed on the take-off table were transferred to the conveyor rack. The job of lifting a core from the machine platform to the take-off table, rotating the box back on the "merry-go-round," then taking the cores from the take-off table to the conveyor required several work motions for the two operators. Although several of these motions were involved in placing cores on and lifting them off the small take-off table, the crew believed that the table was helpful since it revolved 180 degrees from side to side and enabled the operators to take turns carrying the heavy end of the core to the conveyor.

A complete cycle for the single core box on the rollover machine could be accomplished in less than a minute with coordinated team effort. The entire work operation on the blower unit was continuous. The moment a core box came around from the blower, it was pushed onto the rollover machine and the core was drawn. The moment the core was out of the box and placed on the small work table, the rollover machine was rotated back to its original position and another box was made ready. When the rollover workers finished cleaning and replacing the loose metal pieces in the passing core boxes, they worked together pushing the boxes around to the blower operator's position. Thus, the boxes moved continuously around the "merry-go-round" from blower to rollover machine and back again. Exact timing and teamwork were essential features for smooth operations. An operator could perform a job on the blower in a matter of minutes, but it took several days and even weeks to get a crew working efficiently together. Both workers and supervisors agreed that a good crew member was not produced overnight.

BACKGROUND FOR CHANGES ON NUMBER 16

A major cost reduction program was started throughout the Lightner organization early in 1951. Top management designed this program to bring unit prices into line with those of competitors through (1) modernization of equipment and production methods and (2) adjustment of piecework rates and standards on jobs where improvements had been made.

Prior to the introduction of the cost reduction program, certain members of the staff at the Albany plant believed that more accurate and factual time standards and rates were the solution to the problem. George Larrabee, head time-study engineer for the foundry division, often told production supervisors that "the foundry division is behind in setting accurate and factual standards. The sooner we all get behind the new time-study program, the better our cost picture will be." In 1951, the rates department in the foundry division was enlarged, and Mr. Larrabee was placed in charge, with seven subordinates to carry out, as part of the new cost reduction program, the policy of setting more factual and accurate standards and rates.

The production supervisors in all departments of the foundry agreed that changes needed to be made to improve output and that accurate standards were necessary to insure, as James Flint, foundry manager, put it, "a full day's work for a full day's pay." But, as Lloyd Hill pointed out to Mr. Flint and Mr. Larrabee on several occasions, "We need to move with care and make sure that the new rates and standards are correctly determined, or else those of us in line supervision may have trouble enforcing them."

Against this background, major technical changes in production on blower 16 were proposed. Around the middle of August, 1953, the slack production period for the foundry, Mr. Flint called a meeting in his office to discuss the final plans for the proposed changes on 16. Prior to this meeting, both Mr. Hill and Carl Mills had discussed the changes with Mr. Hill's general foremen, David Burke, and Ray Pope, foreman of blower 16. Both of these men had been active in planning the project and had expressed the opinion that the changes would improve production considerably. Also, Mr. Hill and his supervisors had talked with Mr. Larrabee, and the latter had commented that when improvements were carried out on blower 16, it would be possible to set new and, as he put it, "more accurate and factual time standards."

At the beginning of this meeting, Mr. Flint said that he hoped that the final decision for implementing the changes on 16 could be made. He then called on Mr. Mills to outline the manufacturing changes once again to the other men present, Lloyd Hill and George Larrabee. As Mr. Mills spoke, he pointed out several reasons why he believed the changes would improve production substantially on blower 16.

MR. MILLS: Since we have previously talked over this matter together, I'm just going to summarize our plans now. We've all agreed that moving the blower nearer the rollover machine and installing an automatic rollover machine in place of the old Johnson-Smith we now have in there will improve output significantly. Besides installing the fully automatic rollover machine and moving the blower around to the other side, we plan to tear down the old sand elevator which now supplies the blower with sand, and replace that unit with an air-pressured sand delivery system much like those we've installed on some of the smaller blowers. Also, as Jim and Lloyd have pointed out, moving the blower machine away from the gangway side of the department will give us the space we need for the lift trucks. Everyone knows that those lift trucks have been a traffic problem in the department for some time. To give everyone a full picture of the proposed changes, I've sketched them on the blackboard here.[4]

(He turned the blackboard around.)

From the above diagram we can all see that the men will now work much closer together and will be able to coordinate their activities better. The blower machine will be moved around next to the rollover machine and that will place the blower operator much nearer the rollover operators. Each man will be able to see what the others are doing, and they'll be able to help each other with the work a lot more. Also, by moving the blower to this new position we no longer break the flow of core boxes around the "merry-go-round." The boxes can now move around as a unit from the rollover machine to the blower.

Also, the moment a core box is filled with sand, it will move directly onto the new automatic rollover without any delay. Furthermore, the new rollover does not require any clamping at all—it's fully automatic. All the operators have to do is place the box on the machine arm, step back, and push a button, and the machine will swing the core boxes over and place them on the platform for the drawing. The safety guard which will be installed with the new rollover will prevent accidents; the new machine will be much safer than the old one. And, as Lloyd Hill has pointed out, placing the rollover and blower machines closer together will greatly facilitate core-making and the reworking of scrap cores. Core boxes can now be pushed back and forth between the rollover and blower machines. Before, the workers had to remove all the boxes from the "merry-go-round" before the odd cores could be done. That's a major improvement in itself.

[4] See Exhibit 4 for a copy of the diagram sketched by Mr. Mills.

EXHIBIT 4

THE LIGHTNER COMPANY

Proposed Changes on Blower 16

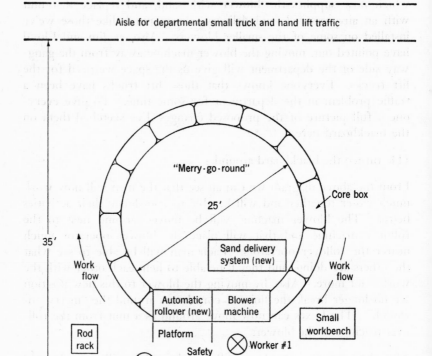

MR. HILL: That's a big difference, Carl.

MR. MILLS: I don't mind telling you that I'm quite excited about the new rollover machine. It's costing a pretty penny, but you'll see what a difference it will make. Also, note that the moment the core is disengaged from the box it can be carried immediately to the racks by the two operators. We no longer need to place cores on

the little revolving take-off table. That entire sequence of work
has been eliminated. The workers can rotate the rollover machine
arm back onto the "merry-go-round" before they move the core
from the platform. Then, all they have to do is remove the loose
metal pieces from around the core, place them back in the box, and
then carry the finished product to the conveyor unit behind them.
The lifting and handling of each core two or three times will no
longer create a bottleneck. And, as I said, the new safety guard
around the machine makes the unit completely safe to operate.
There's no danger now that the rollover arm might swing around
and club one of the workers on the head. (Pause) Well, Jim, all I
can add is that we're ready to go. The new rollover is here and
my men are eager to move as soon as Lloyd Hill says he's ready.
The changeover will take about a week and can best be done during
the coming shutdown.

MR. HILL: Carl, as I've told you before, the changes look very good.
I think you've done an excellent job in layout. I think we are
ready to move.

MR. FLINT: Good, that's why I wanted all of us to get together this
time. The changes will be carried out during the vacation shutdown
period this month.

MR. LARRABEE: Naturally, with these major technical changes, the jobs
on the blower will have to be completely retimed, as provided for
under the contract. That means new standards and new prices
for the jobs.

MR. FLINT: Of course. With these new changes there should be
considerable improvement in production and at less cost per unit.
That's what we are shooting for.

MR. HILL: Production has been pretty high on number 16, but the
cost of producing cores has also been high.

MR. LARRABEE: That's why these changes in production and new
standards will help. As we all know, the rates have been very
loose. We must have more accurate standards to insure that the
workers turn in a full day's work on the job. That's one of the
major reasons why cost is out of line—jobs have not been accurately
time studied in the past. However, when we get these changes in
production methods and work operations, more factual studies can be
made. We'll slowly eliminate this running away with the rates.

MR. FLINT: Of course, we have been trying to improve this situation
by slowly making rate changes and production improvements.

MR. HILL: I think it's important that we look at this situation from
several angles, since we have been encountering resistance from the

workers with these new times studies. I'd like to see the changes and the new rates on 16 move along smoothly. I want to make sure that the rates we set on number 16 are rates my foremen can stand behind. That hasn't always been true in the past, George.

MR. LARRABEE: Lloyd, both you and I know that when new equipment is introduced and improved production layouts are made, we can expect more of the workers. They can produce more because they have improved work methods and equipment. It's just like buying a new car; you expect more from the new one than from the old one which you traded in.

MR. HILL: I just don't want to get caught in a situation where we have to accept and stand behind something that we aren't sure is right. Ever since these more factual time studies started about two years ago, my foremen have complained many times to me that the studies are taken under ideal conditions and that no real working situation ever approaches them. I've told Jim here and I've told you on several occasions, George, that these time studies are basically theoretical. Sometimes, I don't think some of the guys you send down to clock these jobs really know the actual work that is involved in performing the jobs. We all know that the work in this foundry is essentially human variable time—that is, determined by the worker—and not machine consistent time—that is, controlled by machines.

MR. LARRABEE: We've been over all this before, Lloyd. We'll get accurate and fair standards. I've worked out a method for timing 16 that is perfect. I intend to time every work motion that is involved in making each core. In that way, my department will give you exact and tight standards and rates. These will be rates that the workers won't run away with as they have done in the past.

MR. HILL: I don't think anyone in the front office can say that we don't do an honest day's work here in the foundry. As I was saying, if some of your time-study engineers would lift one of those cores and see the effort it takes to make cores all day long, then they might allow something for human fatigue. I don't want a study made after these changes go in and then discover that we have got to make another study. That's been the case in many departments here in the foundry, and it hasn't helped morale one bit. As I've told you before, often you set standards so high that a worker just can never make them. You take that job on the grinder unit in my department. I've had some thirty men on that job in the past year, and only two workers have even come close to the standards you set. Many of my foremen say that the study did not include many important factors. I just wonder if your studies include factors in a normal day's work like patching a core, for instance. That's part of the job, and time should be allowed for such contingencies.

MR. LARRABEE: We will give that job a thorough check the moment the work operations are set up and are operating smoothly. It's up to line supervisors to see that the most efficient work methods are used.

MR. HILL: Yes, but remember, you fellows set standards; we in supervision have to enforce them. There's a difference.

MR. LARRABEE: Don't worry. We'll work this out to everyone's satisfaction.

MR. FLINT: I'm relying on all of you to work together in getting the operations changed.

MR. LARRABEE: And another thing, Lloyd, about the fatigue factor you mentioned. A worker gets in condition over months of work. We wouldn't expect a new man to make the standards at once. He needs to develop the necessary skills and muscles first. Since many standards in the past have been too low, we are setting them up sufficiently so that a worker will have to put out over a day to make the rate. For instance, a worker at about seven in the morning should work at approximately 120 per cent efficiency and hit a peak around nine o'clock. By late afternoon, just before quitting time, this same worker is probably working at about 80 per cent efficiency. Thus, when the two extremes are averaged out, he'll be working at 100 per cent efficiency for the day, that is, provided he is putting out normal effort.

MR. HILL: Yeah, I suppose so, but that "normal effort" concept is a difficult thing to get across to the workers at times. It's been constantly changing in the last couple of years with this drive on setting tighter standards.

MR. FLINT: There is some evidence that you can only go so far with setting tighter rates.

MR. LARRABEE: Of course, you'll receive certain complaints and gripes. That's what the canvassing is for. If the worker doesn't like the job and doesn't want to work, he can transfer.

MR. HILL: Some of these rates have been so difficult for the workers to make that we've had slowdowns. You know yourself of several such situations right here in the foundry. After new rates were set in the departments a couple of months ago, the workers started putting out less than they did before. I don't see how these new standards help when things like that happen.

MR. LARRABEE: We are a service department and we are here to help you. The company wants accurate standards and we are doing our best to provide them.

MR. HILL: We all want accurate standards, but we must also remember that an estimate of workers' efficiency on the job is a subjective judgment, and what you say is normal effort, my foremen have said is far above normal.

MR. FLINT: Well, I guess we are agreed. These differences will be ironed out as we move along with the changes and set new rates on blower 16. I'm asking Mills to go ahead with the production changes. Immediately after they are installed and the work methods are established, George Larrabee and his men will time the jobs. This should help us considerably to improve production and cost on blower 16.

The afternoon following the meeting in Mr. Flint's office, Lloyd Hill told David Burke and Ray Pope that the decision had been made to begin the technical changes on the work unit the following Monday morning. Both supervisors talked about the improvements and expressed the opinion that accurate and factual standards and rates must be set on the operation in order to insure success. "But, we've had changes before," Mr. Burke said, "and when the time-study engineers set new rates on the job, then we start having trouble with the workers." Mr. Pope nodded in agreement.

Later, when Mr. Pope explained the proposed changes to the crew on 16, Pete Kowalski, the operator, made the following comments:

MR. KOWALSKI: Yeh, well, how come? We get the work out without any trouble now, don't we? The price is right as it stands.

MR. POPE: The new changes will help you get the work done better. When they're made, the job goes on no price[5] until the new production standards are set.

MR. KOWALSKI: In the past, changing things around has meant a cut in price. Is that going to happen on this job?

MR. POPE: That's for the time-study engineers to decide when they time the job.

TOM MURDOCK (the rollover operator): I told you, Pete, that if we made too much money, they'd cut the rate out here.

MR. KOWALSKI: Shut up. (Turning back to Mr. Pope) I don't like it.

[5] The period between the cancellation of an old rate and the setting of a new one was referred to as a "no price" condition. Under the contract provisions, during this period workers were paid a flat hourly rate based on their occupational classification.

The Lightner Company (B)

I_N August 1953, management at the Lightner Company proposed major changes in equipment and work methods on blower 16, a three-man core-making operation in the core room of the foundry division of its Albany plant.[1]

The technical changes for blower 16 were designed by the chief production engineer, Carl Mills. Mr. Mills said that the changes "will improve efficiency and output significantly and, at the same time, raise the quality of the cores and eliminate excessive work motion for the crew."

When the technical changes were in the planning stage, Pete Kowalski, blower operator, and Bob Bartnik and Tom Murdock, rollover operators, made up the day crew on the machine.[2] These men had nearly 10 years' experience in the foundry division, most of which had been acquired in working on blower machines in the core room. Mr. Kowalski was the senior operator on the crew and had broken in both Mr. Bartnik and Mr. Murdock on the machines. The crew worked as a team, frequently helping each other in their work. Management regarded the crew's output as "good," but believed that with improved methods and new machines a considerable increase in production was possible. George Larrabee, head of the foundry rates department, believed that previous production standards on the job were "too loose" and that the changes in equipment and production methods and new time standards would result in greater output at a lower cost per unit.

Ray Pope, the foreman of blower 16, explained the situation to the crew and described the technical changes to be made. Mr. Kowalski had replied that "he didn't like the idea" because, as he put it, "every time they make changes on jobs here, down go the rates." Mr. Pope

---

[1] See the Lightner Company (A), p. 456, for additional details pertaining to this case.

[2] Consult Exhibit 1 in case (A), p. 458, for an organizational chart.

told the men to wait and see what happened.   After he left the work area that day, Mr. Kowalski talked to his coworkers.

MR. KOWALSKI: They've done this before on other jobs, and you guys know what has happened.   Every time they get a notion to change equipment around, they come in here and retime the job and lower the price.

MR. MURDOCK: I told you, Pete, if you got careless and started turning in too much money, something would happen.   About three years ago I used to average about $120 a week.   That wasn't too bad. Now with these new tight standards, we've got to watch out. Men like Nat Clark have ruined the jobs for everyone else.   He just ran away with the rate, and after they came out here and retimed his job, it wasn't worth anything to anyone.

MR. BARTNIK: That's just about it.

MR. KOWALSKI: You guys can take it lying down if you want to, but I'm not going to.   If they cut the price, I'm getting off.

MR. MURDOCK: There was a time when the company used to care about us—that was before all these smart time-study men came in and changed everything around.   A man's got to have a little free time to rest now and then.   We can push hard in the morning —both of you know that—but in the afternoon we've got to have a little time to coast.   That doesn't mean we hit the showers a half hour early like some of these guys do around here, but it does mean we have to have some free time.

MR. BARTNIK: That's what happens these days.   You give the best years of your life to the company and when you aren't good enough to keep up the pace, you get a job sweeping the floors.   That's no way to treat us.   Leo Hansen over there worked for years on the bench making cores.   Now he's old and can't keep up on these new time studied jobs, so what happens?   They give him a broom and give the job to a younger guy.   The days when we had a little free time are gone.   Now, they're out to cut the rates.   Just you wait and see.

MR. KOWALSKI: Some of the foremen around here say we brought the whole thing on ourselves.   Remember the time when we used to help Bill, our old foreman, make out the time cards?   We never had much trouble then and no grievances to worry about.   Then we all made about the same money and got along without any trouble.   Bill saw to it that things were fair and right for us.   But some men got greedy and started turning in too much, and so we got this new time-study stuff.

MR. MURDOCK: Well, we're off for a couple of weeks. Let's worry about things when we come back.

During the shutdown, the last two weeks of August, the technical changes were completed on blower 16. When the crew returned to work, the rates on their jobs had been cancelled, as specified under the contract with the union, and line supervisors awaited a new time study and new piecework prices. During this interim period, Mr. Pope worked closely with the crew, as did David Burke, the general foreman, helping them get acquainted with the new work methods and showing them the best ways to operate the new automatic rollover machine. The men seemed quite cooperative and, although production fell considerably, Mr. Pope believed that unfamiliarity with the equipment and the "no price" status of the work accounted for the difference in previous output. He felt sure that when the new piece rates were established, production would improve significantly. However, Lloyd Hill, superintendent of the core room, received complaints from other department heads about the fewer number of cores coming from blower 16. Both Mr. Pope and Mr. Burke had been told by Mr. Hill to keep up as much production as possible during the breaking in and "no price" period on blower 16.

At the end of the third week in September, Mr. Larrabee and his time-study engineers had finished the new time studies on blower 16 and had calculated the rates. As the time study for each of the four types of cores manufactured on blower 16 was finished, Mr. Larrabee submitted the results to Mr. Hill and Mr. Burke for their approval. When Mr. Burke received the new price on the job, he took the figures to the foreman, Mr. Pope. Mr. Pope, in turn, informed the crew members of the results of the time study. Mr. Kowalski reacted for the whole group.

MR. KOWALSKI: They've cut the price. We can't make those standards.
MR. POPE: That's the story that Dave Burke gave me. The time study says that with the new equipment and improved work methods, you fellows can turn out more cores.
MR. KOWALSKI: What's the deal, anyway? You come in here and change a few things around and then cut the price.
MR. POPE: Why don't you give the job a try? With the new automatic rollover, you'll probably do all right. Besides, the good old days aren't here anymore.

For the next few weeks, the crew on number 16 worked under the new price rate but complained frequently to Mr. Pope that they "couldn't make the rate because the prices weren't right." He listened to them but insisted that they should make the attempt. During this same period, he spoke to Mr. Burke about the situation.

MR. POPE: Dave, I'm glad you came by. I want to talk to you about the situation on number 16.

MR. BURKE: What's the trouble?

MR. POPE: It's pretty much the same story we've had before on other jobs. The workers aren't trying on number 16. They're just lying down on the job because they say that the rate is too steep and they can't make out. Also, ever since the new automatic rollover machine has been in, it hasn't worked properly. The men say that the old hand-clamp machine was better, and they're complaining, too, because the table next to the rollover machine has been taken away. I've explained to them why these changes were made and the improvement they will make in the work, but, frankly, production has fallen something awful. I'm getting about half the work I formerly got out of the men.

MR. BURKE: I'll get the engineers over to look at the job. I'll also talk with Lloyd Hill and George Larrabee about the situation. Frankly, I felt a little uneasy when I signed the time studies because I didn't believe those guys in rates allowed enough time for the operation. You know Larrabee, he's always trying to take a study under ideal conditions and setting a tight standard.

MR. POPE: It's not easy to enforce a rate you don't personally believe is right. Ever since these factual time studies started, I've had no end of trouble with the workers. I don't think the study allowed for ordinary difficulties like shaking out loose pieces, adjusting an air hose, or cleaning out when sand gets stuck in the grooves of the core boxes.

MR. BURKE: I know what you mean. When the foreman and time study engineers used to look at a job together, we didn't have these troubles. Now, the rates department does everything.

On several occasions Mr. Burke talked to Mr. Hill about blower 16 and the problem of the rates. Mr. Hill decided to wait to see if there was any improvement in the situation. As the weeks passed, however, output continued to fall on blower 16. An extra night shift had to be put on the job. Production got so far behind that an additional blower had to be retooled and jobs which were normally produced by 16 were transferred to it. On a few occasions, workers in the molding and melting departments were sent home because there were not enough cores from blower 16 for them to cast.

Several meetings were held in Mr. Hill's office to discuss the problem on blower 16. Mr. Hill told Mr. Larrabee about the situation and said that the rates evidently had not been set properly. Mr. Larrabee answered that a careful study had been made and that the rates were correct. He added that it was up to Mr. Hill and his supervisors to see that the workers made the standards. Mr. Hill went to Jim Flint and described conditions on blower 16. Mr. Flint agreed that something had to be done. They wrote a letter to the plant manager explaining the situation and waited for a reply.

In the meantime, the automatic rollover machine was examined, and certain changes were made to make it function better. But production did not improve, and the crew continued to complain to Mr. Pope and Mr. Burke. On the second Monday in October, Mr. Hill suggested to Mr. Larrabee that they call the workers into his office to discuss the situation. Mr. Larrabee was agreeable but added that the chief difficulty lay not in the standards, which he insisted had been accurately set, but in the workers' refusal to do what was expected of them. He added, "It's your job in supervision to see that the work is done properly." Mr. Hill told him that perhaps the meeting might bring out the real cause of the trouble. On the next day, a meeting was held in Mr. Hill's office. In addition to the workers— Pete Kowalski, Bob Bartnik, and Tom Murdock—Dave Burke, George Larrabee, and his assistant, Stephen Wear, were also present. Mr. Hill opened the meeting.

MR. HILL: Men, I've called you in because of the problem we're having on this operation. We in supervision believe that you men are not putting forth normal effort in performing your job. This is clearly indicated by the number of cores that are being produced and by the observations of my supervisors. Even though new equipment has been installed, and improved work methods are being used, production has dropped to about 25 rounds a day. Before, a normal output was around 35 and 40.[3] I've called in the rates department to discuss the new standard with you. We want to get to the bottom of this. I want you men to feel free to say what's on your mind or to make any suggestions about how to improve conditions on the machine.

MR. KOWALSKI: I am doing the best job I can. At least I am working on the job. Ray Pope and Dave Burke say the new rollover machine is faster, but I don't think so. We've had no end of trouble with the machine. The old machine was a lot better. Also, we work so close together, we get in each other's way now.

[3] A completed round referred to the making of 12 cores.

MR. BARTNIK: It's harder to push the boxes around the "merry-go-round."

MR. LARRABEE: But that can't be true. Before, the motion was split in half because of the location of the blower. Now the work flow is uninterrupted from rollover to blower. It's much easier than before.

MR. MURDOCK: You can't make any money.

MR. KOWALSKI: If we get together and work hard to get cores out, what happens? You come out there, and whack goes the price. You are always whacking the price the first chance you get.

MR. LARRABEE: If you mean that we want a full day's work out of you instead of your going to the showers a half hour early, then, yes, we have to "whack the price." The prices now are accurately and factually set. The time studies are right here to prove it, too.

MR. KOWALSKI: I tried to swap jobs with another guy. I wanted off the blower. But when he found out he would have to work on number 16, he didn't want any part of it.

MR. HILL: What's the trouble, men?

MR. MURDOCK: You can't make any money anymore.

MR. LARRABEE: That's just not true. Putting out normal effort, you men can make a fair rate for a fair day's pay. All this reminds me of another situation—an office manager who brought his girls some new electric typewriters. All the girls were very pleased. On the old machines the girls could type only about four or five letters in two hours. When they got the new machines, the office manager told them they would have to produce 10 to 12 letters in that time. He pointed out to them that they could do it with the new equipment. Well, naturally, the girls griped and stewed about the change. But, remember, the company had invested money in new equipment just as we have on blower 16. He wanted some improvement in efficiency just as we do on the blower. Well, to end my story, I recall that the girls eventually started putting out nearly 20 letters in two hours instead of the estimated 12. The same thing applies to your work. We have tried to help you men. But you must help us now instead of laying down on the job.

MR. KOWALSKI: I do my work. Nobody can say I don't.

MR. HILL: Yes. How have the machines been running lately, Dave?

MR. BURKE: Well, there has been some trouble with the automatic rollover machine. It just doesn't seem to want to work right. Most of the changes, however, are very good. The men have to walk less and everything is conveniently located. I think in a little more time we'll get things moving. Ray Pope and I have been working closely with the crew. Isn't that right, men?

MR. BARTNIK: We can't make out. You come out there and change everything around and then cut the rate. There was a time when the job was set up where we could really push and make some money. We can't make anything anymore. If we did, you'd come out there and cut the rate again. Besides, like I told Pete, my back is hurting me more than usual. I'm thinking about transferring, too.

MR. MURDOCK: When the blower was across the way from the rollover, it was better. We haven't any room to work down there anymore.

MR. BURKE: But, Murdock, we've all explained just exactly why the changes were made and the improvements they've made over the old system.

MR. KOWALSKI: We aren't some sort of machine to be changed about.

MR. LARRABEE: I'm glad you brought up that point. No, you're wrong. When everything is properly worked out, the human being is a perfectly timed instrument.

MR. HILL: Well, men. I want to thank you for coming in and telling us straight from the shoulder how you feel. About the price—I think you men can make what you would like if you'll put out good normal effort. If it is not possible then for you to make fair earnings, we'll look into the situation and see what is actually wrong with the price per hundred pieces, that is, if anything. We want your cooperation. Can I count on that?

WORKERS: We'll give it another try.

MR. HILL: That's fair enough. Well, I guess that's that unless someone else has something to say.

After the supervisors and workers had left the office, Mr. Hill asked Mr. Larrabee to remain. The two discussed the results of the meeting.

MR. HILL: What do you think?

MR. LARRABEE: The days of getting something for nothing are gone. We are going to get results, I know. No more of this working hard in the morning and then coasting all afternoon. There's nothing wrong with the rates. You noticed that they gave no valid reasons against the rates. Of course, they are a little sore because we are expecting more of them than before. But with the work changes and the new equipment, that's only fair. They'll see that in time.

MR. HILL: I've said several times that the time studies do not sufficiently consider human variable time in the operation. The fatigue element has got to be considered. Unless we get to the bottom of this situation pretty soon, we'll have to take further action.

MR. LARRABEE: Don't take this too seriously. Remember, I've had considerable foundry experience. When I first came out here, things were pretty disorganized. No one was too interested then in setting factual rates. I can tell you about one job after another where setting accurate rates has resulted in improved production and reduction in cost. Workers don't have the proper attitude. They're a little sloppy and get the idea that they own everything. They become loafers unless you watch them. Oh, I know, they've threatened to meet me outside the gate, but don't worry about that. It won't happen.

MR. HILL: I can cite just as many examples where these new rates have caused more trouble than improvement. There's a limit to how far you can go. Before these new time studies, perhaps we didn't have the most accurate rates, but at least we got production out and with a lot less scrap. In those days, the time-study engineers and foremen used to look over the job together, talk to the worker about some of the problems, and then work together in setting up a standard. But I'm getting all sorts of problems now. We are getting more scrap, less production, and the men are slowing down on the job. It's practically impossible to get their cooperation. Maybe on your paper it looks good, perhaps it looks like we're saving money, but a close examination of the many hidden costs, like our having to put on extra shifts and retool other blowers, might tell a quite different story. We've got a real problem down there in the core department. It's time someone realized that.

MR. LARRABEE: The problem isn't in the rates. There's no problem with my department.

In the week that followed the meeting in Mr. Hill's office, the crew encountered one problem after another with the new automatic roll-over machine. The maintenance department and the production engineers were called into the situation. In spite of their efforts, the machine did not function properly. Finally, Mr. Hill, having listened to complaints about the machine from the crew and foremen alike, ordered Carl Mills to take it out. Two days later, the automatic rollover machine was carted to the basement and an older hand-clamping rollover machine, much like the original Johnson-Smith, was installed. Mr. Mills told Mr. Hill at the time of this change, "I'm sorry this had to happen. Sure, the workers had problems with the automatic machine, but much of that is to be expected with new equipment until it is given a fair try." Mr. Hill explained that under the circumstances he couldn't wait any longer. He told Mr. Mills that other departments were on his neck, since they were being forced to send some workers home because of the poor output on blower 16. "I had to do something. That automatic job looked awfully good on paper, but when it came right down to it, we just couldn't get work out on it."

With the installation of the hand-clamping rollover machine, an extra man joined the crew to work inside the "merry-go-round." His job consisted of clamping the core boxes on the rollover machine, cleaning and inserting rods and loose pieces, and assisting the rollover operators in pushing the box around the "merry-go-round." He became known as the rod man. Mr. Pope assigned Kenneth Hart, a new worker in the department, to perform this job. He also told Mr. Hart to help Mr. Bartnik and Mr. Murdock clean the loose pieces and push the boxes around the conveyor to the blower. When the new man was assigned to the job, the recently established piecework rates were cancelled and the operation was again classified as "no price" until a new study could be taken.

Mr. Hill told Mr. Larrabee that he would like the jobs on number 16 retimed as soon as possible. He pointed out that the molding department was putting pressure on him to get engine cores out: "I can't do anything, until I get a decent rate down there for those men." Both David Burke and Ray Pope believed that with the removal of the automatic rollover machine, production on 16 would improve. Mr. Pope told the case writer, however, that:

MR. POPE: With all these changes it's not easy to get the fellows to work like they used to. There was a time when you could ask the cooperation of your men and get it, but now these fellows have been burned so many times by these rates that they just won't try to cooperate. Take the trouble we had with that automatic rollover machine. In came the maintenance people, the production engineers, the time-study engineers—everybody. Why, at one time, I counted 12 people standing around that machine scratching their heads and trying to figure out what to do next. They tried one thing after another, but nothing seemed to work. Everybody got excited and jumped to one conclusion after another. With all that commotion nobody could work. After nearly five hours those mechanics and engineers finally left with orders for the crew to keep trying. After things calmed down a little, the crew began to put out a little more production, but not enough. They've got to do more, because we are falling farther behind every day.

In the first week in November, a work canvass was taken in the core room. All four workers on blower 16 asked for transfers; two of the men specifically stated that they wanted daywork instead of piecework jobs. Since most of them had sufficient seniority and work experience, they were qualified and entitled under the union contract to other jobs whenever such positions became available. All four men received transfers effective that Friday. Mr. Burke canvassed the remained of the department for replacements for blower 16. All qualified workers refused the openings. At quitting time that evening, Mr. Burke dropped by Mr. Hill's office and described the situation on number 16.

MR. BURKE: I don't know what ought to be done with number 16. Call men back from layoff, I guess. Whenever I think about how little work those men put out and how they laid down on the job, I could swear. They just didn't try. If that happens with the next crew that we get in there, we ought to step in and take disciplinary action.

MR. HILL: I went up to Jim Flint's office just a week ago and we talked about this situation. We both wrote a letter to Henry Nichols and signed it. Both of us said in the letter that if the standards on 16 are accurate and if the rate department will stand behind them, we here in the foundry are ready to take disciplinary action to enforce them. But you know what happened with that. The production rates department refused to take a position; they wouldn't tell us definitely whether the rates were all perfectly accurate. Sometimes, I think we should put a foreman down there over the unit and whenever a worker lays down on the job, reprimand him right then and there.

MR. BURKE: But the trouble is, it's hard to prove whether a man is laying down or not. We'll have the union all over us if we try.

MR. HILL: I know. I frankly think human variable time hasn't been sufficiently considered in setting these new production standards on number 16. That's why George Larrabee and Vernon Tuck won't take a positive position. But we've got to know what is a fair day's work. I believe that eventually we'll get uniform standard data for the whole foundry and we'll lick this problem. But until then, I'm not sure what can be done. I agree with the production rates engineers that we've got to have efficiency, but how can we get efficiency when we have all of these production problems?

MR. BURKE: Three of the men who are leaving are good men. They have nearly 10 years' experience on blowers. Oh, they've laid down on the job for weeks now, but still they won't be easy to replace. The funny thing about number 16 is that a year or so ago workers stood in line to get on that job. Not any more. Not a single worker in this department wanted that job. I guess they think they can't make anything on it. And the damndest thing is that we don't know if they can or not, since none of them have really tried. Well, maybe the new standards and new time study will help.

The Lightner Company (F)

THROUGHOUT the fall and winter of 1953–1964, new equipment and changes in production methods by the Lightner Company were introduced on blower 16 at the Albany plant. This small unit in the core room of the foundry division produced sand cores which were later used by other departments in the manufacture of grey iron castings for gasoline and diesel engines. Following these changes, there emerged problems in output, in operation of new equipment, and in the work crew's morale. In an effort to deal with these problems, management made further modifications in the new equipment, put an extra man on the crew, and retimed the production process. Early in November, Al Dean, a general foreman in the core room, was appointed general supervisor to work with Ray Pope, foreman of blower 16, in clearing up the production problems. Mr. Dean began his supervision of number 16 with a new crew recalled from layoff. The original crew had requested transfers, and no other core-makers in the core room had accepted the job openings.[1]

After the new crew had been given sufficient time to familiarize themselves with the work methods, another time study was taken. When George Larrabee, chief time-study engineer for the foundry division, submitted the production standards and piecework prices for the first core-making job on blower 16, Mr. Dean carefully went over the study and then refused to sign it on the basis that it did not take adequate account of several work motions which he believed were necessary.

To get at the root of these difficulties, several meetings were held among core room supervisors and members of the standards and rates department. The supervisors argued that the basic difficulty was the procedure used by the time-study engineers in setting the production standards and piecework prices. On the other hand, Mr. Larrabee and his assistant, Stephen Wear, stated that inefficient work methods

[1] See Exhibit 5 for a list of the new personnel on blower 16.

479

EXHIBIT 5

THE LIGHTNER COMPANY

*Core Room Partial Organization Chart Showing New Crew and
General Foreman as of November 10, 1953*

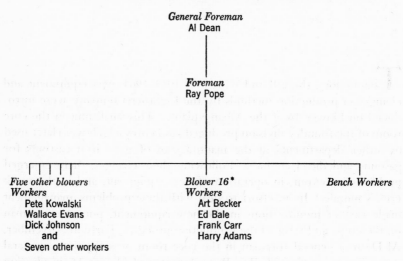

General Foreman
Al Dean

Foreman
Ray Pope

Five other blowers   *Blower 16**   *Bench Workers*
Workers   *Workers*
  Pete Kowalski   Art Becker
  Wallace Evans   Ed Bale
  Dick Johnson   Frank Carr
  and   Harry Adams
  Seven other workers

* *Others affected by blower 16 operations*
  Wayne Curran: Serviceman for blower 16.
  Charles Clark: Union steward in the core room.
  Norman Pike: Dipper who received blower 16 cores.

and lack of worker cooperation were the important factors which had
brought about poor output and scrap.   The latter maintained that the
standards had been fairly and factually ascertained.   Little progress
was made in these meetings to solve these problems.   The workers
continued to complain, and because of the continued low productivity,
an extra shift was put on the blower, and another blower machine was
retooled to supplement production.   Moreover, occasionally workers
on the melting and pouring floor were sent home or were moved to
other jobs because of the difficulties on blower 16.

When Mr. Larrabee was transferred to the machine repair division,
Bill Duncan replaced him as chief time-study engineer for the foundry
division.   Mr. Duncan had been on the job only a short time when he
requested a few meetings with Lloyd Hill, superintendent of the core
room, and Mr. Dean concerning the latest time studies on blower 16.

After these meetings, both Mr. Hill and Mr. Dean believed that for the first time in some months, a time-study engineer was trying to understand their problems concerning the administration of new production standards. Mr. Hill told Mr. Dean that "at least Bill Duncan is willing to say that we might have a problem in the core room with the enforcement of these production standards. He's been very cooperative in sitting down and discussing time studies with us. I believe things have begun to look up."

Mr. Dean agreed. He added, "I hope so. Duncan's a hundred per cent better than George Larrabee, that's for sure. Larrabee had only one point of view—to him everyone else was wrong."

During the second week in December, Mr. Dean and Bill Duncan discussed ways of timing the operations on blower 16. Mr. Dean was assured that if the new production standards did not work out, there would be a recheck of the jobs. Mr. Duncan agreed that possibly there might still be a problem of work allocation to attend to. However, after new rates were developed based on the time studies made under the supervision of Mr. Duncan, Mr. Dean reported to Mr. Hill that he believed the rates were not accurately set and that the crew could not meet the standards.

Additional discussions between the rates department and core room supervision followed. On December 19th, Mr. Duncan agreed to have the work operations carefully rechecked over an eight-hour production period by his time-study engineers. At the time this decision was made, the crew on blower 16 signed a round robin grievance in which they stated that they believed the "rates to be unfair and unreasonable." The grievance was taken over by the union and processed for management's attention. Mr. Dean felt that it was unfortunate that the grievance was submitted at the same time he had negotiated a recheck on the blower 16 jobs. "I'm afraid that now the union has come into the picture, the rates department might get tougher. Also, it will look like the union got the action since that grievance was submitted just the day before Duncan agreed to recheck the job. But, in fact, I had gotten the action taken before the grievance was ever processed. That's one of the troubles—the union again seems to be the hero in the case."

After the recheck had been made over a full work shift, Mr. Duncan and his assistant, Steve Wear, talked with Mr. Dean and Mr. Hill. Vernon Tuck, manager of the plant rates department, also attended one of these meetings. The discussions again focused on the procedure which had been adopted in timing the jobs and setting the piecework prices. The recheck did reveal, Mr. Duncan told the group, that crew members accumulated a considerable amount of idle time. Mr. Wear insisted that this time should be blocked from the study. He pointed out that each worker waited, at one time or another, for his co-workers to complete a certain operation before another operation could be started.

Time study personnel and core room supervisors differed in these meetings on the reasons for this idle time. On the one hand, Mr. Wear held to his original position that the idle time was attributable to the differences in the individual workers' efficiency and to certain improper work methods which, he insisted, supervisors should correct. He added that he had drawn factors to Mr. Dean's attention on numerous occasions during the time studies. On the other hand, Mr. Dean took the position that the efficiency of three of the workers on the blower crew was determined largely by the efficiency of the fourth worker, the second rollover operator.[2] He said that the speed and efficiency with which this second man operated the rollover machine determined the rate of the work flow for the remaining members.

As these discussions continued, Mr. Duncan admitted that Mr. Dean had struck on an important factor which previous time studies had failed to consider; however, Mr. Wear was reluctant to agree. Both Mr. Dean and Mr. Hill insisted that blower 16 was a group operation and that any attempt to consider each individual worker's efficiency as a separate entity, as Larrabee had done, would not work. Mr. Dean finally stated, "If the jobs could be retimed with this new concept in mind, I'm sure an accurate standard could be gotten."

Mr. Duncan and Vernon Tuck talked over the new idea further and agreed that a better method of timing the blower operation was needed. They decided that the jobs would be retimed using the second rollover operator's efficiency as the determining factor. Mr. Wear finally agreed to follow Mr. Duncan's decision to retime the job according to the new concept, although he still insisted that the previous method of timing blower 16 was more accurate. A few days later, he requested vacation leave.

Later Mr. Dean explained the new procedure for timing the jobs to Herbert Lockwood, the case writer:

> Following the recheck, both Duncan and Tuck saw that the second rollover man's efficiency was the controlling factor in the whole operation. They timed his efficiency and made it uniform for all the other crew members. We've gotten some changes in the rates as a result. Now we have rates that the crew can make

[2] See the Lightner case (A) for details on work procedures on blower 16.

if they want to put out some effort.   No more of this figuring each individual work element for each worker.   That was George Larrabee's idea, and it just never worked.   With Bill Duncan in the driver's seat, the attitude of the rates department has changed a lot.   Before, when Larrabee ran the time studies, we supervisors couldn't get any standards readjusted regardless of how bad they were.   Larrabee used to time the jobs, cut the prices to the bone, and then leave us holding the bag, since we had to enforce impossible standards and rates.

During the first two weeks in January 1954, the new rates set by Mr. Duncan were in effect.   Mr. Dean still received complaints from his foreman, Mr. Pope, that the workers were insisting that the standards were not right.   Mr. Dean talked to the crew members on various occasions and pointed out to them the difference in the way the jobs were timed and how much better the new prices were.   He told them that if they went to work, they would make out.   One afternoon, Ed Bale, the second rollover operator, spoke to Mr. Dean about the standards.

MR. BALE: We worked all day on the 4426 job and didn't make out, Al.   There isn't enough time allowed for changing the blower plate and making the morning setup.
MR. DEAN: Let me ask you, isn't the 4426 job much better with the new rates?   You must admit that a good take-home is now possible if you fellows get going.
MR. BALE: We only make a little over what we made with the other rate.   We need to make more.
MR. DEAN: Just keep with it.   You'll be all right.   The rates are set right now.   I'm fully satisfied with them.

During the last half of January and the first two weeks in February, several changes in personnel were made on blower 16.   Art Becker left for California, and Ed Bale requested a transfer to another job.   New workers were brought in to replace them.   At about the same time, the foundry had a temporary production curtailment and the less senior men were laid off while others were transferred within the core room.   Because many men with low seniority worked on blower 16, there were more changes in personnel.[3]   During the next three-week period, several new men worked on the blower.   These workers' attitudes were expressed by Horace Stewart, a grinder, who worked as a

[3] Consult Exhibit 6 for the names of workers who worked on blower 16 for short periods of time.

EXHIBIT 6

THE LIGHTNER COMPANY

*Personnel Changes on Blower 16 from January 20 to
February 15, 1954*

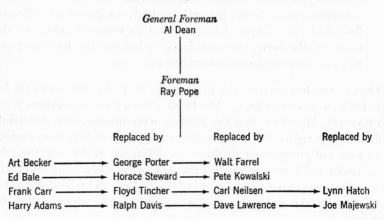

General Foreman
Al Dean

Foreman
Ray Pope

	Replaced by	Replaced by	Replaced by
Art Becker ⟶	George Porter ⟶	Walt Farrel	
Ed Bale ⟶	Horace Steward ⟶	Pete Kowalski	
Frank Carr ⟶	Floyd Tincher ⟶	Carl Neilsen ⟶	Lynn Hatch
Harry Adams ⟶	Ralph Davis ⟶	Dave Lawrence ⟶	Joe Majewski

rollover operator for four days before transferring: "You just can't make out, because everybody's sour on this job." In addition, George Porter, a core-maker, stated after he received his transfer: "Well, I don't know about the job. Maybe a good take-home could be made if the fellows would work together. But having to break in a new man on the job practically every day just makes it too hard. I'm still glad I asked for a transfer."

Due to the seniority layoff procedure, Pete Kowalski was assigned to work on blower 16. He had been the blower operator on the original crew when the initial production changes had been implemented on blower 16.[4]

"Tomorrow morning," Mr. Hill told Mr. Dean, "Pete Kowalski goes on 16. Tell him that he either takes an opening on that job or he takes a quit. There's no other place for him in the department with all the transfers and layoffs we've had lately." The next morning, Mr. Dean told Mr. Kowalski that he was to work on blower 16. "How come?" Mr. Kowalski asked. "I was promised I wouldn't have to work that job anymore." Mr. Dean explained to him that his name had come up on the seniority list. Later Mr. Dean told Mr. Hill, "Kowalski got pretty mad when I told him. He said he had been

[4] See Exhibit 1, p. 458, Lightner Company (A) case.

promised he wouldn't have to work blower 16 anymore. Of course, that isn't true. He went to work, however."

On the first day that Mr. Kowalski was on blower 16, he worked inside the "merry-go-round" as the rod man. The crew turned out 17 rounds during an eight-hour shift. The night crew had done 29 on the previous shift. When Mr. Dean heard about this the next morning, he went down to the work area and told the crew how poorly they had done in comparison with the night crew. Mr. Kowalski answered for the crew.

MR. KOWALSKI: Nobody can make out on this job anymore. You've taken away all the gravy.

MR. DEAN: How do you account for what the night shift did?

MR. KOWALSKI: I don't believe it.

Later that day, Mr. Kowelski talked to Charlie Clark, the union steward, about his assignment to blower 16.

MR. KOWALSKI: I told Lloyd and Al that I didn't want to work on 16. Why do I have to?

MR. CLARK: They say one thing and do another, I know. But your name came up for 16 on the seniority list. That's why you're here, Pete.

MR. KOWALSKI: I don't like it. I was promised I wouldn't have to work on this job anymore. Nobody can make out.

MR. CLARK: Okay, I know that. Why don't you fellows sign a grievance stating just that? Nobody wants this job. Nearly fifteen guys have worked it in the past five months. There was a time when men got in line to work on blower 16. Now, with the rate cut, no one wants it.

MR. KOWALSKI: I just want off, that's all.

Mr. Kowalski worked inside the "merry-go-round" while the other crew members worked the blower and rollover machines. The only worker he knew on the job was Walt Farrel, the first rollover operator. Later that week, the blower operator, Carl Neilsen, and the second rollover operator, Dave Lawrence, transferred. They were replaced by Lynn Hatch and Joe Majewski. Mr. Kowalski and Mr. Farrel knew Joe Majewski from previous jobs. At the time of these personnel changes, Mr. Kowalski moved right inside the "merry-go-round" to his old position on the blower machine. Mr. Hatch, who had less experience than the other men, went inside as the rod man. Mr. Farrel continued as the first rollover operator, and Mr. Kowalski told Joe Majewski to work the second position on the rollover. At this time, Mr. Kowalski began to push the work faster and production began to improve. He told the crew that he wanted a good take-home regardless of what happened. He insisted that he would not be outdone by the night shift crew. He explained to them how long he had worked on blower 16 before they had cut the rates, indicating that the crew was to take orders from him. The men went along with the suggestion and strained on output. Mr. Hatch complained the most about Mr. Kowalski to the others, but they paid little attention to his remarks.

As the men put out more cores on the blower, their scrap rose significantly. Mr. Majewski told Mr. Kowalski several times about the scrap cores, but Mr. Kowalski told him to do his own work and mind his own business. However, Ray Pope considered the number of scrap pieces being made excessive. He cautioned the crew on several occasions that they must stop making so much scrap or they would be forced to rework the pieces. "We want production, that's right," Mr. Pope told the crew, "but if you don't put out good cores, what's the use of all this production?" Mr. Kowalski nodded his head and said that the crew would be more careful. The number of scrap cores, however, did not decrease.

"All they want is production and the biggest pay check possible," Mr. Pope told Mr. Dean. "They're hungry for money and won't watch their scrap." Mr. Dean replied, "If the scrap situation doesn't improve, they will have to rework the cores at a straight classification pay."

Near the end of February, the crew's scrap record was particularly bad. Mr. Dean told Mr. Hill about the situation, and the two decided that the crew had to be taught a lesson. "Tell Ray Pope to take the crew down to the receiving area and have them rework their scrap pieces. We are not going to tolerate that kind of work," Mr. Hill said.

Mr. Dean and Mr. Pope went over to blower 16 and told the crew to stop work.

MR. POPE: Okay, men, stop your work. I've warned you on several occasions about the scrap. Now, you're going to go down to the receiving area and rework the mess you've made. This is not going to continue.

MR. KOWALSKI: Don't tell me that, Pope. I'll take a shower first. Where's the union? Get Charlie Clark.

MR. DEAN: I'll get Clark, but the contract is all laid out on Ray's desk.

Go over and read it—article 5, section 22. It clearly states that all excessive scrap due to the worker's fault must be reworked. Get the contract for them, Ray. I'll get Clark. Let's make this legal.

When Mr. Dean returned with Mr. Clark, Mr. Kowalski asked him about the situation. Mr. Clark answered, "That's right. You made the scrap and you've been warned about the problem by the foreman. Go do the rework." The crew started for the receiving area. Mr. Kowalski turned and said, "Just who wrote that contract? I had nothing to do with it."

About 45 minutes later, the crew returned to blower 16 to resume their work. At quitting time, the men commented briefly about what had happened that day. Mr. Kowalski was still talking about the disciplinary action when he went into the shower room with the other crew members.

During the next week when Mr. Lockwood was in the work area, Mr. Pope told him that the scrap problem had subsided considerably.

> Oh, they didn't like the idea of reworking the cores very much, but it did the trick. Of course, they aren't quite making the standard, yet, but their production is coming right along. They slowed down a little after the scrap incident, but if they can't put out good cores, they will have to slow down until they can. (Pause)
>
> I think they are a little better to get along with. Naturally, that Kowalski fellow isn't easy. He's always yelling that someone is out to get him. The men fight among themselves a lot, too, about the work. Kowalski jumps on them when they hold him up on the blower machine. He just gets hopping mad. I've tried to show them how they can work together better. They aren't doing too badly, but they think we are out to get them or something. I'm getting pretty sick of their telling me every time they have a little problem that they're in a breakdown allowance condition.
>
> With all this pressure for production on me, I've told the crew they had better straighten up and fly right. I can't keep on taking a licking on my cost sheet. In fact, I've told them I'm not going to.

When Mr. Lockwood was in the work area that afternoon, he made the following observations.

Joe Majewski had exchanged jobs with Mr. Kowalski for a couple of hours. At one point in his operation of the blower machine, Mr.

Majewski stopped and looked up under the magazine. Mr. Kowalski called to him.

MR. KOWALSKI: All right, let's get with it. What's wrong anyway? Do I have to work the blower machine too?

MR. MAJEWSKI: This blower isn't safe. I don't want to work on it until that valve is fixed. You see, when I release the sand into the core box, that valve spits air and sand. If I were in front of the machine, I might get hurt.

MR. KOWALSKI: Okay, a breakdown. Let's stop. Get the foreman.

Mr. Majewski went after Mr. Pope while the other workers stopped work and lit cigarettes. Mr. Pope came over immediately.

MR. POPE: What's wrong? Why aren't you guys working?

MR. MAJEWSKI: It's like I told you. I'm not working the blower until it's fixed. The valve right over the blower is spitting sand. It could hit me.

MR. KOWALSKI: Let's get the maintenance boys.

MR. POPE: Just a minute now. Show me what the trouble is, Joe.

Mr. Majewski put a core under the blower and released the sand valve. A small amount of sand came out from the blower.

MR. POPE: That's nothing. Do it again.

Majewski repeated the operation.

MR. POPE: You don't stand in front of the machine anyway when you blow a core. Get with it, fellows. We have to use up that extra sand because there's no second shift on the blower today. I don't want to get caught long on sand.

MR. KOWALSKI: The machine isn't safe. We are in allowance condition.

MR. POPE: There's nothing wrong with the machine. Go ahead with your work. Those are my orders. Any time you lose won't be breakdown allowance. Joe doesn't have to work in front of the machine. Besides, there's practically no sand coming out. I'll call the maintenance department, but you don't have to stop.

MR. KOWALSKI: We aren't going to work until that machine is fixed.

MR. POPE: Ther's nothing unsafe about the machine. I said you're on. I won't take any more lickings on cost because of you guys.

MR. KOWALSKI: I'm not asking for any favors from you. I'll call maintenance if you won't.

MR. POPE: Go to work.

Mr. Pope walked off to check another operation. Mr. Kowalski went over to Mr. Pope's desk and called the maintenance department. When, Mr. Pope returned to the blower about five minutes later, the crew was still standing around.

MR. POPE: I said, you men are on. Every minute you lose comes out of your own pockets. This doesn't go on the time cards. I've put up with this scrap and breakdown stuff long enough.

When the maintenance men arrived in the work area to examine the machine, Mr. Pope told the crew that their downtime started then and not a minute before. The maintenance men looked at the valve and said it was loose, but perfectly safe to operate. They made some quick adjustments and the crew went back to work. The maintenance men and Mr. Pope stood near the work area discussing the situation.

MR. POPE: Thanks, fellows. I knew that the machine was perfectly safe, but I'm glad to hear you fellows agree.

At quitting time, Mr. Pope went over to blower 16 to check the workers' time cards. Mr. Kowalski was leaning against a core box making out the crew's time cards while the other workers cleaned up the work area.

MR. POPE: How much downtime did you have, Pete?
MR. KOWALSKI: None.

The other workers stood near the machines listening to the exchange.

MR. POPE: What do you mean—none? That's not right. You have some coming. I told you when the maintenance men arrived that your downtime started then.
MR. KOWALSKI: We don't expect anything from you. You don't owe us anything.
MR. POPE: I know I don't owe you anything. Okay, then, if that's the way you want it, you won't get anything.

After the workers left, Mr. Pope commented to Lockwood about the situation.

MR. POPE: How do you like that? The maintenance men told me that there was no reason why the workers couldn't operate the machine. I've tried to treat this crew right. More than once I've gone out of my way to help them, but I draw the line when they pull something like this breakdown stuff. They knew I had to get that sand used up because there isn't a second shift today.

The Lightner Company (G)

Following the introduction of technical changes in the work methods and production standards on blower 16 at the Albany plant of the Lightner Company, problems arose in output, in operation of the new equipment, and in morale. Several meetings were held among core room supervisors and members of the standards and rates department to discuss the procedure for timing and setting production standards and piecework prices for this unit which produced sand cores. Following several conferences, Al Dean, general foreman of blower 16, and Bill Duncan, the new chief time-study engineer for the foundry, agreed on a new procedure for timing the jobs on blower 16. A new time study was taken of each of the core-making jobs, and production standards were released which satisfied both Mr. Dean and his foreman, Ray Pope. They both believed that with these standards and piecework prices, the production problems on blower 16 would rapidly improve.

There were fewer worker requests for transfers following the release of the new production standards; however, the scrap problem became acute. The work crew was warned by Mr. Pope on several occasions about the scrap. When the problem persisted, Mr. Dean took disciplinary action by making the crew rework their scrap cores. Both supervisors believed that the disciplinary action helped considerably, and although the crew was not yet making the standard, they believed that there would be a "breakthrough" in the situation soon. Mr. Pope suggested at several times, however, that the crew was still difficult to work with and that getting their wholehearted co-operation was still a big problem. Mr. Pope even suspected that at times the crew insisted on allowance compensations for machine difficulties and breakdowns which he believed could easily have been avoided.

In the first week of March 1954, Lynn Hatch, the rod man in the newest position on the crew, insisted on transferring at the first opportunity from blower 16. The week that Mr. Pope took him off, Andy Cameron, a core-maker from the department, was put on the job. Mr. Cameron had known Messrs. Kowalski, Majewski, and Farrel from previous jobs, and he told Mr. Pope that he thought they were all good workers. When Mr. Cameron came on the unit, Mr. Majewski pointed out to him that Mr. Kowalski was the boss. Mr. Cameron nodded in agreement, and the crew went to work. Mr. Kowalski told him to work Mr. Hatch's job inside the "merry-go-round," and the other workers maintained their original positions.

During Mr. Cameron's first two weeks on the crew, Mr. Lockwood, the case writer from Northwestern University, noticed little change in this crew's attitude or in the way they worked together. Mr. Pope reported to Mr. Dean that there had been a slight improvement in both output and quality of the cores. Both men restated their opinion that the rate could be made if the workers were willing to put out some effort.

"I've worked pretty hard getting these new rates," Mr. Dean told Mr. Pope, "and they are right this time. Just tell the crew to go to it and they'll make out." Frequently, both men visited the blower operation and encouraged the crew to make the standard. On these visits, Mr. Kowalski spoke for the whole crew in complaining about the rotten deal they had gotten. He told Mr. Pope that he wanted off the job whenever there was a decent opening, but that he didn't want a daywork job like the one given Lynn Hatch. The other three workers also told Mr. Pope that they wanted off at the first opportunity.

During the noon breaks, the crew sat around the blower eating their lunches and discussing their problems. At times, when Mr. Pope and Mr. Dean came by and listened to some of their complaints, they pointed out that the standard could be made if they would do less griping and more work. Mr. Kowalski usually interrupted them with the remark, "I don't care what you say, you can't make out. You've taken all the gravy out of the jobs and left us with the bones." When Mr. Dean got tired of these complaints, he told Mr. Pope to see to it that the crew put in a full day's work. "I've heard enough," he said. "I'm not going to coddle them anymore."

Mr. Lockwood observed that the men worked fairly independently and that when there were mistakes or delays, they blamed one another for them. Mr. Kowalski insisted on more and more production and pushed the core boxes out from under the blower faster and faster, sometimes jamming the rollover operation. Mr. Majewski and Mr. Farrel frequently rebelled at this treatment and told Mr. Kowalski that if they weren't moving fast enough for him, he could do their work himself. When Mr. Kowalski became angry as a result, Mr. Cameron would lean over from inside the "merry-go-round" and joke with him. Often he helped out if Mr. Kowalski or Mr. Farrel had trouble moving the core box from the blower onto the rollover table. At first Mr. Kowalski resented his help and told him to stop. Later, however, he began to call on him for assistance.

One afternoon in the third week of March, when Mr. Farrel was absent, Mr. Pope assigned a day worker to the blower. Mr. Kowalski told the newcomer to work inside the "merry-go-round" and invited Mr. Cameron to come outside and work on the rollover machine next to him. As the work day progressed, Mr. Cameron pointed out that one thing which slowed up the operation was that Mr. Majewski had to wait for the inside worker to clamp the rollover arm shut before he could roll the core box over for the shake out. He added that when he and Majewski were ready to roll and shake the core, the inside man was usually busy doing some other job and they had to call him over. Mr. Kowalski immediately started to jump on the new worker for being so slow when Mr. Cameron reached over with his long arms and clamped a box into place himself. This new work method was employed during the rest of that day. When the shift was over, Mr. Majewski commented that the work had gone easier with Mr. Cameron locking the rollover machine from the outside; Kowalski nodded in agreement.

The following morning, Walt Farrel returned to his job as rollover operator, and Mr. Cameron resumed his old job inside the "merry-go-round." During the next four days, the work went as before—there was continued strain among the workers, with Mr. Kowalski attempting to push the blower operation faster and faster. The crew again seemed to be working at cross-purposes.

During a lunch break in the fourth week that this crew worked on the blower, Mr. Cameron sat listening to the others complaining about the jobs and the rates. Finally, he interrupted the conversation.

MR. CAMERON: We won't make out on this job until we work together. We can make out if we pull and help each other more.

MR. KOWALSKI: Nobody knows more about these machines than I do. But it's no use; the good prices are gone.

MR. CAMERON: Okay, maybe you're right, but the good old days are gone, too, Pete. There just aren't any gravy jobs any more. The company expects more, but we can still make out if we pull together.

MR. MAJEWSKI: I'm interested. Just tell me how.

MR. KOWALSKI: I could push cores out faster if the rollover machine didn't slow me down. What do you think I've been yelling about for the last month?

MR. CAMERON: I say that what slows us down so much is my having to come over every time and clamp the rollover arm shut before Walt and Joe can swing and draw the core. This is only an idea, but if I worked the first position on the rollover, I could clamp that lock shut by reaching over from the outside position. You remember, we worked it that way last week and it was better?

MR. KOWALSKI: That's Walt's job. Besides, I don't think it'll help.

MR. CAMERON: Well, let's give it a try anyway.

MR. FARREL: Wait a minute. Joe told me about what you did last week when I was out sick. I'm willing to try it that way. I've worked inside before, and what Andy says about that clamping slowing us down is right, Pete. Andy's taller than I am, and he can reach the clamp from the outside. I could never do that.

That afternoon, Mr. Farrel and Mr. Cameron changed work positions, and Mr. Cameron started working on the rollover machine with Mr. Majewski. Each time a core box came from under the blower and onto the rollover machine, he reached over and clamped the box into place. Mr. Majewski immediately engaged the levers and swung the box for the draw. For the next day or so, little difference was noticeable in the crew's output, but Mr. Lockwood observed that there was far less yelling from Mr. Kowalski. In fact, he began to listen and to follow many of Mr. Cameron's suggestions about improvement in the work.

When Mr. Pope first observed the crew's new work method, he brought up the question of safety. The workers showed him that they could do the job in the new way without any danger. Their cooperative spirit pleased Mr. Pope and he heartily approved the change. Gradually, production improved and he told Mr. Dean that for the first time in weeks the crew was not complaining about the standards. On the fourth day after Mr. Cameron had started on the rollover machine, the crew made the standard on the job. Both supervisors and work crew were pleased. Whenever Mr. Dean came by the operation, he told the men how well they were working together, and the crew worked even faster as a result.

As Mr. Cameron and Mr. Majewski continued working together on the rollover, Cameron showed Majewski how to develop a little running step when carrying the cores to the racks. When the two carried out this operation, the cores went on the racks faster. During this same period of exploring new ways to do the jobs, the workers learned that on certain jobs, Majewski could operate the blower machine better than Mr. Kowalski and that he was much better on the rollover machine than Mr. Majewski. The men talked about it among themselves and agreed that Mr. Majewski would operate the blower and Mr. Kowalski would work with Mr. Cameron on the rollover. With Mr. Cameron clamping the rollover machine from the outside and helping Mr. Kowalski and Mr. Majewski with certain other operations, such as cleaning loose pieces in the boxes, Mr. Farrel was free inside the "merry-go-round" to keep the boxes moving around at an even pace to the blower machine. This even pace in the work flow enabled the blower man to put one core box after another under the magazine without any delay or need to move from his work station to pull boxes into position.

The pace set by the workers became contagious. Mr. Cameron increased his efforts on the rollover machine with Mr. Majewski and Mr. Kowalski. He carried the heavy end of the core to the racks, and to speed up that operation with Mr. Kowalski, he taught him the little running step that he had taught Mr. Majewski. The other crew members saw how Mr. Cameron worked and began to help too. Mr. Kowalski told Mr. Cameron that he was not always to carry the heavy end of the cores. He swapped with him, and although Mr. Majewski complained at times, Mr. Kowalski made him change frequently with Mr. Cameron on carrying the heavy cores to the racks.

Mr. Dean described to Mr. Lockwood his understanding of the changes on blower 16:

> We've finally got some men who are willing to put out production. These men are making their rates for the first time since they went into effect. I told Bill Duncan about the changes in output here, and he said that the workers were earning every bit of their pay.
>
> I think the big change came when the men decided that they would stop complaining and start working. Of course, that new work method of Andy Cameron's on the rollover machine helped an awful lot. Now, the inside worker is free to keep the boxes clean and moving around the "merry-go-round" at an even pace. You see, the rollover operators don't have to wait on the inside man to lock the machine in place now. I told George Larrabee way back when the original time study was taken that the inside man just couldn't be in a dozen places at once.
>
> Kowalski still complains frequently, but he's still on the job and hasn't mentioned lately that he wants off. I hope he doesn't leave, because he knows his business down there. He and the rest of the crew are really going at it. Go down and take a look if you want to.

In April Mr. Lockwood recorded the following observations of the work group:

MR. CAMERON: Let's go there, Pete.   Push that box through.
MR. KOWALSKI: Okay, here it comes.

The moment the box moved onto the rollover machine arm, Mr. Cameron reached over and with one movement clamped the box into place.   Immediately, Mr. Majewski tripped the valve and the core box swung over for the shake-out.   Mr. Cameron walked over to the blower machine to speak to Mr. Kowalski.

MR. CAMERON: How are we doing?
MR. KOWALSKI: Not bad.   That makes nearly thirty rounds for the morning.

Mr. Majeswski and Mr. Farrel joined the group and looked at the chart over Mr. Kowalski's machine.

MR. KOWALSKI: What's this, a convention or something?   Let's keep up the work.   We'll show them yet that we can make a real rate. Let's put four cores on every rack.

The crew returned to work.   While Mr. Majewski and Mr. Cameron took a core to the racks, Mr. Kowalski came from around the blower machine to help Mr. Farrel pull the boxes away from the rollover and to replace the loose pieces in them.   The two workers pushed the boxes around the "merry-go-round" conveyor to the blower.   Then Mr. Kowalski ran swiftly back to the blower and started preparing the next core box.   Mr. Cameron usually came over to the machine and made the blow for him.   After he was through, Mr. Kowalski put a metal plate on top of the core box and the two pushed it on to the rollover machine.   Immediately, Mr. Cameron locked the box into place and Mr. Majewski again tripped the lever which rolled and shook the core free from the box.   This cycle was repeated again and again.

MR. FARREL: That's another core.
MR. MAJEWSKI: Don't push too fast, Pete.   Remember I've got to watch the draw.   You know what Al Dean said about scrap cores.
MR. KOWALSKI: Okay, you're right, Joe.   We want to put out good stuff.   Did you fellows fix up those bad cores during that extra time we had?
MR. CAMERON: Sure.
MR. KOWALSKI: Let's go then.   We want fifty rounds today, don't we?

The workers laughed and returned to work.   Mr. Cameron clamped; Mr. Kowalski blew cores; Majewski turned the rollover machine; and Mr. Farrel cleaned and pushed the boxes around.   Shortly before lunch time, Mr. Kowalski stopped the team.

MR. KOWALSKI: That does that job.   Let's make up for the scrap cores we made today.   I know just how many we junked.   I kept track of every one of them.

MR. CAMERON: Anything you say, boss.

The first core that the crew remade came out with broken edges. Mr. Kowalski stepped down to examine the core with Joe Majewski.

MR. KOWALSKI: What's the trouble?

MR. MAJEWSKI: The core is sticking to the box.   The loose pieces aren't coming out right, either.

MR. KOWALSKI: Go down and work the blower, Joe.   Andy and I will try to fix the loose pieces.   I know a couple of tricks about these old boxes that might help.

The two workers exchanged work positions.   Mr. Cameron worked alongside Mr. Kowalski.   Under his direction, Mr. Cameron clamped the box and the two men carefully swung it and applied the air vibrators.

MR. CAMERON: That's it Pete.   Easy now with the loose pieces when they come off.

MR. KOWALSKI: How's that?

MR. CAMERON: Perfect.

The others smiled at one another as another box was pushed onto the rollover machine.

Later that day, the union steward, Mr. Clark, came by and watched the crew for a few minutes.   He spoke to Mr. Kowalski.

MR. CLARK: You guys are working like madmen.   Don't you know you can't keep up this pace?   If you do, the job will be ruined for anyone else when you leave.

MR. KOWALSKI: Hello there, Charlie.

MR. CLARK: What are you trying to do?   Kill yourselves or something?

MR. CAMERON: We're trying to make a rate on a job that's been whacked to pieces.   Dean and Pope say it can be done and we're just trying to find out.

MR. CLARK: You won't make out on this job.

MR. CAMERON: We might be able to. We've made the rate for nearly a week now. Sure, the job doesn't pay like it once did—but what job around here does, Charlie?

MR. CLARK: Okay, you'll see. No one else has been able to make out. There's been nearly fifteen guys on that machine.

MR. KOWALSKI: I know, Charlie; I was one of the first.

MR. CLARK: You guys might make out because you work and are good at it. But what happens when you leave the job?

MR. CAMERON: We might not leave.

MR. KOWALSKI: Look, Charlie, we're trying to work. Don't bother us now.

During a rest break on one of the afternoons that Mr. Lookwood was around the work area, Andy Cameron described his understanding of the situation this way:

MR. CAMERON: It's like I've told the others, we kind of pull together. That way it's easy for all of us. You've got to help on this job; otherwise you work yourself to death and don't make much either. I came to work over here because I knew these fellows and knew that if we worked together, we'd make out. At first, that wasn't too easy with Pete being mad and all that. But in time we all got together and tried to work things out. We found out that some of us can do certain jobs better than others and so we swapped around. In that way, everyone does what he's best at.

No sir, no one lays down on the job unless he wants to hurt himself and us too. Once I worked on a job where some of us got different pay, and that led to a lot of hard feelings. Here we all do our share because we all get the same pay. Of course, we have problems and the foreman jumps on us and then, but, like I told Pete and the others, he's got things on his mind and he gets told off by his boss, I guess. When he gets mad, he doesn't necessarily mean everything he says. Pretty soon, we've noticed, he gets over it and is willing to joke with us. Pete tells me that Ray has settled down a lot in the last few weeks, and I think he's right.

After the crew finished work that day, Mr. Cameron talked further with Mr. Lockwood about the crew and the way it worked together:

I call us the team on 16, and that's what we are, you know. We all get along fine together. What will make Pete laugh and work isn't the same thing that goes with Walt or Joe. Each of them is different, and you've got to treat them just right.

And we work, too. Like I told Pete, maybe the rates aren't what they once were, but there just aren't any gravy jobs anymore. We can make these rates if we'll work, and on that score, I think both Ray and Al are right. They've shown us how to get the work going, and that's okay by us.

You know, now none of the fellows down here wants to leave the blower. We'll stay as long as we can work together. But if they bring in new people, that will make the work too hard. We've told Ray that we don't want any others on this job. We're all willing to put out. I don't know about others, but we've got an understanding.

And another thing, if one of the fellows can't make it to work, he tells us about it in plenty of time if he can. He doesn't just fail to show up and leave us holding the bag as some of the workers do around here. We appreciate that, and I know Ray Pope does too. We don't want to be absent, because that makes it hard on the others. (Pause)

Well, I don't know much more. We just get the work done, and at the end of the day we get the hell out of here. A foundry isn't the best place in the world to work in, maybe, but it's not as bad as some might think. I had better run—I see the others are heading for the showers. If I don't keep up, I'll miss my ride home with Joe. See you around sometime.

On Wednesday, April 19th, Pete Kowalski came down with a bad cold and failed to show up at work. He telephoned Mr. Cameron and told him that he was running a temperature and that the doctor had said that he might be laid up for a week or two. During the next few days, another man was put on the operation to work with the group. Although the three regulars cooperated on the blower and rollover machines and put the new man inside the "merry-go round," production suffered. The regulars worked harder than usual and attempted to show the new man the "ropes," but as they later told Mr. Pope, "No one knows as much about the blower operation as Pete Kowalski."

On the following Monday morning, Mr. Kowalski unexpectedly made an appearance in Mr. Hill's office and demanded to be put back to work on blower 16. He pointed out his long service with the department and how much he was needed on the job.

"I was simply amazed," Mr. Hill told Mr. Lockwood the next day. "I could hardly believe that this was the same worker who had raised so much hell on that unit a few months ago. Naturally, I told Pete how much we had missed him and that the crew had missed him, too.

I said that nothing would please me more than to have him come back to work, but that first I had to have a release slip from the plant's medical department. Pete listened to all of this and for a moment became quite angry. Then, his face brightened and he walked out of my office."

After Mr. Kowalski's conversation with Mr. Hill, he went by the blower and told the men he was coming back to work the next day. That afternoon, Mr. Hill received a phone call from the medical department stating that Mr. Kowalski had been there all morning demanding to be examined to see if he was capable of returning to work.

"Frankly," Mr. Hill commented the next day, "I had though of calling the medical department when Kowalski came in, but I could never have swung that myself. But Kowalski went over on his own initiative and raised so much hell that he convinced the staff doctors that he was fit to work. He passed the examination with flying colors and today brought me the release slip. How about that? I would normally have expected him to stay out at least a week. The doctors believed he was that sick."

When Mr. Kowalski got back on his old job on the blower, the team again began to function smoothly. Mr. Pope was glad to see Mr. Kowalski back and told him so. He remarked later to Mr. Lockwood that there has been many changes on blower 16.

> It's like I've told Al Dean—the fellows on blower 16 have settled down a lot. For instance, Pete Kowalski has been known around here as a troublemaker for a long time. He used to complain almost every day that no one could make any money in the foundry, and when he was assigned to blower 16, he couldn't wait to get off. The others were more or less the same way— all of them were asking to get off the job. Now, none of them wants off. Isn't that something?

The crew and the foreman laughed.

A couple of weeks later, during an afternoon in the second week of May, there was a major power failure on the conveyor unit which carried the racks to the ovens. There was a shutdown for nearly two hours while the electrical power system was being repaired. During this time the crew on blower 16 was in a period of cessation. Regardless of what they did, they would be paid an average of the rate they would earn for normal operations for that period. Since the conveyor system was not working, they were not expected to continue work. Mr. Pope thought about telling the crew to clean up the machines and work area.

But before he could do this, he noticed that the workers were continuing to make cores anyway. Mr. Pope told Mr. Lockwood later, "Those fellows didn't have to go on, since legitimately they were in a period of work cessation. But damn it all, they did. They put six cores on every rack down the whole length of the department. At times, Pete and Andy had to carry some of them nearly half a block to find an empty shelf. Some of the workers from the receiving area came up and told the blower crew to stop working. They said that they would have twice as much work to do when the conveyor did start up. Kowalski told them to go to work and stop complaining. That shut them up.

"It's something," Mr. Pope continued, "to see those guys work together. Of course, I knew all the time that Kowalski wanted to change the blower plate and get the next job set up, and that's why the crew put all those cores on the racks. But, they've had blower plates to change before, and they've never carried cores that far before."

Mr. Pope got out his reports and showed Mr. Lockwood some of the changes there had been in production and quality during the past few weeks. He concluded his conversation about the crew in this way:

Of course, we still have scrap, but I only have to make a comment about it, and the fellows watch their work more closely. They even patch up some of the cores during their break time without my saying anything. The disciplinary measures we took awhile back helped some. They know we aren't going to let them get away with making a lot of scrap, so they pay more attention to the quality of the cores.

Andy Cameron told me that the fellows don't want anyone else on the job. They want to work on blower 16 as long as the four of them can stick together. Last week, because of some layoffs, I had to juggle some work to keep senior men from bumping this crew off their jobs. The senior men didn't want to bump these fellows off that job, and when I took the canvass slip around, they refused the jobs and took something else. Sometime, however, we'll probably have to put some others on the job. I hope that isn't too soon. For, frankly, that's not going to make my job any easier. Now, all I have to do is tell Andy Cameron or Pete Kowalski something and they see to it. There was a time when I had to explain things over and over again to those workers and go by the blower six or seven times an hour. Now they run the job themselves. I go over there when I'm needed.

Cold-Air Corporation (A)

THE Cold-Air Corporation manufactured commercial and home refrigeration equipment. Before the Second World War it specialized in refrigeration equipment for hotels, wholesalers, and rolling stock, but after 1946 the company began to increase production of 6 to 12 cubic foot sizes. In the spring of 1948, in order to add family-size deep freezers to their product lines, the company expanded its assembly lines and hired 200 new employees.

At the time of this expansion, a few experienced foremen were hired from outside the company, and a number of qualified workers were promoted to supervisory rank. In addition certain technical and personnel changes were made in the line which assembled the working parts for the "Cold-Master" refrigerator, one of the fastest-selling models. Francis Gillespie, foreman on the Cold-Master line, was put in charge of a new deep-freeze section, while Tony Mastico, who had been assistant foreman for three years on another line, was brought in to supervise the Cold-Master assembly, which consisted of the Cold-Master line and two small subassembly lines that fed parts to it.[1]

The main Cold-Master line consisted of 32 workers divided into three sections, each with a group leader, and four inspectors under an inspection group leader.[2] The group leaders, Therese Petrie, Peggy Frates, and Hilda Bennett, constituted the first line of supervision. In addition to filling minor positions on the line, they acted as emergency operators, handled minor questions of discipline, and were the first people called upon by an operator who was having difficulty on her job. They were responsible to the foreman, who also dealt directly with the operators. One inspector worked in the line at the end of each section, while Ruth Henry, the inspection group leader, had the final position on the line next to inspector number three. Ruth reported to John Steen, who was in charge of inspection on all the assembly lines.

[1] See Exhibit 1, p. 502.
[2] See Exhibit 2, p. 503.

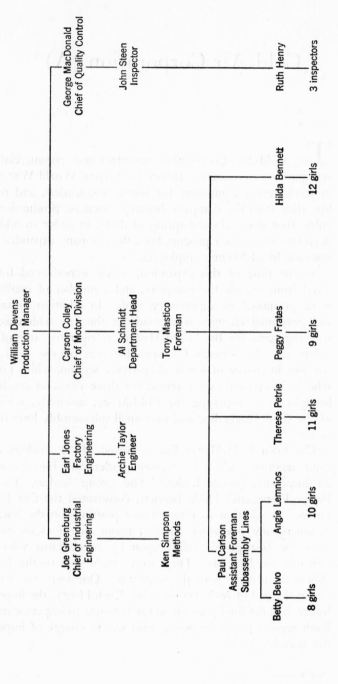

EXHIBIT 1

COLD-AIR CORPORATION

Partial Organization Chart

EXHIBIT 2

COLD-AIR CORPORATION

Cold-Master Line: Layout

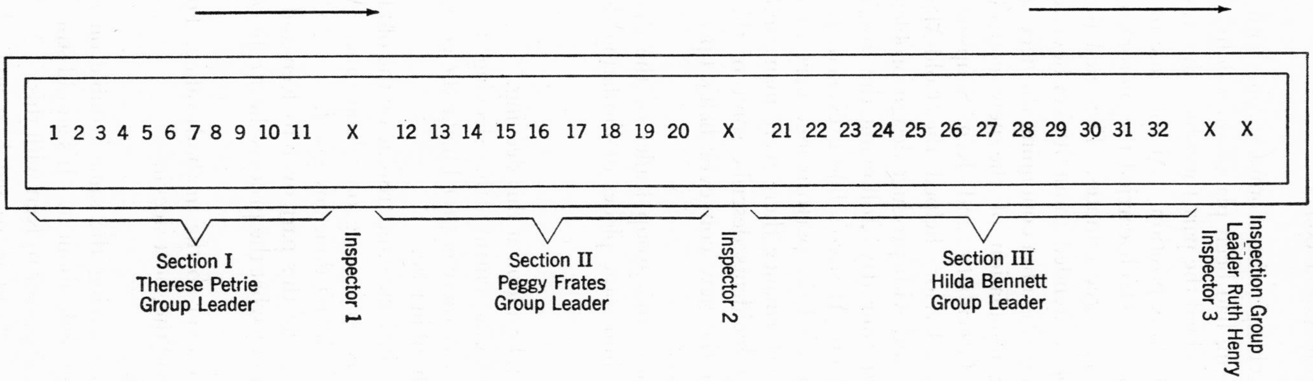

1 2 3 4 5 6 7 8 9 10 11 X 12 13 14 15 16 17 18 19 20 X 21 22 23 24 25 26 27 28 29 30 31 32 X X

Section I
Therese Petrie
Group Leader

Inspector 1

Section II
Peggy Frates
Group Leader

Inspector 2

Section III
Hilda Bennett
Group Leader

Inspection Group
Leader Ruth Henry
Inspector 3

Before the change, the wound stator, with which the assembly of the motor began, had been placed on a dolly when it entered the line. Each operator added the part for which she was responsible and pushed it along to the next position. At the time of the change a conveyor belt was installed, which carried the motors to position at the rate of about one every three minutes. Designed to allow for expansion of the line, the belt extended about 30 feet beyond the final position. At each work place was a bin containing the necessary parts.

During the installation of the new conveyor, two industrial engineers, Joe Greenberg and Ken Simpson, and a factory engineer, Archie Taylor, helped the Cold-Master motor department head, Al Schmidt, with product design problems that arose.

For the first four days following the installation of the new conveyor belt, Tony Mastico's line exceeded the scheduled output. Al Schmidt considered the performance very successful, but to maintain this level of performance there were many difficult problems to solve. The following incidents describe some of the problems faced on the fourth day of the new conveyor belt's operation as witnessed by an outside observer.

Hilda Bennett, the group leader of the third section, called Tony over to show him some pieces of insulating sleeving in one operator's bin.

HILDA: Tony, take a look at this sleeving.

OPERATOR: They're cutting the sleeving too short. Look at how much bare wire there is after I make the connection.

TONY: That shouldn't be.

OPERATOR: We had the same trouble on the old line.

HILDA: This has been going on a long time. We complained about it to Ken, but it hasn't done any good.

TONY: Let me take this part over to Ken and a piece of the sleeving, and I'll find out what the process sheet calls for.

On the way over to the methods office, Tony met Al and showed him the part and the short sleeving.

AL: We'd been having the same trouble on the old line. I couldn't get anything done about it. It's an old story.

TONY: I was going over to Ken with this.

AL: Yeah. Go ahead in to see Ken and ask what the specifications are for this on the process sheet. (Smiling) Yeah. You do that. Go ahead in and see what the specifications are.

Tony walked into the methods office and found Ken seated at his desk, which was piled high with process sheets. Ken seemed to be quite busy.

TONY: Say, Ken, this sleeving is too short, and it's a hot circuit and leaves the wire bare. That's bad. Al told me it's an old story. What is the size called for on the process sheets?

KEN: What does the lead wire measure, and what does the sleeving measure?

TONY (after measuring them on a rule): It's $1\frac{3}{4}''$ for the lead wire on each side and $\frac{7}{8}''$ for the sleeving. That's too short.

KEN: Well, maybe they're not cutting it right in subassembly. Why don't you check with Paul Carlson (foreman of the subassembly lines)?

TONY: First I'd like to know what the process sheet calls for.

KEN: All right.

TONY: I'm sorry to take your time if you're busy, but I'd like to get this straight once and for all.

KEN: Well, I'm pretty busy now, but I'll look it up. (Impatiently.) What's the part number?

TONY: I don't know.

KEN: It looks like it's part number 1303-B. Let me look it up. Yeah. Here it is. Part number 1303-B. It should be $1\frac{1}{2}''$ for each of the lead wires, not $1\frac{3}{4}''$. I guess this is something they've just done in subassembly. Go out and check with Paul on this.

TONY: Look, Ken, you come out with me. I want to get this straight once and for all. Al just told me it's an old story.

KEN: What do you mean, old story? (Angrily.) You go out and see Paul. I haven't got time. I'm busy working on these process sheets.

Tony walked over to the subassembly work area and saw Paul. He explained that the lead wires were too long and not according to the specifications on the process sheet. Paul got his copy of the process sheet; he agreed that the lead wires were longer than specified. At this point Ken came over.

PAUL: This must have just been changed.

KEN: No, it hasn't. There haven't been any recent engineering changes put through.

PAUL: Wait, I'll call my group leader over and see what she says about it.

He called his group leader over and explained the problem.

GROUP LEADER: Oh, I remember now. You see this part number 1303-A down here on the sheet. Well, we couldn't get them, so they told me to substitute 1303-B's for it, and I cut it to the specifications of the A's. That's 1¾". See it here. I was told these parts are interchangeable. I guess they took B's that were cut for A's and used them in another position. Wait and I'll get you a handful of B's with 1½" lead wire.

KEN: Yeah. I see it now. They're used interchangeably.

The group leader returned with the parts and gave them to Tony. Tony returned to the line. When he had left, Ken said to the observer, "Look how complicated Tony made that thing. If he had used a little initiative, he could have used the 1¾" leads just by having the operator make an extra size larger connection and bending the wire upward as it leads out of the part. That would have taken care of the problem. Instead, he wants me to make changes on the process sheet; that gets involved in a lot of paper work, and it would take too long to come through. You see, if he had only taken the trouble to think about it. I wish he'd use some common sense and work these things out on the line himself. Then he wouldn't have all this trouble."

A little later Ruth Henry called Tony.

RUTH: Tony, look at how this lead wire is dressed. It's terrible, and I've been telling the girls about it.

TONY: Whose operation is that?

Ruth told Tony the name of the operator responsible for the operation and Tony cautioned her about it and pointed out the problem to the operator's group leader. Just then Ken came walking by and Tony called him over.

TONY: Look, Ken, I'm having trouble with this lead dressing. I want to work out a system for controlling that. Come on over to Ruth with me and see if we can straighten this out.

They walked over to Ruth.

KEN: Now what's the trouble with this lead dress business, Ruth?

RUTH: This is terrible. We have to do something about it. These wires are touching and they're all going to short out.

Just then, Archie Taylor, the factory engineer, came by, and Tony left Ken and Ruth while he went to speak to Archie.

TONY: Archie, I want to work out a system on this lead dressing business.   Can we get together tomorrow on that?
ARCHIE: Sure. That's a good idea. We should get after that.

Ken watched Tony and Archie talking for a moment and then he wheeled around and left the line in a huff, saying, "What is this? You call me over on the lead dress and while you're talking about it, you walk over to somebody else. I came over here to help you, and if this is what you're going to do, I'll go back to the office. I'm busy and got plenty of things to do over there." Tony hardly noticed what Ken said, and he continued talking to Archie. Then Ruth called out to Tony again.

RUTH: Tony, come over here and take a look at this. They're getting the plugs bent on these units. Can't you do something about it?
TONY: Ken was supposed to bring some brackets over to hold up the assembly bases. He's got some over here now, and I believe more are coming.

John Steen came up to the line, and Ruth showed him the bent plugs. John commented, "Methods was supposed to bring those brackets over a long time ago. They're sure taking their time about it." Ruth went back to her inspection positions and a few minutes later called out to Tony again.

RUTH: Look at this. They're putting in the pins reversed. We've got a whole line of completed units now like that.
ARCHIE: Oh, that's serious. That can cause a lot of trouble. (To Tony.) You'd better get that straightened out.
TONY: I told the pin-up operator about it. He shouldn't be doing it that way.

Tony, Archie, Ruth, and John went over to the pin-up operator's position.

TONY (to the operator): You're putting the pins in wrong. Didn't I show you how they were supposed to go in?
OPERATOR: You told me? I'm doing it the way I was shown. No one told me different. It goes like this: (pointing) 1, 2, 3, 4.
ARCHIE: No, you're reversing the pins.
TONY: I told you that.
OPERATOR: You did not! No one told me to do it different than I am.
RUTH: Tony, why don't you get him a pin-up chart? How's he supposed to remember where they go?

TONY: All right. I'll go over to the office and get him one, and I'll bring some extras back for you.

Ken reappeared on the line, and he immediately spoke to Tony angrily.

KEN: What's the idea of calling me over to check on the lead dress and then leaving me in the middle to go over to somebody else? I'm busy over at the office, and I take my time off to help you, and you haven't got the manners to stay with me. You run off. That's what I call being impolite.

TONY: How can you say that, Ken? I just walked over to Archie to see if we can get together tomorrow to work out a system on this lead dress. I didn't mean to be impolite, but if you think I was, I'm sorry. I apologize. I didn't think I was impolite.

KEN (raising his voice): Well, what else would you call it but impolite? That's what it was, wasn't it?

TONY: Well, I'm sorry, Ken. I didn't mean to be impolite. I went over to Archie about that lead dress.

ARCHIE: That's right, Ken. We all ought to get together tomorrow morning on that.

Ruth came up to the group again.

RUTH: Tony, I thought you promised to bring a pin-up chart for the operator.

TONY (raising his voice in anger): Now wait a minute, Ruth. Stop putting words in my mouth. I did not say I'd bring a pin-up chart over. I said I'd *try* to get it.

RUTH: Well, I said you told me that you'd try to bring it over.

TONY: I never promised anything like that. I said I'd try.

RUTH: Well, now I have to go all the way down the line and change the pins. (Ruth started to walk away. John followed her.)

JOHN: Ruth, you will not change those pins. That's not your job, and I don't want you to do that.

TONY: I'll go down to the office and get those pin-up charts. (He left.)

JOHN: Boy. They call this supervision. This line is getting all fouled up.

ARCHIE: Now wait a minute, John. Don't say that. Give Tony a break. He's just getting started.

JOHN: Well, nobody's giving me a break. I was in Devens' office (production manager), and he gave me hell about the quality. No one's going to take the rap for me.   By God, this has got to change. We're going to get quality out of this line, or else.

ARCHIE: Well, don't blame Tony.   He'll be all right.

JOHN: Okay, Archie (smiles), let's you and I cooperate.   Do you want to cooperate with me?

ARCHIE: Sure, we'll cooperate.   (Laughs.)

Tony returned with several pin-up charts.   He gave one to Ruth and one to the operator at the pin-up station.   Tony then came over to where John and Archie were standing.   Ruth then called Tony, John, and Archie and showed them a unit with a reject tag containing a long list of rejects.   Ruth read off the rejects one by one and she showed John a questionable piece of work.

JOHN: Ruth, reject it!   Reject everything like that.   Don't take any chances.   We're going to tighten up now.

Tony walked away without comment and he was rejoined by John and Archie.   Ruth then came over with the pin-up chart that Tony had given her.

RUTH: This looks like the pin-up chart for the other lines.

TONY: Aw, I'm sorry.   I didn't look and brought the wrong chart. I'm sorry.

ARCHIE: Look, Tony, I'll take a walk over to the office and get you some charts for your lines.

TONY: Would you do that, Archie?   Gee, thanks a lot.   And while you're there, would you get me some extra charts?   Get about 7 of them so that I have them, will you?

ARCHIE: Sure, Tony.

A little later, Tony spoke to the observer.   He said, "I don't know why Ken got sore and called me impolite.   I guess he's still mad about that sleeving business this morning."

During the day's operations, tests of the motors in the test department indicated a technical deficiency in design.   The change was of minor importance in terms of the operations affected, but it was of an emergency nature.   Product engineers soon determined the cause of the problem, and a minor design change affecting the connection of one of the parts was found necessary.   Earl Jones, head of factory engineering, informed production manager William Devens of the predicament.   Mr. Devens decided that the situation warranted the changes without going through the usual paperwork, and later that afternoon told the motor division chief, Carson Colley, to take charge personally. Mr. Devens also saw that methods was informed, so that a new process sheet could be written up for the operation.

In discussing the proposed changes with the observer, Carson Colley stated, "Devens really asked me to handle this so that we wouldn't lose our shirts due to production downtime. These changes are the darnedest things. They just knock hell out of our production. Now I've got to decide whether to authorize overtime for about 12 repairmen or whether to shut down the line and put all the girls on modification work. This company hates to lose money, and I have a hunch that the girls can do the job with suitable instruction. Anyway, come on down to the line first thing tomorrow, and we'll see if we can make the changes without getting the girls all upset. I'll probably let Al Schmidt handle a good part of it, because he's worked with most of these girls for a long time."

About 9:00 A.M. the next morning, Al and Carson Colley arrived on the line and told the workers that the change would have to be installed immediately. Ordinarily, in the case of such a minor change, Ken Simpson, an industrial engineer, would have instructed the few operators affected while the line was running. In this case, however, Carson and Al decided to modify the units that had been completed the day before and that were still on the conveyor. When Carson and Al arrived at the line, Tony was at the far end, and he remained where he was. Ken, Earl Jones, and Archie Taylor were also present to help carry the change through. Al and Carson spoke rapidly and made some quick decisions.

CARSON: This change is very delicate, and we have to be careful about it. Now I want this done right the first time. If it isn't done right, we'll have to do it all over again and we'll be in a hell of a mess. I want it done right this time and avoid trouble later. Now let's get Ken, Earl, Archie, and everybody else connected with this to come in on it. We'll supervise it ourselves.

Al called for these three men. Tony was still at the end of the line, and no one called for him.

AL: Look, the best way to get this done is to shut the line down completely for a half-hour and to throw all the girls to making the modification of all the completed units on the line. That'll be much better than having repairmen come in for overtime tomorrow. And that'll only confuse us. It's simpler to get the thing done once and for all.

CARSON: That's right. We'll shut the line down, and get this over with. (Ken, Earl, Archie, and Al agreed with this.)

AL: Okay. Now let's get all the group leaders over here. Therese, Peggy, Hilda! Over here. (The group leaders assembled.) We're putting in a modification on one of the circuits. We have to change all the completed units on the line. Now, we'll shut down the line for a half-hour, and all the girls will go right down to the units and change the lead. Do you get me? All right now. Ken, Earl, and Archie, will you instruct the group leaders on this change and then the girls? (They nodded.) Okay. Now shut the line down. Oh, wait a minute. The girls over there; be sure they've completed the unit in front of them. That'll save some confusion. Now, this is a very tricky change, so we have to be careful and see that the girls do it right.

CARSON: All set? Well, I'll leave now. Remember, I don't want to have to see this job done over again.

Carson left and Tony came down to the group assembled around Al. No one addressed him or otherwise acknowledged his presence. He in turn offered no comments.

AL: Okay. Shut the line down.

Earl, demonstrating on one of the units on the line, explained the modification and change to the group leaders. The line was stopped and the girls rapidly completed the work on the units in front of them. The group leaders then called the girls down to the end of the line where the instruction and modification were to take place. Tony, meanwhile, walked back and forth from one group to the next, but he still said nothing. The group leaders and Earl, Ken, and Archie began the instruction. There was some confusion because the girls had not brought their hand tools with them, so they were told to go back to their work stations for these tools. Then some of the girls called out that there were no soldering irons available at the last half section of the line, and this caused further confusion.

Tony was then spoken to for the first time. "What about the soldering irons, Tony?" He did not answer. Someone suggested that only a few soldering irons be brought down and spaced evenly along the section of the line where the work was being performed. Tony called for one of the repairmen and told him to bring up some soldering irons and to plug them in along the last half of the line. The repairman looked confused, shook his head and went for the irons. Therese commented to the observer, "What a mess! This goes on all the time. What can you do?" The girls who were awaiting instruction sat at their work places, and there was considerable joking and laughing. One of the girls commented, "Gee, this is fun. I hope the line stays shut down for a while."   Another girl spoke up, "This makes time go by faster." The instruction proceeded and soon all the girls were busy modifying units.

One of the operators came up to Tony with four soldering irons that were still hot. "Tony, what should I do with these"? Tony took them and when Peggy came over he handed two of them to her, holding the others. They held the irons for a moment and then Peggy started to giggle. "Look at me holding these soldering irons. Am I supposed to hold them all day"? Tony walked over to the other side of the aisle and laid the irons he was holding on a roller conveyor. Peggy followed him and did the same.

Tony said to the observer at the time the modification was being performed, "This isn't my idea. Aw, this is terrible. I wouldn't do it this way. They come up here and tell me to shut the line down. They say only half an hour. It'll be at least an hour. Then I'm going to lose all those units. Hell, they won't want to know from nothing in the front office. All they'll ask is where's the production. That's where I'll get it in the neck."

The girls completed the modification work in a little more than an hour. As each girl completed her work, she returned to her position and sat down at her chair. Soon all the girls were seated and resumed their laughing and joking. No one gave the order to start the conveyor until a little later. About 1 hour and 20 minutes had elapsed since the belt was stopped.

After the line resumed operations, Tony calculated that he was 15 units off schedule. He set out to make up this deficiency. He asked Therese to help out at the last position to "push" the units off, and spent most of the day after the line started up again at the last position helping Therese "push out" the units.

Therese helped Tony but she did not like it. She told the observer, "Tony asked me to help push the units out. It shows you how I have to move around. I don't mind doing it today, but I'm not going to do it anymore. Tony said to me how much I was helping him out, and he said, 'Don't worry, Therese, I won't forget this. I'll take care of you!' Take care of me! Hah! I've had more promises made like that than I can remember, and I know damned well they forget about it. They expect me to do everything around here, and yet I get the same pay as other group leaders. That isn't right."

At 10 minutes before quitting time, Therese came over to the observer and reported proudly that the line had succeeded in completing 120 units, which was in excess of its quota for the day. This output was met despite the line stoppage of 1 hour and 20 minutes. Therese showed the observer the daily input-output record for the line. It indicated that 90 units were put into the line that day, while 120 completed units were taken off. The observer was puzzled, and he was about to ask Therese to explain the discrepancy in the input and output figures when Al appeared. He asked Therese how the line made out in the day's production. Therese reported, "We got 120 out even though we were shut down. But the only way we could get it out was to fill in with the units on the repair table." The observer than asked Al what Therese had meant. He said, "Oh, we had units piled back to back on the line, and that's what she meant." The observer later discovered that units waiting for repair were not counted in the day's production until the repairs were completed. There had been a backlog of units on the repair tables, and Therese had "pushed" the repairmen to complete them for entry into the day's quota.

The observer saw Carson during that day and asked him to explain the nature of the change introduced on the line. Carson replied, "You saw that we had to shut down the line. Well, what could we do? I guess it's just the nature of the beast and we just have to live with it. Well, anyway, when they came to me about the change, I figured there were two ways of handling it. One, we could have authorized overtime for about 12 repairmen tomorrow all day. That would have meant overtime pay and even then I'm not sure that the work would have been completed. The other way, and that's what we did, we could shut down the line for half an hour and throw all the girls over on the modification and have it cleaned up once and for all. Well, I explained it to Devens and he bought it. Well, what else could he say? I mean there it was. Unless he could think of a better idea, that's all he could do—buy my way. So that's how it was."

Cold-Air Corporation (B)

IN the second week following an expansion of its assembly lines by the Cold-Air Corporation in 1948, the workers on the new Cold-Master mechanized conveyor line began to have trouble keeping up with the conveyor. It did not take Tony, the foreman, long to figure out that he would lose one unit of production for every few minutes the conveyor was stopped. During the first week after the installation of the new conveyor, Tony did not seem concerned that the conveyor was being stopped when a girl got out of position. Indeed, the first week ended with the line having exceeded its quotas each day.

During the second week, however, as production quotas were raised toward the assigned standards, the girls experienced considerable difficulty in keeping up with the belt. Consequently, if a girl did not complete her operation in the allotted time, she moved along with the belt until she had done her job. The operator in the next position then had to move down the line in order to start her work. As a result, when a girl once got out of position, a vicious spiral was started which made it increasingly difficult for anyone on the line to catch up.

On Wednesday of the second week, the girls were out of position and began pressuring to have the conveyor shut down. Some of them kept insisting to Peggy, their group leader, that she should shut down the conveyor. Peggy kept repeating at each request, "Tony doesn't want the line to stop." Because several girls were absent from Peggy's section, she was busy on the line helping fill-in operators, and she took positions herself until a fill-in operator could be assigned. At one point in the day, while the girls were far out of position, Peggy called for Tony.

PEGGY: Tony, Bertha is out of relief. You better shut down the line. She shouldn't be away.
SEVERAL OPERATORS: Oh, Peggy, what's the matter with you? Why don't you keep quiet? Can't a girl go to the bathroom?

OPERATOR 22 (to the observer): How do you like that? What's a girl supposed to do if she has to go to the bathroom? Do they want her to get sick?

OPERATOR 18: God, this place is worse than Alcatraz. You can't move. It's worse than Alcatraz. (In a loud voice.)

TONY: What did you say?

OPERATOR 18: I said it's worse than Alcatraz here. You can't even go to the bathroom. And it's true.

TONY: I want to see you. (To Peggy.) Relieve her when you're through. I want to talk to her. (Tony walked away.)

The girls started to laugh when Tony was out of earshot.

AN OPERATOR: Oh, you're going to get a talking to. (Laughter.)

ANOTHER OPERATOR: You're going to get it now.

THE OPERATOR: Oh, I had a talking to once. He said to me, "Don't worry. Have faith in me. I'll take care of things."

There was considerable laughter at this remark.

OPERATOR 18: Yeah. He'll bawl me out and tell me to have faith in him. (Laughing.)

AN OPERATOR: Oh, Peggy, can I go to get a drink of water?

SECOND OPERATOR: Me too, Peggy; I'm so thirsty.

THIRD OPERATOR: Peggy, can I go to the bathroom?

There were screams of laughter as the teasing continued.

PEGGY: Oh, shut up, will you?

The next day, conditions on the line seemed worse than the previous day. There were several absentees, and Therese had to work on position 1 until a fill-in could be found for the operator who was absent. The line was shut down for a while in the morning. The observer spoke to some of the operators.

OPERATOR 9: Oh, God, I hate this work. I'm so tired of working. I wish I had a million dollars so I wouldn't have to work anymore. I would just sleep and take it easy.

OPERATOR 10 (laughing): Stop dreaming, Operator 9. What do you have to worry about anyway? You're married.

OPERATOR 9: What? Do you think I work for the fun of it? Boy, I need the money. Oh, how I hate this! I don't know what's the matter with me. I'm so nervous. I don't know what's happened to me. I used to be able to keep up. It's only since I've been on this line that I haven't been able to keep up. Ever since

I've been working on these units. I worked over in——(another division) and I never had any trouble there.

OPERATOR 10: You know why you're nervous, Operator 9? You know what's wrong? It's these bosses. They're so mean and cold-blooded. They don't have any feeling for you. That's what's wrong, Operator 9.

A little later on, when the line had started up again the girls began to get out of position again. Peggy spoke to the observer.

PEGGY: You see what I mean, Observer. Look at how the girls are out of position. They can't work like that. They have to keep moving back and forth for parts. Oh, this is terrible. It never used to be this way. We never had trouble like this with the old line. And when I try to explain it to Tony, he won't listen to me. He should shut down the line to give the girls a chance to get straightened out. But he won't do it. This is terrible, and the girls keep complaining to me, but what can I do? It's Tony. I won't say anything to him any more! I can't work with the girls if I can't help them. If you expect them to cooperate with you, you have to cooperate with them. But I can't do anything about it.

Tony came over to Peggy a few minutes later.

PEGGY: Tony, look at how the girls are out of position. Why don't you shut the line down for a little while so the girls can get back into position?

TONY: Look, Peggy, we can't shut the line down. That's out. The reason they're out of position is that we have two operators on position 11. That means the girls should overlap only one unit. That's all.

PEGGY: Oh, Tony, that isn't true. They're out one position now, but mark my word, before the day's over they'll be out three or four positions.

TONY: How do you figure that way, Peggy? They'll overlap only one position because there are two operators on position 11. You wait and see. But we can't shut the line down. I have to meet a schedule, and whenever the line shuts down you lose units. I can't afford to let that happen.

PEGGY: All right, Tony. Have it your way, but we'll see who's right. They'll be out three or four positions this afternoon. Wait and see. And, Observer, you'll be my witness. You remember what I said and we'll see who is right.

Tony left.

PEGGY: You see what I mean, Observer? You can't talk to him. He just won't listen when I talk to him. I don't know what's the matter with Tony. He talks so you hardly know what he's talking about. How did he get only one position? What's that mean? Honestly, I don't know what he's talking about half the time. Well, you heard what I said, Observer; you'll be my witness and we'll see who's right, Tony or me.

Later in the morning Peggy and Hilda were discussing the situation. They came over to the observer.

PEGGY: Observer, we want to get your opinion on something. You've been standing here watching, and we'd like to get your opinion on something.

HILDA: Look, Peggy and I were talking, and we think that it would be better to stop the line for a few seconds as soon as one girl begins to get out of position and then start it again. Instead we have to wait until the girls are four or five units behind and then they stop the line. That way we lose more units than if we stopped the line right away for a minute or so. Don't you think so?

OBSERVER: You mean stop it right away?

HILDA: Sure. We would lose less time that way and get more production out, too.

PEGGY: We'd just like to get your opinion on this, Observer.

OBSERVER: Well, I really don't know, Peggy. You're so close to it.

PEGGY: I see what you mean. We're so close to it we can see what's happening better.

HILDA: Sure. Well, we thought you might have an opinion on this. But you see what we mean, don't you?

OBSERVER: Sure I do, Hilda.

The situation continued to get worse. The girls were moving out of position more and more as the morning progressed. Operator 9, who had complained earlier of being nervous, started to cry. She reached for her handbag and left the line. Operator 10 stopped the conveyor. The observer walked over to Operator 10.

OPERATOR 10: Operator 9 just left, so I had to stop the line. Gosh, she's nervous because she can't keep up. Where's Therese? I want to tell her.

Therese was sitting at Tony's desk at the end of the line. Operator 10 went over to her. The girls in the first section soon had their work completed and they sat down. The girls started talking about Operator 9.

INSPECTOR 1: Oh, she's so nervous. She couldn't keep up, so it got her nervous.
OPERATOR 11: That's what happens to you around here. Everybody gets like that.

Therese came walking down with Operator 10 and she asked which way Operator 9 had gone. Therese went after her. Tony came over.

TONY: Who shut the line?
OPERATOR 10: I did. Operator 9 had to leave.

Tony then tried to get Operator 10 to take Operator 9's position. After much giggling, she complied, and Tony started the line up again. The girls farther up the line watched the events with interest. Some of the girls commented, "This is awful. This work gets you so nervous. I can hardly wait until this day's over so I can go home and forget about this place."

Therese succeeded in calming down Operator 9, and she returned to her position. At the rest period, Operator 10 said to the observer, "Tony wanted to fire Operator 9 because she left her position. You're not allowed to do that. She's better now. But Therese went after her and wouldn't let Tony fire her. Wasn't that mean of Tony? But Therese is good that way. She takes care of the girls."

Therese told the observer, "Tony said to me that I was the only one besides himself who could shut the conveyor. I just looked at him and wondered if that wouldn't cause dissension with the other group leaders. After all, I'm a group leader the same as they are, and yet he lets only me stop the line."

Peggy reacted to the incident as follows: "You saw Tony shut the line this morning when the first section couldn't keep up. That's what I call showing partiality, because he wouldn't shut it otherwise. He's got it in for me."

Later in the afternoon conditions on the line had not improved. Tony was walking down the line. When he reached Hilda's section he was stopped by several of the girls.

AN OPERATOR: Tony, look how far out of position we are. We can't work this way. (Some of the girls were out by as many as five positions.) We have to walk back and forth for parts. This is awful. Why don't you shut down the line and give us a chance to get back into our regular positions?

OTHER OPERATORS: This is just terrible. I've never seen anything like it before. I don't even know what unit I'm supposed to be working on, or where my parts go. I'm getting all mixed up.

INSPECTOR 3: Look where I am. I'm supposed to be way down there. I don't even have my chart here. It's way down there. How am I supposed to inspect these units.

TONY: What do you need your chart for? How long have you been an inspector?

INSPECTOR 3: Two years, why?

TONY: Two years and you mean to say that you still need a chart to inspect?

INSPECTOR 3: Certainly. I have to look at it once in a while. I can't remember everything on it. You want good work, don't you?

Peggy and Hilda were listening to this conversation.

PEGGY: Tony, I told you this would happen. The girls are way out of position and they say they're getting sick walking up and down while the conveyor moves. Listen, Tony, you're going to have an explosion one of these days unless you do something about it. Why don't you shut the line down and let the girls get back to position?

TONY: I can't shut the line down, Peggy. We'll lose units that way. Why are the girls out of position?

PEGGY: I don't know. It starts down on the beginning of the line where the new girls are. When you get girls absent, it makes it worse.

AN OPERATOR: Why don't you get floaters[1] back on the line?

TONY: Now look. I told you before. You might as well forget about floaters. You're not going to get them, you understand? That's out, so you might as well forget about it. Now look (to Peggy). Now look, you should only be overlapped one unit, because there are two girls on position 11.

PEGGY: Well, look, Tony. They're out 5 positions now. Look for yourself.

TONY: Why are they out 5 positions? I can't understand that. The cycle is 1.8 minutes. One point eight and the line moves a foot per minute. So I even gave you more time to finish the work than you need. Why should you be out?

[1] That is, utility girls who filled in where needed.

AN OPERATOR: Because the line isn't balanced.

OTHER OPERATORS: That's right.

PEGGY: I guess that's the answer, Tony. I don't know.

TONY: Look, Peggy, I've got to find out what the cycle is. Unless I know that, I can't do anything. Now, what's the cycle?

PEGGY: I don't know. Why don't you go over to methods and find out? They'll tell you.

TONY: I can't get the answers from them. Now I figure the cycle is about 1.8 and the line moves a foot a minute, so I gave you extra time.

AN OPERATOR: That's not our cycle. It's 3 point something.

TONY: Who told you that?

THE OPERATOR: I know.

Therese joined the group. Tony addressed her.

TONY: Therese, what's the cycle on this line? You know it. Tell me.

THERESE: Oh no! I don't know anything about it. I'm not going to open my mouth.

TONY: Come on Therese, tell me what's the cycle here. The way I figure it, it's 1.8 minutes and then they split positions. On some positions they've got two operators. So that lowers the cycle.

THERESE: Where the hell do you get that stuff? They split the positions all right, but you begin with a 3.4 minute position, then they add double the work to the position, so you get almost a 7-minute cycle. Then they split the position, but it's still $3\frac{1}{2}$ minutes, isn't it? I don't get this business of the cycle dropping. I didn't want to say anything to begin with, but you asked me, so I told you.

Tony ordered the line shut down. Therese walked away.

TONY (to Peggy): What's the cycle here?

PEGGY: It's just like Therese said, Tony.

TONY: Well, I'll tell you. One of these days I'm going to time the operations and find out the cycle myself.

PEGGY: That's a good idea, Tony. You can do that.

Tony started the line up again. The operators started to complain again. "What's he expect us to do? Does he think we can get back into position in five minutes?" Tony had started the line up because he saw Carson Colley come up to the line. When

Carson left, Tony stopped the line again. The girls continued to complain.

INSPECTOR 3 (to the girls around her): Did you hear what Tony asked me? How long have I been an inspector! I had to hold myself back from asking him how long he's been a foreman, not to be able to run a line right.
AN OPERATOR: Why didn't you?
INSPECTOR 3: I just want to wait. I'll give him a little more rope. He'll hang himself.

Therese was disgusted. She said, "Look at the way this line is shut down. Christ, it makes me sick. And Tony had the nerve to say to me, 'I'm surprised at you, Therese. Why did you say that about the cycle?' Hell, he asked me, didn't he? I didn't want to say anything, but when he kept asking me, I told him. And he told me that Peggy was blaming my section for throwing the line out. How do you like that? Boy, you can't trust anybody around here. I don't know, I should be home minding babies, but instead I'm here."

Tony was worried. He talked to the observer.

TONY: These girls (referring to the group leaders) have me behind the eight ball. I have to depend on them for answers in case Devens calls me into his office, and I don't know whether they're telling me the right stuff or not. They've been on the line longer. So I've just got to wait and get straightened out. Meanwhile, they've got me behind the eight ball and I have to depend on them for answers. When Devens or Carson calls me in, they want a quick answer and it has to be right. It doesn't look right for me to hesitate. So I have to depend on my group leaders, but I'm not sure they're telling me the right answers. I have to find out what my costs are and keep them down. Nobody says anything to me, yet, but I know damned well that they'll call me into the office and ask me why my cost is so high. I want to be ready for them. Today, Greenburg was trying to put me on the spot. He came up to me and asked me how many people I had on my line. I asked him, "What's your question?" He asked me again, "Well, let me put it this way. How many people all told are there on your line?" I said to him, "Well, I really can't say right now." He said to me, "You mean to say you don't know the number of people on your line right now?" Well, then I had to tell him. So I came right out and said to him, "All right, I'll tell you frankly. I've

522 LEADERSHIP AND CHANGE

got 48 people on my line. That's 8 more than I'm supposed to have. You can go right into Devens and tell him now."

You see what he was trying to do? He wanted to get me to commit myself on how many people I had on the line, so he could put me on the spot to Devens. But I don't trust Joe Greenburg, and he don't trust me, but I came out and told him anyway. Then I tried to get back at Joe. I asked him, "What's my cycle on this line?" He'll never give me an answer to that question. I'll keep asking him and he'll never tell me. He'll say, "I'll look it up and let you know." But he never does. That's the trouble. I can't get an answer on what's my cycle. Then you see how they put me on the spot. Ken rebalanced the line. Well, how do I know if it's rebalanced now? They tell me it is, but how do I know that? Yet Joe'll tell Devens that the line is balanced. You see how that puts me on the spot? When they say the line is balanced, then I'm supposed to get my quota out every day, and I can't stop the conveyor.

OBSERVER: You know, Tony, it seems to me that you're supposed to be in charge of the line, yet there are a lot of people who come around and tell you what you're supposed to do.

TONY: Oh no! They can't tell me what to do. I might look like I haven't got authority on my line, but that's only temporary. You see, when we get straightened out here, why it'll be different. I'm sure it'll be different! After all, I'm supposed to be in charge of the line.

OBSERVER: Tony, you've told me a number of times that in your job as foreman you are responsible for production, quality, and personnel. Tell me, what does that mean?

TONY: (Smiling): Well, production means that I'm supposed to get a certain quantity out every day. The schedule . . . .

OBSERVER: Yes, but tell me in your own words.

TONY: (Laughing): Well, methods is supposed to set up the line for me so that I can get out a certain amount. If they don't balance the line or if they don't set it up right, I'm not going to get out the quantity on my schedule. So I'm responsible for that. That means I'm going to get put on the carpet for that. Now, I don't have to let methods come in here to rebalance the line or anything. After all, I'm in charge of the line. But if I don't, then Greenburg is going to see Devens and tell him I don't want to *cooperate*. Now that's going to make me look bad. So I have to cooperate with them. (Laughing.)

You know something? You see a lot of people who come down

to the line and try to tell me what to do.   Look at all the people I
got to confront with.   There's methods, then there's inspection and
engineering, and then I got to confront with my boss.   That means
I got to confront with five different people.   And they don't want
to know the other side of the story.   They only look at their side.
I don't know.   I think things will be all right.   As soon as I get my
costs and find out where I stand, I'll get everything straightened
out.   It's *got* to straighten out!

The next day, Thursday, Tony and Al had lunch together in the
plant cafeteria.   Al handed Tony a quality control report on one of
the two small subassembly lines which were under Tony's jurisdiction.
This line was staffed by 9 or 10 operators.   This week, while Paul
Carlson was on vacation, the line was under the immediate supervision
of a group leader named Angie Lemnios.   Tony ordinarily had few
problems with this line's operation.   He would visit it once or twice
a day and collect the work tickets from Angie or Paul at the end of
each day.

The quality report which Al gave Tony indicated that the quality
of the subassembly units had deteriorated very suddenly.   Al said,
"Look at that quality; it's terrible."   He continued as follows:

AL: We're going to have to do something about it and quick.   I'm
  going to transfer Peggy over to that line.   She'll know what to do
  to take care of it.   Those girls on there will have to get hot.
  They've been giving Angie plenty of stormy weather.   But Peggy
  was on that line once before when quality went down.   She'll
  know how to handle it.   I want you to take Peggy over there and
  talk to those girls.   Tell them that Peggy is Tony over at that line.
  If anyone gets snippy, Peggy shouldn't fool around but report that
  girl to you right away.   This fooling around has got to stop and
  Peggy is the girl to do it.
TONY: (nodding):   Well, Peggy hasn't been doing too good a job for
  me.   I was thinking of transferring her around the different sections.
  She's caused me a lot of problems.
AL: Look, don't worry about Peggy.   You just let me handle her.

Al spotted Peggy in the cafeteria and he motioned for her to join
him.

AL: Peggy, I want you to go over to Angie's subassembly line right
  after lunch.   The quality over there stinks and I want you to fix it.
  You know what to do, don't you?   And I don't want you to take

anything from those girls over there. Get them in line, get me? And get those rejects down!

PEGGY: What about Angie?

AL: She'll come over to the main line. Now Tony'll take you over, so wait for him before you go there.

After lunch and while walking back to the line, Tony seemed very depressed. He said to the observer, "I was going to transfer her over there anyway. I wanted to shift all the group leaders; move them around from section to section."

Peggy and Tony met at the main assembly line.

TONY: Now, you're going over to the subassembly line. I intended to move you over there anyway. I wanted to move you around.

PEGGY: (Excitedly): What do you mean, Tony? Won't I stay over there?

TONY: Who said that? No!

PEGGY: I don't understand. Al told me . . . .

TONY: Wait a minute, Peggy. Never mind. If you'd have listened to me the other day, you would have heard me tell you that I was going to move you around. I said I would move you over to the subassembly line.

PEGGY: You never said that, Tony. You said you'd move me from one section to another on the main line, but not the subassembly line.

Later, Peggy said to the observer, "Did you hear what Tony said to me? He's trying to make me believe that *he* was transferring me to the assembly line and not Al. But *I* know it was Al's idea and *not* his."

Peggy and Tony walked over to the subassembly line together. Tony saw Angie and said, "I'm putting Peggy over here for a while." Angie, who had only recently been appointed as a group leader, became very upset. She slammed down the pliers she had been holding and started to cry. She tried to control herself and said to Tony, "What was I supposed to do? I've had a girl out every day and I've had to fill in a position, so how could I supervise and check the quality?" Tony tried to calm Angie. Then he called all the operators on the subassembly line into a group around him.

TONY: (in a very angry tone): The quality here has been terrible. I got a report from the test department that shows wrong connections, wrong components, and unsolders. Now that's going to stop. We're going to get the rejects down! I'm putting Peggy over here and she's Tony to you! What she says goes! And if anyone doesn't cooperate with her, she'll report to me, and believe me, you'll go right out the door and no questions asked. We're going to improve quality and we're going to do it right away. Now I'm not blaming Angie for this. She's done a swell job, but she didn't get any cooperation from you. Now you know Peggy here . . . .

OPERATORS: Oh, yeah. We know her (laughter). We've had her before.

TONY: Well, she's going to be here. You're going to cooperate with her and get these rejects down right away. Now does anybody have any questions? Speak up and tell me what's on your mind.

OPERATORS: What's the matter with our quality? Nobody's shown me what rejects I've made. I'd like to find out.

TONY: Well, that's what Peggy is going to do. She'll show you your rejects.

Tony told the operators to return to their workplaces. He then told Angie to come back to the main line with him. Peggy protested, "Wait a minute, Tony. She can't go back yet. Give me a chance to learn the line. It's been a long time since I've been over here." Angie joined in, "Who's going to take the position I've been filling today? Somebody's got to be in there. That's been the trouble here. I've had girls out every day." Al joined the group and instructed Tony to send one operator from the main line to the subassembly line. Tony and Angie departed for the main line, leaving Peggy and Al together. Peggy talked as follows:

PEGGY: Al, I don't know what's the matter with Tony. He tried to make me believe that *he* was putting me over here. He said he was going to transfer me around to Therese's section and then to Hilda's section. And you know what he did last Thursday? After work he called me aside and said that unless I got 130 units out he was going to get rid of me. How is it my fault that he can't get out 130 units? After all, I'm in the middle of the line, and I can only put out what I get. Why did he pick on me? All right, if he wasn't satisfied, he should have called all the group leaders together and told us the same thing. Well, afterwards on Thursday, he said to me I misunderstood him. That all he was going to do was transfer me to another section. And you know what else he said to me? "I'm no fool, Peggy. I've got books home and I read them, so I know what's going on!" Imagine saying that!

Al smiled and shook his head while Peggy was talking. When he was about to leave the subassembly line, he said to the observer, "I'm going to have to get rid of Tony."

Later that same day Tony "had it out" with Al. Tony stood at the edge of the aisle talking to Al. He was gesturing and he seemed quite agitated. After Al left, Tony came over to the observer and continued talking.

TONY: Well, I had it out with Al. I really had it out this time, and I told him what was on my mind. I'm tired of everybody coming around here and telling me how to run this line. I'm the one's going to be on the spot when costs don't come down or when we don't meet quota. Then they hit me on quality. Did you see Ruth Henry a little while ago? I'm telling you, she put me on the spot. What's she trying to do? In front of Al, she said, "Tony, I'm trying to keep from marking the rejects on your sheets. I'm trying to help you out." Who does she think she is? Trying to help me out! She's not doing me any favors. I'm running this line. Where does she get off at? Then these methods people! You saw the way I had to shut the line down the other day because methods ordered the wrong component. Is that *my* fault? What do I have to do with that? I'm supposed to use the component they tell me to use. But I don't complain to nobody. I just took it and kept quiet. I was trying to be good about it. So what does methods do? Joe Greenburg goes into Devens and tells him the line is balanced now. Balanced! How do I know that it's balanced? But Devens and Carson expect to get production. The belt should *not* stop now! That's something that's got to change. I'm going to fire the first person that stops this conveyor starting on Monday. That's final! I don't care who it is. No warnings and I'm not taking them to see Al. I'm going to fire them right away. That John Steen! He's supposedly in charge of quality. Now he's trying to run the line. He's always stopping the conveyor. Who does he think he is? Well, that's going to stop. I got to take the responsibility for this line. Nobody wants to admit that they made a mistake. I got to take it! Nobody's big enough to take their own mistakes.
Yeah, I told Al. I said to him, "I'm not excited or nervous. People say I'm nervous, but I'm not. I'm cool as a cucumber and I know what I'm talking about." I'm not excited now, Observer. You can take my blood pressure right this second and you'll see that I'm calm and collected.
Al told me the girls were complaining that I was forcing them to stay overtime. Al said I couldn't force them to stay in overtime. I told Al, "Look, I'm running this line, not you. I'll handle it my

way." Sure! They can call me into the office and say you
shouldn't compel people to stay. You should request. Compel—
request; if I request and they don't stay and things don't get done,
then they tell me, "What kind of a foreman are you that you can't
get people to stay?" I told Al, "These people are working for me,
not you."

Aw, Observer, I'll get things straightened out. Today things got
messed up on the subassembly line. Tomorrow I'm going to figure
my costs. I'll check my cycle and things'll run smooth. It'll be
just like when I was on the other line.

Cold-Air Corporation (C)

At the time of its 1948 expansion of assembly lines, the Cold-Air Corporation installed a conveyor belt in the company's Cold-Master refrigerator line. On Thursday of the third week after Tony Mastico had become supervisor of the Cold-Master assembly, he attempted to figure out whether the conveyor belt operations were really balanced or not. He asked each girl to call out her position number every time she completed her operation on a motor assembly. He explained to the group leader, Hilda Bennett, what he was doing. "I don't want to make them nervous by standing behind them with a stop watch," he said, "so I'm doing it this way. What I'm trying to do is find out why the girls get out of position and who can't keep up. I'm working on your section right now. Will you sit here and keep the tallies for me for a few minutes, because I've been called up to the office about something?"

"Well, I will," Hilda replied, "but you're timing the fastest operators in the place. They're not to blame for the line getting out of position. You should time the girls in the first section."

When Tony returned to the line about 20 minutes later, he found the girls between positions 28 and 32 out of line, and he stopped the conveyor. "The girls were in position while I was watching them," he said to Hilda. "As soon as I left they got out again. Now what happened?"

"I don't know, Tony," Hilda replied. "It's not their fault. Maybe it's the girls up ahead of them."

Tony replied, "I can't understand, Hilda, why this happened. The girls were in position fine, and then I go away for a few minutes and come back and find them out of position. Now how did that happen?"

Hilda repeated her first explanation while Tony kept shaking his head and muttering, "I don't understand why it happened."

About an hour later Inspector 3 called Tony over to the end of the line. "Look where I'm working," she protested. "I'm way out of position. I should be down there." She pointed to a position about 15 feet down the line.

The operator next to her added, "We can't even reach our bins, we're so far out of place here."

"You'll have to stop the conveyor and give us a chance to get back into position," the inspector said.

"I can't stop the conveyor," Tony replied. "We're behind schedule as it is. Now why should you be so far out of line?"

"Our regular girl who puts in the rotor is out today," put in Hilda. "It's a tough position, and we've got an inexperienced operator there today."

"Well, we can't stop the conveyor," Tony repeated. "I lose too much production that way."

"Look where we are. Where will we go?" the inspector inquired.

Tony thought for a minute and then said, "Look, I'll take some units off the end of the line and put them on the repair table. We can finish them over there."

Discussion continued between Tony and the girls. He refused to shut the line down as they requested and ordered half a dozen motors moved from the line to the repair table. While the repair man was doing that, Ruth Henry, the group leader of inspectors, John Steen, her supervisor, and Ken Simpson, the methods man assigned to this line, joined the group.

JOHN: Look, Tony, I want these units taken out of my inspectors' positions right away. Look where my girls are! They've been pushed out of their positions. They can't move their spotlights any further down the line, and I'm not going to have them working in the dark. Now get those things out of their way.

TONY: Wait a minute, John. I'm doing the best I can. I already had six motors moved from the line. What more do you want me to do?

JOHN: I don't care what you do. Just get those units out of the way. It's not my fault your girls can't keep up with the line.

TONY: Aw, listen, John. Don't say that. They're keeping up.

JOHN: Keeping up! What do you call that? Look for yourself. Your last girl is right in my inspector's position. Look at that.

TONY: Now look, John. I have somebody out this morning. That's what's holding the line up.

JOHN: I don't care about that. It's your responsibility to take care of those things. *I* shouldn't be penalized for it.

TONY: Who's penalizing you? I'm doing what I can to get this straightened out. I'm trying to get methods to move the installation of the front end-plate so they'll both be in the last positions and then move your inspectors down. I saw Greenburg and Al Schmidt,

but I can't get any satisfaction out of them. I've been after Greenburg for a week but nothing happens.

JOHN: All right, so you'll have it moved. What I want to know is
what you're going to do now.

KEN: Just a minute here. I heard about moving the end-plate only
last night. What am I supposed to do? I just heard about it, and
you expect me to have it done already.

TONY: I sent Greenburg a work order last week and nothing's been
done yet.

KEN: Well, you didn't tell me. I just heard about it last night.

TONY: I said I told Greenburg.

JOHN: Well, this doesn't help me any. I want those motors moved out
of my inspectors' positions. It's not my fault your line can't keep up.

KEN: They were out of position last night, too.

TONY: Not just last night. It's been that way for a week.

KEN: Well, that makes it even worse.

TONY: Ya, but I've been after methods for a week to move the end-
plate.

JOHN: Look, Tony, are you interested in having inspection?

TONY: Certainly I am.

JOHN: Well, you don't act that way. My girls will have to work
in the dark, and I'm not going to stand for that. You're not cooperating with me.

TONY: Look. Don't say I'm not cooperating with you.

JOHN: What else can I think?

KEN: The line being out of position has nothing to do with methods.

RUTH: Now wait a minute. I know that Tony is bending over back-
wards to help me. The front end-plate should have been moved
long ago.

JOHN: Look, this is getting us nowhere fast. I want those motors
moved, and I'm going to get someone who will see that they are
moved. (Looking around at the others.) All these supervisors
care about is getting production. They don't give a damn about
quality, but I'm not going to let them get away with that.

John left and was back in a few minutes with Al Schmidt. In the
meantime, Tony had stopped the conveyor.

AL: Tony, come over here. You're going to have to stop the line.
Look, you'll have to keep from interfering with John's girls.

TONY: Al, I'm not interfering with John's girls.

AL: Look over there. What do you call that? Now stop the conveyor.

TONY: I have. I've been working all morning on why the girls get out of position.

AL: Look, Tony. They are out of position now, aren't they? Answer me that.

TONY: Yes.

AL: They are over in the inspection positions, aren't they?

TONY: Yes.

AL: You're the supervisor here, aren't you? Well, you're responsible for it, so get your people out of the way of John's girls.

He walked away. In the afternoon Ken came back and moved the end-plate position, as Tony had requested.

At lunch Tony described the morning to a foreman from another part of the factory. "I've been after methods for a week and I couldn't get anything done," he concluded. "I saw Greenburg and Schmidt, and I didn't get any satisfaction. Now they blame me. John says I don't cooperate. Well, they always say that when they want to end an argument. That isn't right." He lit a cigarette. "I am really worried, and I don't know what to do. Schmidt told me yesterday that he wants to speed up the conveyor tomorrow. He has also told me never to stop the belt. Then he comes up this morning and tells me to shut it down. What am I supposed to do? He tells me one thing and then turns around and wants me to do the opposite. That gets me all confused. What was I supposed to do?"

At 3:00 o'clock in the afternoon Tony and his three group leaders reported to the conference room for a meeting of the supervisory training course. This course, called "Human Problems in Supervision," had been organized at the time of the expansion to train the new foremen and group leaders. It was under the direction of Carl French, a member of the personnel department, and met three times a week on company time. The first training group included 25 foremen and group leaders from six production lines. Conference members were given a handbook written by Mr. French which contained short chapters on each of the topics to be discussed at the conferences, plus illustrative material and suggested questions for discussion. The Table of Contents of the manual was a follows:

1. Psychology and the Supervisor
2. Heredity and Environment
3. Emotion and Instinct
4. Physical Conditioning
5. Conflict

6. Learning to Know Your People
7. The Problem of Morale
8. Performance Rating
9. Psychological Tests in Industrial Placement
10. The Functions of the Personnel Department

Hilda Bennett, group leader, arrived first at the meeting and found that a group leader from the adjacent line was the only other person in the room. "Did you see our line this morning?" Hilda asked. "You'd think it was my fault that the girls are getting out of position."

"What happened?" the other group leader inquired.

"Just before I came up here, Tony said to me, 'Unless I get 130 motors tomorrow, I'm going to take you off the line,'" Hilda replied. "That's what he said to me. How can I help it? Do you think it's my fault? I don't see why Tony blames me. He said he would take me off the line if he didn't get 130 tomorrow. How can I help it?"

Therese, coming in just in time to hear the last remark, exclaimed to Hilda, "Boy, are you mad!" The others laughed, and Hilda subsided.

At that point Carl French, the training leader, arrived and opened the session. He commented for a few moments about a large Cold Air ad in the Sunday paper and then reminded the group that the subject for this day's meeting was "Conflict." "Before we begin the discussion," he said, "we ought to understand what we mean by 'conflict' so that all of us will be talking about the same thing this afternoon. As I have defined it for the purpose of these meetings, conflict is any situation involving a disagreement or difference. It could be a disagreement between yourself and another person or yourself and a group, or it might be a situation within yourself. Would any of you like to give illustrations of these types of conflicts? For instance, this is the sort of thing I mean. Supposing your boss came up to you and said, 'I want 175 units out tomorrow and I don't want to know from nothing.' Is that conflict?"

Under her breath Therese muttered, "You hit the nail on the head." Hilda laughed.

"What was that?" French asked Hilda.

"I laughed because she said you hit the nail on the head," Hilda replied. Everyone laughed.

Mr. French smiled. "There are 10 or 12 different ways which individuals may use, consciously or unconsciously, to resolve conflict, no matter whether it comes from inside themselves or from their relations with other people," he went on. "Much of a person's character and personality may be described in terms of which of these techniques he uses. In order to simplify the problem, we may consider that basically they can be grouped into three methods: (1) flight, (2) fighting, (3) compromise." He gave illustrations of each of these methods of handling conflict, ranging from going to the movies as an escape to swearing, brooding, or trying to ignore unpleasant situations. He suggested that one of the ways to avoid conflict was to observe other supervisors and try to imitate methods that appeared to be successful. He warned the group, however, that such imitation required first that they know and understand themselves, since they could copy only those techniques that fit in with their own personalities.

Mr. French concluded, "We have discussed very briefly some of the most commonly used methods of working out conflicts, whether they are within the individual or arise from relations with other people. There are other methods we could talk about, but they are slightly less common, and I feel that we have already devoted sufficient time to this topic. Next time we will try to apply some of these principles of psychology that we have talked about to problems of handling people. For the next meeting will you read the chapter in your handbook called 'Learning to Know Your People.'"

On the way out of the meeting Therese said to Hilda, "Talk about conflict. We really got it on our line. Mr. French didn't know he was getting so close to home. Gee, I could have killed you for repeating my remark. I didn't want Tony to hear it."

"I don't see any reason for covering it up," Hilda replied.

"How could we talk about it with Tony there?" Therese came back. "Anyway, it would have been just talk, so what good is it? But we've sure got conflict on our line."

Tremont Hotel (A)

At 2:30 p.m. on October 22, 1945, the supervisors of the Tremont Hotel attended a meeting called by Mr. Smith, general manager of the hotel (Exhibit 1). The primary purpose of the meeting was to discuss problems of communication with Dr. Robertson, Professor of Industrial Sociology at a nearby university.

Dr. Robertson was familiar with the hotel supervisors and some of their problems. He had first visited the hotel three months earlier, at which time he had arranged to have one of his research workers, Miss Benson, study human relations at the hotel and to have Mr. Stacey, a former human relations research worker, employed as the hotel personnel manager. Dr. Robertson occasionally visited the hotel in connection with this study, and in August he held his first discussion with the hotel supervisors on the problems of dealing with new employees.

The record of the meeting on October 22 which appears below was prepared by Miss Benson.

SUPERVISORS' MEETING, OCTOBER 22, 1945

Mr. Smith opened the meeting by introducing the new chef and new fountain supervisor to the group. After the chef expressed appreciation for the cordial reception and cooperation from department heads, Mr. Smith turned the meeting over to Dr. Robertson.

Pointing to a diagram (below) on the blackboard, Dr. Robertson explained that the organization of any business would roughly correspond to the diagram. He said *A*, *B*, and *C* represented top management, *D* the supervisor immediately responsible for work performance and *W* the workers. He discussed the organization of restaurants in detail. Basing his remarks on a recently completed study, Dr. Robertson observed that all restaurants had many of the same problems of structure and the pressures resulting from it. The diagram did not

534

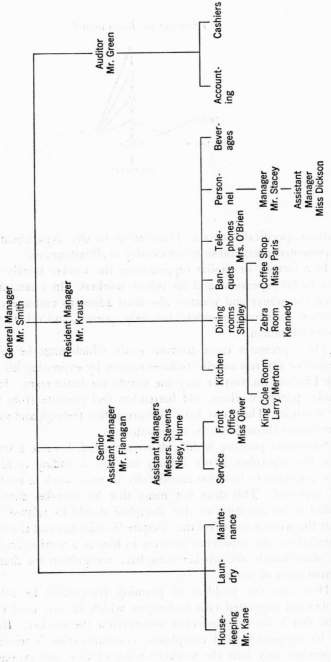

EXHIBIT 1

TREMONT HOTEL (A)

Tremont Hotel Organization Chart* July 1945

General Manager
Mr. Smith

Auditor
Mr. Green

Accounting

Cashiers

Resident Manager
Mr. Kraus

Senior
Assistant Manager
Mr. Flanagan

Assistant Managers
Messrs. Stevens
Nisey, Hume

Housekeeping
Mr. Kane

Laundry

Maintenance

Front
Office
Miss Oliver

Service

Kitchen

King Cole Room
Larry Merton

Dining
rooms
Shipley

Zebra
Room
Kennedy

Coffee Shop
Miss Paris

Banquets

Telephones
Mrs. O'Brien

Personnel

Manager
Mr. Stacey

Assistant Manager
Miss Dickson

Beverages

* This chart was prepared by the research workers as a representation
of the lines of authority as actually in effect in July 1945.

535

Diagram on Blackboard

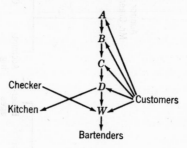

pertain specifically to the Tremont or to any department in it. It represented a general situation existing in all restaurants.

In a factory or similar organization, the worker merely has to adjust to his supervisor and his fellow workers. In a restaurant, however, the waiter and waitress also must adjust to customers, checkers, kitchen workers, bartenders, bus help, porters, and others who work along with them.

These pressures cause nervous strain which must be relieved. A waiter or waitress usually reduces tension by expressing his feelings in the kitchen; the former may use words, the latter tears. In turn, the cooks, pantry workers, and bartenders feel pressure from the waiter or waitress. They, too, have to express their feelings, and so the problems travel throughout the organization.

Sometimes pressure is difficult to withstand, because a worker feels that the supervisor is not helping him but is adding to his burdens. For a worker to function successfully he must work in an *atmosphere of approval*. This does not mean that his mistakes should not be called to his attention or that discipline should be relaxed. It means that the worker must feel that, despite his mistakes and the supervisor's corrections, the supervisor believes in him as a worker and a person. In other words, the worker must have recognition for doing a competent piece of work.

How can this problem of granting recognition be solved? Dr. Robertson suggested two techniques which he saw used effectively. The first is for the supervisor to interview the worker. By listening to his suggestions and complaints, communication is stimulated; the supervisor may hear the worker's point of view and express it to his immediate superior. Eventually it will reach top management. In this way the worker will feel that his ideas are being given proper attention and respect.

The second technique Dr. Robertson suggested was the group meeting. He told of his experiences at a restaurant where he attended such a meeting and watched half the waitresses participate by bringing forth ideas and suggestions.

(At this point Mr. Kraus (Exhibit 1) looked sleepy. Mr. Kane looked bored. Those giving their fullest attention were Mr. Smith, Larry Merton, Mr. Kennedy, Miss Paris, and the chef; in other words, those who were responsible for food departments. The others were listening impassively.)

Dr. Robertson stressed the importance of Mr. C. If D tells C of a good suggestion from a worker and C doesn't act on it or give it adequate attention, D is placed in an impossible position. He is no longer able to encourage his workers to bring suggestions to him, since they gradually will become aware that he cannot do anything about them. Communication must be operating at all levels.

(At this point Mr. Kraus and Miss Oliver exchanged long glances. Miss Oliver smiled and continued to have a half smile on her face for some time. Every now and then Mr. Kraus would whisper something to her, and she'd nod. Her expression was somewhat cynical, while his was enigmatic.)

Dr. Robertson went on to speak of a "system of human relations" which encompassed everyone in a hotel. No one section of the hotel could be isolated for inspection; it had to be regarded as a whole. This is true of all such organizations, not only the Tremont. The attitude of people at all levels in the organization must be taken into consideration.

At this point, Dr. Robertson apologized for talking so long and threw the meeting open to discussion.

MR. SMITH: I guess all of us would like to have an alibi or otherwise defend our positions, at this point. As Mr. A, I'd like to make myself clear in this respect. In a sense, we are in a worse position now than we were in July if our employees are saying, "Well, they did a lot of talking, but what have they done about all these things they talked about?"
I have deliberately stayed away from group meetings in the hotel because it seemed to me that Mr. A, B, and C do all the talking, and Mr. W doesn't get a chance. I find, however, that even when I'm not there, Mr. B and Mr. C are presenting my viewpoints and saying that certain things were what I wanted done. The pressure, in other

words, has all been downward, when what we wanted was some upward pressure.

Now, some suggestions have been made by employees, and they have been ignored or brushed aside. This makes the situation even worse. For instance, in the Coffee Shop: I'm not told that the waitresses have been asking for a water faucet for months now, and I'm just hearing about it. Each time they asked for it they were told that we are to build a new Coffee Shop and don't want to spend money on the old one. Well, that was true a year ago. I was saying that myself, but now I realize that certain things must be done at once to relieve the pressure down there. Our business has increased so greatly that certain adjustments are absolutely necessary if the work is to be done efficiently. This faucet business just goes to show the runaround people get when they have ideas to offer. I want to know what people are thinking about and what they want done.

MR. GREEN: Since I brought this up at the last meeting, I might as well make a report on how Mr. Smith is doing. (Laughter.) You may remember that it was suggested that Mr. Smith speak to employees as he walks through the building. Well, he's doing very well, and it has made a real difference, too. In fact, I received a memo from him myself, commending me for a piece of work I did, and I was so proud that I couldn't talk to anybody for a couple of days.

(Smith beams.)

MR. SMITH: Speaking of things I was to do, I've been working on an organization chart. I know somebody like the chef, here, would benefit by having a chart showing them just what positions the various people around here fill and to whom they should go when they need something done. But business has been changing and growing so fast that I no sooner get something figured out than I have to rearrange the work again. I realize that having this on paper would prevent a lot of false moves, and I still mean to get it done at the first possible moment. Incidentally, I asked each of you at the last meeting to give me a sheet of paper showing the organization of your department, and up to now I've only received three of them. The Personnel Office and Mr. Kane got theirs in to me, and the old chef got in his.

Not to speak of the departed, but sometime I want to show you that chart of the chef's. You would get a good laugh out of it. He showed himself in the middle with spokes going out in all directions from his office.

(General laughter and comments of, "Well, that's where he was most of the time.")

MR. KANE: The question, as I see it, is how can we take off those pressures that Dr. Robertson has been talking about. What are we going to do about them?

MR. SMITH: It seems to me that if Mr. Stacey relieves the pressure, it will only serve to increase pressure in the long run, because Mr. D will tend to resent the interference and will take it out on the worker for going over his head. That would be the tendency, wouldn't it?

DR. ROBERTSON: Suppose Mr. W makes a suggestion to you, and you can't get action on it, what then?

MR. KRAUS: One thing about this place, 99% of the suggestions made by employees are acted upon. None are ignored completely. We always give them consideration.

MR. SMITH: Skillful handling is necessary in cases where bum ideas are brought up. The supervisor certainly shouldn't say, "That's a bum idea," but maybe the same thing can be done by letting the other people in the group challenge it. In other words, if one employee makes a suggestion, get the others to comment on it, and if it is a bad suggestion they can spike it there and then. By the time an idea is passed along to Mr. B and Mr. A, it should not be the idea of one person but the consensus of the whole group.

DR. ROBERTSON: You understand, this is not a common practice in industry. These ideas are being worked out in various places, and we have utmost confidence in them. The problem is: how can we get started on this? Once the pattern is set up, it should be easy to proceed. But, how do we start?

MR. KRAUS: What would happen if Mr. W went straight to Mr. A or B? What should Mr. B do in a case like that?

DR. ROBERTSON: Now, what about a case like that? Do you think the first thing is to ask the employee whether he has spoken to his supervisor? I have seen management people handle it this way. They ask the employee that question, and if the worker says he hasn't spoken to the supervisor, the manager will tell him, "Well, don't talk to me about it, go see your supervisor first." What's wrong with that approach? Isn't it possible that the employee has considered talking to his supervisor and feels that he wouldn't get any satisfaction there? Shooting him back to his own department that way will just block off further communication, wouldn't it? The only thing that could happen which would restore communication in such a situation would be if a union, I might say an active union, steps in, and in that case they would go right to top management; we all know that.

Now, there are several other ways to deal with a thing like this. One way is to talk to the employee and let him blow off steam. Then, when he is finished and has it all off his chest, ask him whether he has seen his supervisor, and, if he hasn't, suggest that he do so. Tell him, if he doesn't get satisfaction, to come to see you again. Meanwhile, you might manage to speak to the supervisor about the matter. Don't just hop on him, of course, but simply present the problem and suggest that he get together with the employee and see what can be done to straighten it out. Now suppose they can't work out something? Then, perhaps, Mr. *A* or Mr. *B* will have to make a solution, but in this situation it is important for Mr. *A* or Mr. *B* not to hand out the solution themselves, but to give it to the supervisor or Mr. *D* and let him officially have the job of handing down the verdict.

Another way I have seen worked sucessfully is to have *A* or *B* call in the worker (Mr. *W*) and supervisor (Mr. *D*) and have them sit down and talk it over. Mr. *D* in that case would have to have prior assurance that any decision he makes will be backed up by Mr. *A* or *B*. After the employee leaves, Mr. *A* might talk further with Mr. *D*, and if he thinks the solution isn't a very good one, he could then suggest that the supervisor think it over some more. He might let the supervisor know that in his opinion trouble will continue until a fairer decision is reached. That leaves the supervisor free to go to the worker and say he has been thinking it over and has changed his mind. This way, Mr. *A* or *B*, whoever is handling the case, is able to encourage upward communication and uphold the position of the supervisor at the same time. Now this way of handling the problem takes a lot of skill, and I don't recommend it as a wholesale procedure. Mr. *A* or Mr. *B* has to be able to prevent excitement when Mr. *D* and Mr. *W* get together in his office, and that's a tough job for anybody. Unless you feel you can control such a situation, it might be better to try one of the other techniques.

MR. SMITH: All this goes back to the fact that you need these meetings. If you have them often enough, the employees can talk up and get things off their chest there and then. It means that *A*, *B*, *C*, and *D* have to keep quiet at these meetings to give the workers a chance. That reminds me of the kitchen meeting that took place after Joe left. I noticed that Mr. Kraus, Mr. Stacey, and myself did all the talking. The employees didn't have a chance. I don't know what we can do about it, maybe we should hold smaller meetings. Now, Mr. Flanagan hasn't had a meeting of his employees for several months, and yet the front office has a great many problems that need to be thought out.

MR. KANE: Isn't that true throughout the house? Not only of the front office, I mean. For instance, I overheard a maid and a houseman having a private meeting of their own in an upstairs corridor the other day. I just wondered how long it has been since they had a chance to express their ideas in a meeting.

MR. SMITH: That's right. And speaking of unions, Kane's department was almost to the exploding point not so long ago. We held a meeting and talked it over, with the result that all they could complain about was the shortage of bath towels. All the time we had plenty of towels; they were just being held in the storeroom. Now, it shouldn't be necessary to go through all of that mess in order to get a need expressed. What the whole organization needs, it seems to me, are more frequent, short meetings.

DR. ROBERTSON: One of the things I've been working on lately is union-management relations. I've been talking to business agents, and they bring out the same fact that Mr. Smith just stated. They say that many things which come to them could have been handled by the immediate supervisor and settled in a few minutes—little things, which become great issues when they aren't dealt with right away. That is the case with most of the grievances which they are called upon to settle. I have heard of a whole factory walking out on strike, and the root of the matter was that certain coat racks had been removed over the employees' protests.

In a case like that, the business agent of the union has to step in and battle for something which he doesn't really want to fight about, something he feels should have been settled right on the spot with no fuss or bother.

MR. SHIPLEY: A year or a year and a half ago, somebody from the outside stepped into our kitchen and settled a dispute for us when none of the people working in the kitchen could see a solution. Sometimes an outsider can see things clearer than the people who work with a problem day after day.

MR. SMITH: Don't you think that depends on the department and the department head? Sometimes that might be true, sometimes not.

MR. SHIPLEY: An outsider can always bring in new ideas and practical suggestions.

MR. NISEY: Mr. Stacey might find out more at those meetings without Mr. *A*, or Mr. *B* present. Maybe the employees are afraid to talk up in front of Mr. *A* or Mr. *B*.

MR. SHIPLEY: Same thing goes for Mr. *D*, doesn't it? Take the Coffee Shop, for instance. Maybe those girls would talk up sooner without their supervisors present. How would it do for Mr. Stacey or Miss Benson to run those meetings?

MR. SMITH: Mr. Stacey and Miss Benson are just interested observers. It isn't their job to run the meetings, but to help the supervisor run them.

MR. KRAUS (to Miss Oliver in a stage whisper): Professors!

MR. SHIPLEY: Well, couldn't they just record the suggestions, and then those which are good could be put into use?

MR. SMITH: How would you feel if Mr. Stacey conducted a meeting in your department? You wouldn't feel so good. If department heads know their own business, they should be able to run the meetings.

MR. SHIPLEY: A lot of the trouble around here is that, no matter what a person asks for, we have to tell them they can't have it until after the hotel is rebuilt.

MR. SMITH: Well, there's some truth in that. And that reminds me, I want to tell you something about the improvements and changes we are planning to make around here, so you can understand some of the stuff you are reading in the papers.

He then proceeded to tell in detail about certain changes, most of them affecting the kitchen, dining rooms, and the lobby.

Mr. Kane continued to nod sleepily as Mr. Smith talked.

MR. SMITH: I realize that we often have stalled people off on making improvements on the ground that we were going to rebuild, but now we realize that some things cannot be delayed any longer without serious loss of efficiency. Our business has grown so large that we can't accommodate people without making some adjustments. For example, our business so far this month is 35 per cent larger than in August; August's business was 35 per cent better than January's; January's was 35 per cent better than the January before. The kitchen is so jammed up that they can't do a good job down there any more. We hope to start on the new kitchen and Coffee Shop in March. I suggest that in the various catering departments, people think in terms of permanent things and temporary things.

MR. GREEN: Looks to me like what we are all driving at is the need for cooperation and coordination.

DR. ROBERTSON: This remodeling program opens just the kind of topic around which to start employee meetings. If we can get the employees themselves to take an interest in it and say what things they would like to see changed or improved, that might be a way to begin our program.

I'd like to say here that I've been hoping Miss Paris would tell us about her meetings, but she's too bashful to tell you of the good job she's doing there. She has been holding group meetings for several weeks now, and from our observations it appears she has been doing a good job there.

MR. SMITH: The thing to be stressed is that an expanded hotel means a chance for all of us to expand with it. Now, Larry, for instance, will have a King Cole about twice as big as the present one. That means he'll have twice as big a job, doesn't it? And not only a bigger salary but more assistants to help him, too, thus making his management better and easier. Tell your employees about this, because an expanded hotel means more jobs, and we hope to move old employees up and put the new ones on the bottom jobs.

MR. O'BRIEN: Will we get a new switchboard, Mr. Smith? You didn't mention any improvement for us. We have the oldest switchboard in the state.

MR. SMITH: We'll take care of the switchboard, don't worry about that.

MR. SHIPLEY: Do you have the oldest telephone supervisor in the state? (Jokes about Ann's age which she takes well.)

MR. KRAUS: I've been sending memos around telling supervisors to have roll call meetings of their dining room employees. How many have done it? Larry, how about you? Now, I want you to have one every day and not every other day.

LARRY MERTON: Well, it isn't as easy as that. We have to consider the time.

MR. SMITH: You'll have to sit down and figure out how many meetings are necessary. There should be a conference between Mr. Kraus and the department head; it shouldn't be decided by one person. We don't want meetings just for the sake of having meetings. We want to accomplish something. Meetings should be planned ahead, and you should know just what ground you want covered and what you plan to say. Another thing: there is a difference between roll calls and meetings. Maybe we need roll calls every day and meetings once a week. That's something we must figure out.

Now, last Saturday is a case which will illustrate our difficulty. We decided to open all the bars and restaurants early because of Homecoming Week, and memos were supposed to go out to everybody. At the last minute it turned out that the accounting office was never notified, and no checkers or cashiers were on the job.

MR. KRAUS: I sent memos to all of them, accounting too. It was the checkers' own fault; I let them know ahead of time.

MR. GREEN: I want to defend the checkers on that score. Those girls were told the bars were to open "early." Now, how were they to know what early meant? They were on the job a little after eleven, but nobody knew they were supposed to be there before that.

DR. ROBERTSON (interrupting): Before this meeting breaks up, I want to state again just what Mr. Stacey's and Miss Benson's jobs are. Mr. Stacey is supposed to help you stimulate upward communication, and he will be glad to consult with you on plans for group meetings or any other technique that might aid toward that end. I don't think it would be a good idea for him to set up a new channel of communication by having the employees come to him with their suggestions. That way the supervisor would not know what was going on in his own department. What we want to do is to send ideas right up the line from Mr. W up to Mr. A, by the way of Mr. B, Mr. C, and Mr. D, and down the line the same way.

Miss Benson will help by interviewing the workers separately to get them interested and encouraged in expressing their ideas. If it seems wise, perhaps Mr. Stacey or Miss Benson or Miss Dickson can sit in on a group meeting and give suggestions for making them more effective.

MR. STACEY: I think we all realize that different departments have different problems. We don't mean to subscribe one cut-and-dried formula for curing all of our ills. Maybe some departments will want a meeting once a week; another may want them oftener, another less often. Some may not want them at all. We must consider each problem separately and work together on its solution. Our job is to oil, to lubricate, the line organization.

DR. ROBERTSON: Miss Benson may be able to fit in another way, too. If you feel your group meetings aren't clicking, the employee might not want to tell you how they feel about it, but they might tell Miss Benson. She can follow up on group meetings and let you know how the employees are reacting. Then she can tell Mr. Stacey her impressions, and he can tell the supervisor, who can take suitable action. Mr. Stacey would not tell Mr. A or Mr. B but would go straight to the supervisor with such information and help him plan future meetings with those facts in mind.

MR. KRAUS: About these group meetings, should Mr. A or Mr. B be present, or not?

DR. ROBERTSON: Well, I don't know, suppose we think about that? I should think that usually it might be well to limit the meetings to Mr. *D* and Mr. *W*. But occasionally it might be a good idea to have Mr. *A* or Mr. *B* present, especially when they have something nice to say to the group, some request to grant. It's my feeling that usually it is better if the top management consults the supervisor and gives him their suggestions and criticisms, rather than to speak directly to the rank-and-file employees.

MR. KRAUS: Usually I participate in all the meetings.

DR. ROBERTSON: Umhmm. Well, occasionally it is an excellent idea to give the employees a chance to talk to you in a group that way, but ordinarily it could get to be quite a burden if you had to take charge of all the group meetings. Another thing I want to point out here is that this atmosphere of approval should extend all up and down the line organization. Mr. *D* needs to feel his superiors have confidence in him just as much as Mr. *W* does.

MR. KRAUS: What if you don't have any confidence in Mr. *D*?

Ripples of laughter throughout the group. Mr. Kraus flushes.

DR. ROBERTSON: Well, there again, the employee, whether he is Mr. *W* or Mr. *D*, needs to feel that if he needs correction, he gets it. But, at the same time, it is absolutely necessary for him to feel the moral support of his superior if he is to turn in a good job. If he feels Mr. *B* doesn't have confidence in him, then he will fail even more tragically than before. If an employee is worth keeping on the payroll at all, he should feel that the supervisor thinks him capable of doing an acceptable job.

MR. SMITH: This meeting is getting too long, but before we break up I want to announce that Miss Dickson has been promoted to the position of Assistant Personnel Manager. We hope that position will not only make the Personnel Office run better, but will help you people in getting what you want, too.

Well, this meeting has gone on too long, but it would help if you got here on time. We will have another meeting in this room one week from today.

That will be all.

Allmetal Steel Corporation

In the fall of 1958, Mr. Arthur Bentley, manager of the Los Angeles District Sales Office, requested the assistance of the Executive Training and Development Division of the Personnel Department in examining the job effectiveness and training needs of LADSO[1] salesmen.

Allmetal Steel Corp. was a large, integrated producer of steel, with headquarters in Chicago, production facilities in the Northeast and Midwest, and warehouses and sales offices in all major cities of the United States and some foreign countries. The more common grades and alloys of steel were sold either by the Central Sales Office in Chicago or by the warehouses, depending on the quantity involved. Special steels, such as stainless, on the other hand, were sold by district sales offices such as the one based in Los Angeles. A group of salesmen, 11 in the case of LADSO, worked in a prescribed territory within 50 to 100 miles of the district sales office. Some of these salesmen had specific territories that they serviced, while others specialized in certain industries, such as architecture or electronics.

In the past five years, in an effort to offset the inroads being made by plastics and aluminum into the traditional markets of steel. Allmetal had considerably increased its plant capacity to produce special alloy steels in general, and stainless steel in particular. In late 1958, the steel industry was suffering from a condition of overcapacity, and Allmetal was specifically concerned with the idle capacity of its comparatively new and efficient stainless steel plants.

In addition to the Central Sales Office, there were various other departments located at Allmetal headquarters in Chicago whose task was to render technical, design, and other services to customers, directly or through the salesmen working from the sales offices. Thus, a salesman could call on the Metallurgical Laboratory to furnish certain information regarding dimensional stability or thermal characteristics of a special alloy steel which was being considered for use by a customer. Often, an engineer would accompany a salesman to the

[1] Los Angeles District Sales Office, hereafter to be referred to as LADSO.

customer's plant to discuss special problems. At other times, a large company might contact the Laboratory directly to ask for technical information. Applications Engineering or Sales Service might likewise be contacted by a district office salesman or a customer.

Organization of LADSO

Each salesman in LADSO had an Order Processor—sometimes referred to as "back-up-girl"—who carried on most of the paperwork for the sales made by the salesman. She would answer requests about materials and procedures, would write up sales orders in proper company format, and would in general help the salesman in any way possible. Officially, the Order Processors were under the supervision of the Office Manager, but in practice they worked most closely with a salesman (see Exhibit 1). Although Mr. Bentley and the Assistant Manager were in charge of the 11 salesmen, most of the time the latter worked quite independently; often they worked with people from various headquarter departments.

The idle capacity alone was not responsible for Mr. Bentley's request to have LADSO studied. For some years he had been curious about the components of job effectiveness of his salesmen. He wanted to have a clearer understanding of the variables that determined the relative success or failure of salesmen working at LADSO. By such a study he hoped to formulate training programs, both for the present sales force and for future trainees.

The Executive Training and Development Division was a part of the Personnel Department, which was located at Allmetal central offices in Chicago. This group was available for assisting company departments in the areas of personnel and human relations research and developing training programs for supervisors and executives. Furthermore, this group was in charge of continuing training programs that served the company as a whole. At the time of his request, Mr. Bentley did not intend to institute a training program similar to those already in existence. Instead, he wanted a study to help interpret salesmen training needs as these related to job effectiveness. He did, however, ask for training recommendations from the research group.

The material in this case study was taken from the report submitted to Mr. Bentley by the Executive Training and Development Division, following three months of intensive participative study. The researchers observed the LADSO organization in operation,

EXHIBIT 1

ALLMETAL STEEL CORP.

LADSO Organization Chart

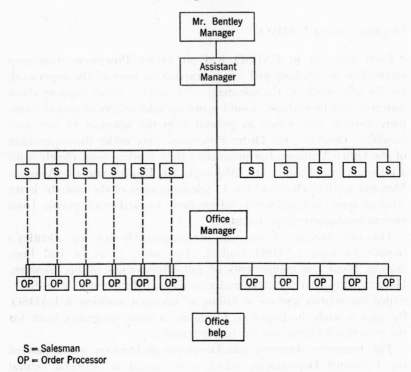

S = Salesman
OP = Order Processor

accompanied salesmen on their sales trips, interviewed all the personnel in LADSO, including Order Processors, and, in general, "lived with" the salesmen.

THE JOB OF A SALESMAN IN LADSO

An Over-all View

As Figure 1 suggests, the salesman has to operate with two significant characteristics of his job in mind in order to satisfy the varied and numerous demands made on him: he is the only continuous and ultimate link between the entire Allmetal organization and the cus-

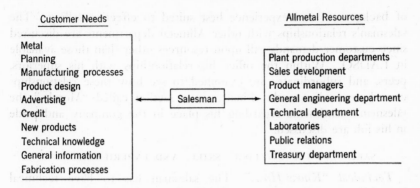

Figure 1

tomer, and he cannot satisfy the customers' needs without relying in varying degrees on other people in his organization. These two job characteristics influence his performance in a number of ways.

Men from other sales service departments may have more of a "hit and run" type of relationship with customers. They arrive on the scene for varying periods of time, bringing highly specialized skills and knowledge; but the salesman has to go on "living with" his customer after the expert moves on to something else.

And yet, as the following section of this report will try to illustrate, he needs the experts and many others if he is to maximize the amount of service he can offer his customers. He is, in fact, in the position of having to administer a complex set of relationships in order to meet a complex set of demands made on him by a large variety of customers. He is, in other words, a business manager vis-à-vis his customers in the widest and fullest sense of the term.

Factors Affecting the Salesman's Performance

Given a situation in which the salesman has to cope with complex demands, questions of resourcefulness arise. "What are the demands made upon the salesman in the situation?" "What resources does he have to meet these demands?" "How does he acquire these resources?" "To what extent is he forced to use his own resourcefulness, and to what extent does he use the resourcefulness of others?"

This section attempts to answer these questions. The salesman's own competence is examined from the point of view of this kind of background and experience best suited to effective selling. The salesman's relationships with other Allmetal departments are discussed since customer demands call upon resources other than those available in LADSO. Within the office his relationships with his superiors, peers, and subordinates are examined to see how these relationships contribute to his work. Finally, in a section called "Morale," the salesman's sentiments regarding his place in the company and pride in his job are discussed.

SALESMAN'S KNOWLEDGE, SKILL, AND EXPERIENCE

Technical "Know-How." The salesman has to have technical knowledge to sell stainless steel. He has to have knowledge about alloys, their properties, forming characteristics, applications, costs, shop practices, and so on. The salesmen are particularly conscious of the importance of technical knowledge and experience. A theme which runs through all their remarks on the subject is the following: "I don't want to be embarrassed by not being able to answer the questions my customers ask me. I don't want to look the fool in front of my customer."

How does the salesman get this technical "know-how"? One point of view, held by people both in and out of the company, is that a salesman should be a trained engineer. Many salesmen felt that the management of LADSO would like to see a greater number of sales engineers in the office. As a company, Allmetal has traditionally filled many of its responsible positions with men with engineering training. Because salesmen need technical competence, it is to be expected that many become engineers.

The answer to questions of technical competence, however, is not as simple as saying. "One has to be an engineer to sell stainless steel." In talking about their own competence and how they came to acquire it, the salesmen place a great deal of emphasis on experience as a significant factor. One salesman pointed out that three salesmen with the most experience "have learned more about stainless steel sheet in (their) basement workshops than anywhere else. . . ." All three of these men stress the importance of being as familiar as possible with the working of metal, and, wherever possible, they underscore the desirability of having a man perform as many operations as possible. Salesman *H*, an engineer and a person considered quite knowledgeable in such matters, is so considered because of his years of plant experience, and not so much for his engineering training. He says himself, "What a salesman needs is training in how metal is formed—not engineering training."

TABLE 1

*Formal Education of Salesmen Listed in Order of
"Perceived Helpfulness"**

"Perceived Helpfulness"	Salesmen	Formal Education
1. (mentioned most often)	K	High school
2.	J	Engineering degree
3.**	I	High school plus
3.**	H	Engineering degree
4.	G	High school plus
5.**	F	Engineering certificate
5.**	E	Naval Academy plus
5.**	D	Degree plus (nontechnical)
6.**	C	Degree (nontechnical)
6.**	B	Degree (nontechnical)
6.**(mentioned least often)	A	Degree plus (nontechnical)

* "Perceived helpfulness" is defined by the number of times a salesman was mentioned in response to the question "Who among the salesmen in LADSO provides the most help to salesmen?"
** Ties indicate those salesmen who were mentioned an equal number of times.

The formal qualifications of the 11 salesmen themselves do not settle the question of how competence is best acquired. Two of the 11 salesmen are trained engineers. Although three other salesmen are technically trained formally, such training is limited to first-year university courses in science and not to specialized courses that might help them sell stainless steel. Some evidence relating to the question of formal training is indicated in the salesmen's responses to the question: "Who among the salesmen in LADSO provides the most help to salesmen?"[2] Their responses are indicated in Table 1, which lists the salesmen in order of number of times mentioned as a source of help. Thus it may be seen that salesmen *K* and *I* (nonengineers) are at least comparable, if not superior, in perceived helpfulness to salesmen *H* and *J* (engineers). Since *K* and *I* are more experienced than *H* and *J*, one cannot infer relative merits of formal training and of

[2] It was felt by the observers that this criterion of "helpfulness" was the best single criterion of competence as defined by the salesmen themselves. While it may be argued that other people in the Sales Department may judge other criteria to be more important, the salesmen's own definitions of competence were felt to be of primary importance inasmuch as the study is concerned primarily with the salesmen.

TABLE 2

Salesmen's Experience in the Company and in LADSO Related to Number of Times Mentioned as Source of Help

	Number of Times Mentioned as Source of Help	
	0 to 1	2 plus
Service within company		
5 years or more	2	4
Less than 5 years	4	1
Service within LADSO		
3 years or more	2	3
Less than 3 years	4	2

experience as means of acquiring competence. In other words, one can only speculate on which salesmen would be seen as providing the most help if years of experience were the same for both the engineers and the nonengineers. One can say, however, that whatever their formal training, salesmen need extensive on-the-job training in order to acquire competence.

Table 2 indicates the importance of experience more clearly. It relates experience both in Allmetal and in LADSO with the number of times mentioned as providing most help. As may be seen in the table, the more experienced salesmen are mentioned most frequently as providing the most help. Four of the six salesmen with five or more years of experience in the company are mentioned two or more times as sources of help, as compared to only one out of five salesmen with less than five years' service in the company. Also, three of the five salesmen with three or more years' experience in LADSO are mentioned two or more times as sources of help, compared with two out of six salesmen with less than three years' experience.

Table 3 documents some of the salesmen's concern for technical training on the job by listing their preferences for the training of experienced salesman. Of the 26 suggestions made, 18 have to do with technical aspects of their work in one form or another. The opportunity to keep abreast of technical developments seems to be vital. Even the idea of providing a senior salesman with a junior to train (discussed in detail later) is seen as providing additional time

TABLE 3

Tabulation of Salesmen's Preferences for Training
Experienced Salesmen

I. Technical developments
   Fabrication clinics (5)*
   Courses from sales development (3)
   Assignments in plants (2)
   Refresher courses
      (a) Similar to welding course and forming course (1)
      (b) Technical developments (2)
   Plant visits (1)
   Films (1)
   Architectural application course (1)
II. Appraisal and development from supervisor (3)
III. Visits to other sales offices (or get-togethers) (3)
IV. Nontechnical training courses
   Human relations (1)
   Administration (1)
   Selling techniques (1)
V. Extra time available for reading and self-improvement (1)

---

* Numbers in parentheses indicate number of times recommendation mentioned.

for the senior salesman to get around to see developments, read up on the latest information in technical magazines or journals, and, in general, to extend the scope of his competence.

The use of engineers in LADSO requires a further qualification: not all engineers have the kind of work interests which selling demands. The stereotype of the engineer sitting at a drafting board, spending weeks on a development problem for a customer, has no place in a sales office. Whatever the advantages of having a top engineering specialist in the sales office might be, and there are many such advantages, some salesmen feel that engineers who are eager for development work do not have the opportunity to utilize their training. The nature of the job is such that the salesman must always be prepared to drop whatever he is doing and pick up the phone, call a customer, or consult his order processor. He cannot take time out to develop a process or design a product which an engineer's qualifications would equip him to undertake. At the present time in LADSO the salesman is outside the office consulting with the customer or with people in the Allmetal organization.

One salesman described the situation as follows:

> . . . I can't sit down and work exclusively on one problem for several weeks or months, but men in product managers' departments and sales development departments can . . . they're set up for just that sort of thing. I've got to see customers . . . be out of the office . . . take care of day-to-day paperwork, etc. Of course, I haven't got the experience and training for working on such problems, but even if I had, I just wouldn't be able to give several weeks or months of uninterrupted attention to one single problem. Some people seem to feel that's the type of man who should be filling some of the jobs around here. I don't think so. I don't think we could attract that type of man, and if we could, we'd lose him, precisely because he wouldn't be able to use the tremendous training and experience some people want him to have. If we have to be out of the office, we have to be out of the office. . . . We can't do that and long range desk work too . . . . Look what happens when someone gets to be as expert as——did on——. We lose him to another department where he can be of help to the company as a whole and not just to one sales office.

Skills in Working with People. The description of the salesman as a business manager in the first section of this report highlights another area of knowledge, skill, and experience which the salesman needs to acquire. As the only continuous link between the customer and the entire Allmetal organization, the salesman has to have the right answers to the customer's questions. He has to relate himself to the customer and to people in Allmetal in such a way that the customer's expectations are met. In the face of conflicting ideas about what these expectations are and how they should be satisfied, the salesman is often faced with a difficult task.

A number of incidents mentioned in this report will make reference to these somewhat intangible skills of working with people. Perhaps one of the most dramatic examples observed where the salesman's skills in working with others "paid-off" was the case of a salesman's handling of a large account. In this particular company it was the practice for the planning division to draw up blueprints and requisitions which had to be initialled by a great many people before they went to the purchasing department. There they were retyped on different forms, checked and initialled by another group of people. By the time Allmetal got the sales order necessary to start producing the steel, there was a delay of three to four weeks. The salesman wanted to reduce this delay. When he approached the chief buyer, the latter said, "These shipment delays are raising Cain. We've got to do something without making any basic changes now." The salesman felt that in order to reduce the delay, he needed the buyer's active support. He decided to draw up a forward picture of sales to the company for five years instead of the usual one year. He showed this to the chief buyer, who agreed with the figures. The salesman then asked: "Well, if we're going to be in the same mess for the next five years, why don't we do something now?" The customer accepted his argument and together they sat down with representatives from the Allmetal planning department. As a result of these efforts, a delay in deliveries of two to three weeks was eliminated.

Somehow this type of skill is not associated with being a "fund of technical knowledge," and yet it seems to produce benefits which accrue to the customer.

SALESMAN'S RELATIONSHIPS WITH OTHER ALLMETAL DEPARTMENTS

Being human, the salesman cannot always match the customer's expectations. There is a limit to his own competence. Because there are many people in the company who have specialized technical knowledge useful to the customer, the salesman is under pressure to utilize these resources in order to meet the customer's demands. Contrary to generally held beliefs that the salesman "should stand on his own feet," salesmen feel they need help from other departments in the company.

The salesmen's comments reflect this dependence. For example, salesman B:

> I've been wanting some publicity on X product for a long time and several people have suggested that I write an article about it for the public relations department. If I were to say to sales development that I'm going to initiate an article on X product it would be humorous, since they have been working on the testing and development of it for years. The best thing for me to do is get to know the guy in sales development who has worked on the product and see what I can learn from him. . . .

Later he went on to say:

> . . . We refuse to admit that there are other people who know more about the XYZ product in the XYZ industry than

we do. This gets us into trouble. *A* and *B* over at sales development have been working on this for a long, long time, and they really know what's happening. Their boss considers it one of his pet projects. They can even get special grade stainless for it whenever they ask for it. I'd be crazy not to work as closely with them as they'll let me. . . .

Salesman *G*:

I have to see a lot of people in quite a few departments in order to take care of my customers properly—and I think I know stainless steel pretty well. Take the technical department, for example. As far as customer *X* is concerned, I couldn't get along without the boys in technical. They are my referees and lawyers on differences of opinion with the customer concerning quality, finishes, packing, shipment, specifications—on all sorts of tolerances. There are several people who work for customer *X* (a large corporation) who are hell on wheels when they are inspecting our products. The boys in the Technical Department have much more specialized knowledge than I do—they are active in a whole bunch of technical societies setting standards, like the American Society of Metals, the American Foundryman's Society, etc., and they speak with more authority than I do. . . .

Salesman *J*:

. . . I'm not a technical man myself, but the guy who lives with his customers day in and day out can teach the technical boys quite a few things. On the other hand, they work exclusively on one product for years sometimes, and I'd be lost without them.

Even a salesman who says he doesn't need help gets it, as illustrated in the following incident:

Salesman *Y* and the specialist for *X* products in the office were discussing a date on which the two men were to see one of *Y*'s customers. After the specialist left, *Y* said, "I work pretty closely with our *X* product expert. He helps me sell *X* products." Further questioning revealed that *Y* went to six people in the technical department, nine in sales development, two in treasury, one in pricing, and six in LADSO. Previous to this, when asked: "Who do you go to in LADSO and elsewhere in Allmetal for help?" he had replied: "I don't see hardly anyone. I work pretty much alone."

Further data illustrative of the extent of the salesman's dependence upon other Allmetal departments was obtained by counting the number of contacts[3] which the salesmen made with other people. These data are summarized in Table 5, which shows the total number of contacts made by all salesmen during the period of observation, as well as the people whom the salesmen contacted. The salesman made a total of 139 contacts with people in other Allmetal departments and works, or 24 per cent of the total number of contacts.

TABLE 5

Contacts Made by All Salesmen While Observed in Their Offices

People Contacted	Number of Contacts	Per Cent of Total Contacts
Order processors and office staff	181	31
Customers	167*	29
Other Allmetal departments and works	139	24
Other salesmen	60	10
Personal (nonbusiness calls)	20	3
Immediate supervisors	16	3
Total contacts	583	

* It was estimated that the salesmen spent at least half their time outside the office on customers.

It is rather difficult to evaluate the figure 24 per cent by itself as a measure of the salesman's dependence upon other Allmetal departments. To highlight the meaning of this figure, it may be compared with another figure very close to it in magnitude, namely the percentage of total contacts made with the order processors and other office staff (31 per cent). The order processor is very important to the salesman. Since a description of the order processor's job will be given later in the report, it is only necessary to mention here that it involves the detailed processing of the customer's order for products. This includes writing the order, writing quotations, cancellations,

---

[3] A single contact was recorded whenever a salesman talked with another person, either by telephone or in face-to-face conversation. Duration of conversations was not designated; both long and short conversations were counted as single contacts. A single contact was recorded whether or not the salesman initiated the conversation.

handling of complaints regarding delivery, shipment dates, and so on, while the salesman is away. In short, the processor is virtually the salesman's "right-hand man." Therefore, the fact that the frequency of salesman contact with the other departments is comparable to his contact with his order processor makes the former substantial in degree.

Areas of Conflict and Tension between LADSO and Other Allmetal Departments. Despite the recognition on the part of salesmen of their function in utilizing the resources of Allmetal to help meet customer problems, there are a few areas of possible conflict between the Sales Office and other Sales Departments. Before stating what these conflicts are, the following two incidents will indicate the context in which conflicts tend to develop:

> A meeting was held for the purpose of negotiating a sales contract with an important customer for a fairly large tonnage, delivery of which would be stretched over a period of nearly a year. Representatives from a sales service department, LADSO, and the customer were in attendance at the meeting. When price quotations were discussed, the sales service department representative answered: "Price will remain firm." Because of the seniority of the sales service representative, the salesman remained quiet even though he thought there were dangers in such an assurance. A little later a price increase was announced and the customer lodged a strong protest with the salesman, the man who processed the order. The salesman could only say: "Well, we thought it was going to be firm at that time." Essentially, the sales service department created a problem which the salesman had to cope with.

While the above incident refers to relationships involving sales service personnel, the areas of conflict were not limited to these departments. For example, the following incidents involved the office management.

> One day a salesman received a call from one of his largest accounts. The customer said he heard a rumor that there was going to be a price increase on stainless steel bar. He was extremely interested in this, for he wanted to know how much the price rise would be on Allmetal semifabricated products. The salesman said he didn't know, since no information concerning a price rise had been given to him by his superiors. Some time later, the customer called one of the salesman's superiors and received the information regarding the price increase.

Not long after this, the salesman had occasion to call the customer again and the customer reported that he was changing his prices on the basis of the Allmetal change. The salesman said: "How are you going to do this?" whereupon the customer said: "I'm not sure if I'm supposed to tell you this, but stainless steel bar will be going up x cents a pound. I received the information from one of your superiors."

This did not make the salesman happy, as he thought he should be in the position of communicating the price change to his customer. He thereupon went to see the superior to complain about the incident, but his superior did not feel that the salesman had any reason to be disturbed.

These incidents generate feelings which indicate the salesman's concern with doing his job. This concern is not simply a question of being on good terms just for the sake of good terms. For the salesmen, there are some fundamental issues at stake, which concern some of the important aspects of his work. The following are some of these issues, supported either by actual quotes or by inferences identified in their comments:

The salesman feels his relationship with the customer is impaired. "We sit down together to negotiate a contract, and then the customer puts the screws on me because I can't keep a promise on a firm price, which wasn't my making."

The salesman feels personally embarrassed. "Imagine being told by your *customer* that the price of your own product has gone up x cents."

The salesman feels there is a danger of his being relegated to the job of order taker, when the customer, in effect, says: "I told the men from sales service [your bosses] that I needed the XY specialist."

The salesman feels that his job satisfaction is being undermined. "The greatest source of satisfaction is my customer. I have a very important job [outside]. I represent a big company. I take my customers out to lunch. All this is being threatened."

The salesman feels that the organization stands to lose by undermining the continuous link with the customer. "Before my boss let out the news about the price increase, my customer used to deal only with me. Now he knows he can call on other people in Allmetal. Maybe he'll phone in his next order to sales development. What gripes me is that they don't have to live with the customer. I do!"

The salesman feels that the development of salesmen, particularly the senior salesmen, is being hampered. "We expect that senior men in the office will get ahead in the company through promotions and transfers to more responsible jobs. We think the company sees things the same way. But how can we build up experience to qualify for better jobs when we can't exercise responsibility for the jobs we have now?"

An objective appraisal of conflict situations is always difficult to obtain, because by their very nature, feelings cannot always be adequately reflected. It is also important to recognize that since only the salesmen were studied, there are many "other sides to the stories" that were not heard. Furthermore, analysis of these conflicts is the proper concern of the training program itself, and this report is primarily concerned with reporting the situation; it highlights the conflicts as being areas that bear on the effectiveness of the salesman's performance.

In spite of these dangers, however, a number of observations may be made about some of the factors leading to conflict.

First, many of the people in service departments with whom the salesman works are people with experience as salesmen. In some cases they know customers very well because they have sold steel to them for many years. Such people find it only natural to maintain their relationships with customers although another salesman has taken over responsibility for the account.

This tendency to maintain a relationship with the customer is particularly strong if the salesman is new to the territory and perhaps even new to selling. The man whom he replaces is older and more experienced—he "knows the ropes" about the customer's expectations, needs, and eccentricities. For the good of the customer, the new salesman, and the Allmetal organization, the older man feels it isn't proper to just "drop" the territory when he moves into a new job.

There is also the feeling that managers and sales service personnel crave some of the satisfactions to be derived from "active" selling. There is an understandable desire to get together with the customer who, after all, is the "raison d'être" for all the activities carried on by the company. The sales service personnel particularly would like to learn about the wider aspects of steel sales, rather than concentrate only on their own field of specialization.

By the same token, the salesmen often feel they would like to participate, to some degree, in the administration of the office and in the designing and developing of products and markets leading up to the actual placement of the order. If they are cut off from these dimensions of selling, they tend to feel that they are being deliberately relegated to the category of "order takers."

The suggestion is often made in such conflict situations that the "organization needs to be changed." It is argued that "lines of demarcation" should be set up, with specifications about what jobs or functions ought to be carried out by various people. For example, "selling" is seen as being the job of the salesman and "developing" as the job of the sales service departments.

From their comments, it was inferred that many salesmen and men in service departments feel that there are satisfactions to be derived from being involved in both the sale and the development of the product. They also feel that it is quite arbitrary to establish a line of demarcation, because it would be different for every order received. Responsibility for conflict, according to these people, rests not on the nature of the organization but rather on the individuals involved in a particular situation. The following comment from a salesman illustrates this point of view:

> It seems to depend on who is filling a particular job. The man who had the job *A* has now (in charge of a sales service department) used to feel that he was there to help us (LADSO) and all the other sales offices. *A* looks at it quite differently. He seems to feel that I work for him and he never feeds out information or data of any sort. He thinks it should all be channeled in to him. When you come right down to it, maybe I do actually work for him, even if he doesn't pay my salary. After all, he controls price, delivery, and scheduling. What else is there? I don't blame my superiors for trying to keep *A* from "taking over" . . . and yet I can't ignore him if I'm going to get my job done. . . . I have to pump him for information so that *I* can find out what's going on. . . . My boss expects me to know what's going on, but he also expects me not to get too close to *A*. . . . I spend most of my time trying to "keep the peace."

Given the above forces tending to induce conflict and tension, two results seem inevitable. In fact, they are occurring according to the salesmen's comments: either a "strong man" in a service department dominates the salesman (who resigns himself to the situation) or LADSO tries to become independent by informally setting up its own services.

In many instances, however, salesmen and men from other departments do work together, a fact which is made significant when one considers the nature of the forces tending toward tension and conflict. The incidents described on pages 555 and 556 of this report

indicate that mutually benefitting relationships exist. Several salesmen appeared to have worked on their own with their counterparts
in sales service departments. Both shared in performing and enjoying the various "staff" and "line" tasks required to sell steel to the
customer.

In one case, a number of salesmen mentioned that *R* (sales service)
was a "terrific guy." They said that he "kept everyone informed of
what he was doing. He seems to route us copies of everything he
does." This relationship was so positive that during the course of
conversation with a salesman one day, in between calls, the salesman
said this:

> Take the *XYZ* industry. I know nothing about the problems
> at all. I called *R* the other day and told him that the next
> time that he was out in my territory he should take me along,
> as I would like to get to know some of the customers.

Thus, the salesman did not consider the fact that this person was
seeing customers in his territory a threat. He wanted to learn from
the experience of the sales service personnel.

In summary, many salesmen seem to feel: "I don't think it's any
one department and it's not the way we're set up—it's the man in the
job."

SALESMEN'S RELATIONSHIPS WITH ONE ANOTHER

In addition to the salesman's own knowledge, skill, and experience,
and the resources of other Allmetal departments, other salesmen in
the office are a potential source of help. That this potential is
recognized has been shown in Table 2, page 552, in which "perceived
helpfulness" was related to experience both in the company and in
LADSO.

The notion that a salesman can learn a great deal within the office
was also indicated by their answers to questions about which salesmen
were sources of help. Salesman *F* said about Salesman *G*:

> . . . a source of great help on general fabricating knowledge.

about Salesman *H*:

> . . . he gives sound guidance and seems sound as a rock in
> his particular field. . . .

Salesman *J* stated about Salesman *K*:

> . . . with his plant experience he is a good deal of help. . . .

However, this potential for help is not realized in fact. The salesmen seem conscious of a lack of teamwork as evidenced by the following remarks. Salesman *L*:

> . . . the salesmen keep me informed informally about what's going on in their territories which is concerned with my work (specialty) but I do not think this type of informal information I get from salesmen comes often enough or is accurate or reliable enough. . . .

Salesman *N*:

> . . . when I first came here I was surprised that the salesmen just didn't see one another. . . .

Salesman *O*:

> . . . There's no feeling of working together in this office. . . . Everyone seems to be "on his own" . . . . There are three or four of the men who have lunch together quite regularly, but that's all. . . . If a man has a luncheon engagement with a customer cancelled, he usually makes no effort to pick up one or two salesmen for lunch if he's around the office. . . . It's a funny setup. . . .

Salesman *Q*:

> . . . the esprit de corps around here seems exceptionally high, especially when you consider the fact that salesmen hardly ever see one another. . . .

In addition to possible informal contact, a regular sales meeting in the office provides another form of interaction. These meetings, held approximately every two weeks for about two hours, are set up to disseminate news, to share experiences, and to raise and discuss common problems. Although potentially well suited to the building of teamwork, the sales meetings were not considered by some salesmen to provide the interaction with one another which they felt to be lacking. Salesman *R*:

> . . . the sales meetings don't seem to give us as much esprit de corps as they might. . . . Maybe if we discussed more specific problems we might have more spontaneous discussion. . . .

Salesman *S*:

> . . . about the only time we get together is at the sales meeting, and we don't really get a chance to exchange ideas there. . . .

It's more of a presentation of news to us, and I don't feel that if we discuss something we'll ever change anything . . . so what's there to discuss?

In the absence of a sense of esprit de corps, the division of the group on the basis of experience (as outlined in Table 2) apparently resulted in an actual division on the basis of friendships. There appears to be the beginning of a subgroup among the more senior men, which to the newcomer may appear as an obstacle to drawing upon valuable experience in the office. The presence of a subgroup was suggested by the salesmen's answers to the question: "Who are your friends in LADSO?" Figure 2 summarizes the salesmen's answers in graphic form.

Of particular interest in Figure 2 are the double-headed arrows, indicating mutual friendship choices. Assuming that mutual friendship choices indicate closer friendships than unresponded choices, a subgroup is indicated in the office, as shown in Figure 2. Salesmen *A*, *B*, and *E* form a relatively stable triangle, with salesman *I* being one of the group to a lesser extent. These four salesmen are among the most experienced in the office. It is significant to note that salesmen *B*, *E*, and *I* do not choose as their friends salesmen outside this group of four.

Figure 2 also indicates that salesmen *F*, *D*, and *C* apparently work independently of the others and that salesmen *J* and *K*, with their

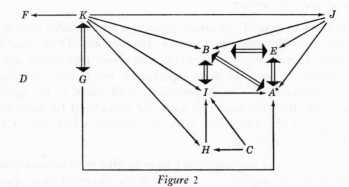

Figure 2

A single-headed arrow designates a choice of one salesman by another as a friend.
A double-headed arrow designates mutual friendship choices.
* Although salesman A said: "Everybody is my friend," it was observed that A spent more time with salesman B and E than with the others. Consequently these two friendship choices have been added to the figure.

comparatively high number of choices, seem to be trying to "break into" the group of more experienced men.

In summary, there is evidence to suggest that subgrouping is beginning to occur among the salesmen. This may result in making more difficult the possibility of less experienced salesmen obtaining help from those who have the most experience.

SALESMEN'S RELATIONSHIPS WITH SUPERIORS

The salesman's superior is another source of help. In addition to his own personal experience, the superior is the salesman's representative to higher management, and the communicator of messages pertaining to the salesman's future in the company. As a superior he has responsibility for delegating work and for appraising the salesman's performance as well as his potential for other jobs. He is in a position to give considerable direction to the salesman's efforts. The salesman increases or diminishes his efforts in certain directions. This depends on how his superior supports and coaches him in these efforts.

From what some salesmen said, it was apparent that they did not see the ideal role of supervisor in terms of either "mollycoddling" or "spoon-feeding" on the one hand, or of "washing hands" on the other. The ineffectiveness of such extremes was noted by one salesman as follows:

> I knew one supervisor who, if you went to him for help, took over the problem from you before you've got half a dozen words out of your mouth. He started telephoning, dictating letters, etc. On the other hand, there was another supervisor who looked out the window when you tried to capitalize on his long years of service and experience. . . . What was the sense of going to see either of those birds unless you absolutely had to?

His reflections seemed particularly relevant to the situation because, by and large, the salesmen seemed to want an atmosphere somewhere between the extremes represented in the above quote.

Management Administrative Philosophy. No specific attempt was made to interview the managers of LADSO for the purpose of defining how they saw their administrative roles. However, an implicit management philosophy or approach to administration was indicated to the observers through informal discussions with the managers while the study was in progress. This philosophy is best expressed in the statement that good administration permits a maximum degree of freedom to the salesmen. This point of view is based on the premise that, in the last analysis, the salesman must be prepared to meet the customer's expectations promptly and effectively. This means (1) spending as much time as is practicable on calling on customers personally and (2) answering the customer's questions on the spot, rather than later or indirectly through someone else. The salesman must be prepared to meet the demands of his job. Thus, according to this point of view, he must be given the freedom to equip himself for the job as he sees fit.

Justification for this position of maximizing the salesman's freedom of action seems to lie in a heightened level of motivation on the part of the salesman. Supervision is not considered "looking over the salesman's shoulder" but rather displaying trust in him, since the salesman, more than anyone else in the office, knows what kind or degree of effort constitutes a day's work. Self-motivation is thought to be not only more productive in most situations, but a necessary condition for effective selling. Only the salesman himself can learn how to be prepared to meet the complex demands of his job.

Initial Reactions to Administration in LADSO. The salesmen's reactions to management philosophy are best illustrated in their comments about their training experiences. The salesmen were asked: "What parts of (your initial) training were most helpful?" The following were some of their answers. Salesman *L*:

> . . . the first three months were a dead loss. . . . I must admit I had a chip on my shoulder for six months, and this hindered my development considerably. The (bosses) should map out a course on the basis of past experience of the individual. You have to give a fellow a sense of direction. In this company there is a tendency to toss a fellow into the pool and see if he can swim. . . . There have been times when I thought I was going to have a nervous breakdown with nothing to do (during his first six months in LADSO). I went through six months of purgatory here. I didn't know where I was going. I don't think anybody should be put in that position.

Salesman *N*:

> . . . looking back, the whole thing was pretty half-hearted, and (Plant *A*) and (Plant *B*) are the only two places where anyone knew I existed and where anyone took the trouble to teach me anything. . . .

By contrast, salesman *O* speaks of his initial experiences as follows:

> . . . I was earmarked for a specific job from the very beginning and went to (Plant *A*) for two months. . . . *X* (a former

ALLMETAL STEEL CORPORATION 567

head of sales service department) would give me specific projects to work on and I would return to Los Angeles from time to time for long discussions with him after I'd completed each of the projects he assigned to me. . . . I found it all pretty helpful.

Salesman P:

. . . I think we ought to get some help from our senior people regarding selling techniques if there are any and some coaching gathered by their experience. . . .

Salesman Q:

. . . there was quite a bit of time waiting around. . . . You could work on your own initiative, but you really didn't know what you needed to know. . . . I considered the changeover when I got my job to be very, very poor. . . . I wasn't prepared for it, and (my predecessor) left too quickly. . . . I began to think my new job was hopeless. . . . A trainee should have his training appraised as he goes along, to tell him how he is doing or where he needs aid. . . . A new salesman needs an explanation of the office . . . what goes on, the purpose of it all. . . . Take the man to the specialists, introduce him around. . . .

Salesman R:

. . . I got no training whatsoever for my work here. I came in 1954, and prior to that visited a couple of plants. . . . Any week-long visits were not tied in with any particular projects or questions or focused in any way. . . . I got no training here from anyone of a specific type for selling . . . nothing on policy or anything else. . . . You have to find out completely on your own whom to see about what. . . . I think we should have occasional reviews with our superiors and with the specialists about what we have covered and what we are supposed to know. . . .

In short, in the initial stages of working in LADSO the salesman sees management's role in his work situation as one of noninterference at best, and complete indifference at worst. If the salesman feels that there is little or no help forthcoming from his superiors, he tends to lean more heavily on others for assistance. These others may be fellow salesmen or people in other Allmetal departments. In spite of a management philosophy which expects him to "stand on his own two feet," the salesman finds pressures operating which push him into developing relationships with people who can give him effective help.

Even the customer contributes his share of effective assistance to the untrained salesman. Salesman X says:

> . . . the highest point of training in my job has been and still is . . . (one of my largest customers). . . .

Another salesman put it in roughly the same manner:

> . . . when are we going to stop asking the customers to train our salesman?

And still another salesman says about his job, after several years:

> . . . most of the time ideas come from the customers, not the other way around. . . .

Adjustment to LADSO. If the newcomer survives his "training" period he becomes a salesman. He gets caught up with his work—dictated by his customers' demand—and he learns where and how to go about getting the help and assistance he needs. In this phase, he tends to appreciate the atmosphere of noninterference to a greater extent than he did initially because he feels he can use his discretion in interpreting the beliefs of management. Because of the permissive behavior of his superiors, he does not have to take too literally the "be out on the road every minute you can" belief of management. He can ignore, as he must, the "don't go running around asking other people for help." His justification is that, in the final analysis, his customer has to be served, regardless of whether the salesman handles the account himself or whether he stays inside the office to do it. If his superiors ask him to make "cold calls,"[4] the noninterfering administration enables him to duck such calls if he believes he shouldn't make them.

In summary, some salesmen think that management does not provide enough effective support and coaching to them so that they can deal with the problems they face. Some salesmen, in fact, believe that management's urging of self-motivation through self-development of their own resources is an attitude of noninterference, and in few cases a matter of indifference.

Actually, the salesman comes to appreciate some of the latitude which is given to him, provided that he is able to "work through" the training phase in the office. Challenged by the customers' prob-

---

[4] A first call on a customer not previously contacted.

lems and aided by other people in the Allmetal organization, he learns to sell stainless steel.

The administrative relationship described above between the salesman and his supervisor is duplicated to some degree between the order processor (or "back-up girl") and the salesman in LADSO. While being in a subordinate position to his boss, the salesman is at the same time in a somewhat supervisory position to a person who is practically an indispensable part of his activities. Consequently, the salesman is in a position to appreciate the problems of supervision being both a receiver and initiator of administrative action.

The Job of Order Processor in LADSO. The main job of an order processor is to process the orders which a customer makes for Allmetal products. At one time this job was performed by salesmen-in-training, but at the time that the study was conducted, most of the order processors were women. To process an order, the "back-up girl" must "write it up" according to the specifications which a customer presents either verbally or in writing. She may also be required to write change orders involving changes in specifications, tonnages, or prices. Occasionally she will be required to write up quotations to a customer and also to cancel orders.

Processing of an order may take from 10 minutes to a number of days. In the case of a large customer ordering a large variety of products, the financial calculations may take a considerable period of time. On the other hand, a routine order for a commodity which had been ordered many times before will involve a few minutes to simply hand-write the order on a form. After the order has been written, it goes to checkers who check to insure that the order meets specifications as to price, etc. The order is then typed and a copy is returned to the processor for her files.

To write up an order requires a knowledge of procedures, including knowledge of customer code numbers, prices, specifications, delivery dates, credit information, and various kinds of special information concerning special orders and customers. She may have to solicit help from the pricing division (in Chicago) or teletype plants concerning prices or delivery dates. She may even suggest alloys or applications to a customer, and she invariably has to have extensive knowledge of the availability of products.

She is the salesman's representative when he is out of the office. As such, she answers telephone calls, handles complaints, and provides information. She may be required to initiate a certain amount of correspondence, both in answer to customers' queries and as a normal procedure in writing an order.

Teamwork between Order Processor and Salesman. The job of order processor is of crucial importance to the salesman's performance. After all, she actually services his customers, and the service the customer receives is, in the final analysis, the main determinant of the salesman-customer relationship. By her behavior on the telephone, by the accuracy and promptness of her reactions to customers' requests, and by her ability to produce what the salesman has promised in terms of the necessary paperwork, she can make a donkey out of her boss or help to build the reputation of both the salesman and the company. Some of the goodwill which she may generate can be shown by a case in which no less than six customers had asked a salesman at various times to have the opportunity of meeting his order processor, since she had done such a magnificent job for them. On another occasion, a customer took an order processor out to an extremely lavish luncheon just prior to her marriage.

Although the order processor works for the salesman, her boss is the office manager who reports to the manager of LADSO. This is a situation which apparently accounts for the fact that many salesmen feel they have no responsibility for her work.

Most of the salesmen had no idea of their order processor's salary, when they got their last increase, how they were rated, whether they needed time off, and so on. And yet these same salesman naturally expected this kind of interest from their own superiors.

There were some incidents which suggested that occasionally a salesman expressed a sense of responsibility and interest in his order processor beyond that which was formally required. At times a salesman conferred with the office manager about the girl's salary, time off, performance, and so on. In some instances such matters were discussed with the order processors themselves. There were even occasions when a salesman recommended a salary increase for his girl, or he took the initiative in getting her a visit to a plant with which she dealt daily by telephone and teletype.

There were, on the other hand, instances in which the behavior of the salesman did not always leave the order processor in a "happy" and responsible frame of mind. The following incident illustrates the point.

Order processor X went up to salesman Y to ask him some questions about their work. He was browsing through a plant newspaper—not reading it—just thumbing through it. She asked him a question and received no reply. After repeating her question twice and receiving no acknowledgement, she reached over, placed her hand over the newspaper he was looking at, and said, "Please."

He looked up and asked her what she wanted. She repeated the same question again. He muttered a short reply and while she was in the process of asking him to elaborate a little, he picked up the phone without a word and began dialing a number.

She threw up her hands in the air and said: "I'll have to wait until salesman Z comes in!"

Apart from the obvious frustration which X experienced in this relationship, it is significant that salesman Y prided himself on delegating responsibility to his "back-up girl." His attitude toward their relationship was expressed as follows:

> . . . I don't mess around with that stuff (paperwork). . . . I turn it all over to her and let her carry the ball. . . . That's the way she'll learn. . . . I don't want to be telling her what to do every five minutes. . . . I believe in delegating responsibility. . . . If she can handle it, okay; if she can't then we'll need to get someone else. . . .

For her part, she saw his behavior quite differently:

> . . . salesman Y just can't be bothered. . . . He couldn't care less, and I hate working for him. . . . It's such a favor when he even answers you. . . . He just doesn't care about this end of the work . . . and if he doesn't I wonder why I should. . . .

In a situation where the closeness of their work relationship leads the salesman unofficially to "supervise" his order processor, the salesman finds himself with some of the same superior-subordinate problems mentioned in the previous section of this report. As his supervisor "sets the tone" in his relationship with the salesmen, so does the salesman govern his relationship with the order processor. The system of delegating responsibility which he works out does not always meet the expectations of those working under him.

The result is that service to the customer may be impaired. For example, salesman Y, who is mentioned above, on one occasion had to apologize to a customer because a quotation for a fairly large order had not been supplied by the requested date. Although this had been given to the processor to do, she had not made the quotation because she was unable to obtain the help she thought was necessary.

MORALE IN LADSO

Unlike the factors affecting the salesman's performance discussed thus far, statements about the salesman's morale are probably the least objective and in a sense the most intangible. It is necessary to highlight this fact because, in describing a person's morale, it is easy to say that he is being "unreasonable." Other people can grasp, for example, an understanding of a salesman's background of experience and how it contributes to his work. His interactions with his associates and customers can be observed and any inferences about such interactions may be checked and hence made convincing. But in describing a person's state of mind, one is within the realm of attitudes, where the observers' data often seem less convincing. Because attitudes are subjective phenomena, it is easy to attribute "unreasonableness" to the person expressing them; one tends to feel that the person "is in a bad mood," "has a chip on his shoulder," "is hard to get along with," perhaps even "disloyal." The effect of such reactions to attitudes is to disregard their significance.

The point to be made here is that states of morale are real and sincere, no matter how "unreasonable" they may seem to an outsider. They do make a difference in a worker's ability to do his job. People are inclined to take drastic action depending, for example, on their pride of belonging or pride of workmanship. A competent worker may resign his position for something he may call "lack of job challenge," a statement which those around him may fail to understand. On the other hand, people may marvel at someone who is able to deal with a difficult situation on the basis of something he may call "pride of doing a job."

In keeping with the variety of connotations associated with the word "morale," the discussion to follow will report the salesmen's attitudes along a number of dimensions, rather than in terms of a single concept. Four such attitude areas will be discussed: namely, recognition of experience, involvement in the company, pride in working in LADSO, and pride in serving the customer. While these four titles may be incomplete in relation to notions popularly held about what constitutes morale, they are chosen here for their relevance to the salesmen. Other attitudinal factors were not mentioned by the salesmen as being important to them.

The reader should be warned at this point that some of the comments expressed represent strong negative feelings. On some matters the salesmen feel that they "are being let down badly." The tendency upon reading such comments is to wonder how the salesmen can remain in the situation if they feel so strongly.   One might expect them to seek other jobs.   The reader is to be assured, however, that the salesman has positive rewards in the situation—he does not feel compelled to leave.   The nature of these incentives will be indicated near the end of this section under the subtitle "Pride in Serving the Customer."

Recognition of Experience.   Mention has already been made in this report of the fact that the salesmen tend to differentiate themselves as either "junior" or "senior" on the basis of experience.   Thus the more experienced salesmen are seen as providing the most help in the office (page 552) and as interacting more with one another than with the junior salesmen (page 564).   This informal status is acknowledged because it is felt that it represents accumulated experience and skill in dealing with customers and sales situations.   The "seniors" in particular feel that a newcomer to LADSO cannot acquire such background automatically, no matter what his previous experience happens to be.

While this informal status is acknowledged by all salesmen, and hence is some source of pride to them, the senior salesmen feel that this status ought to be given more formal recognition by management. They point out that officially all but two of the salesmen are given the formal job title of "senior salesmen," which means, in effect, that many newcomers assume that title automatically upon arrival.   The result is that this lack of recognition of experience is interpreted as depriving the men of a feeling of having progressed with LADSO.   As a senior salesman put it:

> . . . I think that as far as prestige is concerned, the best job stops at *X*'s job (assistant manager).   I think there is no particular job below *X*'s and *Y*'s (manager) which carries any greater amount of prestige than any other job in the office.   We just don't run the type of operation which allows any one job to have more prestige than any other job below *X*'s.   An Allmetal salesman is on quite a high pedestal outside the company—people think we are pretty important in other companies—but inside the company one salesman is the same as any other.

When asked: "What does a newcomer to LADSO have to look forward to by way of job advancement and promotion?" he replied:

> A job as a salesman in LADSO.   Following that he would have to leave LADSO for promotion, since our policy is not to promote to assistant manager or manager within the same office.

> Some people tell me that the job I have now is a senior job. I don't see it that way. I think *I'm* senior, but I don't think my job is.

The salesmen themselves do not aspire to the senior positions in the office as a line of advancement in the company. They were asked: "What kind of job are you looking forward to getting in the future?" Only one of the salesmen mentioned any of the senior jobs. Even he qualified his answer by saying that one of his own accounts was equally challenging and had "tremendous scope."

Perhaps the best reflections of the senior salesman's wish for the recognition which he feels his seniority has earned him are to be found in his recommendations for training. The three most senior men stressed emphatically that a newcomer to LADSO should be assigned to one or more of them as an assistant salesman—for training and evaluation. They feel that one way that management might give them some extra recognition is to use their accumulated experiences more fully. Management could, they feel, by its behavior, give some formal significance to the informal title of "senior salesman." As it is now, they say management seems to communicate the message that years of experience with the company and with LADSO are worth little or no extra recognition.

The following are the salesmen's own words. Senior salesman *P*:

> . . . assign him (sales trainee) to a senior salesman. . . . Let him apprentice under a senior salesman, go visit customers and plants together. Give him a few of the more routine accounts and make those his responsibility to look after. The senior salesman will check with those customers from time to time, but let the apprentice carry the ball. . . . As a salesman he should not have a sales trainee assigned to him until he becomes a senior salesman. . . . During the apprentice period I visualize the junior and senior salesmen working very closely together. The senior salesman would also be evaluating his performance and should be consulted by management regarding his performance, assignments, etc.

Senior salesman *Q*:

> . . . some way should be found for a newcomer to profit from the experience of the older and more senior men like *P*, *R*,[5] and myself. The newcomer should learn from the older and more

[5] The other two senior salesmen.

senior men the complexity of the job—they should guide him along until he gets his bearings. Do not leave him to his own devices. . . .

. . . it is up to (the sales manager) and others at that level to use (a man) more specifically. He should be encouraged to work along those lines where he is best and most interested. Management has certain responsibilities along the line. They should see in him and discover in him what his best abilities, tendencies, and inclinations are—these might be outside of sales work altogether. . . . They might be in labs or some other place. In any case he must be helped . . . otherwise he may be wasted. He will get browned off. Give him some encouragement, work assignments. Management has the responsibility to help him . . . to help bring out what he's got.

Senior salesman *R*:

. . . we should be asked for our opinion and for our advice on whether a sales trainee is ready to go out on the road. . . . We should have something to say about this. . . .

This same salesman also made the point that:

. . . there would be quite a bit of incentive created by mentioning some of the efforts of the salesmen in the sales reports . . . when they have done something outstanding. . . . It would give us something which I consider almost tangible. . . . It's quite a thrill, you know, to sign up an order for x millions of pounds of y at one fell swoop. . . .

Involvement in the Company. Mention has been made of the salesmen's feeling that they lack direction in the company. Part of the section on "Factors Affecting the Salesman's Performance" describes their feelings about training. The attitude that management can be more helpful in providing leadership is shown in other areas besides training. Salesmen seem to feel that they are not given a sense of developing and growing in the company. They do not have a feeling that others in management ranks are concerned about their accomplishments or involvement in matters of company policy. The following remarks illustrate some of these feelings.

Salesman *X* was asked, "How satisfying is it for someone to work as a salesman in LADSO?" He replied:

Most of the time it is very satisfying, although sometimes you get fed up. You want to have a sense of accomplishment. You don't depend on commissions, you get your check every month. I realize you can't get a raise every year, but it is sometimes very frustrating if I am not asked about my territory for six months. I like to feel that somebody is taking an interest in me and the job, even if it is to blame me for not doing something right. A sense of accomplishment promotes application and carry through . . . and is usually a group effort. Most of the time ideas come from customers, not the other way around. You have to be alert for ideas. You cannot tell customers what to do, and the big thing is to know people so that they tell you. You go through a regular cycle . . . when it is all new it is fun, then you get discouraged because it is all routine . . . , then you get to know customers and talk about their problems, and it becomes interesting again. Often, we need a little more criticism. . . . There is plenty of responsibility here and financial incentive. The (job) is your own, you can hang yourself or succeed. The only thing that bothers me is whether anybody knows whether you are hanging yourself or succeeding.

Salesman *Y*:

. . . nobody asks me or tells me what my possibilities might be or where I go from here. . . .

Salesman *Z*:

. . . I think the bosses should review with the new man (and with older salesmen also) his work, his progress, and the areas where he needs more information and guidance. . . . I think there should be a closer contact between us and the sales manager. . . . We can always go in to see him, but I think it is wrong for him not to initiate the contacts. After all, he is the kingpin here in our life, and he should call us in.

Salesman *T*:

. . . It would be nice to have a bit of encouragement and support when you do something a little outstanding. I think it helps tremendously to know that your efforts are appreciated. . . .

Salesman *W*:

. . . our bosses should try to get to know people more. . . . It is difficult occasionally in our office to know who to go to and quite difficult to communicate. Sales meetings are 50 per cent effective . . . (because we don't get the opportunity to) give the boss an idea of what we think about policy. . . . We should have some encouragement to discuss policy and questions about policy. . . . (The practice) of letting people do what they want tends to throw people into separate units. I would aim to make it a more cohesive team so that one guy knows something about what the other guy is doing. As it is now, he never sees the other guy so he doesn't know what anyone else is doing. We could be encouraged, for example, to write up experiences and route them around and learn from these. Really be part of a team.

Salesman V:

. . . I just received a raise today and I feel pretty good about it, particularly since this is the first time in my memory that I have been told in advance that I was receiving a raise. This seems to me to be better than opening your check and learning that you received a raise. You usually find the salesmen around here opening checks when they receive them to see whether they got a raise this month. I even caught myself doing this after a while.

Most of the above comments were directed toward immediate supervisors in the office. That the salesmen's feelings concern company management in general is indicated in the following comments. Salesmen S:

. . . We are beginning to be asked about price increases on various prices and commodities. We never used to be asked or consulted in any way. Maybe this means that some top management people in the company are beginning to appreciate the customer via the salesman. This is, to me, the way top management can indicate its concern with the customer, by backing up the salesman, keeping him informed and supporting him in general. . . . There are too many areas and levels of sales activity where you find men with no actual selling experience—who do not realize that a customer writes a salesman's efficiency report . . . who can put himself in the customer's shoes. . . .

Salesman Q:

. . . we are much too far apart from our seniors. I have never been introduced to X [a sales executive]. I used to see Y [another sales executive] once in a while but I feel that if your job changes then that is the end . . . you will probably never see him again. I don't see why we shouldn't be able to at least shake hands once in a while with our senior people. I have a feeling sometimes that no one knows you are working here. . . .

Pride in Working in LADSO. The salesmen were critical of their office facilities. One might debate whether their criticisms stem from a preoccupation with the office or whether they are symptoms of being disturbed with other factors mentioned above. Whatever the source of their criticisms, however, their feelings seem particularly strong, as evidenced by the following remarks. Salesman *P*:

> . . . offices are too noisy and crowded. . . . There should be a little privacy and a chance to get something done quickly . . . and a place to receive customers. . . . We are overcrowded here, and the place looks filthy. . . .

Salesman *Q*:

> . . . improve the actual accommodations. The existing office facilities are very depressing, littered with junk and filthy dirt. It is a most awkward layout, climatic conditions are terrible, and I would be quite ashamed to bring a customer into this place. I do think that physical conditions affect the way you feel, which in turn affects productivity. . . .

Salesman *M*:

> . . . I've been told not to worry about the offices because I'm supposed to be "on the road" most of the time. . . . Well, I don't spend too much time at home, but that doesn't mean I want my home to look like a pigsty. . . .

Salesman *Z*:

> . . . something has to be done to make the salesman feel he's important. There is an attitude around here that salesmen don't need good office facilities or a place to call home. . . . We should convince people that we work for the best. . . . I would like to have a little nook or corner that's quiet where I could do my work. . . .

Pride in Serving the Customer. In spite of the critical nature of the above comments, it would be a gross error to say that the salesman does not enjoy his work. Pride in serving the customer is by far the greatest source of satisfaction to the salesman and appears to be quite sufficient to compensate for the negative attitudes which he expresses.

To his customer, the salesman is a "very important guy." He feels important because he is the representative of a company enjoying a great deal of prestige and reputation in the country—and in many parts of the world. The Allmetal organization is set up to supply the customer's needs, and the salesman is the only continuous link between Allmetal and the customer. He is able to take the customer out to good lunches in high-prestige restaurants. He is able to bring to the customer the services of engineers, metallurgists, physicists, chemists, and all the other technological facilities of a large corporation. He feels important because to the customer he *is* an important person.

His card is a "passport" to see practically anyone he cares to see in the customer's organization. Many salesmen commented on the feeling of prestige they enjoyed when calling upon the executive of a large company, something which virtually never happens in their own organization. On one occasion a salesman was invited to lunch by a customer who had a substantial contract with Allmetal. The luncheon party included the president, vice president, and secretary-treasurer of the company. The salesman remarked that he was "treated lavishly." Another salesman remarked on the feeling of importance he experienced when a a customer asked to see an Allmetal engineer about a special project. The engineer was in a very responsible position, and was the head of a section consisting of 15 engineers. The customer saw the salesman as providing him with some very "high-powered" talent.

These status satisfactions which the salesman derives affect the way he sees his role in the customer's organization. Not only does the salesman derive his major source of satisfaction from his customer, but for practical purposes he comes to feel a part of the customer's organization as well as his own. As one salesman put it:

> . . . if you're really going to be a good salesman you have to be company-oriented more towards your customer's company than toward your own. . . . I feel I have to represent my customer. Who's going to go to bat for him if I don't?

Because he receives his check from Allmetal and because he feels he has a chance to develop himself into a more responsible job in the Allmetal organization, the salesman has an attachment to his company. But these are almost incidental to the satisfactions he derives from serving the customer. He may feel he could do almost as well or better working in another company or in another job. He knows that he has to compete with a great many people in Allmetal for recognition. He may feel he has to "fight" to get ahead. But outside the company he has no peers and no superiors. He is a business manager to the customer, a person whose importance merits extra consideration. His biggest source of satisfaction is outside the Allmetal organization.

Training

The aim of training is to help salesmen serve their customers more effectively. The preceding pages have indicated some of the factors related to effective selling—factors which form the agenda to which a training program needs to be directed. Before discussing specific training issues, the discussion of the preceding pages will be summarized.

SUMMARY OF FINDINGS

The main feature of the salesman's job is his responsibility to act as the continuous link between the customer and Allmetal. He brings to bear on the customer's problems his own resources as well as the resources of the Allmetal organization and, in so doing, acts as a business advisor to his customers.

The significant factors affecting the way the salesman performs his job are:

(1) His technical competence.
(2) His skills in working with his customers.
(3) His relationships with people in other departments of the company.
(4) His relationships with his associates in the office, including the other salesmen, his superiors, and his order processors.
(5) His sense of pride and accomplishment in his work.

One of the demands placed upon the salesman is that he assist the customer in technical matters, and the inability to do this is a potential source of embarrassment to him. Most salesmen feel that the technical competence required to sell is acquired from practical experience rather than from formal training. Although there is some logic to the idea that the salesmen should be trained as engineers, many salesmen emphasize the need to select trainees who prefer the "active selling" rather than the "development" aspect of serving the customer.

The salesman is expected by his superiors to operate independently, on the assumption that effective selling demands a situation in which he is given a maximum degree of freedom to develop his own resources and capabilities. However, there is an obvious limit to the salesman's own competence. Because there are many people in the Allmetal organization who have specialized technical knowledge of use to the customer, the salesman tends to utilize these resources in order to meet the customer's demands.

In his role of bringing to bear the resources of the Allmetal organization on the customer's problems, the salesman finds himself more as "a member of a team" than as a "lone wolf." The observers noted many striking examples of successful work accomplished by the salesmen when they displayed the skill of working effectively with people in other Allmetal departments, and when, rather than "standing on their own feet," they succeeded in relating themselves to, and capitalizing on, the accumulated "know-how" of others within Allmetal.

When a salesman obtains help from people in other departments of the company, he sometimes is in a situation in which he feels others are "cutting in" on his territory. Such situations tend to create conflicts; the salesman feels that his relationship with the customer is impaired; he feels personally embarrassed at the danger of being relegated to the job of "order-taker"; his job satisfaction is being undermined.

Although the salesmen recognize that potential help exists in the Los Angeles District Sales Office, there is little evidence of exchange of such help. This is particularly important to the newcomer who apparently sees the more experienced group of salesmen as "keeping to themselves."

The order processor is indispensable to the salesman's work, and to a large extent her performance determines the reputation which the salesman and the company possess. The problems the salesman has of working with his superior are at least in some measure duplicated in his relationships with his order processor. The system of delegating responsibility which he works out does not always meet the expectations of the processor working for him.

The salesman's feelings of satisfaction in his job are mixed. On the one hand, he is proud to serve the customer. To the customer the salesman's job is an important one, and the salesman reacts with a sense of involvement in the customer's company, just as if he were a member of that customer's organization.

These are the findings of the study. They indicate the problems to which a training program needs to be directed. Many of the factors affecting salesman performance concern day-to-day relationships between people. In terms of training procedures such problems imply informal rather than formal procedures, "approaches" to working together rather than specific practices, long-term effects rather than short-run gains, and exploration rather than established methods.

But questions of formal training need to be dealt with. Attempts to modify working relationships cannot be left solely in terms of wish fulfillments. They must be brought down to concrete realities of "What shall be done about training?" at least exploratory fashion of trial and error and retrial. It is also to be recalled that many salesmen made specific suggestions about training, and these demand careful consideration.

RECOMMENDATIONS FOR TRAINING

Training for New Salesmen

(i) It was recommended that trainees be assigned to work with the more experienced salesmen in the office. This would help the trainee become accustomed to the job, facilitate the use of the senior man's knowledge and experience, and give the senior salesmen some administrative responsibility and more prestige in the office.

Perhaps the salient feature of training as perceived by the salesman is the interest which those who are doing the training take in him. While this applies to all phases of training, it seems particularly important after the initial period of orientation and before the trainee has cut out a place for himself in the office. If the trainee is motivated to learn, the chances are he *will* learn, and in large measure this motivation will reflect the interest that he believes the company is taking in him. As far as the trainee is concerned, the person immediately concerned with his development is probably the most important person in the company. An experienced salesman would seem to be the person best qualified to show this interest. He knows "selling," he knows the company, he understands some of the frustrations of breaking in, and he wants to help.

(ii) It was recommended that training programs be arranged according to the experience and interests of the trainee rather than according to a standard pattern for all trainees. This implies involving the trainee in planning his own program.

It would seem inapplicable to attempt to train a liberal arts graduate who has spent most of his life in the railroad industry in the same manner as an individual who has an engineering degree and has spent a number of years in a technical department. Similarly, the type of training which an individual would receive if he were thoroughly familiar with the properties of stainless steel, having worked on it in his workshop, must be quite different from that which might be received by someone who, although technically competent, had had little experience with stainless steel per se. This notion of individual training extends to on-the-spot experiences as well. It may be that after a trial period the trainee will be judged unsuitable for a particular job, and other arrangements will have to be made.

(iii) It was recommended that plant visits for trainees be arranged after some initial office experience, rather than before.

If this were done, the trainees would gain some understanding of the types of problems which they might come up against in their territories, and the applicability of fabrication routines and capacities to the salesman's job. It would be more meaningful to them if they knew what to look for. They probably would gain a greater understanding of why deliveries of certain fabricated items might take three to six months. They might understand the way sales office personnel view plant personnel and then compare these perceptions with those of the people at the plants.

(iv) It was recommended that an effort be made to occupy the trainee's time more effectively. It is understandable that a trainee cannot be given responsibilities comparable in scope to active selling, but, on the other hand, the salesmen complained of training experience which left them feeling they had nothing to do.

If training is to be effective, there should be some goal in terms of the experience which the trainee will have. If the trainee has no idea where he will be, whether he will be a specialist or territory salesman, whether he will be working in sales administration or sales development, then certainly the type of material he assimilates will be very different. His experiences will be more meaningful, and training will be more effective, if there is some goal, even if only a limited one, in terms of future assignment.

Providing a variety of training experiences may also help to maintain the trainee's sense of being useful, since, by grasping the total picture of the sales department operations, he may "find himself" more easily. For example, he may be assigned to both territory and specialist positions, and perhaps from one senior salesman to another. He may spend some time working as an order processor, or he may be asked to investigate and write a report on a specific problem with which he is unfamiliar.

Training for Experienced Salesmen

(i) It was recommended that opportunities be provided for the salesman to improve their competence, particularly in the technical aspects of their work. Such training should be directed toward advancement within the company as well as toward serving for the customer more effectively. The actual suggestions for formal course content have been listed on page 553 (Table 3).

Most salesmen place a high value on receiving technical information that may be of use on their jobs. The opportunity of keeping abreast of technical developments is apparently of vital importance. Thus, giving a senior salesman a junior salesman to train would not only add to the prestige of the former's job, but might also allow him additional time to read professional magazines, to enlarge his business contacts, or to do creative sales work, depending on his particular interests. The opportunity afforded the senior salesman of meeting people in other or competing industries would undoubtedly increase his effectiveness. He might want to visit other geographical areas and developments with the aid of salesmen in other sales territories. It would give him the opportunity to train and manage the work of a less experienced person.

(ii) It was recommended that a forming clinic be established similar to the welding clinic at Detroit. Such a clinic would provide training not only for trainees and experienced salesmen, but for the customers as well.

In a sense, these suggestions are illustrative only, since there may be other suggestions implicit in the report which were not picked up by the observers. No observer or manager can approach the intimate knowledge of selling which the salesman himself has, and for the purposes of instituting changes such knowledge would seem essential. Consequently, it would appear that consulting salesmen regarding training problems would be helpful.

Informal Training. In addition to the suggestions indicated, the report raises issues which are not amenable to easy change. These issues involve working with people and call for skills which cannot be taught too easily, if at all. In discussing such problems it is possible to describe situations and to designate factors and relationships. In effect, this is what the report attempts to do. But our comprehension of how to change behavior or how to act effectively is still largely at the intuitive level. We may recognize effective or ineffective behavior without knowing how it may be made effective or ineffective.

In spite of efforts to make "reasonable" the behavior and attitudes of those mentioned in the report, the reader may tend to blame certain people. The reader may say, "Why doesn't he do (such and such)? Why doesn't he do things differently? If I were in his shoes I would know exactly what to do!" In defense of the person blamed, it is to be noted that this kind of attitude is not too helpful. No one can articulate to a manager how he is to become "more interested" in his salesmen, or to take another example, how the salesmen can delegate responsibility without displaying disinterest. Such skills are delicate and difficult to grasp even when observed to occur.

Whatever their origin may be, however, it appears that skills in working with people develop in a setting which permits expression of opinion and feeling, where the people concerned may explore various alternative ways of acting. What kind of setting is necessary is debatable, but it is suggested that a group situation in which the salesmen and their manager are seriously concerned about the problems will provide sufficient emotional support to those in the group to make such an attempt reasonably successful.

The intent of suggesting that the salesmen be consulted is to point up those instances mentioned in the report in which salesmen succeeded in working through apparently difficult situations. After all, whatever the tone of the report may suggest, the salesmen are not in a state of chaos in relating themselves to others in the company. People with conflicting interests do work together, and by examining these incidents of effective work relationships a great deal may be learned. Furthermore, effective administrations calls for not only responsible leadership, but responsible "followership" as well. Perhaps the greatest contribution of the salesmen may be in "building upon" those experiences in which they were able to work out effective relationships with others.

List of Cases

Agricultural Equipment Company, 119
Allmetal Steel Corporation, 546
The Briggs Box Company, 154
Cold-Air Corporation (A), 501
Cold-Air Corporation (B), 514
Cold-Air Corporation (C), 528
Community Church (A), 314
The Crandell Watch Company, 41
The Eastern Electronic Company: A Problem in Liaison, 51
Grosvenor House, 282
Howard Atkins and Joseph Wexler, 259
The Lightner Company (A), 456
The Lightner Company (B), 469
The Lightner Company (F), 479
The Lightner Company (G), 490
Margaret Mahoney and Richard Carleton, 266
New England Markets, Inc., 401
Observations and Interviews with a Small Group of Workers, 63
Spofford Fabricated Products Company (B), 10
Tremont Hotel (A), 534
The Watkins and Worster Agency (B): A Study of Interpersonal Relations in an Advertising Agency, 325
The Webbing Line, 15

301.15
Z22

Date Due

65944

AP 23'68	OC 22'68			
'68				